P9-DTK-444

HEALTH CARE MANAGEMENT

WILEY SERIES IN HEALTH SERVICES
Stephen J. Williams, Sc.D., Series Editor

HEALTH CARE MANAGEMENT
A TEXT IN ORGANIZATION THEORY AND BEHAVIOR

SECOND EDITION

Stephen M. Shortell, Ph.D.

A.C. Buehler Distinguished Professor of Hospital
and Health Services Management
Professor of Organization Behavior
J.L. Kellogg Graduate School of Management
Professor of Sociology
Member, Center for Health Services and Policy Research
Northwestern University
Evanston, Illinois

Arnold D. Kaluzny, Ph.D.

Professor
Department of Health Policy and Administration
School of Public Health
Research Associate, Health Services Research Center
University of North Carolina at Chapel Hill
Chapel Hill, North Carolina

and Associates

A WILEY MEDICAL PUBLICATION
JOHN WILEY & SONS
New York • Chichester • Brisbane • Toronto • Singapore

Chapter 9: quote. Andrew Rooney, excerpted from *A Few Minutes with Andy Rooney.* Copyright © 1981 Essay Productions, Inc. Reprinted with permission of Atheneum Publishers.

Copyright © 1983, 1988 by John Wiley & Sons, Inc.

All rights reserved. Published simultaneously in Canada.

Reproduction or translation of any part of this work beyond that permitted by Section 107 or 108 of the 1976 United States Copyright Act without the permission of the copyright owner is unlawful. Requests for permission or further information should be addressed to the Permissions Department, John Wiley & Sons, Inc.

Library of Congress Cataloging in Publication Data:

Health care management.

   (Wiley series in health services) (A Wiley medical publication)
   Includes bibliographies and indexes.
   1. Health services administration.   I. Shortell, Stephen M. (Stephen Michael), 1944–
II. Kaluzny, Arnold D.   III. Series.   IV. Series: Wiley medical publication.   [DNLM: 1. Health Services—organization & administration.

W 84.1 H4364]
RA393.H38   1987   362.1′068   87-14786
ISBN 0-471-85111-6

Printed in the United States of America

10   9   8   7   6   5   4   3   2

To Odin Anderson and George Bugbee
S.M.S.

To Richard Griffith and Daniel Katz
A.D.K.

For stimulating and nurturing our interest in the field

and to

Susan, Stephanie, and Juliana
Barbara, Melissa, Carrie, and Don

Who provide organization and balance to our lives

Contributors

Jeffrey A. Alexander, Ph.D.
Associate Professor
Graduate Program of Hospital and Health Services Administration
School of Community and Allied Health
University of Alabama
Birmingham, Alabama

Thomas S. Bateman, D.B.A.
Associate Professor
Graduate School of Business
University of North Carolina
Chapel Hill, North Carolina

Selwyn W. Becker, Ph.D.
Professor of Behavioral Sciences
Graduate School of Business and
The Center for Health Administration Studies
University of Chicago
Chicago, Illinois

James W. Begun, Ph.D.
Associate Professor
Department of Health Care Administration
Medical College of Virginia
Virginia Commonwealth University
Richmond, Virginia

Lawton R. Burns, Ph.D.
Assistant Professor
Department of Management and Policy
College of Business and Public Administration
University of Arizona
Tucson, Arizona

Martin P. Charns, D.B.A.
Associate Professor of Organizational Behavior and Health Care Management
Boston University
Boston, Massachusetts

Karen S. Cook, Ph.D.
Associate Professor of Sociology
Department of Sociology
University of Washington
Seattle, Washington

David Greenberger, Ph.D.
Assistant Professor of Management and Human Resources
College of Business
Ohio State University
Columbus, Ohio

S. Robert Hernandez, Dr.P.H.
Associate Professor
Graduate Program of Hospital and Health Services Administration
School of Community and Allied Health
University of Alabama
Birmingham, Alabama

Robert W. Hetherington, Ph.D.
Professor
Department of Sociology
University of Alberta
Edmonton, Alberta
Canada

Arnold D. Kaluzny, Ph.D.
Professor
Department of Health Policy and Administration
School of Public Health
Research Associate, Health Services Research Center
University of North Carolina at Chapel Hill
Chapel Hill, North Carolina

John R. Kimberly, Ph.D.
Professor
Department of Management
Department of Health Care Systems
The Wharton School
University of Pennsylvania
Philadelphia, Pennsylvania

James M. Klingensmith, Sc.D.
Assistant Professor
Health Administration Program
Graduate School of Public Health
University of Pittsburgh
Pittsburgh, Pennsylvania

Peggy Leatt, Ph.D.
Professor
Department of Health Administration
Faculty of Medicine
University of Toronto
Toronto, Ontario
Canada

Roy J. Lewicki, Ph.D.
Associate Dean, College of Business
Associate Professor, Department of Management and Human Resources
Ohio State University
Columbus, Ohio

Carol A. Lockhart, Ph.D.
Executive Director
Greater Phoenix Affordable Health Care Foundation
Phoenix, Arizona

Beaufort B. Longest, Jr., Ph.D.
Professor and Director
Health Administration Program and Director, Health Policy Institute
Graduate School of Public Health
University of Pittsburgh
Pittsburgh, Pennsylvania

Roice D. Luke, Ph.D.
Professor and Chairman
Department of Health Administration
Medical College of Virginia
Virginia Commonwealth University
Richmond, Virginia

Laura L. Morlock, Ph.D.
Associate Professor
Department of Behavioral Sciences and the Health Service Research
    and Development Center
School of Hygiene and Public Health
Johns Hopkins University
Baltimore, Maryland

Fred C. Munson, Ph.D.
Professor
Department of Health Services Management and Policy
School of Public Health
University of Michigan
Ann Arbor, Michigan

Constance A. Nathanson, Ph.D.
Professor
Department of Population Dynamics
School of Hygiene and Public Health
Johns Hopkins University
Baltimore, Maryland

Thomas G. Rundall, Ph.D.
Professor and Chairman
Department of Social and Administrative Health Sciences
School of Public Health
University of California
Berkeley, California

W. Richard Scott, Ph.D.
Professor
Department of Sociology
Stanford University
Stanford, California

Stephen M. Shortell, Ph.D.
A.C. Buehler Distinguished Professor of Hospital
    and Health Services Management
Professor of Organization Behavior
J. L. Kellogg Graduate School of Management
    and the Center for Health Services and Policy Research
Northwestern University
Evanston, Illinois

David Starkweather, Dr. P.H.
Professor and Director
Health Services Management
School of Public Health and School of Business Administration
University of California
Berkeley, California

Stephen Strasser, Ph.D.
Associate Professor
Division of Hospital and Health Services Administration
Ohio State University
Columbus, Ohio

Howard S. Zuckerman, Ph.D.
Associate Professor
Department of Health Services Management and Policy
School of Public Health
University of Michigan
Ann Arbor, Michigan

Foreword

Change is occurring at a dizzying rate for managers of health care; it seems depressingly slow for many outside the system. This reflects two commonplace but crucial facts. Organizations look different from varying vantage points and the multiplicity and complexity of perspectives is a crucial aspect of the managerial challenge. Health care organizations must not only strive to attain reasonable levels of efficiency, quality, and even equity, but also convince their publics that they are doing so. If directing an organization was simply a technical task, management would be a snap. But all organizations, and especially those dealing with human services, must function in changing social and symbolic contexts that affect internal processes as well as the environment and increase uncertainty and the importance of personality, leadership, and politics.

For the student seeking a blueprint for management, neither this nor any other book is likely to meet expectations. Undoubtedly, many books so advertise themselves, but those who accept such claims are simply foolish. There are, of course, technical issues to be mastered and skills to be acquired. An effective manager, however charismatic or persuasive, must understand clearly the objectives of the organization and the processes consistent with them. Managers must be clear on lines of communication and decision making, the design and supervision of work processes, and the means for successful coordination. But there is no single path to organizational effectiveness. Managers "satisfice"—to borrow a term from Herbert Simon—because they have neither the wits nor the time to find optimal solutions.

Having experimented from time to time with the roles of organizational theorist and manager, I have come to believe that the value of studying organization theory and behavior comes less from any specific applications and more from how it shapes the way managers come to think about their jobs and the range of options to be considered. Appreciation of the theory of organizations thus results less in a set of principles to be applied to concrete problems—although there are some—and more to enhancing one's breadth of possibilities.

I had the opportunity to consider the applications of organization theory when thrust into the position of organizing a major university reorganization, creating a new unified faculty of arts and sciences from five constituent college faculties each with its own history, traditions, commitments, centers of power and influence, and autonomous budgets. In addition to melding these five faculties into a single unit fiscally and administratively, encompassing more than a thousand faculty members and all the support staff and facilities that go with them, we had to physically move hundreds of individuals to achieve the necessary physical consolidation of disciplines. It is commonly quipped that moving faculty is equivalent to moving a graveyard, and there was no shortage of prophesies for disaster. Yet, we successfully completed the task with unexpected harmony and were able to strengthen significantly the opportunity of our faculty to position itself for the future.

In taking on this reorganization, I naturally considered what wisdom I could muster from what I knew of the management sciences and organization theory, but I must confess that from day to day I was less guided by organizational hypotheses and empirical findings and more by the need to clearly define our objectives and monitor the volatile and changing environment in which we were functioning. Organization theory suggested checkpoints, processes, cautions, and, at times, options—never blueprints. And that is as it should be, because at crucial points there is nothing more important than judgment. This book, and the valuable open-systems theory it espouses, can contribute significantly to developing and sharpening the critical capacities of the manager and, if properly mastered, will help nurture informed judgment.

Health institutions are being subjected to fundamental changes in organizational alignments and financial arrangements. The external environment as reflected in changing science and technology, the aging of the American population and the growth of the oldest-old subgroups, the impending excess of physicians, and newly emerging power configurations among doctors, managers, regulators, and a better-informed public all contribute to uncertainty for health managers. The expanding base of science and technology, and the growing organizational complexity of care, require more technical expertise of the manager than ever before. Economic constraints, increased competition among health professionals, and perceived loss of power especially require the manager to maintain morale and commitment and deter unproductive conflict. The changing environment provides abundant opportunities to innovate or to blunder in setting the organization's course. Successful health care executives have to understand from where we have come but, even more, they require a reasonable conception of how systems of care are evolving.

The approach of this book is exemplary and its organization reflects the large and varied tasks to which a manager must attend. The detailed chapters reviewing work on the cutting edge of organizational theory and investigation have much to teach, but their meaning also lies in their relationship to the larger whole that constitutes the manager's field of action, which is imaginatively conceptualized in the organization of chapters.

Health is an exciting arena offering incredible challenges. It also provides many opportunities, whether in the private or public sector, to address major national concerns about access to care, protecting the 35 million Americans without health insurance, building a framework of long-term care, and maintaining and enhancing the nation's health. Those who understand and practice the principles taught in this book will find that they have acquired the means to do good while doing well.

David Mechanic, Ph.D.
Rene Dubos Professor of
Behavioral Sciences
Director, Rutgers University
Institute for Health, Health
Care Policy, and Aging
Research
New Brunswick, New Jersey

Preface

This second edition of the text retains most of the distinguishing features of the first edition. These include:

- Recognition that the manager's world is a world of action.
- The importance of understanding the behavioral and social sciences that underlie organization theory and behavior and, in turn, managerial practice.
- Emphasis on the centrality of the managerial role in relation to organization performance.
- A systematic, integrative treatment of individual, group, and organization-wide issues.
- A broad exposure to the organization theory and behavior literature in addition to the literature specific to health services organizations so that readers can see commonalities as well as differences.
- Treatment of a wide variety of health services organizations including hospitals, multi-institutional systems, nursing homes, ambulatory care group practices, health maintenance organizations, health departments, and clinics.
- Discussion questions and suggestions for additional reading.
- Sets of managerial guidelines included with many of the chapters.
- A future orientation.

Based on feedback from students, faculty, and other readers, this second edition also features:

- Increased attention to the proactive nature of the manager's role in influencing the environment and creating the organization's future.
- Increased discussion of the population ecology/natural selection perspective on organizational survival and particularly its relation to strategic planning.
- Increased attention given to multihospital systems and related organizational coalitions, networks, federations, and affiliations.
- Incorporation of the growing literature on negotiation and bargaining. The challenges facing health care managers today place a premium on negotiation, bargaining, and conflict resolution skills.
- Expansion of the content on strategic management.

• Increased use of short stories, vignettes, and mini-case studies to serve as examples and illustrations of key concepts, principles, and guidelines.

In addition, each chapter has been updated to reflect state-of-the-art management theory, research, and practice. We believe the net result is a text which is both readable, relevant, and interesting as well as theoretically and empirically grounded.

This book takes an open-systems and contingency perspective on the management of health organizations while at the same time noting the many contributions of other perspectives. The overall approach is presented in Chapter 1, followed in Chapter 2 by an extensive discussion of the managerial role. These chapters should be read first. After that, the sections on motivating and leading people, operating the technical system, and renewing the organization are developed in succession, concluding with a section on charting the future. For the most part these sections deal with individual, group, and organization-wide issues, respectively. While we believe these are logical building blocks, others may wish to use them in a different order depending on personal preference, course objectives, and student mix.

The book is written primarily for graduate students taking a course in health services management. For the most part, it assumes that students have already taken an introductory course in organization theory and behavior. But because the text integrates much of the fundamental literature in the field, it can serve equally well as a text for students exposed for the first time to graduate-level instruction in organization theory and behavior. Undergraduate programs may also find the text of value.

The book is not limited to students formally enrolled in programs in health services management. Rather, it is intended equally for students of medicine, nursing, pharmacy, social work, and other health professions who will assume managerial responsibilities or who want to learn more about the organizations in which they will spend the major portion of their professional lives. Because of the many examples, short case studies, and questions raised, the text is particularly relevant to experienced managers who are involved in continuing education or extended-degree programs or who are simply interested in being exposed to the state of the art and beyond of health services management in a systematic, rigorous, and behaviorally based fashion.

We do not claim that the text can be used alone. Instructors will want to supplement the text with articles, case studies, and other materials. In recent years, a number of useful casebooks and books of readings have been developed which can be used to supplement the material contained in this text.

Neither do we claim to have eliminated all redundancy or repetition among chapters, a major challenge for any book that includes over 20 different authors. In some cases we have deliberately encouraged redundancy. This has been done where we felt it important to show the flow of ideas from one chapter to another; where the concepts were so important that they deserved mentioning throughout the text; where the concepts were relatively difficult to grasp such that repetition was useful; or where the concepts could be further explicated by the use of different examples in different chapters. We have opted for effectiveness rather than efficiency—clearly a managerial decision. Nonetheless, we believe that unnecessary redundancy and repetition have been eliminated and that reading is further facilitated by common terminology and frequent cross-references to related chapters, ideas, and research.

Finally, it should be noted that the managerial guidelines presented should not be interpreted as blueprints or prescriptions. Rather, they are best considered as sensitizing statements based on the best and most recently available evidence regarding where managers might first focus their thinking on a given issue.

Once again, we have been fortunate to work with talented colleagues. Each has contributed his or her special expertise. We have also learned from each other in such a way as to make the collaborative nature of this second edition particularly rewarding.

Stephen M. Shortell
Arnold D. Kaluzny

Acknowledgments

This second edition has benefited greatly from students and faculty throughout the country who took the time to provide many thoughtful suggestions and comments. As indicated in the preface, we have incorporated many of these suggestions.

In addition, appreciation is expressed to numerous colleagues who commented on specific chapters. These include Alexandra Burns, Ron Andersen, Charles Bidwell, Gordon Brown, Thomas D'Aunno, Geoff Gibson, The W. K. Kellogg Foundation staff, David Mechanic, Dennis Pointer, and Amjit Sethi.

For clerical assistance and related support, appreciation is also expressed to Lee Bolzenius, Donna Cooper, Binne Douglas, Susan Harris, Britta Jenkins, William Kahn, Paul A. Kinkel, Kris Olson, Marie Taylor, Kit Simpson, and Jean Yates (deceased).

Stephen M. Shortell
Arnold D. Kaluzny

Contents

xxi

HEALTH CARE MANAGEMENT

PART ONE

Organizations and Managers

Young people today will have to learn organization the way their forefathers learned farming.

Peter Drucker

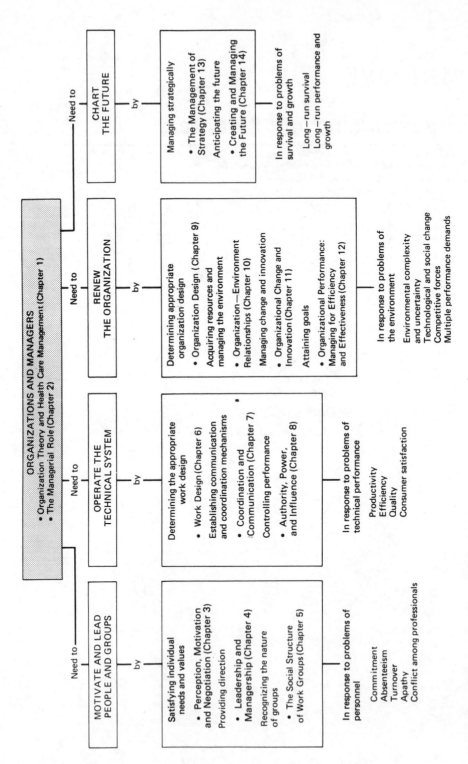

ORGANIZATIONS AND MANAGERS
- Organization Theory and Health Care Management (Chapter 1)
- The Managerial Role (Chapter 2)

Need to

MOTIVATE AND LEAD PEOPLE AND GROUPS

by

Satisfying individual needs and values
- Perception, Motivation and Negotiation (Chapter 3)

Providing direction
- Leadership and Managership (Chapter 4)

Recognizing the nature of groups
- The Social Structure of Work Groups (Chapter 5)

In response to problems of personnel

Commitment
Absenteeism
Turnover
Apathy
Conflict among professionals

Need to

OPERATE THE TECHNICAL SYSTEM

by

Determining the appropriate work design
- Work Design (Chapter 6)

Establishing communication and coordination mechanisms
- Coordination and Communication (Chapter 7)

Controlling performance
- Authority, Power, and Influence (Chapter 8)

In response to problems of technical performance

Productivity
Efficiency
Quality
Consumer satisfaction

Need to

RENEW THE ORGANIZATION

by

Determining appropriate organization design
- Organization Design (Chapter 9)

Acquiring resources and managing the environment
- Organization—Environment Relationships (Chapter 10)

Managing change and innovation
- Organizational Change and Innovation (Chapter 11)

Attaining goals
- Organizational Performance: Managing for Efficiency and Effectiveness (Chapter 12)

In response to problems of the environment

Environmental complexity and uncertainty
Technological and social change
Competitive forces
Multiple performance demands

Need to

CHART THE FUTURE

by

Managing strategically
- The Management of Strategy (Chapter 13)

Anticipating the future
- Creating and Managing the Future (Chapter 14)

In response to problems of survival and growth

Long–run survival
Long–run performance and growth

The nature of organizations: Framework for the text.

The delivery of health services has become largely an organizational process. This is evidenced by the growing numbers of physicians practicing in groups, the growth of alternative delivery systems, the increasing number of hospitals joining multiunit systems, and the continuing regionalization of health services. These developments and others place a premium on effective management. The two chapters in this first section take up this challenge by laying the groundwork for the remainder of the book.

Chapter 1, Organization Theory and Health Care Management, focuses on the following types of questions and issues:

- What is the composition of the system? How many different kinds of health care organizations exist, and what are their characteristics?
- In what ways are health care organizations different from other organizations? In what ways are they similar?
- What characteristics can be used to differentiate key health care organizations?
- What major theories of organizations can provide a framework for the study and management of health care organizations?
- What do the different theories have to say about such important issues as efficiency and effectiveness, conflict and change, survival and growth, and the organization's ability to influence its environment?

Chapter 1 concludes with an action-oriented framework around which the text is organized.

Chapter 2, The Managerial Role, focuses on the following kinds of questions:

- What do managers do?
- What are the main characteristics of the managerial role?
- In what way is the managerial role different for health care managers than for managers of other organizations? In what way is it similar?
- To what degree is the managerial role different for managers of multi-institutional systems than individual organizations?
- What is currently known about the health care manager's role?
- What are the advantages and disadvantages of different role conceptions?
- In what ways is the health care manager's role expanding to meet new demands?

Upon completing these two introductory chapters, readers should be able to:

- Know the different kinds of health care organizations, particularly in terms of size, distribution, and the role they play in the health care system.
- Understand the ways in which health care organizations are similar to many other kinds of organizations, but also appreciate the ways in which they are different.
- Distinguish hospitals, ambulatory care group practices, nursing homes, and health departments on a number of dimensions, such as environment, mission and goals, time orientation, specialization, decision making, and manager–physician relationships.
- Define and distinguish between closed-system and open-system models of organizations and rational-system and natural-system approaches.

- Summarize what the different approaches have to say about efficiency and effectiveness, conflict and change, social integration and coordination, and organizational maintenance and adaptation to the environment.
- Define and distinguish among the universalist, organizational, and political conceptions of the managerial role.
- Identify the interpersonal, informational, and decisional roles of managers.
- Know the differences in managerial roles at different levels of the organization.
- Define and distinguish among the production/support function, the maintenance function, and the adaptation function of the organization and know the implications of these functions for the manager's role.
- Identify the effects that an organization's age and size have on the manager's role.
- Summarize the main findings from the studies of health care managers' roles.
- Integrate the universalist, organizational, and political role conceptions to develop a personal managerial philosophy.

CHAPTER 1

Organization Theory and Health Care Management

Stephen M. Shortell
Arnold D. Kaluzny

The American health care system is large and complex. By 1990, expenditures are expected to be $640 billion, comprising 11.3% of the gross national product (1). The portion of the gross national product (GNP) allocated to health care has nearly doubled over the past 25 years. In addition, the health care system is one of the largest employers in the country, employing over 7 million persons (2). It is *the* largest employer of women; one of every six women in the labor force holds a position with a health care organization (3).

The system is characterized by a diversity of providers. Professional providers include physicians (both allopathic and osteopathic), dentists, nurses, podiatrists, chiropodists, chiropractors, pharmacists, social workers, optometrists, physical therapists, and others. They are organized in a variety of ways and practice in a number of settings, including private practice, group practice, health maintenance organizations, emergency rooms and outpatient clinics, hospitals, nursing homes, health departments, and home health agencies. There is also great variation within these settings. For example, there are many different kinds of hospitals, including tuberculosis hospitals, psychiatric hospitals, children's hospitals, hospitals for the physically or mentally disabled, teaching hospitals, and the short-term, general, acute-care hospital. Hospitals may range from 20- to 30-bed institutions that provide only the simplest kind of care to 1,000-bed teaching hospitals with the most advanced specialties and services.

The complexity suggested above is in large part associated with the shift in the delivery of health care from an individual to an organizational process. Consumers increasingly look to organizations and groups for health care services, such as ambulatory care centers, emergency rooms, satellite clinics, and health maintenance organizations, rather than to individual providers. Associated with the shift are a number of challenges. Consider the following:

- Can the rising costs of care be contained without seriously compromising the quality of care or access to needed care?
- Can the public's apparent demand for a broader array of preventive services be met?
- Can constructive and humane ways be found to provide services to an increasing elderly population?
- Can health services be coordinated and integrated with the larger social/human service delivery system?
- Can the special needs of the underserved among certain minority groups and in rural areas be met in a more cost-effective fashion?
- Can the frequently competing interests and demands of health professionals be managed in a way that promotes better patient care?

Our ability to deal with these challenges will be largely determined by how well organizations function. As described by Bowers et al. (4):

> Neither the individual nor society as a whole resolves problems of this size and scope. Society survives or fails, thrives or deteriorates on the effectiveness of its organizations. These problems and many others make it patently clear that the American society simply must find a ready, transferable way in which to make its component systems—its organizations (health service organizations)—more effective. Much must be accomplished for comparatively less input. Less must be wasted, more must be wisely used and more of high quality must be generated.

In short, a premium is being placed on knowledge of how organizations work, their potential for growth and change, and their contribution toward providing more cost-effective health services. For these reasons, knowledge of organization theory and behavior has become a sine qua non of modern health care management.

This chapter provides a summary of the different types and numbers of health care organizations, classifies a number of them on relevant criteria, describes the major theories of organizations through which managers can gain perspective on their task, and provides an integrative framework for the remaining chapters of this text.

THE ECOLOGY OF HEALTH CARE ORGANIZATIONS

A DESCRIPTIVE PROFILE

The health services industry is large and diverse. The more important organizations are classified below by type of service rendered. The intent is not to provide an in-depth description of each, but rather to give sufficient background for subsequent discussion throughout the text.*

---

*For a detailed description of hospitals see Dowling, 1987 (5); for nursing homes see Kane and Kane, 1987 (6); for HMOs see Anderson et al., 1986 (7); for hospices see Torrens, 1985 (8); for mental health services see Scott and Black, 1986 (9); for public health departments see Shonick, 1987 (10); for municipal primary care centers see Ginzberg et al., 1985 (11); for hospital-sponsored group practice see Shortell et al., 1984 (12); and for emergency services see Georgopoulos, 1986 (13).

INPATIENT SERVICES

Hospitals and nursing homes are traditionally classified as institutional providers. As presented in Table 1.1 there are approximately 6,872 hospitals in the United States. The majority of these institutions are nonfederal, short-term hospitals, accounting for approximately 92.8% of all admissions (14). The remaining hospital facilities are either federal or nonfederal specialty-type institutions, which have been declining in number since 1960, except for a slight increase in nonfederal psychiatric hospitals.

A significant and fairly recent development is the growth of multihospital systems.

TABLE 1.1. Inpatient Services, 1950–1985

	Year	
Type of Organization	*1980*	*1985*
Hospitals[a]	6,965	6,872
Federal	359	341
Nonfederal psychiatric, TB, research, other long-term	692	717
Nonfederal short-term, general, other specialized	5,904	5,814
Nongovernment, non-profit, community hospitals	3,322	3,351
Investor-owned (for profit) community hospitals	730	786
State/local government community hospitals	1,778	1,622
Multihospitals systems[b]	267; 256 [1981]	243
Total hospitals	1,797; 1,877 [1981]	1,958
Total beds	341,383; 351,408 [1981]	365,914
Nursing homes[c]	18,900 [1977]	25,849 [1982]
Nursing home beds	1,402,400 [1977]	1,642,067 [1982]

Nursing Home Ownership	*Nursing Homes*	*Number of Beds*
Total	25,849 [1982]	1,642,067
Proprietary	21,132	1,194,000
Nonprofit	3,606	335,514
Government	1,111	112,553
By certification[d]		
Medicare or Medicaid (SNF)	7,032	855,096
Medicaid	5,564	442,277
Not certified	5,643	212,881
Unknown	7,610	131,813

[a]SOURCE: American Hospital Association. *AHA guide to health care field.* Chicago, IL: American Hospital Association, 1985, Table 1, pp. 4–7.

[b]SOURCE:: American Hospital Association. *Directory of multi-hospital systems* (4th ed.). Chicago, IL: American Hospital Association, 1984, Tables 2–3, pp. 92–93.

[c]SOURCE: National Center for Health Care Statistics. A. Scirroco: An overview of the 1982 national master facility inventory survey of nursing and related care homes. Advance data from vital and health care statistics No. 111. DHHS Pub. No. (PHS) 85-1250. Hyattsville, Md.: Public Health Service, September 20, 1985.

[d]Facilities classified as SNF and intermediate care have been classified as SNF.

Defined as two or more hospitals with a common form of ownership, approximately 35–40% of all U.S. community hospitals belong to systems comprising approximately 40% of all beds. In 1984, 243 systems were reported as operational, a decline from the 256 reported in 1981 (15). But, most significantly, the total number of hospitals involved in a multiunit system increased from 1,877 to 1,958 in 1984, suggesting that fewer systems managed or owned more hospitals.

Finally, the total number of nursing homes and of beds has steadily increased since 1963. By 1982 there were a total of 25,849 certified nursing homes with a total bed complement of 1,642,057 (16). The majority of these institutions were proprietary and were providing intermediate care (16).

AMBULATORY SERVICES

Many health services are provided on an ambulatory basis. As shown in Table 1.2, the organizational setting for much of this care traditionally has been the physician's private office. The number of group practice organizations, however, has grown steadily, doubling between 1960 and 1980, with a recent surge in 1984 to 15,485 (17).

A growing form of group practice is the prepaid group practice plan. These organizations combine delivery and financing, and provide comprehensive services for a fixed, prepaid fee. As shown in Table 1.2, 393 were operational in 1985, in contrast to 243 plans in operation in 1980 (18). These plans take a variety of forms. *Staff model* prepaid plans are characterized by a close relationship between plan administration and the medical staff. The physicians are usually salaried by the plan. *Group model* prepaid plans are characterized by a greater autonomy given to the medical staff vis-a-vis plan administration. Here the plan typically contracts with the medical group but is not part of the overall administrative structure of the group practice. *Independent practice associations* (IPAs), physicians in private offices, are paid on a fee-for-service basis by the prepaid plan to deliver care to enrolled members. *Network model* plans involve a relationship between the central plan administration and a number of multispecialty group practice clinics that provide care on a prepaid basis to a defined group of enrollees.

A more recent development is represented by preferred provider organizations (PPOs). This type of arrangement operates similarly to IPAs in that contracts are de-

TABLE 1.2. Ambulatory Services, 1950–1985

| | Year | |
Type of Organization	1980	1985
Physician office-based practice	247,554 [1979]	296,658 [1982][a]
Medical group practice	8,483 [1975]	15,485 [1984][b]
Prepaid health plans	243 [1974]	393 [6/1985][c]
Surgicenters		521 [1986 proj.][d]

[a]Eiler, M.A. *Physician characteristics and distribution in the U.S.* Chicago: American Medical Association, 1985, Table 61.

[b]*Medical groups in the U.S. 1984.* Chicago, Il.: American Medical Association, Survey and Data Resources Division, 1985.

[c]*HMO survey.* Excelsior, MN: Interstudy, June 1985.

[d]Henderson, J. Surgery centers may double: Consultant. *Modern Healthcare*, June 7, 1985.

veloped with private practice physicians, but here fees are usually discounted to 80% of usual and customary charges. In return, physicians are guaranteed prompt payment. These plans, like the IPAs, are most relevant in areas of high competition among physicians where there is an incentive to join in order to hold on to or expand one's current patient base.

Finally, a growing number of freestanding ambulatory centers have developed. These include surgery centers, urgent care centers, primary care centers, and imaging centers. As seen in Table 1.2, for example, it is estimated that there are 521 surgicenters and it is expected that this number will rise to 682 facilities by 1990.

COMMUNITY-BASED SERVICES

Community or public health services focus on treatment of the community rather than the individual. The historical focus of these organizations has been on control of infectious agents and provision of preventive services. There were approximately 3,061 local health departments in 1982 and 55 state health departments (19).

Of the funds allocated to local health departments, 53.6% are for personal health services, including maternal and child health, communicable diseases, crippled children, and mental health. Environmental services represent 10.1% of the monies allocated, and allocations for health resources represent 5.9% of the total. The local departments are permitted to designate their own use for an additional 22.5% of the total dollars not designated for categorical programs (19).

OTHER SERVICES

While hospitals, nursing homes, health departments, and ambulatory care organizations represent the primary service-delivery agencies, it is important to note the development of a number of other organizations that may be institutionally located or freestanding within the community. For example, Table 1.3 presents information on hospices and various home health agencies. Home health agencies may be hospital based, public health department based, skilled nursing facility based, or voluntary on a profit or non-profit basis. The number of home health agencies has steadily increased from 874 in 1950 to 5,964 in 1986, with the majority being profit and hospital based (20).

Hospices, which originated in England and provide care to the terminally ill, represent another developing organization that may be located in a hospital or local health department or may be freestanding within the community. They are a relatively recent development in the United States. The National Hospice Organization reported in 1984 more than 410 in various stages of development and 935 fully operational (21).

Finally, the number of self-help/self-care organizations have been increasing over the past 30 years. These organizations take a variety of forms and are defined by Lurie and Shulman (22) as follows:

As an organization of peers (who may be consumers of a health service) organized for the purpose of pursuing self-interest, mutual support, and aid . . . most self-help groups seek to raise the conscientiousness of the community about the nature of a specific physical or emotional disease. Significantly, it is a self-directed group. Although professional staff may be utilized, the decisions concerning policy, procedures, and action are determined by group members. . . .

TABLE 1.3. Community Based Services, 1950–1985

Type of Organization	Year	
	1980	1985
Hospice (933 operational, 2 FP, 410 under plan)		1,345 [1984][a]
Home health agencies		5,964[b]
Voluntary		518
Official (Health Department)		1,217
Combination		57
Rehabilitation facility based		20
Hospital based		1,260
Skilled nursing facility		129
Proprietary		1,927
Private not-for-profit		831
Unclassified		5

[a]*The 1984 guide to the nation's hospices.* Washington, D.C.: National Hospice Organization, 1984.

[b]*Report.* Washington, D.C.: National Association for Home Care, January 3, 1986.

Reliable information on the number of groups or chapters for any particular year are difficult to obtain. A number of self-help clearinghouses are located throughout the United States. These organizations have attempted to monitor the number and forms of self-help groups within their communities. For example, it is estimated that in Chicago 15,000 self-help/self-care organizations are listed for 352 medical conditions. This represents a 32% increase in the number of groups operational in 1983. Similar increases are reported for other large metropolitan areas.

SUPPORTIVE AND ANCILLARY ORGANIZATIONS

Organizations involved in the direct provision of health care are influenced by a number of other organizations whose operations have a significant effect on provider organizations as well as on the overall performance of the health system. These organizations include regulatory or quasi-regulatory/planning agencies, various third-party financing organizations, professional associations, pharmaceutical and medical equipment supply corporations, and various educational and training organizations.

REGULATORY AND QUASI-REGULATORY/PLANNING AGENCIES

A typical health care organization is subject to surveillance and control by a range of regulatory and quasi-regulatory planning agencies. These agencies may be private or public; they influence decisions involving captial construction, cost and charges for services, personnel standards, quality and working conditions, and so forth. Two mechanisms which have been particularly significant in the past, although their future role is in doubt, are certificate of need (CON) programs and professional review organizations (PROs).

Certificate of need programs are state regulatory mechanisms for review and approval by health planning agencies of capital expenditures and service-capacity expansion by hospitals and other health care facilities. There is a great deal of variability among states as well as uncertainty about the future funding of the program at the federal level. Initially funded in 1975 when Congress passed the National Health Planning and Resources Development Act of 1974, seven states have repealed the CON laws (Idaho, New Mexico, Minnesota, Utah, Arizona, Kansas, and Texas) and a number are scheduled to expire in 1986–1987. However, even where states have repealed the CON (except for Arizona, Utah, and Texas), they have enacted either a moratorium on new hospital construction and expansion or have adapted what is termed "Section 1122" programs— that is, a federally funded, state-optional form of CON providing for planning agency review and approval for Medicare and Medicaid reimbursement of capital expenditures proposed by health care facilities. Moreover, a close review of existing state provisions indicate that even if all the states with CON laws scheduled to expire in 1986–1987 did not enter into a new Section 1122 arrangement or adopt a moratorium on construction, 41 states and the District of Columbia would continue to have some form of health facility regulation (23).

Peer review organizations (PROs) are under contract to the Health Care Financing Administration to monitor hospital use and quality of care of Medicare patients. There are currently 54 such organizations which, with the exception of Idaho, meet the criteria: of demonstrating either physician sponsorship, defined as 10% of physicians in the area, or physician access (i.e., involvement of representatives of at least 17 of the 23 generally recognized specialties). Moreover, the PRO could not be affiliated with the health care facility or association of facilities or with third party payors. Most PROs are transformed PSROs (professional standards review organizations) which were initially established in 1972, and with the awarding of the last three PROs in 1984 the last PSRO was phased out (24).

THIRD-PARTY FINANCING ORGANIZATIONS

The government, through such financing mechanisms as Medicare and Medicaid, represents the single largest third-party organization involved in health services. In 1983 it represented 39.7% of all expenditures for personal health services (25).

Private health insurance carriers, which largely account for the remaining expenditures, are composed of nonprofit and profit-making components. In 1984, there were 67 Blue Cross plans and 67 Blue Shield plans (25). Of these, 67 were joint plans, providing a total of 90 Blue Cross and Blue Shield plans. Commercial insurance companies such as Metropolitan, Prudential, and Aetna represent the profit sector. At year-end 1983 over 800 such organizations provided health insurance coverage to 111 million people (25).

Blue Cross and Blue Shield and the commercial insurance companies accounted for 31.9% of personal health expenditures (25). Of the total benefits paid in 1983, approximately 48% were provided by commercial companies and 52% from Blue Cross/Blue Shield and other hospital medical plans.

PROFESSIONAL ASSOCIATIONS

Service-delivery organizations and individual health care providers all have associations to protect their interests. The following is a list of professional associations that represent various categories of health care personnel and organizations:

Physicians.   American Medical Association (AMA); American College of Physician Executives (ACPE); American Academy of Medical Directors (AAMD)

Administrators.   American College of Health Care Executives (ACHCE); American College of Nursing Home Administrators (ACNHA); Association of Group Medical Administrators (AGMA); Medical Group Management Association (MGMA); American Society of Hospital Personnel Administration; Association of Mental Health Administrators

Dentists.   American Dental Association (ADA)

Nurses.   American Nurses Association (ANA)

Allied health personnel.   American Society of Allied Health Professions (ASAHP)

Health professionals at large and schools of public health.   American Public Health Association (APHA)

Hospitals.   American Hospital Association (AHA)

Medical schools.   Association of American Medical Colleges (AAMC)

Academic health science centers.   Association of Academic Health Science Centers (AAHC)

Group health organizations.   American Group Practice Association (AGPA)

These associations operate at the local, state, and federal level and provide a number of functions, including protection and social support, training, and maintenance of standards. In addition to the more traditional professional associations there is increasing interest in the development of unions for physicians and other health care workers. For example, the California based Union of American Physicians and Dentists (UAPD) currently reports 17 state-affiliated groups and a membership of approximately 42,000 physicians and dentists. Similarly, other health care workers are involved in joining and/or forming unions. The Service Employees International Union (SEIU), for example, represents approximately 200,000 health care workers and reports a significant increase in requests for assistance in organizing unions in a variety of health care organizations (26).

PHARMACEUTICAL AND MEDICAL EQUIPMENT SUPPLY CORPORATIONS

In 1984, 6.7% of medical care expenditures were allocated to drugs, medical supplies, and equipment (27). The primary suppliers of these items were the 1,281 drug manufacturing companies, which employed 306,600 persons and in 1984 listed total domestic sales of $17,095 million and foreign exports of $10,411 million of ethical pharmaceuticals (28).

EDUCATIONAL AND TRAINING FACILITIES

The provider organizations are staffed with a wide range of professionals educated in a variety of educational and training facilities. These settings include schools of medicine, nursing, dentistry, pharmacy, business, public health, social work, and allied health, and undergraduate and graduate programs in health administration. Each of these institutions socializes students into the norms and values of its respective profession. The different professional identities that result from this process represent a pervasive source of conflict and change within health care organizations. Moreover, the schools are involved in various associations that represent their particular interest and constituency.

Schools of public health: Association of Schools of Public Health (ASPH)

Programs/departments of health services policy and administration: Association of University Programs in Health Administration (AUPHA)

Medical schools: Assocation of American Medical Colleges (AAMC)

Nursing: National League of Nursing (NLN)

Pharmacy: American Association of Colleges of Pharmacy (AACP)

Dentistry: American Association of Dental Schools (AADS)

ARE HEALTH CARE ORGANIZATIONS UNIQUE?

Health care organizations are often described as unique or at least different from other types of organizations; in particular, different from industrial organizations. Further, these differences are felt to be significant in the management of health care organizations. Among the most frequently mentioned differences are the following:

1. Defining and measuring output are difficult.
2. The work involved is felt to be more highly variable and complex than in other organizations.
3. More of the work is of an emergency and nondeferrable nature.
4. The work permits little tolerance for ambiguity or error.
5. The work activities are highly interdependent, requiring a high degree of coordination among diverse professional groups.
6. The work involves an extremely high degree of specialization.
7. Organizational participants are highly professionalized, and their primary loyalty belongs to the profession rather than to the organization.
8. There exists little effective organizational or managerial control over the group most responsible for generating work and expenditures: physicians.
9. In many health care organizations, particularly hospitals, there exist dual lines of authority, which create problems of coordination and accountability and confusion of roles.

Upon careful examination, it is possible to refute or at least question each of these allegedly distinctive attributes. For example, universities have equal difficulty in defining and measuring their product. Is it the number of students graduated or the number of credit hours produced? Is quality measured by grade point average? If so, how much of that is the contribution of the student or of the faculty? How do you measure the "value added" of a university education?

A number of other organizations are concerned with highly variable, complex, emergency work, including, for example, police and fire departments. Other organizations also have limited ability to tolerate errors or ambiguities: for example, air traffic controllers. Are work activities any more interdependent in health care than in a symphony orchestra? What about the high degree of specialization of activities in a large legal firm? As for control over professional members, do universities or research institutes have any more control over their faculty or investigators than health care organizations have over hospital-based or hospital-affiliated physicians? Finally, many business and industrial organizations have dual lines of authority. In fact, as discussed in Chapter 9, many firms have institutionalized dual authority structures through matrix organization designs. Further, the concept of uniqueness can be harmful if it leads health care managers to believe that their job is so much more difficult or different from others that relatively little can be done to improve performance.

On the other hand, health care organizations may be unusual if not unique in that many of them possess all of the characteristics stated above *in combination*. It is one thing to have little control over professionals when they do not need to interact frequently with others in the organization, (for example, the situation with a number of research and development units in industry). But it is different when physicians, nurses, and other health professionals are highly dependent on each other in providing and coordinating patient care. The independence of professionals from managerial control is also less of a problem in situations where output is readily defined and measured. It is different when clear performance criteria do not exist and yet external bodies hold the organization responsible for the activities of the relatively independent group of professionals. Thus it is the confluence of professional, technological, and task attributes that make the management of health care organizations particularly challenging. Further, as Hasenfeld and English (29) note, all human service organizations are highly involved with values on a daily basis. For example, cost containment, which is valued by society at large, may frequently conflict with individual client values, such as the desire to recover one's health at almost any cost. In other cases, such as abortion, outcomes valued by different parties may be in conflict. Further, as Friedson notes:

> In the human services of medicine, education, welfare, and law, the aim is not merely to "turn out" a measured product of a given quality at a given cost but to serve human beings in need of help. . . . Responsiveness and recognition, of themselves, may constitute the service and its benefit: without it, the encounter is dead and the service provided to a mere object, albeit not one of fiber, plastic, or metal (30).

A TYPOLOGY OF HEALTH CARE ORGANIZATIONS

A useful way of understanding some of the characteristics of health care organizations is to consider a typology based on a number of important attributes. Table 1.4 presents such a typology for hospitals, ambulatory care group practices, nursing homes, and health departments. These four types of health care organizations are compared along 13 attributes, including their environment, mission and goals, degree of goal congruence, technology, time orientation toward patients, organization structure, degree of professionalism, degree of specialization, degree of task interdependence, concentration of decision making, coordination, reward systems, and the nature of the relationship between managers and physicians.

The typology is intended as a heuristic device to stimulate thinking about differences and similarities between health care organizations and their associated managerial implications. As such, several warnings are in order. First, it is important to recognize that there is substantial variation within hospitals, ambulatory care group practices, nursing homes, and health departments in size, ownership, location, and related factors. These differences are in turn associated with differences in regard to the organizational attributes. Teaching hospitals, for example, are more highly specialized and professionalized than community hospitals. Similarly, a large city health department is likely to have a more diffuse decision-making structure than a small rural county health department. Thus what is presented represents "average" expected characteristics of many hospitals, ambulatory group practices, nursing homes, and health departments.

Second, it is important to note that the four types of organizations are compared *relative to each other*. The descriptions are based largely on judgment and experience, since there has been relatively little systematic research on health care organizations other than hospitals. The descriptions, therefore, are not "correct" in any absolute sense, but rather should be accepted as having some degree of face validity. Certainly, the orderings might be reversed in a number of cases, and readers are encouraged to think of the characteristics in light of personal experience. After reading the remaining chapters of the text, a number of which use examples from a wide range of health care organizations, the reader may want to return to the typology to make possible changes. In brief, the typology serves as a learning exercise.

While Table 1.4 compares the four organizations on all 13 attributes, it is particularly instructive to highlight the following eight criteria: environment, mission and goals, goal congruence, time orientation toward patients, degree of specialization, degree of task interdependence, concentration of decision making, and manager–physician relationships.

ENVIRONMENT

As Table 1.4 indicates, the environment of hospitals is highly complex and dynamic. Health departments and nursing homes also face fairly complex and dynamic environments. Ambulatory care group practices, largely because they are not faced with many external regulations, have somewhat less complex and dynamic environments compared to the other types of organizations. However, this is changing, as competition among physicians and between some physicians and some hospitals grows. At present the demands of the environment may be heaviest for hospital administrators and somewhat less so for managers of the other organizations. Hospitals, therefore, call for a somewhat different set of management structures and processes to deal with the environmental influences and exchange relationships required than do the other kinds of organizations. Some of these are discussed further in Chapter 10.

MISSION AND GOALS

The organization's mission and associated goals are its reason for being. They ordain the major tasks to be carried out and the kinds of technologies and human resources to be

TABLE 1.4. A Typology of Four Health Care Organizations

Attribute	Hospitals	Ambulatory Care Group Practices	Nursing Homes	Health Departments
External environment (complex/dynamic)	Environment highly complex and dynamic; large number of external regulations and high degree of competition	Somewhat less complex environment, but competitive and regulatory factors increasing	Fairly complex environment due to state regulations and third party financing	Complexity limited primarily to wide variety of federal and state funded programs
Missions and goals	Primarily treatment oriented	Primarily individual diagnosis, treatment and prevention-oriented	Maintenance and social supported oriented	Community-wide prevention, diagnosis, and treatment oriented
Goal congruence (similar and well-integrated goals)	Goals not particularly well integrated or congruent	Relatively high degree of goal congruence	High degree of goal congruence centered around maintenance and social support	Somewhat lower degree of goal congruence and integration due to wide range of services typically offered
Technological sophistication	Highly sophisticated	Relatively highly sophisticated depending on specialty composition of the group	Less technologically sophisticated due to social support maintenance function	Technological sophistication depends on type and range of services offered
Time orientation toward patients during a usual encounter	On average, six days	Minutes	Months/years	Hours
Complexity of organization structure; number of hierarchical levels	Highly complex	Typically less complex, although varies by size of practice	Less complex	Moderately high complexity

16

	Highly specialized	Degree of specialization dependent on the number of different specialties in the practice	Least highly specialized	Highly specialized depending on range of programs and services offered
Degree of specialization; percentage of organizational participants in different job classifications	Highly specialized			
Degree of task interdependence; degree to which two or more people or units must work together to accomplish their objectives	High degree of task interdependence	Relatively low interdependence	Moderate interdependence	Task interdependence a function of number of programs or services that must be coordinated
Concentration of organizational decision-making influence; degree to which decisions are typically concentrated in one or a few people or groups versus diffused among many people or groups	Low level of concentration; decision making diffused	Decision making most highly concentrated in the patient's physician	Decision making moderately concentrated	Also low level of concentration; decision making diffused among the various programs
Coordination mechanisms most frequently used	Multiple standards, plans, informal adjustment	Primarily standards and plans	Primarily standards	Multiple but primarily standards and plans
Rewards most frequently used: materialistic, purposive or solidarity[a]	Primarily purposive goal-oriented behavior	Combination of materialistic, purposive, and solidarity	Primarily purposive and solidarity	Primarily purposive and solidarity
Nature of manager–physician relationship	Impersonal; structured	Personal; unstructured	Distant; transitory	Peer to peer

[a]Materialistic rewards involve monetary compensation including fringe benefits; purposive rewards involve recognition for a job "well done" and goal attainment; solidarity rewards involve the satisfaction from being part of a group and benefiting from group interaction. See Clark, P. M. & Wilson, J. Q. "Incentive systems: A theory of organizations." *Administrative Science Quarterly*, 1961, 6, 1290–166.

employed. As shown, the hospital's mission and goals are primarily treatment oriented; ambulatory care group practices combine treatment, prevention, and diagnosis-oriented goals; nursing homes are primarily maintenance and social-support oriented; and health departments are more community prevention, diagnosis, and treatment oriented. Given these fundamental differences, it follows that the kinds of technological and human resources employed will be different and that these will have different managerial implications.

GOAL CONGRUENCE

The organizations also differ in the degree to which their goals are congruent; that is, the degree to which goals are relatively similar and well integrated. In this regard, nursing homes probably have the highest degree of goal congruence, followed by ambulatory care group practices, health departments, and hospitals. The managerial task, particularly in regard to resource allocation and coordination (see Chapter 7), becomes more difficult when the goals of the organization are not well integrated, as is frequently the case with the patient care, teaching, and research activities of hospitals or the activities of health departments, which range from primary and secondary prevention in maternal and child health to direct provision of long-term care for the elderly poor.

TIME ORIENTATION

The four types of organizations also reflect distinctly different time orientations toward patients, ranging from months and years in the case of nursing homes to minutes and hours in the case of ambulatory care group practices. This has implications for the speed with which decisions need to be made (see Chapter 4), the amount and type or organizational resources that are required for providing care, and the way in which the organization socializes people into patient roles.

SPECIALIZATION

Another key dimension along which health care organizations differ is the degree of specialization, which is defined as the number of people holding different occupational positions. Hospitals are the most highly specialized, followed by health departments, ambulatory care group practices, and nursing homes. While specialization has the advantage of concentrating expertise on given problems, it also has disadvantages in that the work of the different specialists needs to be coordinated (see Chapters 6–8).

TASK INTERDEPENDENCE

The degree to which tasks are reciprocally interdependent (two or more persons or units depend on each other for carrying out a work activity) is another key attribute. Where such interdependence is high, as in the case of hospitals and often of health departments, special coordination and control mechanisms may be needed to promote better performance (see Chapters 7, 8, and 12). Where interdependence is somewhat lower, as in the case of ambulatory care group practices and nursing homes, simpler and more direct communication, coordination, and control mechanisms may be used.

DECISION MAKING

The degree to which decision making is concentrated in a few groups or individuals or dispersed throughout the organization is another differentiating attribute. Hospitals, with their multiple coalitions of individuals involving the governing board, administration, medical staff, nursing staff, and others, have the most diffuse organizational decision-making process, although this varies depending on a number of other variables, including, in particular, the leadership and decision-making style of the chief executive officer. Decision making is more concentrated in nursing homes and in ambulatory care organizations in the patient's personal physician. Organizational decision making is also fairly concentrated in health departments, despite the wide variety of programs and services typically offered. The managerial implications of these and other aspects of decision making are discussed further in Chapter 4.

MANAGER–PHYSICIAN RELATIONSHIPS

Finally, it is of interest to consider the nature of manager–physician relationships across the four kinds of organizations. In hospitals the relationship is in general relatively impersonal and highly structured, operating through numerous board, administration, and medical staff committees. At the same time, it is characterized by an assortment of interest groups that often pursue conflicting objectives.

In ambulatory care group practices, on the other hand, the relationship is likely to be much more personal, direct, and informal because of the relatively small size of most groups and the need to take relatively quick corrective acton. In health departments, where for the most part the director's role is filled by a physician, the relationship with other physicians in the community is primarily one of ambiguity and some distrust. In part, this is based on the different perspectives of curative medicine and public health.

The relationship between managers and physicians is probably most difficult to describe in nursing homes, where physicians, for the most part, are not actively involved on a day-to-day basis. This relationship is probably best described as somewhat distant and transitory. These different relationships suggest that there are different ways in which managers and physicians influence each other's behavior. Some of these are discussed further in Chapters 8, 11, and 12.

In sum, it is important to recognize that health care organizations differ in a number of important characteristics that hold implications for the nature of the health care manager's role, as will be discussed in Chapter 2. The discipline of organization theory and behavior provides several useful perspectives for thinking about these differences.

ORGANIZATION THEORY: PAST, PRESENT, AND FUTURE

Everyone has a theory of how organizations function. From personal experience, we create certain mental maps of how organizations operate. Organization theory is based largely on the systematic investigation of the different kinds of mental maps or concepts of how organizations work. The two major approaches involve the closed-system and open-system models. The *closed-system* approach is based on the assumption that the most important features of organizations have to do with their internal structures and processes, which are relatively isolated from the external environment. The *open-system* approach assumes that an organization's behavior is best understood by taking into account its environment and that the organization's structure, process, and performance are centrally influenced by the nature of the inputs taken in from the environment and the outputs produced.

Following Scott (31), these two models may be further divided into rational- and natural-systems approaches. The *rational-system* approach stresses goal-oriented behavior, in which criteria are explicitly measured and the organization is rationally designed to attain measurable goals and objectives. The *natural-system* approach stresses the importance of unplanned, emergent, spontaneous processes and events that occur in settings in which goals cannot be explicitly agreed upon or measured and in which the primary emphasis is on coalitions of individuals concerned with their own growth and development and the basic survival of the organization. The following sections describe some of the major closed- and open-systems models of both the rational and natural perspectives.

CLOSED-SYSTEM MODELS

Rational Approaches

Closed-system models involving rational approaches are best represented by the early works of Taylor (32), Gulick and Urwick (33), and Mooney (34). Together they contributed to the "principles of management" approach to organizations found in many modern textbooks. The focus of these early classical theorists was on span of control, unity of command, appropriate delegation of authority, departmentalization, and work methods. For example, Taylor's emphasis on "scientific management" consisted of (1) programming the job, (2) choosing the right person to match the job, and (3) training the person to do the job. Much of the early work on job design (see Chapter 6) is derived from Taylor's approach. In similar fashion, modern work methods and operations research approaches can be viewed as stemming from the scientific management tradition. These approaches have found increasing acceptance in health care organizations, including the development of nurse staffing models and patient flow admission models.

Weber's (35) theory of bureaucracy is consistent with the closed-system rational model approaches described above. He constructed an "ideal type" based on five characteristics: (1) the organization is guided by explicit, specific procedures for governing activities, (2) activities are distributed among office holders, (3) offices are arranged in a hierarchical authority structure, (4) candidates are selected on the basis of their technical competence, and (5) officials carry out their function in an impersonal fashion. Weber and others alleged that the principal advantage of the bureaucratic form of organization was its technical superiority over other forms. However, Merton (36), Gouldner (37), and Selznick (38) among others, have pointed out the dysfunctional consequences of bureaucracy, including lack of individual freedom, rigidity of behavior, and difficulty with clients. Modern-day theorists have highlighted its limitations in dealing with the environment. Nonetheless, most health care organizations are organized to some degree along bureaucratic lines. The manager's challenge is to decide which organizational components might best be organized along bureaucratic lines and which might best be organized in other ways. Chapters 9–12 examine this issue in detail.

Natural Approaches

Natural-system approaches developed as a reaction against the rational approaches. The early approaches are best described as the "human relations" school of management.

The main emphasis of the human relations school was on the individual. Satisfaction of individual participants in the organization was seen as a worthy goal in itself and not merely as a means of achieving other organizational goals. The human relations school is best represented in the early works of Chester Barnard (39), the Hawthorne Western Electric studies of Roethlisberger and Dixon (40), and the somewhat more recent work of Douglas McGregor (41), Chris Argyris (42), and Rensis Likert (43). The emphasis in all these studies is on the importance of the individual, the usefulness of participatory decision making, which involves the individual in the organization, and the role of intrinsic self-actualizing aspects of work. These writers represent the foundation for much of modern organizational development efforts and individual microlevel approaches to organizational change (see Chapter 11). They also form part of the foundation for the recent interest in Japanese-style management, which emphasizes the integration of individual and organizational goals through the development of a common culture conducive to both (44, 45). The human relations perspective on organizations has also received widespread attention in health care organizations, particularly in recent years as more employees are laid off, unionization efforts increase, nurse turnover rises, and various health professional groups continue to battle over roles and responsibilities. A number of these issues are explored further in Chapters 5, 6, and 8.

OPEN-SYSTEM MODELS

Rational Approaches

Stimulated by the general systems work of von Bertalanffy (46) and the social psychological systems perspective of Katz and Kahn (47), a number of writers in the 1960s developed open-system perspectives on organizations, which focused on the relationship between the organization and its environment, particularly in regard to technology. The most important aspect of the open-system perspective is that it has led to the development of a number of contingency theories of organization suggesting that, contrary to most of the closed-system approaches, there is no one best way to manage. Rather, how the organization is structured depends on the nature of its task, technology, and environmental factors, such as the degree of competition and regulation the organization faces.

Most open-systems theorists focus on the inputs the organization takes in from its environment, the transformation process by which the organization produces its products or services, and the outputs the organization exports back into the environment. The organization is seen as a set of interdependent parts which contribute something to and receive something from the whole which, in turn, is interdependent with larger forces in the organization's environment.

Contingency Theory. Burns and Stalker (48), Woodward (49), Lawrence and Lorsch (50), Thompson (51), and Perrow (52). are among the principal early developers of the contingency tradition, with additional contributions by Khandwalla (53) and Becker and Gordon (54). In general their writings and findings suggest that a more bureaucratic or "mechanistic" form of organization is more effective when the environment is simple and stable, the task and technology are routine, and a relatively high percentage of nonprofessional workers are employed. In contrast, a less bureaucratic, more "organic" form of organization is likely to be more effective when the environment is complex and dynamic, the task and technology are nonroutine, and a relatively high percentage of professionals are involved. The more organic organizational form involves decentralized decision making, more participative decision making, and greater reliance on lateral

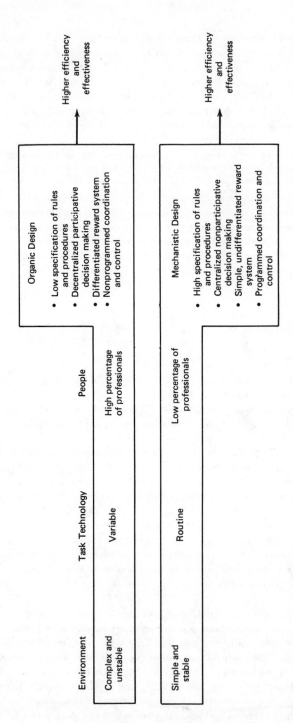

Figure 1.1. Summary of mechanistic and organic design characteristics. (Adapted from Shortell, S. M., The role of environment in a configurational theory of organizations, *Human Relations*, 1977, *30*, 289.)

communication and coordination mechanisms to link people and work units. Some of these distinctions are summarized in Figure 1.1.

Building on these foundations, Hage (55, 56) and Shortell (57) have developed a number of propositions specifically relating various kinds of organizational designs and processes to environmental factors, to each other, and to performance outcomes. The underlying rationale for the differentiation between mechanistic and organic forms is essentially that complex environments and nonroutine technologies make greater demands upon the organization for information, expertise, and flexibility; thus the more organic kinds of designs are better able to respond to these needs. In contrast, where no such demands are being made, there is less need for flexibility and the more traditional bureaucratic approach is likely to be more efficient and effective. Contingency theorists do not advocate an either/or approach but rather view the process as a continuum from more or less bureaucratic (i.e., mechanistic) to more or less organic. Furthermore, it is recognized that different subunits of the organization may be organized differently depending on the specific environments and technologies with which they are involved. It is also important to note that the empirical support for contingency theory ideas is mixed, depending upon whether one is studying the organization as a whole, particular subgroups, or specific individuals (58). Nonetheless, given the differences between and within health care organizations, the open-systems rational contingency models have wide application for health care managers. Additional concepts, ideas, findings, and examples are presented in Chapters 9–12.

Decision-Theory Approach

Consistent with the open-system rational perspective is the work of Simon (59), Cyert and March (60), and Alexis and Wilson (61), who emphasize decision-theory approaches toward organizations. Organizations are viewed as systems of decision-making individuals and units. The key concept is *bounded rationality*, the idea that people as problem-solving organisms can attend to only a small part of the information they receive and the environment in which they function. For this reason, organizations display characteristics such as delegation, decentralization, specialization, and so on. In addition, organizations and the individuals in them often do not have enough information, time, or certainty of consequences to make optimal decisions. As a result, "satisfactory" as opposed to optimal solutions are sought. These satisfactory solutions depend on the ability of the organization and its members to engage in effective search strategies for obtaining information and learning about the environment. These ideas lend still another perspective to the managerial role and the nature of health care organizations. They are discussed further in Chapters 9, 12, and 13.

NATURAL APPROACHES

Resource Dependence/Political Negotiation/Strategic Contingencies

Resource dependence and the related approaches of political negotiation and strategic contingencies focus on successful recruitment of resources from the environment. Key resources represent "strategic contingencies." Not only do organizations negotiate externally for such resources, but organizational members also compete internally for influence and control over the resources. Organizations desire to maintain their autonomy and remain relatively independent of their environment, but at the same time recognize that certain coalitions or networks may be needed to pool resources and reduce transaction costs. Organizations that can procure needed resources over time are more likely to survive and thrive. The resource-dependence perspective, unlike the population-ecology perspective discussed below, assumes that managers can actively influence their environment to reduce unwanted dependencies and enhance survivability. Among the major contributions to this perspective are Hickson et al. (62), March and Olsen (63), Pfeffer and Salancik (64), Williamson (65), Ouchi (66), Tushman and Nadler (67), Provan (68, 69), and Scott and Meyer (70).

Population Ecology

The population ecology model argues that the environment "selects out" certain organizations for survival. Based on theories of natural selection in biology, the focus is on a given population of organizations rather than an individual organization. Whether a given organization will succeed depends on where it stands in relation to the population of its competitors and the overall environmental forces influencing that population. As environmental pressures increase, only the stronger, more dominant organizational forms will survive; the weaker forms will cease to exist or will survive only as markedly different forms of organization. In the population-ecology approach, there are severe limits on the ability of the organization to adapt, involving a high degree of "structural inertia." Thus, in this approach, the ability of managers to successfully influence their environments is minimal. The major contributors to this approach are Hannan and Freeman (71, 72), Aldrich (73), and Carroll (74). Alexander et al. (75), explored the implications for the health care industry.

The population-ecology approach is based on the principles of variation, selection, and retention. Variation involves the continuous development of new organizational forms which add to the variety and complexity in the environment. In health care, examples include freestanding surgery centers, urgent care centers, birthing care centers, diagnostic imagining centers, and fitness centers.

The selection principle states that some of the new organizational forms will fit the external environment better than others. They will be better able to exploit the environment for resources and will move in the same direction that the environmental trends are moving. In health care, ambulatory surgery centers serve as an example given that more surgical procedures are being reimbursed on an outpatient basis and there appears to be a growing trend wherein consumers prefer quicker, more accessible, and convenient services.

Retention involves the preservation and ongoing institutionalization of the new organizational form. Those that are valued by the environment in the long run will be retained while others will fall by the wayside. In health care, ambulatory surgery centers may experience relatively long survival (at least until it becomes more possible to do most surgery in the patient's home), whereas urgent care centers, faced with stiff competition from physician providers, hospital emergency rooms, and growing regulatory requirements, face a less certain future. The winners may be those that manage to carve out specialized market niches where they are seen as complementary to other provider forms of organization and where they can act as noncompeting feeders of patients to other providers.

As health care organizations are faced with increasing cost containment and competitive pressures, the issues raised by the population-ecology perspective become particularly important. In recent years an increasing number of hospitals and health maintenance organizations have "gone out of business" and a variety of new organizational forms have arisen, such as satellite emergency rooms, birthing centers, hospices, occupational health centers, and sports medicine clinics. In addition, the hospital industry has become transformed from a largely cottage industry of individual hospitals to the development of large multiunit hospital systems. These systems, both investor-owned and not-for-profit, are working to find specific niches in the market place, focusing in particular on the development of regionally and locally integrated systems of care. While the population-ecology perspective tends to minimize the manager's role, it adds an important dimension and challenge to the effective management of health care organizations by emphasizing the importance of networking and coalition building and of developing favorable market niches—specific products and services for specific population segments in which the competitive market forces and related pressures are less threatening.

SUMMARY OF MAJOR THEORETICAL APPROACHES

A useful way of summarizing the approaches discussed above is to apply them to fundamental organizational issues. These issues include organizational efficiency, effectiveness, conflict, change or innovation, social integration and motivation, coordination, and maintenance or adaptation to the environment. Table 1.5 summarizes in some detail each theory's general conception of these issues. A few of the more salient differences will be highlighted along with a number of questions for consideration.

EFFICIENCY AND EFFECTIVENESS

In terms of efficiency and effectiveness, positions range from the classical theorists' emphasis on rules, procedures, and job designs; to the human relations emphasis on worker involvement, recognition, and autonomy; to the contingency perspective that elements of both are needed in varying degrees depending primarily on the environment and task technology; to the open natural-system approach's essential rejection of efficiency and effectiveness and focus on basic survival needs. From the health care manager's viewpoint, the following questions are worthy of consideration:

1. How does the importance of efficiency and effectiveness as goals differ for hospitals, health maintenance organizations, nursing homes, and health departments?
2. What hospital departments would be best managed by developing a bureaucratic form of organization and why? What departments would be hampered by a bureaucratic form of organization?
3. How would the development and implementation of a patient scheduling system differ for the inpatient hospital admitting department versus the ambulatory care clinic?
4. It has been said that the specific goals of health care organizations are difficult to define and even more difficult to measure. To the extent that this is true, what implications does it have for the "resource dependence/political negotiation" approach to organizations? What kinds of managerial skills are particularly important with this approach as opposed to the other approaches?

TABLE 1.5. Summary of Theoretical Perspectives on Organizational Issues

| Organizational Issues | Closed System | |
	Rational Approaches	Natural Approaches
	Classical Bureaucratic Theory (Taylor, 1911; Gulick & Urwick, 1937; Weber, 1947; Mooney 1947; Gouldner, 1954)	*The "Human Relations" School* (Barnard, 1938; Roethlisberger & Dickson, 1939; McGregor, 1960; Argyris, 1966; Likert, 1967).
	Classical/Bureaucratic Theory Position	*Human Relations Position*
Efficiency	May be obtained through application of work-study methods and predetermined principles of "good" management. Maximized through a hierarchically ordered chain of positions and specified procedures for operation.	Best brought about by integrating individual aspirations with organizational goals. Involve workers in their job through participatory decision making, job enlargement, job enrichment, etc.
Effectiveness	As above.	In addition to profit, growth, and quality, individual member satisfaction in the organization is viewed as a major goal in its own right.
Conflict	Should be avoided. This can be accomplished by constructing appropriate departmentalization, chains of command, and span of control. Minimize potential for conflict by having a rule or procedure for everything.	Is generally viewed as dysfunctional, but should be managed and confronted openly when it occurs.
Change (innovation)	Handle by means of rational accommodation and intervention, establishment of new rules and procedures.	Must be accommodated through changes in the informal structures of the organization as well as the formal structures.

| | *Open System* | |
| *Rational Approaches* | *Natural Approaches* | |

| (Burns & Stalker, 1961; Woodward, 1965; Lawrence & Lorsch, 1967; Thompson, 1967; Perrow, 1967; Katz & Kahn, 1966; Becker & Gordon, 1966; Hage, 1965, 1980; Khandwalla, 1974; Shortell, 1977; Simon, 1965; Cyert & March, 1963; Alexis & Wilson, 1967) | (Hickman et al., 1971; March & Olson, 1976; Meyer & Rowan, 1977; Pfeffer and Salancik, 1978; Williamson, 1981; Ouchi, 1980; Tushman & Nadler, 1978; Provan, 1983, 1984; Scott & Meyer, 1983) | (Hannan & Freeman, 1977, 1984; Aldrich, 1979; Carroll, 1984; Alexander et al., 1986). |

Contingency/Decision Theory Position	*Resource Dependence/Political Negotiation/Strategic Contingencies*	*Population Ecology*
May be attained in several ways depending on the nature of the tasks involved, the people involved, and external environmental circumstances. Depends on the quality of the decisions made under uncertainty.	Overall objective is not efficiency per se but system survival. As such, political as well as economic transactions become important.	Concern is with the overall survival of a population of organizations and not the efficiency of a given organization. Environmental forces are more important than internal managerial efficiency.
As above; in addition, one way that organizations survive is by expanding or changing their goals to meet new demands from the environment. Emphasis is on goal attainment.	As above. Emphasis is not on goal attainment but on obtaining resources and balancing internal political considerations of those vying for power in order to survive.	Environmental factors largely determine which organizational forms are more or less effective. Effectiveness depends on how well positioned the organization is within the overall population of organizations of interest.
Not necessarily viewed as dysfunctional. Can promote creativity and innovation. The problem is to minimize disruptive conflict. Attending to different goals at different times may be helpful.	Viewed as a natural consequence of internal negotiations over power, given the strategic contingencies the organization faces.	Conflict is accepted as one of the reasons for structural inertia—the inability of individual organizations to successfully adapt to external pressures. Competing interests and aspirations of organizational members make it difficult to initiate significant organizational change.
Can occur either from within or without the organization. Again, depends on nature of tasks, people, and environment. Some evidence to indicate that more loosely structured organizations are more innovative in an "inventive" sense but that more tightly structured organizations may be better at implementing and diffusing the innovation. Ability to change or innovate is also a function of organization learning over time.	Comes about both through external demands and internal political adjustments to those demands. Those who can most influence the type, pace, and direction of change at one point in time may not be most influential at another point in time as the organization's environment changes and its need for different kinds of expertise changes accordingly.	As above. The population ecology approach assumes there are limits to the ability of organizations to change their goals, technology, forms of authority, and market relationships. Small changes may be made but these are not sufficient to resist environmental pressures stemming from overall population dynamics.

27

TABLE 1.5 (Continued)

Organizational Issues	Closed System	
	Rational Approaches	*Natural Approaches*
Social Integration/Motivation	Can be attained through appropriate structural mechanisms (unity of command, span of control, etc.). Little attention given to the individual.	Achieved through the informal system of relationships among workers. Emphasis on nonpecuniary rewards, such as intrinsic job satisfaction and opportunities for personal expression and growth.
Coordination	A primary goal of the organization. May be achieved through appropriate departmentalization, hierarchy, and specification of rules and procedures.	Little attention given to it. Again, emphasis is on the informal work group as a coordinative mechanism.
Maintenance (adaptation to environment)	Essentially not considered.	Essentially not considered.
	Limitations	*Limitations*
	1. Incomplete motivational assumptions.	1. Many of the studies upon which the theory is based have been poorly designed.
	2. Little appreciation of nature or role of conflict.	2. Limited view of human motivation—assumes all individuals want more participation and involvement.
	3. No consideration of the limitations of individuals as information-processing beings.	3. Essentially no consideration of the environment.
	4. Essentially no consideration of the environment in which organizations function.	4. A "one best way" approach.
	5. A "one best way" approach: the "only way" to manage.	

Rational Approaches	*Natural Approaches*	
May be achieved in a variety of ways including both intrinsic and extrinsic factors contributing to job satisfaction. The emphasis is on *role*—getting people to function in their role and understanding each other's roles.	Is achieved through internal accommodation among competing groups that agree to go along with the dominant coalition at the time because it is in their best interest to do so.	Not a key factor. Again, the population ecology approach assumes that social integration is problematic for organizations and is one of the reasons for the organization's inability to deal with population/environmental pressures.
The more specialized the organization and the greater the degree to which tasks are interdependent, the greater the need for coordination. May be achieved through committees and task forces as well as informal organization.	Primary reliance is placed on informal and emergent processes rather than on formal rules, procedures, or committees. Coordination is achieved through negotiation and bargaining.	Not a key factor. As above, it is assumed that organizations have limited ability to develop effective means of coordinating work due to structural inertia and related factors.
Crucial to understanding organizational behavior. The organization must "negotiate" its environment by engaging in search procedures, dealing with uncertainty, and structuring itself to meet the demands of the environment.	Of primary importance. Those in leadership positions must manage the organization's environment as well as the internal structures and processes. Leaders must seek to "enact" their environments in addition to simply "reacting" to them.	As above. Basic thesis is that there are severe limits on the ability to adapt. Managers can do relatively little to successfully influence the environment.

Limitations	*Limitations*	*Limitations*
A conceptually sound approach for the study of organizations; but requires much more research to replicate some of the early findings and define further the nature of the interaction between an organization and its environment. Problem of measuring the environment; perceptual versus nonperceptual measures.	There has been little empirical study to date of the open natural systems approach. The approach may also be somewhat of an overreaction to the rational contingency approaches. A middle ground would suggest that organizations survive in the long run through some degree of goal attainment in which certain kinds of organization designs and processes provide a structural framework for channeling internal political negotiations. In brief, some degree of goal attainment would appear necessary in order for the organization to maintain sufficient credibility to continue to attract needed resources.	1. May somewhat overstate the importance of environmental and population pressures. 2. Tends to ignore the ability of individual organizations to influence organization populations in the larger environment through networking, coalition building, and other macro political strategies. 3. Relatively little empirical work to date and existing findings may be largely a function of the industries studied (e.g., newspapers). 4. More attention has been paid to organizational deaths than births. In health care, the factors behind the proliferation of new organizational forms deserve particular attention.

CONFLICT AND CHANGE

In regard to conflict and change, the approaches vary from denial and/or attempts to handle conflict through established rules and regulations to active encouragement and management of conflict and change through internal contingency adjustments or political negotiation and accommodation. The population-ecology perspective highlights the inability of organizations to adequately deal with conflict and change issues. The following questions deserve consideration:

1. What factors might influence the degree to which change focuses on individuals versus changes in organizational structure?
2. In what way might the increasing introduction of computers and sophisticated management information systems into health care organizations alter the concept of 'bounded rationality'? How might it specifically affect the manager's role (see Chapter 2)?
3. In general, would teaching hospitals find it more difficult than community hospitals to develop a preferred provider organization? Why or why not?
4. It has been suggested that the relatively organic organization structure may be best for the generation and initial adoption of new ideas but that more bureaucratic mechanistic structures are needed for ongoing effective implementation. Do you agree or disagree with this statement and why? What other factors might influence this relationship? Do you believe it is equally true for introducing change into hospital settings and into nursing home settings?

SOCIAL INTEGRATION AND MOTIVATION AND COORDINATION

The different schools also take different positions on issues of social integration and motivation and coordination. The classicists place emphasis on structural mechanisms; the human relations school on informal systems; the contingency theorists view each as dependent upon the nature of environmental demands, the degree of task uncertainty, and the kinds of people involved; and the resource dependence/political negotiation proponents stress the informal and emergent processes but link them directly to the opportunities, problems, and constraints faced by the organization. Population ecologists tacitly assume that these are part of the problem of structural inertia. Relevant questions for consideration include:

1. Which of the above views on social integration and coordination best fits hospitals, ambulatory care group practices, nursing homes, and health departments. Why?
2. Which of the above approaches would you find most useful as the manager of a new HMO? As the chief executive officer of a long-established community hospital? As the director of a health department faced with significant cutbacks in programs and services as a result of changes in Medicaid financing?
3. Which approach or approaches would give you the most insight in trying to establish more cooperative and collaborative work relationships between nurses and physicians?
4. Suppose you are putting together an executive management team for a 300,000 member HMO. Which approach to achieving coordination and social integration would provide you with the most insight? Why?

ORGANIZATIONAL MAINTENANCE AND ADAPTATION

Finally, each of the approaches takes a different view on organizational maintenance and adaptation to the environment. The classicist and human relation schools, which are essentially closed-system approaches, have little to say about this issue. The contingency theorists argue that organic approaches are more appropriate when the environment is complex and unstable, whereas mechanistic structures are more appropriate where the environment is routine and stable. The resource dependence/political negotiations approach notes the rational adaptation perspective described above but also stresses the importance of organizations actively manipulating their environments on the one hand and, on the other, despite these attempts being actively selected out by environmental conditions. In contrast, the population-ecology approach argues that there are limits to such attempts and that organizations end up being "selected out" by environmental forces. Relevant questions for consideration include:

1. Hospitals are increasingly becoming a part of multiunit hospital systems. How would the resource dependence and population approaches account for the growth in multiunit systems? In what ways would their explanations differ?

2. In recent years, pharmaceutical companies (e.g., Monsanto and Searle) and hospital supply companies (e.g., Baxter-Travenol and American Hospital Supply Corporation) have merged. What do you think are the main factors behind these mergers and which of the theoretical approaches or combination of approaches best explain such merger activity?

3. Not-for-profit hospitals, both freestanding and those belonging to systems, have increasingly turned to affiliations and coalition arrangements to better meet their needs. Examples include the Voluntary Hospitals of America (VHA) for the freestanding institutions and American Healthcare Systems (AHS) for those belonging to systems. What are the main factors behind such arrangements and which of the approaches discussed above or combination of approaches provide the most insight into these relationships?

4. Do either of the open systems approaches—rational or natural—provide an explanation for the increased vertical integration of health care organizations (for example, hospital–ambulatory care center linkages or hospital–nursing home linkages)? If so, what is the nature of the explanation?

ORGANIZATION THEORY AND BEHAVIOR: A FRAMEWORK FOR THE TEXT

As indicated in the preface, this text takes an open systems perspective—that the nature of the managerial role is to motivate and manage people and groups to carry out technical tasks for the attainment of organizational goals and at the same time to renew the organization for long-run survival and growth and chart the organization's future. These dimensions of the managerial challenge are outlined in Figure 1.2, which provides a basic framework for the book.

The book is divided into five sections. The first is an introductory section that provides

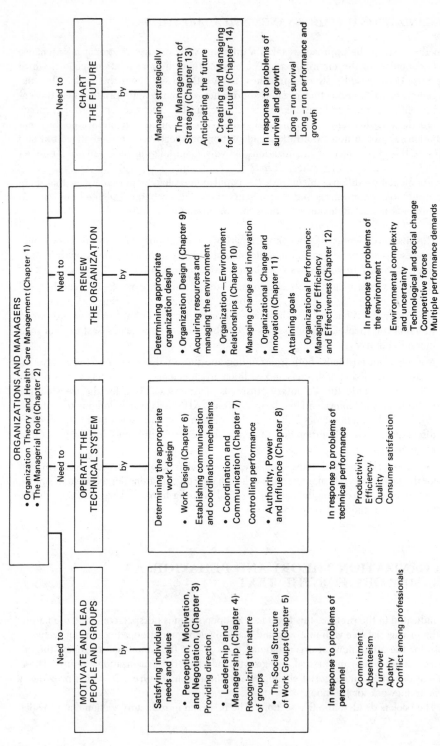

ORGANIZATIONS AND MANAGERS
• Organization Theory and Health Care Management (Chapter 1)
• The Managerial Role (Chapter 2)

Need to

MOTIVATE AND LEAD PEOPLE AND GROUPS

by

Satisfying individual needs and values
• Perception, Motivation, and Negotiation, (Chapter 3)
Providing direction
• Leadership and Managership (Chapter 4)
Recognizing the nature of groups
• The Social Structure of Work Groups (Chapter 5)

In response to problems of personnel

Commitment
Absenteeism
Turnover
Apathy
Conflict among professionals

Need to

OPERATE THE TECHNICAL SYSTEM

by

Determining the appropriate work design
• Work Design (Chapter 6)
Establishing communication and coordination mechanisms
• Coordination and Communication (Chapter 7)
Controlling performance
• Authority, Power and Influence (Chapter 8)

In response to problems of technical performance

Productivity
Efficiency
Quality
Consumer satisfaction

Need to

RENEW THE ORGANIZATION

by

Determining appropriate organization design
• Organization Design (Chapter 9)
Acquiring resources and managing the environment
• Organization—Environment Relationships (Chapter 10)
Managing change and innovation
• Organizational Change and Innovation (Chapter 11)
Attaining goals
• Organizational Performance: Managing for Efficiency and Effectiveness (Chapter 12)

In response to problems of the environment

Environmental complexity and uncertainty
Technological and social change
Competitive forces
Multiple performance demands

Need to

CHART THE FUTURE

by

Managing strategically
• The Management of Strategy (Chapter 13)
Anticipating the future
• Creating and Managing for the Future (Chapter 14)

In response to problems of survival and growth

Long – run survival
Long – run performance and growth

Figure 1.2. The nature of organizations: Framework for the text.

32

an overview of health care organizations (Chapter 1, Organization Theory and Health Care Management) and an analysis of the role of management in these organizations (Chapter 2, The Managerial Role). This is followed by four sections corresponding to the managerial activities of motivating people and groups, operating the technical system, renewing the organization, and charting the future.

Managers must motivate people in response to personnel problems of commitment, absenteeism, turnover, apathy, and conflict. This is accomplished by satisfying individual needs and values (Chapter 3, Perception, Motivation, and Negotiation), by providing direction (Chapter 4, Leadership and Managership), and by recognizing the nature of work groups within organizations (Chapter 5, The Social Structure of Work Groups).

Managers must operate the technical system in response to problems of technical performance involving productivity, efficiency, quality, and satisfaction. This is accomplished by determining the appropriate work design (Chapter 6, Work Design), establishing communication and coordination mechanisms (Chapter 7, Coordination and Communication), and by controlling performance (Chapter 8, Authority, Power, and Influence).

Organizations operate within a constantly changing environment and managers must renew the organization by determining appropriate organizational design (Chapter 9, Organization Design), by assessing and managing the environment (Chapter 10), by acquiring resources and managing change and innovation (Chapter 11), and by attaining organizational goals (Chapter 12, Organizational Performance: Managing for Efficiency and Effectiveness).

Finally, organizations function through time and managers must be responsive to problems of long-term survival and growth of the organization. This is accomplished by managing strategically (Chapter 13) and anticipating the future (Chapter 14). The framework presented in Figure 1.2 is intended as a departure point, not a point of closure, for the reader's own synthesis of the material that follows.

DISCUSSION QUESTIONS

1. Select two health care organizations other than a hospital, ambulatory care group practice, nursing home, or health department and compare them along the following dimensions: environment, mission and goals, goal congruence, time orientation, specialization, task interdependence, decision making, and manager–physician relationships.
2. What would be the advantages and disadvantages of organizing and managing a group-model HMO along an open systems rational approach?
3. State one characteristic of health care organizations that is of particular interest to you (e.g., high percentage of professionals involved). Discuss this characteristic from the perspective of at least two approaches examined in this chapter.
4. Do you agree or disagree with the following statement? "For the most part, health care organizations are no different from most other organizations." Indicate the specific reasons for your agreement or disagreement and develop at least two reasons in addition to those presented in the chapter.

SUGGESTED READINGS

Cummings, L. L., & Dunham, R. B. *Introduction to organizational behavior: Text and readings.* Homewood, Ill.: Richard D. Irwin, 1980.
Provides an excellent set of readings on the correlates, determinants, and consequences of behavior in organizations. Many of the readings are classics. Provides a psychological and social-psychological perspective to complement the more sociological approach of Scott's book, noted below. Particularly useful for students with little background in organization theory and behavior.

Daft, R. L. *Organization Theory and Design* (2nd ed.). St. Paul, Minn: West Publishing, 1986.
A very good introduction to macro issues of organization design, change, innovation, and organization–environment relationships. Many good examples and case illustrations.

Griffin, R. W., & Moorehead, G. *Organization Behavior.* Boston: Houghton Mifflin Company, 1986.
Well documented current text which provides excellent coverage of basic organization behavior issues. Good complement to the Cummings and Dunham reader noted above.

Scott, W. R. *Organizations: Rational, natural and open systems* (2nd ed.). Englewood Cliffs, N.J.: Prentice-Hall, 1987.
Provides an excellent elaboration and synthesis of the major approaches to organizational analysis described in Chapter 1. Students with little or no previous coursework in organization theory or behavior would be well-advised to read many of the chapters in this text.

REFERENCES

1. U.S. Department of Health and Human Services, Health Care Financing Administration. *Health care financing review,* Washington, D.C., Spring, 1986, 7, 2.

2. U.S. Department of Health and Human Services, Public Health Service. *Health United States, 1981.*

3. Shortell, S. M. Organization of health services. *Courses by newspaper.* San Diego: University of California Press, March, 1981.

4. Bowers, D., Franklin, J., & Tecorella, P. A. *Taxonomy of intervention: The science of organization development (Technical report).* Ann Arbor: University of Michigan, Center for Research on the Utilization of Scientific Knowledge, May, 1973, p. 2.

5. Dowling, W. L. The hospital. In S. J. Williams & P. R. Torrens (Eds.), *Introduction to health services* (3rd ed.). New York: John Wiley & Sons, 1988.

6. Kane, R. L., & Kane, R. The nursing home: Neither home nor hospital. In S. J. Williams & P. R. Torrens (Eds.), *Introduction to health services* (3rd ed.). New York: John Wiley & Sons, 1988.

7. Anderson, O. W., Herold, T. E., Butler, B. W., Kohrman, C. H., & Morrison, E. M. *HMO development: Patterns and prospects.* Chicago: Pluribus Press, 1986.

8. Torrens, P. R. (Ed.) *Hospice programs and public policy.* Chicago: American Hospital Publications, Inc., 1985.

9. Scott, W. R. & Black, B. L. (Eds.) *The organization of mental health services: Societal and community systems.* Beverly Hills: Sage Focus Editions, January, 1986.

10. Shonick, W. Public health services: Background and present status. In S. J. Williams & P. R. Torrens (Eds.) *Introduction to health services* (2nd ed.). New York: John Wiley and Sons, 1984.

11. Ginsberg, E., Davis, E., & Ostow, M. *Local health policy in action: The municipal health services program.* Totowa, N.J.: Bowman and Allaheld, 1985.

12. Shortell, S. M., Wickizer, T. M., & Wheeler, J. R. C. Jr. *Hospital–physician joint ventures: Results and lessons from a national demonstration in primary care.* Ann Arbor: Health Administration Press, 1984.

13. Georgopoulos, B. *Organization structure, problem solving and effectiveness: A comparative study of hospital emergency services.* San Francisco: Jossey-Bass, 1986.

14. American Hospital Association. *Hospital statistics.* Chicago: American Hospital Association, 1985.

15. American Hospital Association. *Directory of multihospital systems.* Chicago: American Hospital Association, 1985, Table 1, pp. 4–7.

16. National Center for Health Statistics. A. Scirrocco: An Overview of the 1982 Master Facility Inventory Survey of Nursing and Related Care Homes. Advance Data from Vital and Health Statistics. No. III. DHHS Pub. No. (PHS)85-1250. Hyattsville, Md.: Public Health Service, Sept. 20, 1985.

17. *Medical groups in the U.S. 1984.* Chicago: American Medical Association, Survey and Data Resources Division, 1985.

18. *HMO survey,* Excelsior, MN: Interstudy, June 1985.

19. *Public health agencies 1982: Volume 1, expenditures and sources of funds,* Association of State and Territorial Health Officials, June 1984.

20. *Report.* Washington, D.C.: National Association for Home Care, January 3, 1986.

21. *The 1984 guide to the nation's hospices.* Washington, D.C.: National Hospice Organization, 1984.

22. Lurie, A., & L. Shulman. The professional connection with self-help groups in health care setting. *Social Work in Health Care,* 1983, *8,* 69–70.

23. Simpson, J. B. State certificate-of-need programs: The current status. *American Journal of Public Health,* 1985, *75*(10) 1225–1229.

24. Dans, P. E., Weiner, J. P., & Otter, S. E. Peer review organizations: Promise and potential pitfalls. *New England Journal of Medicine,* 1985, *313*(18), 1131–1137.

25. Health Insurance Association of America. *Source book of health insurance data, 1984–1985.* Washington, D.C.: Health Insurance Association of America, 1985.

26. Tames, S. Physician unions for a changing market. *Medicine and health.* Washington, D.C.: McGraw Hill, (February 24, 1986.)

27. Bureau of Census. *Statistical Abstracts of the United States: 1986* (106th ed.). Washington, D.C.: 1986.

28. Pharmaceutical Manufactures Association. *PMA annual survey report, 1983–85.* Washington, D.C.: 1986.

29. Hasenfeld, Y., & English, R. A. Human service organizations: Conceptual overview. In Y. Hasenfeld & R. English (Eds.), *Human service organizations.* Ann Arbor: University of Michigan Press, 1977.

30. Friedson, E. *Doctoring together: A study of professional social control.* New York: Elsevier, 1975.

31. Scott, W. R. Developments in organization theory, 1960–1980. *American Behavioral Scientist*, 1981, *24*, 407–422.

32. Taylor, F. *Scientific management.* New York: Harper & Row, 1947.

33. Gulick, L., & Urwick, L. *Papers on science of administration.* New York: Columbia University Press, 1937.

34. Mooney, J. E. *Principles of organization.* New York: Harper and Row, 1947.

35. Weber, M. *The theory of social and economic organization.* Glencoe, Ill.: Free Press, 1964.

36. Merton, R. K. Bureaucratic structure and personality. In *Social theory and social structure.* New York: Free Press, 1957.

37. Gouldner, A. *Patterns of industrial bureaucracy.* New York: Free Press, 1954.

38. Selznick, P. *TVA and the grass roots.* New York: Harper & Row, 1966.

39. Barnard, C. I. *The functions of the executive.* Cambridge, Mass.: Harvard University Press, 1938.

40. Roethlisberger, F. J. & Dickson, W. J. *Management and the worker.* Cambridge, Mass.: Harvard University Press, 1939.

41. McGregor, D. *The human side of enterprise.* New York: McGraw-Hill, 1960.

42. Argyris, C. *Integrating the individual and the organization.* New York: John Wiley & Sons, 1964.

43. Likert, R. *The human organization.* New York: McGraw-Hill, 1967.

44. Ouchi, W. *Theory Z, how American business can meet the Japanese Challenge.* Reading, Mass.: Addison-Wesley, 1981.

45. Pascale, R. T., & Athos, A. G. *The art of Japanese management: Applications for American executives.* New York: Simon & Schuster, 1981.

46. von Bertalanffy, L. General system theory: A critical review. In J. Litterer (Ed.), *Organizations*, Vol. 2. New York: John Wiley & Sons, 1969.

47. Katz, E., & Kahn, R. *The social psychology of organizations.* New York: John Wiley & Sons, 1966.

48. Burns, T., & Stalker, G. M. *The management of innovation.* London: Tavistock, 1961.

49. Woodward, J. *Technology and organizational behavior.* Oxford, England: Oxford University Press, 1970.

50. Lawrence, P., & Lorsch, J. *Organization and environment.* Cambridge, Mass.: Harvard University Press, 1967.

51. Thompson, J. D. *Organizations in action.* New York: McGraw-Hill, 1967.

52. Perrow, C. A framework for the comparative analysis of organizations. *American Sociological Review*, 1967, *32*, 194–208.

53. Khandwalla, P. M. Mass output orientation of operations technology and organizational structure. *Administrative Science Quarterly*, 1974, *19*, 74–97.

54. Becker, S. W., & Gordon, G. An entrepreneurial theory of formal organizations. *Administrative Science Quarterly*, 1966, *11*, 315–344.

55. Hage, J. An axiomatic theory of organizations. *Administrative Science Quarterly*, 1965, *10*, 289–320.

56. Hage, J. *Theories of organizations: Form, process, and transformation.* New York: John Wiley-Interscience, 1980.

57. Shortell, S. M. The role of environment in a configurational theory of organizations. *Human Relations,* 1977, *30,* 275–302.

58. Mohr, L. B. *Explaining organizational behavior.* San Francisco: Jossey-Bass, 1982.

59. Simon, H. *Administrative behavior* (2nd ed.). New York: Free Press, 1965.

60. Cyert, R., & March, J. *A behavorial theory of the firm.* Englewood Cliffs, N.J.: Prentice-Hall, 1963.

61. Alexis, M., & Wilson, C. *Organizational decision-making.* Englewood Cliffs, N.J.: Prentice-Hall, 1967.

62. Hickson, D. J., et al. A strategic contingencies theory of intra-organizational power. *Administrative Science Quarterly.* 1971, *16,* 216–229.

63. March, J. G., & Olsen, J. P. *Ambiguity and choice in organizations.* Bergen, Norway: Universitetsforlaget, 1976.

64. Pfeffer, J., & Salancik, G. R. *The external control of organizations.* New York: Harper & Row, 1978.

65. Williamson, O. E. The economics of organization: The transaction cost approach. *American Journal of Sociology,* 1981, *87,* 548–577.

66. Ouchi, W. G. Markets, bureaucracies, and clans. *Administrative Science Quarterly,* 1980, *24,* 129–141.

67. Tushman, M., & Nadler, D. Information processing as an integrating concept in organizational design. *Academy of Management Review,* 1978, *3,* 613–624.

68. Provan, K. G. The federation as an interorganizational linkage network. *Academy of Management Review,* 1983, *8,* 78–89.

69. Provan, K. G. Interorganizational cooperation and decision-making autonomy in a consortium multihospital system. *Academy of Management Review,* 1984, *9,* 494–504.

70. Scott, W. R., & J. W. Meyer, The organization of societal sectors. In J. W. Meyer, and W. R. Scott (Eds.), *Organizational environments.* Beverly Hills: Sage Publications, 1983.

71. Hannan, M. T., & Freeman, J. H. The population ecology of organizations. *American Journal of Sociology,* 1977, *82,* 929–964.

72. Hannan, M., & Freeman, J. H. Structural inertia and organizational change. *American Sociological Review,* (April 1984,) *492,* 149–64.

73. Aldrich, H., *Organization and environments.* Englewood Cliffs, N.J.: Princeton Hills, 1979.

74. Carroll, G. Organizational ecology. *Annual Review of Sociology,* 1984, *10,* 71–93.

75. Alexander, J. A., Kaluzny, A. D., & Middleton, S. Organizational growth, survival and death in the U.S. health care industry: A population ecology perspective. *Social Science and Medicine,* 1986, *22* (3), 202–308.

CHAPTER 2

The Managerial Role

Fred C. Munson
Howard S. Zuckerman

The features of the health care industry described in the opening chapter offer health care managers an array of challenging opportunities. Because of the industry's size and growth, opportunities for mobility and for rapid increase in responsibility are great. Because of the diffuse and shifting distribution of power some managers may continually complain of a lack of authority. However, self-confident managers with strong interpersonal skills may see it as an opportunity to build relationships based on respect and trust, rather than on formal authority. David Everhart, Chief Executive Officer of Northwestern Memorial Hospital, responded to a question concerning the always difficult problem of administrator relations with medical staff by describing his role as that of a respected consultant, and urged that new health managers develop their own relations with physicians with this basic assumption of mutual dependence in mind (1). Because of their vital social role, the managers of health care organizations have a social trust to honor as well as a business to operate. Walter McNerney, documenting his view that "precious few in the health field seem to have a clear and reasonably uncommitted view of what improves morbidity and mortality" went on to say that

> The implications for the hospital are clear. Unless it puts medicine in a broader perspective, geared less to the technical and more to the humanistic and holistic, it will be subordinated to a larger idea and a different organizational framework. The administrator who responds to those ideas will at times be pitted against entrenched clinical interests; the administrator who does not may be guilty of administrative malpractice. (2)

These views highlight the managerial challenge in health services. It is an industry with considerable internal complexity and with significant power and influence exerted by the professionals who produce its services. It stands high on a scale of social importance, creating on the one hand a socially meaningful role for managers but on the other, a strong pressure to achieve social ends through external regulation. And to complicate the picture still further, it is constantly changing.

How can such organizations be managed effectively? We summarize the major approaches below and then describe two answers to this question that assume there is one best way to manage all organizations. Two studies of what managers actually do are then reviewed, which challenge these universalist answers to the question of how to manage effectively. We then describe an organizational conception of the managerial role and review seven role studies of health managers that make use of this more complex answer to the question of what managers actually do. Finally we describe a personal/political conception of management that is not fully captured in either the universalist or organizational models, and conclude by highlighting important issues facing health managers today.

THREE MANAGERIAL ROLE CONCEPTIONS

The literature on management is rich beyond measure. Much of the early writings viewed management as a set of skills or activities that applied universally to all organizations. Barnard caught this view nicely:

> A university president tells me that his principal organization difficulty is the "following, which, of course, is peculiar to universities." He then describes a problem I have encountered a hundred times, but never in a university. (3)

This is a *universalist* conception of management, a well-known and widely accepted managerial model. It contains two distinct schools, the traditional and the human relations models of management. Though at present neither of these models is popular, much wisdom and much of importance is contained in them, as is evidenced by the continuous flow of articles and books that reclothe their core truths in new words and phrases.

A continuing problem of universalist conceptions is that, by necessity, they deemphasize differences in managerial roles. Among important differences are those that exist in managerial roles at different levels in the organization, in organizations of different size, and in organizations in different environments, both cultural and economic/political ones. The most important of these differences can be accounted for by recognizing differences in the organizations that managers operate. The last two decades, which have seen significant growth in our understanding of organizations, have also seen a growing emphasis on an *organizational* conception of the managerial role.

This conception is not the opposite of the universalist conception. Rather, it emphasizes that organizations create role demands for the manager. These demands will not be identical between large organizations and small ones, young organizations and old ones, or protected organizations and unprotected ones. Among the important differences between organizations are those arising from the use of different work processes, or technologies, and those arising from different environments. For example, Woodward's (4) path-breaking work associated span of control with type of technology employed, and Burns and Stalker's (5) research showed an association of management style with stability in the organization's environment.

A third conception of the managerial role is a *personal/political* one. It is not the opposite of either the universalist or organizational view; it simply emphasizes the centrality of power and personal tactics in understanding the manager's role. The modern version we will call the "managerial strategist." It draws heavily on advances in our understanding of organizations and their environments. James Thompson, one of the few who stand with Barnard in breadth of vision and contribution to our understanding of management, highlights an aspect of this view:

> The "pyramid" headed by the single all-powerful individual has become a symbol of complex organizations, but through historical and misleading accident. The all-powerful chief can maintain such control only to the extent that he is not dependent on others within his organization; and this is a situation of *modest complexity*, not one of a high degree of complexity. (6)

A more common form of the political model is the "heroic manager." It has a much longer history, and it draws not on the organization but the individual in accounting for power. Such names as Winston Churchill, George Washington, and Napoleon Bonaparte, come to mind; it was clearly this conception that Machiavelli had in mind when instructing the prince. Self-help books, from *Horatio Alger* to *Up the Organization Ladder* (7), and discussions of type A personalities (8) all reflect this idea that individuals do make a difference.

These three conceptions are all true in the sense that each captures an important reality about the manager's role. They are also useful, for each draws attention to a body of knowledge or associated tactics that is relevant to managerial action. An understanding of the managerial role is furthered by emphasizing what the different schools have contributed, rather than by quarreling about what each has left out.

THE UNIVERSALIST CONCEPTION

MINI-CASE: AN UNTRADITIONAL PERSON USING A TRADITIONAL MANAGERIAL MODEL

No question about it—some managers are better organized than others, but how often have you run into a really well organized manager—I mean *really* organized? MacGregor, who at the time was manager of one of the largest refineries in the country, was the last of more than 100 managers I had interviewed in the course of a study I was doing on participative management. When I called to schedule the interview, he answered himself and told me to come anytime except Thursday between 10:00 A.M. and noon. I took MacGregor at his word and drove over immediately. His secretary—who, when I arrived, was knitting busily,—greeted me and nodded me into his office without dropping a stitch. MacGregor was standing by the window peering absently into space. He turned slowly when I entered his office and said, "You must be Carlisle. The head office told me you wanted to talk to me about the way we run things here. Sit down on the sofa and fire away."

"Do you hold regular meetings with your subordinates?" I asked.

"Yes, I do," he replied.

"How often?" I asked.

"Once a week, on Thursdays between 10:00 A.M. and noon; that's why I couldn't see you then," was his response.

"What sorts of things do you discuss?" I queried, following my interview guide.

"My subordinates tell me about the decisions they've made during the past week," he explained.

"Then you believe in participative decision making," I commented.

"No—as a matter of fact, I don't," said MacGregor.

"Then why hold the meetings?" I asked. "Why not just tell your people about the operating decisions you've made and let them know how to carry them out?"

"Oh, I don't make their decisions for them and I just don't believe in participating in the decisions they should be making, either; we hold the weekly meeting so that I can keep informed on what they're doing and how. The meeting also gives me a chance to appraise their technical and managerial abilities." Skeptical, I arranged to speak with Johnson, one of MacGregor's eight subordinate managers. All of them were chemical engineers.

I walked over to Johnson's unit and found him to be in his early thirties. "I suppose MacGregor gave you that bit about his not making decisions, didn't he? That man is a gas."

"It isn't true though, is it? He does make decisions, doesn't he?" I asked.

"No, he doesn't; everything he told you is true."

Then I asked Johnson whether he ever tried to get MacGregor to make a decision and his response was:

"Only once. I had been on the job for about a week when I ran into an operating problem I couldn't solve, so I phoned MacGregor. His response was instantaneous: 'Good, that's what you're being paid to do, solve problems,' and then he hung up. But I didn't really know any of the people I was working with, so because I didn't think I had any other alternative, I called him back. When I insisted on seeing him about my problem, he answered, 'I don't know how you expect me to help you. Ask one of the other men. They're all in touch with what goes on out there.' I didn't know which one to consult, so I insisted again on seeing him. He finally agreed—grudgingly—to see me right away.

"He asked me to state precisely what the problem was and he wrote down exactly what I said. Then he asked what the conditions for its solution were. I stumbled through the conditions that would have to be satisfied by the solution. Then he asked me what alternative approaches I could think of. I gave him the first one I could think of and then several others; he wrote each one down as I gave it and asked me what would happen if I did that. Then he asked me if my answer met the conditions I had specified. None did, though the outcome of the last alternative I had given came close. MacGregor then asked me if I could combine any of the approaches I'd suggested. I replied I could use the first and fourth alternatives, and then saw that the resultants would indeed satisfy all the solution cconditions I had set up previously. When I thanked MacGregor, he replied, 'What for? Get the hell out of my office; you could have done that bit of problem solving perfectly well without wasting my time. Next time you really can't solve a problem on your own, ask the Thursday man and tell me about it at the Thursday meeting.' "

I asked Johnson about Mr. MacGregor's reference to the Thursday man.

"He's the guy who runs the Thursday meeting when MacGregor is away from the plant. I'm the Thursday man now. My predecessor left here about two months ago."

"Where did he go? Did he quit the company?" I asked.

"God, no. He got a refinery of his own. That's what happens to a lot of Thursday men."

After speaking with another subordinate and getting much the same story, I went down to the head office and visited the operations chief for the corporation. When I told him I had met MacGregor, his immediate response was, "Isn't he a gas?" I muttered something about having heard that comment before and asked him about the efficiency of MacGregor's operation. He said, "Oh, MacGregor has by far the most efficient producing unit."

"Is that because he has the newest equipment?" I asked.

"No. As a matter of fact he has the oldest in the corporation. His was the first refinery we built."

I went back to the refinery with a few last questions for MacGregor. His secretary had made considerable progress on her knitting and her boss had resumed his position by the refinery window.

"I understand you were downtown. What did they tell you about this place?"

"You know damn well what they said—that you have the most efficient operation in the corporation."

"Yup, it's true," he replied, with no pretense of false modesty.

"I understand you have quite a control system here. How does it work?" I asked.

"Very simply," said MacGregor. "On Wednesdays at 2:00 P.M., my subordinates and I get the printout from the computer, which shows the production men their output against quota and the maintenance superintendent his costs to date against the budget. If there is an unfavorable gap between the two, they call me about 3:00 P.M. and the conversation goes something like this: 'Mr. MacGregor, I know I have a problem and this is what I'm going to do about it.' If their solution will work, I tell them to go ahead. If not, I tell them so and then they go and work on it some more and then call back. When I came here, I worked out a computer-based production control system in conjunction with a set of quotas I negotiate each year with each of my operating people and a cost budget with the maintenance man. Then I arranged for Wednesday reports. Sometimes it takes a bit of time to renegotiate these quotas—and I've been known to use peer pressure to get them to a reasonable level—but these performance objectives really have to be accepted by the individual before they have any legitimacy or motivational value for him.

"I do a lot of reading related to my work. That's why, when they call me with proposed solutions, I can usually tell accurately whether or not their proposals are going to work out. That's my job as I see it—not doing subordinates' work but, rather, exercising supervision."

"Is there anything else you do?" I asked.

"Well, I look after community relations. One more thing—I work on these." He stepped over to the engineer's file cabinet in the corner of his office. "In here are manning and equipment tables for this plant at five levels of production—at one-year, two-year, five-year, and ten-year intervals. That's what I see as being an upper-level manager's job. These sorts of decisions are way in the future and are terribly difficult and expensive to reverse once they are embarked on. I plan, listen to Wednesday reports and Thursday decisions, and play golf."

"Do your subordinates help you make these planning decisions?" I asked.

"No," said MacGregor. "They gather some of the information and I show them how I go about making up the plans. They all know how to do it after they've been here a couple of years. The actual decisions, though, are made by me. If they are wrong, I have to take the blame—and if they are right," he said with a smile, "I take the credit. Now, I have a most important golf game scheduled. If you have any further questions, just come in any time except Thursday between 10:00 A.M. and noon. I don't have much to do except to talk to visitors."*

---

*Adapted, by permission of the publisher, from "MacGregor," by Arthur Elliot Carlisle, *Organizational Dynamics,* Summer 1976, pp. 51–58, © 1976 American Management Association, New York. All rights reserved.

THE TRADITIONAL MODEL

The standard conception of the role of management can be described by the acronym PODC. The letters stand for Plan, Organize, Direct, and Control.

1. *Planning* is determining the mission of the enterprise, its programs and objectives, and working out methods and procedures to accomplish the purpose of the enterprise.
2. *Organizing* is the establishment of a formal structure of authority and division of labor through which administrative subunits are defined and coordinated to carry out the plans.
3. *Directing* is the continuous task of leadership and supervision in the guidance and instruction of personnel toward organizational objectives.
4. *Controlling* is ensuring that operating results conform to planned results. This involves the establishment of standards, comparison of actual results against the standard, and corrective action when performance deviates from the plan.

These management functions, which Henri Fayol first described, can be divided differently, with some splitting Organizing into Organizing and Staffing (POSDC), or with further refinements into POSDCORB (Planning, Organizing, Staffing, Directing, Coordinating, Reporting and Budgeting). Whatever the division, the traditional model assumes that these basic management activities will be performed in any organization, and that they represent the key contribution of management. Indeed, the pure form of the model asserts that these activities *are* the definition of management. Newman, for example, noting that administrators do other things as well, states that "strictly speaking, the performance of nondelegated duties such as meeting customers is not a part of administration . . . " and concludes that they need not be emphasized in a book on administrative action (9).

A notable quality of the traditional model is that it permits formalization of managerial and technical functions, thus permitting the full armamentarium of scientific methods to be applied to management. Frederick Winslow Taylor has been called the father of scientific management and his work exemplifies this development, but so do the more recent and continuing contributions from operations research and management science. The relevance and applicability of many "tool courses" such as finance, accounting, quantitative analysis, and quality assurance rest in turn on the continued relevance of this model.

The relation between these functional skills of management and the traditional management model is sometimes not recognized, and in the last 30 years there has been a tendency to poke fun at this rather formal conception of the managerial role. One major criticism is that it is more a description of the objectives of managerial work than it is a description of the work itself. Another criticism centers on the prescriptive tone that permeates such writings, setting norms for what managers ought to do, with relatively little emphasis on what they actually do. A third criticism is that, because of its concentration upon the formal aspects of organizations, it tends to ignore or distort the task of managing external relations and the informal aspects of the administrator's role.

Because of these criticisms and the popular growth of open systems theories of management, PODC and the traditional school are currently out of fashion. This creates difficulties, for the famous quadrivium does indeed catch an important truth about the formal aspects of the internal component of the manager's role. The report of the Com-

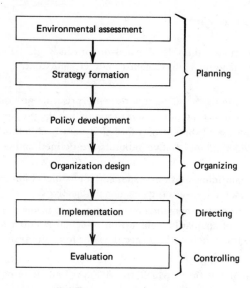

Figure 2.1. Model of the role of the CEO.

mission on Education for Health Administration chose to emphasize this aspect strongly in their definition of the process of health administration:

> Health Administration is planning, organizing, directing, controlling, coordinating and evaluating the resources and procedures by which needs and demands for health and medical care and a healthful environment are fulfilled, by the provision of specific services to individual clients, organizations, and communities. (10)

Some of the recent writing on the health manager role retains the formal structure of the traditional model but acknowledges the importance of environmental factors as well. Longest uses the traditional model in his article "The Contemporary Hospital Chief Executive Officer" (11). He describes the tangible things that hospital chief executive officers (CEOs) can be expected to do by use of a model developed by Newman and Logan, which coincides closely with the PODC model (Fig. 2.1).

As is apparent from the model, Longest emphasizes the planning function, and within that function he emphasizes the major significance of an accurate environmental assessment. This must include assessment of the environment itself and the impact the changes in that environment will have on the hospital. In his discussion of organization design and implementation, he highlights the importance of such factors as the informal organization, organizational climate, and the motivation of individuals. It seems clear that this traditional model of management remains a helpful and indeed powerful tool for understanding the role of health care managers.

THE HUMAN RELATIONS MODEL

A second perspective that emphasizes the universal nature of managerial action does not attend to planning, organizing, directing, and controlling, but rather focuses on the immensely difficult task of motivating individuals to the achievement of organizational ends. The spirit of the human relations school is captured perfectly by McGregor's principle of integration:

> The essential task of management is to arrange organizational conditions and methods of operation so that people can achieve their own goals *best* by directing their *own* efforts towards organizational objectives. (12)

The focus of the human relations school is always on persons, more specifically on their social behavior. The social needs of individuals and the way they are met at work becomes an important part of the understanding and knowledge required for effective management. Roethlisberger and Dickson's study, *Management and the Worker* (13) enriched our understanding of group processes and provided a far more sophisticated understanding of the needs that individuals bring with them to the workplace. In such a context, the informal organization is not an unofficial, irrelevant, and occasionally troublesome element of the organization. Quite the contrary, it is a centrally important element, a necessity without which the system could neither adapt nor survive. Thus the human relations model is focused on the managerial obligation of creating and sustaining effective work groups, an atmosphere of openness, trust, and supportiveness, and above all, a system of participation in decision making:

> Every aspect of a firm's activities is determined by the competence, motivation, and general effectiveness of its human organization. Of all the tasks of management, managing the human component is the central and most important task, because all else depends on how well it is done. (14)

It is no accident that among all of the schools of management, only human relations is referred to as a "movement," for like the labor movement, it is strongly colored by an ideology. It is an ideology that focuses on the importance of individuals and the moral and economic benefit that flows from allowing them to share in shaping their own destiny. When this is done, then individuals may desire to adopt the organization's goals for their own and to give their life and energy to the organization. Substantial experimentation during the past 50 years has provided a number of appropriate management tactics to build this motivational force, particularly in the area of leadership processes, group-building processes, the development of intrinsic rewards, communication processes, and participative decision making.

The human relations model, like the traditional model, specifies what managers ought to do, and is, therefore, prescriptive in tone. But why should anyone criticize an effort to specify how managers should act? Professional health managers do management, not research; their goals are results, not knowledge. There is often a tendency among academics to treat "prescription" as something undesirable, when in fact professional schools should be in the business of prescribing behavior that will improve performance in their profession. The real problem of the universalist model is that in much of the writing, prescriptions are based primarily on common sense and conventional wisdom, and are usually supported with anecdotes and illustrations. This is an unsatisfactory basis for any profession, particularly when authors who support it suggest that their prescriptions of how managers should act are also descriptions of how they do act. It is not surprising then that perceptive students of management should ask, "Yes, but what do managers *do?*"

TWO MAJOR ROLE STUDIES

Two of the best-known answers to the question, "What do managers do?" are provided by Henry Mintzberg and Rosemary Stewart. Both Mintzberg and Stewart sought to avoid a prescriptive bias in their data collection, and followed a method of letting their substantive categories develop from the data they found.

Henry Mintzberg's Nature of Managerial Work

Mintzberg's work (15) considerably sharpens our understanding of what managers do. He examines closely questions such as: What are the distinguishing characteristics of managerial work? What kind of activities does the manager perform? What basic roles can be inferred from a study of the manager's activities? He identified ten managerial roles, three dealing with interpersonal relationships, three with the transfer of information, and four with decision making. Mintzberg based his writing on a review of managerial role studies and on direct week-long observation of five managers. While the data base is limited, the insights derived are compelling.

The three interpersonal roles are that of figurehead, leader, and liaison. As *figurehead*, the manager carries out social, inspirational, legal, and ceremonial duties. In the *leader* role, the manager directs subordinates, defines the milieu in which the subordinates work, motivates them, and takes responsibility for hiring, training, and promoting them, seeking to ensure that the organization functions as an integrated unit. The final interpersonal role is the *liaison* role, in which the manager develops a network of contacts outside the organization, trading information and favors for mutual benefit.

The three informational roles of the manager are monitor, disseminator, and spokesman. As a result of the interpersonal contacts within the organization and outside it, the manager is able to serve as a nerve center of the organization's information system. The unique access to subordinates and outside sources provides a powerful data base of external and internal information. The manager as *monitor* seeks and obtains information from many sources in order to develop a thorough understanding of the organization and its environment. The manager uses this information to detect changes, to identify problems and opportunities, and to acquire a feeling for context for decision making purposes. In the *disseminator* role, the manager sends external information into the organization and internal information from one subordinate to another. Finally, as *spokesman*, the manager transmits information to various external groups. Acting in a public relations capacity, the manager lobbies for the organization and keeps influential individuals informed.

Information that is unused is useless. The informational roles provide the knowledge base for the four decisional roles of entrepreneur, disturbance handler, resource allocator, and negotiator. The manager as *entrepreneur* initiates and keeps track of many of the planned changes in the organization that respond to identified problems and opportunities. The manager as entrepreneur is not a specialist designing the details of the new program. Mintzberg points to two aspects of the entrepreneurial role of much relevance to health care managers:

> First, these projects do not involve single decisions. . . . [T]hey emerge as a series of small decisions and actions sequenced over time. Apparently the chief executive prolongs each project so that he can fit it . . . [into a] busy, disjointed schedule . . . and gradually come to comprehend the issue, if it is a complex one.

Second, the chief executives I studied supervised as many as 50 of these projects at the same time. (16)

The manager must also assume command when the organization meets an unexpected problem for which there is no programmed response. It is in this sense that the role of *disturbance handler* is to be understood. As *resource allocator*, the manager oversees the allocation of all forms of organizational resources. Evidently, some resource allocation decisions can be programmed or formalized, as in capital budgeting decisions; participation in these formal processes is a less important part of the chief executive's resource allocator role than giving final approval to the outcomes of these processes and making ad hoc decisions. Mintzberg describes the manager's resource allocation decisions as "incredibly complex," but his reference is only to the intrinsic complexity of the problem. The choice process is cerebral, making more use of scratch pads and conversations than of operations research and management science.

The last of the four decisional roles is that of *negotiator*. This is a skill that is drawn upon whenever agreements need to be reached with parties who have different and sometimes conflicting interests. In many cases negotiations are with outside groups, but in large health care organizations negotiations with internal groups or individuals are also common.

Some of Mintzberg's findings deserve special emphasis. Keep in mind that these are findings about what managers do, not about what someone says they ought to do.

1. *The roles are interlocked.* The manager's interpersonal roles provide a basis for securing information, and the information becomes a foundation for the decisional roles. The whole forms a gestalt that can be subdivided among different individuals only with great difficulty.

2. *Managerial activities are characterized by brevity, variety, and discontinuity.* Managers are not reflective or systematic planners; they work at an unrelenting pace, moving rapidly from one topic and problem to another and keeping themselves constantly open for inputs from diverse sources as a way of tracking and influencing the many streams of organizational action.

3. *The manager is imprisoned by a set of duties that must be performed.* These duties, however, are not well described by planning, directing, organizing, and controlling. The ceremonial role is an important one; one manager described his job as seeing visitors, "so that everyone else can get his work done" (16). Other "chores" are connected with the monitor, leader, and negotiator roles. They are chores in a literal sense: perhaps repetitive and unexciting, but essential, inherent in the role, and not easily delegated.

4. *The manager works largely with informal and soft data.* The point is not that hard data such as cost reports, budget projections, and productivity analyses are irrelevant. On the contrary, they may be in place and available because of much executive labor. Once complet., however, they can be handled by staff specialists while the managers go on to the other problems or opportunities to which they must be continually alert. Aggregated abstractions seem of little use to a manager, who looks instead for specific, current, and concrete tidbits of data which, in Richard Neustadt's words, "illuminate the underside of issues put before him." (17)

5. *Managers emphasize linking their organization with its environment.* The picture of the manager that emerges from Mintzberg's research is that of a boundary spanner

as well as an organizational leader. This is evident in the figurehead role, in the role of entrepreneur, and very much in the role of monitor.

Although Mintzberg's role study included the CEOs of a consulting firm, a technology company, a hospital, a consumer goods company, and a school system, he found no need to distinguish among the managerial roles he found. The managerial role he portrays is quite different from that of the traditional or the human relations model of management, but this best-known part of his work does reflect a universalist conception of the managerial role.

Rosemary Stewart's *Managers and Their Jobs*

Stewart's study (18) of managerial roles draws on a much larger sample than Mintzberg's, the diaries of 160 middle- and upper-level managers of British firms obtained over a four-week period. From the collected data, the average time that a manager spent on a particular activity was calculated. Managers were then descriptively divided according to activity into five groups: emissaries, writers, discussers, troubleshooters, and committeemen. Stewart's research design as well as the sample size made it easy for her to identify differences in the management role. Indeed, her data led her to conclude that because these differences were great, it was misleading to talk about *the* managerial job or about how typical managers spend their time. Her five categories are empirically based on the proportion of time that managers spent in different kinds of activities.

The *emissaries* were outward oriented; their workplace and their contacts were often outside the company. They worked longer hours than managers in any other group, mainly because of travel and entertainment requirements, and they tended to have a less fragmented working day with fewer fleeting contacts. The most numerous representatives of the group were sales managers and the next most numerous were chief executives.

The *writers* spent about half their time doing solitary paperwork. Though they spent significant amounts of time in contact with other people, it was usually in talking with one other person. They spent the least time in group contacts, such as committee meetings, and tended to work shorter hours than managers in the other groups. The kind of managers belonging to this group were primarily staff specialists; the next most common were middle managers.

The next three groups spent much of their time in supervising or coordinating the work of people within the organization. They differed from each other primarily in the nature of their contacts. The *discussers,* who in some respects were the most typical of the total sample, spent a relatively high proportion of their time with colleagues. The group included a wide variety of middle-level functional managers, such as product engineering, personnel, accounting, and sales managers. It included no chief executives. The group Stewart called the *troubleshooters* spent nearly all their internal contact time with subordinates. They experienced significantly higher fragmentation of their work schedule because of fleeting contacts and having to deal with crisis situations. This group included most of the plant managers, some production managers, and a few chief executives of small companies. The final category, the *committeemen,* had a wide range of internal contacts with people in other departments and in a variety of different levels in the organization. They spent far more time than members of any other group in discussions and committee meetings and had the widest range of internal contacts. Managers in this group often worked for large companies, most commonly in line positions at the middle level.

Stewart's role study is important to our understanding of managerial roles. Her inclusion of other than chief executives has helped emphasize the differences in managerial work at different levels of the organization. But her data also show that the roles of top managers differ from each other as well. Elsewhere she has noted the importance of this for management education:

> From Henri Fayol, with his all-too-often quoted functions of management, to Henry Mintzberg, with his refreshingly different approach to managerial roles, the emphasis continues to focus on the common aspects of management. [Yet the behavioral demands vary considerably.] We need to develop courses that take account of differences other than levels in the hierarchy. (19)

Stewart's study leads us directly to a consideration of the proposition that managers' jobs are shaped by the organizations in which they work. As the organization and its environment changes, so does the managerial role. (20)

ORGANIZATIONAL CONCEPTION OF THE MANAGERIAL ROLE

MINI-CASE: CHANGED ORGANIZATIONS BRING DIFFERENT MANAGEMENT PROBLEMS

The new forms of national investment [in medical research which began in the late 1940s] were meant to expand and strengthen medical research and hospitals. That they did. But they also changed the careers of thousands of physicians and in other, unexpected ways altered the postwar development of medical care.

NIH research grants helped to build new research centers, especially in the West, and training grants provided the stipends for an enlarged corps of investigators. The growth of subspecialities broke down the old pyramidal pattern, since a larger number of residents could now rise to senior posts. As the demand for academic physicians rose, so did their income. And, like other academics in the postward period, medical school professors also became more geographically mobile. One key consideration in attracting faculty became the provision of research space and clinical facilities. This increased the interest of medical schools in expanding their network of affiliated hospitals and acquiring land in local neighborhoods, tearing down residential buildings, and replacing them with institutes, clinics, and hospitals.

[Inevitably, these developments have changed the role of the dean.] The role of the dean . . . has evolved from an academic function with a circumscribed administrative responsibility to a much broader executive function. Most medical school deans retain the academic role . . . but because of the growth in size and complexity of the organization and the enormous influence of the outside environment on its programs, the deanship has assumed a function that is more fully executive and managerial. There are other "executives" in the center—hospital directors, vice-presidents, department chairmen, to name a few principals. How these positions interrelate as the power bases change or are modulated by external forces has captured the attention of the university leadership and particularly the governing boards in a number of universities. It is not unusual that the medical school is a very significant portion of the university budget. With university ownership of a teaching hospital, the center budget may be one-third to one-half of the university budget. Further, the medical school is frequently a major link to the community through the provision of medical care, a not inconsequential issue for the university administration. [The Dean] . . . has become an essential boundary person between the medical school and its social and economic environment.*

*Adapted from *The Social Transformation of American Medicine* by Paul Starr. Copyright © 1982 by Paul Starr. Reprinted by permission of Basic Books, Inc., Publishers. Adapted from Wilson, M. P. and McLaughlin, C. P., *Leadership and Management in Academic Medicine.* San Francisco: Jossey-Bass, 1984.

We now shift from the generic-role emphasis characteristic of the universalist model, and view managers as having a role pressed upon them by their organization or its environment. This produces a different and more complex picture of the manager than is suggested by McGregor's principle of integration or Fayol's four functions. Common experience tells us that all successful managers do not act alike, and in this conception we look to organization and environmental differences to find patterns in this diversity among managerial roles. Specifically, five ways that organizations may differ are considered, three of which are directly influenced by the organization's environment. The five are the organization's age, its size, the technologies employed in producing its goods or services, the requirements for maintaining an effective human organization, and the requirements for keeping a match between what it does and what outsiders want it to do.

An organization's age has very direct effects on the manager's role, although the difference is pronounced only between very young organizations and all others. Older organizations have faced and solved more problems than young ones and thus have a larger repertoire of tested behaviors to draw from. Both advantages and disadvantages flow from this added knowledge. On the one hand, managers are less often faced with problems that require innovative solutions; they have more time to plan and control, since they need to spend less time in organizing and directing. On the other hand, a steady dependence on using tested behaviors is habit forming, and habits are sometimes hard to break. We may summarize these twin results of organizational age by saying that organizations tend to formalize task behaviors over time, and that formalization leads to efficiency in constantly repeated organizational activity but creates difficulty in adopting innovative solutions when such are required. This paradox is worth emphasizing. New organizations will not survive unless their managers can achieve a measure of formalization; old ones may not survive if their managers are unable to change these hitherto-successful practices when necessary. This point receives further attention in Chapter 9, Organization Design.

Organizational size also has direct, and more obvious, effects on the managerial role. The greater specialization characteristic of larger organizations has the effect of increasing the need to coordinate, and specialized staff units develop that specialize the managerial role itself. Thus in very small organizations a manager may be a true generalist, deciding salaries, determining the need for new services, and negotiating reimbursement levels. In large organizations this breadth of hands-on practical skills is less relevant. Attention must focus instead on two major issues, maintaining the effectiveness of the human organization and managing the organization's relation with its task and larger political environment.

The next three organization attributes identify different ways the organization is linked to the larger social setting in which it operates, whether through the technology it uses, the human resources it employs, or the goods and services it exchanges. Readers will recognize these attributes as characteristic of an *open-systems* view of organizations, and it will be useful to place them within this theoretical framework.

Early work by Parsons distinguished three levels in formal organizations: technical, managerial, and institutional (21). The emphasis is not on hierarchy or formal authority, but on the qualitatively different functions of each level. The *technical level* is concerned with those activities that produce the organization's outputs. It is at the technical level in a given organization that the work gets done. The focus of this level is within the organization. Exigencies to which the suborganization are oriented are those imposed by the nature of the technical task, the physical, cultural, or human resources, and the kinds of cooperation required to get the job done. The *managerial level* administers the internal operations of the organization and mediates between the technical level and its immediate environment by procuring the necessary financial, human, and physical resources and by finding customers for organizational products or services. The *institutional level* is that subset of the larger society from which the organization must secure its resources, its markets, and its legitimation (22).

Of particular interest are the points of articulation between the levels. For example, although decisions made at the managerial level control operations at the technical level, the relationship is not unidirectional, particularly in organizations with a professional component. That is, at the interface between technical and managerial levels in a health care organization, professionals have much to say about managerial decisions as a result of their professional and technical competence. While managers may be able to hold professionals responsible for the consequences of their decisions or to veto their recommendations, they may be unable to propose alternative or meaningful changes. Health care managers often function as a rubber stamp for highly work-related decisions such as new nursing procedures or professional department promotions. Technical decisions are made in the professional departments—what is to be done and who is to do it are decisions often made by professionals. Further, technical experts at the professional level may be members of both the managerial organization and the technical system, but the allegiance of such professionals goes beyond either subsystem to a reference group, which has the effect of reinforcing the internal influence of the professional.

In its external relations, the managerial level is concerned with markets for disposal of products and with procuring the resources necessary to perform its functions. There are, however, other problems, in that organizations deal not only with customers or sources of supply but also with "organized" superior agencies. At issue is managerial responsibility, given that it is not possible to perform the function of focusing legitimation and community support for the organization while at the same time serving as the active management of it. Thus a board acts as a mediating structure between the affairs of the organization at the managerial level and the public. Parsons draws our attention to problems arising at the interface, problems in the relationship between levels:

> . . . not only does such an organization [a formal organization] have to operate in a social environment which imposes the conditions governing the processes of disposal and procurement, it is also part of a wider social system which is the source of the "meaning," legitimation, or higher level support which makes the implementation of the organization's

goals possible. Essentially, this means that just as a technical organization (at a sufficiently high level of division of labor) is controlled and "serviced" by a managerial organization, so in turn is the managerial organization controlled by the institutional structure and agencies of the community. (21)

Parsons helps us locate the health service manager as part of the managerial level and as such responsible for meshing the sometimes conflicting requirements of survival that arise from within and without the organization.

Building upon the conceptual foundation of Parsons, Katz and Kahn have defined several subsystems of activities necessary to organization survival. These are the production, supportive, maintenance, and adaptive subsystems (23).

The *production*, or technical, subsystem includes those activities that produce the products or services of the organization. Within this subsystem there is an emphasis on technical proficiency, on efficient production methods, and therefore on specialization of the work process and stability in the production cycle.

The *supportive* subsystem carries on environmental transactions by procuring input, disposing of output, or aiding these processes. This subsystem aids the production system directly by importing material to be worked on or by exporting finished products, and indirectly by maintaining a favorable environment. The supportive subsystem is concerned with sustaining the production cycle as it exists.

The *maintenance* subsystem focuses not on the material worked on but on the patterned human behavior that is the "equipment" used to get the work done. It functions to maintain the fabric of independent behavior necessary for task accomplishment by maintaining stability and predictability within the organization. Concerned with inputs for preserving the system, important mechanisms in this subsystem include appropriate selection of personnel, socialization practices, and reward and sanction systems.

While most of the other subsystems tend to face inward, the *adaptive* subsystem is concerned with sensing relevant change in the environment and translating the meaning of these changes to the organization. Major functions within this subsystem include market and product research, long-range planning, and research and development. Similar in purpose to the maintenance function, this subsystem aims at constancy and predictability by seeking to attain control over the environment and modifying organization structure and/or processes to meet external changes.

Katz and Kahn add a fifth subsystem, the *managerial*, but it is also possible to think of this as the coordinating and directing of other subsystems, resolving conflicts between hierarchical levels, and coordinating external requirements with organizational resources and needs. As such, the managerial subsystem cuts across the other subsystems and is concerned with preservation of the entire structure. For example, change emanating from the adaptive subsystem typically is implemented through the managerial structure, since such change may affect the entire organization and responsibility for such basic modification cannot be delegated without transforming the organization itself. Likewise, the authority structure or adjudicative mechanism is designed to maintain the organization as an entity.

ORGANIZATION SUBSYSTEMS

The organization functions described by Parsons and by Katz and Kahn define organization requirements above and below as well as at the managerial level. We will combine these functions into three general categories: production/support, organization maintenance, and adaptation activities. Think of them as creating the managerial tasks of managing production, maintaining the organization, and managing external relations. The organizational impact on the managerial role is best addressed by concentrating on these three functions.

The first is the *production/support* function, which involves managing for technical efficiency and includes those supportive activities necessary to sustain the production process. Securing necessary resources, allocating and using these resources, producing goods or services, and disposing of outputs are involved in the production/support function. If the technology is well understood and easily routinized (or perhaps mechanized or even automated), the manager's role is quite different than if the technology is both complex and potentially variable in its application to each client or object worked on. Consider the difference in the hospital functions of room cleaning and patient treatment. In the latter case the "production" of treated patients is sufficiently complex and problematic that only persons competent in using the technology (i.e., professionals) are able to coordinate and direct the required activities for each patient's treatment. This technologically determined requirement may require managers in such organizations to share the managerial role with persons whose tasks are primarily "production."

The second function is *maintenance*, which is concerned with the human organization. The focus is on maintaining stability and predictability of behavior among individuals as well as within and between units of the organization. Managers of organizations with stable technologies in placid environments will be less affected by the requirements of this function than those that must maintain a significant measure of stability in the human organization in the face of changing conditions. It is worthwhile to note that this function presents some of the most challenging managerial problems in developing societies, where modern organizations are often breaking new ground, and prospective employees are neither trained nor socialized to accept prescribed organization roles (26).

Adaptation, the third function, focuses on the organization's ability to adapt to a changing environment and on its efforts to influence that environment to provide ample resources. As such, adaptation is viewed as both reactive and proactive. Some of the activities in this function can be routinized and given to nonmanagers (marketing specialists, lobbyists, product engineers), but fundamentally this function lies close to the heart of management of any organization facing significant changes in its technology or task environment (25). The onset of aggressive competition among hospitals, the shift from cost-based to prospective case-based payment, and the introduction of drug therapy in psychiatric treatment are three examples of events in the environment of health care organizations that illustrate the importance of the adaptive function, and suggest how central it is to the managerial role.

AN ILLUSTRATION OF THE ORGANIZATIONAL CONCEPTION OF THE MANAGERIAL ROLE: PERROW'S VALLEY HOSPITAL STUDY

This detailed study (24, 27) of a hospital discovered that different tasks were critical at successive stages of its 75-year history. Perrow hypothesized that as different tasks became critical to the organization's survival, those groups best able to perform them would become influential in directing the organization's course and development. The critical tasks can be identified as follows:

1. Securing needed resources, particularly capital and operating income, and also community acceptance, or legitimation.

2. Providing the necessary skills, particularly if the organization engages in nonroutine or highly specialized activities.
3. Coordinating the activities of members and the relationship of the organization with other organizations and with clients and consumers.

Perrow notes that all of these are important, but not equally important at any point in time. The relative emphasis on a particular task depends on the nature of the work of the organization, the technology appropriate to that work, and the stage of organizational development. During the hospital's early history, when, financial needs and legitimation were primary, it was the trustees who dominated. At this stage, the manager had limited power or prestige and was little more than a business manager. At a later stage, when the technology of medicine had improved greatly, then technical skill and medical excellence became primary and it was the medical staff that dominated. At this stage, the role of the manager was minimized and the administrative viewpoint on operative goals neglected. Policy matters were defined as medical in nature by the doctors, and neither trustees nor administrators were viewed as qualified to have an equal voice in policy formation. Perhaps the key point to be made is that as these shifts occurred within the organization, the role of the manager changed accordingly.

As the organization became increasingly complex and interdependent, the need for cooperation and coordination emerged. As this occurred, the importance of effective management increased. Perrow argues that this growing complexity, interdependence, and need for interorganizational linkages is best handled, through experience and training, by managers. These activities often impinge upon the physician at many points, providing a basis for management control over physicians and also leading to commitments in which trustees may have to acquiesce. By controlling some matters that affect physician demands for status, deference, and convenience, by maintaining supervision over employees, by promoting the independent basis for competence of nonphysicians, and by supporting employees in conflicts with the physicians, the manager may mitigate the high functional authority of physicians. Further, by controlling communication between trustees and physicians, the manager may prevent these two groups from allying.

Perrow contends that managerial dominance, based on complexity of activities rather than on a medical service role, may lead to an operative orientation toward fiscal solvency, efficiency, and budget control. An alternative possibility is that professional managers may act as professional health care managers, still technically equipped to handle administrative matters easily, but committed to leading the organization toward a broader medical and social role involving organizational and financial innovations in delivering care. The manager may even be able to bring some areas of medical standards under management control within the formal system. Perrow concludes by arguing that rather than any one group dominating, there may be a form of multiple leadership with several stable, well-known centers of power, without a single ultimate power.

HEALTH MANAGER ROLE STUDIES

Perrow's insights come from the intensive study of a single organization, but consider all 75 years of its history. The seven studies summarized below examine many organizations, but at a single point in time. These role studies of health service managers give us information about how they spend their time, the forms of communication they use, what activities they undertake, and what activities they consider important.

When one asks a manager "What do you do?" the answers may be of three kinds:

1. Behavioral answers (e.g., I write memos, attend meetings, talk on the telephone).
2. Skill-utilizing answers (e.g., I lead, monitor, act as spokesperson).
3. Organization function answers.
   a. General functions (e.g., I plan, organize, direct).
   b. Specific functions (e.g., I recruit professionals, deal with planning agencies, obtain corporate and malpractice insurance).

The kinds of answers received are of course framed by the survey and interview methodology. Mintzberg (20) received skill-utilizing answers, Stewart (18) and Weaver (28) received behavioral answers, and the Allison et al. (29), Kuhl (30), Morita et al. (31), Johnson et al. (32), Johnson and Forrest (33), and Kaiser (34) role studies all used questions designed to receive specific-function answers. Although some studies (notably Johnson et al.) used multiple methods, we will direct our primary attention to data on specific functions.

Weaver (28) studied 46 health care facilities in a metropolitan area of southern California. His sample was a diverse mix of institutions, including 16 convalescent hospitals and at least 13 short-term general hospitals. His activity categories included such items as attending meetings, correspondence and telephone, and preparing reports. His analysis appears to draw more extensively on interviews than on his survey of activities.

In the first of two studies directed by Dowling, Allison (29) studied the role of 24 health administrators in four different types of delivery organizations: hospitals, long-term-care facilities, multispecialty group practice clinics, and health maintenance organizations. Allison interviewed the chief executives in six of each of these organizations, who also completed questionnaires. The Allison role study made an explicit linkage to open-system theory, using the Katz and Kahn subsystem typology both in the design and analysis of the data. We have followed this lead in drawing together the findings of the health manager role studies. Allison developed 46 items describing specific management functions and asked his respondents to indicate level of involvement, time spent, and degree of importance of each. This method of defining the health administrator role was used in all of the subsequent studies.

Kuhl (30) used a questionnaire based on Allison's, which was mailed to a national sample of hospital chief executives and to the administrators of all prepaid group practice health plans that were known to exist. In both cases the response rate was about two-thirds, producing a sample of 149 hospital chief executives and 42 HMO chief executives. Although Kuhl's basic activities list was similar to that of Allison's, the method of forming groups of executive tasks differed. Kuhl used content analysis, which produced 23 groupings that were then placed in four broad areas that represented components of the executive role. These areas were internal management, organizational development, external relations, and environmental surveillance. The large majority of the activities appeared in the internal management area, which was subdivided into organizational design, personnel management, financial management, logistical management, service delivery, and legal work.

In 1976 Morita et al. (31) reported a study of the roles of the Medical Group Management Association (MGMA) members, to which 583 group practice administrators responded. In addition, some responses were received from medical directors and board chairmen of the same organizations. The MGMA study took considerable pains to develop an appropriate set of specific-function items. Starting with a 350-item task list, they reduced this to 141 activities and grouped them within a modified Katz and Kahn subsystem typology. This study reported data by size of group practices and payment mechanism, whether fee-for-service or prepayment.

The most extensive health service manager role studies were undertaken at the University of Wisconsin. The first of these, by Johnson et al. (32), included a national sample of 755 hospitals and 148 long-term care institutions (LTCs) and an additional sample of 31 clinics and 9 HMOs from midwestern states only. The study used several methods for gaining a perspective on the managerial role. A description of Mintzberg's ten roles was provided to the respondents, and they were asked to rank the importance of them. In addition, they described their activities in detail by use of a standard list of 46 specific functions.

In 1979 Johnson and Forrest (33) reported on a second study, concerning the role of community mental health and human services administrators, that adopted the same framework as used in the health administrators study two years earlier but did not include the Mintzberg items. A total of 181 Wisconsin community mental health facilities were surveyed, including 42 clinics, 35 day care centers, 30 departments of social services, 26 group homes, and 19 sheltered employment agencies. No psychiatric hospitals were included, and it appears from some of the data that social workers were the most common professional group within the organizations.

A study of 16 North Carolina local health departments by Kaiser, reported in 1978 (34), included among its 136 respondents 12 agency directors. The study is methodologically the most sophisticated of the role studies reviewed. It made use of 104 specific function items and used internal analysis to validate its theoretically derived categories.

The findings of these studies provide some support for the universalist models of the manager's role. All save Weaver's document the presence of health-related general administration activities as well as organization-building human relations activities. As Ray Brown said a decade ago, "the field [of health services management] is different as a whole and not by its parts" (35). Yet in addition to these general similarities, there were also clear differences. Kuhl concluded that the generic role was most evident at a very general and abstract level. As one looked more concretely at the role of the manager, some differences became evident. We can use the five categories developed in the preceding section to illuminate these differences and the organizational attributes which appear to account for them.

AGE

There are two relevant aspects of age: the age of the organization itself and the newness of the organization type it represents. Kuhl comments on this variable with respect to HMOs:

> It would seem that prepaid health plan executives are profoundly constrained by the scarcity of information. Many prepaid health plans are organizations without memories. . . . In comparison to hospitals, health plans are few in number and structurally varied. Standard industry practice exists only to a limited degree. Most health plans have been in operation for a short period of time and are undergoing rapid growth. (30)

Kuhl notes that her study was not designed to tap the significance of age, and this is true of other studies as well. Johnson and Forrest had also studied a set of young organizations in their group of community mental health facilities. The authors note that one of the two major themes that emerged from their study was that "the last ten to fifteen years have seen major changes in the system . . . [and that the time has come] for a period of stabilization and standard operating procedures so that administrators can judge the accomplishments of the past and make creative decisions about future operations. Continual change over a lengthy period is ultimately destructive. . . . " (33). The scanty evidence that we have supports the most common expectation about youthful organizations in new industries: that the organizations have low levels of formalization. Managers face more uncertainties and perform tasks that in older organizations have been routinized and delegated to others.

SIZE

Three characteristics of the health manager's role appear to be directly influenced by larger size of the managed organization:

1. Lesser involvement in technical functions as the firm grows in size, with direction setting rather than task performance being the major activity.
2. Greater involvement in relations with the external environment.
3. Greater emphasis on building an effective human organization.

The most apparent effect of small size is to involve the manager with more activities at a more detailed level than is true in large organizations. Managers of larger organizations report that their involvement is at the policy level; the manager of a small organization is likely to be that unit's long-term planner, personnel officer, controller, chief accountant, emergency room supervisor, and general maintenance person as well. The Morita et al. study (31) of group practice managers shows this clearly. The degree of personal involvement of the chief executive in the 141 discrete tasks was calculated, distinguishing between small and large organizations. Of the 39 tasks for which statistically significant differences were found, for 37 of them the executive in large organizations had less direct, personal involvement. The Wisconsin study of hospital executives (32) confirms this finding for hospitals. Time consumed in activities such as financial management, personnel management, and coordinating department operations was significantly greater in small than in large hospitals, while the reverse was true for such activities as facility planning, government-related activities, and other outside activities. Rather curiously, the conclusions Kaiser draws from his data on local health department directors (34) do not support this clearly, although his data would seem to. Perhaps this is because the nature of his sample (12 directors, 124 subordinates) caused him to emphasize the differences between the directors and other health department personnel.

We now turn to the three central sets of organization activities that revolve around producing the organization's output, maintaining the organization as a viable system, and influencing the environment or adapting the organization to it.

THE PRODUCTION/SUPPORT SUBSYSTEM

This organizational subsystem contains much of the actual work of the organization. It includes the core diagnostic and treatment services, the necessary professional and technical support services such as nursing, housekeeping, and dietary, and the administrative support services such as accounting, purchasing, and payroll.

A distinctive feature of health service organizations is the degree to which the core diagnostic and treatment services are both performed and controlled by the professional staff. This is most true in the hospitals, clinics, and HMOs. In the Morita et al. study (31) of group practices, none of the 530 medical group managers identified maintaining quality standards of medical care as one of their five most important tasks. This is an extreme example; Allison (29) found that among his four managerial types, only clinic managers did not rate "developing systems to control quality" as crucial. But developing systems is not the same as having effective direction; all save one of the studies note what Allison describes as "the very real phenomenon of the dual hierarchy in which physicians and other professionals dominate the delivery subsystem within health organizations" (29).

In respect to professional and technical support activities, the constraints are less severe. Particularly in hospitals, some support activities have professional attributes that limit the manager's influence. Yet even here Weaver found, for example, that in problems with nursing staff the key difficulties were not with internal operations but with recruitment and retention. In a hospital these essential support services add significantly to the administrative burden but also add to administrative influence. In long-term-care facilities, they are also essential but less diverse, and therefore more easily managed. The clinic, HMO, and community health facility are all ambulatory or preventive activity settings, and in such facilities professional and technical support services are less central.

The conventional and traditional role of the health service manager is in the direction of the administrative support services. Fundamentally this is the role of the business manager, and it is one that a surprisingly large number of managers play. For example, Johnson et al. (32) reported that among the top 11 tasks of clinic managers, seven are such activities as solving cash-flow problems, negotiating leasing agreements, and analyzing expenditures. The MGMA study opens the summary of its results with strong corroboration of this finding:

> The professional administrator is responsible for a majority of a group's administrative activities, but these tasks are not usually of a high decision-making level. Administrative tasks that involve high-level policy making or that are related to the medical aspects of the group are not included among the chief responsibilities of the professional administrator. (31)

The summary goes on to note that managers are in fact influential in policy decisions, but that the focus of their day-to-day activities is clear.

Johnson et al. (32) report that long-term-care managers reported performing directly fewer administrative support activities, and that hospital managers reported the least of all. In common with many technical support services, such tasks can be routinized and therefore controlled from above. While hospital managers do not perform these tasks, they do clearly have responsibility for them. Instead of managing tasks, they set directions and manage the human organization.

By all odds the most important activities in administrative support services deal in one way or another with money. Two quite different sets of activities are associated with the finance area for health care institutions, only one of which is included in administrative support services. This has to do with making sure the bills are paid, budgets are prepared and adhered to, receivables kept under control, and so forth. The activities look almost entirely inward and are directed toward efficiency. The second set of activities includes raising capital, adjusting charges ("cost shifting"), maximizing revenue and minimizing tax liabilities, and other forms of creative financing that take advantage of the opportunities facing the organization. These activities are part of the adaptive subsystem and look outward toward survival and growth.

THE MAINTENANCE SUBSYSTEM

This subsystem is directed toward maintaining the effectiveness of the human organization. The activities necessary to achieve some aspects of effectiveness, like those in the professional and technical and administrative support components, can be routinized. Among such activities are recruitment, selection, training, indoctrination, and discipline. Once routinized, such activities effectively become part of the administrative support system. In some of the health care organizations studied, these activities were not routine and therefore remained a problem area for the managers. This appears to be the case in many community mental health facilities. Johnson and Forrest (33) noted the difficulties clinically oriented managers had in delegating responsibilities and performing these technical administrative tasks. Their respondents identified this area as a key element in appropriate career preparation.

The achievement of other dimensions of effectiveness is problematic in all the organizations studied. Reward systems, leadership styles, and structures for decision making are difficult to design and maintain in any organization, and particularly difficult in organizations that both require and encourage diverse value systems in different parts of the organization. As noted earlier, this is characteristic of human service organizations, and it can create a major challenge for the manager. Johnson et al. (32) conclude from their study that human relations is in fact the single most important skill required by hospital executives, more important even than skills in finance. Allison found that the focus on the maintenance function was also strong in long-term-care facilities, and the MGMA study found that this was important, but particularly so in the larger organizations. The authors noted that "smaller groups can perform fewer maintenance tasks because their size allows the groups' managers to become aware of trouble spots early and to correct them personally without the need for any formal structures" (31). Among the system-maintenance activities that were rated as crucial in all four organization types (hospital, long-term care facility, clinic, HMO) in Allison's study were the following:

1. Decisions concerning professional and managerial salaries.
2. Motivating and directing immediate subordinates.
3. Dealing with personal and interpersonal problems.
4. Making changes in the decision or authority structure.

Only managers of long-term-care facilities did not rate as crucial the activity "arbitrate between policy making groups." This suggests again that the manager of a long-term-care facility operates in a setting in which power is concentrated at the apex of the organization.

There is little question that in the hospital, maintenance of an effective human organization is a challenging task. Nowhere is this more evident than in university teaching hospitals, where the values of the academic community are held by the medical staff and bureaucratic values are held by the administrative organization. Weisbord has suggested that the problem of creating an effective decision-making structure is caused not only by the differing emphasis placed on the goals of teaching, research, or patient care, but in a more fundamental way by these differing value systems. "In medicine, professionals believe in their bones that procedures an organization needs for its survival will be inimical to theirs" (36). Maintaining an effective human organization made up of such participants can become the major challenge facing the manager.

THE ADAPTIVE SUBSYSTEM

We have discussed the production/supportive and maintenance subsystems first in order to emphasize that the health services manager does indeed have major tasks in these two internally oriented systems. Human service organizations also are strongly interdependent with their environments. The function of influencing the organization's environment or adapting the organization to it must be performed by managers as well.

It is useful to think of an organization as requiring resources from the environment to survive; for health care organizations, the four crucial resources are patients or clients, money, personnel, and necessary approvals. In obtaining these resources health care executives play both an external political negotiator role and an internal adaptive role. The former may involve coalition building and networking with the organizations. The latter may involve the development of new programs internally. Leonard Cronkhite, then president and "Mr. Outside" of Children's Hospital in Boston, described one of his key functions as that of initiating and protecting programs that he believed the hospital's community needed and should be offered, and when they were self-sufficient, folding them back into the regular hospital operation (37). This is closely akin to Mintzberg's entrepreneurial role; Cronkhite notes that four or five such projects might be started in a year, the overriding reason for all of them being that "institutions like the Children's Hospital have to equate their long term survival with their responsiveness to the community . . . " (37).

These influences from the external environment have had four types of impact on the health service manager's role:

1. They have created a greater emphasis on long-term and strategic planning. As Longest noted (11), the essential first steps of strategic planning are to understand the forces in the environment and to estimate the impact they will have on the organization.
2. They have shifted the attention focus of the executive toward events that are occurring outside the organization. This is most true in large hospitals whose size and visibility has required the chief executive to pay particular attention to external threats to the survival of the organization. In smaller organizations, the chief executives must still give substantial attention to internal efficiency and the maintenance of the organization.
3. They have augmented the role of the board. The health services manager must give attention to the development and effectiveness of a strong board, somewhat paralleling their earlier emphasis on the development of an effective internal organization.

4. Finally, and paradoxically, the growing importance of the external environment has increased the relative influence of the manager within the organization, because so many of the critical resource dependencies are best handled by professional managers.

It is fair to say that the external environment leads, perhaps by several years, the administrative response to it. The role studies conducted in the mid to late 1970s still found that hospital managers and local health department directors were concerned primarily with managing the internal affairs of their organization; this was more true for long-term-care facilities and even more so for clinics. Perhaps the HMO manager gave the strongest emphasis of all to the external environment.

A PERSONAL/POLITICAL CONCEPTION OF THE MANAGERIAL ROLE

This conception of the managerial role is not readily apparent in existing studies. Possibly the effort to secure a description of specific organization functions cannot evoke information about the charisma of individuals or about the politics of power, what has been called "the organization's last dirty secret." Yet this conception is important. It encourages us to consider what it is that managers do when they are given, or seek out, the task of managing inherently unmanageable situations.

A paradigm suggested by Scott (38) to illuminate different orientations of organization theory is useful for placing this conception of management within differing schools of organizational thought. A property common to both the traditional and human relations conception of management is the strong inside-the-organization emphasis both have. They differ sharply in the emphasis they place on structural versus psychosocial variables. The organizational approach differs from both in rejecting the assumption that the boundaries of the organization are also the boundaries of the managerial role, but is similar to the traditional model in its emphasis on structural variables. The personal and/or political conception of the manager's job uses neither the closed system assumption that it is inside the organization, nor the structuralist assumption that the job can be treated independently of the individual who is in it. Thus the personal/political model fills the empty cell of the matrix, as shown in Figure 2.2. In fact, this conception of the managerial role contains two themes, one resting on individual and the other on organizational sources of power. The individualist, or heroic, conception of the manager

	Closed system emphasis	*Open system emphasis*
Structural attributes	Traditional manager	Organizational manager
Psychosocial attributes	Human relations manager	Political manager (managerial strategist)

Figure 2.2. Fitting managerial role conceptions within orientations to organization theory.

THE HEROIC MANAGER

MINI-CASE: A TIME FOR HEROICS: LEE IACOCCA MOVES TO CHRYSLER

Before . . . [my first day at Chrysler] was over, I noticed a couple of seemingly insignificant details that gave me pause. The first was that the office of the president, where Cafiero worked, was being used as a thoroughfare to get from one office to another. I watched in amazement as executives with coffee cups in their hands kept opening the door and walking right through the president's office. Right away I knew the place was in a state of anarchy. Chrysler needed a dose of order and discipline—and quick.

Then there was the fact that Riccardo's secretary seemed to be spending a lot of time taking personal calls on her own private phone! When the secretaries are goofing off, you know the place has dry rot. During the first couple of weeks in a new job, you look for telltale signs. You want to know what kind of fraternity you've joined. These are the signs I remember, and what they told me about Chrysler made me apprehensive about what I was getting myself into.

It turned out that my worries were justified. I soon stumbled upon my first major revelation: Chrysler didn't really function like a company at all. Chrysler in 1978 was like Italy in the 1860s—the company consisted of a cluster of little duchies, each one run by a prima donna. It was a bunch of mini-empires, with nobody giving a damn about what anyone else was doing.

What I found at Chrysler were thirty-five vice-presidents, each with his own turf. There was no real committee setup, no cement in the organizational chart, no system of meetings to get people talking to each other. I couldn't believe, for example, that the guy running the engineering department wasn't in constant touch with his counterpart in manufacturing. But that's how it was. Everybody worked independently. I took one look at that system and I almost threw up. That's when I knew I was in really deep trouble . . .

There was so much to do and so little time! I had to eliminate the thirty-five little duchies. I had to bring some cohesion and unity into the company. I had to get rid of the many people who didn't know what they were doing. I had to replace them by finding guys with experience who could move fast. And I had to install a system of financial controls as quickly as possible.

These problems were urgent and their solutions all pointed in the same direction. I needed a good team of experienced people who could work with me in turning this company around before it completely fell apart. My highest priority was to put that team together before it was too late . . .

Fortunately, the cancer at Chrysler did not reach all the way down. Although I had to replace almost all the officers, there was plenty of dynamic young talent beneath them. As we started getting rid of the less competent people, it was a lot easier to find the good ones. To this day, I can't believe that the former management didn't notice them. I'm talking about people with fire in their eyes: you can practically tell they're good just by looking at them . . .

One of the luxuries we had to eliminate was a large staff. Ever since Alfred P. Sloan took over the presidency of General Motors, all management functions in our industry have been divided into staff and line positions—just like the Army. Line guys are in operations. They have hands-on involvement and specific responsibilities, whether it's in engineering, manufacturing, or purchasing . . .

With all the firings, we ended up stripping out several levels of management. We cut down the number of people who needed to be involved in important decisions. Initially we did it out of the sheer necessity to survive. But over time we found that running a large company with fewer people actually made things easier. With hindsight it's clear that Chrysler had been top-heavy, far beyond what was good for us. That's a lesson our competitors have yet to learn—and I hope they never do!*

*Quoted, with permission from the publisher, from Iacocca, Lee, with William Novak, *Iacocca*. New York: Bantam Books, 1984, pp. 152, 165–66, 170–71, 190–91.

The individualist theme is the oldest, and we believe still the most popular, conception of the manager. Many organization theorists have the same respect for this model as physicians have for chiropractors. However, the strength of this view, with its recognition of the importance of leadership, endures. The common theme is the resources of the manager, whether they come from nature, nurture, or faith.

An early expression of this view appears in Exodus, as Moses, "without eloquence and slow of speech and tongue," is nevertheless the leader who brings his people out of Egypt. The Exodus is a story of heroic leadership, of a man and his brother called to build a nation from a community that scarcely ceased objecting to the process for 40 years. Jethro's famous advice to delegate responsibility is less representative of this saga than the continual focusing on Moses as the one true spokesman of the Lord. "Now go; I will help you speak, and will teach you what to say" (Exodus 4:12).

Machiavelli provided a different kind of instruction to the prince, but the importance of the leader is equally clear. Three pieces of his advice catch both the unswerving goal orientation and the amoral qualities we associate with his name (39):

- In taking a state the conqueror must arrange to commit all his cruelties at once, so as to be able, by not making fresh changes, to reassure people and win them over by benefiting them.
- A wise prince will seek means by which his subjects always and in every condition have need of his government. . . .
- (A prince) ought to be feared and loved, but, . . . it is much safer to be feared than loved, if one of the two has to be wanting. . . . Men have less scruple in offending one who makes himself loved than one who makes himself feared. . . .

The belief in the capacity of individuals to overcome personal, social, or organizational constraints is also a theme in the general self-help literature and in some writings of the women's movement, where the barriers to success for women in management are described as not only political but cultural as well. Bird describes women who have reached top positions as "the loophole women," identifying their careers by the types of loopholes they have found in male defenses of positions of power. But such women have some qualities in common:

The careers of successful women are uncharted. There is not, as there is for men, a clearly marked path, so success goes almost exclusively to individuals who can create their own opportunities. The adjectives "practical," "realistic," and "expediential" dotted our notes on interviews. Men sometimes become successful by cutting themselves off from whole areas of common experience; but there was not a single impractical dreamer among the successful women we saw. (40)

The heroic conception does not reject the possibility that management education is useful, but often views it with suspicion. Livingston (41) argues that management education has limited value and suggests that the ability to find the right problems to work on and a natural management style are two critical abilities, neither of which can be taught in management programs. Livingston carefully avoids the "great managers are born" position, though his descriptions of the personal qualities needed to manage effectively do identify rather deep-seated characteristics. These are: (1) the need to manage, or the enjoyment of influencing the performance of others; (2) the need for power, that is, finding pleasure in the competitive battle to reach the top and in the fruits of victory; and finally (3) capacity for empathy, sensing the emotional state of others while remaining able to deal with it productively. Zaleznik goes somewhat further: he builds his discussion on a distinction between managers and leaders and notes that "there are no known ways to train 'great' leaders" (42). Zaleznik's conception of a leader is someone with a mission who is willing to use organizations to achieve it, though it may mean destabilizing the organization and ignoring what we have called the maintenance function almost entirely.

Discussions of entrepreneurship, particularly case studies describing the growth and development of firms marketing new products, often point to the individual qualities associated with success in these new ventures, such as a strong sense of purpose and a distaste for bureaucracy (43–45). We must reemphasize that this is not a conception of the manager's job that is in conflict with the organizational model; rather, studies until recently have treated entrepreneurship quite separately from the manager's role. But it need not be treated separately, as an increasing number of scholars are recognizing. As will be evident to the reader, it fits comfortably with the idea of an organization's age affecting the manager's role, and it does no violence to the notion of entrepreneurship to recognize that opportunities are influenced, for example, by the stage of development of a technology, or by the openness of a market to new entrants.

A common theme in both prescriptive and descriptive writings about the heroic manager is the requirement for a certain hardness and unswerving purposefulness in the behavior of the manager. It is this, as much as anything, that establishes the distinction between the heroic and the human relations model. The heroic manager is purpose oriented, the human relations manager is people oriented.

Almost without exception, the writings on the heroic manager are prescriptive, and they use examples rather than evidence to support their position. Few empirical studies have assessed the contribution of leadership relative to other organizational predictors of performance. Perhaps one exception to this is a study by Lieberson and O'Conner (46), who found that much of the variance in three measures of performance—sales, earnings, and profit—could be explained by factors other than leadership variance. Yet such studies are often ignored or rejected by those who live within organizations, for a thousand such studies may not convince persons who have seen a hospital change dramatically under the personal qualities of a new manager (or chief of staff, or board chairman) whom they believe "made it happen." Clearly, what is required here is a capacity to deal comfortably with both the personal resources a manager can bring to a situation *and thus change it,* and the situational forces which operate on managers *and thus change the manager's behavior.* This complex and intriguing problem of disentangling "leadership" and "managership" is addressed directly in Chapter 4.

THE MANAGERIAL STRATEGIST

MINI-CASE: A TIME FOR STRATEGY: MICHAEL BICE REORIENTS LUTHERAN HEALTH SYSTEMS

The genesis of the ongoing organizational transformation activity in Lutheran Health Systems can be traced to the summer of 1982. At the time, I was the System's chief operating officer and had arrived at several conclusions about the organization. I believed it had very significant potential, but it did not have either the will or the resources to be an effective long-term player. It had an organizational structure which was relatively unchanged for 30 years; an organizational overhaul was clearly called for. It had a strong historical culture which served primarily as a barrier to change. It was a "society of administrators" with a major norm of conformance. Finally, it was slow to react to environmental changes, and thus, was not perceived to be in the mainstream of healthcare . . .

I carefully sought out support from the young future leaders of the organization, many of whom were disgruntled with the old order. I recruited members of senior management from outside of the organization who were at least open to organizational change. Consultants—external auditors, attorneys, and strategic planners—were used judiciously in an effort to lay the groundwork and present a case for large-scale cultural change. The "old guard" wasn't ignored. Rather, I sought out long-time employees who, while loyal to the organization, also were frankly concerned about where it was heading.

I then spent most of the next eighteen months building my knowledge base of corporate culture change and also selling the concept to our Board of Directors, Corporate Officers, field managers, and department heads. During this period of time, I made approximately 25 presentations on my assessment of the Society's culture. Support for organizational change grew and put me in a increasingly combative posture relative to the incumbent President. The matter came to a head in June of 1984, when I was promoted to the position of President and Chief Executive Officer. Upon reflection, the field generally supported this change, but still had no clear understanding of the implications of my program of organizational transformation . . .

In a rapidly changing healthcare environment, leverage to move the organization forward was not hard to find. In 1984, the introduction of a new Medicare payment system accelerated the decline in usage of many of our rural facilities, and we ended the year in poor financial shape. Eight facilities were earmarked for divestiture. The impact of changes in farming and energy have placed many of our communities in severe economic distress. Thus, changes in Federal healthcare payment, together with economic decline, have been used to convince field managers that they must change their behavior if they are to survive. Market, and not operational orientation, has been stressed as a pathway to the future . . .

It's clear that from this point forward, the field can make or break this effort. No amount of cajoling or negative incentives will lead to the widespread acceptance of this transformation. Rather, the field managers need to perceive this program as in their best interests as well as the corporation's. In fact, they should see it as representing an appropriate response to a rapidly changing environment. Fortunately, many do. The remainder will come on board, given time, and given a continuing commitment to the program by the senior management of the company.

Large-scale cultural change is an imposing undertaking and substantive change will not come about overnight. The chief executive officer must make a multiple year commitment to the effort. Enormous amount of time and travel are involved, and to the extent possible, the individual should embody the desirable attributes of the new culture. Continuing, personal, hands-on involvement is essential . . . *

*Courtesy, Michael O. Bice from an article entitled "The Organizational Transformation of Lutheran Health Systems."

The heroic manager model is free of any reference to organizations in its fundamental assumptions. Not so the managerial strategist model, which has gained popularity with the recognition that some organizations are inherently unmanageable in the traditional sense. Consider an organization that has widely diffused power, strong dependency on elements in its environment, an uncertain technology, and ambiguous and shifting goals. One could say with some logic that planning, organizing, directing, and controlling are impossible in such a setting. Yet we see in the patterns of health industry development a movement in just these directions.

Health organizations are made up of multiple influential decision makers, each with their own interests, values and goals, which often, and perhaps inevitably, conflict. The question is how an organization's objectives are defined in such a conflict situation. Cyert and March's bargaining model specifies that objectives are defined by a process of continuous bargaining among changing coalitions of such influential participants (47). They note that participants will have different amounts of influence, or power, in different situations and on different issues. Such bargaining among coalitions does not necessarily lead to a set of consistent rational objectives for the organization. Bucher and Stelling argue that this model is particularly relevant in professional organizations (48), in which a variety of professional groups each work in their own direction and seek to implement their own professional values. To the extent that any integration occurs in such a situation, it occurs under conditions of diverse values and competing interests, and only through a continual political process. That is, members of these various professional groups seek out allies in attempting to bring to bear sufficient power to influence organizational policy. Through concerted political activity, the various allies and factions seek to influence events so as to protect their vital interests and implement their professional values. Which persons and groups have the most influence in setting goals and practices in professional organizations is a complex and fluid phenomenon. Power to influence policy is diffused and the locus and balance of power often shift in response to different issues and as different persons and groups move through the organization.

For the manager, this means first that it is necessary to understand the sources of power in an organization (e.g., control of scarce resources, control of communication, knowledge, or technology, formal positional authority, and power which accrues from one's own personality or style (49). Managers must also understand the implications of this bargaining model so as to effectively balance conflicting points of view, coordinate activities of various subgroups, and develop their own strategies. The manager must be able to identify who is likely to be influential and active in a given situation, what outcomes each group is likely to want in a particular instance, what demands these influential groups are likely to make, what it is they are likely to support or oppose, and what amounts and sources of power each group is likely to have in a given situation. The manager must be able to anticipate what coalitions are likely to form and be able to design a negotiating strategy which may serve to offset the power of some influential groups while strengthening the power of others. Managers must also develop their own sources of power. In so doing, they may have to actively line up support for certain positions by forming coalitions, perhaps going outside the organization (e.g., to accrediting agencies, third-party payors) to gather sufficient support.

The Cyert and March (47) bargaining model of managerial decision making was among the first to frame this setting usefully, and it was adopted by Thompson (6) in his description of a coalitional model of management. Thompson moves beyond the idea of a coalition as a group containing those persons with a strong power base, pointing out that there may be hundreds of such individuals in a large, complex organization. His observations suggest that an inner circle develops, and in this context, he describes the role of the manager:

> It seems clear, then, that in the highly complex organization, an individual can be powerful, can symbolize the power of the organization, and can exercise significant leadership; but we would predict, as in the case of the inner circle, that he can do so only with the consent and approval of the dominant coalition. Thus the highly complex organization is not the place for the dictator or commander to emerge. In the highly complex organization, in our opinion, neither the central power figure nor the inner circle (nor their combination) can reverse the direction of organizational movement at will. . . .
>
> Without the "superb politician," metropolitan school systems, urban governments, universities, mental hospitals, social work systems, and similar complex organizations would be immobilized. (6)

How does one describe the role of a "superb politician"? The heroic manager may be one, but not in the sense described here. The context is strongly organizational, and, as Pfeffer notes, though individual skills and personality can affect the amount of influence a manager has, "power is first and foremost a structural phenomenon, and should be understood as such" (50).

A first attempt at understanding the role of the managerial strategist is to recognize that it is closely linked to the function of the adaptive and maintenance subsystem. However, it rejects the universalist human relations model of McGregor or Likert as the means of achieving a viable human organization, largely because there is no option to introduce "participation." Instead there is an acknowledgement of the need to deal with separate interest groups, each with its own basis of power.

Evidently the construction of coalitions and the ability to create and sustain a viable power base to ensure the manager's membership in the inner circle are both critical skills. Johnson emphasizes the second (51). Describing the chief executive role as "a life of leverages, of using tonal qualities, facial expressions, and body language to buttress their skills in carefully controlling information, agendas, and timing," he suggests that the control and selective use of information can be a foundation of managerial power. The chief executive may be the only common thread among the many committees, departments, the medical staff, the governing board, and critical external groups. Johnson also notes that information can be important to the manager in anticipating and channeling events and sensing and influencing a flow of action at a time when the manager's influence is still decisive. As power is gained, it can be frozen into place by using it to create structural forms that benefit managers (such as having themselves retitled president, or gaining a seat on the board). Power can also be stabilized by creating loyalties. Although granting of favors is moderately effective, nothing creates stronger loyalties than an unbroken chain of successes. Thus, managerial strategists are acutely sensitive to the probable success of a project before deciding to support it, but they become strongly results oriented when their name is irrevocably linked with a project. As another seasoned hospital executive noted, "you don't want to joust with the windmill if you are going to lose" (37).

There is nothing about the managerial strategist model that links it to overarching social values, or that necessarily excludes them. Johnson's power brokers may be building either a true community health facility or monuments to themselves. The managerial strategist model simply accepts the centrality of power to prospering in these partly professional, partly bureaucratic, and partly anarchic organizations.

There is a tendency to accept this most up-to-date model of the health manager's role as the final word on the subject. Our view is that it enriches but does not replace the more conventional models of the health manager's role. Rather it gives further emphasis to the liaison, monitor, spokesman, and negotiator roles identified by Mintzberg, which we consider as characteristic of the adaptive and maintenance subsystems.

We can summarize this position by saying that power is important, perhaps increasingly so, but one must still attend carefully to the universal core of the management process and the attributes which make each organization distinct. In short, none of the three perspectives that have been used to study the managerial role can be rejected, for each gives an emphasis without which the challenge and the variety inherent in the role is diminished.

A Note on Garbage Can Models

The managerial strategist model acknowledges that some organizations are inherently unmanageable in the traditional sense. Nevertheless, some rationality in organization action is assumed by the model, for without such assumptions the concept of management itself is at least ambiguous, and perhaps meaningless. To some degree, assumptions of rationality underlie all the managerial roles we have described. We assume that organizations have (or produce) purposes, that these purposes guide actions, and that managers have enough understanding to select intelligently among actions, and enough power to have that selection make a difference. The heroic manager may bring new purposes, the managerial strategist may concentrate on building a power base, and the other roles may refine or develop different aspects of these assumptions, but the assumptions themselves remain. Indeed, they are so deeply embedded in our thinking that seeing organizations in a different way requires a special effort. To achieve this new perspective, Weick suggests as a guiding principle that we reverse the common assertion, "I'll believe it when I see it," suggesting that we only will be able to see organizations as loosely coupled systems when we believe they can exist. "[They] may not have been seen before because nobody believed in them or could afford to believe in them." (52)

What would we "see" in an organization if these assumptions were relaxed? Certainly the first point to emphasize is that we would "see" nothing until we replaced them with some alternative framework to give meaning to what was observed. Such phrases as "organized anarchies," "loosely coupled systems," or "garbage can models of organizational choice" have been used to describe several quite similar frameworks in which an alternative set of assumptions is used to make sense of observed decision-making events in organizations (53). The garbage-can model has been described as follows (54, p. 17):

> In pure form, the garbage can model assumes that problems, solutions, decision makers and choice opportunities are independent, exogenous streams flowing through a system. They are linked in a manner determined by their arrival and departure times and any structural constraint on the access of problems, solutions and decision makers to choice opportunities. In the absence of structural constraints within a garbage can process, solutions are linked to problems, and decision makers to choices, primarily by their simultaneity.

Our experience in academic settings, particularly in academic health centers, has convinced us that garbage can models do indeed give the observer an alternative framework within which to understand how some complex organizations operate. As yet, it is not clear that this understanding offers a useful basis for specifying a managerial role. One well-known example of an organized anarchy is the American university. Cohen and March describe the university president as " . . . a bit like the driver of a skidding automobile. The marginal judgements he makes, his skill, and his luck may possibly make some difference to the survival prospects for his riders. As a result, his responsibilities are heavy. But whether he is convicted of manslaughter or receives a medal for heroism is largely outside his control." (55, p. 203) Garbage can models illuminate aspects of organizational action and stimulate fresh thinking about "what do managers *really* do?"; they have not yet provided an accepted new dimension to the managerial role.

SIGNIFICANT ISSUES

Does this view of the health services manager as part rationalist, part politician, and part organization analyst help illuminate the challenges that managers of the future will face? Let us consider several major trends that seem to be taking shape in our industry and consider the impact they may have on the manager's role.

One of the basic, continuing changes in the health care industry is the move away from free-standing autonomous institutions to a set of interdependent multiunit organizations. These organizations have evolved for several reasons—to cope with an increasingly turbulent and complex environment, to acquire scarce and valued resources, to enable growth and, in some cases, survival, and to gather sufficient size and strength to influence the environment. Thus multiunit systems are both reactive to constraints and contingencies imposed by the external environment and also proactive in their efforts to influence the environment. As multiunit organizations develop, they increasingly involve linkages with other organizations. Such linkages, which may be extreme, as in the case of mergers, or which may be more loosely coupled, as in coalitions, networks, or strategic alliances, require greater attention to the adaptive function on the part of the manager.

These developments emphasize the two-way nature of the organizational–environmental interaction. That is, the organization is affected by its environment but also has the opportunity to influence its environment. This suggests that the place of strategic planning will grow in importance (see Chapter 13) as managers seek to assess the opportunities and threats posed by the environment and to identify the strengths and weaknesses of their organizations in order to adapt to and influence the environment.

This question of organizational and environmental interaction is discussed in greater detail in Chapter 10. However, it is important to note that the role of managerial strategist, as described in the political conception, is heightened.

Another likely development in the creation of multiunit organizations is a potential redistribution of power within the organization, with a shift away from the professional component and toward the managerial component. As the environment becomes increasingly constrained, as we are faced with increased regulation and competition, the skills and knowledge of the manager become increasingly important and central to the organization's ability to cope. The increasing numbers of physicians available over the next decade, which will change the balance of supply and demand, may further shift the balance of power toward the managerial component. How these shifts are handled becomes a crucial managerial question. It is likely that we will see increasing competition between physicians and health care organizations in the provision of services. A truly effective manager, however, will seek to integrate physicians into the organization, recognizing the mutuality of interests that exists and the growing interdependence of clinical and managerial decision making. This integration will undoubtedly include new roles for physicians in management. Such physician-managers will be key players in the development and implementation of emerging organizational strategies, in the nurturing of effective relationships with physicians and medical staffs, and in the management of programs and resources.

Growing complexity within the organization brings forth an additional set of issues. As the number of occupational groups within the organization continues to grow, we will witness increasing competition, overlapping of professional domains, and, most importantly, differing professional cultures and loyalties among these various occupational groups. Needed will be coordination among these groups as well as the management of the inevitable conflict that will arise.

Emerging multiunit organizations are no longer simply horizontally integrated, but are vertically integrated and diversified as well. As such increasingly complex organizations evolve, the various subunits may well move in different and potentially conflicting directions. The coordination and control of such wide-ranging organizational activities becomes a growing challenge for managers within the system. Further, the necessity of balancing the interests, priorities, and concerns of the various subunits becomes a key concern of system management (56). Evolving multiunit organizations also bring with them a more complex set of internal interrelationships, notably those among and between corporate management and governance vis-a-vis local or institutional management and governance. In such relationships issues inevitably arise as to allocation of resources, decision-making responsibilities, domains of authority, and accountability. These issues suggest the need for greater attention to the maintenance function in order to provide for organizational stability and predictability.

In many ways, multiunit organizations have brought with them a greater degree of specialization, that is, one finds growing emphasis placed on such functional areas as finance, strategic planning, marketing, risk management, information systems, and management engineering. What is likely to be the impact on the organization of such functional specialization? What does the growing emphasis on such specialization mean with regard to the requisite skills and knowledge for those who serve as "generalist managers"? Will this emphasis on specialization lead to different types of career patterning? In other industries it is not uncommon to find that, depending upon the stage of development and needs of a given organization, the general manager may well have emerged from a functional area such as finance or marketing. Within health care organizations, particularly not-for-profit hospital organizations, the pattern has been for generalist managers, typically former hospital managers, to become high-level corporate executives. Might we expect patterns from other industries to become more prevalent within health care, and if so, what are the implications?

Growing concern over issues of costs, capacity reduction, and utilization, emanating not only from government but from industry and labor as well, will focus increased attention on the production function within the hospital. Issues of productivity, cost control, and other concerns in the realm of technical efficiency will grow in importance. We must also be reminded that the pressures for efficiency may involve countervailing forces. That is, to what extent does focus on cost affect quality? To what extent are organizations and their managers prepared to deal with the possibility of rationing services? How do managers deal with potential conflict between organizational values and pressures for efficiency? Pressures to deal with these issues will cause organizations to come under growing scrutiny, requiring concern with organizational efficiency and fostering the growth of integrated management and clinical information systems. Thus a set of external factors will force attention to be given to what we have defined as the production function. In this context, we are reminded that the traditional school, with its focus on the rational manager responsible for technical performance, continues to be a basic imperative.

An important question is whether the changing structure of the field of health services brings with it a *fundamental* change in the role of the manager. We think not. We would agree that increasingly complex and diversified organizations do indeed bring new challenges to managers and may well call for shifting emphases. Such shifts are likely to take place within the context of the management role as described in this chapter. Indeed, the major changes may require growing attention to enabling the organization to adapt internal structure to a changing environment, and seeking to integrate the various parts of the organization in pursuit of organizational goals (56).

These emerging issues lead to a conclusion that there will be new challenges for managers in responding to the adaptive, the maintenance, and the production functions of their organizations. This is not to suggest that a single individual will find his or her role expanded in all three areas. Rather it suggests that the generic role of manager is enhanced and expanded by these external and internal developments. The problem will be to focus attention on all of these managerial requirements, which may involve splitting the role among individual managers. Yet in order to work, it will also require an effective way of reintegrating these functions to create what Mintzberg referred to as a gestalt of roles.

For health care managers of the future this integrating requirement may be the greatest challenge: being responsive to the vision of a healthy society without becoming an irrelevant dreamer, and finding pathways to organizational survival without losing the vision that makes survival worthwhile.

SUMMARY

In summary, this discussion of alternative managerial roles suggests the following guidelines or precepts.

MANAGERIAL GUIDELINES

1. All conceptions of the manager's role are potentially useful to future executives. There are some common features to the role (i.e., universalist school); there are some important differences, which exist because of variations in organization size, age, environment, technologies, and related factors (i.e., the organizational view); and aside from either universalist or organization views, the personal/political/strategic role of the manager is increasingly important.

2. As health care organizations become more diverse, the importance of the organizational conception of the manager's role becomes more important.

3. As the environment of health care organizations becomes more turbulent, the personal/political/strategic role of the manager increases in importance. This is particularly true at higher-level managerial level positions.

4. Entry-level managerial positions are primarily focused on production or technical subsystem activities; intermediate-level managerial positions are primarily focused on system support and maintenance; and top-level executive positions are primarily focused on strategic adaptation, organizational renewal, and transformation. Different types of skills and orientations are required for each.

5. Managerial roles are constantly being refined as a function of daily interaction between the organization and its many stakeholders both internal and external. There is great need for organizational leaders who can integrate the various roles into a coherent whole.

6. The emphasis in the future is likely to be on *management teams* that complement each other in skills, orientations, and roles so as to produce needed synergy for organizational survival and growth.

DISCUSSION QUESTIONS

1. Do you know any managers whose behavior seems to fit one of the five managerial role models?

2. In what kind of organizations would managerial strategists be most common? Heroic managers?

3. Take a poll of the class to determine which kind of managerial role your classmates would most like to have. Listen carefully to the reasons, then debate this proposition: "Managers will reconstruct their job to fit their preferences, and not vice versa."

4. Develop a description of three health organizations: one that has serious problems in the production/supportive function, one that has serious problems in the maintenance function, and one that has serious problems in the adaptive function. How will the managerial role differ in these organizations?

SUGGESTED READINGS

Allison, R., Dowling, W. & Munson, F. The role of health services administrators and implications for educators. In J. P. Dixon, (Ed.), *Education for health administration* (Vol. II). Ann Arbor: Health Administration Press, 1975.

Provides further elaboration of some of the issues raised in this chapter, with particular reference to the education of health managers.

Cronkhite, L. HCMR interview: Mr. Inside and Mr. Outside. *Health Care Management Review,* 1 (2), 1976, 77–88.
Provides an interesting discussion of the different roles and responsibilities of CEOs who must deal with the external relationships of the hospital and those who must deal primarily with internal operating issues.

Mintzberg, H. *The nature of managerial work.* Englewood Cliffs, N.J.: Prentice-Hall, 1973.
A classic work on what it is that managers actually do. Among the key findings are that managers spend very little time on any one activity and that current information, such as what can be obtained by phone and through face-to-face interaction, plays an important role in decision making.

Thompson, J. D. The administrative process. In *Organizations in action.* New York: McGraw-Hill, 1967, Chapter 11.
Highlights the importance of "co-alignment" of people, technology, structure, and environment. Emphasizes that while the administrative process must reduce uncertainty, it must search for flexibility at the same time. This is particularly important as organizations in society become more interdependent.

Wegmiller, D. C. Management issues in the development and maturation of multihospital systems. *Health Care Management Review,* 10 (2), 1985, 9–17.
Describes the stages of development of multihospital systems, and explores the demands and challenges to managers as systems develop and mature.

REFERENCES

1. Everhart, D. L. HCMR interview: David L. Everhart of Northwestern Memorial Hospital. *Health Care Management Review,* 1978, 3 (2), 97–105.

2. McNerney, W. J. The role of the executive. *Hospital and Health Services Administration,* 1976, 21, 9–25.

3. Simon, H. A. *Administrative Behavior* (2nd ed.). New York: Macmillan, 1961.

4. Woodward, J. *Industrial organization: Theory and practice.* New York: Oxford University Press, 1953.

5. Burns, T., & Stalker, G. M. *The management of innovation* (2nd ed.). London: Tavistock, 1966.

6. Thompson, J. D. *Organizations in action.* New York: McGraw-Hill, 1967.

7. Townsend, R. *Up the organization: How to stop the corporation from stifling people and strangling profits.* Greenwich, Conn.: 1970.

8. Freidman, M. *Type A behavior and your heart.* New York: Knopf, 1974.

9. Newman, W. H. *Administrative action: The techniques of organization and management* (2nd ed.). Englewood Cliffs, N.J.: Prentice-Hall, 1963.

10. Dixon, J. P. *Education for health administration* (Vol. I). Ann Arbor, Michigan: Health Administration Press, 1975.

11. Longest, B. B. Jr.; The contemporary hospital chief executive officer. *Health Care Management Review,* 1978, 3 (2), 43–53.

12. McGregor, D. A. Managerial responsibilities: The human side of enterprise. *Proceedings of the Fifth Anniversary Convocation of the School of Industrial Management*, Massachusetts Institute of Technology, Cambridge, Massachusetts, April 9, 1957, pp. 23–30.

13. Roethlisberger, F. J., & Dickson, W. J. *Management and the worker*. Cambridge, Mass.: Harvard University Press, 1947.

14. Likert, R. *The human organization: Its management and value*. New York, McGraw-Hill, 1967.

15. Mintzberg, H. *The nature of managerial work*. Englewood Cliffs, N.J., Prentice-Hall, 1973.

16. Mintzberg, H. The manager's job: Folklore and fact. *Harvard Business Review*, 1975 53 (4), 49–61.

17. Neustadt, R. E. *Presidential power*. New York: John Wiley & Sons, 1960.

18. Stewart, R. *Managers and their jobs*. New York: Macmillan, 1967.

19. Stewart, R. To understand the manager's job: Consider demands, constraints choices. *Organizational Dynamics*, 1976, 4 (4), 22–32.

20. Mintzberg, H. *The structuring of organizations*. Englewood Cliffs, N.J.: Prentice-Hall, 1979.

21. Parsons, T. *Structure and process in modern society*. Glencoe, Ill.: Free Press, 1960.

22. Mouzelis, N. P. *Organization and bureaucracy: An analysis of modern theories*. Chicago: Aldine Atherton, 1968.

23. Katz, D., & Kahn, R. *The social psychology of organizations* (2nd ed.). New York: John Wiley & Sons, 1978.

24. Perrow, C. The analysis of goals in complex organizations. *American Sociological Review*, 1961, 26, 854–865.

25. Urmy, N. B. "Flight or fight: Managing hospitals in an increasingly controlled environment. Reprinted in A. R. Kovner and D. Neuhauser (Ed.). *Health Services Management; Readings and Commentary;* (2nd eds.). Ann Arbor: Health Administration Press, 1983.

26. Psacharopoulos, G. Assessing training priorities in developing countries: Current practice and possible alternatives. *International Labour Review*, 1984, *123* (4), 569–583.

27. Perrow, C. Goals and power structures. In E. Freidson (Ed.), *The hospital in modern society*. New York: Free Press, 1963.

28. Weaver, J. L. *Conflict and control in health care administration* (Vol. 14). Beverly Hills, Cal.: Sage Publications, 1975.

29. Allison, R. F., Dowling, W. L., & Munson, F. C. The role of health services administrators and implications for educators. In J. P. Dixon (Ed.), *Education for health administration* (Vol. II). Ann Arbor: Health Administration Press, 1975.

30. Kuhl, I. K. *The executive role in health service delivery organizations*. Washington, D.C.: Association of University Programs in Health Administration, 1977.

31. Morita, E. K., Hodapp, R. D., Slater, C. H. *Group practice administration: Current and future roles*. Medical Group Management Association, Final Report for Contract No. NO1-MB-44176. Bureau of Health Manpower, Health Resources Administration, Public Health Service, U.S. Department of Health, Education, and Welfare, Center

for Research in Ambulatory Health Care Administration, Denver, Colorado, June 30, 1976.

32. Johnson, A. C., Forrest, C. R., Mosher, J. *An investigation into the nature, causes, and implications of health care administration.* University of Wisconsin-Madison, Final Report for Contract No. 231-75-0004. U.S. Department of Health, Education, and Welfare, Public Health Service, Health Resources Administration, Bureau of Health Manpower, March 31, 1977.

33. Johnson, A. C., Forrest, C. R. *The roles and relationships of mental health human services administrators.* University of Wisconsin-Madison, Grant No. ST23MH15017-02. Center for State Mental Health Manpower Development, Division of Manpower and Training Programs of the National Institute of Mental Health.

34. Kaiser, D. L. *An empirical examination of administrative roles in local health departments.* Monograph 7, Chapel Hill, North Carolina, Department of Health Administration, School of Public Health, University of North Carolina at Chapel Hill, 1978.

35. Brown, R. C. Training for health services management. *Hospital Administration,* 1973, 11–23.

36. Weisbord, M. R. Why organization development hasn't worked (so far) in medical centers. *Health Care Management Review,* 1976, 17–28.

37. Cronkhite, L. HCMR Interview: Mr. Inside and Mr. Outside. *Health Care Management Review,* 1976, 77–88.

38. Scott, W. R. Introduction to part one: Theoretical perspectives. In M. W. Meyer, et al. (Eds.), *Environments and organizations.* San Francisco: Jossey-Bass, 1980.

39. Machiavelli, N. *The Prince and the Discourse.* New York: Carlton House (n. d.).

40. Bird, C. *Born female* (rev. ed.). New York: Pocket Books, 1971.

41. Livingston, J. S. Myth of the well-educated manager. *Harvard Business Review,* 1971, 79–89.

42. Zaleznik, A. Managers and leaders: Are they different? *Harvard Business Review,* 1977, 55 (3), 67–78.

43. Kimberly, J. R. Issues in the creation of organizations: Initiation, innovation and institutionalization. *Academy of Management Journal,* 1979, 437–457.

44. Quinn, J. B. Technological innovation, entrepreneurship and strategy. *Sloan Management Review,* 1979, 3, 19–30.

45. Murray, J. A. A concept of entrepreneurial strategy. *Strategic Management Journal,* 1984, 1–13.

46. Lieberson, S., & O'Conner, J. Leadership and organizational performance. *American Sociological Review,* 1972, 37, 117–130.

47. Cyert, R. M., & March, J. G. A behavioral theory of organizational objectives. In M. Haire (Ed.), *Modern organization theory.* New York: John Wiley & Sons, 1959.

48. Bucher, R., & Stelling, J. G. *Becoming professional,* Vol. 46. Beverly Hills, Calif.: Sage Library of Social Research, 1977.

49. Dowling, W. L. *Objective setting and policy-making in hospitals.* U.S. Army Medical Field Service School, Fort Sam Houston, Texas, April 5, 1972.

50. Pfeffer, J. *Power in organizations.* Marshfield, Mass.: Pitman Publishing, 1981.

51. Johnson, R. L. The power broker—Prototype of the hospital chief executive? *Health Care Management Review,* 1978, 67–73.

52. Weick, Karl E. Educational organizations as loosely coupled systems. *Administrative Science Quarterly*, 1976, *21*, 1–19.

53. Cohen, M. D., March, J. G., & Olsen, J. P., A garbage can model of organizational choice. *Administrative Science Quarterly*, 1972, *17*, 1–25.

54. March, J. G., & Olsen, J. P., Garbage can models of decision making in organizations. In *Ambiguity and command: Organizational perspectives on military decision making.* J. G. March & R. Weissinger-Baylon (Eds.). Marshfield, Mass.: Pitman, 1985, p. 17.

55. Cohen, M., & March, J. *Leadership and Ambiguity: The American college president.* New York: McGraw Hill, 1974.

56. Wegmiller, D. C. Management issues in the development and maturation of multi-hospital systems. *Health Care Management Review*, 1985, *10* (2), 9–17.

PART TWO

Motivating and Leading People and Groups

People are the organizing principle.

Robert Theobold

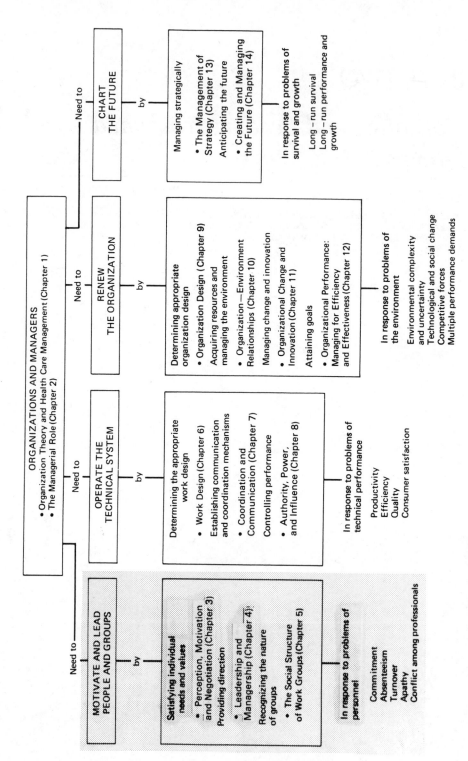

ORGANIZATIONS AND MANAGERS
• Organization Theory and Health Care Management (Chapter 1)
• The Managerial Role (Chapter 2)

Need to → MOTIVATE AND LEAD PEOPLE AND GROUPS

by →

Satisfying individual needs and values
• Perception, Motivation and Negotiation (Chapter 3)
Providing direction
• Leadership and Managership (Chapter 4)
Recognizing the nature of groups
• The Social Structure of Work Groups (Chapter 5)

In response to problems of personnel

Commitment
Absenteeism
Turnover
Apathy
Conflict among professionals

Need to → OPERATE THE TECHNICAL SYSTEM

by →

Determining the appropriate work design
• Work Design (Chapter 6)
Establishing communication and coordination mechanisms
• Coordination and Communication (Chapter 7)
Controlling performance
• Authority, Power, and Influence (Chapter 8)

In response to problems of technical performance

Productivity
Efficiency
Quality
Consumer satisfaction

Need to → RENEW THE ORGANIZATION

by →

Determining appropriate organization design
• Organization Design (Chapter 9)
Acquiring resources and managing the environment
• Organization – Environment Relationships (Chapter 10)
Managing change and innovation
• Organizational Change and Innovation (Chapter 11)
Attaining goals
• Organizational Performance: Managing for Efficiency and Effectiveness (Chapter 12)

In response to problems of the environment

Environmental complexity and uncertainty
Technological and social change
Competitive forces
Multiple performance demands

Need to → CHART THE FUTURE

by →

Managing strategically
• The Management of Strategy (Chapter 13)
Anticipating the future
• Creating and Managing the Future (Chapter 14)

In response to problems of survival and growth

Long – run survival
Long – run performance and growth

The nature of organizations: Framework for the text.

Whether considered a hassle or an opportunity, the need to motivate and lead people and groups within the organization is critical to the management process. Motivation and leadership are needed to satisfy individual needs and values and to provide overall direction.

Chapter 3 deals with perception, motivation, and negotiation. The objective of this chapter is to consider each of these concepts and its application to understanding individual behavior within health care organizations. Individuals spend a great deal of time in organizations. In addition to specific work accomplishments, individuals have needs for affiliation, self-worth and identity, and to negotiate successfully in a variety of situations. Understanding the motivation and perception of individuals in the organization and the negotiation process among individuals and groups is critical to successful management.

This chapter gives attention to the following questions:

- Why do individuals perceive certain things yet ignore others?
- What can individuals do to minimize perceptual bias?
- What motivates individuals to act in certain ways?
- Is it possible to affect individual motivation and behavior to enhance performance?
- How is it possible to reconcile the legitimate (and not so legitimate) viewpoints of individuals?

Chapter 4 considers leadership style and managership. The chapter begins with a review of leadership from the perspective of psychological and organizational theory. The psychological perspective gives attention to personality traits, behavior, and style; the organizational perspective focuses on the structural environmental contexts of the organization and emphasizes the broad set of activities that leads to the formalization and implementation of decisions.

These distinctions are considered within the context of health care organizations, with emphasis on different levels of management. In considering these issues attention is given to resolving the following questions:

- What is the difference between managership and leadership within organizations?
- How can the health care manager's role be restructured to provide better leadership for the organization?
- What are the roles of management in strategic planning?

Chapter 5 outlines the basic characteristics of the work group. Attention is given to understanding the importance of different types of work groups in the operations of the organization and to considering both structural and process characteristics and implications for effective management. The chapter centers on the following questions:

- What is the differential contribution of structural versus procedural characteristics on work group performance?
- Among structural characteristics, what are the primary determinants of various aspects of work group performance?
- What are the roles of size and technology in the design of work groups?
- What functions must be performed by the group to ensure its survival?

Upon completing these three chapters students should be able to:

- Identify factors that influence their perception of various aspects of the organization as well as identify perceptual biases.
- Understand the types of behaviors that organizations need or desire from their members to enhance their overall performance.
- Identify and apply techniques that will stimulate motivation and facilitate desired behaviors.
- Understand the negotiation process, the factors affecting the process, and the strategies available to the manager.
- Distinguish between managership and leadership.
- Identify situations in which management or leadership is appropriate for the effective allocation of resources.
- Understand the importance of work groups within the organization and identify critical structural and process characteristics associated with work group performance.

CHAPTER 3

Perception, Motivation, and Negotiation

David Greenberger
Stephen Strasser
Roy J. Lewicki
Thomas S. Bateman

This chapter focuses on three major topics in health care management: perception, motivation, and negotiation. Ideas and concepts from social and organizational psychology and learning theory are utilized to explain perceptual and motivational processes and their application to the practice of effective health care management. These can then be applied to better understand the negotiation process.

Motivation, perception, and negotiation are closely related topics. They are important areas of study for a variety of reasons. The study of perception concerns the process by which people derive their own view of the world from the multitude of stimuli within themselves and their environment. The study of motivation deals with ways in which the individual behaves in response to these perceptions. Finally, all health care managers are involved to varying degrees in negotiations. This has become especially true in light of an environment characterized by increasing competition over existing resources. A manager's effectiveness in negotiation will depend in part on the accuracy of the manager's self-perception and the perception of others.

By studying the perception process, health care managers can develop (1) a greater awareness of how their own behaviors, attitudes, impressions, and decision-making styles are formed; (2) a better understanding of why they and other organizational members view the health care setting the way they do; and (3) greater insight into the biases that may exist within their own and others' perceptual systems. This third point has special significance, for biases in an administrator's perceptual system can easily lead to poor decision-making practices and a wide variety of other maladies, such as nonproductive attempts at conflict management and low-quality interpersonal relations with staff. Just as important are the personal and professional frustrations administrators experience that result from their inability to perceive themselves and other accurately.

By studying the motivational process, health care managers can develop *(1)* an awareness of why they are or are not motivated to work effectively; *(2)* a better understanding of how to motivate others in the health care setting; and *(3)* insight into how to sustain over time the motivational levels of employees. Each of these areas can translate into increased managerial effectiveness.

The first part of this chapter focuses on the perception process. First, the concept of perception is formally defined. Second, a model of the interpersonal perceptual process is presented. The model gives current and prospective health administrators a general framework from which specific practical applications can be made. Third, a number of considerations essential to the further understanding of the perceptual process are discussed: *(1)* the levels of analysis in perception; *(2)* the selective nature of perception; and *(3)* the notion of perception as functional reality in management. Fourth, building on this foundation, some of the perceptual biases health care managers are prone to and the problems biases cause within the health management context are addressed. Finally a number of suggestions of how the health care manager can deal with biases are offered. A major theme throughout the section on perception is that health organizations have a variety of contextual factors which impact adversely on the health administrator's ability to perceive himself and others accurately.

The next part of the chapter focuses on the motivation process. First, a set of behaviors (for example, good performance) which a health manager should want to motivate are identified. Second, the issue of how to stimulate and facilitate desirable behaviors is addressed. Third, the consequences of behaviors (rewards or punishments) are explored, with attention given to the impact of positive and negative reinforcers on employee behavior and motivation. Throughout this analysis the costs and benefits associated with various motivational strategies are considered; the role of learning theory as it applies to motivation is also explored. Finally, a model of employee work behavior outlined at the beginning of the motivation section is completed in detail.

The last section looks at the nature of the negotiation process. First, the nature of this process is defined. Second, the keys to negotiation strategy are explored. Last, the sequence of events which negotiations typically follow is outlined.

Effective health care management requires a thorough understanding of the individual in the organization. Studying how individuals perceive themselves and the world around them and exploring why they are motivated to behave in the way they do helps develop this understanding. This knowledge might then be applied to improving the manager's ability as a negotiator.

PERCEPTION

Consider what a health care manager sees, hears, and does on a given day. When one thinks about the number of meetings attended, phone calls made, letters answered, reports reviewed, plans considered, and individual people seen, one is struck by the magnitude, variety, and complexity of the external and internal stimuli directed at the manager. The way in which the manager puts meaning to these stimuli is the perception process. The exact meanings an individual attaches to stimuli is perception. Nisbett and

Ross (1) further narrow this definition in terms of some of the activities the perceiver performs:

> The perceiver is an active interpreter, one who resolves ambiguities, makes educated guesses about events that cannot be observed directly and forms inferences and associations and causal relationships. . . . (1)

A brief scenario may give greater clarity to this definition:

> The director of the Memorial Hospital pharmacy department realizes that a shortage of personnel is badly delaying production and delivery of prescriptions to hospital medical-surgical inpatients. He knows from past experience that top management will listen sympathetically to a request for additional personnel but will point out that the hospital's uncertain fiscal position makes his manpower problem a very low priority concern. Management's lack of concern is not shared by the nursing staff, who are increasingly upset by delays in filling orders for medication. Caught between management's inflexible stand and the demands of the ward service, the director complains to the assistant director: "I have had it with administration. They say they understand my problem, but they do nothing about it. I guess they really don't care. Going to talk with them would be just another waste of time. You know, I always feel I lose when I meet with those people. They can't see beyond their sacred budgets—they're all that way."

In this scenario the director of the pharmacy has developed a perception of hospital managers as short-sighted individuals. He has, in fact, stereotyped managers. The stimuli that led him to this conclusion are mostly external to the director; his stereotype is based on past experiences with administrators. However, there are also stimuli internal to the director that contribute to his views. For example, one might speculate that the director is emotionally incapable of accepting responsibility for current problems and, as a result, finds a significant or convenient other to whom to attribute blame. In sum, the director's perception of hospital executives is a function of the way he interprets rather explicit external stimuli and, less explicitly in this scenario, his own internal stimuli (such as need structure, cognitive processes, and so forth). Figure 3.1 illustrates this type of interpersonal perception and the role of internal and external stimuli/factors on it.

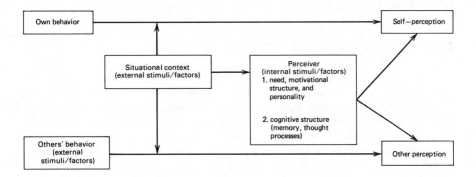

Figure 3.1. A model of the process of interpersonal perception.

A FRAMEWORK FOR UNDERSTANDING PERCEPTION

In the model of interpersonal perception perceivers develop perceptions of themselves and others through the influence of several sources of stimuli. As shown in Figure 3.1, these may be external (contextual) or internal to the perceiver. The meaning the perceiver attaches to the stimuli is the *perception*.

EXTERNAL STIMULI/FACTORS

External stimuli comprise all things which exist outside the perceiver. They may be objects, things we see, sound, odors, people, their behaviors, and so forth. The combination and configuration of these stimuli comprise the context from which many of our perceptions are shaped.

The role played by external (contextual) factors in the perception process can be illustrated in two brief scenarios:

1. The setting is the center of the hospital's visiting area for families of obstetrical patients. The executive vice president (perceiver) sees Dr. Welsh berating Nurse Smith. In a loud voice, Dr. Welsh blames Nurse Smith for delay in reporting sudden change in the condition of one of his patients. His emotional outburst draws the attention of all the visitors and all the staff members working at the nursing station.

2. The setting is the private office adjoining the nursing station where Dr. Welsh is screaming at Nurse Smith. The clinic manager (perceiver) enters the office by opening the door from the working area. On hearing the violent outburst the manager hastily closes the door, only knowing that Nurse Smith is receiving a reprimand.

In the first scenario the manager might consider Dr. Welsh's behavior reprehensibly unprofessional. The manager might imagine each new or prospective father saying to himself, "I hope Nurse Smith is not on my wife's case." In the second scenario the manager might believe that Dr. Welsh's behavior is inappropriate but that Dr. Welsh has shown good judgment in venting his outrage in private. Even though in both cases Dr. Welsh is violently reprimanding Nurse Smith, the first context leads to a perception of Dr. Welsh as unprofessional; the second leads to a less negative perception.

INTERNAL STIMULI/FACTORS

Internal stimuli exist within the perceiver and influence perception. One source of internal stimuli which influences our perceptions is our need structure. While this will be discussed in greater depth later, the following example illustrates the point: People need to maintain feelings of self-worth, self-esteem, and competence. These needs, for example, influence how we perceive our personal contribution to successful outcomes (2–4). When perceivers' egos are vested in a given outcome, they tend to attribute successes to their own internal attributes, such as ability, whereas they may be more likely to attribute their failures to external phenomena such as luck or the behavior of others. This may have been a part of the director of pharmacy's perception of managers. Unable to accept responsibility for his own department's problems (because such acceptance would be ego threatening), he instead blamed a convenient other: management. As another example, consider the perceptions of bad sports, who typically blame everything but themselves for their loss.

A second source of internal stimuli lies in the perceiver's cognitive qualities and capabilities. Based in part on the work of Tversky and Kahneman (5, 6), it has become clear that internal information processing systems (our cognitive orientation) influence what we perceive. Perceptions are often influenced, for example, by the accuracy of memory or the saliency individuals place on information received (7). Motivational or need structure (such as maintainance of ego strength) and cognitive information processing systems represent two broad classes of internal factors (or stimuli) that influence perceptions. They most probably operate in tandem in the formation of our perceptions.

OTHER PERCEPTIONS AND SELF-PERCEPTIONS

Figure 3.1 also distinguishes between "other perception" and "self-perception," as discussed in detail by Schneider, Hastorf and Ellsworth (8) and Nisbett and Ross (1). In the Dr. Welsh scenarios, the type of perception the hospital manager develops is different from the perception the bad sport has of the reasons for losing. In the former case the hospital manager has an impression of another (Dr. Welsh is insensitive). This is termed *other perception;* the bad sport's perception of losing (I lost because of bad luck, I'm really a better player) represents *self-perception.* When individuals make judgments of others, as when they attribute causes to their behavior or stereotype someone as a "typical" doctor, lab technician, or nurse, they are involved in the process of "other perception." Conversely, when individuals make attributions of the cause of their own behavior, or see themselves as "good" persons, better tennis players, and so forth, the process is termed "self-perception." Both internal and external stimuli will affect how we form self- and other perceptions.

Although self-perceptions and other perceptions differ in kind, the work of Bem (9–11) suggests that the way in which we develop perceptions of *others* may be quite similar to the way we develop *self*-perceptions. When we perceive others, we observe their behavior within a given context. Bem argues that we develop our own self-perceptions in a similar way. We observe (as another outside perceiver would do) our *own* behavior and infer from that behavior the attitudes, values, and beliefs that must have caused it. For example, the director of nursing services may observe himself getting up earlier every day to get to work sooner (the behavior) and may infer from that behavior that he enjoys his work (the self-perception/attitude). A critical component of the process is that we tend to use our own behavior or the behavior of others (10–12) to infer our own attitudes (self-perceptions), if we begin by experiencing vagueness or lack of saliency about our attitudes, feelings, or emotions. Hence, when we have no explanation (12) or unimportant information about our own internal dispositions, our behavior or some environmental stimulus helps us identify our attitudes and emotions (for example, the employee saying, "I've been working here for 20 years; I must like it here"). When individuals can explain their own feelings, attitudes, or perceptions they may be less dependent on their own or others' behavior to define their perceptions (12).

When we have little or unclear information about the internal disposition of others, we as observers develop our *other* perceptions through the actor's behavior and the context in which it occurs. One might hypothesize that when we do have an understanding of another person's internal dispositions we may be less dependent on their behavior (or a single episode of it) to develop our other perceptions. Perhaps, the relative strength of internal and external stimuli will dictate which predominates in the development of our self and other perceptions (8).

Bem's (10, 11) conceptualization of self-perception formation represents only one view of the process. Festinger (13) offers another in his theory of cognitive dissonance.* This theory suggests that when a person perceives inconsistencies in feelings, beliefs, and behaviors, he or she experiences dissonance (an uncomfortable state) and hence is motivated to reduce it: "The presence of dissonance leads to action to reduce it just as, for example, the presence of hunger leads to action to reduce the hunger . . ." (13). Following this line of reasoning, perceivers may attempt to see things in a way congruent with their own attitudes, beliefs, and self-expectations. When noncongruency exists, dissonance occurs, and the perceiver acts to minimize it. For instance, a health manager accused of inequity in her treatment of employees experiences dissonance because she perceives herself as an equitable person. To resolve the dissonance between the accusations and her self-perception the manager attempts to "restore consistency between cognitions" (15). There are many ways the manager can accomplish this. For example, she can: (1) alter her original self-perception ("unfortunately, managers need to be inequitable sometimes"), or (2) find new information in the environment to self-justify the behavior ("I know they treat employees this way at other hospitals") (15).

Festinger's formulation might help explain how other perceptions are formed. Suppose you just hired a new chief financial officer for your HMO. It was a difficult choice because there were many excellent candidates. You still have nagging doubts. However, once the new CFO comes on board you note that you evaluate enthusiastically everything she does. Upon reflection, you realize that you probably have inflated your assessment. Why did you do this? The answer lies in your desire to remove dissonance (conflicting feelings). Perceiving the CFO as a superstar makes your beliefs about her consistent with your decision in hiring her.

Important differences between the Bem and Festinger theories emerge. In the former, perceptions are formed not from an internal motivational basis but from a cognitive one (a perceiver sees himself or herself as an observer would). In the latter, perceptions are formed from a motivational basis to minimize feelings of internal dissonance.

In sum, the formation of self and other perceptions is a complex process. They are based on many factors. Clearly, the interplay of internal (cognitive and motivational) and external factors are important in the formation of perceptions.

SPECIFIC COMPONENTS OF THE PERCEPTION PROCESS

Levels of Analysis—From Snap Judgments to Attribution

An important aspect of the perception process has to do with the *level of analysis* we give to our perceptions—the complexity and depth of our perceptions vary. A new director of a state health department may walk into her office for the first time and observe the elderly receptionist curtly saying to a visitor, "Can't you read the index of offices next to the elevator—the well baby vaccination clinic is on the third floor." From

---

*A third theoretical approach to the formation of self and other perception is offered by Jones and Nisbett (14). The perspective has different implications and is discussed in more detail in a later section.

this observation the director may simply say to herself, "That is a cold, hard woman," and leave it at that. Alternatively, the director might say to herself, "That is a cold, hard woman—I guess that she must be frustrated or burned out with her job, after so many years."

The level of analysis is different for each of these two perceptions. The first represents a snap judgment. The director forms an immediate impression. According to Schneider et al. (8), "snap judgments do not involve complex hypotheses about the intentions and motives of the stimulus person or the cause of behavior. . . ." The second instance represents a more cognitively complex perception. Here the director goes beyond the snap judgment and attempts to find reasons for the receptionist's behavior. Social psychologists would argue that the director *attributes* a cause to the receptionist's behavior. Research designed to understand the nature and patterns of such attributions has been an important topic in the social psychology literature and has been frequently referred to as attribution theory research. While we all make attributions in a variety of circumstances, Wong and Weiner (16) suggest that perceivers frequently engage in "attributional search" (asking why something happened) when they experience (1) frustration or failure, (2) an unexpected event, or (3) personal tragedy.

What is the value to the perceiver of making snap judgments and attributions? More generally, what is the value of any kind of perception? Frequently snap judgments or attributions help us make rational sense of the world around us. Perceptions of any kind and at any level can allow us to integrate, often into meaningful wholes, the infinite number of stimuli which we confront. Second, snap judgments permit us to expedite the perception formation when time is at a premium. Third, snap judgments and attributions allow us to predict the behavior of ourselves and others (8). The predictive capability is extremely useful in facilitating our ability to work, interact socially, and simply survive in organizations and society. While our perceptions are sometimes inaccurate, as will be discussed later, the process can nonetheless be extremely functional.

The Selective Nature of Perception

Perception is a highly selective process. If it were not, we would be overwhelmed by the infinite number of stimuli to which we experience and are exposed. The fact that we select only a relatively small number of stimuli to process as perceptions allows us to function, cope, and create order out of what would otherwise be a chaotic world.

Health care managers in the course of daily routine find themselves surrounded by examples of this selective process. For instance, a manager might notice a perinatal intensive care unit nurse who is oblivious to all the infants crying in the unit but responds immediately to a missed heart beep from the cardiac monitor. Or the manager might observe himself at board of trustee meetings, tuning out discussion of details of a capital expenditure project but immediately hearing and actively listening to the comments of the board president. More generally, most people experience conflict situations in which they find themselves emotionally committed to one side of the argument. Such ego involvement can blind individuals to information that undermines their chosen position and lead them to perceive only that information which enhances their committed view.

People do perceive particular things and ignore others. On this aspect of human behavior, Harold Leavitt makes the following comment:

> People's perceptions are determined by their needs. Like mirrors at the amusement park, we distort the world in relation to our own tensions. Children from poorer homes, when

asked to draw a quarter, draw a bigger than actual one. Industrial employees, when asked to describe the people they work with, talk more about their bosses (the people more important to their needs) than about peers or subordinates, and so on. (17)

The nature of our cognitive abilities and limitations also affects our perceptions. Given our information-processing constraints, we cannot realistically manage all the stimuli we encounter. Persons must take short cuts in perceiving the world around them. Hence the interplay between our cognitive orientation and our personal needs and motivational structure dictates what we do and do not perceive.

From the health care manager's perspective, the selective nature of perception is truly a double-edged sword. On the positive side, managers are able to cope with the complexities of their organizational role by filtering out redundant, low-value stimuli. On the negative side, the filtering process may be systematically defective. Managers may omit or distort exactly those stimuli that would result in better management. The importance of this point should not be minimized, as the following example indicates. Many hospital CEOs have the opportunity to select members of their own top management staff upon entering their position. And, as is true with many of us, we have a strong need to affiliate (18): to be around people we like and feel comfortable with. Research conducted in the early 1960s by Byrne (19) and Byrne and Nelson (20) indicates that we tend to like others who are similar to ourselves in attitudes, values, and beliefs. If the CEO has a high need for affiliation and manifests the tendency to like or hire similar people, it is not hard to imagine virtual clones of the CEO moving into the top administrative positions. In essence, the CEO's need for affiliation creates a selective perceptual bias as it applies to critical staffing decisions. The manager perceives prospective co-workers primarily on the basis of affiliation rather than on additional criteria such as potential productivity and performance. Projecting into the future, it is not difficult to imagine the problems associated with uncreative group decision making or "group think" (21). In fact, research on the group-polarization phenomenon indicates that the attitudes of individuals in work groups may move in the direction of increasing risk or conservativeness because the individuals are exposed to only one type of argument in the group (22). Clearly, the health manager's cognitive awareness of both the functional and dysfunctional sides of the selective nature of perception is an important first step in becoming a better manager.

Perception, Reality, and Multiple Realities in Health Care Management

The perceptions people have of themselves and others form their reality—their notion of what is. Whether or not these perceptions of reality are in fact congruent with some absolute reality is a secondary issue within a managerial context. One important implication of people's *perception—reality equivalency* is that two people can observe an object or some set of behaviors and arrive at two completely different conclusions about what they saw (23). To each observer, what is perceived is their reality, though two quite different realities are reported. In addition, they may well behave on the basis of their own reality. Given that individuals' internal need states and cognitive processes are both different and transitory and that they dictate what we perceive, multiple realities can emerge in almost any situation.

The concept of multiple realities is demonstrated in a study by Shapiro and Dessler (24). These researchers first asked a group of administrators to assess their own performance and then asked the supervisors of this group to evaluate the administrators' per-

TABLE 3.1. Comparison of Self and Superior Ratings: Total Sample

	Self-Rating		Superior's Rating	
Performance Rating	Actual Number	Percent	Actual Rating	Percent
Outstanding	15	11.3	17	12.8
Highly satisfactory	79	59.4	47	35.3
Fully satisfactory	39	29.3	53	39.9
Minimally satisfactory	0	0	14	10.5
Unsatisfactory	0	0	2	1.5

SOURCE: Shapiro, G., & Dessler, G. *A comparison of hospital administrators' self and superior performance ratings.* A paper presented at the 42nd Annual Meeting of the Academy of Management, New York, August 1982, p. 10. Reprinted with permission.

formance. As shown in Table 3.1, the subordinates' self-perceptions were generally more favorable than their supervisors' perceptions. In fact, these self-versus-other perceptions showed very low congruency; the two sets of ratings are poorly correlated ($r = .09$).

Problems with multiple realities arise most frequently in organizations that are *(1)* highly specialized along functional and technological dimensions; *(2)* highly status and role differentiated; and *(3)* highly goal differentiated. As indicated in Chapter 1, health organizations meet all three criteria. High levels of technical and functional specialization are exemplified by the multitude of allied medical professions represented in hospitals and larger health departments. Status and role differentiation, common in many health settings, are demonstrated by the power accorded the physician in patient care settings. Within nursing departments, different status is often given to baccalaureate nurses compared to diploma or associate degree nurses, even though all three categories are state certified as registered nurses.* Finally, high levels of goal differentiation may well result from technical and status differences. Clearly, the surgeon's quasi-organizational affiliation to the hospital creates a perception of organizational goals different from that of the full-time administrator. In essence, there are a wide variety of professional and nonprofessional employees in health care organizations with heterogeneous need structures and differing education levels, value systems, and desired goals for themselves and their organizations. The probability of multiple realities emerging on any one issue dramatically increases because of this.

A related implication of the perception—reality equivalency and the multiple realities that stem from it is that many managers often find it difficult to accept the existence of more than one truth. Supporting this point, Ross states that:

> Laymen tend to perceive a "false consensus," that is, to see their own behavior choices and judgments as relatively common and appropriate to existing circumstances while viewing alternative responses as uncommon, deviant, and inappropriate. (25)

False consensus perceptions—"the tendency to see one's own behavior as typical" (26)— has received empirical support. Ross et al. (27) found that on a given behavior, those

---

*It should be noted that the licensing requirements for the RN degree may be changing in the next few years.

who engaged in it believed that others were more likely than not to also engage in it. The same finding held for those who rejected the same behavior; they felt that others too would be more likely than not to reject it.

Within a managerial context the result of this may often be reflected in the administrator's unwillingness or inability to see the other's point of view. The implications of this for adversarial versus constructive conflict management is obvious.

In settings where multiple realities always coexist, effective management requires that health administrators understand the perceptual reality of others. The moment health managers believe their perceptions represent absolute truth is also the moment they begin to run into trouble. While the so-called political behavior of organization members is often viewed pejoratively, health managers must have certain political capabilities in order to survive. If political behavior is based on the manager's desire to recognize, accept, and work with multiple realities, then few ethical or moralistic problems should arise with being a "politically oriented" administrator.

PERCEPTUAL BIASES PERTINENT TO EFFECTIVE HEALTH CARE MANAGEMENT

Health care managers may predictably and systematically distort or select stimuli in such a way as to bias their perceptions of themselves and others. This section discusses a number of biases and the adverse impacts they can have on the management process within health settings. Suggestions on what managers can do to minimize perceptual biases are presented in later sections.

Halo Effect

We sometimes perceive a single positive or negative characteristic in another person and allow that to influence other traits we ascribe to that individual. For example, when a manager perceives how sensitively an X-ray technician handles a frightened child and from that perception concludes, "I just know this technician is also a generous, sharing, and professionally committed person," the *halo effect* has occurred. When the same manager observes the director of planning insulting a subordinate in public and says to herself, "I bet this guy would walk over his mother to get to the top," a negative halo effect has occurred (28).

From a managerial perspective the key issue is whether or not these assumed correlations are real, idealistic, or unrealistic. While some halo effect perceptions may, in fact, be valid (reality based), much research suggests that often these extrapolations are unfounded (29), representing what Chapman and Chapman (30) refer to as the "illusionary correlation."

When health managers fall into the trap of false generalization, they note a few things about an employee and from these make inferences or projective associations about the employee's complete personality or motivational structure. They may be generalizing in an effort to understand, predict, and order the stimuli in their environment. Naturally, the manager's inaccurate conclusions based on halo effect can cause problems. Zalkind and Costello (28) note the employee's performance appraisal as an example. Supervisors who allow one positive or negative aspect of an employee's behavior to color the rest of the assessment may generate an erroneous evaluation that will (1) not give the employee the quality feedback that is needed; (2) reward behaviors that are inappropriate;

(3) alternatively, fail to reward behaviors that are appropriate; or *(4)* undermine supervisory credibility in the eyes of the subordinate and others.

A second situation in which the halo effect may present problems is in job interviews. The job interview environment may well activate the interviewer to fall into the halo effect bias. Under these circumstances, time pressure to form an evaluation of the interviewee is high. This pressure can stimulate the interviewer to allow one particular trait to influence their other perceptions about the applicant. For example, if an applicant interviewing for a health care management job only wears a tie and jacket—rather than a three-piece suit—the interviewer could well conclude that the applicant has neither the drive nor interpersonal skills to perform the job. In this and other cases the probability of making an erroneous evaluation is greatly increased.

The Jones-Nisbett Model and the Fundamental Attribution Error

Jones and Nisbett (14) offer a perspective on self- and other-perception which has been termed the actor–observer effect. These researchers suggest that "there is a pervasive tendency for actors to attribute their actions to situational requirements whereas observers tend to attribute the same actions to stable personal dispositions." Along the same lines, Ross (25) argues that when we observe others, we tend to overemphasize the role that dispositional characteristics play in determining their behavior. This is termed the *fundamental attribution error*.* Ross states there is a "tendency for attributors to underestimate the impact of situational factors and overestimate the role of dispositional factors in controlling behavior. . . ." of others. Interestingly, a recent study by Gilbert and Jones (26) suggests this phenomenon may be even stronger than social psychologists originally thought.

As an example, reconsider Dr. Welsh's indelicate public reprimand of Nurse Smith. As observers, we may be too willing to attribute his behavior to dispositional factors (for example, "Dr. Welsh is a mean and angry man"). We may not be as likely to consider alternative external or contextual factors for his behavior (he may be ill, or his children kept him up all night and he is fatigued).

The actor–observer effect from the actor's perception might best be exemplified by unwillingness to accept personal blame for a failure, and too readily attributing the failure to external or contextual factors (such as bad luck). However, the actor–observer effect, despite its robustness, may be reversed when the actor willingly takes personal credit for success (14). In the next section, these issues will be discussed in more depth. Students of health care management should also note that there is some controversy over the validity of actor–observer effect. For example, Jellison and Green (32) have data suggesting that actors do "depict themselves as having a greater tendency to locate causality internally. . . ." (32). While this effect may not be supported under all circumstances and contingencies, there is probably sufficient theoretical and empirical support to justify its utility under certain circumstances.

From a health manager perspective, the actor–observer effect or the fundamental attribution error can lead to misattributions of cause for self- and other perceptions. The potentially negative impact on effective decision making, equitable treatment of employees, and development of sound interpersonal relationships is noteworthy.

---

*Current thinking suggests the term "error" may be a "misnomer" and that "bias" should replace it (26; 31, pp. 75–76).

Ego Defense and Egotism*

Egotism is defined by Snyder et al. (4) as the "tendency to make attributions that put oneself in the best possible light." In recent years much attention has been paid to studying the attribution process of success and failure situations (4). The research on how actors and observers perceive their own and other's task successes and failures suggests the following:

1. Generally, actors tend to attribute successes internally to factors such as ability and failure (3) externally to factors such as bad luck (3, 34, 35). Miller (3) and Snyder et al. (4) indicate that these attributions are particularly strong when actors are ego-involved in a task or their self-esteem is at stake. (Again, note that in the instance of personal failure the actor–observer effect appears to operate. In the instance of personal success the actor–observer effect may become reversed.)

2. As ego-involved observers, we tend to attribute an actor's or competitor's success (the observers' loss) less to the actor's skill and more to the actor's luck (4). Here the actor–observer effect is again reversed.

3. As one study suggests, non–ego-involved observers can make internal attributions of actors' successes and external attributions of their failures (36). In these instances the actor–observer effect may be operating under the success contingency but not the failure contingency.

4. In general, the research finding that actors tend to attribute their successes to dispositional factors is stronger than the finding that actors externally attribute the cause of their failures (31).

It is probably most important to focus on conditions where ego involvement is present. When our self-esteem is at stake we, as actors, internalize success and externalize failure. As ego-involved observers we may begrudge the success of others. While alternative explanations are plausible (8), there is evidence to indicate that we often behave in a self-enhancing fashion. These perceptual tendencies are often motivated by our "egotistical" (4) desire to protect our own self-esteem and look good publicly.

What are the important managerial implications of this kind of bias? The first is that the accurate diagnosis of organizational problems may not be easily reached. If, in an effort to protect their own egos, health managers refuse to consider themselves as possible causes of an unsuccessful venture, an inaccurate assessment of the causes of failure will be more likely to occur. If misdiagnosis does occur, then selected ameliorative interventions will, likewise, be misspecified. The waste in economic and human resources might be substantial.

A second implication of this bias involves perceptions about organizational rewards. If a manager tends to overattribute her successes to ability, then her expectations about equitable remuneration for her successes may be overinflated. As a result, the manager may perceive herself to be treated inequitably when the rewards she receives are less than what she feels is fair. Naturally, the reverse argument holds for managers who are ego-involved in failure experiences. In this case, a manager may feel that she is inequitably

---

*Readers interested in further exploring this topic should read an article by Thompson and Kelley (33), who discuss the "self-centered bias"—where the actor tends to take more credit for jointly produced outcomes regardless of their success or failure.

treated in receiving no reward for behaviors for which she does not feel responsible. If, in either of these two instances, the reward giver is either threatened by or in competition with the manager, the manager may feel even greater inequity.

Certain factors inherent to health settings affect ego involvement. For example, professionals tend to be extremely ego-involved in their work. Clearly, this tendency does lead to the professional commitment necessary for high-quality patient care. However, though much is said about peer review and "honest feedback," health professionals may not be enthusiastic about having their own expertise questioned. Thus health managers need to be fully aware of the ego defense bias and its potential negative impact on effective management when assessing themselves and others.

To muddy the waters, the ego defensive (protective) bias may be manifest in a counterintuitive way. For example, some successful actors might publicly disclaim personal causation for their success and take direct responsibility for failure (Reiss et al., 35). This "self-presentation" effect may be an effort on the part of some actors to "look good" publicly, though in their minds they may perceive the reverse. (Some people, however, may not be so manipulative.) Expressing modesty about a success—"It was really a team effort"—is one example. Taking personal blame for a failure may soften the negative consequences forthcoming—"At least he was honest enough to admit failure; I'll give him a second chance."

Stereotyping

Although there is some question about the definition of stereotyping (37), social and organizational psychologists tend to view this perceptual process as judgments of others based on their group affiliations. Stereotyping behavior occurs when, over time, perceivers develop a set of traits, dispositions, attitudes, and behaviors that define a group of people for them. They use the set of characteristics to reach certain conclusions about an individual if that person belongs to the previously defined group. The following scenario clarifies the point:

> A hospital CEO tells one of his colleagues that "All nurses are absolutely resistant to change. I see this time and time again." When the colleague asks how the new director of nursing is getting along at the hospital, the CEO responds, "Fine, but I know she will be just like all nurses. Whenever I want to change something she will create problems."

As long as perceivers can aggregate people into logical groups, stereotyping will occur. As a result, we have stereotypes about professional groups (doctors, nurses, laboratory technicians), nationalities (Germans, French, Canadians), ethnic groups, religious groups, and so forth. In addition, people develop stereotypes about groups classified around demographic factors such as education, marital status, and age. One study with direct managerial implications looks at age stereotypes (38). Subjects were randomly given equivalent information about a young and an elderly employee and were then asked to make a managerial decision about a work-related issue that involved members of both age groups. The results indicated that older workers were more often the recipient of negative stereotypes. In addition, such stereotypes led to "administrative actions that were clearly damaging to the career well-being and career progress of older workers . . ." (38). While the laboratory features of this research make one cautious about applying these findings to actual work settings, the implications are nonetheless noteworthy.

While stereotypes may at times be valid, the evidence of misperception is also quite strong (28, 29, 32). The frequency of such misperceptions may be a consequence of the functional nature of stereotyping. It reduces the complexity of human behavior to a unique common denominator. It permits the perceiver to expediently wade through infinite stimuli that innumerable others present. However, as with any generalization process, the variant cases will be misinterpreted.

Within health organizations three factors can contribute to the probability of developing stereotypic perceptions: (1) the complexity of roles and functions; (2) the need to make quick decisions (thus stereotyping offers a short cut); and (3) the vast number of clearly identifiable groupings already present in health organizations. These three factors may operate in a complementary fashion. Given the complexity of health settings and the need to make speedy decisions, perceivers may be easily seduced into depending on (or developing) stereotypes to organize the mass of stimuli into meaningful wholes simply and quickly. The presence of clearly identifiable, highly differentiated groups makes this task easier. As a result, health managers, perhaps more than their industrial counterparts, need to be cognizant of how their environment may trap them into excessive stereotyping.

It should not be assumed that stereotypes can be only negative or derogatory. Stereotypes may be extremely positive and include characteristics that are socially desirable. Still, positive stereotypes can create as many misperceptions and managerial problems as negative ones. For example, the naive administrator of a long-term-care facility may stereotype all of his nursing aides as committed, altruistic, and sensitive. When he learns that two nursing aides are caught stealing patient gifts, his stereotype may act to distort or even deny the information (40). If this occurs, the quality of his subsequent managerial actions (such as disciplinary measures, additional security) may be adversely affected.

Finally, stereotyping may be a natural consequence of belonging to a group (41). Brewer (41) concludes that persons naturally tend to develop more positive stereotypes of members of their in-group, and negative stereotypes of those in out-groups. Interestingly, the polarized stereotypes made between in-groups and out-groups are due primarily to the positive stereotypes made by persons about their own in-group—"All members of my group are hardworking, bright, and very capable."

Other Types of Judgmental Errors—Representativeness and Availability*

Perceivers obviously do make errors. Sometimes errors are motivationally based. For example, perceivers may be unwilling to admit an error so that they need not look bad to themselves or others. At other times errors are purely cognitive in nature. Such errors result from the way we process the stimuli or information with which we are confronted. The errors are somewhat analogous to a perceptual short circuit rather than a result of conscious or unconscious motivations such as our need to look good in the eyes of the boss. Tversky and Kahneman (5, 6) identify two classes of cognitive inaccuracies in judgments: representativeness and availability.

Representativeness. Representativeness is "an event [that] is judged probable to the extent that it represents the essential features of its parent population or generating

---

*The reader is urged to read Tversky and Kahneman (6), particularly the discussion of "Adjustment and Anchoring" (pp. 1128–1130).

process . . ." (5). Typically, such an error occurs when the perceiver does not consider the role of simple probability theory or statistics in making judgments. For example, Tversky and Kahneman (6), cite the phenomenon of the "gambler's fallacy." Here, the typical roulette player believes that after red comes up a few times in succession the probability that on the next spin black will appear is increased, although in reality the odds for the next spin have not changed. Viewing this in terms of representativeness, gamblers believe that "black is now due, presumably because the occurrence of black will result in a more representative sequence than the occurrence of an additional red. . ." (6).

The law of small numbers represents a second example of the representativeness process (42). Here, observers tend to make unduly broad generalizations about a group of people based on impressions formed after observing or interacting with only a small subset of group members. This may be somewhat analogous to stereotype development (43).

The "illusion of validity" (6) represents a third example of this process and may have more direct managerial applications. In this instance, perceivers express confidence in their prediction or classification judgments when the information with which they are presented is congruent with the judgment. The better the ostensible fit between the available information and their judgment (the greater the representativeness), the greater the perceiver's confidence in that judgment. This phenomenon occurs even if information is "scanty, unreliable, or outdated" (6). The examples these researchers cite of the confidence people have in their stereotyping decisions or job interviewers have in their predictions, in spite of their knowledge of the frequent invalidity of such predictions, are noteworthy. In essence, if two pieces of a puzzle seem to fit together, then the perceiver may believe that they do fit, without worrying about the possibility that other pieces may actually fit better. This observation receives considerable support in a study by Pyszczynski and Greenberg (44). When study subjects were exposed to events they expected, they conducted much less "attributional processing" (information seeking as to why the event occurred) than when confronted with unexpected events. The authors concluded that when people observe expected events, they may forego relevant information and risk an inaccurate appraisal of the causes of such behavior and the dispositions of the actors involved" (44).

Availability. Judgmental errors frequently result from the *availability* of information to the perceiver. For example, perceivers may overestimate the frequency with which certain objects appear in the environment only because the objects in question have distinctive features that make them easier to remember (5). Perceivers may temporarily overestimate their chances of having an automobile accident if they have recently witnessed a crash scene (6). In this instance, the perceiver's subjective belief in the probability of having an accident might be overstated because of the recent experience and also because of its cognitive saliency. Hence, the ease with which information is remembered, its saliency, and its immediacy in the perceiver's memory may all act to interject bias into the perceiver's judgments and perceptions.

Transferring these findings from social and cognitive psychology to management may best be accomplished in a decision-making perspective.* Clearly, health managers will

---

*See Schwenk's (45) excellent discussion on "commitment to a course of action" for a further discussion on this issue.

compromise the quality of their decision making unless they are aware of the kind of cognitive traps into which they may fall. Since these traps are characterized by improperly processed information, spurious relationships, and inaccurate assessments of probabilities, the decisions that arise from them will be less than optimal. Three brief scenarios illustrate cognitive-trap situations into which managers may fall:

1. "The last two times we took such a substantial risk we did quite well. I don't think we should take the same risk a third time—we can't win three in a row."
2. "I just spoke with the CEO of Memorial Hospital. The only way they got their capital expansion bonds to sell was at an interest rate of 21%—the debt service will kill them. Since the same thing could happen to us, I suggest we use some other revenue-generating mechanisms for our expansion program."
3. "He's sensitive, caring, intelligent, and calm. You know he'll make a great patient advocate."

In each scenario, the judgment may in fact be accurate. However, in each decision, judgmental biases might have crept in. Judgment 1 is suggestive of the gambler's fallacy. The first two successes may have no bearing on the chance that a third event will result in a negative outcome. Judgment 2 is suggestive of saliency and proximity of events and how they may in the short run increase the subjective probabilities of the event's happening to the administrator. Judgment 3 suggests the illusion of validity. The employee's characteristics could fit the interviewer's stereotype of an effective patient advocate. However, the stereotype might be wrong (good patient advocates might be aggressive or assertive). Or the interviewer may have the right stereotype but fail to see that the real characteristics of the interviewee are different than what was originally perceived.

We have repeatedly pointed to the negative effects resulting from perceptual biases. However, not all stereotypes are inaccurate; perceivers do not always manifest the halo effect, not all attributions of success and failure are evoked to protect the perceiver's self-esteem, all actors and observers do not misspecify the locus of causality and all people are not ignorant of statistical principles (46). Many of these processes may, in fact, be accurate assessments of ourselves and others and, in addition, may permit us to cope and adapt to the complexities of our environment. Health managers do not always have the time and information to arrive at fully rational or objective assessments of their own behavior or that of others. Our tendencies to generalize and approximate, for example, with stereotyping or the unconscious deployment of the halo effect, allow us to cope, in part, with these limitations. Nonetheless, perceptual errors do occur. Actions health managers can take to minimize them are discussed in the next section.

SUGGESTIONS FOR IMPROVING PERCEPTUAL ACCURACY

In managers' attempts to minimize perceptual biases, the perceiver's willingness to recognize his or her biases is always a necessary precondition to effective action.

Cognitive Awareness

Managers must recognize the possibility of bias in their perceptual systems. The manager must learn to recognize those situations in which biases are most likely to emerge. Under conditions of job stress and time pressure the health manager may be susceptible to making expedient judgments by stereotyping or making judgments based on the halo effect. Or, with high ego involvement in a success/failure situation, the ego defense bias may emerge.

The health manager can develop cognitive awareness through use of a self-monitoring system grounded in the following kinds of questions: *(1)* Am I being fair and equitable in my judgment? *(2)* Is a lack of information biasing my judgment? *(3)* For what reasons are other people perceiving the same event differently? *(4)* Why might this situation (or person) be atypical of this category or class of situations? *(5)* Am I honestly considering alternative or even "opposite explanations" (47)? Employing this type of checklist in a systematic fashion may minimize the emergence of biases.

Two limitations prevent cognitive awareness from completely eliminating inaccurate and biased perceptions. First, perceivers in the process of examining themselves for judgmental biases, may in their self-monitoring be prone to the same, or other, perceptual biases (1). In other words, the perceptual process of cognitive awareness can itself be biased. Managers may ask themselves if the ego-defense bias influenced their external attribution of blame for a project's failure. The way in which the manager makes that self-judgment (perception) could also be prone to bias. Second, even if perceivers are able to identify bias in their original perception, recognition of this does not guarantee that they will overcome the bias (1). Despite these limitations, however, the safeguard mechanism of cognitive awareness represents a useful first step in minimizing bias in perceptions.

Feedback and Reality Testing

Zalkind and Costello (29) argue that misperceptions can be minimized if perceivers receive feedback from some other person on the accuracy of their perceptions. In other words, perceivers can use others in the environment to reality test their perceptions.

This approach to improving perceptual accuracy can be a mixed blessing. On the positive side, the other person(s) may increase the accuracy of the perceiver's views by forcing the perceiver to validate his or her perceptions (for example, by playing the role of devil's advocate) and offering additional clarifying information the perceiver might have selected out. In addition, research has shown that if the other person is the object the perceiver is attempting to understand, feeding back the meaning of messages improves the accuracy of interpersonal communication (48). On the negative side, the other person can interject his or her own biases, which may further exacerbate the perceiver's inaccurate views and judgments. Also, because of pressures to conform, the other person may provide a socially acceptable response—which may simply repeat (echo) the original person's bias—rather than provide bias-free (nonnormative) feedback (49). Hence the success of the feedback approach is dependent upon *(1)* the other person's ability to contribute to the accuracy of the perceiver's views, *(2)* the other person's willingness to tell the perceiver that her perceptions are inaccurate, and *(3)* the perceiver's willingness to accept alternative perceptions as representing a better reality. If administrators recognize these qualifications, then they can benefit from this reality-testing approach.

Observing Behavior

Many of our perceptual errors are the result of having insufficient information. Perceivers who make expedient snap judgments, instantaneous attributions, and quick stereotypic classifications often do this because they do not possess adequate data to develop and make more complex perceptions. To overcome this error health managers must make conscious efforts to observe systematically the behavior of those they are perceiving.

Based on our knowledge of the perception process and the biases that are likely to arise, it seems beneficial to the health manager to adhere to the following sampling guidelines:

MANAGERIAL GUIDELINES

1. Observe the behavior of yourself and organizational members over significant periods of time.
2. Observe the behavior of yourself and others under various *structural* circumstances (e.g., one-on-one meetings, group settings, board meetings, performance evaluation conferences).
3. Observe the behavior of yourself and others under various *psychosocial* circumstances (e.g., high stress and low stress conditions, high ego involvement and low ego involvement situations).
4. Consider the observations of others to reality test your own.

These sampling guidelines may help to minimize a number of the perceptual biases.

Training

There is some evidence that formal training can help to reduce certain perceptual biases. For example, research by Ivancevich (50) and Bernardin and Ponce (51) shows that formal training does reduce halo effects and leniency errors (overly favorable ratings). Research by Thornton and Zorich (52) suggests that the accuracy of one's observations can be increased through training programs. Fay and Latham (53) indicate that training significantly reduces rating errors (halo effect) and first-impression errors.

For training to be effective at minimizing perceptual biases, a number of conditions need to be met. Clearly, the manager must recognize a need for training and be motivated to learn. In addition, the trainer must be knowledgeable and competent. However, less obvious are two other conditions necessary for effective training. First, the trainer should avoid prescriptions about what the trainee should and should not perceive. For example, to suggest to trainees that no more than 40% of their workers should get the highest performance appraisal rating may simply replace one skewed perception with another (53). Hence the most appropriate role of the trainer may be to teach the manager *how* to think, not *what* to think. Second, training programs may lose their positive influence over time. Ivancevich (50) found that the positive influence of halo-effect training erodes after 6 months. As a result, for training to make a difference it may be necessary to use a continuing education approach (50).

Training can make a difference. In fact, Nisbett and Ross suggest that:

> statistics and probability theory should be taught at least as early as secondary school, and curricula should feature discussion of the contrast between formal and intuitive strategies. Providing concrete and anecdotal examples of intuitive errors and teaching judgmental maxims also should be helpful. (1)

In sum, perceptual biases can be minimized. While it is difficult to change people's perceptions, attitudes, beliefs, and biases, the suggestions made here may nonetheless be helpful. Finally, as noted earlier, managers should recognize that unless the individual perceives a need for change and is motivated to change, the beneficial effects of these strategies will be minimal.

PERCEPTION AND MOTIVATION

The discussion of perception has focused on both the adaptive and maladaptive aspects of the process. The selective nature of perception aids us in coping with the complexities of our environment, but our selectivity may lead to overly quick, biased, and erroneous judgment. By understanding the perceptual process from a managerial perspective, the health manager may maximize the adaptive and useful components of the perception process and minimize its inherent pitfalls.

Related to the subject of perception is another key area—the nature of individual motivation. Human motivation is not distinct from perception. These areas are interrelated, so that the understanding of one clearly facilitates the understanding of the other. The nature of this interrelationship and conceptual overlap occurs at two levels: (1) mutual dependency and (2) process similarity.

Mutual Dependency

Motivational and perceptual processes operate in a mutually dependent fashion (see Fig. 3.2). On the one hand, what a person perceives is often a function of what he or

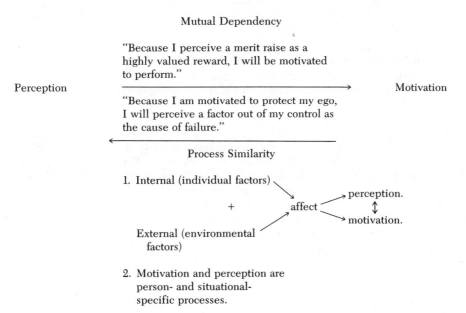

Mutual Dependency

"Because I perceive a merit raise as a highly valued reward, I will be motivated to perform."

Perception ⟶ Motivation

"Because I am motivated to protect my ego, I will perceive a factor out of my control as the cause of failure."

Process Similarity

1. Internal (individual factors) + External (environmental factors) affect perception. ↕ motivation.

2. Motivation and perception are person- and situational-specific processes.

Figure 3.2. The mutual dependence and conceptual overlaps between perceptual and motivational processes.

she is motivated to see. Thus, the perception is a causal outcome of the individual's motivational state. A brief vignette illustrates the relationship:

> A public health nurse realizes that, through her own carelessness, she has vaccinated twenty healthy babies with the wrong Polio Serum. Unable to internalize responsibility for this unfortunate act, she states, "If the mothers had kept their brats from screaming this would not have happened."

Clearly, the public health nurse is motivated to minimize her own feelings of failure which in turn causes a perception of others (the mothers) as responsible for the error.

On the other hand, what motivates one person's behavior is often a function of how that person perceives the relative value of certain consequences or outcomes. For instance, some employees perceive a merit raise as highly rewarding, whereas others value the opportunity for promotion more than money. Or, the merit pay system may not be perceived as such by employees if they believe that raises are actually based on politics more than true merit; consequently, they will not be motivated to perform at higher levels. Hence, perception can dictate (cause) the activation of motivated behavior.

Process Similarity

Motivational and perceptual processes are similar in two ways (see Fig. 3.2). First, both are influenced by internal (personal) and external (environmental) factors. The perceptions people hold of another person, for example, may be influenced by the perceiver's need (the internal dimension) to see the other in a certain light. In addition, the context (the external dimension) in which one observes the other's behavior also influences perception. From a motivational perspective, employees' internal attributes may influence the extent to which they manifest high or low levels of motivated behavior. For example, individuals with a high internal need for achievement may be willing to exert an extraordinary amount of effort in attaining a particular work goal. In addition (and this is true of the perceptual process, as well) the context or environment plays a critical role influencing motivated behavior. For example, many employees may have a high need for achievement, but external organizational obstacles to task accomplishment may frustrate them into low motivation.

Second, both processes tend to be person- and situation-specific. In the same way that people often perceive the same event or occurrence in different ways, people are often not identically motivated by the same things. Certainly, there are numerous instances in which perceptual agreement occurs or motivators influence a group of people similarly. However, individual differences do exist. The concept of individual difference has significant implications for effective management. This issue is discussed in greater depth later in the chapter. In short, we believe that by gaining an understanding of the conceptual interrelationships and similarities, health care managers can develop more effective perceptual systems and create more motivating work environments for their employees.

MOTIVATION

Why do individuals behave the way they do? In other words, what motivates people to act in certain ways? Can managers ever really understand why their people act the way they do—why some employees work hard whereas others don't even show up for work, why some perform at record levels whereas others (even some conscientious employees) chronically show below-par performance levels? Can a manager predict what employees are going to do in response to carefully planned motivational strategies? When will a given motivational technique work, and when not? Is it possible to change employee motivation, behavior, and performance? These questions are explored in the next section.

UNDERSTANDING AND CHANGING BEHAVIOR

Exploring these questions requires that we attempt to take some complicated theories and practical knowledge and integrate them into a coherent and integrative framework that is simple enough to be manageable and useful. Our starting point lies in the basic equation formulated by the social psychologist Kurt Lewis (54): $B = f[P,E]$, that is, human behavior (B) is a function of individual characteristics of the person (P) and of characteristics of his or her surrounding environment (E). Understanding employee behavior thus has two basic elements, person and environment. Efforts to change employee behavior can focus on either, but characteristics of the work environment are more under the health care manager's control than are employees' personal characteristics. This section of the chapter will concentrate on ways in which the work environment can be changed for maximum benefit to the employee and the organization.

To ground these general statements in more concrete, usable terms, we will build, through a series of analytical stages, a coherent, integrative framework (Fig. 3.3). The primary purpose of the framework is to provide an easily remembered, portable model useful for understanding, predicting, and changing employee behavior. *Behavior* refers to any work-related activity of interest to the health care manager, and *employee* refers to any member of the health organization—professional or nonprofessiona, medical or nonmedical, chief executive officer or part-time operative-level worker.

Most generally, the model incorporates Lewin's statement that behavior (B) is a function of both environmental (E) and personal (P) characteristics. Furthermore, the model suggests two primary components of the person's work environment: the *antecedents* and *consequences* of the behavior. As proposed by operant theorists in behaviorist psychology and recently applied in the management literature (55), *behavior* is "sandwiched" between a prior (antecedent) environmental situation and an environmental consequence. And, usefully, the antecedent-behavior-consequence sequence provides a handy mnemonic (ABC) for the practicing manager.

The sections that follow describe in more detail *(1)* the various employee behaviors of interest; *(2)* the antecedents of behavior that can stimulate and facilitate desired behaviors; *(3)* the consequences of behavior that further motivate employees to engage in

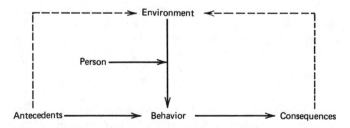

Figure 3.3. A general model of work behavior.

these behaviors; and *(4)* personal characteristics of employees that interact with the antecedent and consequent work environment to predict and affect behavior more completely. We conclude by presenting a more detailed version of the model to help generate points of action for the practicing manager to bring about constructive change in employee behavior.

BEHAVIORS THAT NEED TO BE MOTIVATED

The first step toward motivating employees involves identifying the types of behaviors that the organization needs or desires from its members. There is seemingly an infinite number of behaviors that a single nurse or health care manager exhibits on the job. There are also many different jobs and employees throughout any given organization. The multiplicity of behaviors and jobs makes organizational behavior seem very complicated to many managers. Yet managers can achieve great simplicity, and therefore a useful starting point, by subsuming these myriad behaviors into five broad categories around which many more specific behaviors are organized. Health care managers need to motivate people in the following ways:

Entering the Organization

Crucial to the survival of the organization is the ability to attract good people. This statement implies two things. First, adequate numbers of employees must be motivated to join the organization. Second, these employees must have the needed skills and abilities, or at least the aptitude or potential, to respond positively to formal and informal training. Custodians, physicians, technicians, nurses, administrators, and others need to be motivated to choose your organization from among many other options as they graduate from school or leave another employer. Some organizations are better than others at the recruiting function. In fact, many hospitals employ nurse and/or physician recruiters exactly for this reason. Many things contribute to this ability, and the inability to motivate competent people to join is harmful to any organization.

Remaining in the Organization

An organization must attract personnel; then it must motivate people to continue their employment relationship with the organization. When employees are motivated to seek employment elsewhere (or to drop out of the profession altogether, as has been the case with many nurses), the turnover may have tremendous direct and indirect costs to the organization, including quality of patient care. Many hospitals have invested money and time in attempts to curb tremendous rates of turnover, and it is essential that these resources be allocated in ways that will most efficiently and appropriately motivate retention. Again, as with motivating people to enter the organization, the goals of retention are twofold. A critical mass of people must be maintained, and those who are most motivated to remain within the organization will, hopefully, be the best employees (56).

Attendance

Employees must be motivated to come to work regularly, punctually, and predictably. Poor attendance creates staffing problems, quality-of-care problems, frustrations, cost overruns, and other negative repercussions. What seems to be a simple issue—getting people to come to work—is often a source of administrative headaches.

Performance

Job performance is typically conceptualized along the dimensions of quantity of output (productivity) and/or quality of work. Good attendance rates by themselves do not ensure high or even adequate levels of performance. Employees hired to do a job are expected to do it well. Moreover, to the extent that tasks are interdependent, the performance of one employee may positively or negatively affect the performance of others. In health care organizations, performance is even more critical than in many other organizations, because poor performance may be not only financially costly but also dangerous. Clearly, it is essential to motivate organizational members toward high levels of individual, group, departmental, and organizational performance.

Citizenship Behaviors

Quantity and quality of job performance are not the only dimensions of behavior that employees exhibit or fail to exhibit while at work. Katz and Kahn (57) discuss a much wider array of behaviors that are not an explicit part of the job description but that loyal, committed organizational members might be motivated to exhibit: cooperation; altruism; making positive statements about work; protecting fellow employees and organizational property; avoiding waste, complaints, and arguments; and generally going above and beyond the call of duty. Such prosocial, pro-organizational gestures might be referred to as citizenship behaviors (58), because they probably make the manager's job easier and contribute to smoother departmental and organizational functioning. Citizenship behaviors are perhaps less obvious and measurable than job performance per se, but they are of value to any organization.

This classification scheme summarizes the types of behavior that health care managers need to motivate. Many specific behaviors are assumed to belong in one or more of these five categories. How, now, do we begin to understand employees' motivation to engage or not engage in these critical behaviors?

THE ANTECEDENTS OF BEHAVIOR

All behavior takes place in some context; there are always some environmental events or characteristics that exist prior to the onset of behavior. The behavior of picking up the telephone is preceded by the ringing of the phone; the behavior of stopping the car is preceded by the traffic light turning red; the behavior of going out for a drink is preceded by a friend's invitation; the behavior of studying is preceded by an instructor's announcement of an impending examination.

Employees in a health care organization are likewise exposed to environmental stimuli that either prompt or fail to prompt performance-related behaviors. In other words, the work situation may provide *cues* as to the relative importance of various employee behaviors. According to one of the most widely known theories of worker motivation, Vroom's expectancy theory (59), employees' perceptions of the work environment are crucial to their behavior. In essence, these perceptions or beliefs form the hidden, perceptual antecedents to behavior, which the manager can influence primarily through the use of controllable, visible antecedents in the work environment.

In brief, expectancy theory holds that employees are motivated to behave (perform) to the extent that they believe that (1) their efforts will result in the required behavior, (high performance), and (2) the resulting behavior (performance) will lead to the attainment of valued rewards and avoidance of punishments. The first belief is termed *expectancy*, and the second is termed *instrumentality*. The stronger these two beliefs, the higher the motivation.

To increase employee perceptions of expectancy and instrumentality, managers can provide a number of useful, pertinent cues in the work environment. The following two sections discuss some environmental characteristics that can (1) stimulate motivation and (2) facilitate desired behaviors such as job performance, often by means of increases in instrumentalities and expectancies.

Antecedents that Stimulate Behavior

A manager can use a number of techniques to convey the possibilities of eventual rewards and punishments (instrumentalities of behaviors) and thereby stimulate motivation.

Performance Appraisal.   Most organizations employ formal systems of employee evaluation. If it is clear to employees that the evaluation is used as a basis for allocation of valued rewards such as pay raises and promotions, they will be motivated to do well on the appraisal—its instrumentality is high. On the other hand, to the extent that this evaluation is seen as having low instrumentality (as when all employees receive the same pay raise regardless of performance, or, for whatever reason, promotion is seen by the employee as an impossibility) motivation to excel on the appraisal diminishes.

Assuming that the appraisal is viewed as instrumental to the attainment of valued rewards, an issue arises regarding which behaviors are most instrumental to achieving high evaluation. Generally, those dimensions of behavior evaluated on the appraisal have high instrumentality, whereas those behaviors that are not a part of the appraisal do not. This may sound like an obvious statement, but organizations often say they want people to do something (for example, train and develop their subordinates), but never formally evaluate the behavior. If certain organizationally desired behaviors are not appraised, their instrumentality is reduced and employees may never be motivated to make any effort in those directions.

Managers also need to minimize subjectivity in performance appraisal. The more subjective the process, the more likely that another class of behaviors will be viewed as more instrumental to the attainment of a good appraisal, leading in turn to other desirable rewards. Subjectivity in appraisals fosters organizational politics (behavior not sanctioned by the organization and/or aimed at achieving organizationally unsanctioned goals) (60). Motivation to engage in political behaviors detracts from the energy devoted to better job performance and can hinder organizational effectiveness. The power of performance appraisal systems as antecedents to employee behavior, either in desired or undesired directions, such as politicking, has led to the development of a vast management literature in appraisal design and implementation.

Goals.   An impressive literature has been accumulated to demonstrate the motivational impact of specific performance-related goals. Clearly defined, challenging, but attainable goals stimulate effort and provide standards around which work activities can be organized (61, 62). In addition, recent research demonstrates that task performance is affected by the degree to which employees accept the goals and the feedback they are given about how they are progressing toward the goals (61).

Goals may be identified in the periodic performance appraisal as well as in the well-known, organization-wide, management-by-objectives (MBO) systems. Goals may also be used in department- or unit-wide goal-setting programs, or informally on an individual basis. The research evidence is clear: appropriate use of goals is a much stronger antecedent to work motivation than the lack of specific goals or even admonitions to "do your best."

Accountability. Both performance appraisals and goal setting create accountability, or responsibility, for the employee. A number of other techniques are very commonly used to communicate accountability for the appropriate instrumental behaviors, including job descriptions, verbal orders and requests, memos, and so forth.

Deadlines. Deadlines add another important dimension, time, to accountability. Most of us can attest to the impact on motivation of a rapidly approaching deadline. Deadlines should probably not be administered arbitrarily or with unduly short notice. However, as with goal setting, the use of specific deadlines probably prompts action much more reliably than suggestions to "get it done as soon as you can."

Modeling. Behavioral modeling refers to the process of learning new behaviors through the observation of others (63). Modeling is undoubtedly a pervasive process in organizations, as employees observe the behavior of their bosses, coworkers, or others who seem to be doing what it takes to survive or get ahead in the organization. Of course, people may model inappropriate behaviors too, as when drinking is encouraged within a group of administrators, cutting corners in patient care becomes the norm in a nursing home, or the successful pilfering of drugs by an orderly encourages others to do the same. A good health care manager establishes herself as a positive role model to others, and organizational employees who wish to do well often benefit from selecting such a model as a mentor. Whether the impact is positive or negative, the observation of others often acts as a powerful stimulus to subsequent behavior.

Socialization. Socialization is the process by which employees learn attitudes, behaviors, and values expected of them in a new organization or in a new job within the same organization. Socialization may be formal, as in the use of organizationally sanctioned training programs, literature, and so forth, or informal, as when supervisors or (more commonly) co-workers communicate the workings of the department or organization. The importance of early socialization should not be underestimated; the environmental cues a new employee absorbs have a major impact on subsequent job behavior.

The above list of behavioral antecedents is hardly exhaustive. It does, however, suggest some organizationally relevant processes that stimulate employee behavior. Effective health care managers and organizations can analyze the current work environment they provide their employees and maintain or change socialization practices, performance appraisal systems, and other cues to stimulate desired behaviors and discourage less desired behaviors.

Antecedents that Facilitate Behavior

While the emphasis on environmental cues that stimulate employees is essential, health care managers must recognize that although high motivation will probably contribute to higher levels of performance on the job, motivation and performance are *not* synonymous. In addition, we have not yet discussed the ways in which *expectancies*—employee beliefs that their efforts can accomplish the desired behaviors—can be influenced by the employee's antecedent work environment.

The distinction between motivation and performance (64) can easily be illustrated by considering that some students who study hard do poorly on exams, whereas others make excellent grades despite little studying. Experienced managers know that some employees put forth much time and effort at work (in other words, are highly motivated) but have less-than-satisfactory performance levels. At the same time, other employees perform quite well despite minimal levels of effort.

This distinction is important, among other reasons, because managers often attribute different performance levels to different levels of motivation. This tendency is related to the problem of perpetual bias. To the extent that managers simplistically attribute high performance to high motivation and low performance to low motivation, they may overlook other important factors that influence performance levels.

Although environmental antecedents of work behavior, such as deadlines, goals, and performance appraisals, affect instrumentalities (and indirectly motivation), other environmental features also indirectly affect performance through their impact on expectancies (and therefore motivation). Furthermore, these factors can also influence performance more directly, regardless of motivation levels. Specifically, the presence or absence of various needed resources can account for great differences in levels of job performance.

One of the more recently popular and valid theories of leadership, House's path–goal theory (65), suggests that a key function of a leader is to reduce any frustrating barriers that block the path to higher performance. The effective manager is one who makes sure that subordinates have the resources they need to accomplish their tasks. In other words, a manager should view his or her role as one of facilitator—a path clearer—of subordinate performance.

Some key environmental resources that effective managers might provide include such things as:

1. *Tools and equipment.* In any job, from custodian to radiologist, up-to-date, functioning equipment extends human capabilities in such a way that performance is vastly improved.

2. *Budget.* Clearly, money is a scarce and needed resource and its lack can directly impede effectiveness. The effective health care manager attempts to attract adequate funds to his or her department or organization and distribute them to optimize departmental performance levels.

3. *Information.* Ranging from sophisticated management information systems for decision making to simple feedback of performance data, the information needs of people and jobs must not go unmet if performance levels are to be improved or maintained.

4. *Personnel.* If staffing needs are unmet, regarding numbers or competence levels of employees, it may be impossible for individuals, groups, or entire organizations to attain performance standards.

5. *Authority.* A common complaint of health care managers and some practitioners is that they are given responsibilities that exceed their available authority for getting the necessary cooperation or compliance of others.

6. *Time.* Truly a finite resource, time pressures usually motivate people to work hard,

but often at the expense of performance. Because lack of time is a real constraint on performance, deadlines that are intended to motivate people should be realistic.

Besides these possible environmental constraints on performance, managers must realize that more personal factors also have positive or negative effects in facilitating or impeding desired behaviors. The model formulated by Porter and Lawler (64), for example, explicitly recognizes at least two such potential performance inhibitors: employee traits and abilities, and role perceptions. *Traits and abilities* may define an upper limit to performance. Lack of intelligence, physical strength, analytical abilities, social skills, or whatever specific attributes are relevant may prevent success at a task even when motivation and effort are high. On the other hand, extremely high ability levels may render good performance so easy as to be relatively effortless. In both cases motivation can continue to have an effect on performance, but ability levels are important as well.

Role perceptions are an employee's understanding of the way his or her role is to be performed. The person needs to understand performance requirements and how those requirements can best be met. If misunderstandings exist, high effort may be channeled in the wrong direction, in which case the necessary performance remains unfacilitated and unrealized. A doctor may exert a lot of effort to cure a patient, but a misdiagnosis leads to unsuccessful treatment. A hospital manager may spend a great deal of time trying to forecast bed utilization accurately, but many uncertainties may lead to major errors in prediction. Even seemingly mundane jobs may be poorly performed by highly motivated employees if some fundamental tactic or procedure for effective accomplishment is misunderstood.

As lack of ability or erroneous role perceptions hinder performance, expectancy levels decrease. Managers must be attuned to these problems and attempt to correct them through proper selection and placement practices, skill training, and communication of role requirements.

In sum, the availability of these and other environmental and personal resources directly facilitates or hinders performance. Over time, inadequate resources ultimately act as indirect detriments to performance, by decreasing the expectancy that the desired performance levels are attainable.

Recently, Greenberger and Strasser (66) suggested that a high expectancy in itself may be rewarding to the individual. In their model of personal control in the organization, they state that personal control, the employees' ability to affect a change in a desired direction in his or her work environment, is something desired by most persons (2). They indicate that abundant research points to a variety of negative consequences associated with a perceived loss of control: increased stress (67–69); depression (70); and decreases in performance (71–73).

Because the presence of personal control is a crucial contribution to the employee's well-being it may be an important source of motivation in the individual health service employee. When persons see that their actions result in expected outcomes, personal control will probably be perceived as high and they will be content. They should be motivated to engage in similar types of behaviors because they expect that they will accomplish the task, and thus feel in control. However, when persons are unable to accomplish the tasks they desire, they will be motivated to obtain more control. This desire for control will have positive consequences for the health care organization if the organization establishes accomplishable outcomes which are consistent with the organizational goals. The desire for control will have negative consequences for the organization if these acceptable outcomes are not present or are not achievable. Finally, if health care employees persist in perceiving that they cannot attain sufficient levels of performance and/or desired consequences, they will experience extremely low levels of control. They may stop trying altogether and may even experience symptoms associated with a state of learned helplessness (74). In this state the employee may reason, "What's the use of trying anymore if I cannot accomplish what I want."

In sum, the availability of these and other environmental and personal resources directly facilitates or hinders performance. Over time, inadequate resources ultimately act as indirect detriments to performance, by decreasing the expectancy that the desired performance levels are attainable. The effective health care manager will therefore (1) realize that performance levels are not solely attributable to motivation levels; (2) identify the important resources for effective performance; and (3) facilitate performance by doing whatever is possible to provide appropriate levels of those resources. While the latter suggestion may not always be possible, good managers will do what they can to find a way.

THE CONSEQUENCES OF BEHAVIOR

We have identified various behaviors that health care managers desire from their personnel and some of the environmental antecedents that stimulate and facilitate those behaviors. The next step toward understanding why people behave the way they do is to think about the environmental *consequences* of their behavior. On balance, people allocate their behavior in ways that help them maximize their positive consequences and minimize their negative consequences.

Thorndike (75), a pioneer in behavior analysis, in 1911 articulated one of the most simple, fundamental, and far-reaching statements about behavior. His *law of effect* states that behavior that is followed by positive consequences is more likely to recur. Conversely, behavior followed by negative consequences is less likely to recur.

Positive Versus Negative Consequences

The many possible consequences of a behavior can be categorized into four basic types. *Positive reinforcement* refers to the application of a positive consequence that increases the likelihood that the behavior will be repeated. Examples might include praise from a supervisor, thanks from patients, successful completion of a task, documentation of improvement in financial performance, or receiving a pay raise for outstanding performance. *Negative reinforcement* involves the removal or withholding of an undesirable consequence. Examples include employees who cut corners because it reduces an aversive work load, or who work hard so the supervisor will get off their backs.

These two outcomes—receiving a positive consequence and avoiding or escaping from negative consequence—are "good" for the employee. Their occurrence therefore motivates the employee to continue to exhibit the behaviors that led to these outcomes.

Two other types of consequences are undesirable for the employee. *Punishment* is the administration of an aversive consequence. Examples include a reprimand from the supervisor, an unattractive work assignment, or a poor performance evaluation. *Extinction* refers to the lack, or withdrawal, of any significant reinforcing consequences—the supervisor may fail to notice an employee's good job, a certain co-worker may never return favors, or successful performance on a routine, boring job may provide no sense of accomplishment. If a behavior is followed by either of these outcomes—punishment or the lack of any reinforcing consequence—the employee becomes less motivated to exhibit the behavior in the future.

Using Extinction and Punishment

Two behavioral consequences—extinction and punishment—reduce the likelihood that an employee will engage in behaviors that led to them. Both of these processes occur in organizations, and both represent viable strategies for dealing with employees. They also have certain specific implications that the health care manager must consider before using them.

Two particular problems surround the use of extinction. First, managers need to be aware that they may be unwittingly extinguishing good performance. All too often, the supervisor fails to acknowledge a job well done, or high performers do not receive pay raises significantly higher than the raises received by poor performers, or promotions are made on the basis of politics, not capability, or conditions preventing high performance are allowed to persist. In all of these cases, there is no reason (no reinforcement) for the employee to strive to improve performance.

A manager's understanding of the way in which extinction operates makes it less likely that appropriate work behaviors will go unreinforced. At the same time, a manager can cease reinforcing inappropriate behaviors (for example, politics, extreme conformity) and thereby extinguish them. However, an overreliance on extinction may lead to the second problem surrounding its use: the conscious application of extinction may not have its intended effects, because once a manager accepts the importance of behavioral consequences in influencing employees, he or she must realize that many of these consequences do not result from the manager's actions. Simply because the manager does not reinforce a certain behavior does not mean that the behavior is not reinforced in some other way. For example, the undesired behavior of failing to report to work may not be extinguished if the supervisor ignores the behavior or refuses to reinforce it. Similarly, a head nurse's refusal to laugh at or otherwise encourage horseplay may not completely extinguish that behavior. In these and many other instances, the behaviors are reinforced in other ways (getting a day off and having a few laughs with co-workers, respectively) and therefore continue to occur.

In situations like these, extinction alone will not serve as a viable influence strategy. One possibility is to provide reinforcement for desirable behaviors that are incompatible with the unwanted behavior, e.g., reward good behavior.

Alternatively, the administration of punishment appears to be a logical method for reducing behavioral problems. Punishment is, of course, commonly used in organizations. Unfortunately, it is also probably used to a greater extent than it should be. When supervisors reprimand an employee, they usually receive some type of reinforcement: the employee may apologize, or say that the behavior won't happen again, or quickly cease the undesired behavior and behave more appropriately. Thus, the person who punishes is immediately reinforced for applying the strategy. Furthermore, many supervisors view punishment as the most available means of influence—they lack the authority to use merit pay, for example, as a positive reinforcement, but can use punishment. Finally, punishment is often used for emotional as well as rational reasons, as when a manager reacts in anger to some aggravation caused by a misbehaving employee, or believes that one bad turn deserves another.

Unfortunately, these reasons for the use of punishment often overshadow a number of nonobvious effects that suggest the undesirability of a strong reliance on punitive techniques. Punishment usually only temporarily reduces undesired behaviors; since the tendency to behave in such ways persists, the behavior often begins with renewed intensity once the threat of punishment disappears. Thus, threat of punishment must be more or less continually achieved through costly surveillance of subordinates. Furthermore, the use of punishment may cause resentment and even hatred from employees.

This possibility alone may disturb managers who care what their employees think of them; but even if such interpersonal factors are not of concern to a manager, hostilities may manifest themselves in concerted efforts by employees to get back at their supervisor. Sabotage, output restriction, and a host of other negative repercussions may cause serious difficulties for the manager or organization that relies too much on punishment to control employee behavior.

It is not being suggested that punishment should be discarded as a method for reducing unwanted employee behaviors. In situations where extinction is ineffective or positive reinforcement for incompatible behaviors is impractical (such as when the appropriate behavior never occurs), punishment may be quite useful. However, the use of punishment should be restricted to those circumstances in which less negative approaches have failed, and when punishment is used, the manager should be cognizant of some of its nonobvious, long-term potential repercussions.

The Prevalence and Importance of Inappropriate Reinforcements

Let us consider how far a focus on consequences can take us toward explaining why people behave the way they do. We are often faced with people who frustrate us because, seemingly inexplicably, they behave in ways that are different from or opposite to the ways in which we want them to behave. These unexpected or undesired behaviors often become understandable as soon as their consequences are considered. Even more important, many undesirable behaviors come about precisely because of the backwards system of rewards and punishments created by the person or organization trying to control these behaviors. In other words, hoped-for behavior is often inadvertently punished, and undesired behavior is often inadvertently rewarded (76). The following examples illustrate the effects of inappropriate reinforcements:

1. Absenteeism is a behavior that organizations typically want to reduce. With this goal in mind, absenteeism policies are often created to punish employees for absences exceeding some specified number. Thus absence rates within the allowable limit go unpunished. This policy virtually assures that many employees who would otherwise come to work more frequently will use up all their allowable absences. Because programs designed to decrease absenteeism may actually encourage it, programs that reinforce attendance, rather than punish excessive absenteeism, may be more useful (77).

2. Students receive rewards in the forms of entrance to college or graduate school, scholarships, good jobs, and so forth on the basis of classroom grades. Unfortunately, classes are often structured so that grades come from performance on multiple-choice or rote essay exams. The rational strategy for a student may well be to cram the night before the exam and memorize the material. Cramming and memorizing are two techniques well known not to facilitate real, long-term learning. Ideally, students are supposed to learn in school, but they are too often rewarded for other behaviors.

3. Professors are exposed to the same kind of paradox. The traditional role of professor is to perform well as a classroom teacher, but institutions often provide little reward for teaching and maximum reward for research, publication, and obtaining grants.

4. Budget allocations are designed to keep spending within reasonable limits. However, it is common knowledge among managers that successfully staying under budget may result in a lower allocation next year, whereas excessive spending may guarantee a higher budget for the next period. Thus prudence is punished and spending rewarded.

5. Politicians present us with a recurring source of frustration and aggravation as they rarely answer questions or describe programs in concrete terms. This vagueness is, in fact, perfectly rational. More frankness and specificity is likely to antagonize blocks of voters, whereas general, harmless policy statements, while a bit frustrating, will offend no one. Thus generalities and evasiveness are more likely to be rewarded with an election victory, whereas the honesty and straightforwardness that voters claim they value are actually punished with election defeats.

6. Upward communications such as suggestions or constructive criticisms to higher management from employees can be very helpful in improving organizational functioning. Managers say they want their subordinates to speak up when they disagree with something the boss says or does. But in practice, when subordinates speak out the boss holds a grudge and finds a way to punish the "troublemaker," or at the very least fails to consider the employee's viewpoint. These responses punish or extinguish upward communications.

7. Long-run costs and opportunities should be attended to by managers of all health care (and other) organizations. Often, however, pay raises are given and jobs are lost or kept on the basis of short-term results. The rational behavior, then, is to sacrifice the long-term for short-term rewards. While such a strategy does not constitute the most appropriate management outlook, it usually does maximize chances for personal survival.

8. In group meetings managers may say they want everyone to participate—"Let's get input from everyone." When a reticent employee ventures forward and speaks up, the manager tells him, in a humiliating way, "That may be the worst idea ever presented." Later the manager wonders why this employee and *others* say nothing at the meetings he chairs.

The list of similar examples is almost endless. People basically behave in ways that maximize their rewards and minimize their punishments. Many unwanted behaviors (unwanted, that is, from the perspective of the person doing the observing) are actually a result of the reward structure (the environment) created by the social organization. In essence, in each case we hope the person behaves in one way but we reinforce some other behavior.

This basic analysis of the reward structure of a person's situation will go a long way toward helping us understand behavior; it also points out that, once we know what behaviors we want a person to exhibit, we need to make sure that those behaviors, not others, are reinforced.

The Complexity of Behavior Consequences: Building on the Law of Effects

Despite the power of behavioral consequences to predict behavior, the simplicity of the law of effect must not cause us to overlook practical complications that exist in organizational environments. First, it is not possible for a supervisor or manager to be continually available to punish (or extinguish) every undesirable behavior and provide reinforcement for every desired behavior. Second, the law of effect, as originally formulated, implies a one-behavior–one-consequence sequence that ignores three aspects of employee behavior: (1) interactions between the health care manager and employees occur over very long periods of time; (2) employees exhibit multiple behaviors and are exposed to multiple consequences over time (and even at any single time); and (3) many behavioral consequences experienced by the employee derive from a number of different sources and therefore are not under the control of the manager.

Two useful concepts are pertinent to these issues. *Schedules of reinforcement* address the inability to administer appropriate consequences continually and the long-term nature of the employer–employee interaction. The *matching law*, a revised version of the original law of effect, addresses the issue of multiplicity of behaviors and consequences and the existence of rewards and punishments that emanate from sources other than the employee's boss and the formal organization.

Schedules of Reinforcement. The original law of effect refers to the consequence that occurs as a result of a given behavior. Schedules of reinforcement concern the administration of a series of consequences over time. The schedule by which reinforcements are administered has an important and predictable impact upon behavior. There are five basic schedules of reinforcement: *continuous schedules*, under which a person is reinforced each time he or she exhibits the appropriate behavior, and four subtypes of *intermittent schedules*, under which the person is reinforced less frequently.

Continuous Schedules. Under a continuous schedule every desired behavior is followed by a reinforcement. As examples, a teacher may give daily quizzes, in which case every incident of adequate study behavior results in a good grade (or avoidance of a bad grade); and a manager who strongly believes in the power of praise as a reinforcer may unfailingly tell people that they are doing a good job. The behavioral effects of these schedules over time are quite predictable. The student or employee learns very quickly that a particular behavior will be reinforced; learning is fastest with this schedule, leading to dramatic increases in motivation and behavior. However, effectiveness may diminish in the long run as the reinforcement loses its value after repetition. After repeated quizzes, or incessant praise, these reinforcers may become less potent. Furthermore, motivation drops off rapidly if the reinforcement stops, as when the manager stops praising employees for high performance.

While this long-term feature of continuous schedules appears to be a drawback, in practice it has positive implications, in that a manager need not be (indeed, should not be) available to continuously apply reinforcement to employees. Furthermore, as we shall see, intermittent schedules (which require less availability, time, and surveillance of employees) are in fact more powerful over time.

Intermittent Schedules. As shown in Figure 3.4*a*, the four subtypes of intermittent schedules are differentiated along two dimensions—interval versus ratio, and fixed versus

Frequencies based on:

		Interval (time)	Ratio (behaviors)
Reinforcement Schedules	Fixed	*Example:* Paychecks every 2 weeks Cell #1	*Example:* Small bonus every time an employee is on time for work for 5 days in a row Cell #2
	Variable	*Example:* Time varied managerial visits to the nursing units Cell #3	*Example:* Slot machine payback schedules which vary Cell #4

(a)

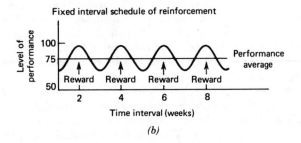

(b)

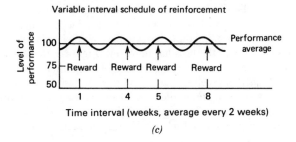

(c)

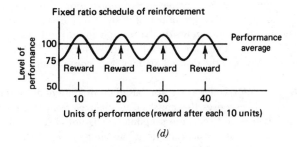

(d)

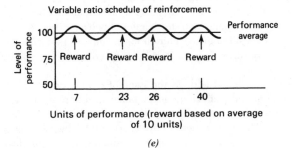

(e)

Figure 3.4. The effects of various schedules of reinforcement on performance. (Organ, D. W., & Hammer, W. C. *Organizational behavior: Applied psychological approach* (2nd ed.). Plano, Texas: Business Publications Inc., 1982, p. 76. Reprinted with permission.)

variable. *Interval schedules* involve reinforcers administered on the basis of the passage of time, whereas *ratio schedules* are based purely on the occurrence of behavior. *Fixed schedules* are those in which the reinforcement (whether based on time or behavior) is administered on a regular, predictable basis; under *variable schedules* the reinforcements are administered on an irregular, unpredictable basis. Some examples, and descriptions of their impacts on behavior, should clarify these distinctions.

Fixed interval schedules (cell #1) exist when reinforcers are administered at some constant, specific time period if the desired behavior has occurred within that period. The most widely used example is that of the regular paycheck, which comes on a predictable basis as long as the employee lives up to the minimally acceptable conditions of employment. The best example of the behavioral effects of this schedule is when a manager drops in on subordinates at the same time every day during the course of making rounds. Employees will be motivated to be productive when the manager is present at that (implicitly) specified time, but will have much less motivation to produce once that time has passed and the boss has departed. Figure 3.4b shows the weakness of this schedule in maintaining a high, steady level of motivation (15).

Variable interval schedules (cell #3) are also based on the passage of time, but the time period is less constant, or unpredictable. If the manager in the above example continues to drop in on workers five times a week but varies the times, the lowered predictability of this variable interval schedule results in higher, steadier performance levels (Fig. 3.4c).

Fixed ratio schedules (cell #2) involve the administration of the consequence after the occurrence of some established number of desired responses. Programs to reduce absenteeism may specify various rewards that are given on the basis of a person's attendance rates. Motivation levels are generally high with ratio schedules, because the more an employee behaves in the desired manner, the more rewards he or she receives (Fig. 3.4d).

Variable ratio schedules (cell #4) are also based on the rate of desired behavior, but the number of desired responses that must occur changes from one reinforcer to the next. In other words, unlike fixed ratio schedules, it is not clear which behavior will result in a reward. The most classic example is gambling, such as with a slot machine, when a gambler never knows which coin and pull of the lever will produce a jackpot. This example of gambling behavior may make it clear that variable ratio schedules are the most powerful at maintaining high steady rates of behavior (Fig. 3.4e). Supplementary monetary bonuses, days off, and recognition for exemplary performance or attendance provide examples of rewards that can be administered on such a schedule to enhance motivation.

Schedules of reinforcement address the issue of reinforcement administration over time, and different schedules affect employee behavior differentially. The power of variable ratio schedules in particular obviates the need to administer appropriate consequences continually. The next sections of this chapter introduce a revised version of the law of effect to aid the health care manager in thinking about complexities caused by multiple employee behaviors, multiple consequences, and the lack of formal control over all sources of rewards and punishments.

The Matching Law. Each employee in an organization has at least two major personal resources at his or her immediate disposal—time and effort. The problem of employee motivation may be considered a problem of personal resource allocation. Just as money managers discuss allocation of finite financial resources, marketing managers discuss resource allocation in terms of product mix, and microeconomists discuss production functions and the optimal allocation of capital and labor, we can talk of motivation as the process by which people allocate, among various alternatives, their finite resources of time and effort. We are effectively managing the motivational process if our employees are allocating optimal levels of their time and effort on behalf of the organization. The question now becomes, upon what bases do employees allocate these resources?

In almost any situation, an individual can engage in any of a number of possible behaviors. While the law of effect focuses on a single behavior and its consequence, the matching law goes a critical step further by considering the simultaneous existence of alternative behaviors, with their respective consequences. This feature clearly makes the analysis more realistic.

The matching law suggests that personal resources (time, effort) will be allocated on the basis of the distribution of rewards that exist across alternatives (78). Assume, for example, that a person can choose from between two possible behaviors in a given situation. As Figure 3.5 illustrates, the proportion of resources allocated to an alternative will equal the proportion of rewards it brings. In equation form:

$$\frac{B_1}{B_1 + B_2} = \frac{R_1}{R_1 + R_2}$$

in which B_1 represents the amount of personal resources allocated to the first alternative, B_2 represents the resources allocated to the second alternative, and R_1 and R_2 represent their respective amount of resulting rewards. If multiple behavioral alternatives are available, the matching law generally becomes:

$$\frac{B_1}{B_1 + B_2 + \ldots B_n} = \frac{R_1}{R_1 + R_2 + \ldots R_n}$$

The two denominators are, respectively, the sums of all the resources that are allocated and all the rewards they produce.

The matching law demonstrates how people allocate their behaviors across alternatives. The net level of reward (R_1) offered by organizationally desired behaviors (B_1) relative to the net reward (R_2) of undesired behaviors (B_2) should bear some relationship to the way behavior is allocated across those alternatives. For example, if B_1 represents the choice to join an organization and B_2 represents the choice to join a different organization, the perceived net level of rewards $(R_1$ vs. $R_2)$ will help predict the success of recruiting efforts. The relative rewards of going to work on a given day (B_1) versus not going to work (B_2) will be related to absenteeism. Similarly, staying with the current employer (B_1) versus quitting (B_2) should be a function of R_1 and R_2. Organizations that offer minimal rewards and/or substantial punishments compared to not being at work or to working elsewhere are more likely to have personnel who exhibit undesirable behavior patterns (recruiting difficulties, absenteeism, turnover) than organizations that provide relatively greater levels of positive net rewards for desirable behavior.

Employees allocate some proportion of their resources (time and effort) to the organization in the form of maintaining their membership, attending on some reasonable percentage of working days, and spending some adequate number of hours per week at the job. Within the work sphere, they may allocate resources across two basic alternatives: performance (B_1) and nonperformance (B_2). As indicated earlier, a person's attendance doesn't necessarily imply anything about his or her job performance. The

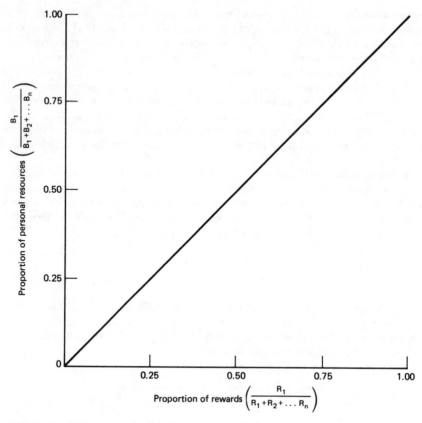

Figure 3.5. The matching law.

distribution of rewards and punishment between performance-related behaviors and non-performance-related behaviors pertains to the relative level of personal resources allocated toward performing well on the job. To the extent that high performance levels result in higher levels of reward and/or lower levels of punishment, the employee will be motivated to expend more resources toward performing than toward not performing. On the other hand, if good performance does not result in relatively greater levels of net reward than nonperformance (recall the earlier examples of how people may inadvertently reinforce the wrong behaviors), employees will be relatively less motivated to devote their time and effort to performance.

Sources of Rewards and Punishments

Any useful extension of the matching law and the notion of resource allocation across alternatives must take into account the existence of multiple sources of reward and punishment. Figure 3.6 portrays a focal employee who is exposed to a variety of these sources. Even excluding nonwork sources of influence, such as the family, numerous entities within the organizational context generate a wide variety of potential rewards and punishments:

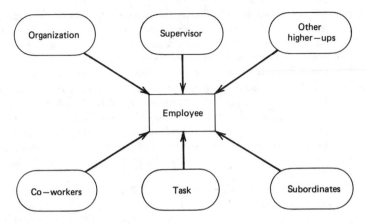

Figure 3.6. Employee reward structure (sources of rewards).

1. The immediate *supervisor* often evaluates performance, provides important feedback, has input into promotions and transfers, gives or withholds favors, allocates work responsibilities, and is the direct or indirect source of countless other important outcomes for employees.

2. *Higher-level managers* have less day-to-day contact with a given employee than the immediate supervisor, but their personal recognition, praise, reprimands, as well as the more consequential outcomes over which they have control, may have even greater meaning than those emanating from an immediate boss.

3. *Formal organization policy* covers important determinants of employee behavior, ranging from benefits and pay plans to work-shift policy and patient-care procedures.

4. The *peer group* provides social rewards and punishments, such as friendship and ostracization, and work-related rewards and punishments, such as informal helping or frustrating incompetence.

5. *Subordinates* can work hard, goldbrick, complain, stay extra hours, provide friendship or animosity, and generally exhibit or fail to exhibit the job performance, attendance, and citizenship behaviors that can make the manager's or supervisor's job rewarding or punishing.

6. The *task* itself can be a crucial source of reward or punishment. Boring, repetitive, degrading work can be psychologically, if not physically, punishing to engage in. The pioneering work of Herzberg (79) established the advantages of building motivators into tasks to make them more intrinsically, or inherently, rewarding. Improving the work itself through added responsibility, recognition, and opportunities for personal growth, advancement, and feelings of achievement constitutes the foundation of popular job enrichment programs. Since Herzberg's early efforts and subsequent criticisms of his work (80), other researchers have furthered the goals of improving the work itself by postulating some specific practical guidelines for creating the core task characteristics of variety, feedback, significance, autonomy, and identity. According to the job characteristics model (81), positive task characteristics result in motivating and satisfying psychological states.

We can predict that people will allocate their personal resources according to the mix of consequences that derive from these various sources. People will have to make trade-offs at different times, but over time they will spend time and exert effort to exhibit those behaviors that will, to the extent possible, maximize their net outcomes.

From a managerial perspective, the ideal situation is one in which each entity in the employee's set of sources of reinforcement either punishes nonperformance or reinforces performance. In such circumstances, the employee would truly be highly motivated to perform (indeed, too motivated, in that work would become life's sole means of reinforcement). However, this situation is rare if not impossible, and the opposite situation— one in which there exists, on balance, too little net positive reinforcement for performance-related behaviors—is more likely to be the problem because of the lack of employee motivation it engenders.

Quite likely, the various consequences to which the worker is exposed will conflict with one another. This conflict hinders motivation and acts as a distinct source of stress for the worker. For example: *(1)* a laboratory technician is paid to work extra hours by the organization, but the task she must complete is boring and frustrating; *(2)* a department head is told by her supervisor that she must work her people harder, but her subordinates criticize her efforts to comply; *(3)* a nurse is given one set of work priorities by the supervisor and a different set of demands from doctors; *(4)* a custodian is reprimanded by an administrator for drinking on the job but co-workers encourage the same activity; *(5)* organizational policy provides a large number of paid absences, yet supervisor and co-workers expect higher attendance in order to help with the workload. The classic example of conflict created by a nonwork influence is when the family demands less work time and more leisure time while the organization or supervisor demands high amounts of work time. In these and many more situations, whatever positive source of performance motivation exists is partially or completely offset by some form of reinforcement for nonperformance.

Figure 3.6 also clearly indicates another important point: that the supervisor or manager does not represent his or her subordinates' only source of reinforcement and punishment (82). This fact suggests two practical considerations. First, the manager must recognize that there are certain other factors in the work environment that affect employee behavior, that may not be under the manager's control, and that may inhibit the success of any direct attempts to change the employee. Secondly, and more optimistically, each factor represents a point of leverage, an additional source of reinforcement the manager or organization can attempt to use in order to influence employee behavior indirectly. In other words, changes in these factors constitute changes in the work environment that affect the behavior of the employee.

Finally, we stress the large array of potential rewards that are available to managers and organizations. Table 3.2 is a partial list of rewards that may positively influence employee behavior. Extensions to the list may be situation specific but are also limitless, given adequate managerial forethought, insight, and creativity.

What is Rewarding?

Although it is generally clear that rewards and punishments influence employees, different people value different things. It is therefore logical that the same "reward" applied to two different employees may serve as a positive reinforcer for one but have no effect or a negative effect on the other.

As discussed earlier in this chapter, behavior is a function of both characteristics of

TABLE 3.2. Examples of On-the-Job Rewards

Contrived On-the-Job Rewards				Natural Rewards	
Coffee-break treats	Desk accessories	Office with a window	Money	Friendly greetings	Job with more responsibility
Free lunches	Wall plaques	Piped-in music	Stocks	Informal recognition	Job rotation
Food baskets	Company car	Redecoration of work environment	Stock options	Formal acknowledgment or achievement	Early time off with pay
Easter hams	Watches	Company literature	Movie passes	Invitations to coffee/lunch	Work on personal project on company time
Christmas turkeys	Trophies	Private office	Trading stamps (green stamps)	Solicitations of suggestions	Use of company machinery or facilities for personal project
Dinners for the family on the company	Commendations	Popular speakers or lecturers	Paid-up insurance policies	Solicitations of advice	Use of company recreation facilities
Company picnics	Rings/tie pins	Book club discussions	Dinner and theater tickets	Compliment on work progress	
After-work wine and cheese parties	Appliances and furniture for the home	Feedback about performance	Vacation trips	Recognition in house organ	
Beer parties	Home shop tools		Coupons redeemable at local stores	Pat on the back	
	Garden tools		Profit sharing	Smile	
	Clothing			Verbal or nonverbal recognition or praise	
	Club privileges				
	Special assignments				

SOURCE: Luthans, F., & Kreitner, R. *Organizational behavior modification.* Glenview, Ill.: Scott, Foresman, 1975, p. 101. Copyright © 1975 by Scott, Foresman and Co. Used with permission.

the environment and characteristics of the person. Environmental characteristics include, among other things, behavioral consequences, schedules of reinforcement, and various sources of reinforcement. An understanding of the importance of these environmental factors aids the manager in understanding why employees behave the way they do and in determining ways in which to change employee behavior. Our analysis is not complete, though, without considering the role of personal characteristics as they interact with environmental factors.

The Role of Personal Characteristics. Psychologists have long analyzed individual differences. Several theorists have been influential in the management literature through their identification of various human needs. Below, in summary form, is a list of major needs, condensed from the theories of McClelland (83), Maslow (18), and Alderfer (84). Each of these need dimensions has particular relevance to the work setting and implications for determining whether or not a particular behavioral consequence will act as a reinforcer for a given employee. There is some conceptual overlap among the various needs, but each can independently contribute some separate insight into the personality differences which exist among people.

Existence needs, according to Alderfer, include all the various forms of material and physical desires. Maslow's *physiological* needs (food, water, sex, and shelter) and *safety* needs (freedom from danger, threat, and deprivation) can be subsumed under this category.

Social needs have been defined by Maslow to include love, friendship, acceptance, and belonging. Social needs also constitute a major component of Alderfer's *relatedness* needs, defined as the need for relationships with significant others.

Power needs have been described by McClelland as the need to exert influence or control over other people. These needs can be expressed in personalized desires (power over others) or socialized power (the use of influence on other people's behalf).

Ego needs (Maslow) can be satisfied in various ways, including feelings of independence, self-worth, and personal effectiveness.

Achievement needs (McClelland) pertain to a strong desire to strive for and meet high standards of task performance. This may be considered one subset of Maslow's ego needs but has received much attention in the management literature as a separate need that typifies most effective managers.

Growth needs are satisfied when a person can find ways to utilize his or her abilities and develop new talents. According to Alderfer, growth needs include both Maslow's needs for achievement and *self-actualization* (the realization of one's full potential).

This list represents a compilation of important dimensions along which employees may be expected to differ. For some employees social needs may be more potent than power needs, for example; for such employees, characteristics of the social environment may have more of a motivational impact than an opportunity for power. For other employees, the reverse may be true. People with strong achievement needs, according to McClelland (83), thrive in environments that provide performance feedback, challenge, and moderately difficult goals. Those with high growth needs are most likely to respond positively to increases in core job characteristics (task variety, autonomy, and so forth). In sum, the extent to which any given reward will serve as a reinforcer and therefore motivate behavior depends upon its ability to satisfy the needs that are generally important or currently operative for the employee under consideration.

The Role of the Situational Context. Individuals differ in personal needs and general predispositions. It is also useful to keep in mind that the motivational impact of a potential reinforcer depends in part on the context within which it becomes available. Reinforcement theorists (85) highlight at least two specific situational considerations: the effects of deprivation and relativity. Additionally, social psychologists suggest the pertinence of the social context when they invoke equity theory (86) to explain how we interpret rewards received within social contexts such as organizations. These situational contexts, which help predict how individuals may differ in their responses to organizational rewards, will be discussed in turn.

Deprivation effects refer to the power of rewards of which the person has been deprived over time. Most of us are aware of the powerful motivating impact of such things as food, sex, money, friendship, or positive performance feedback after having been deprived of them over significant periods of time ("significant" depending upon the specific reward involved). On the other hand, many theoretical analyses suggest the other extreme, that reinforcers lose their effect over time if they are presented too frequently. As examples, the physiological psychologists speak of "saturation"; Maslow indicates that a satisfied need no longer motivates; and the earlier discussion of continuous schedules of reinforcement suggests that lack of deprivation renders an initially powerful reinforcer impotent over time.

Nonetheless, there may not be such a simple linear relationship between actual deprivation and the need satisfaction potential of a reward. A logical derivation of the deprivation notion might be that receiving some reward reduces deprivation and therefore reduces the future power of the reward to motivate. However, an initial taste of a novel reward may, like an appetizer before a fine meal, whet the appetite for more by creating a felt deprivation where none previously existed. For example, just such a process may occur upon the introduction of task variety and autonomy into a job.

Relativity effects refer to the fact that virtually no behavior and its set of behavioral consequences occurs in a vacuum; the strength of motivation to behave in a particular way depends not only on the absolute level of rewards resulting from the behavior but upon the level of rewards relative to the sum total of all rewards available in the situation. A seemingly trivial level of reward may maximally motivate a behavior as long as the rewards are greater than those available for other potential behaviors. Brown and Hernstein (85) provide the example of sophisticated people battling rudely and pettily for a seat on the subway—in the context, there exists little else in the way of reward. In the organizational context, a poor job that has little appeal to the worker may make little things like the supervisor's compliment or the cooperation of a co-worker very important aspects of the workplace. Anything that limits the range of rewards in a situation intensifies the power of the remaining rewards. Conversely, seemingly generous rewards may have minimal effect if a situation is rich with other rewards.

This relativity effect is also implied in the *matching law*. The person is predicted to allocate behavior according to relative gain. The rewards that provide the relative gain, furthermore, depend upon the personal needs that are relevant to the individual in the given situation.

Equity theory (86) suggests that we interpret the rewards we receive on the basis of how fairly we feel we have been treated compared to other people. The consequences, or outcomes, we receive from our efforts (and other inputs) are judged against the inputs and outcomes of others. We perceive the existence of equity if our outcome/input (O/I) ratio is equal to the O/I ratio of other employees. If employees' O/I ratios are lower than those of other employees against which they compare themselves (for example, when an employee feels that his inputs have been higher than others' but his outcomes are not; or when an employee's inputs are the same as others but he perceives his outcomes to be less), there exists a dissatisfying state of inequity. As such, a given level of reward (consequence, outcome) can have differing motivational impacts depending upon the recipient's perceptions of equitable treatment.

In sum, a given reward or reinforcer has differential value for different employees. People differ in their most generally prevalent needs, their changing and temporary levels of deprivation of various needs, their relative situational contexts as they affect the power of a reward, and their perceptions of equitable treatment. These factors, when taken into consideration, help explain and predict how different individuals will respond to various organizational rewards.

In fact, Deci (87), in his Cognitive Evaluation Theory, and others have demonstrated that the application of extrinsic rewards—money, a promotion—may actually undermine intrinsic motivation. How can this occur? The answer while complex, may lie in an application of Bem's theory of self-perception. Suppose that a person motivated by the sheer joy of successfully performing the task itself begins to receive extrinsic rewards for it. Whereas he previously attributed his high level of performance to the intrinsic rewards he received, he might now infer that the reason he engages in the task is because of the extrinsic rewards. Thus the monetary reward given as a consequence of the high performance serves as a better and more immediate explanation for his performance and he may now start to discount the role of intrinsic rewards. If the extrinsic rewards are stopped, the effectiveness of intrinsic rewards—which have been discounted—for motivation, are now reduced. Hence there is less remaining to motivate the employee.

As noted by Fiske and Taylor (31) the logical implications of this are disconcerting:

> The implications of the overjustification effect are, of course, staggering. Our entire economy runs on the assumption that rewards improve the quality and quantity of subsequent performance, assumptions that must now be questioned, at least under some circumstances (p. 59).

Yet, the negative impact of extrinsic rewards on intrinsic motivation does not always occur (88). Deci argued, in fact, that extrinsic rewards will not diminish intrinsic task motivation if the rewards are presented as a symbolic representation or statement of the employee's competence—rather than as an effort to control the employee's behavior. In addition, intrinsic motivation will not diminish if the organization makes salient the employee's sincere interest (intrinsic rewards) in the tasks. Fiske and Taylor (31) identified research supporting these assertions.

The lesson for managers is clear. Extrinsic rewards are not always a perfect answer to low motivation. In fact, they may diminish motivation whenever intrinsic motivation is present. Intrinsic rewards should be encouraged and made salient to the health care employee. However, if these are not sufficient to motivate the employee—and some jobs simply cannot be made high in intrinsic motivation—extrinsic rewards should be made to signal competence and success.

Rewards and Professionalism. It is typically argued that health care workers, both professionals and nonprofessionals, gain tremendous intrinsic rewards through their careers in a helping profession. There is little doubt that this is true in many instances. Being a part of an endeavor designed to make sick people well or prevent illness from occurring is indeed a reward in itself. It is also argued that health professionals are inherently dedicated, committed, and motivated to perform high-quality work. Again, there is little doubt that for many this is true. However, health care managers should not be seduced into naively thinking that these considerations alone will keep physicians, nurses, dietary workers, and other employee groups highly motivated.

Social comparisons, for example, will be made. And if a group of health care employees feels that another institution can pay them at a rate closer to what they feel they deserve, turnover to the new setting may occur. Twenty years ago the words "unionization" and "health care employee" would never be uttered in the same context. Today, nurses participate in collective bargaining, health care workers go on strike over pay, and medical residents engage in work slowdowns over working conditions. Equity considerations and extrinsic rewards can make a difference in influencing the motivational levels of professionals as well as nonprofessionals. Effective health care managers need to consider these rewards in addition to the inherently motivating ideals and values professionals and nonprofessionals hold.

BACK TO THE ABCs

We have gradually added complexity to our analysis of employee behavior. We began by defining the various types of behaviors that employees must be motivated to exhibit in order for the organization to survive and prosper; we then noted that all behavior takes place in some stimulus situation; and we described some antecedent stimuli that can increase motivation to behave in organizationally desired ways, usually through increased expectancies and instrumentalities. We then described the original law of effect and refined and extended it to include the role of time (schedules of reinforcement), the various organizational sources of rewards and punishments, and some of the important personal and situational attributes that help determine what is rewarding and what is not.

To help us integrate and summarize what has been established thus far, Figure 3.7

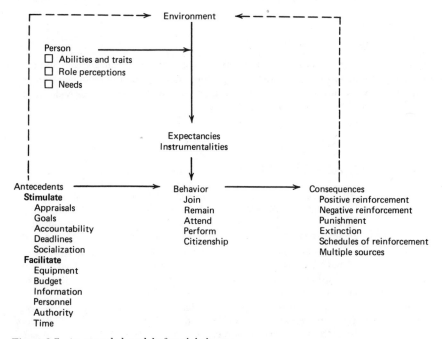

Figure 3.7. An extended model of work behavior.

displays a refined version of the basic model of employee behavior presented at the beginning of the motivation section of this chapter. Again, behavior is considered to be a joint function of the person and his or her environment, and is influenced by a set of antecedents and a set of consequences. The resulting mnemonic—the ABCs of ante-cedents–behavior–consequences—provides an easily remembered, portable model of employee behavior consistent with established theory yet maintaining a practical ori-entation.

The model highlights the categories of variables the health care manager can consider and, if necessary, change in order to improve employee motivation and performance. Employee behavior can be observed, measured, appraised, and pinpointed for strengths and weaknesses. Collecting performance data, possibly conducting an organization-wide performance audit, creates an awareness among managers of performance problems. Such actions also may help define for employees the dimensions of performance that are considered important by management.

Once performance requirements are identified, there are several factors that influence behavior. First, the manager should provide stimuli (antecedents) that instigate or mo-tivate performance (e.g., set goals, create accountability, etc.) and that facilitate per-formance (e.g., provide adequate resources). Second, the consequences (various rewards and punishments) that result from appropriate behavior should be analyzed and maxi-mized to the extent possible. Finally, these environmental characteristics should be considered in light of personal characteristics of individual employees (need, skills, etc.) and how they might influence the two primary perceptual antecedents of behavior: expectancies and instrumentalities.

The basic foundations for this integrative framework, as well as some real world complications, have been discussed in the preceding pages. An understanding of these contingencies, then, paves the way for the constructive change of employee behavior.

Analyzing Behavioral Problems

Figure 3.7 suggests a set of action points through which a manager can implement strategies intended to improve employee performance. While the following framework of questions is a summary approach rather than an exhaustive list, it provides a useful guide to practical behavior analysis and change:

MANAGERIAL GUIDELINES

Question 1: What is the behavioral discrepancy?   Why do I think there is a mo-tivation problem? What is the difference between what is happening (performance, absenteeism, turnover, etc.) and what is supposed to be done? Have I collected the pertinent data?

Question 2: Have the behavioral requirements been specified and otherwise stim-ulated?   What are the important behaviors? Have specific goals been established? Is the employee held accountable? Has the performance appraisal been adequately communicated?

Question 3: Are there obstacles to performing; can I facilitate performance? What prevents the employee from performing? Does the employee have the necessary resources: the money, the equipment, the per-sonnel, the information, the authority, the time? Is the employee restricted by outdated policies? What can I eliminate or provide to aid performance?

Question 4: *What is the employee's "balance of consequence"?*   On balance, is desired performance more rewarding than nonperformance? What are the employee's sources of rewards and punishments: organizational policy? the job itself? you? co-workers? what else? What are the schedules of reinforcement? Which of these rewards and punishments conflict with one another? Which are more important than others? Is it somehow punishing to perform? Is it somehow more rewarding to not perform? Are there adequate levels of reward for performing? Is the wrong behavior somehow being inadvertently rewarded? How are organizational rewards evaluated by employees? Are they equitable? adequate? Is there adequate performance feedback? How often? From what source: you? the job itself? available data? Is the feedback only negative, or is it positive as well?

Question 5: *Is it a skill deficiency?*   Does the employee have the ability, or at least the potential, to perform well? Does the employee have the knowledge to use the resources (information, equipment, etc.) at his or her disposal appropriately? Does the employee understand the job and how to do it?

Question 6: *Have individual differences among employees been taken into account?*   Have their needs been adequately considered? Are organizational rewards geared to these needs? Are the same rewards used uniformly for all people, even though the people differ?

Question 7: *Which solution is best?*   What strategies might solve the problem as you have defined it? Which is the easiest? the cheapest? Which would yield the most positive results? Might there be any unanticipated problems? On balance, what are the ratios of costs to benefits?

NEGOTIATION IN HEALTH CARE ORGANIZATIONS

In the past, when one thought of "negotiation" in health care organizations, several images came to mind: a purchasing manager attempting to strike a deal with a supplier for a new piece of equipment, a hospital CEO seeking to acquire a tract of land for facilities expansion, or a nurses' union negotiating with management for an improved compensation and benefits package. Indeed, health care managers do use negotiating skills in these situations. But to see negotiation as ONLY occurring in these "formal" settings is a limited view of the key role that negotiation skills play in a manager's everyday job performance. Instead, as we shall point out, health care managers, like most other public and private sector managers, negotiate all the time. Consider the following examples:

• Today, the health care manager's negotiation arena extends far beyond just the boundaries of the hospital. Health care managers are consistently negotiating with other organizational representatives on issues pertaining to shared service agreements, management contracts, and joint entrepreneurial ventures.

• The corporatization of American health care has witnessed a consolidation of hospitals into corporate or multihospital configurations. Today's hospital manager now negotiates for resources with a new level of management . . . the corporate level.

• In the last 5 years there has been enormous growth in alternative care delivery systems. The emergence of urgent care centers and home health care organizations are characteristic of this. Medical staff–management relationships now extend far beyond those of the traditional hospital setting. The negotiations that now must occur between the managers of these new delivery organizations and the medical personnel who staff and cover them may present new sets of issues unique to these types of health care organizations.

In this section, we describe some of the key aspects of the negotiation process and their relevance for health care managers. We begin by defining what we mean by "negotiation" and the nature of the negotiation process. We then discuss several key factors that affect all negotiations and the way that managers negotiate and examine two major types or styles of negotiation—cooperative and competitive—and describe how each may be used to exert influence and resolve conflict successfully. Finally, we briefly describe the process needed to prepare for an upcoming negotiation. The treatment of negotiation in this chapter and volume is by necessity limited, and only scratches the surface of what health care administrators should know about the negotiation process. A list of supplementary books and readings is offered at the end of this chapter for those who wish to read about the negotiation process in more depth.

DEFINITION OF NEGOTIATION

We begin by attempting to define our terms. There are probably as many different definitions of negotiation and bargaining as there are books and articles on the subject. (In this chapter, we use the terms "negotiation" and "bargaining" interchangeably, although "negotiation" sometimes connotes a more formal deliberation process, while "bargaining" is more often used to describe the "haggling" one might use to buy a used car.) To begin, we offer the following two definitions of negotiation:

Interaction that occurs when two or more parties attempt to agree on a mutually acceptable outcome in a situation where their preferences for outcomes are negatively related. (89)

The use of information and power to affect the other party's behavior within a web of tension. (90)

What do these two definitions (and others like them) have in common? The following distinctions can help to clarify the essence of the process called negotiation (adapted from 89):

1. Negotiation is minimally a two-party process. While it is possible that an individual can "negotiate with himself" (i.e., debate in his mind how he is going to spend a free Saturday morning or which new stereo system to buy), the negotiation process as we describe it occurs between two or more individuals.

2. The two parties are interdependent. One major characteristic of situations that require negotiation is that the parties are interdependent—that is, they have to work together with someone else in order to get their own needs satisfied. A person who is independent can get what he/she needs without the help of others. Thus a self-employed

person can earn as much salary as his time, efforts, and current business conditions allow. A person who is dependent must rely on someone else to get what he/she wants; when one works for an organization, one must do the job as required or face not getting paid. Two parties who are interdependent must work to meet each other's needs—party A provides certain goods and/or services, and party B provides certain goods and/or services in return.

3. The two parties are divided by a conflict of interest. Although they are interdependent, the parties frequently disagree as to what (or how much) goods and services each one deserves or will provide for the other. This disagreement is termed a conflict of interest. Each party has a set of *preferred outcomes* that he/she wants to achieve from the interdependence. Moreover, at least one or both parties believe that it is not possible for both of them to simultaneously attain their most preferred outcomes. Thus the two parties must search for ways to resolve their conflict: who will perform which activities and how much each will receive as a result of their efforts.

4. Negotiation is a voluntary relationship. Parties are seldom required to negotiate— that is, that their ONLY option is to determine how to work together to manage their interdependence and resolve their conflict of interest. More commonly, parties also have the choice of resolving their conflict by each going his/her separate way—that is, by becoming independent—or by establishing an interdependence with someone else who is more sympathetic to their needs. The very fact that parties perceive themselves as having options or alternatives to striking a bargain with the current adversary is essential to understanding the negotiation process. The willingness to abandon an unfavorable negotiation with an opponent in favor of independence or interdependence with an alternative partner gives a negotiator considerable strategic power.

5. The process of negotiation creates expectations that each side will engage in "give and take"—that is, compromise and concession making. When they enter into a process called "negotiation," parties expect that each side will make initial demands and requests for what they would like, but not what they actually expect to receive as a settlement. The heart of the negotiation process, therefore, is the strategy and tactics that each side uses to get the other side to move away from their initial demands and requests—to resolve the conflict of interest so that the negotiators' preferences for outcomes are compatible rather than incompatible. The expectation of give and take is very strong, and creates several important consequences. First, because negotiators expect to make some concessions, they may actually inflate their initial demands to build in "giveaways" for the concession-making process. They will also have to decide what settlement is minimally acceptable if their initial objective cannot be reached. Determining these giveaways and minimally acceptable settlements is a key part of the negotiation planning process.

Second, adversaries who do not make concessions from their initial positions are seen as negotiating unfairly, as not "playing the game by the rules." In labor relations, making a salary offer to labor and refusing to negotiate that offer has been called "boulwarism," and ruled illegal by the National Labor Relations Board (91); making "one and only one" offer in more informal negotiations is frequently perceived by opponents as inflexible and arbitrary. Failing to engage in systematic give-and-take can also create major psychological problems for negotiators. Cohen (90) relates the story of a man who walked into an antique store and saw a clock that he really liked. The posted price on the clock was $350. After some discussion about the clock with the shopkeeper, the man offered $175, to which the shopkeeper immediately said, "Sold!" The man walked out with his clock, but felt tremendously unsatisfied with the deal because of the way the shopkeeper acted. This lack of satisfaction is best explained by our last definitional point.

6. The negotiation process traditionally includes two kinds of activity: the division of resources, or who will receive how much of the money, goods, or services at stake in the conflict of interest, and the resolution of the psychological concerns and dynamics that are present whenever people engage in conflict. The resources are frequently called the "*tangibles*" of negotiation, and include the price to be paid for a certain item, a rate of interest that might be paid, the terms and conditions of a contract, or the rights and obligations of a specific agreement or settlement. In contrast, the "*intangibles*" of negotiation encompass the psychological dynamics and personal motivations that frequently arise as people engage in conflict—competing, cooperating, winning, losing, beating an opponent, looking good to an audience, maintaining one's principles, preserving a reputation, being fair, being tough, setting a precedent, and saving face.

Most theory and research has been directed toward how the negotiation process goes about achieving agreement on the tangibles. Yet as we saw in the clock example, the intangibles also play a very important role. First, how satisfied one feels about a negotiated settlement is a very subjective phenomena. What might be a highly satisfactory settlement to one negotiator will not be to another. This psychological satisfaction is derived both from the specific outcome one attains relative to the goals one set before negotiation AND to the relative harmony of the processes used to achieve that outcome. Since two different negotiators achieving the same actual outcomes may have started with different goals and/or had more or less harmonious negotiating experiences with their opponents, their feelings of satisfaction will vary considerably based on their goals and experience. In the clock example, had the shopkeeper countered with an offer of $325, and had they haggled for half an hour and agreed on a price of $250, the buyer would have actually paid more but might also have felt far more satisfaction with the deal he worked hard to get. Second, negotiations that are unsuccessful, that lead to anger and hostility, communication breakdowns, legal action or strikes, frequently fail because of the intangibles. Parties may have negotiated for weeks, made considerable progress and be relatively close to settlement on the tangibles, but cannot agree because of the intangibles: building frustration and irritation; perceptions of the other side as inflexible, unreasonable, or irrational; refusal to make further concessions, and so on. Many international and labor negotiations have collapsed because the intangibles have overriden the tangibles and precluded the parties from reaching agreement.

In summary, negotiation is a process in which two or more parties are interdependent upon one another and must at least partially rely on the other person to achieve their own objectives (although they usually have the option of "going it alone" or striking a deal with someone else). The task before the parties is to resolve some conflict of interest by a process of inventing options and/or making compromises on the issues in conflict. This process requires the parties to set goals for what they would optimally like to achieve, but also to expect that they will have to make concessions away from this optimum. At best, each party hopes to maximize his/her negotiating goals; but each is also aware that he will probably have to agree to something less than the maximum. Finally, each party must define some minimally acceptable outcome, a point beyond which they would rather walk away than agree. As we stated earlier, the process by which negotiators set these maximums and minimums, and develop strategies to achieve them, is at the heart of the negotiating process. We will now turn to a discussion of that goal setting and strategizing process.

GOALS, PERCEPTION OF GOALS, AND RESOURCES—THE KEYS TO STRATEGY

As we described in the previous section, negotiators differ in the goals they set—both tangible and intangible. Tangible goals are the specific outcomes they hope to achieve through the negotiation (rate, price, terms, specific contract, etc.); intangible goals are the psychological objectives they hope to achieve. Since negotiating parties are interdependent, however, a negotiator cannot achieve his goals on his own; whether he achieves his goals, and how he achieves them, also depends on his opponent's goals, whether the two sets of goals are actually compatible or not, and how each party perceives the goals. These factors determine whether negotiators tend to pursue *cooperative* (win–win) or *competitive* (win–lose) strategies.

Optimal conditions for COOPERATIVE strategies are likely to occur when the following are true:

- The tangible goals of both negotiators are to attain a specific settlement that is fair and reasonable.
- There are sufficient resources available in the environment for both sides to attain their tangible goals, more resources can be attained, or the problem can be redefined so that both sides can actually "win".
- Each side believes (perceives) that it is possible for both of them to attain their goals through the negotiation process.
- The intangible goals of both negotiators are to establish a cooperative relationship and work together toward a settlement that maximizes their joint outcomes.

Thus cooperative (win–win) negotiation occurs when parties have clear, specific, and reasonable goals; when there are sufficient resources available (or acquirable) for both parties to achieve these goals; and when the parties perceive the situation as win–win— that is, they believe a cooperative settlement is possible and are motivated to work toward it. In contrast, optimal conditions for COMPETITIVE strategies are likely to occur when:

- The tangible goals of both negotiators are to attain a specific settlement or to get as much as they possibly can.
- There are insufficient resources available for both sides to attain their goals, or their desires to get as much as possible makes it impossible for one or both parties to actually attain their goal.
- Both sides perceive that it is impossible for both of them to attain their goals.
- The intangible goals of both sides are to beat the other, keep the other from attaining his goals, humiliate the other, or refuse (for various reasons) to make concessions in one's own negotiating position.

Thus competitive (win–lose) negotiation occurs when the parties want to get as much as they possibly can, when the situation is such that it is impossible for both sides to achieve their goals, when the parties also believe that it is impossible for them to achieve their goals, and/or when the parties are motivated to defeat, conquer, or humiliate an opponent and defend against his comparable tactics rather than establish a positive working relationship.

Note that we have described situations which maximally lead to cooperative or competitive negotiating strategies. In fact, most negotiating situations we encounter are not "purely" one or the other, but some combination of the two. For example, the parties' goals may actually be compatible, but they perceive them as incompatible, and thus drift toward a competitive approach when in fact it is unnecessary. Similarly, one negotiator often intends to behave cooperatively but misperceives the situation (and/or his opponent's behavior) as competitive and assumes a competitive strategy, thereby turning his cooperative opponent toward competition in retaliation. In general, the more one or both parties tend to espouse competitive goals or motivations, perceive their opponent as competitive, and believe that only one party can attain his goals successfully, the more competitive the negotiation will become. Parties may move toward cooperative strategies by changing their own goals and motivations, correcting their perceptions, working to change those of their opponent, or attempting to improve communication. In extreme situations, neutral third parties such as judges, arbitrators, and mediators may be necessary to help the parties rebuild and convert their working relationship.

THE COMPETITIVE BARGAINING STRATEGY

The competitive bargaining strategy has often been called the "win–lose" or distributive bargaining strategy (92, 93). Negotiators adopt this strategy when they believe that resources are fixed and limited so that both parties cannot achieve their objectives, when they are interested in maximizing their outcomes at the expense of the other party, and/or when they possess some personal animosity or distrust of their opponent. In competitive bargaining, each negotiator must assess the costs and benefits of staying in the negotiation and using tactics to persuade his opponent to yield versus dropping out of the negotiation in order to attain objectives by some other means. To make this assessment correctly, each negotiator must determine:

1. A *target point,* or a settlement with which he would be reasonably satisfied.
2. An *opening bid,* or what he will initially ask for (but not really expect to get, since he knows that he will have to make concessions).
3. A *resistance point,* walk-away point, or bottom line—a point below which he will not make any further concessions and would rather walk away from the negotiations than accept an inferior settlement.
4. *Options or alternative settlement* possibilities with other negotiators in other contexts. These options are frequently called BATNAs—Best Alternative(s) to a Negotiated Agreement (94)—and represent the best alternative deal a bargainer can make should he fail in his efforts to reach agreement with the current opponent. A competitive negotiator will then use a variety of tactics (bluffs, threats, pressure tactics, emotional ploys, etc.) to manipulate his opponent into accepting a deal as close to his target point as possible. (See Karass (95) and Levin (96) for descriptions of these tactics).

THE COOPERATIVE BARGAINING STRATEGY

The cooperative bargaining strategy has often been called the "win–win" or integrative bargaining strategy (92, 93). Negotiators adopt this strategy when they believe that resources are not limited so as to preclude both parties achieving their objectives, when they want to work together with the opponent to achieve the best possible joint settlement, and when each party believes that the other person is fundamentally trustworthy and credible. In cooperative bargaining, the parties do not take a hard line with regard to opening bids and walk-away points. Instead, the parties attempt to define their problem as some form of common, shared, or joint goal that both want, and then develop a strategy to achieve that goal. In cooperative bargaining, parties attempt to understand the other party's real needs and objectives, to promote a free flow of information and exchange of ideas, to emphasize the things they have in common rather than their differences, and to search for solutions which meet the needs of BOTH sides.

In contrast to the competitive, warfare-like tactics of competitive bargaining, cooperative bargaining is much like joint problem solving. Parties first attempt to achieve a joint definition of the problem. Next, they diagnose the problem and understand the impact of the problem on both sides. Third, they search for possible alternative solutions—settlements which might be acceptable to one or both sides. Fourth, multiple issues and possible solutions are "packaged together" so that each side maximizes its outcome by virtue of the combination of settlements. Each of these packages is evaluated, and parties modify the packages to shape the final solution. Finally, the parties plan for implementation. Additional strategies for improving the effectiveness of cooperative negotiation may be found in Fisher and Ury (94), Pruitt (97) and Pruitt and Rubin (98).

ELEMENTS OF STRATEGY—THE FLOW OF NEGOTIATIONS

Whether one is engaged in competitive or cooperative bargaining, negotiations tend to proceed through time in a fairly predictable sequence of steps and activities. Numerous authors have written about this sequence and flow (99, 100). While these and other authors disagree somewhat as to the exact number of steps and how to label them, it is safe to say that negotiation tends to proceed (from inception to conclusion) according to the following phases:

1. A *preparation phase*, during which negotiators assess the nature of their conflict of interest, set their own goals and priorities, analyze their opponent, and determine what strategy they are going to use.

2. An *entry phase*, during which negotiators make their initial contact with one another, set an agenda and discuss rules and procedures for negotiation, and make a presentation of their initial goals and priorities.

3. An *elaboration and education phase*, during which negotiators elaborate upon their stated goals and priorities, and try to learn more about their opponent's stated goals and priorities.

4. A *bargaining phase*, when negotiators attempt to question their opponent's goals and logic, defend their own goals and logic from attack, and search for ways to make compromises and tradeoffs and invent alternative solutions.

5. A *closure phase*, when negotiators seek to arrive at a basic agreement, consolidate all issues together in a package, record the agreement so that all agree, and plan for implementing the agreement.

An analysis of the key strategic elements of competitive and cooperative negotiation in each of these phases is presented in Table 3.3. In negotiations which are neither purely cooperative nor competitive, a mixture of the two sets of tactics may be used, and both strategies may be used in larger negotiations where both cooperative and competitive issues or perceptions are present. Negotiators approaching an upcoming bargaining session may use the questions presented in the right-hand column of Table 3.3 to determine what kind of strategy they may want to use in any given negotiation.

CONVERTING COMPETITIVE OPPONENTS TO COOPERATION

Negotiators frequently find themselves in the position of saying, "I would like to use a cooperative strategy in an upcoming negotiation, but my opponent is going to be competitive. Can I protect myself against my opponent's competitiveness and even convert my opponent to a cooperative strategy?" The answer is clearly "yes!" While no single tactic is guaranteed to change your opponent's behavior, the collection of tactics described below have a high likelihood of producing change or at least giving you much clearer signals about your opponent's true intentions (92, 94, 98).

MANAGERIAL GUIDELINES

1. Attempt to verify your perception that your opponent intends to behave competitively. Because of the competition, mistrust, and miscommunication fostered by conflict situations, negotiators often misperceive their opponent's intentions. They assume or expect that their opponent intends to behave competitively because of the opponent's past behavior, conflict dynamics in the current situation, or sheer lack of information and communication. This leads negotiators to behave competitively, which elicits competitive behavior from their opponent, thereby confirming the negotiator's perception that the opponent is competitive—a complete self-fulfilling prophecy. Negotiators can avoid this trap by attempting to verify how their opponent intends to approach the negotiation.

2. Be explicit about your own preferences for approaching the negotiation as a cooperative process and searching for a win–win solution. Negotiators can be "up front" about their own desires to achieve a win–win agreement simply by beginning the negotiation with a statement of their intentions and desires. Openly state that you would like the negotiations to be as cooperative as possible, that you would like to minimize or eliminate any competitive tactics and destructive behavior, and that your desire is to achieve a win–win agreement. Ask the other side whether that is acceptable to them, and how they would like to approach the negotiation—in fact, you are "negotiating" with the other about how you will negotiate.

3. Be willing to openly raise and discuss "breakdowns" of the cooperative process if and when they occur. This should not be done with any accusation or blame, but simply a comment that "we seem to be getting angry at one another" or "I'm not sure we are being as candid as we need to be to understand one another's point of view," followed by suggestions about how the negotiations can get back on track. Negotiators frequently do not discuss how the negotiations themselves are proceeding, and these comments can legitimize such a discussion.

4. Focus on what you are truly interested in, rather than developing some hard-line "position." If you're negotiating a starting salary for a job and you've decided you want $25,000 a year, you probably would be willing to take $24,900 if other things about the job were attractive. Therefore, it's probably not useful to tell yourself that you wouldn't accept less than $25,000. Instead, what you are

truly interested in is a "fair and reasonable" starting salary and a good overall compensation package; that's your real interest in the negotiation.

5. Listen to the other side's positions and arguments carefully. Developing good win–win agreements depends heavily on understanding the other's point of view. Until both negotiators understand what the other is really interested in, it is difficult to invent options and alternatives that meet both sides' needs. Therefore, make sure that you know what the opponent really wants.

6. Propose ways for both sides to have their needs met. Competitive negotiations tend to deteriorate into "mine vs. yours" arguments. In fact, there are usually ways for both negotiators to get what they want, and AT WORST to compromise so that each gets something. Once a negotiator has effectively listened to what each side wants, he/she can begin to invent solutions, compromises, or "package agreements" by which both negotiators achieve significant positive gain.

SUMMARY AND CONCLUSIONS

The purpose of this chapter has been to give health care managers a better understanding of perceptual, motivational, and negotiation processes. An effort has been made to identify those things managers can do to understand and manage their own and others' perceptual systems and create a more motivating work environment. We have identified pitfalls (such as perceptual biases or the rewarding of undesirable behavior) that health care managers should avoid in the conduct of their jobs. Understanding effective negotiation represents a logical outgrowth of initially understanding human perception and motivation.

A CONTINGENCY THEORY PERSPECTIVE OF PERCEPTION, MOTIVATION, AND NEGOTIATION

One major theme we have focused on is the diversity and multidimensionality of individual perceptions and behaviors in health care settings. Different employees often perceive the world in different ways. Similarly, different employees may not be motivated to behave in exactly the same way given their different personal makeups, their respective work environments, and their unique perceptual schemas. A manager's decision to rely on any of a variety of negotiation strategies may also depend on the kind of personality he or she possesses and the situation confronted.

The recognition of these differences and this diversity tends to insert a great deal of complexity and uncertainty into the manager's role. The manager should not despair, however, because it is exactly this diversity and complexity that generate effective, innovative, and exciting organizational functioning. If health care managers can view perception, motivation, and negotiation from a contingency perspective (101), they may be able to eliminate some uncertainty while maintaining the benefits inherent in individual differences among organizational members.

The contingency perspective, as it applies to motivating employees, begins with a recognition that a given motivational program may not be equally effective with all employees. Rather, employee-specific motivational strategies may need to be developed by managers within the constraints imposed on them. The health care manager may

TABLE 3.3. Differences Between Cooperative and Competitive Bargaining

Phase	Competitive Bargaining	Cooperative Bargaining	Key Strategic Questions
Preparation	Set specific goals, bottom lines, and opening bids. Develop firm "positions" and competitive tactics to attain those goals at the expense of the other.	Develop general goals and broad objectives. Cultivate good options (BATNAs). Cultivate good relations of trust and openness with opponent to promote effective problem solving.	Is this going to be a fundamentally competitive or cooperative negotiation? How broadly or narrowly should I state my goals? Should I prepare competitive or cooperative tactics?
Entry-problem identification	State the problem in terms of one's own preferred solution. Publicly disguise or misrepresent own needs and goals; don't let the other side know what's really important.	State the problem in terms of the underlying needs of all parties. Represent own needs accurately to the other party; listen carefully to understand their needs.	How can I state the problem as broadly as possible while still protecting my own interests and preferences?
Elaboration/education	Disclose only that information necessary to support our position and have the other side understand it. Hide possible vulnerabilities and weaknesses.	Disclose all information that may be pertinent to a problem, regardless of whose position it supports. Expose vulnerabilities in order to protect them in the joint solution.	How much information should I disclose? What should be the "timing" of this sharing process? How can I present a complete case, as opposed to only the "most positive" case.
Bargaining	Include false issues, "dummy" options, or issues and options of low personal priority in order to trade them away for what you want. Make an early public commitment and stick to it.	Minimize the inclusion of false or "dummy" issues and stick to the major problems and concerns. Avoid early and public commitments to preferred alternatives in order to give all options full consideration.	Do I confine the definition of the problem and issues to only those things that I am most concerned about, or that we are both concerned for? How hard should I stick to, and fight for, the solution that I think is best?
Closure	Maximize own utilities while not caring about the other's. Overvalue concessions to other; undervalue gains one achieves. "Nibbling" strategy of taking issues off the table as one achieves a favorable settlement.	Maximize solutions that have joint utility; be honest and candid in disclosing preferences. "Nothing is ever final until all issues are settled" strategy.	How fully do I disclose what are my true priorities and preferences, and what I stand to gain by particular outcomes? Should I try to negotiate issues one at a time or strive for a joint package?

find it useful to identify, on as individualized a basis as is reasonably possible: *(1)* those stimuli and facilitators that encourage desired behavior; *(2)* those reinforcers that are valued by the employee and that improve the probability of desirable behaviors reoccurring; and *(3)* the personal attributes of the employee. In short, effective motivational strategies are contingent on a wide array of environmental and personal characteristics of the employee.

The contingency perspective, as applied to the perceptual process, begins with an understanding that what we perceive is contingent upon both our internal makeup and disposition and the environmental context. Recognizing these contingencies allows the manager to understand the principle of individual differences inherent in perception. These differences occur because employees are not all dispositionally identical and the situational contexts in which organizational members find themselves are not all the same. Given these differences, multiple realities sometimes emerge in the health setting, and health managers must cope with these and ultimately reconcile them. Understanding the contingency basis of perception formation should help health care managers develop greater tolerance and respect for the diversity of perceptions they and their colleagues hold.

Finally, health care managers need to realize they have available not one, but a set of negotiation strategies to employ. Their task becomes one of matching a given negotiation strategy to the situation they face. The ability to understand human perception and motivation in oneself and others should increase the likelihood of selecting the optimal negotiating approach to the situation confronted.

DISCUSSION QUESTIONS

1. What characteristics unique to health care organizations tend to exacerbate the development or use of perceptual biases?
2. While perceptual biases may serve certain utilitarian functions, they can also create problems for the health care manager. What steps can a manager take to overcome the problems of these biases? Are these methods foolproof?
3. Reinforcers are often used inappropriately in attempts to influence behaviors. What are some instances from your own life (home, work, school) in which the use of rewards resulted in unplanned or unexpected behaviors? What might you have done differently to have prevented this from occurring?
4. Choose any behavior, in a school environment or a job you may be familiar with, and use the model of work behavior to suggest some specific strategies that can be applied to increase the occurrence of the behavior.
5. Look back at a negotiating situation in which you were involved. Did you use a collaborative or competitive approach? Did the approach you used fit the situation you were in? What improvements in your negotiating style might you now incorporate?

SUGGESTED READINGS

Aronson, E. The rationalizing animal. *Psychology Today*, May 1973,
This article presents an excellent discussion of the theory of cognitive dissonance.

Research findings supporting the theory as well as limitations are provided. The impact of the perceiver's self-esteem on dissonance is explained. This article can help the health administration student better understand the perception process.

Folberg, J., & Taylor, A. *Mediation.* San Francisco: Jossey-Bass, 1984.

Goldberg, S., Green, E., & Sander, F. *Dispute Resolution.* Boston: Little-Brown, 1985.

Kerr, S. On the folly of rewarding A, while hoping for B. *Academy of Management Journal,* 1975, *18,* 769–783.

This article illustrates how managers and organizations often unwittingly motivate people to do the wrong things. The author provides numerous examples of desired behaviors that are unrewarded or even punished and undesired behaviors that get rewarded. Data from two organizations also serve to stimulate the reader to consider the shortcomings of management practices in his or her own organization.

Lawler, E. E. The individualized organization: Problems and promise. *California Management Review,* 1974, *17* (4), 31–39.

Throughout this chapter we have pointed to the individual differences that exist among employees' perceptions and motivational structures. This article further clarifies this issue as it applies to job design, pay systems, training, selection, and leadership. The way the organization can meaningfully respond to motivational differences among employees is discussed. The notion of universal theories of management is challenged.

Moore, C. W. *The Mediation Process.* San Francisco: Jossey-Bass, 1986.

Porter, L., & Lawler, E. E. *Managerial attitudes and performance.* Homewood, ILL.: Irwin-Dorsey, 1968.

This book provides a comprehensive and useful model of managerial performance. Motivation is viewed as only one of several important influences on performance. As the title implies, the focus of the book is on managerial levels, although the model is generally applicable to levels throughout the organization. A well-known book among academicians, it is also easily read and well suited to the needs of practitioners.

REFERENCES

1. Nisbett, R., & Ross, L. *Human inference: strategies and shortcomings of social judgment.* Englewood Cliffs, N.J.: Prentice-Hall, 1980.

2. White, R. W. Motivation reconsidered: The concept of competence. *Psychological Review,* 1959, *66,* 297–333.

3. Miller, D. T. Ego involvement and attributions for success and failure. *Journal of Personality and Social Psychology,* 1976, *34,* 901–906.

4. Snyder, M., Stephan, W. G. & Rosenfield, D. Egotism and attribution. *Journal of Personality and Social Psychology,* 1976, *33,* 435–441.

5. Tversky, A., & Kahneman, D. Availability: A heuristic for judging frequency and probability. *Cognitive Psychology,* 1973, *5,* 207–232.

6. Tversky, A., & Kahneman, D. Judgment under uncertainty: Heuristics and biases. *Science,* 1974, *185,* 1124–1131.

7. Taylor, S. E., & Fiske, S. T. Salience, attention and attribution: Top of the head phenomena. In L. Berkowitz (ed.), *Advances in experimental social psychology,* Vol. 11. New York: Academic Press, 1978.

8. Schneider, D., Hastorf, J. & Ellsworth, W. *Person Perception.* 1979.

9. Bem, D. J. Self-perception: The dependent variable of human performance. *Organizational Behavior and Human Performance,* 1967, *2,* 105–121.

10. Bem, D. J. Self-perception: An alternative interpretation of cognitive dissonance phenomena. *Psychological Review,* 1967, *74,* 183–200.

11. Bem, D. J. Self-perception theory. In *Advances in experimental and social psychology.* New York: Academic Press, 1972.

12. Schacter, S., & Singer, J. E. Cognitive, social and psychological determinants of emotional state. *Psychological Review,* 1962, *69,* 379–400.

13. Festinger, L. *A theory of cognitive dissonance.* Stanford, Cal.: Stanford University Press, 1962.

14. Jones, E. E., & Nisbett, R. E. The actor and the observer: Divergent perceptions of the causes of behavior. In E. E. Jones et al. (Eds.). *Attribution: Perceiving the causes of behavior.* New York: General Learning Press, 1972.

15. Organ, D. W., & Hamner, W. C. *Organizational behavior: An applied psychological approach.* Plano, Texas: Business Publications, Inc., 1982.

16. Wong, P. T., & Weiner, B. When people ask "why" questions and the heuristics of attributional search. *Journal of Personality and Social Psychology,* 1981, *40,* 650–653.

17. Leavitt, H. J. Perception: From the inside looking out. In *Managerial Psychology* (4th ed.). Chicago: University of Chicago Press, 1958.

18. Maslow, A. H. A theory of human motivation. *Psychological Review,* 1943, *50,* 370–396.

19. Byrne, D. Interpersonal attraction and attitude similarity. *Journal of Abnormal and Social Psychology,* 1961, *62,* 713–715.

20. Byrne, D., & Nelson, D. Attraction as a function of attitude similarity: The effect of topic importance. *Psychonomic Science,* 1964, *1,* 93–94.

21. Janis, I. Group think. *Psychology Today,* November 1971.

22. Myers, D. G., & Lamp, H. The group polarization phenomenon. *Psychological Bulletin,* 1976, *83,* 602–627.

23. Vallone, R. P., Ross, L., & Lepper, M. R. The hostile media phenomenon: Biased perception and perceptions of media bias in coverage of the Beirut massacre. *Journal of Personality and Social Psychology,* 1985, *49* (3), 577–585.

24. Shapiro, G., & Dessler, G. A Comparison of Self & Superior Performance Ratings. Paper presented at the 1982 *National Academy of Management Meetings,* Division of Health Care Administration, New York, August 1982.

25. Ross, L. The intuitive psychologist and his shortcomings: Distortions in the attribution process. In L. Berkowitz (Ed.). *Advances in experimental social psychology.* (Vol. 10). New York: Academic Press, 1977.

26. Gilbert, D. I., & Jones, E. L. Perceiver-induced constraint: Interpretations of self-generated reality. *Journal of Personality and Social Psychology,* 1986, *50,* (2), 269–280.

27. Ross, L., Green, D., & House, P. The false consensus effect: An egocentric bias in social perception and attribution processes. *Journal of Experimental Social Psychology,* 1977, *13,* 279–301.

28. Freedman, J. L., Carlsmith, J. M., & Sears, D. O. *Social psychology* (2nd ed.). Englewood Cliffs, N.J.: Prentice Hall, 1974.

29. Zalkind, S. S., & Costello, T. W. Perception: Implications for administration. *Administrative Science Quarterly*, 1962, 7, 218–235.

30. Chapman, L. J., & Chapman, J. P. Genesis of popular but erroneous psycho-diagnostic observations. *Journal of Applied Psychology*, 1969, 72, 193–204.

31. Fiske, S. T., & Taylor, S. E. *Social cognition*. New York: Random House, 1984.

32. Jellison, J. M., & Green, J. A self-presentation approach to the fundamental attribution error. *Journal of Personality and Social Psychology*, 1981, 41, 643–648.

33. Thompson, S. C., & Kelley, J. J. Judgment of responsibility for activities in close relationships. *Journal of Personality and Social Psychology*, 1981, 41, 469–477.

34. Fitch, G. Effects of self-esteem, perceived importance, and choice on causal attributions. *Journal of Personality and Social Psychology*, 1970, 16, 311–315.

35. Reiss, M., Rosenfield, D., Melburg, V., & Tedeschi, J. T. Self-serving attributions: Biased private perceptions and distorted public descriptions. *Journal of Personality and Social Psychology*, 1981, 41, 224–231.

36. Frieze, I., & Weiner, B. Cue utilization and attributional judgments for success and failure. *Journal of Personality*, 1971, 30, 591–605.

37. Brigham, J. C. Ethnic stereotypes. *Psychological Bulletin*, 1971, 76, 15–38.

38. Rosen, B., & Jerdee, T. H. The influence of age stereotypes on managerial decisions. *Journal of Applied Psychology*, 1976, 61, 428–432.

39. Campbell, D. Stereotypes and the perception of group differences. *American Psychologist*, 1967, 22, 817–828.

40. Haire, M., & Grunes, W. F. Perceptual defenses: Processes protecting an organized perception of another personality. *Human Relations*, 1950, 3, 403–412.

41. Brewer, M. B. In-group bias in the minimal inter-group situation: A cognitive motivational analysis. *Psychological Bulletin*, 1979, 86, 307–324.

42. Tversky, A., & Kahneman, D. Belief in the law of small numbers. *Psychological Bulletin*, 1971, 76, 105–110.

43. Quattrone, G. A., & Jones, E. E. The perception of variability within in-groups and out-groups: Implications for the law of small numbers. *Journal of Personality and Social Psychology*, 1980, 38, 141–152.

44. Pyszczynski, T. A., & Greenberg, J. Role of disconfirmed expectancies in the instigation of attributional processing. *Journal of Personality and Social Psychology*, 1981, 40, 31–38.

45. Schwenk, C. Information, cognitive bias, and commitment to a course of action. *Academy of Management Review*, 1986, 11 (2), 298–310.

46. Kruglanski, A. W., Friendland, N., & Farkash, Z. Lay person's sensitivity to statistical information: The case of high perceived applicability. *Journal of Personality and Social Psychology*, 1984, 46, (3), 503–518.

47. Lord, C. G., Lepper, M. R., & Preston, E. Considering the opposite: A corrective strategy for social judgment. *Journal of Personality and Social Psychology*, 1984, 47 (6), 1231–1243.

48. Haney, W. V. A comparative study of unilateral and bilateral communication. *Academy of Management Journal*, 1964, 7, 128–136.

49. Levine, J. M. Reaction to opinion deviance in small groups. In P. Paulus (Ed.), *The psychology of group influence.* Hillsdale, N.J.: Earlbaum, 1980.

50. Ivancevich, J. M. Longitudinal study of the effects of rater training on psychometric error rating. *Journal of Applied Psychology,* 1979, *64,* 502–508.

51. Bernardin, J. H., & Ponce, E. G. Effects of rater training: Creating new response sets and decreasing accuracy. *Journal of Applied Psychology,* 1980, *65,* 60–65.

52. Thornton, G. C., & Zorich, S. Training to improve accuracy. *Journal of Applied Psychology,* 1980, *65,* 351–354.

53. Fay, C. H., & Latham, G. P. Effects of training and rating scales on rating errors. *Personnel Psychology,* 1982, *35,* 105–115.

54. Lewin, K. *Field theory in social science.* New York: Harper, 1951.

55. Luthans, F., & Kreitner, R. *Organizational behavior modification.* Glenview, Ill.: Scott, Foresman, 1975.

56. Dalton, D. R., Todor, W. D., & Krackherdt, D. M. Turnover overstated a functional taxonomy. *Academy of Management Review,* 1982, *7,* 117–123.

57. Katz, D., & Kahn, R. L. *The social psychology of organizations.* New York: John Wiley & Sons, 1966.

58. Bateman, T. S., & Organ, D. W. Job satisfaction and the good soldier: The relationship between affect and employee citizenship. Paper presented at the Academy of Management Conference, New York, 1982.

59. Vroom, V. H. *Work and motivation.* New York: John Wiley & Sons, 1964.

60. Mayes, B. T., & Allen, R. W. Toward a definition of organizational politics. *Academy of Management Review,* 1977, *2,* 672–678.

61. Locke, E. A., Shaw, K. N., Saari, L. M., & Latham, G. P. Goal setting and task performance: 1969–1980. *Psychological Bulletin,* 1981, *90,* 125–152.

62. Salancik, G. R. Commitment and the control of organizational behavior and belief. In B. M. Staw & G. R. Salancik (Eds.), *New directions in organizational behavior.* Chicago: St. Clair Press, 1977.

63. Bandura, A. *Social learning theory.* Englewood Cliffs, N.J.: Prentice-Hall, 1977.

64. Porter, L. W., & Lawler, E. E. *Managerial attitudes and performance.* Homewood, Ill.: Dorsey Press, 1968.

65. House, R. J. A path–goal theory of leadership effectiveness. *Administrative Science Quarterly,* 1971, *16,* 321–328.

66. Greenberger, D. B., & Strasser, S. The development and application of a model of personal control in organizations. *Academy of Management Review,* 1968, *11,* 164–177.

67. Averill, J. R. Personal control over aversive stimuli and its relationship to stress. *Psychological Bulletin,* 1973, *80,* 286–303.

68. Miller, S. M. Controllability and human stress: Method evidence and therapy. *Behavior Research and Therapy,* 1977, *17,* 287–304.

69. Thompson, S. C. Will it hurt less if I can control it? A complex answer to a simple question. *Psychological Bulletin,* 1981, *90,* 89–101.

70. Abramson, L. Y., Seligman, M. E. P., & Teasdale, J. Learned helplessness in humans: Critique and reformulation. *Journal of Applied Psychology,* 1978, *67,* 472–479.

71. Bazerman, M. H. Impact of personal control on performance: Is added control always beneficial? *Journal of Applied Psychology*, 1982, *67*, 472–479.

72. Glass, D. C., & Singer, J. E. *Urban Stress: Experiments on Noise and Social Stressors*. New York: Academic Press, 1972.

73. Greenberger, D. B., Strasser, S., Durham, R. B., & Cummings, L. L. Personal control, locus of control, and performance. Paper presented at the 1986 National Academy of Management Meetings, Chicago, Illinois.

74. Seligman, M. E. P. *Helplessness: On depression, development, and death*. San Francisco: Freeman, 1975.

75. Thorndike, E. L. *Animal intelligence*. New York: Macmillan, 1911.

76. Kerr, S. On the folly of rewarding A, while hoping for B. *Academy of Management Journal*, 1975, *18*, 769–783.

77. Stephens, T. A., & Burroughs, W. A. An application of operant conditioning to absenteeism in a hospital setting. *Journal of Applied Psychology*, 1978, *63*, 518–521.

78. Baum, W. M. The correlation-based law of effect. *Journal of Experimental Analysis of Behavior*, 1973, *20*, 137–153.

79. Herzberg, F. *Work and the nature of man*. Cleveland: World Publishing Company, 1966.

80. House, R. J., & Wigdor, L. A. Herzberg's dual-factor theory of job satisfaction and motivation: A review of the evidence and a criticism. *Personnel Psychology*, 1967, *20*, 369–389.

81. Hackman, J. R., & Oldham, G. R. Motivation through the design of work: Test of a theory. *Organizational Behavior and Human Performance*, 1976, *16*, 250–279.

82. Mawhinney, T. C., & Ford, J. D. The path–goal theory of leader effectiveness: An operant interpretation. *Academy of Management Review*, 1977, *2*, 398–411.

83. McClelland, D. C. *The Achieving Society*. Princeton, N.J.: Van Nostrand, 1961.

84. Alderfer, C. P. An empirical test of a new theory of human needs. *Organizational Behavior and Human Performance*, 1969, *4*, 142–175.

85. Brown, R., & Hernstein, R. J. *Psychology*. Boston: Little, Brown, 1975.

86. Adams, J. S. Inequity in social exchange. In L. Berkowitz (Ed.), *Advances in experimental social psychology* (Vol. 2). New York: Academic Press, 1965.

87. Deci, E. L. *Intrinsic motivation*. New York: Plenum, 1975.

88. Boal, K. B., & Cummings, L. L. Cognitive evaluation theory: An experimental test of processes and outcomes. *Organizational Behavior and Human Performance*, 1981, *30*, 289–310.

89. Rubin, J., & Brown, B. *The social psychology of bargaining and negotiation*. New York: Academic Press, 1975.

90. Cohen, H. *You can negotiate anything*. Secaucus, N.J.: Lyle Stuart, 1980.

91. Kochan, T. A. *Collective bargaining and industrial relations*. Homewood, Ill.: Richard D. Irwin, 1980.

92. Lewicki, R. J., & Litterer, J. *Negotiation*. Homewood, Ill.: Richard D. Irwin, 1985.

93. Walton, R., & McKersie, R. *A behavioral theory of labor negotiation*. New York: McGraw Hill, 1965.

94. Fisher, R., & Ury, W. *Getting to yes*. Boston: Houghton-Mifflin, 1981.

95. Karrass, C. *Give and take*. New York: Thomas Y. Crowell, 1974.

96. Levin, E. *Levin's laws*. New York: M. Evans, 1980.

97. Pruitt, D. Achieving integrative agreements. In M. Bazerman and R. J. Lewicki (Eds.), *Negotiating in organizations*. Beverly Hills: Sage Publications, 1983.

98. Pruitt, D., & Rubin, J. *Social conflict: Escalation, stalemate, and settlement*. New York: Random House, 1985.

99. Kennedy, G., Benson, J., & McMillan, J. *Managing negotiations*. Englewood Cliffs, N.J.: Prentice Hall, 1982.

100. Nierenberg, G. *Fundamentals of negotiation*. New York: Hawthorne Books, 1973.

101. Strasser, S. The effective application of contingency theory in health settings. *Health Care Management Review*, Winter 1983, *8*, 15–23.

CHAPTER 4

Leadership and Managership

Lawton R. Burns
Selwyn W. Becker

The literature on leadership can be segmented into two camps: *(1)* discussions of "managership" and *(2)* discussions of "leadership." Research on managership, conducted primarily by psychologists, examines the role of middle- and lower-level supervisors. These studies focus on various elements of the supervisor–subordinate relationship (e.g., supervisory styles and behaviors, situational characteristics, subordinate perceptions and attributions) and their impact on employee satisfaction and productivity.

Studies of leadership, conducted primarily by organizational theorists, analyze the role of top administration. These studies focus on the relationship of chief executives to the people and the systems they direct as well as to the external environment in which their systems operate. The key executive activities include strategies to mobilize internal and external support, efforts to develop employees, decisions regarding the purpose and direction of the organization, assessments of external threats and opportunities, and responses to those threats and opportunities. These activities are viewed as critical to the organization's survival, legitimacy, and goal attainment.

Until recently, the literature was dominated by discussions of managership. In the past 5 years, however, researchers and practitioners have begun to direct their attention to issues of leadership. Research suggests that both institutional leadership, defined by Selznick (1) as the making of critical decisions regarding the development and maintenance of the organization, and transformative leadership, defined by Burns (2) as the elevation of both leader and led to higher levels of motivation and morality, may be most essential for organizations in highly complex, uncertain, and turbulent environments (3, 4). Leadership may also be extremely important for organizations confronted by challenges to their legitimacy (5). All of these environmental characteristics describe the context in which health organizations currently operate.

Hospitals, for example, are faced with restricted access to capital markets, the proliferation of high-cost technology (e.g., nuclear magnetic resonance equipment) and allied health professionals, a shift to prospective reimbursement for both inpatient care and capital costs, a multiplication of regulatory bodies, the growing economic leverage of federal and state governments as major purchasers of health care, the rise of negotiated relationships in third-party payment, growing economic competition from their own medical staffs, increasingly active consumers, and the development of new delivery systems (6–8). Hospitals are also encountering growing challenges to: (1) their performance, such as criticisms about escalating costs and inadequate patient access; (2) the missions they serve, such as leveling of demand for inpatient care and growing demand for ambulatory and preventive care; and (3) their administrative coherence, owing to the growing web of inconsistent regulations imposed from outside (7). Such environmental conditions impose a variety of constraints and contingencies on the hospital's operations to which Chief Executive Officers (CEOs) must adapt. They also present a variety of choices and opportunities from which CEOs must select.

Institutional and transformative leadership in health care—the steps hospital executives take in response to these conditions and challenges—may well determine the organization's ability to survive and function effectively (9). Given the complexity of hospitals and the environment in which they operate, CEOs will be confronted with a number of important institutional issues. These include:

- Developing an internal consensus on organizational priorities
- Enlisting internal and external support for the organization's purposes
- Selecting an optimal service and patient mix
- Locating responsibility for the organization's direction and performance
- Developing effective planning strategies
- Selecting competitive strategies to pursue
- Managing conflicts between economic and professional interests
- Negotiating reimbursement with third parties and the government

In resolving these issues, CEOs may engage in the promotion of organizational values, the resolution of moral questions, the invocation of various symbols, the management of internal and external coalitions, the assessment of environmental constraints, and the search for opportunities and choices within those constraints. Such issues, and the types of leadership decisions that may be required, are the major concern of the latter part of this chapter.

This chapter is divided into five sections. The first discusses the various definitions of leadership proposed by researchers and draws a formal distinction between "managership" and "leadership" that helps to sort out the different theoretical and empirical approaches. The second section outlines the major psychological approaches to the study of leadership and the observed findings in health care settings. This review indicates that the psychological studies are really discussions of managership rather than leadership. The third section outlines the major organizational approaches to the study of leadership and suggests that, over time, organization research has devoted more consideration to leadership issues. The fourth section integrates the psychological and organizational perspectives. Drawing on several recent studies of successful companies and executives, this section shows that leaders are adept at both dealing with subordinates and handling organizational/environmental issues. The final section discusses leadership issues as they pertain to the management of health care organizations. Our remarks here indicate the types of decisions health executives may be required to make, as well as the types of leadership questions for which new knowledge is required.

WHAT IS LEADERSHIP?

According to James McGregor Burns, "leadership is one of the most observed and least understood phenomena on earth " (2). Leadership is an essential factor whenever co-ordinated efforts of people are desirable. It is as necessary an ingredient in the modern corporation as it was in primitive tribal situations. It is quite likely that leadership has been a subject of interest, discussion, or research since language was developed. After motivation, it is still the most researched area in psychology (10). This research interest is testimony to both the importance of the subject and the difficulty of understanding what it deals with.

We are interested in leadership in the setting of formal organizations, particularly in the subset of formal organizations that comprises the health care field: hospitals, nursing homes, ambulatory care centers, and the like. Theories of leadership must be linked to the organizational context in which it occurs (11). Similarly, the practical skills of leading an organization must be related to the organizational problems a leader is called on to solve (12). Furthermore, we are interested in leadership wherever in the formal organization it might be relevant. It should, therefore, be useful to look at def-initions of leadership within the setting of a formal organization to see if some of the dimensions are more relevant than others and to determine if the dimensions of leadership have differential relevance to various parts of the system.

Some researchers consider leadership to be either synonymous with managerial be-havior (13) or a subset of it (14). Mintzberg (15), for example, views leadership as one of 10 roles that managers play. Other researchers see a distinction between the two. Bavelas (16) distinguishes leadership as (1) an organizational function from (2) a set of personal abilities. Leadership as an organizational function refers to the distribution of decision-making powers throughout the organization. Organizational leadership consists of making choices to reduce uncertainty. Such choices are made according to rational calculations with the aim of maintaining organizational efficiency. Personal leadership, on the other hand, involves the ability to innovate and take risks—attributes that disappear as organizations grow larger and more bureaucratized. This distinction between orga-nizational and personal leadership is thus related to the distinction between management and entrepreneurship (17). Indeed, Bavelas seems to equate organizational leadership with middle management functioning and personal leadership with top administrative functioning.

Similar distinctions are made by other researchers in contrasting managership with leadership. Zaleznik (18) argues that organizational systems are inherently conservative and that only conservative managers are successful within such systems. Managerial cultures in these systems are characterized by tradition, inertia, collective decision mak-ing, risk avoidance, and maintenance of the status quo. Zaleznik contrasts this managerial culture with leadership in three respects:

1. *Leaders* adopt personal and active attitudes toward goals, shaping ideas and estab-lishing objectives.
2. *Leaders* attempt to develop fresh approaches to long-standing problems, to open issues to new options, and to generate excitement in work.
3. *Leaders* relate to people in intuitive, empathetic ways. Leaders concentrate on what decisions to make and on what such decisions and events mean to participants.

We find the same distinctions drawn in the health care literature. Sheldon and Barrett (19) describe the types of leadership needed to bring health care organizations into alliance with one another. They state that managership is the efficient solution of today's *today* problems, while leadership is the identification of tomorrow's problems and the estab- *tomorrow* lishment of mechanisms today that will be needed to solve them. Leaders must thus adopt a proactive stance toward internal and external problems, developing the long-range plans, resources and competencies necessary for future operation. Hutchens (20) likewise defines managers as caretakers of something that is defined and ongoing to ensure the status quo. Leaders, on the other hand, are concerned with action, change, and novel solutions to problems.

Summarizing these and other writers (2–4, 21, 22), we may characaterize the differences between managers and leaders in terms of *(1)* what they do and *(2)* how they do it (the basis of power). These differences are outlined in Table 4.1.

We have highlighted the distinctions between managership and leadership because we feel they lend perspective in evaluating the various conceptual approaches and empirical studies. In subsequent sections we review the psychological and organizational approaches to the study of leadership and the supporting empirical evidence. These approaches are seen to be studies of managership and leadership respectively.

THE IMPORTANCE OF LEADERSHIP

The organizational approach to leadership emphasizes the importance of various institutional decisions and activities for organizational survival. These include setting goals, inculcating values and moral purposes in the organization, managing symbols and organizational legitimacy, mobilizing employees, mediating coalitional conflicts, managing environmental demands, and altering environmental constraints.

In handling these activities, top executives may have a tremendous impact on the organization's continued operation and performance, perhaps even greater than that exerted by lower-level supervisors (23). As Pfeffer (24) notes, "If leadership has an impact on organizations, it should certainly be more evident at higher organizational levels, where there is more discretion in decisions and activities." In a later essay, Pfeffer (25)

TABLE 4.1. Differences Between Leaders and Managers

Leadership	Managership
What they do	
Critical decision making	Routine decision making
Strategic decisions	Tactical decisions
Option widening	Uncertainty reduction
Opportunistic surveillance	Problemistic search
Goal setting and changing	Goal achieving
Prospective	Retrospective
Proactive	Reactive
Elevate employees	Exchange with employees
Shape the organization's culture	Work within the organization's culture
How they do it	
Emergent	Designated
Personal	Structural
Moral	Rules and regulations
Consensual, catalytic	Hierarchic
Empower people	Control and influence people

attitude

suggests that the "symbolic" actions and decisions of leaders may have much stronger effects than their "substantive" actions and decisions.

Research on organizational innovation illustrates the importance of leadership. Daft and Becker (26), for example, report that superintendents' attitudes toward innovation have strong positive associations with innovation adoption among school districts. Within health care settings, Hage and Dewar (27) and Nathanson and Morlock (28) find that the social change values held by the elite are more powerful predictors of innovation than are structural variables. Their results suggest that elite values may have a tremendous impact on the organization's direction and goals. The impact of leadership on innovation in health settings may, again, be greater in periods of institutionalization (29).

Moreover, several researchers indicate that leadership is becoming more important as the environment becomes more turbulent. Gilmore (30) argues that leadership is concerned with the management of boundaries between the organization and the environment, and between the leader and those led. Increased rates of change and interdependence with the environment increase the leader's task of managing these boundaries—identifying what the boundaries are and regulating the transactions across them. Similarly, Lippitt (31) states that several trends (e.g., expectations of shared power, the need to maintain quality with fewer resources, more people required for problem solving, integrating technological with human resources) will effect changes in leadership roles. The challenges that will increasingly face leaders are (1) to respond proactively to change, (2) to achieve a balance between centralization and decentralization, (3) to build teams out of diverse personnel, (4) to balance a technological work focus with a human work process, and (5) to mobilize resources, ideas, and support.

Hall (23) and Kimberly (32) suggest that the potential impact of leadership is greater in organizations that are smaller, younger, and less bureaucratized. These findings substantiate the arguments presented earlier that leadership may be more important in periods of institutionalization (1) and change (5) and in organizations that have simple structures (33). Inversely, older, larger, and more bureaucratic organizations may diminish the impact of leadership.

In summary, we suggest that discussions of leadership should shift much of their attention from the supervisor—subordinate relationship to the executive—organization and executive—environment relationships. Concomitantly, these discussions should focus less on supervisory styles (managership) and more on institution-wide decision making (leadership). Institutional leadership may be critically important for organizational survival during periods of institutionalization and in complex environments that pose uncertainties and challenges. These conditions characterize the health care system at present. The discussion of leadership in health care settings may, therefore, be richly informed by considering the institutional decisions and activities described above.

PSYCHOLOGICAL APPROACHES: THE STUDY OF MANAGERSHIP

PERSONALITY TRAITS AND LEADERSHIP

The early psychological studies focused on personal traits associated with effective leadership. This line of inquiry was vigorously pursued from 1904 through 1970 (34) despite critical reviews in the 1940s that questioned the fruitfulness of searching for one or two key leadership traits (35–37).

The search for the unique set of traits associated with leadership began with biographical studies of prominent political leaders. Such studies were soon complemented by more formal searches for traits that distinguished leaders from followers, effective from ineffective leaders, and higher- from lower-level leaders. Bass (34) lists 16 personality traits that have been positively correlated with leadership. Dominance and self-confidence are most frequently related to leadership; emotional control, independence, and creativity are the next most frequent. Social skills, such as sociability and administrative ability, have also been associated with leadership.

To be sure, many studies reported negative evidence for these relationships. Other evidence suggests that such traits have a limited ability to explain differences in leadership effectiveness. Finally, as Gibb (38) points out, "Traits of leadership are any or all of those personality traits which, in any particular situation, enable an individual to (i) contribute significantly to group locomotion in the direction of a recognized goal, and (ii) be perceived as doing so by fellow group members." In effect, Gibb concludes that the traits associated with leadership are contingent upon the nature of the task, the goal pursued, and the characteristics of group members.

Recognizing the difficulties in documenting universal traits of leaders, many researchers turned to other strategies. The new lines of inquiry were behaviorally oriented. The basic research question changed from "Which trait is associated with leadership?" to "What behaviors are associated with leadership?" and "What functions do leaders perform in effective groups?"

BEHAVIORAL APPROACHES

The early behavioral research was not guided by a theory of leadership; that is, by a specification of the relevant variables and their functional relationships. The early studies instead searched for dimensions to use to classify leadership behavior patterns and for the most effective leadership style.

Consideration and Initiation of Structure

The behavioral approach was inaugurated in the late 1940s by researchers at Ohio State University and the University of Michigan. At Ohio State, factor analytic studies of data obtained from use of the Leader Behavior Description Questionnaire (LBDQ) revealed two different factors of leader behavior patterns: "consideration" and "initiating structure." Bass (34) describes these patterns as follows:

Consideration.   This factor comprised the extent to which a leader exhibited concern for the welfare of the other members of the group. Considerate supervisors expressed appreciation for good work, stressed the importance of job satisfaction, maintained and strengthened self-esteem of subordinates by treating them as equals, made special efforts for subordinates to feel at ease, were easy to approach, put subordinates' suggestions into operation, and obtained approval of subordinates on important matters before going ahead. The inconsiderate superior criticized subordinates in public, treated them without considering their feelings, threatened their security, and refused to accept suggestions or to explain actions.

Initiation of Structure.   This second factor referred to the extent to which a leader initiated activity in the group, organized it, and defined the way work was to be done. The initiation of structure included such behavior as insisting on maintaining standards and meeting deadlines, deciding in detail what will be done and how it should be done. Particularly relevant were defining and structuring the leader's own role and those of the subordinates toward goal attainment.

These leadership behavior patterns were not seen as opposite ends of a continuum but rather as two distinct patterns that a leader could exhibit.

Researchers at Michigan and elsewhere drew similar distinctions between employee-centered versus production-centered (39, 40), democratic versus autocratic leadership (41), group-maintenance-oriented versus goal-achievement-oriented (42), and participative versus directive (43). Many researchers identified three or more dimensions. Mann (44) stated that leader behavior comprises three skills: human relations, technical, and administrative. Bowers and Seashore (45) developed four factors: interaction facilitation, giving support, work facilitation, and goal emphasis. Regardless of the labels used and the number of factors specified, these dimensions are similar in content to one or the other of the Ohio State dimensions ("consideration" and "initiating structure") and are highly intercorrelated with them (34, 46).

Leadership Style

Once the basic dimensions of leader behavior were specified, the next step was to determine their most optimal mix. Optimal or effective leadership styles were sought by statistical association with (1) subordinate satisfaction, (2) subordinate performance, such as productivity or low turnover, and (3) evaluations of leader performance (47). If this research was guided by any theory, however, it was implicit rather than explicit.

Early studies of consideration and initiation of structure found that effective leaders scored high on both dimensions (48–50). "The successful leader," according to Jago (47), "was one who developed good rapport and two-way communication with subordinates and who, at the same time, took an active role in planning and directing group activities." More recently, Blake and Mouton (51) have incorporated this school of thought into a normative training program called "management by grid."

In contrast, researchers investigating the democratic versus autocratic continuum suggested that democratic leaders were the most effective. Jago (47) claims that their hypotheses were based heavily on the "presumed benefits of participative decision-making and power-sharing." Indeed, two of the most widely known proponents of participative leadership, Douglas McGregor and Rensis Likert, were rooted in the human relations school of management (see Chapters 1 and 2) and subscribed to Maslow's (52) argument that employees were motivated by needs for self-actualization.

McGregor (53) described the consequences of employing one or another of two management styles: theory X and theory Y. Theory X style was directive, authoritarian, and coercive. This style was based on the belief that subordinates dislike their work and will avoid doing their jobs. The application of this style, however, was thought to lead to employee dissatisfaction and, ultimately, to low productivity. Theory Y, on the other hand, elicited participation from subordinates in all areas of decision making. This style was based on the belief that subordinates are motivated to work and have the capacity to assume responsibility. Participation was viewed as a means of allowing subordinates to achieve their own goals by accomplishing the objectives of the organization. In this manner, participation contributed both to higher satisfaction and productivity.

Likert (54) developed a theoretical model of how to improve worker productivity and satisfaction. His model was based on four different systems of interpersonal relationships: (1) exploitative autocratic, (2) benevolent autocratic, (3) consultative, and (4) democratic.

Likert claimed that productivity and satisfaction increase as organizations shift from autocratic to democratic systems. Thus, while McGregor's work had normative implications, Likert's theory was explicitly normative: organizations should move toward the democratic system.

More recently, Misumi and Peterson (55) delineated four types of leadership style using the two behavioral dimensions: leaders who emphasize production (P), employee maintenance (M), both (PM), and neither (pm). The PM leaders are not necessarily extremists on either dimension, however, unlike Blake and Mouton's model (51).

Empirical Findings

The behavioral approaches summarized above generated a lot of empirical research. It became evident, however, that the most effective leadership style depended on the characteristics of the workers, leaders, tasks, and organizations studied (56, 57). Similar assessments were made about the literature on participative leadership styles (58, 59). Research in Japanese organizations has been less equivocal. Studies of lower-level supervisors clearly show that the PM style of leadership is superior in promoting worker productivity and satisfaction (55). When contrasted with U.S. research findings, these studies suggest that the appropriate style may also depend on culture.

Research on behavioral styles in health care organizations has been conducted primarily in hospital settings and primarily examines the satisfaction and productivity of nursing personnel. The findings here are also mixed. Some researchers, for example, report that nursing supervisors who combine high levels of initiating structure and consideration promote the greatest satisfaction and technical performance among their subordinates (60). One study examined the behavioral styles used by nonnursing personnel (61). When asked to consider various managerial situations, mental health professionals (MDs and PhDs) suggested the most effective way to deal with each situation was to combine high levels of both behaviors. Others find that this combination is optimal only in certain kinds of hospitals (62) or at certain supervisory levels (63). For the most part, high consideration by nursing supervisors is associated with nurse satisfaction (63–66), high levels of performance (67), and reduced job tensions (62, 67). Initiating structure, on the other hand, has been found to promote satisfaction at lower supervisory levels rather than higher (63), and at higher levels rather than lower (44). Initiating structure is also reported to reduce performance (64). Evidence regarding the effects of participation are too scanty and mixed to permit generalizations (68, 69).

CONTINGENCY APPROACHES

When it became apparent that the behavior appropriate for good leadership in one situation might be antithetical to it in another, researchers turned their attention to contingency or situational approaches. The contingency approaches attempted to specify when and under what conditions each of the earlier approaches was most applicable. It is interesting to note that the same theoretical developments were occuring in organization research at the same time and for the same reasons (70, 71).

The two major variants of this new approach were Fiedler's contingency model (72, 73) and the 'path–goal' model proposed by Georgopoulos et al. (74), Evans (75), and House (76, 77). Fiedler's research attempted to specify the conditions under which certain leader traits were effective; path–goal models attempted to identify the conditions under which consideration and initiating structure behaviors were effective (47, 78).

Fiedler's Contingency Model

Fiedler's model is as normative as Likert's. The difference between the two is that Likert said that an organization should always have democratic interpersonal relationships, while Fiedler said that leaders should be either relations or task oriented, depending on how "favorable" the situation is for the leader. This orientation, according to House and Baetz (78), referred to which of two needs or motivations was dominant in the leader's personality: (1) concern for good leader–subordinate relations, and (2) concern for task success and task-related problems. These two motivations were considered to be polar opposites (unlike the behavioral styles of consideration and initiating structure) and were measured by the leader's score on a Least Preferred Co-worker scale. The leader described, using a set of bipolar adjectives—unpleasant versus pleasant, unfriendly versus friendly, and so forth—the person with whom he or she could work least well. The scores for each item were then added to yield the least preferred co-worker (LPC) score. Jago (47) clarifies the meaning of this score quite nicely:

> Interpreting your LPC score hinges on the assumption that your descriptions of your co-worker says more about *you* than about the person you have described. In essence, it is assumed that everyone's least preferred co-worker is about equally "unpleasant" and that differences in descriptions of these co-workers actually reflect differences in an underlying personality trait among the people doing the describing.

Situation favorability is defined by three variables: (1) the quality of leader–member relations, (2) the degree of task clarity and structure, and (3) the amount of power vested in the leader's position. The situation is most favorable for the leader when leader–member relations are good, the task is structured, and the leader has strong position power. Conversely, it is least favorable when relations are poor, the task is unstructured, and the leader's position power is weak.

The essence of Fiedler's contingency model is that leaders with low LPC scores—those who are task-motivated—will be most effective when the situation is extreme (most or least favorable). Intermediate situations, neither highly favorable nor highly unfavorable, require leaders with high LPC scores (relations-motivated leaders) for group effectiveness.

Path–Goal Model

The leader's task in the path–goal model is to increase the personal payoffs to subordinates for achieving work goals, to clarify the paths to these payoffs by coaching and direction, and to increase the opportunities for subordinate satisfaction, contingent on effective performance (58). In sum, leaders act to influence subordinates' perceptions of the clarity of paths to goals and the value of attaining those goals. The path–goal model differs from Fiedler's in that Fiedler's leader affects group effectiveness directly, while the path–goal leader enhances subordinates' motives to produce and their satisfaction with work.

The path–goal model is a contingency approach because the effectiveness of these leadership functions depends on the characteristics of the task (e.g., structured versus unstructured) and characteristics of the subordinates (e.g., perceived ability, perception that rewards are contingent on their own rather than another's behavior). For example, the model hypothesizes that when tasks are unstructured and ambiguous, leader initiating structure serves to clarify subordinates' work roles and facilitate successful task performance. This enhances subordinates' satisfaction by meeting the intrinsic demands of the task and by clarifying the probabilities of obtaining rewards for successful performance. When tasks are highly structured, on the other hand, leader initiating structure is viewed as redundant and overly restrictive. In such situations, leader consideration is most effective by providing extrinsic rewards that reduce subordinates' dissatisfaction with routine, highly structured tasks (79).

RELATED APPROACHES

The path–goal model was based on the earlier finding that consideration and initiating structure were statistically independent factors. This led naturally to the search for conditions under which one or the other of the independent factors was most strongly correlated with effective leadership. It also led to the mindset that the two factors were independent when considering personal styles of leadership. That is, a person as a leader was primarily one type or the other, high on initiating structure or on consideration, but not both. It soon became clear that leadership was a dynamic variable which operated in a changing environment. At one point in time, a leader could be effective by initiating structure and at another by concentrating on consideration. Further, environmental situations could be encountered where leaders must be high on both types of behavior to be successful. One of the most succinct statements of this position is that made by Hersey (80). In paraphrasing his and his collaborators' earlier work, Hersey states that appropriate leadership behavior depends on the followers' readiness and willingness to perform the work of the group.

This work is compatible with other recent approaches to leadership which focus on leader–group interactions and which also examine the causes of leader behavior. Osborn and Hunt (81, 82), for example, argue that leadership behavior constitutes an adaptation to environmental conditions and a reaction to subordinate demands. Similarly, Graen and Cashman (83) argue that leadership must be understood as a dyadic exchange between the supervisor and each subordinate. Leaders exchange resources, support, and trust for subordinate commitment and work behavior. Leadership behavior is not assumed to be uniform over the entire group; rather, leaders develop different types of exchanges with different subordinates. Leadership is thus viewed as a developmental process in which roles and exchanges become defined.

A different type of interactionist approach is presented by Calder (84), who suggests that the important interaction deals with perceptual processes (see Chapter 3). Calder argues that leadership is a label that group members apply to the behavior of others. This attribution process consists of a series of stages. Group members first observe the behavior of others and the effects of that behavior. If the observed behavior is viewed as (1) distinctive, (2) consistent with members' implicit theories about how leaders should act, (3) important enough to imply leadership qualities, and (4) the result of these leadership qualities, and if the one observed is perceived to have goals compatible with the observer, then there will be a stronger tendency to attribute leadership.

According to Hunt (85), leadership is an attribution that people use to make sense out of organizational events that are otherwise unexplainable. These attributions are made because people have a need for meaning—a preference for simple causal explanations of complex phenomena (e.g., organizational success and failure)—and a desire to believe in the effectiveness and importance of individual action. Leadership is thus largely a construct of the mind.

There seems to be consensus on several points. One, that initiation of structure or task oriented behavior and consideration or relations-oriented behavior are both important dimensions of leadership. Two, these dimensions alone are sufficient to explain either effective group behavior or subordinate satisfaction. Three, it is also necessary to consider task complexity or subordinate competence vis-a-vis the task as well as subordinate motivation and expectations about appropriate leadership behavior. The functional relations between these contingencies and appropriate leader behavior and group performance and satisfaction are not yet well-specified.

Empirical Findings

The studies purporting to test Fiedler's model of leadership effectiveness have been subject to controversy on statistical as well as conceptual grounds. By 1970, 38 field studies and experiments had been cited in support of parts of the model, with only nine yielding opposing findings (86, 87). In the last decade, however, the empirical work has provided little basis for major advances or changes in Fiedler's theory (88).

The path–goal model has been tested in a variety of settings, including hospitals. Earlier reviews of the literature (89) suggest general support for the model: structuring is most effective for ambiguous tasks, while consideration is most effective for structured tasks. Later reviews (10, 90) cite more mixed results. Mitchell (10) concludes that the findings of the path–goal model "are stronger for the consideration hypotheses than the structuring hypotheses and stronger for satisfaction as a criterion than for performance."

Most of the hospital-specific studies have been conducted by Szilagyi and Sims (64, 91). In one study, they found that initiating structure for associate nursing director activities reduced role ambiguity, clarified the path to goals, and improved satisfaction. For head nurses, who performed more structured tasks, initiating structure was unnecessary and reduced satisfaction. In another study of administrative (e.g., assistant department heads), professional (e.g., nurses, therapists), technical (e.g., LPNs, lab technicians) and hotel groups, they reported that leader initiating structure and subordinate satisfaction were positively correlated in the administrative group and negatively correlated in the hotel group, while the other two groups showed insignificant negative associations. They also reported that role ambiguity increases with occupational level (e.g., from hotel to administrative groups). Thus, at the higher managerial levels, initiating structure served to clarify the work tasks and improve satisfaction; at the lower support levels, initiating structure was perceived as excessive control and hence dissatisfying.

In contrast to the findings about initiating structure, Szilagyi and Sims found that leader consideration and satisfaction were positively correlated for all groups. In addition, initiating structure and subordinates' satisfaction were negatively correlated for all groups. These findings are contrary to the predictions of the path–goal model.

In one other path–goal study, Alpander (92) found that the degree of congruence in role conception among supervisors and their superiors about the supervisor's job function was positively correlated with the supervisor's job satisfaction and expectations that their efforts would lead to successful task accomplishment. These findings tend to support the path–goal model hypothesis that reducing role ambiguity enhances job satisfaction and task performance.

leadership - within
~ motivation.   *empowerment*

Leadership and Managership   153

Assessment < Skills - taught ~experimentation
\ reading ~reflection.
- recording

MANAGERIAL GUIDELINES: IMPERATIVES OF MANAGERSHIP

1. A manager must be adept at both leadership behaviors: initiating structure and consideration. The manager must be able to both structure the tasks to be performed and provide support and feedback to employees to ensure task achievement.
2. The manager must understand the complexity of the task to be performed in relation to the competency of those who are to perform it. The manager must also understand the strength of employee commitment and motivation to accomplish the task, and whether that motivation is intrinsic or extrinsic to the task.
   a. When workers are poorly trained or lack sufficient ability to perform a complex task, managers must provide structure. Workers may also be unsure of their own abilities and thus may also require managerial support and feedback.
   b. When workers are trained or perform familiar tasks but lack internal commitment, managers must provide relationship support but little structure.
   c. When workers are well-trained and intrinsically motivated, they require little structure and relational support. Managership takes the form of checking whether targets are met and acknowledging employee accomplishments.

SUMMARY

The various approaches to leadership have generated mixed empirical results. None is supported without some contradiction, so it is important to examine more closely what is being measured and where.

Looking only at what has been measured, rather than at what the various approaches state, it seems clear that these are discussions of managership rather than leadership. The approaches purportedly refer to leadership, yet the independent variables associated with leaders' traits and behaviors are almost exclusively those of initiating structure and consideration. Initiating structure deals with defining and structuring roles, scheduling work, reducing uncertainty, adhering to rules and regulations, and achieving goals. Consideration deals with two-way communication, consultation on decisions, positive feedback, and reducing tensions and pressures. These activities relate more to organizational self-maintenance and the accomplishment of objectives that have been set by those above, than to the establishment of new courses or objectives for the organization to pursue.

The outcomes that leadership is supposed to affect are group productivity (effectiveness), satisfaction, and turnover. These variables are typically measured among small work groups or departments in large organizations. Most groups are located at lower levels of the organization, although a few studies examine middle-level management. None of the studies examine leadership at the top levels of organizations.

We suggest that the approaches concern managership rather than leadership and thus have been tested at appropriate levels in formal organizations. Still, the results are mixed; we don't even have good theories of managership. Why? The contention here is that the approaches are too simplistic. Leadership and managership are complex behavioral processes not explainable by two- or even four-factor models. Fiedler's model, for example, is not so much incorrect as it is incomplete. As such, it is correct only in those situations in which the variables in his model predominate. The same can be said for the other approaches. It is exceedingly difficult to develop a comprehensive theory that includes all of the relevant variables. This problem is exacerbated by a lack of data that might permit investigators and managers to conceptualize by inductive reasoning functional relationships between variables.

Psychological studies of leadership are beginning to incorporate the characteristics and behaviors of leaders, those led, and the tasks performed. Future studies may consider how organizational and environmental characteristics affect interpersonal relations, influences, and attributions.

If leadership is based on the attributions of others, then perhaps House's (93) reintroduction of the term "charisma" into the literature may be an important contribution. Members attribute to charismatic leaders both extraordinary traits and a transcendent, radical mission. Charismatic leaders articulate ideological goals, build images of the organization's mission, develop member support for that mission, and build images of their own special abilities. In Zaleznik's (18) terms, we might easily associate charisma with leadership rather than managership. Indeed, Tosi (94) states that charisma is the base of leadership as opposed to managership.

Once these system-wide variables are included in leadership studies, perhaps the focus will shift to leadership and decision making. This topic has been almost totally ignored in the psychological literature that studies leadership as an influence process. The organizational literature, on the other hand, has squarely addressed this topic. It is to this literature that we now turn.

ORGANIZATIONAL APPROACHES: TOWARD THE STUDY OF LEADERSHIP

The development of organization theory, like that of the psychological literature, exhibits several important paradigmatic shifts. Scott (95) has conveniently classified these major paradigms as the rational-, natural-, and open-systems perspectives of organizations:

The rational system perspective—which encompasses the scientific management, classical administration. Weberian, and decision-making schools of thought—emphasizes the need for obtrusive and unobtrusive bureaucratic means to control the behavior of organizational participants.

The natural system perspective—which includes the human relations school, the institutional approach of Selznick and Barnard, and Parsons' social system theory—emphasizes the importance of the organization's internal climate, its purposive and moral character, and its external maintenance activities.

The open system perspective, finally—reflected in contingency theory and resource dependence theory, among other schools—emphasizes the importance of strategic adaptation to and manipulation of the organization's environment.

These schools of thought, which are described in detail in Chapter 1, suggest different organizational imperatives that must be satisfied and, by implication, different leadership functions that must be performed. As organization theory has evolved from the rational-systems perspective of machine bureaucracies to the natural- and open-systems views of organizations as organic and adaptive systems, the description of leadership has changed from an internal maintenance and control activity to an external maintenance, strategic, and symbolic activity.

Thus, returning to the basic distinction proposed in this chapter, we suggest that the evolution of organization theory has been accompanied by a transition from strictly managership studies to leadership studies. Indeed, a small number of natural- and open-systems theorists have explicitly considered the role of the chief executive or institutional level of the organization in relation to both the external and internal environment. These theorists describe the executive's role in dealing with a number of important questions, including the organization's survival, legitimacy, goals, values, morals, and internal politics. Such analyses direct our attention to some of the key functions of leadership.

The sections that follow consider various schools of organization theory that encompass the three major paradigms. The intention is to trace not the evolution of organization theory but its conceptualization of leadership functions. Greater emphasis is given those schools that explicitly address the role of leadership.

LEADERSHIP IN THE RATIONAL-SYSTEM PERSPECTIVE

Rational-system theories construct mechanical models of organizations, complete with formalized relationships and predetermined goals. These arrangements are viewed as the most efficient means to accomplish specified ends. The "rational" character of the organization inheres in the formal structure itself, in the orchestration of activities that represents the most efficient means of goal attainment. The development of these efficient methods constitutes the role of leadership.

The classic school of administration, exemplified by the writings of Fayol (96) and Gulick and Urwick (97), derives a broad range of universal administrative principles to guide managers in structuring their organizations and running them in a rational, efficient manner. The scalar principle, span of control, departmentalization, and other principles serve as normative guidelines for the inspection and modification of the organization's structure. Clearly, the role of the manager is to (1) assess how closely the organization meets these principles and (2) align the organization in accordance with them. The classic school also identifies basic managerial functions that contribute to maximum efficiency. These include Fayol's five elements of administration, (forecast/plan, organize, command, coordinate, control) and Gulick's POSDCORB activities (planning, organizing, staffing, directing, coordinating, reporting, budgeting).

Weber's (98) bureaucratic model exhibits several similar elements. The characteristic features of bureaucracies—the hierarchy of authority, division of labor, formalized rules, and so forth—are structural devices that impose strict discipline and order and contribute to the stability of the organization and predictability of its performance. Bureaucratic organization is also the most rational means of controlling the arbitrary behavior of managers and workers. What makes bureaucratic administration "rational" is that the exercise of control is based on technical knowledge, on the formal training and experience of higher officials. Within the bureaucracy, the role of leadership is the imposition of these structural controls and the invocation of rational rules to regulate the functioning of the organization on the basis of knowledge. Bureaucratic leadership is thus concerned with the implementation of policy in the most efficient manner.

The decision-making school, illustrated by the work of Simon and his colleagues (99–101) argues that organizations need to control not only the arbitrary behavior of their members but also the premises of their decision making. In general, in Simon's view, "organizations both simplify decisions and support participants in the decisions they need to make" (95). One method of simplifying decisions is to establish a "means–ends" hierarchy, in which the means of achieving general goals become factored into subgoals for lower hierarchical levels. This hierarchy promotes rational organizational behavior by ensuring some consistency in the activities and decisions of different organizational levels. The role of leadership is to decide on the general goals and priorities of the organization and to delegate responsibility for their accomplishment. Goal setting and planning are not continuous leadership functions in Simon's view, however. As Perrow (46) notes:

> Once established, the goals remain quite stable because of such things as the high cost of innovative activity, "sunk cost," and "sunk assets." . . . Even planning is difficult, for "daily routine drives out planning." (101)

In addition to this formal restriction of decision-making activity, organizations also employ unobtrusive methods such as standard procedures, communication channels, and programs to reduce uncertainties in the decision-making process. Superiors thus employ both obtrusive and unobtrusive means to structure the tasks and perceptions of organization members beneath them. The emphasis of leadership is clearly on stability and routine, not planning and change.

In sum, rational-system theories place a strong emphasis on structure, rationality, and efficiency. Organizations are described as rational instruments to control the behavior of their members and coordinate it toward the accomplishment of specified goals. The primary role accorded leadership is to develop the most efficient structural means for implementing predetermined goals. Institutional questions—such as the selection of goals, the survival and legitimacy of the organization, its relations with the environment— are either not discussed or not considered to be problematic.

LEADERSHIP IN THE NATURAL-SYSTEM PERSPECTIVE

Natural-system theories do not view organizations as instruments that can be manipulated to achieve predetermined goals in the most efficient manner. On the contrary, as Scott (95) notes, they are "social groups attempting to adapt to and survive in their particular circumstances." The natural-system perspective considers the organization's internal and external environment as problematic. On the one hand, the behavior of organizational participants is strongly influenced by work group and professional norms and sentiments. On the other hand, the environment is not assumed to be given or stable, but instead contains resources and support capacities for which the organization must negotiate. The dynamic character of the environment also requires adaptations by the organization to maintain itself. These conditions create potential problems of survival, goal attainment, and legitimacy.

Given their view of the organization's internal and external environment, the natural-system theorists are led to consider those institutional questions that the rational-system theorists ignored. Such questions, in turn, lead to the first explicit consideration of leadership functions. Not all of the natural-system theories discuss leadership in the same terms, however. The psychologically oriented human relations school (53, 54, 102–104) and much of the psychological literature reviewed above, describe leadership as supervisors' motivation of and influence over their subordinates. The other natural-systems theories, by contrast, focus on the executive level and describe leadership as a policy-making, morality-creating (i.e., inculcating organizational values and purposes), and legitimizing or symbolic role. It is to these latter theories that we turn our attention.

Barnard (105) characterizes organizations as cooperative systems held together by common purposes and an organizational morality. These common purposes must be moral purposes: they must reflect the long-term interests, purposes, and values of the organization. A key function of the executive is the establishment and inculcation of these moral purposes throughout the organization and its participants. This function is necessary for the survival and legitimacy of the organization.

Barnard also views organizations as systems of decision making. In this context, the executive is responsible for formulating the broad purposes and making the key decisions that determine the organization's direction. Barnard recognizes the dynamic character of the external environment but devotes little discussion to this topic.

Selznick (1) goes beyond Barnard in considering the problematic characteristics of the internal and external environment, as well as their implications for the organization and its leadership. For Selznick, organizations are "institutions"—organisms that adapt to pressures from without and from within. Organizations are limited in their degree of rationality by (1) their environment, which may deflect the organization's purposes and constrain future actions, and (2) their participants, who develop or bring to the organization their own particular commitments and interests that may be at variance with organizational purposes.

Selznick argues that there is a close connection between these institutional aspects of organizations and the functions that leadership must perform. In fact, he comes close to advocating a contingency theory of leadership by suggesting some of the conditions under which leadership is or is not important. In so doing, he draws a clear-cut distinction between leadership and management.

Leadership is most essential in those organizations and during those periods of organizational life in which the goals and functioning of the organization are not strictly determined by technical considerations, but rather are open to internal and external influences. In such instances, organizations undergo a process of adaptation and "institutionalization," that is, they take on values, commitments, goals, and repertoires of action that are considered important for their own sake (1). Leadership is responsible for guiding this process of institutionalization. This task involves making "critical decisions" concerning the development and maintenance of the institution:

1. The leader must define the role and mission of the organization.
2. The leader must enact a social structure that embodies the key values and commitments of the organization.
3. The leader must legitimate the organization's values and distinctive competences before the external public and the organization's members.
4. Finally, the leader must regulate internal rivalries by reaching an accommodation between organizational goals and group interests.

Leadership thus involves the promotion and protection of values, the setting of policy, and political negotiation. The importance of these activities increases as one ascends the organization's administrative hierarchy.

Management, by contrast, is more relevant to periods characterized by stability. In such instances, the existing formal and informal structure is adequate to solve operational problems with only minor adaptations. The essence of management is routine decision making and the concern for efficiency. These activities are performed at lower administrative levels and encompass the variety of supervisory styles and human-relations techniques mentioned in the previous section (1).

Parsons (106, 107), finally, also examines the organization in relationship to its environment. The basic orientation of the organization is its system of values, which focus on legitimizing the organization's goals in the eyes of both its external environment and its internal membership (106). Responsibility for this articulation of values rests with the top layer—or "institutional" level—of the organization. Institutional activities thus include the set of policy decisions that commit the organization to certain purposes. The managerial level of the organization, on the other hand, is responsible for administering the organization's technical functions and for mediating its input/output exchanges with the environment.

These natural-system theories tend to agree that organizations are adaptive systems that seek to survive and gain legitimacy in their internal and external environments. In contrast to most rational-system theorists, who view goals as predetermined, the natural system theorists consider the determination of goals as the organization's central concern. Organizational leadership performs a creative function—establishing and disseminating the organization's purposes—rather than a maintenance function. Leadership is also tied directly to critical decision making, directing the organization in its environment.

LEADERSHIP IN THE OPEN-SYSTEM PERSPECTIVE

Open-system theories view organizations as systems that are "loosely coupled" both internally and externally (108, 109). Internally, the organization's structural elements, activities, and members may be only loosely connected to each other and therefore semiautonomous in their behavior. This poses difficulties in achieving concerted action among organizational groups. Externally, the organization is subject to, but not completely determined by, the constraints and uncertainties in its environment. The organization may respond by adapting itself to environmental demands or by attempting to manipulate its set of environmental dependencies and exchanges.

These considerations lead open systems theorists to a broader conceptualization of leadership. Leadership is concerned not only with infusing values into the organization, defining the organization's goals, making the critical decisions, and establishing the organization's legitimacy, but, also include managing internal coalitions, mobilizing employees toward a common purpose, monitoring and adjusting to the environment, and modifying the environment. These functions are depicted in the contingency theories and resource dependency theories of organizations.

Contingency Theories

Leadership in organizational contingency theories may be distinguished by the nature of the contingency. Some theories argue that the type of leadership is contingent upon the environment. Others claim that leadership is contingent upon hierarchical level or organizational type. These different theories are outlined below.

Hirsch and Andrews (5) present a contingency theory of leadership that closely resembles the work of Selznick. The authors summarize their argument in the following four propositions:

1. The type of leadership behavior appropriate for given situations varies with the legitimacy context in which an organization is located.
2. These contexts are subject to change.
3. An important aspect of administrative leadership consists of knowing which set of symbols to invoke and which type of authority to exercise at different points in time.
4. Organizations embody efforts to maintain and adapt to external, institutional value complexes and in turn, convey corresponding cultural symbols to their members and the world at large.

The authors take issue with the treatment of leadership in traditional theories of organization and administration—particularly in the rational-systems perspective. They suggest that these theories examine leadership in a "stability frame" in which such institutional issues as the organization's goals, purposes, or legitimacy are not considered to be problematic.

In periods of social change and in unstable environments, however, institutional questions become more problematic. According to Hirsch and Andrews, the organization may be confronted with "performance challenges" and "value challenges" to its legitimacy. Performance challenges call into question the organization's ability to accomplish the goals that define its mission and justify its claims for external support. Value challenges call into question the organization's mission and *raison d'être*.

These challenges require administrators to act more like leaders, to invoke various symbols and values that legitimate the organization's position in its environment. In the face of performance challenges, leaders may *(1)* offer alternative indicators of the organization's performance or goal attainment, *(2)* rationalize their organization's poor performance, *(3)* emphasize that better days are ahead, or *(4)* serve as scapegoats for poor performance and be replaced. In the face of value challenges, leaders may *(1)* radically alter the mission and structure of the organization or *(2)* aggressively defend them (5). In each instance, leadership serves to mediate the organization's relationships to its environment through the use of "symbols, stances, and behavior called for by particular conditions and surroundings" (5).

Bass (3) presents another environmentally based contingency theory of leadership that builds on Burns' (2) work. Burns distinguishes transactional leadership, based on exchanges between leaders and led, from transformative leadership, which elevates both leaders and led to higher levels of morality and motivation. Transactional leaders recognize what employees want from their work, exchange rewards for employees' efforts, and respond to employees' self-interests if they can be met by accomplishing the task. Transformative leaders, on the other hand, arouse and satisfy higher needs which transcend self-interests and induce extraordinary effort among employees. This distinction is equivalent with the managership versus leadership dichotomy presented above. According to Bass, transformative leadership is likely to emerge during times of crisis, change, and high uncertainty in the environment, and when the goals and structure of the organization are neither predetermined nor clearly articulated.

Bradford and Cohen (4) offer a similar contingency theory. Managership models are appropriate when organizational tasks are simple and characterized by low interdependence, when employees are relatively unskilled, and when the environment is stable.

Leadership, on the other hand, is suited to complex and highly interdependent tasks, skilled employees, and a constantly changing environment.

Another line of contingency theory focuses on the hierarchical level of the leader. As noted above, studies of managership and leadership are distinguished by the level of the managerial hierarchy they focus on. Some researchers have explicitly recognized the vertical level in the hierarchy as a contingency. Katz and Kahn (110) state that higher managerial levels are associated with a broadening of perspective and less concern with technical knowledge. Among the top echelon, the leader's cognitive emphasis is on the total organizational system and its environment. At the same time, charisma is an important characteristic of leaders. Among lower supervisors, on the other hand, the emphasis is on technical knowledge, understanding rules and policies, and concern with equity in the use of rewards and sanctions.

Mintzberg (15) also states that there are differences in managerial work across hierarchical levels. Mintzberg identifies 10 different managerial roles, grouped into three categories: interpersonal, informational, and decision making. Several roles (liaison, spokesperson, figurehead) link the organization to its environment. According to Mintzberg, CEOs focus much of their attention here. Lower-level managers, in contrast, focus on certain internal roles (disturbance handler, negotiator) which deal with maintaining the work flow and handling daily operational problems. Empirical research on Mintzberg's model suggests some different patterns, however. The available evidence indicates that both external and internal roles increase in perceived importance to managers as one ascends the hierarchy (111–114).

Mintzberg and Waters (33), finally, argue that organization type poses a contingency for the emergence and type of leadership. In organizations with simple structures, the leader is an entrepreneur—setting the organization's vision, deciding strategy, and molding the organization to his/her own initiatives. In machine bureaucracies, the organization's systems, procedures, planning methods, and structure take precedence over the exercise of entrepreneurial leadership. The leader here is a planner who both encourages the organization to respond to environmental change and tries to buffer it from external disruptions.

Resource Dependence Theories

Resource dependence theories suggest that a key problem for organizations is ensuring their survival. According to Pfeffer and Salancik (109), organizations survive to the extent that they are "effective"—able to acquire the resources and mobilize the support necessary for their continued operation. Effectiveness in obtaining resources and support has both an internal and external focus.

Internally, an organization is a loosely linked coalition of interest groups headed by a dominant coalition of representatives from the key groups. Leaders, themselves members of this dominant coalition, must be able to manage the competing demands of other members in such a way as to satisfy group interests and elicit group support in the pursuit of organizational objectives. Leadership thus encompasses the use of political and negotiation tactics in averting coalitional conflicts.

The organization is also a system of patterned activity. Effectiveness requires that this activity be perceived by organization members as meaningful, legitimate, and consonant with prevailing social norms and values (25). A key administrative task, therefore, is to develop explanations and rationalizations for the organization's activities. This task involves the use of language, symbols, and rituals to construct and maintain systems of shared beliefs and meanings (25, 115, 116).

Externally, organizations must also manage the demands of environmental groups and coalitions of support. According to Pfeffer and Salancik (109), leadership can perform a variety of important functions, both actively and passively, in handling these demands. Leadership can play a "symbolic" role, for example, by serving as a focal point of personal responsibility and control over the organization's performance. Internal and external groups thus attribute organizational successes and failures to acts of leadership. By investing top positions with symbolic value, the organization *(1)* enhances its own stability by emphasizing the importance of organizational self-control and self-determination, and *(2)* develops a mechanism to deal with performance challenges, such as replacing the administrator. Leadership may also play an active symbolic role by managing the organization's social legitimacy. Strategies here include *(1)* promoting beliefs in the organization's distinctive competencies (25), *(2)* designing formal structures that adhere to institutionalized, prescriptive rules—such as arranging medical care facilities for a large employer's work force or developing environmental protection programs (117)—and *(3)* meeting the various reactions to value challenges noted by Hirsch and Andrews (5).

In addition to these symbolic activities, leadership may play a "responsive" role by adapting the organization to environmental demands and constraints. In contrast to some contingency theories, which suggest an isomorphic relationship between the environment and the most effective organizational structure, the resource dependence theories suggest that a number of activities and structures may be consistent with effective performance. The critical role of the leader, therefore, is to determine which sets of demands the organization should respond to. Leadership thus involves making key decisions among choices. More importantly, however, leadership involves making an assessment of the environmental context—"being aware of the situation of interdependence and the demands of those with whom the organization is interdependent"—and an assessment of alternative responses. Pfeffer and Salancik (109) thus describe this role as more "information gathering and processing" than "decision making."

Finally, leadership may play a "discretionary" role by actively manipulating and enacting the environments in which the organization operates. Rather than adapting to environmental constraints and dependencies, leadership attempts to alter them. Such attempts include "merging, lobbying, co-opting, and doing all the various things that alter the interdependencies confronted by the organization" (109). This leadership role requires the same assessment of environmental constraints but assumes a more proactive and opportunistic stance.

In summary, the open-system perspective extends the conceptualization of leadership presented by the natural-system theorists. This conceptual development is tied to an increasingly sophisticated and explicit consideration of organization–environment relations. Recognition of the various external demands and constraints imposed on organizational performance emphasizes the need for leadership to monitor and adapt to the environment. Recognition of the loose coupling between the organization and environment suggests that leadership may employ a repertoire of symbolic and strategic activities to manipulate environmental constraints. Finally, recognition of the loose coupling between organizational components emphasizes the need for political, charismatic, and symbolic leadership skills in mobilizing support for organization-wide objectives and reconciling divisive group interests.

It is not the intent of the preceding discussion to highlight the importance of leadership at the expense of managership, however. As Mintzberg (15) and others have pointed out, the difference between the two is partly a matter of degree. The following section pulls together these two perspectives into a more comprehensive model of leadership that accords each its due place. This model is then illustrated with a variety of case materials (personal biographies, organizational histories) and survey findings from large corporations.

RECONCILING THE PSYCHOLOGICAL AND ORGANIZATIONAL PERSPECTIVES: A NEW MODEL OF LEADERSHIP WITH ILLUSTRATIONS FROM CORPORATE BUSINESS

At first glance, the psychological and organizational perspectives seem not to share common ground. The psychological approach focuses on the traits and behaviors of lower-level supervisors, the exchanges between supervisors and employees, and the attributions of leadership made by employees. The organizational perspective, in contrast, examines the chief executive officer, the decisions he makes, the values he imparts to employees to mobilize their efforts, and the direction he charts for the organization in the environment. One can nevertheless synthesize the two approaches in a useful model to guide leadership action.

One avenue for achieving this synthesis is to examine how the independent variables identified in managership research (traits, behaviors, exchanges, attributions) play a major role in describing the activity of CEOs. That is, how does an analysis of the CEO's traits, supervisory styles, transactions with subordinates, and cognitive attributions of his or her leadership help us to understand the CEO's institutional and transformational leadership.

ELEMENTS OF A NEW MODEL OF LEADERSHIP

As a starting point, we propose that the two supervisory styles of initiating structure and consideration are essential ingredients to the CEO's defining, inculcating, and defending the organization's mission and values. The leader employs both supervisory styles to establish the mission and values. Congruent with an initiating structure style, the leader:

- Makes decisions at the top (not shared).
- Emphasizes the goal to be achieved.
- Lets people know what is expected of them (standards).
- Expects unquestioning compliance among employees.
- Insists on strict attention to detail.

Congruent with a consideration style, the leader:

- Develops a basis of cooperation, mutual understanding, and morale.
- Serves to inspire and motivate employees.
- Focuses on the "social" environment of the organization—employee loyalties, commitments, and norms of behavior.

- Makes use of informal communication channels.
- Decentralizes the responsibility for adherence to organizational standards.

Similarly, the inculcation of the organization's mission and values among employees may be understood as a process of social exchange and influence between leader and led. The CEO does not exchange tangible rewards to employees in return for their task performance. Instead, the CEO communicates a vision to employees about what the organization stands for, where it fits in the wider, societal division of labor, and in what direction it is headed. The CEO who communicates a compelling organizational vision draws employees to himself and fosters an identification process. Moreover, the CEO must delegate the responsibility and authority to employees to translate this vision into reality. One can pinpoint some of the essential exchanges between CEOs and their employees as processes of communication, identification, and empowerment.

Successful transactions between leaders and led, moreover, depend on certain leadership traits on the part of the CEO. For employees to embrace and identify with an organization's mission and values, they must first identify with the CEO who establishes them. The personal character and morality of the CEO are reflected in the organization's standards and values. The CEO's traits and personal example thus perform an important role in fostering allegiance to the mission and values of the organization. For instance, as the CEO displays the trait of self-confidence, he may elevate employees' perceptions of their own ability to uphold the organization's standards and achieve its transcendant mission. Similarly, the CEO's example of consistency, determination, and assertiveness in pursuit of the organization's mission and values may be crucial for employees' internalization of them.

Finally, we propose that attributions of leadership are not merely romanticized perceptions of otherwise unexplainable events, but instead reflect the presence of charismatic authority. According to Weber (98), this authority rests on the followers' perception that the leader possesses extraordinary traits and a transcendant mission. This perception, in turn, is based on certain traits and behaviors exhibited by the leader (93).

The implications of this view of charismatic leadership are profound. The first is that charisma is not necessarily an inborn characteristic but may be developed as one takes on certain attitudes, dispositions, and actions. The charismatic leader, moreover, shapes the attitudes, perceptions, and actions of followers and elevates them to a higher plane (3, 118). This process is central to transformational leadership. The ultimate effects of this leadership are loyalty and commitment to the leader and the mission he espouses, identification with the leader and imitation of his example, and heightened goals of followers and their conviction that they can successfully attain the organization's mission (93).

CASE ILLUSTRATIONS: PERSONAL BIOGRAPHIES AND ORGANIZATIONAL HISTORIES

A few years ago, Mintzberg (119) took the managership approach to task for failing to uncover any significant empirical findings about leadership. Mintzberg argued that leadership is an essential ingredient in organizations, but is intractable to conventional research methods because it is difficult to define and measure empirically. Researchers have floundered in trying to understand leadership analytically rather than intuitively.

Consultants and professional managers, on the other hand, have a more intuitive understanding of the subject, and they have pursued some unconventional research methods in recent years to provide a rich description of leadership. These methods include personal biographies of CEOs and organizational histories of successful firms. Their unstructured observations of leader traits, behaviors, and decisions provide case illustrations of the new model of leadership just outlined.

"EXCELLENT FIRMS"

The most prominent of these descriptions is found in Peters and Waterman's examination of "excellent firms" (120). Based on interviews with executives in 43 high-performing companies, the authors found that all companies shared eight attributes, some of which can be ascribed directly to the CEO. For example, one attribute is "value-driven organization." Almost every successful firm had a strong CEO and an organizational culture that incorporated and institutionalized the values of the CEO. The values gave a purpose and stability that underlay all of the policies and actions of the firm. When one examines the values of some of these firms, one can recognize the tint of the two supervisory styles on them. The initiating structure style is evident in such corporate values as "We want to be the best at what we do" (set standards of achievement), "We do the job well" (pay attention to detail), and "Superior quality and service" (set strict standards of performance). The consideration style is evident in other values, such as "Importance of people as individuals" (person-oriented), "Informality enhances communication" (be open and approachable), and "We want innovators at all levels of the organization" (allow employee participation, initiative, and growth). Corporate values thus indeed serve the dual purpose of (1) setting standards for employees to rigidly adhere to and (2) inspiring and motivating employees.

A second attribute of these firms, "simultaneous loose-tight properties," also reveals how the two supervisory styles are essential ingredients to the CEO's inculcation of organizational values. The organizations Peters and Waterman studied are tightly structured in terms of strongly-held values: everyone's actions must line up with these values, which thus provide a new system of discipline and control. Deviations from these values are not tolerated. However, because employees are expected to adhere to these values, there is less need to supervise them overtly. This yields a loosely-structured environment that permits autonomy, flexibility, and experimentation. The organization thus builds the initiating structure and consideration styles into its structure as well as its values.

Several other attributes serve to enhance this "looseness." One is "autonomy and entrepreneurship:" allow people to make decisions and innovate. Another attribute is "productivity through people." These activities constitute illustrations of the CEO's empowerment of employees, granting them the responsibility for translating the organization's vision into reality.

MINI-CASE: "EXCELLENT DEPARTMENTS"

Bradford and Cohen (4) reached similar conclusions about the leadership of excellent departments. Based on results from a training program for middle and upper-middle managers, the authors outline three components of successful leadership:

1. Build a team with a sense of shared responsibility for management of the department, its decisions, and its performance. Shared responsibility fosters greater commitment to departmental success and informal peer control.
2. Promote continuous development of individual skills. Employees need opportunities to learn on the job and must be trusted to take responsibility.
3. Determine and build a common vision into the department. This vision serves to inspire, unite, and motivate employees to give extra effort. It also sets standards by which to evaluate decisions and actions.

Leadership in excellent departments is thus centrally concerned with the articulation and inculcation of a mission and a set of values. To accomplish this, leaders engage in a particular exchange with followers: leaders empower them. By giving followers responsibility and authority, leaders increase employee commitment and motivation to the departmental vision, and thus gain a measure of control over them.

MINI-CASE: "SUCCESSFUL CEOs:" STRATEGIES FOR TAKING CHARGE

Bennis and Nanus (21) state that leadership is the pivotal force behind successful organizations (i.e., organizations that can survive and adjust to environmental disturbances). Based on interviews with 60 successful CEOs and 30 outstanding leaders from the public sector, they derive four "kernels of truth about leadership" which may be alternately considered four strategies for taking charge of one's organization. These include:

1. Attention through vision: develop a compelling vision and agenda that draws people to the leader, challenges them to perform, and instills confidence that they can accomplish the desired goals.
2. Meaning through communication: use symbols to communicate the organizational vision and to enable employees to understand abstract principles and objectives. Also, institutionalize new meanings and interpretations of organizational life among employees that are shared and that facilitate coordinated activity.
3. Trust through positioning: through his actions and example, the leader defines what is right and what is necessary for the organization to do. Leaders establish a set of morals and ethics and model them for employees to emulate. Leaders also demonstrate a persistence and dedication to the firm's mission and values. In this manner, leaders establish an integrity and sense of trust inside the organization that facilitates accountability, predictability, and reliability.
4. Deployment of self through positive self-regard: leaders demonstrate positive self-images and thoughts (e.g., embrace positive goals, look forward rather than behind, avoid rationalizing mistakes or dwelling on shortcomings).

According to the authors, the effect of these four strategies is empowerment of employees. Leaders tap and harness the energies and talents of employees by granting them responsibility. They also articulate and embody a set of values and principles that attract employees to them and motivate them by identification. Empowerment is thus the end result of institutional and transformational leadership: leadership that articulates transcendant goals and elevates employee motivations and morality.

___

TRANSFORMATIONAL LEADERSHIP AND PERFORMANCE BEYOND EXPECTATIONS

Bass (3) conducted several studies and surveys to determine the components of transformational leadership. A pilot study consisting of open-ended interviews with top industrial executives, and a survey of 104 senior U.S. Army officers revealed three major components: charisma, individualized consideration, and intellectual stimulation. Transformational leaders are above all charismatic: they inspire followers to give extra effort and to believe in great causes, they build confidence in the ability to achieve them, they build enthusiasm for work, and they lead followers to expect they will do well. They generate enthusiasm, in part, by instilling a common vision in the minds of followers and by demonstrating a consistent, determined adherence to that vision. According to Bass, the traits such leaders need to be charismatic are self-confidence, self-esteem, self-determination, and inner direction.

Second, transformational leaders exhibit individualized consideration (i.e., they treat each person individually). The leader makes the most of whatever talents employees have, gives them as much responsibility as they can handle, and expresses appreciation for work well done. The leader also serves as a role model and mentor for employees: counselling, coaching, and teaching. Indeed, the leader places a premium on the careful selection and training of employees.

Third, the transformational leader increases the intellectual capacity of followers. This occurs by increasing employee awareness, conceptualization, and discernment of organizational problems and methods to solve them. Leaders also spur the thinking and imagination of followers, and arouse or change their beliefs and values. Indeed, the intellectual contribution of the transformational leader is found in his generation, interpretation, and elaboration of symbols. Leaders project abstract ideas and corporate values and ideals by means of symbols. Symbolic images enable leaders to communicate clear messages and meanings that motivate employees to give extra effort and elevate their organizational behavior to a higher moral plane. Bass reports that these three components are all positively correlated with employee satisfaction and leader effectiveness.

CEOs AND THE SUCCESSFUL REJUVENATION OF ORGANIZATIONS

Levinson and Rosenthal (121), finally, argue that leadership is responsible for organizational success and failure. The revival of stagnating organizations depends on leadership that provides direction, allocates power, and evolves an adaptive structure that generates ideals to give new life and vision to the organization. The authors examine the biographies of six prominent CEOs who rebuilt their organizations. Their summary of the components of successful transformational leadership can be expressed in terms of a handful of traits and behaviors.

The constituent traits of corporate leadership include an infusion of values and morals, a preoccupation with detail, and intellectual capacity. Above all, the leader gives meaning to the organization by articulating a set of personal values (e.g., "We stand for quality," "We're all in this together") which establish a collective purpose and morality. This morality is shared by both the leader and followers with the leader setting a personal example by holding himself out as a role model, and then strictly insisting on employee adherence to it. Role modeling and the articulation and reinforcement of values are continuous activities performed by the leader. Part of the CEO's example is a penchant for both personal and organizational details. Attention to detail is seen as a requirement for maintaining high standards of quality and performance. According to the authors, these CEOs see themselves as stewards who act in the interests of the owners, the employees, and the public. As stewards, they devote much time to careful consideration of ideas and information before taking decisive action. To modify Peters and Waterman, they are both thinkers and doers.

The behaviors most often associated with their transformative leadership include: taking charge, delegating authority, interacting with people, and developing subordinates. The CEO is in the forefront during crises—defining the problems, mapping out ways to solve them, and making the final decisions. The leader is a risk-taker as well, charting the organization's course in new and unfamiliar directions to ensure its survival, without compromising its values and identity. To accomplish this, the leader delegates authority and the permission to take risks. The integrity of the whole is never sacrificed, however; departments are held accountable for performance and must develop the perspective of the organization, not of an autonomous unit.

Leaders also spend much of their time interacting with and developing subordinates. Chief executive officers develop a large network of personal relationships in order to (1) get to know their people and their needs, (2) foster identification with the leader, (3) keep informed about activities throughout the organization, (4) elicit ideas and information relevant for decision making, and (5) promote a family atmosphere of teamwork. This concern for the individual is reflected in the CEOs' personal involvement and concern with succession. Leaders see themselves as mentors and teachers of younger managers. Great attention is therefore paid to selecting, developing, testing, and appraising subordinates. Younger managers are viewed as the key asset of the organization and the key to its future survival.

SUMMARY

This section has sketched a model of leadership that synthesizes elements of the psychological and organizational perspectives. According to this model, the key activities of leadership include the articulation and inculcation of organizational values, the enactment of a social structure that embodies those values, the definition of the organization's mission, and the elevation of employees to a higher level of morality and motivation. These activities, as described in the preceding section on the organizational perspective, constitute the essence of institutional and transformational leadership. To carry out these activities effectively, however, the leader must exhibit certain traits and engage in certain behaviors and exchanges identified by the psychological perspective. These include: (1) the traits of self-confidence, determination, assertiveness, positiveness, self-esteem, intellectual capacity, and detail-mindedness; (2) such behaviors as initiating structure and consideration; and (3) such activities as delegation of authority, empowerment, role modeling, mentoring, and employee development, which are exchanged for greater employee commitment to the organization's goals and vision, accountability for performance, innovation, and identification. Attributions of leadership follow on the heels of the manifestation of such traits, behaviors, and exchanges.

This model is supported by several recent studies of corporate leadership. These studies agree that good leadership is the key to organizational success and reach consensus on the components of successful leadership. The strength of these studies lies partly in their methodology: they examine the personalities, behaviors, and decision-making styles of successful executives and corporations. As a result, they uncover the "how" of leadership: what executives do to be successful.

The next section outlines several ways in which this leadership model can be applied to health care organizations. Specifically, the material identifies several institutional issues that face health executives and shows how this model may help in dealing with them.

MANAGERIAL GUIDELINES: IMPERATIVES OF LEADERSHIP

The Leader must:

1. Make explicit the values of the organization.
2. Ensure that these values are communicated to organization members in a variety of ways—personally (both verbally and as a role model) and symbolically.
3. Elicit employees' trust, cooperation, and team behavior through the use of several mechanisms—challenge, responsibility, and positive attitudes and rewards for performance.

INSTITUTIONAL LEADERSHIP IN HEALTH CARE ORGANIZATIONS

As we stated in our introduction, health care executives are confronted with several institutional issues that require resolution. Such issues, and the types of decisions CEOs may need to make, can be classified into three groups: moral, symbolic, and proactive. These groupings can be roughly defined as follows:

1. *Moral Issues.* The need for commonly held values and principles that define the organization's mission and resolve conflicts among competing, but legitimate, ends.
2. *Symbolic Issues.* The need for symbols and stances that legitimate the organization's claims for support from internal and external coalitions and that provide a sense of organizational stability and self-control.
3. *Proactive Issues.* The need for long-term planning and strategic responses to maintain organizational autonomy within turbulent environments.

It is evident that these groups are not entirely orthogonal. Each set of issues and decisions has important implications for the others; for example, the symbols invoked by CEOs to legitimate the organization's continued operation can also serve to define its moral purposes and mission. These issues do, however, reflect the major concerns of leadership described above. The three sets of issues, and the leadership opportunities they present, are discussed in detail below.

MORAL LEADERSHIP AND THE PROMOTION OF ORGANIZATIONAL VALUES

The health care executive serves a variety of interests simultaneously (122). In the hospital, the CEO is:

1. Entrusted by the board to manage the organization efficiently.
2. Expected by physicians to honor their autonomy in clinical decision making and to provide the necessary facilities and working conditions for high-quality care.
3. Responsible for upholding the rights of patients.
4. Required to conform with various standards and statutes enacted by government and other agencies.
5. Expected to address the health and welfare needs of the community and society at large.

The diverse range of interests poses a number of problems for CEOs. First, the claims of different groups—such as the board's interest in cost containment and the medical staff's desire for the latest technology—may seriously conflict (123). In an era of fiscal retrenchment, the shortage of resources may exacerbate such conflicts over the institution's priorities. Second, the CEO faces tremendous environmental uncertainty and lacks the necessary information to analyze the costs and benefits of the various priorities. Thus CEOs must decide upon priorities in the face of conflicting claims and ambiguous tradeoffs.

The decisions CEOs reach in balancing these priorities are moral decisions. As Callahan (122), Hitt (124), and McGeorge (125) note, they differentially affect the interests of the various groups and reflect some judgment about what is best for the organization. Decisions concerning how resources are to be allocated or what services will be developed will be more acceptable to some groups than to others. Such choices also entail various risks and costs and commit the organization to some future course of action.

The moral process of selecting among the various priorities may be either haphazard or systematic. On the one hand, choices may be based on personal gains or short-term advantages. This course typically leads to intense departmental rivalries and organizational drift (126). On the other hand, choices may be based on the appeal to some higher authority (127) (i.e. some set of explicit values and principles shared by all of the groups involved.) These values lend meaning and consistency to the decisions reached and allow organizational activities to be evaluated in terms of their contribution to broad organizational purposes. The promotion and maintenance of these values in organizational decision making is the essence of moral leadership.

A number of people have described the importance of moral leadership. Levinson (22) writes that health organizations must change from their present "role-oriented" structure to a "task-oriented" structure. The former organizational type emphasizes roles, procedures, and regulations; the latter emphasizes tasks, values, and goals. This transition has important implications for the health care executive. "The basis of his activity must be a reorientation of his perspective. He must realize that leading an institution is more than administration . . . he must acquire *leadership* skills as contrasted with administrative skills" (22). One such skill involves articulating a "publicly-stated transcendant purpose" that serves as a standard for judging organizational decisions and activities and defines a common goal toward which individual actions can be directed. A related skill is consolidating the various groups around a mutually agreeable set of values that transcend particular interests.

Peters (128) also describes the role of top management in terms of "value promotion" and "transforming leadership." The mission of the chief executive is to shape "robust institutional values" that define the direction of the organization and allow an orderly determination of goals, options, and policies. Such leadership may transform the organization by introducing a new set of values over time. According to Meyer (129), shared institutional values are important and appropriate for health organizations because they lack objective measures of performance, because they pursue vague and abstract goals, and because their goals permit considerable latitude for interpretation. Institutional values thus provide a basis of cooperation, coordination, and control in loosely coupled organizations (130).

One of the most significant shifts in values in the health care field today is the transition from the product and selling concepts to the marketing concept (131). As Goldsmith (9) writes,

> health care organizations and their managers tend to be production-oriented. That is, they take the organization's current service offerings, and their quality, accessiblity, and other important variables, for granted. To the extent that they engage in marketing activities, they tend to be oriented toward selling the product to a customer whose needs are, more often than not, defined in a self-serving way.

There are signs, however, that a marketing orientation—identification of consumer needs and wants, and delivery of services to meet them—is beginning to emerge. In a recent survey of hospital marketing executives (132) over three-quarters described their institutions as "market-driven." This trend is evident in the growing involvement of hospitals in ambulatory care and alternative delivery systems. Such a transition constitutes a redefinition of the organization's purpose and raison d'être.

Another emerging value system in health care is "entrepreneurship." Entrepreneurship is concerned with enhancing the organization's competitive position and maintaining its fiscal solvency. The entrepreneur's task is to initiate innovative programs to raise census levels, generate new sources of revenue, and be a visionary of unmet patient needs and emerging technologies (133, 134).

The emergence of a new system of values, such as the marketing orientation and entrepreneurship was triggered primarily by increased competition in the health care sector. Competitive pressures may also force a reconsideration of a number of other institutional values. Heyssel (135) suggests that a competitive marketplace for health care may have deleterious consequences for the quality of care, the availability of specialty and emergency services, the equitable distribution of services, and the operation of residency training programs. These values were vigorously pursued in an earlier period of expansion, when there were fewer choices or the choices were easier to make. Such may not be the case in the future. For example, the incentives of cost competition might motivate CEOs and physicians to limit the provision of services (particularly those that are expensive to maintain and render), the introduction of new technology, and the types of patients and patient problems treated. Under competitive conditions, then, CEOs will be forced to weigh their product goals versus their contribution to community health needs and societal goals of access, equity, and training. The choices made will reflect changes in the values and purposes that health organizations pursue.

These developments concern many health care observers. According to Levey and Hill (127), health executives find their traditional service mission besieged by commerical, bottom-line ideologies. As a result, there is considerable temptation to compromise standards of care and ignore patient interests (136). This concern has led observers to emphasize the need for a set of personal and organizational ethics to guide health care decision making (127, 137, 138). This need must be addressed by the health care executive. The health care CEO has the major influence on organizational ethics, values, and culture (139, 140). Ethics committees, which exist in 60% of all hospitals, typically concern themselves only with life support issues or case review (141).

SYMBOLIC LEADERSHIP AND FITNESS FOR FUTURE ACTION

Health care organizations are thus confronted with a complex decision-making environment and various challenges to their legitimacy. During periods of environmental instability and transition, these organizations require some sense of purpose and direction toward which their energies can be channeled. The promotion and maintenance of organizational values constitutes one leadership strategy to provide this direction. In addition, health organizations require new symbols and leadership stances to help legitimate their continued operation before the public. They also require some sense of self-control and self-determination amidst the various external pressures (109, 142). Chief executive officers, by virtue of their positions of high visibility among internal and external groups, may logically serve as the focus of the organization's stability, control, and peformance. This role defines the symbolic aspect of institutional leadership.

Within the organization, symbolic leadership is important for demonstrating that top management has control of the situation. According to Levinson (22), organizations need to be led and directed, rather than administered. While these requirements provide opportunities for CEOs to assert themselves, they are often thwarted by the current conceptions and content of the CEO's role. Numerous observers suggest that this role is neither well defined nor well understood (143, 144). Divergent conceptions of this role have formed largely as a result of the multiple bases of control and authority that have emerged in health organizations (126, 145). Trustees see hospital management as responsible for maintaining efficient operations and guiding the activities of support personnel. Physicians see hospital management as responsible for providing facilities and services necessary for high medical performance. Management often views its own role as one of compromise and negotiation between the interests of other groups. The lack of specificity in the manager's role is also a consequence of changes in the functions that must be performed. Growing problems in financing, reimbursement, regulation, and marketing have increased managerial responsibilities in areas that affect the organization's survival and performance. Hospital executives have thus assumed responsibility for managing the myriad external relations in addition to internal operations. These expanding responsibilities were documented in Chapter 2 and receive further attention in Chapter 10.

There seems to be some discrepancy, therefore, between the roles executives are expected to play and the functions they actually perform. Some observers suggest that the prestige of the health executive needs validation (143). Others suggest that the executive's role is in need of restructuring. According to Steinle (146) and Ewell (147), it is important that the executive be designated and recognized by both trustees and physicians as the chief executive officer of the organization. In this manner, the executive's office becomes invested with greater leadership qualities and responsibility for the organization's direction. Johnson (148) argues that the institution needs to strengthen its leadership in an increasingly competitive environment.

> In a highly competitive marketplace the abilities of the chief executive and the senior management of the hospital are going to determine the success or failure of the institution. . . . In addition, chief executives are going to need much more authority so they can make decisions and implement them at a speed that is in keeping with the rapidly changing external environment. From time to time, they may have to exercise their authority even though it may run counter to the desires and thoughts of the medical staff or hospital personnel. To wait until all parts of the hospital organization are in agreement may mean missing opportunities in the marketplace (148).

Johnson (149) and Wren and Hilgers (150) suggest that such titular changes also clarify the executive's role to the external agencies and groups that interact with the organization but are unfamiliar with its operations.

The establishment of corporate management structures in health organizations is one such solution that is growing in popularity (151). Executives are given the title "president" or "chief executive officer" and placed in charge of planning and external affairs; they also sit on the board and may even be president of it. Reporting to the president are vice-presidents for finance, operations, nursing, and medical affairs who are responsible for internal activities. According to Todd (152–154) and Pfeffer (155), restructuring is a symbolic, attention-focusing process that emphasizes a change in the organization's operations and the growing importance of the administrative function within it. Whether these kinds of posturings improve the organization's ability to survive and compete in its environment is unclear. Survey data indicate that executives perceive some benefits. Kauffman's (156) study found that 64% of executives believe that changes in job titles help them to perform their duties and responsibilities more effectively. Todd's (155) survey found that 40% of executives believe that title changes grant them the respect and equal status of their peers in the community and allow them to relate on a meaningful basis. The significance of restructuring thus lies in the identification of the health executive with other business executives who have responsibility for the leadership and performance of their organizations.

The transition to corporate models and executive roles will likely encounter physicians' opposition. Physicians often view these developments as representing the rise of corporate medicine, the loss of their clinical authority, and the growing emphasis on cost control rather than patient care. Actual or anticipated opposition by physicians is often sufficient to deter corporate restructuring (150). Chief executive officers may therefore have to rely on other symbols in assuming this new leadership role. For example, some observers suggest that CEOs avoid declarations of their ultimate authority over everything that occurs within their organizations. Instead of attempting to demonstrate "who's in charge," CEOs should seek to clarify "who's in charge of what" (157). Similarly, these observers suggest that CEOs consider the symbolic content of the strategies they propose to improve efficiency:

Thus the physician for whom the words "cost containment" may evoke an image of meager resources, if not cut corners, might be perfectly comfortable with the concept of "cost effectiveness," which considers cost in the context of acceptable care. (157)

The management of symbols will also be important for health executives in dealing with their internal and external coalitions. For example, as the capital base of hospitals erodes and inpatient care declines in importance relative to other product lines (9, 158), hospital executives must be able to demonstrate the fitness of their institutions for future action (71). Chief executive officers must convey to their boards and medical staffs the new realities facing the hospital: increasing needs for capital and changing markets (159). Chief executive officers must also convince these groups that the new realities must be addressed and must recommend viable strategies for the institutions to pursue. The strategies proposed must emphasize that the interests of the various groups are tied to the survival of the institution. One such strategy—the development of hospital-based ambulatory care programs—can be marketed within the hospital as a solution to such problems as declining census, specialty referrals, and primary health care needs in the community. The growing supply of physicians has led to greater competition among providers—both physicians and hospitals—for the more profitable surgical and ancillary services that can be provided in ambulatory settings (9). To confront this competitive challenge, CEOs must emphasize the distinctive competencies and resources of their institutions for initiating ambulatory programs and they must thereby enlist the participation of physicans in joint ventures.

Chief executive officers must also demonstrate the fitness of their institutions to sources of environmental support. For example, CEOs may need to demonstrate the credit worthiness of their institutions in order to obtain capital from financial institutions or local governments to meet needs for expansion, modernization, or replacement of facilities. Executives may point to a number of indicators—the quality of management, operating statistics and trends, competitive advantages over neighboring institutions—that reflect their organizations' financial health and prospects. Executives may also influence bond ratings, which determine the cost of borrowed capital, by upgrading the hospital's image and reputation (160). In this manner, they can strengthen their institutions' claims on needed resources (161).

Hospital executives also need to demonstrate to patients that their institutions are concerned about both the cost and quality of care they provide. High costs, the growing incidence and size of malpractice awards, and increased consumerism are primarily responsible for the current erosion in the hospital's image and legitimacy (162). These problems must be addressed through vigorous efforts to serve the patient. Such efforts include comprehensive risk management programs and involvement of patients in their own care.

In addition, CEOs often resort to a number of face-lifting strategies—such as management reorganization and innovation, physical remodeling, and development of affiliations—to ensure continued accreditation, recruitment of managerial and professional personnel, and patient satisfaction. These strategies are ultimately designed to enhance the prestige and professional image of the organization.

Finally, executives may seek to manage public policy and public opinion by releasing statements to the media concerning their institutions' positions on proposed legislation, by developing personal links with legislators and providing them with information needed to formulate legislation, by speaking in public about their institutions' improvements in management and efficiency, or by advertising (163–166). Such strategies are largely symbolic efforts to improve public relations. The quality of the institution's public relations and reputation in the community may influence occupancy rates, CON decisions, and market positioning (160).

PROACTIVE LEADERSHIP AND ORGANIZATIONAL PLANNING

Perhaps the most significant and difficult function for health executives to perform is long-term planning. On the one hand, strategic planning can enhance moral and symbolic leadership by defining general values or objectives to be followed in the future and by closely identifying planning activities with the administrator's role. On the other hand, strategic planning may present several challenges to executives. One challenge is dealing with the increasingly turbulent character of the health care environment. The withdrawal of Certificate of Need (CON) legislation and cost-based reimbursement, the rise of investor-owned firms and multihospital systems, limited access to capital, the rise of alternative delivery systems, and the future increase in number of physicians will foster tremendous competition in the marketplace for patients and resources. These developments will cause great uncertainty about capital investment decisions, future sources of patient revenues and operating capital, and the franchise for hospital services. Chief executive officers will thus have to make important decisions under highly ambiguous conditions.

A second challenge is that current decision-making patterns in hospitals frustrate strategic planning efforts. Given the balance of power among trustees, physicians, and executives, sucessful planning has often been based on the short-term maintenance of organizational harmony rather than the long-term achievement of objectives (126, 145, 167). Long-term planning leads to conflicts of interest that may threaten the established prerogatives and powers of the various groups. Perrow (126) concludes from his case study of Valley Hospital that (126)

> only the "something for everyone" plan could succeed, and this had to avoid the assessment of long-range consequences. Outwardly the hospital might prosper, but perhaps for reasons that had little to do with its avowed goals, and even at the expense of those goals. By avoiding the question of what is its distinctive competence and its responsibility, the organization is no longer a means for achieving goals that are rationally established and publicly offered for community inspection and support.

A third challenge is that members of the dominant coalition in hospitals may have little interest in or understanding of the planning process. Bander (168) conducted interviews with executives, medical directors, and trustees in 10 voluntary teaching hospitals. She found that medical directors believe that planning is too time-consuming and lengthy a process (from initiation to implementation). Most directors do not appreciate the need for planning and lack interest in regulatory or legal issues. Trustees, on the other hand, may be interested in planning but perceive difficulties in applying business techniques and planning models from the for-profit sector to the teaching hospital.

Fourth, the various activities that comprise planning can be neglected by executives or handled in piecemeal fashion (144). In an early survey of 434 general hospitals, Perlin (169) found that hospital executives spend less than one-eighth of their time on planning. Moreover, nearly one-third of the hospitals that engage in long-term planning do so on a one-time basis. In a study of 15 community hospitals, Mankin and Glueck (167) found that

- 93% of the executives report that the strategic changes implemented in weekly meetings constitute reactions to, rather than preparations for, a changing environment.
- None of the executives report having a specific individual or department responsible primarily for planning.
- None of the executives evaluate the effectiveness of the strategies pursued.

More recent evidence suggests that strategic planning is becoming widespread among hospitals. Results show that roughly three-quarters of all hospitals have strategic plans, and two-thirds have a full-time planner. The majority adopt a long-term planning horizon (5 years or more) and revise their plans annually (170).

A fifth and final challenge of strategic planning is that, even in those institutions where it is practiced, the strategies employed may be misguided. Rynne (171) suggests that long-term planning is gaining greater acceptance among hospitals and their executives as a necessary activity. He criticizes current planning efforts in several areas, however. First, strategies are typically based on linear growth projections rather than the possible need for retrenchment:

> A linear growth presumption not only prevents hospitals from anticipating nogrowth situations, but it also prevents hospitals from eliminating some services, functions, and products that have outlived their usefulness. . . . Hospital planning usually focuses on what is new and does not give adequate attention to what is old, in decline or no longer productive.

Second, strategies are typically based on a mixture of "product" and "selling" concepts (131), which emphasize provider interests in developing and selling a high-quality product—patient care. This planning approach ignores consumers' health care needs and perceptions of quality care.

The various challenges described above suggest that there is a critical opportunity and need for sound, long-term planning in health care organizations. This suggestion is echoed by numerous observers of the health care field (167, 172). These observers prescribe an array of conceptual models to assist executives in the planning process, such as management by objectives, the marketing concept, and program planning, budgeting, and control systems. Each of these conceptual approaches requires a definition of the organization's objectives; an assessment of future demands, constraints, and opportunities in the environment; an assessment of the organization's resources and competencies to match environmental conditions; the selection of specific strategies; the redesign of organizational capabilities to pursue these strategies; the appraisal of organizational performance in key result areas; and the re-evaluation of organizational objectives in light of results achieved.

Chief executive officers must therefore assume a more responsive and discretionary stance toward the organization's environment (109). They must gather extensive information—both quantitative and qualitative—on social, political, and economic forces that affect the organization: for example, regulatory and reimbursement trends, population trends, physician and consumer utilization patterns, physician needs and attitudes, and market threats and opportunities (133). Recent evidence suggests that one-half to two-thirds of all hospitals now rely on national and local market research studies to formulate their strategic plans (170, 173). Chief executive officers must screen this information to identify relevant problems and needs in the environment and select some subset to which the organization will respond. Finally, they must decide upon specific strategies that will enable the organization to adapt to these external requirements or to modify them aggressively, and they must decide quickly.

Chief executive officers are beginning to adopt a number of strategies to manage their environments actively. These strategies are designed to buffer health organizations from the uncertainties they face and to limit their dependencies on external elements. Diversification strategies, for example, constitute attempts to develop more flexible organizational structures that can take advantage of new marketing opportunities and reduce dependence on single product lines (e.g., inpatient care). Vertical integration strategies attempt to extend organizational control over ambulatory services that supply inputs (e.g., refer patients) to the organization. The restructuring of health organizations into holding companies is designed, in part, to escape legal and regulatory constraints on the development of revenue-generating activities (9). Horizontal combination strategies such as the formation of coalitions, management contracts, and multihospital systems represent attempts to improve the organization's access to capital markets, to increase its bargaining power in the purchase of supplies, to increase its influence in the local community, to exert greater power in relation to external agencies such as regulatory groups and third-party payers, and to improve financial management and operating efficiency (174–176).

These develoments in organizational planning signal the emergence of proactive leadership in the health care field. With increasing competition and the growing need for formal planning at the organizational level, CEOs may grasp the opportunity to assert the autonomy and integrity of their organizations. These and related ideas concerning strategic planning and management are further elaborated in Chapter 13.

SUMMARY

This chapter has addressed three topics. First, we have discussed the meaning of leadership in the context of formal organizations. We suggested at the outset that leadership is a complex, multidimensional concept. We argued further that the various dimensions of leadership might have greater or lesser relevance in different parts of the organization. The literature on leadership has two very different perspectives: the psychological view and the organizational view. Despite the tremendous diversity of approaches within each, in general the two perspectives examine different phenomena at different levels in the organization. The psychological perspective focuses on interactions and influence processes between supervisors and their subordinates; the organizational perspective, on the other hand, focuses on decision making at the highest levels. Following a number of other writers, we have characterized these phenomena as "managership" and "leadership." It is thus evident that managership and leadership are associated with qualitatively different types of activities.

Second, we showed how theories of managership and leadership have been applied to health care organizations, particularly hospitals. Studies of managership typically examine the relationship between a nursing supervisor's style (e.g., consideration, initiating structure) and the satisfaction or turnover of subordinates. Studies of leadership, in contrast, examine the role of the chief executive in directing the hospital in its environment.

Third, we have argued that a comprehensive model of leadership encompasses elements of both managership and leadership. Leadership requires certain traits, behaviors, and exchanges with subordinates in order to be successful at enacting institutional values, defining the institutional mission, and obtaining internal and external support.

At present, most discussions of leadership in health care organizations focus on managerial issues. While we acknowledge the importance of managerial activities in achieving the organization's goals, we suggest that executives and researchers devote more attention to leadership issues. The myriad of external problems that confront health organizations and the potential impact of administrative decisions in handling these problems indicate that leadership will become increasingly important in the future. Executives may be required to perform a number of institutional and transformational leadership activities to ensure the organization's survival and development, and to mobilize internal support for the orgnaization's goals. We have described these activities in terms of the moral, symbolic, and proactive roles that executives can play. We believe that successful performance of these roles may be an increasingly important factor influencing organizational performance (see chapter 12).

DISCUSSION QUESTIONS

1. What kind of training will health care leaders need in the future? How does their training differ from health care managers? Can leaders in fact be trained?
2. What role should health care leaders play in the daily administration and management of their organizations?
3. This chapter has argued that leadership is more important under some conditions (e.g., during periods of institutionalization or challenges to legitimacy) than others. What are some other situations in which leadership might be essential? Why?
4. What are some specific strategies health care leaders might employ to infuse their organizations with value or meaning?
5. How might the leader's role differ as a function of the health care organization that he or she leads? Specifically, compare and contrast leadership roles in hospitals, HMOs, and public health departments. What similarities and dissimilarities do you observe?

SUGGESTED READINGS

Bass, B. *Leadership and performance beyond expectations.* New York: Free Press, 1985. *Transformational leadership is required for high levels of organizational performance and individual effort.*

Bennis, W., & Nanus, B. *Leaders: The strategies for taking charge.* New York: Harper and Row, 1985 *Examination of 90 leaders from diverse fields. Highlights the importance of creating, communicating, and implementing a sense of vision.*

Bradford, D., & Cohen, A. *Managing for excellence.* New York: John Wiley & Sons, 1984. *Distinguishes between the manager as technician, as orchestrator, and as developer. Emphasizes the importance of the developer role. Several excellent illustrations.*

Levinson, H., & Rosenthal, S. *CEO: Corporate leadership in action.* New York: Basic Books, 1984.

> *Organizational success and failure are due to the quality of leadership, not to the organization's structure or environment. Case studies of six chief executive officers of successful corporations reveal a consistent pattern of institutional and transformational leadership.*

Pfeffer, J. Management as symbolic action: The creation and maintenance of organizational paradigms. In L. Cummings, B. Staw (Eds.), *Research in organizational behavior* (Vol. 3). Greenwich, Conn: JAI P ress, 1981, pp. 1–52.

> *Management has a potentially greater impact on symbolic outcomes (values, attitudes, legitimacy) than on substantive outcomes (resource allocation, sales).*

Selznick, P. *Leadership in administration.* New York: Harper & Row, 1957.

> *The institutional leader is an expert in the promotion and maintenance of values. The leader defines the institution's role and mission and builds them into the social structure.*

REFERENCES

1. Selznick, P. *Leadership in administration.* New York: Harper & Row, 1957.

2. Burns, J. M. *Leadership.* New York: Harper & Row, 1978.

3. Bass, B. *Leadership and performance beyond expecations.* New York: Free Press, 1985.

4. Bradford, D., & Cohen, A. *Managing for excellence: The guide to developing high performance in contemporary organizations.* New York: John Wiley & Sons, 1984.

5. Hirsch, P., & Andrews, J. Administrators' response to performance and value challenges. In T. Sergiovanni & J. Corbally (Eds.), *Administrative leadership and organizational cultures: New perspectives on theory and practice.* Urbana: University of Illinois Press, 1983.

6. Goldsmith, J. The future corporate structure of the hospital and implications for education for management. *Health Administration Education,* 1985, 3, 93–102.

7. Scott, W. R. Conflicting levels of rationality: Regulation, managers, and professionals in the medical care sector. *Health Administration Education,* 1985, 3, 113–131.

8. Bruton, P. A reasoned approach to hospital planning in an uncertain world. *Health Care Management Review,* 1982, 7, 39–43.

9. Goldsmith, J. *Can hospitals survive?* The new competitive health market. Homewood, Ill.: Dow Jones-Irwin, 1981.

10. Mitchell, T. Organizational behavior. In M. Rosenzweig & L. Porter (Eds.), *Annual Review of Psychology,* (Vol. 30). Palo Alto, Cal.: Annual Reviews Inc., 1979.

11. Miner, J. The uncertain future of the leadership concept: Revisions and clarifications. *Journal of Applied Behavioral Science,* 1982, 18, 293–307.

12. Dubin, R. Metaphors of leadership: An overview. In J. Hunt and L. Larson (Eds.), *Crosscurrents in leadership.* Carbondale, IL: Southern Illinois University Press, 1979, pp. 225–238.

13. Wilpert, B. Various paths beyond establishment views. In J. Hunt, U. Sekaran, and C. Schriesheim (Eds.), *Leadership: Beyond establishment views.* Carbondale, IL: Southern Illinois University Press, 1982, pp. 68–74.

14. Hunt, J., Sekaran, U., & Schriesheim, C. Beyond establishment views of leadership: An introduction. In J. Hunt, U. Sakaran, & C. Schriesheim (Eds.), *Leadership: Beyond establishment views*, 1982, pp. 1–6.

15. Mintzberg, H. *The nature of managerial work*. Englewood Cliffs, N.J.; Prentice-Hall Inc, 1980.

16. Bavelas, A. Leadership: Man and function. *Administrative Science Quarterly*, 1960, *5*, 491–498.

17. Peterson, R. Entrepreneurship and organization. In P. Nystrom & W. Starbuck (Eds.), *Handbook of organizational design*. London: Oxford University Press, 1981.

18. Zaleznik, A. Managers and leaders: Are they different? *Harvard Business Review*, 1977, *55*, 67–78.

19. Sheldon, A., & Barrett, D. The Janus principle. *Health Care Management Review*, 1977, *2*, 77–87.

20. Hutchens, T. Change: The cornerstone of leadership. *Pathologist*, 1979, *33*, 345–349.

21. Bennis, W., & Nanus, B. *Leaders: The strategies for taking charge*. New York: Harper & Row, 1985.

22. Levinson, H. The changing role of the hospital administrator. *Health Care Management Review*, 1976, *1*, 79–89.

23. Hall, R. *Organizations: Structure and process*. (2nd ed.), Englewood Cliffs, N.J.: Prentice-Hall, 1977.

24. Pfeffer, J. The ambiguity of leadership. In M. McCall & M. Lombardo, (Eds.), *Leadership: Where else can we go?* Durham, N.C.: Duke University Press, 1978.

25. Pfeffer, J. Management as symbolic action: the creation and maintenance of organizational paradigms. In L. Cummings & B. Staw, (Eds.), *Research in organizational behavior* (Vol. 3). Greenwich, Conn.: JAI Press, 1981.

26. Daft, R., & Becker, S. *Innovation in organizations*. New York: Elsevier, 1978.

27. Hage, J., & Dewar, R. Elite values versus organizational structure in predicting innovation. *Administrative Science Quarterly*, 1973, *18*, 279–290.

28. Nathanson, C., & Morlock, L. Control structure, values, and innovation: A comparative study of hospitals. *Journal of Health and Social Behavior*, 1980, *21*, 315–333.

29. Burns, L. The adoption and diffusion of decentralized management in hospitals. Ph.D. dissertation, University of Chicago, 1981.

30. Gilmore, T. Leadership and boundary management. *Journal of Applied Behavioral Science*, 1982, *18*, 343–356.

31. Lippitt, R. The changing leader–follower relationships of the 1980s. *Journal of Applied Behavioral Science*, 1982, *18*, 395–403.

32. Kimberly, J. Initiation, innovation, and institutionalization in the creation process. In J. Kimberly & R. Miles (Eds.), The organizational life cycle. San Francisco, Jossey-Bass, 1980.

33. Mintzberg, H., & Waters, J. The mind of the strategist(s). In S. Srivastva (Ed.), *The executive mind*. San Francisco: Jossey-Bass, 1984, 58–83.

34. Bass, B. *Stogdill's handbook of leadership*, (rev. & Exp. ed.). New York: Free Press, 1981.

35. Stogdill, R. Personal factors associated with leadership: A survey of the literature *Journal of Psychology*, 1948, *25*, 35–71.

36. Bird, C. *Social psychology*. New York: Appleton-Century, 1940.

37. Jenkins, W. A review of leadership studies with particular reference to military problems. *Psychological Bulletin*, 1947, *44*, 54–79.

38. Gibb, C. Leadership. In G. Lindzey (Ed.), *Handbook of social pschology*. Cambridge, Mass.: Addison-Wesley, 1954.

39. Katz, D., Maccoby, N., & Morse, N. *Productivity, supervision, and morale in an office situation*. Ann Arbor, University of Michigan, Institute for Social Research, 1950.

40. Katz, D., Maccoby, N., Gurin, G., & Floor, L. *Productivity, supervision, and morale among railroad workers*. Ann Arbor, University of Michigan, Institute for Social Research, 1951.

41. Lewin, K., & Lippitt, R. An experimental approach to the study of autocracy and democracy: A preliminary note. *Sociometry*, 1938, *1*, 292–300.

42. Cartwright, D., & Zander, A. *Group dynamics—Research and theory*. Evanston, Ill.: Row, Peterson, 1960.

43. Tannenbaum, R., & Schmidt, W. How to choose a leadership pattern. *Harvard Business Review*, 1958, *36*, 95–101.

44. Mann, F. Toward an understanding of the leadership role in formal organization. In R. Dubin (Ed.), *Leadership and productivity*. San Francisco: Chandler, 1965.

45. Bowers, D., & Seashore, S. Predicting organizational effectiveness with a four-factor theory of leadership. *Administrative Science Quarterly*, 1967, *11*, 238–263.

46. Perrow, C. *Complex organizations: A critical essay*. Glenview, Ill.: Scott, Foresman, 1979.

47. Jago, A. Leadership: Perspectives in theory and research. *Management Science*, 1982, *28*, 315–336.

48. Hemphill, J. Leadership behavior associated with the administrative reputations of college departments. *Journal of Educational Psychology*, 1955, *46*, 385–401.

49. Halpin, A. The leader behavior and effectiveness of aircraft commanders. In R. Stogdill & A. Coons (Eds.), *Leader behavior: Its description and measurement*. Columbus: Ohio State University, Bureau of Business Research, 1957.

50. Fleishman, E., & Simmons, J. Relationship between leadership patterns and effectiveness ratings among Israeli foremen. *Personnel Psychology*, 1970, *23*, 169–172.

51. Blake, R., & Mouton, J. *The managerial grid*. Houston: Gulf Publishing Co., 1964.

52. Maslow, A. *Motivation and personality*. New York: Harper & Row, 1954.

53. McGregor, D. *The human side of enterprise*. New York: McGraw-Hill, 1960.

54. Likert, R. *New patterns of management*. New York: McGraw-Hill, 1961.

55. Misumi, J., & Peterson, M. The performance-maintenance (PM) theory of leadership: Review of a Japanese research program. *Administrative Science Quarterly*, 1985, *30*, 198–223.

56. Korman, A. "Consideration," "initiating structure," and organizational criteria—A review. *Personnel Psychology*, 1966, *19*, 349–361.

57. Kerr, S., & Schriesheim, C. Consideration, initiating structure, and organizational criteria—An update of Korman's 1966 review. *Personnel Psychology*, 1974, *27*, 555–568.

58. Filley, A., House, R., & Kerr, S. *Managerial process and organizational behavior.* Glenview, Ill.: Scott, Foresman, 1976.

59. Locke, E., & Schweiger, D. Participation in decision-making: One more look. In B. Staw (Ed.), *Research in organizational behavior.* (Vol. 1). Greenwich, Conn.: JAI Press, 1979.

60. Gruenfeld, L., & Kassum, S. Supervisory style and organizational effectiveness in a pediatric hospital. *Personnel psychology*, 1973, *26*, 531–544.

61. Blake, R., & Mouton, J. Theory and research for developing a science of leadership. *Journal of Applied Behavioral Science*, 1982, *18*, 275–291.

62. Oaklander, H., & Fleishman, E. Patterns of leadership related to organizational stress in hospital settings. *Administrative Science Quarterly*, 1964, *8*, 520–531.

63. Nealey, S., & Blood, M. Leadership performance of nursing supervisors at two organizational levels. *Journal of Applied Psychology*, 1968, *5*, 414–422.

64. Szilagyi, A., & Sims, H. An exploration of the path-goal theory of leadership in a health care environment. *Academy of Management Journal*, 1974, *17*, 622–634.

65. Bonjean, C., Brown, B., Grandjean, B., & Macken, P. Increasing work satisfaction through organizational change: A longitudinal study of nursing educators. *Journal of Applied Behavioral Science*, 1982, *18*, 357–369.

66. Gray-Toft, P., & Anderson, J. Organizational stress in the hosptial: Development of a model for diagnosis and prediction. *Health Services Research*, 1985, *19*, 753–774.

67. Sheridan, J., & Vredenburgh, D. Structural model of leadership influence in a hospital organization. *Academy of Management Journal*, 1979, *22*, 6–21.

68. Bragg, J., & Andrews, I. Participative decision-making: An experimental study in a hospital. *Journal of Applied Behavioral Science*, 1973, *9*, 727–736.

69. Wolf, G., Breslau, N., & Novack, A. The effect of delegation on outcomes in the primary care team. *Academy of Management Proceedings*, 1977, 401–405.

70. Becker, S., & Gordon, G. An entrepreneurial theory of formal organizations, part I. *Administrative Science Quarterly*, 1966, *11*, 315–344.

71. Thompson, J. *Organizations in action.* New York: McGraw-Hill, 1967.

72. Fiedler, F. *A theory of leadership effectiveness.* New York: McGraw-Hill, 1967.

73. Fiedler, F., & Chemers, M. *Leadership and effective management.* Glenview, Ill.: Scott, Foresman, 1974.

74. Georgopoulos, B., Mahoney, G., & Jones, N. A path-goal approach to productivity. *Journal of Applied Psychology*, 1957, *41*, 345–353.

75. Evans, M. The effects of supervisory behavior on the path-goal relationship. *Organizational Behavior and Human Performance*, 1970, *5*, 277–298.

76. House, R. A path-goal theory of leader effectiveness. *Administrative Science Quarterly*, 1971, *16*, 321–338.

77. House, R., & Dressler, G. The path-goal theory of leadership: Some post hoc and a priori tests. In J. Hunt & L. Larson (Eds.), *Contingency approaches to leadership.* Carbondale: Southern Illinois University Press, 1974.

78. House, R., & Baetz, M. Leadership: Some empirical generalizations and new research directions. In B. Staw (Ed.), *Research in organizational behavior* (Vol. 1). Greenwich, Conn.: JAI Press, 1979.

79. Schriesheim, C., & Kerr, S. Theories and measures of leadership: A critical appraisal of current and future directions. In J. Hunt & L. Larson (Eds.), *Leadership: The cutting edge.* Carbondale: Southern Illinois University Press, 1977.

80. Hersey, P. *The situational leader.* Escondido, CA: Center For Leadership Studies, 1984.

81. Osborn, R., & Hunt, J. An adaptive-reactive theory of leadership: The role of macro variables in leadership research. In J. Hunt & L. Larson (Eds.), *Leadership frontiers.* Kent, Ohio: Kent State University, Comparative Administration Research Institute, 1975.

82. Hunt, J., & Osborn, R. Toward a macro-oriented model of leadership: An odyssey. In J. Hunt, U. Sekaran, and C. Schriesheim (Eds.), *Leadership: Beyond establishment views,* Carbondale, IL: Southern Illinois University Press 1982, 196–221.

83. Graen, G., & Cashman, J. A role-making model of leadership in formal organizations: A developmental approach. In J. Hunt & L. Larson (Eds.), *Leadership Frontiers.* Kent, Ohio: Kent State University, Comparative, Administration Research Institute, 1975.

84. Calder, B. An attribution theory of leadership. In B. Staw & G. Salancik (Eds.), *New directions in organizational behavior.* Chicago: St. Clair Press, 1977.

85. Hunt, S. The role of leadership in the construction of reality. In B. Kellerman (Ed.), *Leadership: Multidisciplinary perspectives,* Englewood Cliffs, N.J.: Prentice-Hall, Inc. 1984, pp. 157–178.

86. Fiedler, F. The contingency model and the dynamics of the leadership process. In L. Berkowitz (Ed.), *Advances in experimental social psychology* (Vol. 2). New York: Academic Press, 1968.

87. Fiedler, F. The effect of culture training on leadership, organizational performance, and adjustment. *Naval Research Revue,* 1968, 7–13.

88. Schneider, B. Organizational behavior. In *Annual Review of Psychology.* Palo Alto, CA: Annual Reviews, Inc., 1985.

89. House, R., & Mitchell, T. Path-goal theory of leadership. *Journal of Contemporary Business,* 1974, 5, 81–97.

90. Schriesheim, C., & Von Glinow, M. The path-goal theory of leadership: A theoretical and empirical analysis. *Academy of Management Journal,* 1977, 20, 398–405.

91. Sims, H., & Szilagyi, A. Leader structure and subordinate satisfaction for two hospital administrative levels: A path analysis approach. *Journal of Applied Psychology,* 1975, 60, 194–197.

92. Alpander, G. Role clarity and performance effectiveness. *Hospital and Health Services Administration,* 1979, 24, 11–24.

93. House, R. A theory of charismatic leadership. In J. Hunt & L. Larson (Eds.), *Leadership: The cutting edge.* Carbondale: Southern Illinois University Press, 1977.

94. Tosi, H. Toward a paradigm shift in the study of leadership. In J. Hunt, U. Sekaran, and C. Schriesheim (Eds.), *Leadership: Beyond establishment views.* Carbondale, IL: Southern Illinois University Press, 1982, 222–234.

95. Scott, W. R. *Organizations: Rational, natural, and open systems.* Englewood Cliffs, N.J.: Prentice-Hall, 1981.

96. Fayol, H. *General and industrial management.* London: Sir Isaac Pitman and Sons, 1949.

97. Gulick, L., & Urwick, L. (Eds.). *Papers on the science of administration.* New York, Institute of Public Administration, Columbia University, 1937.

98. Weber, M. *Economy and society.* G. Roth & C. Wittich (Eds.). Berkeley: University of California Press, 1978.

99. Simon, H. *Administrative behavior.* New York: Macmillan, 1947.

100. Simon, H., Smithburg, D., & Thompson, V. *Public administration.* New York: Alfred A. Knopf, 1950.

101. March, J., & Simon, H. *Organizations.* New York: John Wiley & Sons, 1958.

102. Roethlisberger, F., & Dickson, W. *Management and the worker.* Cambridge, Mass.: Harvard University Press, 1939.

103. Mayo, E. *The social problems of an industrial civilization.* Boston: Graduate School of Business Administration, Harvard University, 1945.

104. Argyris, C. *Interpersonal competence and organizational effectiveness.* Homewood, Ill.: Richard D. Irwin, 1962.

105. Barnard, C. *The functions of the executive.* Cambridge, Mass.: Harvard University Press, 1938.

106. Parsons, T. Suggestions for a sociological approach to the theory of organizations. *Administrative Science Quarterly,* 1956, *1,* 63–85.

107. Parsons, T. *Structure and process in modern societies.* Glencoe, Ill.: Free Press, 1960.

108. Weick, K. Educational organizations as loosely coupled systems. *Administrative Science Quarterly,* 1976, *21,* 1–19.

109. Pfeffer, J., & Salancik, G. *The external control of organizations.* New York: Harper & Row, 1978.

110. Katz, D., & Kahn, R. *The social psychology of organizations* (2nd ed.). New York: John Wiley & Sons, 1978.

111. Alexander, L. The effect level in the hierarchy and functional area have on the extent Mintzberg's roles are required by managerial jobs. *Academy of Management Proceedings,* 1979, 186–189.

112. Paolillo, J. Role profiles for managers at different hierarchical levels. *Academy of Management Proceedings,* 1981, 91–94.

113. McCall, M., & Segrist, C. *In pursuit of the manager's job: Building on Mintzberg* (Technical Report No. 14). Greensboro, N.C.: Center for Creative Leadership, 1980.

114. Pavett, C., & Lau, A. Managerial work: The influence of hierarchical level and functional specialty. *Academy of Management Journal,* 1983, *26,* 170–177.

115. Pondy, L. Leadership is a language game. In M. McCall & M. Lombardo (Eds.), *Leadership: Where else can we go?* Durham, N.C.: Duke University Press, 1978.

116. Weick, K. Cognitive processes in organizations. In B. Staw (Ed.), *Research in organizational behavior* (Vol. 1). Greenwich, Conn.: JAI Press, 1979.

117. Meyer, J., & Rowan, B. Institutionalized organizations: Formal structure as myth and ceremony. *American Journal of Sociology*, 1977, 83, 340–363.

118. Berlew, D. Leadership and organizational excitement. In D. Kalb, I. Rubin, & J. McIntyre (Eds.), *Organizational psychology: A book of readings.* Englewood Cliffs, N.J.: Prentice-Hall, Inc., 1974.

119. Mintzberg, H. If you're not serving Bill or Barbara, then you're not serving leadership. In J. Hunt, U. Sekaran, and C. Schriesheim (Eds.), *Leadership: Beyond establishment views.* Carbondale, IL: Southern Illinois University Press, 1982, 239–259.

120. Peters, T., & Waterman, R. *In search of excellence.* New York: Harper & Row, 1982.

121. Levinson, H., & Rosenthal, S. *CEO: Corporate leadership in action.* New York: Basic Books, 1984.

122. Callahan, D. Morality in management. In *Ethical issues in health care management.* Proceedings of the Seventeenth Annual Symposium on Hospital Affairs, Center for Health Administration Studies, University of Chicago, 1975.

123. McNerney, W. The role of the executive. *Hospital and Health Services Administration*, 1976, 21, 9–25.

124. Hitt, D. Managerial ethics in practice: An administrator's view. In *Ethical Issues in Health Care Management.* Proceedings of the Seventeenth Annual Symposium on Hospital Affairs, Center for Health Administration Studies, University of Chicago, 1975.

125. McGeorge, K. A call for moral leadership in health services administration. *Health Management Forum*, 1980, 1, 27–30.

126. Perrow, C. Goals and power structures: A historical case study. In E. Freidson (Ed.), *The hospital in modern society.* New York: Free Press, 1963.

127. Levey, S., & Hill, J. Between survival and social responsibility: In search of an ethical balance. *Health Administration Education*, 1986, 4, 225–231.

128. Peters, T. Leadership: Sad facts and silver linings. *Harvard Business Review*, 1979, 57, 164–172.

129. Meyer, A. Reacting to surprises: Hospital strategy, structure, and ideology. *Health Care Management Review*, 1981, 6, 25–32.

130. Howell, J., & Wall, L. Executive leadership in an organized anarchy: The case of HSOs. *Health Care Management Review*, 1983, 8, 17–26.

131. Kotler, P. *Marketing management* (4th ed.). Englewood Cliffs, N.J.: Prentice-Hall, 1980.

132. Steiber, S. Boscarino, J., & Jackson, E. Hospital marketing more sophisticated: Survey. *Hospitals*, 1985, 59, 73–77.

133. Ready, R. K., & Ranelli, F. E. Strategic and nonstrategic planning in hospitals. *Health Care Management Review*, 1982, 7, 27–38.

134. Goldsmith, J. Entrepreneurship: Its place in health care. *Hospital Forum*, 1984, 27, 17–19.

135. Heyssel, R. Competition and the marketing for health care—It won't be problem free. *Hospitals*, 1981, 55, 107–114.

136. Cunningham, R. M. *The healing mission and the business ethic.* Chicago: Pluribus Press, 1982.

137. Seiden, D. Ethics for hospital administrators. *Hospital and Health Services Administration*, 1983, *28*, 81–89.

138. Darr, K., Longest, B., & Rakich, J. The ethical imperative in health services governance and management. *Hospital and Health Services Administration*, 1986, *31*, 53–66.

139. Harrison, F. Values-based management. *Health Management Forum*, 1985, *6*, 4–17.

140. Chown, E. Commentary. *Health Administration Education*, 1986, *4*, 240–243.

141. Ethics committees double since '83: Survey. *Hospitals*, 1985, *59*, 60–64.

142. Murray, R. A reassessment of the CEO's administrative skills. *Hospital and Health Services Administration*, 1978, *23*, 28–38.

143. Ewell, C. Evaluation of administrative and organizational effectiveness in hospitals. *Hospital and Health Services Administration*, 1976, *21*, 9–26.

144. Longest, B. The contemporary hospital chief executive officer. *Health Care Management Review*, 1978, *3*, 43–53.

145. Johnson, R. Revisiting "The wobbly three legged stool." *Health Care Management Review*, 1979, *4*, 15–22.

146. Steinle, J. Consultant's corner. *Hospital Topics*, 1967, *45*, 52.

147. Ewell, C. Organizing along corporate lines. *Hospitals*, 1972, *46*, 59–62.

148. Johnson, R. L. Shoring up the wobbly three-legged stool. Unpublished, 1983.

149. Johnson, E. Continual evolution of the hospital administrator. *Hospital Administration*, 1966, *11*, 47–59.

150. Wren, G., & Hilgers, S. Titles of hospital administrators. *Hospital Administration*, 19, 1974, 68–82.

151. DeWitt, C. Getting down to business. *Hospitals*, 1981, *55*, 76–78.

152. Fuller, G. W., & Beaupre, E. M. Physicians and administrators can work together. *Hospital Financial Management*, 1979, *33*, 14–23.

153. Fisher, B., & Grant, D. A new organizational model: Breaking the three-legged stool. *Hospital Financial Management*, 1980, *34*, 38–42.

154. Heyssel, R. M., Gaintner, J. R., Kues, I. W., Jones, A. A., & Lipstein, S. H. Decentralized management in a teaching hospital. *New England Journal of Medicine*, 1984, *310*, 1477–1480.

155. Todd, C. Hospitals' organizational structure. *Hospitals*, 1971, *45*, 55–59.

156. Kauffman, F. Trends in hospitals—Changing the administrator's title. M.H.A. Research Project, Xavier University, 1970.

157. Cunningham, R. Who's running this place, anyway? *Hospitals*, 1980, *54*, 96–98.

158. Toomey, R., & Toomey, R. Political realities of capital formation and capital allocation. *Hospital and Health Services Administration*, 1976, *21*, 11–23.

159. Brown, M. New leadership needed for future management systems concept. *Federation of American Hospitals Review*, 1976, *9*, 21–23.

160. Rynne, T. Managing the community hospital's reputation. *Health Care Management Review*, 1983, *8*, 57–66.

161. McLaughlin, C. Strategic planning under current cutback conditions. *Health Care Management Review*, 1982, 7, 7–17.

162. Friedman, E. What's eroding the hospital's image? *Hospitals*, 1985, *59*, 76–84.

163. Goates, L. A compelling public relations challenge for American hospitals. *Hospital and Health Services Administration*, 1976, *21*, 47–66.

164. Riggs, F. Managing the impact of public policy. *Health Care Management Review*, 1980, *5*, 59–66.

165. Heatwole, K., & Breindel, C. A political paradigm for the health care administrator. *Health Care Management Review*, 1980, *5*, 67–73.

166. Super, K. Hospital uses editorial page ads to express its opinions on issues. *Modern Healthcare*, 1986, *16*, 86.

167. Mankin, D., & Glueck, W. Strategic planning. *Hospital and Health Services Administration*, 1977, *22*, 6–22.

168. Bander, K. Strategic planning: Reality versus literature. *Hospital and Health Services Administration*, 1980, *25* (Special Issue I), 7–22.

169. Perlin, M. Current practices in long-range planning. *Hospitals*, 1972, *46*, 62–65.

170. Steiber, S. Boscarino, J., & Jackson, E. Finance driving CEOs' strategic plans. *Hospitals*, 1985, *59*, 69–71.

171. Rynne, T. The third stage of hospital long-range planning. *Health Care Management Review*, 1980, *5*, 7–16.

172. Migliore, R. The use of long-range planning/MBO for hospital administrators. *Health Care Management Review*, 1979, *4*, 23–28.

173. Jensen, J. Jackson, B., & Miklovic, N. Two-thirds of hospitals relying on marketing research studies. *Modern Healthcare*, 1985, *15*, 84–85.

174. Brown, M. Changing role of the administrator in multiple-hospital systems. *Hospital and Health Services Administration*, 1978, *23*, 6–19.

175. Zuckerman, H. Multi-institutional systems: Promise and performance. *Inquiry*, 1979, *16*, 291–314.

176. Zuckerman, H., & Wheeler, J. Management contracts: strategy for organizational stability. *Health Care Management Review*, 1982, *7*, 45–51.

CHAPTER 5

The Social Structure of Work Groups

Thomas G. Rundall
Robert W. Hetherington

MINI-CASE: NURSING STAFF STRUCTURE AT COMMUNITY MEMORIAL HOSPITAL

The nursing staff at Community Memorial Hospital is highly qualified and takes pride in their professional abilities. Until recently, ward nurses were technically supervised by head nurses, although in reality the head nurses had little power and authority. The chief clinical nurse at Community Memorial maintained decision-making control and responsibility for supervising and evaluating the work of all the nursing staff, delegating such day-to-day tasks as minimally necessary to run the wards. The chief clinical nurse joined Community Memorial's nursing staff 20 years ago fresh out of her nurse training program and in a short time earned great respect for her administrative skills. She steadily acquired managerial responsibility, and her role in the hospital evolved from direct patient care to the administration of nursing units, culminating in her appointment as chief clinical nurse. In recent years at Community Memorial problems began to surface among the nursing staff. Morale was low and turnover among the nurses was increasing. Head nurses, with little real authority or latitude in decision making, were especially disgruntled. The source of the ward nurses' dissatisfaction, however, had more to do with their sense that standards and performance among the nurses were eroding, and they perceived that the evaluative standards used by the clinical head nurse did not seem appropriate to nursing practice.

After lengthy discussions and problem-solving "retreats" the structure of the nursing service was altered. More head nurses were appointed (about 3 for each 100 beds), and greater authority was delegated to the head nurse position. The position of chief clinical nurse was maintained, but three chief clinical nurses (1 for each 100 beds) were appointed, each selected and promoted from within the nursing staff on the basis of their nursing skills rather than their administrative skills. Each chief clinical nurse and head nurse was granted associate membership in Community Memorial's medical staff, and was generally recognized as a professional colleague of the physician with whom they worked. The former chief clinical nurse was appointed to a new position: Director of Nursing Services. This position held no line authority over the chief clinical nurses or other nurses of each 100-bed unit. The director's job instead involved recruitment and training of clinical nursing talent, evaluation of patient care in the hospital, and the development of new hospital clinical services. The director of nursing services was awarded full medical staff membership and sat on the medical staff executive committee.

Is hospital nursing staff performance simply the sum of the abilities, qualifications, and expertise of the individual nurses? At Community Memorial Hospital it isn't. These individual characteristics are important, but at Community Memorial, as in virtually all organizations, the *social structure* of the work group is a major determinant of *work group* performance. In hospitals, not only nursing services, but such disparate activities as surgery, meal preparation, and contract negotiations all require the coordination of work performed by members of a group who have come together to complete the task. Indeed, it is difficult to think of a substantial task within our modern health service organizations that does not require a team, or work group, for its completion. The purpose of this chapter is to present the concepts and models of work group performance that will enable the reader to understand the problems at Community Memorial Hospital and the rationale for believing that the changes in nursing work group structure at Community Memorial will enhance performance. More importantly, since the concepts and models we present are generalizable, the reader will have a useful set of tools for analyzing and understanding a wide range of work groups across the entire spectrum of health service organizations.

Work groups are important because they provide the social environment within which much on-the-job behavior occurs. A long tradition of research on group processes supports the notion that individuals' behavior and work performance are significantly affected by the behavior of other work group members as well as by others' expectations about the behavior of group members. Ever since the pioneering work of the social psychologist Solomon Asch (1) on conformity, we have been aware that strong group pressure can cause individuals to perform the most simple tasks incorrectly. On the other hand, individuals may also perform tasks beyond their normal limits as a result of pressure to conform to the high performance standards consensually accepted by the group. Thus to get individuals to perform well, an insightful manager will need to understand the structure of and interactions within the work group.

Managers sometimes mistakenly assume that everyone in an organization is working toward the same goals. In fact, individuals are likely to put the satisfaction of their own needs ahead of these goals. Moreover, work groups often set goals for themselves that conflict with or take precedence over the goals of the larger organization. This process has come to be called the *suboptimization* problem, and it is of concern to managers who believe that work groups are performing below their capacity. In her revealing study of hospital care, Millman (2) described just such a situation among a group of doctors treating a patient with a history of tuberculosis and seizure disorder. Although a hospital intern repeatedly suggested that a muscle biopsy be done, the neurologist working on the case failed to arrange for such a test. After 2 weeks of delay and appeals to the patient's personal physician and the hospital's chief of medicine, the biopsy was performed and revealed what they had suspected:

The patient suffered from an autoimmune syndrome that required that her medication of Dilantin (for her seizures) be discontinued, and that she be placed on a regimen of steroids. However, before they could initiate the steroid treatments, they wanted to be certain that her tuberculosis was no longer present, since steroids could activate a dormant tuberculosis condition, and this required obtaining a series of sputum samples.

The house officers confessed that by this time they were very angry with the neurologist and the family physician for keeping them waiting so long for the muscle biopsy. So the house officers, in turn, decided to keep the private doctors waiting for the tuberculosis results. Each morning they would "forget" to obtain the sputum—and since the sputum had to be collected early in the morning before breakfast (and before either of the private doctors was around to check up on the house officers), they kept "finding" it inconvenient to obtain the sample because of other, more pressing duties. (2)

Among this group of physicians, the struggle for power and the emergence of the subgoal of establishing dominance supplanted and inhibited the achievement of the hospital's main goal, the provision of high-quality medical care.

Irving Janus has identified another potential problem with work group processes: "group think." Group think occurs when members of a group engage in mutually reinforcing interaction leading to harmful outcomes such as overconfidence, underestimating the competition, and suspension of critical thinking and the expression of disagreement within the group. Group think may result in group decisions that are overly risky, poorly thought out, and potentially disastrous. Two examples of group think identified by Janus are the Bay of Pigs invasion of Cuba during the Kennedy administration, and decisions by President Lyndon Johnson and his advisors to continue escalating the Vietnam war. Undoubtedly the same process goes on among decision groups in the health services industry such as hospital boards of trustees, corporate boards of multi-institutional health systems, and the policymaking staff of governmental health agencies.

Finally, it should be noted that organizations are not cast as single pieces. Different work groups within a given organization are likely to differ in structure and interpersonal processes. Hence, studies designed to increase our understanding of the way in which organizations work can benefit from a focus on work groups, because there is so much variability to be found among these subunits. Studying the organization as a whole may obscure his variability. For instance, in a study of a hospital, combining the nursing units might place together very different organizational units (e.g., the difference in complexity of the task environments between an intensive care unit and a ward caring primarily for obstetric and gynecological patients).

WHAT IS A WORK GROUP?

Up to now, this chapter has assumed that the meaning of the term *work group* is obvious. But is it? Certainly all would agree that a surgical team in the process of removing a patient's appendix constitutes a work group. The physicians, nurses, and other team members work closely together toward a common goal and are coordinated by one person who is clearly defined as the work group leader. But would the patient be considered a member of the work group? Or the patient's family? Whereas the full-time nurses on a given ward might be considered a work group, would the part-time and temporary nurses be included? Perhaps even more difficult to classify would be all the chief financial officers of hospitals owned by a multi-institutional chain. As we begin to classify different groups of individuals, we also begin to see that the definition of a work group is not intuitively obvious. The fundamental issue at stake is what distinguishes a group from an aggregate of individuals. This, of course, is a question that has bedeviled social psychologists for many years. There is no single, generally accepted definition of what constitutes a group; rather, there are several definitions, each of which emphasizes one or another characteristic. The following section, building on a classification scheme proposed by Organ and Bateman (3), reviews several of the prominent conceptualizations of groups and concludes with a definition of the work group that incorporates essential elements from each of these conceptualizations.

MOTIVATION

Some writers have emphasized that members of a group must be motivated to participate in the group. Forced or unknowning participation, it has been argued, does not constitute group membership. Within this perspective, for instance, Bass (4) defined a group as "a collection of individuals whose existence as a collective is rewarding to the individuals."

PERCEPTION

Other writers on group phenomena have emphasized that group membership is dependent upon the perceptions of individuals. For example, Bales (5) suggested the following:

> A small group is defined as a number of persons engaged in interaction with one another in a single face-to-face meeting or series of such meetings, in which each member receives some impression or perception of each other member distinct enough so that he can, either at the time, or in later questioning, give some reaction to each of the others as an individual person, even though it may be only to recall that the other was present.

INTERACTION

Some observers of groups have emphasized the opportunity for and the frequency of interaction among individuals as the distinguishing characteristics of groups. Homan's (6) definition of a group is typical of this approach:

> We mean by a group a number of persons who communicate with one another often over a span of time, and who are few enough so that each person is able to communicate with all the others, not at second hand, through other people, but face-to-face.

STRUCTURE

Another frequently used conceptualization of a group has been that of an organized social structure. In this approach, aggregates of individuals who form structured relationships and patterned forms of interaction constitute a group. Such a definition, suggested by McDavid and Harari (7), is the following:

[A group is] an organized system of two or more individuals who are interrelated so that the system performs some function, has a standard set of role relationships among its members, and has a set of norms that regulate the function of the group and each of its members.

Each of the above definitions emphasizes one or more of the following important characteristics, which distinguish a group from an aggregate of individuals:

1. Group members are motivated to participate in the group.
2. Group members perceive each other.
3. Group members interact with each other to share information and solve problems.
4. The behavior of group members is to some extent governed by norms.

Building on these essential characteristics of groups, the following definition of a *work group* is proposed: a work group consists of two or more individuals who voluntarily interact in a task-oriented situation in such a manner that the behavior and/or performance of each group member is influenced to some extent by the behavior and/or performance of other members.

FORMAL WORK GROUPS AND INFORMAL GROUPS IN WORK SITUATIONS

Although our definition of a work group does not require that it be so, in practice the vast majority of work groups are formal rather than informal. To avoid confusion, some discussion of the distinction between formal work groups and informal groups existing within the work situation will be helpful.

Organization leaders assign to employees the responsibility to perform tasks. Hence most employees are members of a work group based on their assigned position in the organization: a formal work group. Further refinements of this concept are possible. Sayles (8), for example, distinguished between two types of formal work groups: command groups and task groups. The distinction between these two types of work groups was clarified by Gibson, Ivancevich, and Donnelly (9):

> The command group is specified by the organization chart. The group is comprised of the subordinates who report directly to a given supervisor. . . . A task group is comprised of the employees who work together to complete a particular task or project. For example, the activities of clerks in an insurance company when an accident claim is filed are required tasks. These activities create a situation in which several clerks must communicate and coordinate with each other if the claim is to be handled properly. These required tasks and interactions facilitate the formation of a task group. The nurses assigned to duty in the emergency room of a hospital usually constitute a task group, since certain activities are required when a patient is treated.

Kaluzny (10) has pointed out that both command and task groups in health care organizations are often interdisciplinary, with group members from such wide-ranging disciplines as surgery, nursing, psychology, engineering, and social work. Managing interdisciplinary work groups may require specialized roles (coordinators) or structures (matrix organization) so that members' specialized skills and common tasks are properly integrated and supervised.

Individuals, of course, may also form groups that cut across the formal group boundaries and that may or may not be supportive of formal work group activities. These informal groups arise in organizations to meet a variety of employee needs: friendship, affiliation, and personal goal fulfillment, among others. Since these groupings appear in the work situation in response to social needs, they evolve naturally rather than by organizational design. Informal groups are of two major types: interest groups and friendship groups (8).

Interest groups consist of individuals who may not be members of the same formal work group but who band together to achieve some mutual goal. Many interest groups come together as "coalitions" to influence the outcome of major organizational decisions (11). Coalitions develop around specific issues that arise, and once the issue has been decided, the coalition may dissolve, with individuals realigning themselves in a different fashion when a different issue surfaces. Tushman and Nadler (12) suggest that not all individuals or cliques of individuals in a coalition stand to gain equally from an outcome. Those that stand to gain the most must offer inducements to the others to join the coalition. Hence coalitions tend to be fragile and short-lived as those with the most to gain from an outcome seek to provide the least amount of inducement to the smallest number of others as necessary. Employees who group together to press demands for better working conditions, employer-sponsored childcare and employee car pooling are examples of coalitions that seek to use their aggregate political strength within the organization to get management to agree to their demands.

As the name implies, *friendship groups* are formed by the drawing together of individuals who have something in common, such as hobbies, age, political beliefs, or personal attraction to each other. Such friendship groups, of course, are frequently the source of much interaction and social life for employees during their leisure time. Close inspection of an employee's behavior would almost certainly reveal that he or she belongs to many different and overlapping groups, both formal and informal. The major difference between them is that formal groups are designated by the formal organization and are a means to accomplish organizational goals, whereas informal groups are created by individuals to satisfy basic needs for affiliation and personal goals. Although informal groups are of interest to organizational researchers and managers, of more direct importance to our topic is the formal group. The remainder of this chapter focuses on the formal work group, including both command and task groups.

KEY CONCEPTS IN THE STUDY OF WORK GROUPS

Suppose you are invited to observe at first hand a working session of the utilization review committee of a 200-bed hospital. Although you know that a physician is present, as well as a nurse, an assistant vice president and several staff members of the medical records department, you do not know which person performs which job. Could you properly match each person with his or her job after observing the interaction in this work group for 1 hour? Could you determine what kinds of problems the group finds most difficult to solve and make reasonable guesses about what is causing those difficulties? If you are an astute observer of work group structure and processes, you probably could do these things and perhaps a good deal more. You might observe that the participants behave in quite different ways. The man you ultimately conclude is a medical records clerk is deferential to others and tends to speak only in response to questions asked by others. He tends to report factual statements but not to offer advice or personal opinions.

The woman you ultimately decide must be the physician in the group, however, not only is the recipient of more comments, questions, and pleasantries than the clerk but also initiates much more interaction with other group members. She freely offers her opinions and is quick to argue with the others. You may observe that the committee members become bored toward the end of the meeting and start to apply standard solutions to the utilization issues before them. Indeed, you may observe that much of the work is delegated to the other members by the physician member just before she makes an early withdrawal to attend to other business. If you were to follow her to her next meeting, the weekly medical staff meeting of the hospital, would you observe the same pattern of behavior between her and the other physicians? This depends on the social structure of the medical staff, her status within that structure, the nature of the group processes, and the types of tasks the group must perform.

While psychological characteristics and personality traits are, no doubt, important in social interactions, our focus here is on the structural characteristics of work groups rather than the personal attributes of individuals. We argue that a full understanding of individual behavior in work groups, as well as of the performance of the group as a unit, requires an examination of (1) the social structure of the work group, (2) the interpersonal processes commonly observed within work groups, (3) the nature of the tasks performed by the work group, and (4) the characteristics of work group performance used to assess effectiveness. Since other chapters of this book deal with some of these topics, we comment only briefly on work group processes (see Chapters 6–8), task characteristics (see Chapters 4, 6, and 12), and work group performance characteristics (see Chapter 12). We focus our attention more closely on the social structure of work groups.

BASIC STRUCTURAL CHARACTERISTICS OF WORK GROUPS

The basic structural characteristics of work groups, the building blocks of the more complicated concepts we discuss later, are statuses, roles, norms, and group size. These concepts, which are central to the study of virtually all social systems, describe the characteristics of a group, not merely the attributes of individuals. Certainly individuals have status, perform roles, and conform to norms, but the status structure and the individual's location in it, the type of role behavior, and the shared expectations that constitute a norm are all functions of the group. Take the group away, and the statuses, roles, and norms disappear. Alter the group by changing its size, and the structural characteristics are likely to change as well. Hence, unlike personality, attitudes, or other aspects of individuals that are thought of as relatively enduring personal traits, the concepts of status, role, norm, and size must be considered in the context of a group. Furthermore, these basic structural characteristics of groups serve to emphasize the fact that behavior and interaction in a human group, in our case the work group, are more than the sum of individual personalities.

Status

Every person holds a number of different positions in society; a woman may be a native American, wife, mother, and head nurse in a hospital. In American society, each of these positions, with the rights and duties associated with it, is a status. The more general definition is as follows: A *status* is a position within a social system, with the rights and duties that that position entails.

Some statuses are assigned at birth. In our example above, being a woman and a native American are assigned statuses. A status assigned at birth is called an *ascribed status*. Although there may be important instances in which one's position in a work group is at least in part an ascribed status, by and large most positions held by persons in organizational work groups are the result of something those people have done. The status that is acquired by having done something is called *achieved status*. In our earlier example, the native American became a wife by getting married, became a mother by giving birth to a child, and became a head nurse by completing a formal course of study and performing exemplary work over a number of years in the nursing profession.

Role

Associated with every given status in a social system is a set of behaviors that is expected of persons in that status. Doctors are expected to examine patients, make diagnoses, and prescribe treatment, while patients are expected to seek help from competent physicians and to cooperate in the therapeutic program. A *social role* is the expected behavior associated with a social position.

Although roles are necessary to social systems because they make a good deal of interaction ordered and predictable, they can also cause problems. The most frequently experienced of such problems is role conflict. Because virtually every individual has several statuses and hence several roles, there is the possibility that the expected behaviors associated with two or more roles may conflict (13).

Norms

There also exist in groups more general behavioral expectations that apply to all members. These expectations define for group members what are and are not appropriate behaviors and guide individuals in their interaction with other group members. *Social norms* are general expectations for behavior that, because they are internalized, induce routinization and conformity in simple interaction.

The existence of norms is typically thought to increase group unity. Norms are the social expression of the shared understandings among group members of what behaviors are proper. There is an inescapable ethical component to norms; normative behavior is presumed to be right. Nonnormative behavior is presumed to be wrong, deviant, and subject to punishment. Doctors wear white lab coats; managers do not, for example. A group of physical therapists may develop the norm of treating five patients with ultrasound therapy per day. To treat more would be considered rate busting; to treat fewer would be wrongfully slacking off. In his account of his first year as a Harvard medical student, Charles LeBaron (14) quickly discovered how difficult it is to alter social norms when he and a contingent of other students tried to get the medical school to change the long-established norm of holding Saturday classes:

> "Could you explain why we have Saturday classes?" I said. The others turned around at me with worried expressions. Stone [dean of academic affairs] replied, "As far as I know, we've had Saturday classes since Harvard Medical School was founded two hundred years ago. Up until a few years back, the country had a six-day work week, so students didn't think too much about it. Now many people work five days a week. So I guess that students periodically want to rearrange the whole schedule to fit their desires."
>
> "Is there any reason why we couldn't have Saturday classes on Tuesday or Thursday or Friday?"
>
> "There may be some scheduling conflicts. In fact, there probably are. It would require a tremendous amount of work now that the term has started."

"Are those scheduling problems insuperable?"

Chanesohn [dean of students] spoke up. "All these changes you're asking for represent a good deal of disruption for the school. I'm sure that, as mature people, you're aware of that. So before embarking on anything of that magnitude, we'd like to hear a little more from you exactly why it is so urgent that we change this two-century tradition for you."

Needless to say, the norm of holding Saturday classes at Harvard Medical School continues well into its third century of existence!

Size

The last of the basic structural characteristics we mention is work group size. We can learn a good deal about a group by observing what is perhaps its most obvious characteristic: the number of members in the group. A *dyad*, or group of two, has several unique qualities. It is fragile, since it can be destroyed by the departure of only one member. But because of its fragile nature, the dyad requires close, positive interaction for its maintenance and hence can provide more emotional satisfaction than any other kind of group. Expanding the dyad to a *triad* by adding a third member creates a new set of problems. According to the German sociologist Georg Simmel (15), sooner or later two of the three group members will draw closer together, excluding the third. Increasing group size still further obviates these problems; yet it is generally accepted among students of groups and organizations that increasing the size of the group tends to increase the complexity of the social structure. Boulding (16) has referred to this as "the principle of increasingly unfavorable environment." As Boulding explains,

As the size of an organization or organism increases, it is impossible to maintain the proportional structure of the organism intact. In the biological organism the problem arises because a uniform increase in the linear dimensions of an organism increases its surfaces by the square and its volume by the cube of the linear increases. Thus, doubling the linear dimensions of any object increases all its areas four times and increases all its volumes eight times.

One way of demonstrating the effect of this principle on work groups is to calculate the increase in the number of possible interactions among individual members as a work group increases in size from three to six members (see Fig. 5.1). By doubling the work group from three to six people, the number of possible interactions among group members is increased by a multiple of five. This is a serious problem for growing work groups, as improvements in their structural characteristics and group processes, especially the internal communications system, are essential in order to counteract the principle of increasingly unfavorable internal structure.

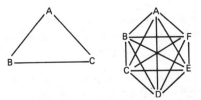

Figure 5.1. Possible interactions within (*left*) a three-person and (*right*) a six-person work group. *Left*, the number of possible interactions is three; *right*, it is 15.

With this overview of the basic structural characteristics of work groups, we now turn to some of the processes that go on within work groups and to some thoughts about how different tasks may affect work groups.

BASIC PROCESS CHARACTERISTICS OF WORK GROUPS

Several other chapters in this text are devoted to group processes, most notably Chapters 6–8. We, therefore, discuss them here only insofar as they contribute to understanding the social structure of work groups.

Leadership

A more complete discussion of leadership appears in Chapter 4; we restrict our presentation to a few major developments. Two leadership patterns identified by Likert (17) appear to have differing effects on work group performance; these styles are referred to as job-centered and employee-centered. The *job-centered* leader practices close supervision and requires subordinates to perform tasks according to specified procedures. The job-centered leader relies on the use of reward, punishment, and legitimate power to influence workers' performance. The *employee-centered* leader, on the other hand, attempts to create a supportive working environment by delegating decision-making responsibility and aiding subordinates' personal growth and achievement.

In a series of studies, the effect of these two leadership styles on work group performance has been examined. For example, in a study of leadership style and performance among various groups of public health nurses, analysis reveals a strong positive relationship between job-centered leadership and both productivity and satisfaction (18). Generally, however, job-centered leadership style has been found to increase productivity in the short run, but at the cost of negative employee attitudes and increased absenteeism and turnover. The conclusions of Likert and other analysts of leadership suggest that in the long run, employee-centered leader behaviors are more effective.

A similar approach to leadership was developed by a group of researhers at Ohio State in the years following World War II (19). The distinctive leadership patterns isolated by these studies are (1) initiating structure and (2) consideration. These closely parallel Likert's job-centered and employee-centered leadership styles.

Finally, Bowers and Seashore (20) attempted to integrate the various available notions of leadership into a four-factor theory of leadership. They proposed that leadership behavior involves four fundamental activities:

1. *Support:* Enhancing followers' feelings of personal worth and self-esteem.
2. *Interaction facilitation:* Encouraging followers to develop close, satisfying relationships.
3. *Goal emphasis:* Motivating followers to achieve high levels of performance.
4. *Work facilitation:* Scheduling, planning, coordinating, and providing resources and technical knowledge to help group members achieve work goals.

All four leadership factors must be present before work groups will experience both high productivity and high worker satisfaction over the long term.

To summarize, the enactment of leadership in a work group is an important process.

Typically, a group member with a highly valued or respected status (shift supervisor, head nurse, vice president) assumes the additional responsibility of group leader. The leader exerts influence over other work group members and can exercise legitimately sanctioned power. But a leader, particularly one chosen by the work group itself, can do much more than reward and punish group members. He or she can enable members to satisfy their own needs and inspire them to perform well. As Alvin Zander (21) has noted:

> As leaders of a group convince members to value pride in their group, their desire for success becomes stronger. Members wish their group to succeed so that they can feel proud of it; the more value members place on pride, the more they desire to succeed.

There can be little doubt that such leadership is an effective approach to organizational productivity and employee morale in health service organizations.

Communication and Coordination

Perhaps the essential point about communication in work groups was succinctly put by Sayles and Strauss (22):

> The basic problem in communications is that the meaning which is actually received by one person may not be what the other intended to send. The speaker and the listener are two separate individuals living in different worlds; any number of things can happen to distort the messages that pass between them.

In general, roles and norms enhance communication in groups by making everyday communications predictable and by freeing people from the burden of developing a new pattern of interaction each time they meet. Expectations may at times also hinder communication. In work groups, the expectations attached to roles and group membership may cause miscommunication. For example, group members may mistakenly think they understand what someone has said or done because they assume that simple role or normative behavior was operating. One example of such miscommunication is the way in which job absenteeism is often perceived by work group members. Although an absent worker is typically presumed to be sick and conforming to sick-role behavior by resting and perhaps seeking professional help, there is a wealth of evidence that supports the notion that much absenteeism is due to low worker morale, boredom, and job frustration.

Finally, it should be noted that group size has an important impact on communication. An increase in size, as we noted before, greatly increases the opportunities for interaction. However, communications that pass through large numbers of people quickly get altered, so that the comment or instruction heard by the last person in a chain probably differs substantially from that heard by the first person. Thus communication among work group members should be structured in such a way that performance is maximized.

In a series of experimental studies conducted during the 1950s and 1960s, following a technique developed by Bavelas (23), the properties of different patterns of communication among group members were explored. The most frequently studied structures are presented in Figure 5.2. The circle and all-channel networks are relatively decentralized communication structures. The chain and especially the wheel are more centralized structures. Most studies have shown that on relatively simple, unambiguous

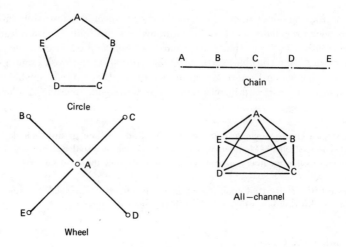

Figure 5.2. Different types of communications networks among five-person groups.

tasks, groups with centralized structures perform better than groups with decentralized structures (24, 25). As tasks become more complex and ambiguous, however, decentralized communication patterns are usually superior to centralized structures (26).

Related to the problem of communication is the difficulty of coordinating the efforts of work group members. In small work groups that perform simple tasks, coordination of activities may be easily accomplished through close working arrangements and frequent communication among members. But as work group size increases and tasks become more difficult, and as statuses and roles become more specialized and lines of communication grow longer, coordination of the activities undertaken by the work group becomes important. Dating from the early work of a French industrialist, Henri Fayol, and two General Motors executives, James Mooney and Allan Reily, coordination has been singled out as one of the central administrative principles. Scott (27) has summarized the traditional approach to coordination:

> The major principles developed to guide coordination activities include: the scalar principle, which emphasizes the hierarchical organizational form in which all participants are linked into a single pyramidal structure of control relations; the unity of command principle, specifying that no organizational participants should receive orders from more than one superior; the span of control principle, which emphasizes that no superior should have more subordinates than can be effectively overseen (theorists were unable to agree on the precise number of subordinates who could be supervised); and the exception principle, which recommends that all routine matters should be handled by subordinates and that the superior should be free to deal with exceptional situations to which existing rules are inapplicable.

As Scott noted, this traditional approach to coordination, emphasizing formal and closely coupled working arrangements, has been criticized on various grounds. The main problem with this approach, however, is its normative quality. Not all work groups are, in fact, coordinated in this way. The traditional approach to coordination is one end of a continuum of administrative processes. At the other end is an alternative set, which emphasizes less formal, loosely coupled working arrangements. Within this approach, often observed in organizations dominated by professionals, individual autonomy, collegial working relationships, and the use of liaison roles (special roles created to help coordinate the work of group members and to resolve conflicts among them) are more common coordination strategies.

Although we have been focusing on the coordination processes within a given work group, we should emphasize that the issue of coordination between work groups is equally important. Again, the major point here is that there is no one best way to coordinate these activities:

> Obviously some organizations effect tighter coupling among their departmental units than do others; and within a given organization we will see variation in the degree of coupling. . . . [T]wo conclusions merit emphasis: first, the extent of interdependence, coordination, or coupling present among any two organizational subunits is a matter for empirical determination, not assumption; second, whether looser or tighter coordination or coupling is adaptive for the organization depends on the specific circumstances confronted, and is also a matter for investigation, not prejudgment. (27)

Influence, Power, and Control

The ability to influence and control work group members is based largely on the perceived power of the leader. Power has been defined as the degree to which an individual has the capacity to obtain performance from other individuals (28). As Gibson et al. (9) noted:

> Power includes personal and positional attributes, while the concept of *authority* involves the use primarily of positionally related power. For example, the firstline supervisor position has authority because of hierarchy rank and not because of person characteristics, such as the charisma of the individual.

A typology of different forms of power—coercive, reward, legitimate, expert, and referent—has been developed by French and Raven (29). The forms of power a group member may possess are defined as follows: *Coercive* is a form of power based upon fear. A group member complies with requests initiated by another because failure to do so could result in some form of punishment.

Reward is a form of power based upon the expectation of receiving a reward—perhaps praise, special recognition, or additional income—for compliance with a group member's requests.

Legitimate is a form of power based upon an individual's status in the group or organizational hierarchy. In a formal work group, for example, the supervisor is perceived to have more power than those persons performing the work tasks.

Expert is a form of power based upon a special skill, expertise, or knowledge. Group members may comply with another's request because they perceive that the individual has special expertise that exceeds their own. Much of the power exerted by physicians, for example, is ultimately based upon their technical knowledge acquired through many years of specialized training.

Referent is a form of power based upon attractiveness or personal appeal. This form of power is frequently referred to as charisma, the ability of one person to lead and inspire others by sheer force of personality, without the aid of material incentives or coercion.

Expert and referent power are, of course, properties of individuals. Coercive, reward, and legitimate power are, however, specified by an individual's role in the work group hierarchy. One interesting aspect of power in work groups is the extent to which it is centralized, or held by a small proportion of work group members.

CHARACTERISTICS OF WORK GROUP TECHNOLOGY

As tasks become more demanding, the social structure of work groups tends to change so as to accommodate the more demanding tasks. In the field of organizations, *technology* is the term that has evolved to refer to the work performed by the organization (see also Chapters 6, 9, 10, 12). Unfortunately, the term has caused much confusion among students of organizations because of the multiplicity of interpretations that have evolved with it. As Scott (27) noted, technology has been variously defined by organizational theorists to include "not only the hardware used in performing work but also the skills and the knowledge of workers, and even the characteristics of the objects on which work is performed." We restrict our discussion of technology to two important dimensions: complexity and uncertainty.

Complexity of work group technology refers to the number of different items or tasks that must be dealt with simultaneously by the work group. As the number of items or tasks increases, the technology is said to become more complex. Hence, nurses assigned to a ward restricted to maternity patients would be thought to have a less complex technology to deal with than nurses assigned to a general medical or surgical ward occupied by patients of all ages in various stages of illness and injury.

Uncertainty, on the other hand, refers to the extent to which it is possible to predict the outcomes of the work group efforts. The variability of the inputs and the number of exceptions encountered in the work process are two frequently used measures of uncertainty.

As indicated above, these variables are of interest because the effectiveness of a given work group structure is likely to change as the complexity and uncertainty of its tasks vary. The notion here is that task situations low on complexity and low on uncertainty will be most effectively dealt with by a hierarchically structured work group with routinized job tasks. Tasks high on complexity and uncertainty will be performed better in collegial work group structures with greater latitude for individual decision making. This notion is often referred to as the contingency model of organizational design and has helped health services researchers to rethink the structure of nursing units (30) and other health services work groups.

A MODEL RELATING WORK GROUP STRUCTURE
TO PERFORMANCE

To this point, we have concerned ourselves with defining work groups and identifying some of their major theoretical characteristics. From a management perspective, however, it is important to go one step further to understand the relationships among variations in work group characteristics and performance of the work group within a health service organization. To this end, the remainder of the chapter is devoted to discussion of a general model which attempts to specify some of these relationships.

Before proceeding, it is useful to alert the reader to several important considerations regarding the model. *First,* the variables in the model are derived primarily from industrial applications. The precise nature of the predicted relationships may not always be directly transferable to a health care setting. For instance, one important difference between the two settings is the relative emphasis in industry on productivity compared with the emphasis in health care on quality. Measures taken in industry to maximize productivity may have to be modified in the health care setting to take into account possible adverse effects on quality of care. *Second,* it is assumed that hypotheses derived from the organizational literature are applicable to work groups. In the final analysis the only difference is in the size of the collectivity involved. Generally, aggregations of 10 or fewer individuals are thought of as groups, and those with more than 10 as organizations. One implication is that groups are more likely to be governed by informal processes than are organizations. This leads to a *third* consideration. Our view is that even though work groups will be greatly influenced by informal processes, one should not underestimate the influence of formal structure on work group performance. Furthermore, an important (perhaps primary) component of management strategy for affecting performance is the manipulation of formal structures. Finally, it is evident that *some* structure is required in all work groups, no matter how minimal it may be. The question is not whether structuring occurs but how much. Thus the model we explore deals with variations in structure as management "means" for attaining organizational "ends."

THE HAGE MODEL

Jerald Hage (31) has developed a model building on means–ends concepts, and it is presented in Table 5.1. Hage chose four variables to represent the structure of groups: formalization, centralization, stratification, and complexity. Values of an organization or group on these variables determine its "structural profile," which is, within limits, the result of management strategy designed to achieve acceptable performance. Organizations and work groups with high values on these variables are said to be mechanistic in nature, while structures with low values on these variables are said to be organic. One constellation of values on these four variables may produce a structural profile suitable for task groups (i.e., tendency toward more mechanistic structures), while a different constellation may be suited to planning groups (i.e., tendency toward more organic structures).

On the performance or effectiveness side, Hage operationalized four variables to represent the four system needs identified in Parsons' (32) functional theory of social systems: adaptation, goal-attainment, integration, and latency. For adaptation, Hage suggested innovation as the performance measure, with the general idea that organic structural profiles are more likely to be receptive to innovations than mechanistic organizations. Parsons' goal-attainment is represented by production, with the overall hypothesis that mechanistic organizations are likely to be more productive than organic organizations. The integrative need of groups is measured as efficiency, again maximized by mechanistic organizations. Latency is represented by job satisfaction or morale, more likely to be found in organizations and groups that are organic in nature.

The great contribution of the Hage model is the specification of relationships. This provides for empirical testing and for the specification of conditions under which relationships do or do not hold. Among the relationships discussed above, for instance, it is likely that contingencies will radically alter the predicted associations. In task-oriented

TABLE 5.1. Hage's Axiomatic Theory: Basic and Derived Hypotheses

---

Propositions

  I.   The higher the centralization, the higher the production.
 II.   The higher the formalization, the higher the efficiency.
III.   The higher the centralization, the higher the formalization.
 IV.   The higher the stratification, the lower the job satisfaction.
  V.   The higher the stratification, the higher the production.
 VI.   The higher the stratification, the lower the adaptiveness.
VII.   The higher the complexity, the lower the centralization.

Corollaries

 1.   The higher the formalization, the higher the production.
 2.   The higher the centralization, the higher the efficiency.
 3.   The lower the job satisfaction, the higher the production.
 4.   The lower the job satisfaction, the lower the adaptiveness.
 5.   The higher the production, the lower the adaptiveness.
 6.   The higher the complexity, the lower the production.
 7.   The higher the complexity, the lower the formalization.
 8.   The higher the production, the higher the efficiency.
 9.   The higher the stratification, the higher the formalization.
10.   The higher the efficiency, the lower the complexity.
11.   The higher the centralization, the lower the job satisfaction.
12.   The higher the centralization, the lower the adaptiveness.
13.   The higher the stratification, the lower the complexity.
14.   The higher the complexity, the higher the job satisfaction.
15.   The lower the complexity, the lower the adaptiveness.
16.   The higher the stratification, the higher the efficiency.
17.   The higher the efficiency, the lower the job satisfaction.
18.   The higher the efficiency, the lower the adaptativeness.
19.   The higher the centralization, the higher the stratification.
20.   The higher the formalization, the lower the job satisfaction.
21.   The higher the formalization, the lower the adaptiveness.

Reprinted from "An Axiomatic Theory of Organizations" by Jerald Hage, published in *Administrative Science Quarterly*, Volume 10, #3 by permission of *Administrative Science Quarterly*.

work groups, it is particularly likely that the nature of the task will make a difference, for instance, as to whether or not increased formalization will result in greater efficiency. It is also relevant, as Hage notes, that there are limits beyond which a linear relationship cannot be expected and in fact may be reversed (e.g., one cannot expect to achieve greater and greater performance improvements through infinite increases in any of the means variables).

The hypotheses of the Hage model are presented in Table 5.1. Although Hage's work (as well as that of the other scholars mentioned in this section) has been directed toward the organization as a whole, we believe that the model may be appropriately applied at the work group level as well. Our effort to apply Hage's model to work groups within hospitals forms the basis for discussion in the remainder of this chapter. The first seven hypotheses are basic propositions derived from the literature, logic, and theory; the remaining 21 hypotheses are derived from these seven.

ORGANIZATIONAL MEANS: STRUCTURAL CONCEPTS

Four structural concepts, the "means" with which organizations or work groups strive to achieve their "ends," are relevant to this discussion: formalization, centralization, stratification and complexity.

Formalization

We suggest a definition that combines that of Price (33) and Aiken and Hage (34): formalization is the degree to which the norms of a social system are explicit and enforced. This incorporates Aiken and Hage's division of the concept into three subconcepts as follows: *Job codification* is "The number of regulations specifying who is to do what, when, where, and why." (35) *Specificity of jobs* is "The degree to which procedures defining a job are spelled out." (35) *Rule observation* is "The diligence with which rules are enforced." (34)

Centralization

Three dimensions of centralization can be identified. The first is the extent to which an employee defers to a supervisor's powers and control. The second is who in the organization makes important decisions. The third is the relative amount of influence that various statuses in the group have at their disposal.

Stratification

Our concept of stratification includes the relative distribution of formal status among functional groups within the larger work group or organization, as well as the pattern of communication between and among these groups. Thus the greater the difference in status between the highest and the lowest functional groups, the greater the stratification. Communication patterns in highly stratified work groups are seen to be primarily top-down (in the form of directives), and where there is upward communication, it is more likely to be unreliable, reflecting the formal requirements of the system or conforming to the perceived wishes of the party to whom the communication is addressed.

Complexity

Perrow (36) referred both to the analyzability of technical problems and to their variability. These two dimensions of task complexity and person complexity are not unrelated, but neither are they the same. In the former, we are concerned with the degree to which tasks are variable, thus borrowing one portion of the Perrow conceptualization and following Hage's use of the term "routineness." In the latter, we emphasize the amount of knowledge (37) brought to bear on the production of services and the difficulty of tasks performed (38).

In addition to the above two dimensions of complexity, a third aspect is suggested by the Perrow concept of analyzability and has been developed in the literature as task uncertainty (39, 40). Uncertainty of tasks is not always identified separately from task variability, which in itself involves a type of uncertainty. In this study, however, the definition of task uncertainty emphasizes amount of thinking time (36) involved in constructing solutions and the extent to which the relationship between activities performed and outcomes expected is known (41, 42).

ORGANIZATIONAL ENDS: PERFORMANCE CONCEPTS

Following Parsons, performance must be assessed in four areas: efficiency, adaptation, productivity, and employee morale. These correspond to the ends portion of the means–ends schema advanced by Hage. Since our orientation is the health care setting, specifically hospital work groups, we reconceptualize certain of these performance areas, without departing from the intent of the original conceptualizations.

Efficiency

Hage defined *efficiency* as the cost per unit of production. Since "units of production" may be difficult to measure in hospital work groups, we use the concept of coordination as an approximation of efficiency; more specifically, the degree or quality of coordination achieved. The fit with Hage's definition is not indisputable, however; although it is difficult to conceive of an efficient group that is uncoordinated, it does not necessarily follow that a highly coordinated group is efficient. Kahn et al. (43) have pointed out that coordination is not achieved without cost to the organization, and at some point it may well become cost ineffective to put forth greater efforts to achieve greater coordination. It is clear that coordinative mechanisms are essential (by definition), but their type and extent must be varied to suit the situation. The definition employed here is based on Georgopoulos and Mann (44): *Coordination* represents the extent to which the various interdependent parts of an organization function each according to the needs and requirements of the other parts and of the total system.

Within this definition, and drawing on the distinctions made by March and Simon (45) and by Parsons and his colleagues (46), Georgopoulos and Mann further subdivided the concept into four parts: regulatory, preventive, promotive, and corrective coordination.

Adaptiveness

The concept of *adaptiveness* used here emphasizes the climate for change in the work group, rather than to the rate of adoption of innovations, which is frequently used in studies of innovation and which is specifically referred to in Hage's work on this concept. We follow closely the work of Duncan (40, 47), which defined climate for change as the "perception of departmental personnel" on four dimensions: need for change, openness to change, potential for change, and participation in dealing with change. The concept as used here includes both the changes inside the hospital and those that are externally induced. Recent work (48–50) suggests that the social change values subscribed to by work group personnel (in particular by the leaders) are closely linked to the rate of adoption of innovations.

Production

In deriving his axiomatic theory, Hage referred to production as the units of output per specified time period, which is decidedly an industrial-organization type of measure. However, he also makes reference to the fact that certain organizations measure their performance primarily in terms of the quality of the product rather than the amount. In the case of hospitals, quality of care is of primary concern (44), and it is this concept that we suggest rather than production. This may lead to reconsiderations of the hypotheses, of course, since factors that are theoretically linked to production may not necessarily be linked to quality. In fact, theory (51) and some evidence (52) lead to the conclusion that in medical settings, beyond a certain level of production the quality of the product begins to decline regardless of the mode of organization.

Without becoming involved in the controversy over whether medical quality should be judged in terms of structure, process, or outcomes (53) or whether technical or interpersonal characteristics are paramount (54), we adopt a definition of quality that parallels that of Georgopoulos and Mann (44): the overall quality of care is equivalent to the average perception of quality by a wide range of personnel in the hospital. It is assumed that respondents, from aides and technicians through nursing and medical staff members will perceive quality of care from a number of perspectives, the average of which will incorporate considerations of technical, interpersonal, and other aspects. Although the judgment of any category of respondent may be biased, it is assumed that an average of perceptions will closely approximate true quality of care.

A second dimension of our definition of quality concerns an aspect of structure: peer review mechanisms. In this respect, we follow Donabedian's thinking about the relationship of structure to quality performance: "structure . . . is relevant to quality in that it increases or decreases the probability of good performance" (51). The definition thus assumes that functioning peer review systems, as one aspect of structure, increase the probability of high quality of care.

Morale

Our concept of morale combines orientation toward both the job and fellow workers. Thus we have adopted a modified version of the Price (28) definition: "The degree to which the members of a social system have a positive affective (and cognitive) orientation

TABLE 5.2. Organizational Performance Concepts and Operationalized Measures

Hage's Organizational Performance Concepts	Suggested Operationalized Measures for Hospital Work Groups
Rate of adoption of innovations	Climate for change Perception of need for change Openness to change Potential for change Participation in changes
Production (units per time period)	Quality of care Average perception of quality Structural mechanisms for quality assurance
Efficiency (cost per unit)	Coordination Regulatory Preventive Promotive Corrective
Morale	Morale—satisfaction with Fellow workers Supervisors and management Pay Workload Tension management

toward membership in the system." Subdimensions included in this concept are orientation toward fellow workers, supervision, rewards, and workload. Within the subconcept of "rewards" we also attempt to reflect the definition employed by Porter and Lawler (55), in which worker morale is conceptualized as the amount of congruency between expectations and experiences.

Translation of the performance variables from the Hage model to assessment of work-group effectiveness in hospitals is summarized in Table 5.2.

THE IMPACT OF STRUCTURE ON WORK GROUP PERFORMANCE

The remainder of the chapter reports some findings from a hospital organization research study designed to test the validity of the Hage model. The study was conducted in clinical departments of an American multihospital system.

DISCUSSION OF RESULTS AND MANAGEMENT GUIDELINES

The Hage hypotheses at the work group level of measurement were verified in 11 out of 17 instances, with only 1 instance in which statistically significant relationships were not found at all, and 5 in which the original hypothesis was reversed.

The basic idea underlying the axiomatic theory is that organizations or work groups that are organic in structure maximize adaptiveness and morale, whereas those that are mechanistic in structure maximize production and efficiency. The problem arising from this conceptualization for managers is evident, because effectiveness must be assessed across all performance dimensions simultaneously, since poor performance on one dimension can affect overall group success, either in and of itself or through its eventual effect on other dimensions. A further aspect of the theory is that groups in complex task environments are thought to be better suited to organic arrangements, whereas mechanical structures work best in more straightforward task environments.

Regarding efficiency, the axiomatic theory predicts greater efficiency among groups that are formalized, centralized, and stratified. The results support the notion that to increase coordination in work groups, it is essential to provide formal and clear-cut specifications of the duties and obligations of the staff. A negative effect of uncertainty on coordination was found. Analyses showed that for work groups confronted by an uncertain task environment, this negative effect on coordination was reduced to nonsignificance by the introduction of controls for formalization and centralization. The implication is that as uncertainty rises, staff members must be clear about their responsibilities (job specification) and about the line of authority (hierarchy of authority). Powerlessness (a subconcept of centralization) and poor communications (a subconcept of stratification) were found to be negatively related to coordination. These negative relationships are not anticipated by the theory, wherein both stratification and centralization are positively associated with efficiency. These findings suggest that further thought and study need to be given to the conceptualization and measurement of the two concepts and to the nature of their effects on efficiency.

Next we consider the correlates of adaptiveness (climate for change). The axiomatic theory predicts that work groups that are formalized, centralized, and stratified will be less adaptive, whereas those involved with complex task structures will be more adaptive. Three of the four Hage hypotheses were supported. One reversal is of interest, in that greater job specification was related to *increased* adaptiveness. The manager should also note that the apparent effect of professionalism on adaptiveness held only under controls for formalization; when controls were introduced for centralization and for stratification, the relationship disappeared. The data suggest that adaptiveness is not so much a function of the level of professionalization of the work group as it is of the degree to which staff are involved in decision making, the degree to which communications flow upward in the group, and the extent of uncertainty in the task environment. This is a reaffirmation of previous research findings on the importance of the structure of relationships in determining organizational performance, regardless of the characteristics of the individuals in those organizations.

Regarding production (quality of care), the axiomatic theory predicts that production will be higher in formalized, centralized, and stratified organizations and lower in complex task environments. Managers should note that the strongest relationship with quality of care was with quality of communications: quality of care rose significantly with improvements in the quality of information passed up and down between staff members and supervisors. A potentially controversial conclusion that better-qualified staff members provide poorer quality of care when they are less subject to formalized procedural specifications requires further examination in a nongovernmental hospital setting. It is, evident, however, that the specification of duties and obligations has a significant and positive impact on the quality of care. These data provide support for the formalization of quality assurance programs. Furthermore, the relationship between job specification and quality was upheld under controls for complexity, indicating that a favorable impact on quality can be made regardless of the nature of the tasks involved or of the qualifications of the personnel.

Finally, we consider morale. The axiomatic theory predicts that morale will be higher in complex task environments and lower in formalized, centralized, stratified organizations. We found that all the hypotheses were supported. In the instance of formalization, the predicted inverse relationship with morale was specified for rules observation and satisfaction with supervision, while the reverse relationship was found (with exactly the same partial r) between job codification and satisfaction with rewards. The strongest relationship ($r = -.662$) was found between perception of powerlessness and satisfaction with supervision; in situations in which staff members do not perceive that they have a meaningful input into decision making and are not delegated sufficient authority to do their jobs well, morale declined precipitously. It is this aspect of participation in decisions—meaningfulness—that had the greatest impact on morale. Hierarchy of authority did not have as strong an impact; neither did the extent of participation. It was not consistently demonstrated that hierarchy of authority has a negative effect on morale.

MANAGERIAL GUIDELINES

Analysis of work group characteristics and performance suggest the following managerial guidelines:

1. As work groups confront increasing uncertainty, effective managers are sensitive to the need for personnel to be clear of their job responsibilities (job specification) and about lines of authority.

2. Effective managers recognize the importance of structure. Perhaps the single most important contribution of effective management is to create structures that assure performance independent of the level of professionalization within the group.

3. Health care managers should actively seek the involvement of professional personnel in decision making. Failure to assure meaningful involvement has negative consequences on morale and eventually on overall work group performance.

SUMMARY

Overall, the data demonstrate that the most important means employed by managers were those concerned with job specification and the quality of communications between supervisors and staff. Among the measures of stratification, quality of communications had the highest partial correlation with all four performance measures; among the measures of formalization, job specification had the highest partial correlation with three of four performance measures. These are important considerations in the structuring of effective work groups. It might be concluded from our information that a decisive consideration in achieving effective job specification and quality of communications is the meaningful involvement of staff in decision making. To this end, the current emphasis in some hospitals on decentralized, relatively autonomous unit management structures is probably well placed.

Finally, we should note that, in our quest to aid in the understanding of work group performance, we have been most successful in predicting performance as measured by morale (average partial r of .453), next most successful in predicting efficiency (.308) and adaptiveness (.309), and least successful in predicting production (.218).

We began this chapter by asserting that work groups are the driving forces within organizations. While our discussion has brought out the complexity of these forces, we have also emphasized that work group functioning is neither idiosyncratic nor unpredictable. There exist patterned and predictable relationships between the social structure of work groups and their performance. The concepts we have presented here, from the rather simple building blocks of work group structure, process, tasks, and performance to the more complicated merging of these concepts into our model of work group bureaucratization, provide health organization managers with a framework with which to better understand their work groups and some suggestions for making them work more effectively.

DISCUSSION QUESTIONS

1. This chapter argued that the behavior of individuals in work groups cannot be entirely explained on the basis of each individual's personality and attitudes. Why is this so?

2. What are the major distinctions between organic and mechanistic work groups?

3. How are the various components of Hage's axiomatic model defined and measured within the context of hospital organizational research?

4. In the study of work groups in hospitals reported in this chapter, job specification and quality of communication were found to be important determinants of work group

perfor.aance. What were the relationships among these two variables and the various measures of performance? What do these findings suggest for the way health service managers organize their work groups?

5. Participatory management of work groups has become popular in recent years. Why is this so? Could participatory management work in hospitals? For what kinds of work groups would such a management structure most likely work?

6. Work groups sometimes conflict with one another. What are the usual bases for these conflicts? How might restructuring the work groups help alleviate conflict?

SUGGESTED READINGS

Bosk, C. L. *Forgive and Remember*. Chicago: University of Chicago Press, 1979.
Insightful ethnographic analysis of two different surgical services at Pacific Hospital. The report centers on how professionals determine their own identity, how they control performance and how they cope with the limits of their own skill and knowledge.

Hage, J. *Communication and organizational control*. New York: John Wiley & Sons, 1974.
Provides a conceptualization, illustration and a test of a cybernetic model of coordination and control. The book presents an excellent discussion of cybernetic control, its assumptions as well as analytical problems. The illustration is based on a case study involving the introduction of a director of medical education in a community hospital, and the test is based on data from 16 social welfare and rehabilitation organizations.

Sayles, L. R., & Strauss, G. *Human behavior in organizations*. Englewood Cliffs, N.J.: Prentice-Hall, 1966.
Comprehensive text presenting "dynamic interplay of people and structures" in organization. Sections deal with individuals, jobs and groups; leadership and motivation; managerial skills.

Wexley, K. N., & Yukl, G. A. *Organizational behavior and personnel psychology*. Homewood, Ill.: Richard D. Irwin, 1977.
Extensive book containing 52 case readings with commentaries, divided into eight sections. Readings include review and discussion articles as well as reports on empirical research.

Zander, A. *Making groups effective*. San Francisco: Jossey-Bass, 1982.
Brief but important volume presenting research issues on group behavior in organizations. Chapters describe organizational situations in which the functioning of groups is crucial to the organizational outcome.

REFERENCES

1. Asch, S. E. Effects of group pressure upon the modification and distortion of judgements. In H. Guetzkow (Ed.), *Groups, leadership, and men*. Pittsburgh: Carnegie Press, 1951.

2. Millman, M. *The unkindest cut*. New York: William Morrow, 1977.

3. Organ, D. W., & Bateman, T. *Organizational behavior.* Plano, Texas: Business Publications, Inc., 1986.

4. Bass, B. M. *Leadership, psychology, and organizational behavior.* New York: Harper & Row, 1960.

5. Bales, R. F. *Interaction process analysis: A method for the study of small groups.* Cambridge, Mass.: Addison-Wesley, 1950.

6. Homans, G. C. *The human group.* New York: Harcourt, Brace, and World, 1950.

7. McDavid, J. W., & Harari, M. *Social psychology: Individuals, groups, societies.* New York: Harper & Row, 1968.

8. Sayles, L. R. Work group behavior and the larger organization. In *Research in Industrial Human Relations* (Publication #17), Industrial Relations Research Association. New York: Harper & Row, 1957.

9. Gibson, J. L., Ivancevich, J. M. & Donnelly, J. H. Jr. *Organizations: Behavior, structure, processes.* Dallas: Business Publications, Inc., 1976.

10. Kaluzny, A. D. *Design and management of disciplinary and interdisciplinary groups in health services: Review and critique. Medical Care Review,* 1985, 42, 77–112.

11. Bacharach, S. R. & Lawler, E. J. *Power and politics in organizations.* San Francisco: Jossey-Bass, 1980.

12. Tushman, M. L., & Nadler, D. A. *Implications of political models of organization* in R. H. Miles (Ed.), *Resource book in macro organizational behavior.* Santa Monica, CA: Goodyear Publishing, 1980.

13. Biddle, B. J. *Role theory: Expectations, identities and behaviors.* New York: Academic Press, 1979.

14. LeBaron, C. *Gentle vengeance.* New York: Penguin, 1982, p. 57.

15. Simmel, G. *Conflict and the web of group affiliation.* Glencoe, Ill.: Free Press, 1955.

16. Boulding, K. E. *The organizational revolution.* New York: Harper & Brothers, 1953.

17. Likert, Rensis. *New patterns of management.* New York: McGraw-Hill, 1961.

18. Hernandez, S. R., & Kaluzny, A. D. Selected determinants of performance within a set of health service organizations. *Proceedings of the 42nd Annual Meeting of the Academy of Management,* August, 1982, 52–56.

19. Stogdill, R. M. *Handbook of leadership.* New York: Free Press, 1974.

20. Bowers, D. G., & Seashore, S. E. Predicting organizational effectiveness with a four-factor theory of leadership. *Administrative Science Quarterly,* vol. 11, 1966, 238–263.

21. Zander, A. *Groups at work.* San Francisco: Jossey-Bass, 1977.

22. Sayles, L. R., & Strauss, G. *Human behavior in organizations.* Englewood Cliffs, N.J.: Prentice-Hall, 1966.

23. Bavelas, A. Communication patterns in task-oriented groups. In D. Lerner and H. D. Lasswell (Eds.), *The Policy Sciences,* Stanford, Cal.: Stanford University Press, 1951.

24. Leavitt, H. J. Some effects of certain communication patterns on group performance. *Journal of Abnormal and Social Psychology,* 1951, 46, 38–50.

25. Guetzkow, H., & Simon, H. The impact of certain communication sets upon organization performance in task-oriented groups. *Management Science*, 1955, *1*, 233–250.

26. Shaw, M. E. Communication networks. In L. Berkowitz (Ed.), *Advances in Experimental Social Psychology* (Vol. 1). New York: Academic Press, 1964.

27. Scott, W. R. *Organizations: Rational, natural and open systems.* Englewood Cliffs, N.J.: Prentice-Hall, 1981.

28. Price, J. *The handbook of organizational measurement.* Lexington, Mass.: D.C. Heath, 1972.

29. French, J. R. P., & Raven, B. The bases of social power. In D. Cartwright and A. F. Zander (Eds.), *Group Dynamics* (2d ed.). Evanston, Ill.: Row, Peterson, 1960.

30. Leatt, P., & Schneck, R. Criteria for grouping nursing subunits in hospitals. *Academy of Management Journal*, 1984, *27*, 150–165.

31. Hage, J. An axiomatic theory of organizations. *Administrative Science Quarterly*, 1965, *10*, 289–320.

32. Parsons, T. *The social system.* New York: Free Press, 1951.

33. Price, J. L., & Mueller, C. W. *Professional turnover: The case of nurses.* Jamaica, N.Y.: Spectrum Publications, 1981.

34. Aiken, M., & Hage, J. Organizational interdependence and intra-organizational structure. *American Sociological Review*, 1968, *33*, 912–930.

35. Shortell, S. M., Becker, S. W., & Neuhauser, D. The effects of management practices on hospital efficiency and quality of care. In S. M. Shortell and M. Brown (Eds.), *Organizational research in hospitals* (Inquiry Monograph–Blue Cross Association), 1976, 90–107.

36. Perrow, C. A framework for the comparative analysis of organizations. *American Sociological Review*, 1967, *32*, 194–208.

37. Hage, J. *Theories of organizations: Form, process, and transformation.* New York: John Wiley & Sons, 1980.

38. Forrest, W. H., Jr., Scott, W. R., & Brown, B. W., Jr. *Study of institutional differences in postoperative mortality.* Stanford, Cal.: Stanford University, Center for Health Care Research, 1974.

39. Van de Ven, A. H., Delbecq, A. L., & Koenig, R. Jr. Determinants of coordination modes within organizations. *American Sociological Review*, 1976, *41*, 322–338.

40. Duncan, R. B. Characteristics of organizational environments and perceived environmental uncertainty. *Administrative Science Quarterly*, 1972, *17*, 313–327.

41. Parsons, T. A sociological approach to the theory of organizations. *Administrative Science Quarterly*, Part I, 1956, *11*, 63–85.

42. Burns, T., & Stalker, G. M. *The management of innovation.* London: Tavistock Publications, 1961.

43. Kahn, R. L., Wolfe, D. M., Quinn, R. P., Snock, J. D., & Rosenthal, R. A. *Organizational stress: Studies in role conflict and ambiguity.* New York: John Wiley & Sons, 1964.

44. Georgopoulos, B. S., & Mann, F. C. *The community general hospital.* New York: Macmillan, 1962.

45. March, J. G., & Simon, H. A. *Organizations.* New York: John Wiley & Sons, 1958.

46. Parsons, T., Bales, R. F., & Shils, E. A. *Working papers in the theory of action.* Glencoe, Ill.: Free Press, 1953.

47. Thompson, J. D. *Organizations in action.* New York: McGraw-Hill, 1967.

48. Aiken, M., & Hage, J. The organic organization and innovation. *Sociology,* 1971, *5,* 63–82.

49. Hage, J., & Dewar, R. Elite values versus organizational structure in predicting innovation. *Administrative Science Quarterly,* 1973, *18,* 279–290.

50. Nathanson, C. A., & Morlock, L. L. Control structure, values, and innovation: A comparative study of hospitals. *Journal of Health and Social Behavior,* 1980, *21,* 315–333.

51. Donabedian, A. *Explorations in quality assessment and monitoring* (Vol. I). Ann Arbor: Health Administration Press, 1980.

52. Hetherington, R. W., Hopkins, C. E., & Roemer, M. I. *Health insurance plans: Promise and performance.* New York: John Wiley & Sons, 1975.

53. Donabedian, A. Evaluating the quality of medical care. *Milbank Memorial Fund Quarterly,* 1966, *44,* 166–203.

54. Brook, R. F., & Williams, K. N. Quality of health care for the disadvantaged. *Journal of Community Health,* 1975, *1,* 132–156.

55. Porter, L. W., & Lawler, E. E. III. *Managerial attitudes and performance.* Homewood, Ill.: Richard D. Irwin, 1968.

PART THREE

Operating the Technical System

The problem before us is not to invent more tools but to use the ones that we have.

Rosabeth Moss Kanter

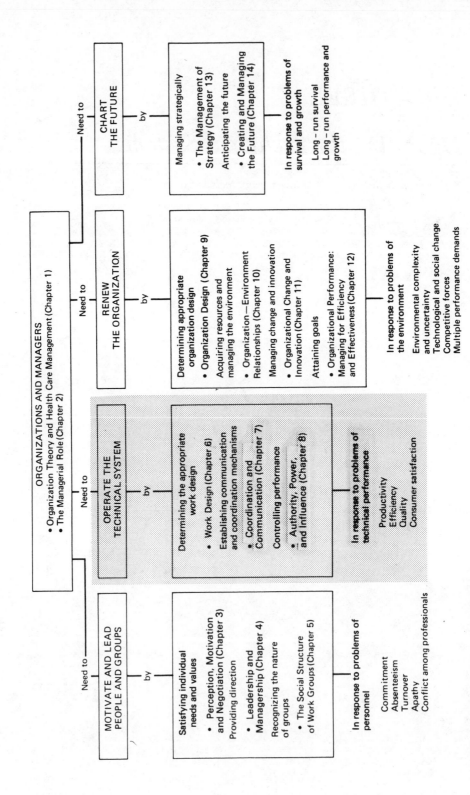

The nature of organizations: Framework for the text.

The three chapters of this section focus on operating critical components of the technical system within health care organizations. This involves determining the appropriate work design, establishing communication and coordination mechanisms, and controlling performance. The following chapters characterize these functions in order to enhance technical aspects of productivity, efficiency, quality, and consumer satisfaction.

Chapter 6 considers the design of work in organizations. The emphasis is on defining different types and components of work and assessing the interconnected nature of work within the organization. The chapter addresses the following questions:

- What is work? Is it different from working?
- What are the effects of autonomy on individual motivation and satisfaction?
- How does work design affect organizational performance?

Chapter 7 deals with coordination and communication. These are the essential means through which managers link together the various people and groups within the organization and link the organization to other organizations. The following questions provide the major focus of the chapter:

- How does the nature of health care organizations affect the need for communication and coordination?
- What is the role of interorganizational coordination? How is it similar to or different from intraorganizational coordination?
- What mechanisms are available to achieve intraorganizational and interorganizational coordination?
- What are the major barriers to communication and how can they be overcome?

The last chapter in this section deals with power, influence, and control (Chapter 8). Attention is given to alternative models of power and influence, their applicability to health care organizations, and the identification of factors that affect power relationships and influence patterns within organizations. The chapter addresses the following questions:

- What is the difference between influence, power, authority, and control?
- What are the sources of power?
- Through what mechanisms is power converted into influence over decisions and activities?
- Why are health care organizations often considered unique in their distribution of power and influence?

Upon completing these three chapters, the reader should be able to:

- Differentiate between work and working and identify different types and components of work in health care organizations.
- Understand the interconnected nature of work within organizational units and specify approaches to ensure the effective coordination of work activities.
- Understand the different types of communication and the basic organizational characteristics associated with each type.

- Distinguish between different types of coordination mechanisms and factors associated with each mechanism.
- Differentiate between intra- and interorganizational coordination.
- Understand the differences between power, influence, and control and their implications for the operations of the organization.
- Identify organizational characteristics and environmental contingencies that determine the balance of power and shape influence patterns within health care organizations.

CHAPTER 6

Work Design

Martin P. Charns
Carol A. Lockhart

MINI-CASE: A TALE OF TWO NURSING UNITS

Unit 5B, a small pediatrics unit in a major eastern teaching hospital, is characterized by high dissatisfaction among the nursing staff and is the target of frequent complaints from residents and attending physicians. Absenteeism among members of the nursing staff is high, requiring that the unit be staffed with nurses from a float pool.

The administration views the unit as its major trouble spot in the hospital. The unit generally appears to be in a state of chaos. Parents of patients on 5B often wander around the unit asking physicians and nurses for information about their children. Parents often complain that they receive conflicting information from the medical and nursing staffs. The largest number of patient complaints received by the administration concern 5B.

The organization of the hospital is similar to that of most major teaching facilities, with the major organizational units representing professional (nursing, social service, dietary) and nonprofessional (housekeeping, security, transportation) departments. Nursing staff members are assigned to units, each geographically located on a wing of one floor. Unit 5B is small. It has 16 beds, of which 12 usually are occupied, and a full-time nursing staff of 17 RNs. Internally 5B uses primary nursing organization. Each RN is responsible for the total nursing care of a number of patients, although when the primary nurse is not at work, other members of the unit's nursing staff perform the nursing activities for those patients. The nursing staff is responsible to a head nurse, who has administrative responsibility for several nursing units. She is located on another floor, separated from 5B activities.

Unit 2-South, also a pediatrics unit in a different eastern teaching hospital, is seen by the nursing and medical staffs and the hospital administration as an exemplary unit. It has the reputation for quality care and responsiveness to both patients and their families. Nurses express high satisfaction about their work and the hospital and frequently take advantage of the organization's liberal educational benefits to attend courses to increase their professional skills. In general, the unit runs smoothly and responds well to routine situations as well as to emergency and unusual cases.

Unit 2-South also is a small unit, with 21 beds, 14 RNs, a head nurse, and 3 nursing assistants. It uses primary nursing but differs organizationally from 5B in several ways. First, the RNs are organized into three groups. When a primary nurse is not at work, a member of her group assumes the role of associate and takes responsibility for providing nursing care and implementing the care plan. Each group has responsibility for the patients of one team of house staff and associated attending physicians. An assignment board, located at the entrance of the unit, indicates for each nursing group the corresponding house staff team, the patients, the primary nurse assignments, and the nurse covering for off-duty primary nurses. On a daily basis primary nurses participate with their corresponding physician group in patient care rounds. The head nurse's major responsibilities are managerial—development of nursing staff, orientation of house staff who are beginning their six-week rotation on the unit, coordination with house staff and attending physicians, coordination of nursing staff, and liaison with other parts of the nursing department and hospital. Her office is centrally located on 2-South. In rare instances she serves as an associate to a primary nurse and is directly involved in patient care.

The differences between the effectively functioning unit 2-South and the chaotic 5B are seen by many administrators and health care professionals as arising from differences in the leadership of the units. Others attribute the differences to the clustering of nurses on 2-South into three groups, allowing them, unlike the 5B nurses, to identify with a small and cohesive group. Still other observers believe that the differences between the two units are most directly related to the competence of the staff or to their motivation. Rarely mentioned is the design of the jobs of the staff nurses on the two units. At first glance, since both units utilize primary nursing, it appears that the nurses' jobs are essentially the same. Further analysis, however, reveals important differences between the design of work on the two units.

APPROACHES TO WORK DESIGN

The work design concepts can be applied at several levels in an organization. In fact, they can even be applied to analyze and design the work of two or more related organizations, such as multi-institutional systems or an organization and its suppliers or referral networks. The focus in this chapter, however, is on single organizations. Attention is directed to the design of work contained within *single jobs* (i.e., job design) and the design of work within organizational units consisting of *several jobs* (i.e., work unit design). The individual job is the basic element of any organization. As such, job design has been a focus of attention in the literatures of organizational behavior and health administration. Contrasting approaches to job design are found in the literature and in practice. In many health care organizations, jobs that reflect these differing perspectives exist side by side. For example, professionals (e.g., physicians, nurses, social workers) generally determine for themselves both what work to do and how to do it. Technicians' jobs, however, are often highly engineered and their activities specified. Yet problems of low productivity, low morale, and dysfunctional individual behaviors, such as alcoholism and drug abuse, exist among both professional and nonprofessional workers. One-dimensional approaches to solving these problems are rarely effective. Instead, it is necessary to consider both the needs of the organization and those of the individual. Since the individual job is the interface of the organization and the individual, it is a critical area for managerial attention. In this chapter different approaches to job design are discussed along with their inherent assumptions, strengths, and limitations. An integration of the concepts and a framework for their managerial application are then presented.

APPROACHES TO JOB DESIGN

There are two major approaches to job design. Each focuses almost exclusively on either job activities or the psychological aspects of workers. Several related approaches are aggregated here under the job activities label.

The scientific management school of thought developed by Taylor (1) and Gilbreth (2) had its genesis in manufacturing organizations and led to the development of industrial engineering. Through examination of job activities in time-and-motion studies, industrial engineers design jobs to most efficiently utilize technology and to minimize wasted human effort. Within a technologically driven work setting, workers most suitable to the jobs are selected and trained. Through experience workers become more proficient at their jobs; and thus specialization and routinization of work activities attempt to take advantage of the individual's learning curve. Since an objective of this approach is elimination of extraneous activities, its success depends upon ensuring that people perform the job as designed.

This approach has made important contributions to management, especially in the automobile industry in the United States. Scientific management approaches have gone beyond manufacturing settings, however, and can be found in both inpatient and ambulatory health care settings. The routine nature of many jobs in support services of hospitals, such as transport, laboratory, laundry, and radiology, allows job activities to be studied from an industrial engineering perspective. However, systems designed in this manner are tailored to meet specific conditions and are inherently unresponsive to change or uncertainty. Since patient needs and emergencies are not always subject to specification, health care employees at *all* levels of the organization are frequently required to use their own judgment, which limits the usefulness of scientific management principles.

There are three assumptions underlying activity-focused approaches to job design. These assumptions suggest that (1) the work can be divided into repetitive routine elements; (2) workers can be trained and motivated to perform dependably, and (3) worker motivation derives primarily from economic rewards associated with doing the work. Although these assumptions have face validity in many situations, they also are inherently limiting. Often the work cannot be divided into elements that can be repetitively performed. In addition, workers frequently seek more than economic rewards from their work and react to routine, repetitive jobs by not performing dependably or by quitting the job. From a purely economic perspective, the cost of repeated recruiting and training often exceeds the benefits believed to be gained from any technological efficiency.

Another more flexible approach to job activities analysis is the job inventory methodology, often used in studies of jobs of health professionals, especially nurses, physicians, and physician assistants. In the mid-1960s a shortage of health workers was predicted in the United States. In response, this methodology was developed to categorize job activities, such as those of physicians and dentists (3–5). Kane and Jacoby (6), for example, demonstrated the feasibility of using physician assistants (Medex) for job activities not requiring a fully trained physician. This methodology provides the basis for current studies to determine the costs of nursing and other health care activities in response to DRGs and the continuing changes in health care financing.

PSYCHOLOGICAL APPROACHES TO JOB DESIGN

In contrast to the job activity approach is the perspective rooted in psychology and organizational behavior. Focusing on worker psychology and motivation, this approach assumes that when individuals perform work that meets their needs for growth and that when jobs themselves are intrinsically rewarding, substantial motivation results. Professional jobs, in which there generally is a strong relationship between an individual's self-concept and his or her work, are examples. On the other hand, routine, repetitive jobs that include only a small portion of a larger task, or jobs that are strictly and narrowly delineated, are difficult for anyone to identify with. They limit the extent of an individual's involvement in work and the motivation to perform well, and therefore productivity suffers.

Sometimes, however, when individuals have *total* discretion over the way they do their work and what work they perform, their motivation may not be directed toward organizational goals. In fact, it may work against the organization's goals. The assumption that motivation will result in organizationally desirable productivity does not necessarily hold. Even so, professional workers are often given complete discretion over what they do and how they do it. This, in fact, is one of the attributes of a profession. In medicine, generally regarded as the prime example of a profession, professional work is typically off-limits to organizational job design analysis.

The issues of cost control and competition have come to dominate the health care system of the 1980s. Health care managers have responded to these issues and to the challenges of a market-driven health care system by moving to make their organizations price sensitive.

Work arrangements that made half-hearted attempts at efficiency in the fee-for-service health care system no longer are viable in a price-sensitive system. Coordination and the management of care have become primary tools for controlling health care costs. No longer is the caregiver—physician, nurse, or other provider—able to choose the course of treatment or the equipment and supplies used to provide that treatment without considering the cost implications of these decisions.

The force of the changes occurring in the health care system is reflected in major shifts in power of physicians and administrators. There has been a relative increase in power and control exercised by management and a relative decrease in power of physicians. These changes have been fueled by the surplus of physicians and the lessening of demand for their services. Managed patient care, HMOs, and other prepaid arrangements demand fewer physicians, as the quantity of care is consciously reduced. Prior to these changes, administrators had limited control of practitioners in their institutions or organizations. Now, however, they can decide whether the productivity and practice style of these practitioners is consistent with the economic survival of the organization. If it is not, physicians and others are being denied contracts, receiving reduced payments from HMOs and PPOs, and facing an array of sanctions never before encountered. The impact of such controls has only begun to be felt.

Through direct efforts, such as utilization management and tying financial considerations to patient care practices, as well as through more indirect efforts, such as by influencing the culture of the organization to be more aware of the cost of care, managers are influencing physician decision making. Although it is difficult to change practice styles developed over many years, physicians to different degrees are changing their behavior. Whether these changes place the patient at greater risk or reduce the quality of care is uncertain. It is a question that will accompany the health care system over the next decade.

Given the opportunity to influence both physician decision making and the quality and cost of health care, it is more important than ever for managers to recognize the potential of work design. How a health care manager chooses to approach this issue is influenced by the range of approaches to work design and their conflicting underlying assumptions.

Often managers become believers in one approach to job design and reject the others, thus limiting their effectiveness and the opportunity to integrate the approaches for maximum advantage. In the multifaceted health care system, no one approach guarantees success.

ANALYSIS OF WORK

WORK AND WORKING

One of the prime reasons for poor management and less-than-optimal performance in health care and other organizations is that managers confuse "work" and "working" (7, 8). They also inappropriately manage the relationship between work and working. *Work* is objective and impersonal. It is energy directed at organizational goals, identifiable separately from the person who does it. It is analyzable. *Working*, on the other hand, is a worker's affective response to work. Far from totally analyzable, it is an individual's personal and subjective reaction. Work affects working, and working affects work.

Writers and managers who follow scientific management and related job activity analysis focus on work and largely ignore working. The workers' affective responses are seen as extraneous elements to be controlled so that they do not interfere with work. In contrast, management of professionals often is based almost exclusively upon attention to working. The result is that work is directed at the goals chosen by the professional. They may or may not be organizational goals. Similarly, managerial efforts to improve working conditions or to humanize work are often pursued with working in mind and with insufficient and inappropriate consideration for the work requirements.

TYPES OF WORK

An analysis of work recognizes that all organizations perform three different types of work: (1) direct work, (2) management work, and (3) support work. *Direct work* is effort that directly contributes to the accomplishment of an organization's goals. In health care organizations, clinical work performed by doctors, nurses, and other care providers generally is direct work. In organizations that have multiple goals, such as teaching hospitals, there is a set of direct work activities for each goal (for example, teaching, research, and patient care). Although an individual may perform more than one type of direct work, the work itself is identifiable and analyzable separate from the person performing it.

Management work includes *(1)* providing the resources and context within which direct work can be performed effectively, and *(2)* maintaining an alignment between an organization and its external environment. Management work is decision making about the organizational context within which other work is performed (8). Since the primary way of influencing decision making is by influencing its premises—the information that is considered in making a decision—management work affects all other work because it influences the premises on which other decisions are made (9).

Support work does not directly result in achievement of an organizational goal, but it is needed for effective accomplishment of other work. For example, support work for clinical work includes such things as maintaining medical records, transporting patients, maintaining the physical surroundings in which care is delivered, and performing laboratory tests. Support work for management work includes providing legal counsel, clerical assistance, data on both internal operations and the external environment, planning and analytical assistance, as well as personnel support.

Recognizing these three major types of work provides the basis for determining the requirements of work. To consider both work and working effectively, a more detailed analysis is needed, one that considers the components of each type of work and their interrelationships. Charns and Schaefer (8) argue that this analysis consists of answering four separate but related questions:

1. What are the component parts of work and the characteristics and requirements of each?
2. How do the component parts inherently fit together?
3. What resources are needed to do the work?
4. What controls are needed to determine and evaluate the performance of the work?

DETERMINING COMPONENTS OF WORK

Miller (10) has suggested guidelines for identifying the primary tasks in an organization. These guidelines continue to provide the best approach to identifying the components of work. Miller suggests that the manager look for the natural boundaries in work that occur along the dimensions of time, technology, and territory. When different work is or can be performed at different points in time, such as on different days or at different times of the day, distinct work components can be identified. For example, patient care given during one office visit is distinguishable from that given during another visit, as is patient care delivered to a patient during different hospital admissions. Similarly, discrete components of work often can be identified by the fact that they are performed in different places (territories), such as in hospital, ambulatory, and home care settings.

Finally, components of work can be identified by the technology involved:

Technology should be considered broadly to include not only hardware, but also skills and training, personality characteristics and interpersonal orientations and different practices associated with performing different work. Such different practices may result from tradition, from regulation of government, licensing agencies, or accrediting bodies, or from professional norms of accepted practice. Thus, for example, the work performed by different professional groups is a natural place to look for inherent boundaries. (8)

In doing so, however, analysis must determine whether differences are real and inherent in the work or are maintained only by tradition.

By taking a broad perspective of technology we can also ask what differences in work are associated with different parts of an organization's environment. For example, do different patients represent different types of work? Do treating different diseases, preventing illness in contrast to treating it, or interacting with people from different ethnic or socioeconomic backgrounds represent the use of different technologies and therefore different work? Often differences in technology overlap with differences in time or territory, but together they help identify discrete components of work.

The task inventory method provides a helpful approach to identifying components of work. When using this method, it is important not to overlook significant but difficult to observe aspects of work. Furthermore, this approach starts with a description of the status quo. To the extent that either an array of jobs or the task inventory does not include important aspects of work which should be present, the analysis will be incomplete.

Galbraith (11) has provided a set of categories for determining the behaviors required for effective task performance. These can be applied to each element of work as well as to the aggregate of elements that comprise a single job. Galbraith's five categories in ascending cumulative order are:

1. Decisions to join and remain in an organization
2. Dependable role performance
3. Effort above minimum levels
4. Spontaneous and innovative behavior
5. Cooperative behavior

In general, all jobs require the first two categories of behavior. Organizations require that people join and remain employed in their jobs and that they perform dependably. These two minimum levels of behavior, however, are often not completely met. Where the work itself or the working conditions do not provide a worker with an acceptable level of rewards—including satisfaction—turnover and absenteeism result. Dependable role performance also does not occur when people either do not know what is expected of them or feel that the work that is expected of them is not equitably balanced with the rewards of the job.

When jobs require more than the first two minimum categories of behavior, the design of the job itself becomes a greater concern. When all elements of the work cannot be anticipated, spontaneous and innovative behavior is required. This requirement can be distinguished from behavior above minimum levels by the frequency with which unanticipated events occur and the degree of innovative behavior required. It is characterized by an individual (1) needing to recognize that spontaneous and innovative behavior is required and (2) having the skills and willingness to act. When in addition the work requires an individual to recognize and be willing and able to work with others to achieve the desired outcome, it requires cooperative behavior.

The five categories of behavior are cumulative and form a scale directly related to the inherent uncertainty of the work. Thus, work that is highly certain and predictable generally requires only the first two categories of behavior. Work that is highly uncertain and unpredictable requires cooperative behavior in addition to all four other categories of behavior.

It is important to identify discrete components of work activities to determine their unique requirements. But before using such an analysis to design jobs or units of an organization, it is also necessary to examine the way in which the components must fit together.

INTERCONNECTEDNESS OF WORK

Once the elements of work are identified by the various methodologies, it is necessary to determine how they fit together to form a coherent whole: to determine for each element of work the other elements essential to its effective performance. At one extreme are elements that can be performed independently of each other. For example, feeding one patient and performing laboratory tests on a specimen from another patient are independent elements of work. In contrast, successful performance of other types of work requires that different work elements occur in sequence or that performance of one element affects a second element, which in turn acts upon the first element. For example, in medical diagnosis, initial diagnosis determines what laboratory and radiologic procedures are required. The results of those studies refine the original diagnosis. At the most complex level, elements of work affect each other simultaneously. Van de Ven et al. (12) have called this "team interdependence," exemplified by the administration of anesthesia and the performance of surgery on a patient.

The concept of interconnectedness of work is critical to effective work design. When interconnected elements of work are performed by different people, components must be coordinated to ensure effective performance. Coordination requires resources from the organization, such as development and use of plans and protocols, supervision of people responsible for interconnected elements, or discussion among those people. Where possible, therefore, it is most effective to design jobs with interconnected elements of work so that the interconnections are not spread over several people. Realistically, this model is not always feasible, because elements are often too numerous for a one-person assignment; because elements are so different from one another that no one individual has the skills, training, desire, or inclination to do them all; or because technological advantages outweigh costs of coordination. When the interconnections cannot reside within one single job, it is best to organize work to contain the interconnected elements within a single work group (8, 13).

DESIGNING INDIVIDUAL JOBS

Underlying the design of any job are assumptions about individuals and the relationship between individuals and their work. These assumptions may be formally stated (as in a labor contract) or not, and they may be recognized by managers or not. The job design literature is based upon the general assumptions that people work to satisfy a broad range of needs, and that how a job is designed affects its ability to meet those needs. Two perspectives can be taken to consider in greater detail the relationship between job design and motivation.

First, consider that people are motivated by unfulfilled needs and that they exert effort to satisfy those needs. If opportunities for meeting a person's needs are provided by the work itself, the person will be motivated to perform the work. Where work itself does not provide opportunities to satisfy individual needs, the person will seek other outlets and may not be motivated to perform the work. Thus, it is important to match people and their needs to jobs and their inherent work requirements. For example, if work requires an individual only to join and remain in the organization and to perform dependably, these behaviors often can be obtained by matching the job to people with economic needs and rewarding them monetarily. When such jobs are held instead by people whose needs are for achievement or other forms of personal growth (14), the individuals most likely will not respond to only monetary rewards and will direct their efforts away from the dependable role performance required by the organization. These people are better matched to jobs that require spontaneous and innovative behavior.

A second perspective on individual motivation is based upon the assumption that people evaluate courses of action to choose among them. The *expectancy model* of motivation (15, 16) posits that individuals exhibit behavior that they perceive will result in outcomes that yield valued rewards. In its simplest form the model indicates that people subjectively evaluate possible behaviors in terms of three elements: *(1)* the probability that a behavior will yield a desired outcome, *(2)* the probability that the outcome will yield rewards, and *(3)* the value of those rewards to the individual. These three elements combine multiplicatively in a person's assessment, so that if any one element is low it is unlikely that the person will choose the associated behavior. Where that behavior is required to perform work effectively, we must ask how the elements in the model are affected by the job.

When work is intrinsically rewarding to individuals—that is, when effectively performing the work itself is inherently rewarding—we can see that there is a direct connection between behavior and rewards. Hackman et al. (17) argue that this occurs when three psychological states are present:

1. *Experienced meaningfulness:* The job is seen as important, valuable, and worthwhile.
2. *Experienced responsibility:* The individual feels personally responsible and accountable for the results of his or her efforts.
3. *Knowledge of results:* The individual understands how effectively he or she is performing the job.

These three aspects of working have a major impact on a person's motivation and are themselves affected both by characteristics of the individual and by the content of the work itself.

Three characteristics of a job contribute to its *experienced meaningfulness:* skill variety, task identity, and task significance. *Skill variety* refers to the variety of different skills and talents required of an individual in performing a job. A job that has *task identity* represents an identifiable piece of work that an individual can perform from beginning to end and that has a visible outcome. *Task significance* refers to the impact a job has on the lives of other people. In general, because health care organizations perform work that directly affects other people, great potential exists for designing jobs with high task significance. Yet by designing isolated jobs in which people cannot see how their work is an important part of a whole effort that helps other people, one can create jobs low in all three core dimensions.

Experienced responsibility for work outcomes is directly affected by the degree of *autonomy* in a job. The components of autonomy are freedom and discretion in scheduling work and in determining procedures to be used in performing it. A considerable degree of autonomy is present in jobs falling into Galbraith's categories of "effort above minimum levels," "spontaneous and innovative behavior," and "cooperative behavior" (11).

Feedback on work performance provides an individual with the third psychological dimension, *knowledge of results*. The most direct feedback is from the work itself, available primarily in situations in which an individual has responsibility for a whole and identifiable element of work. Where job design itself cannot provide direct feedback, it is important to obtain feedback from supervisors or peers.

An additional potential source of feedback is an organization's performance evaluation system. In some organizations performance evaluation is based solely on the subjective appraisal of an employee's supervisor. In others, however, it is based upon achievement of measurable goals. To the extent the goals for assessment of an individual align with the organization's goals, the individual's efforts can be directed at achievement of the organization's goals, in addition to serving as a feedback mechanism. In some organizations, the goals used for performance evaluation are goals of the program or department for which the individual has a major share of responsibility. Although few examples of this arrangement appear in the literature, Kotch et al. (18) provide an excellent description.

To some degree skill variety, task identity, and task significance can substitute for one another, as they all contribute additively to experienced meaningfulness. Together they combine multiplicatively with autonomy (experienced responsibility) and feedback (knowledge of results) in contributing to the overall motivating potential of a job. A job's motivating potential score (MPS) can be expressed as follows:

$$\text{MPS} = \frac{1}{3} \times \left[\begin{array}{c} \text{Skill} \\ \text{variety} \end{array} + \begin{array}{c} \text{Task} \\ \text{identity} \end{array} + \begin{array}{c} \text{Task} \\ \text{significance} \end{array} \right] \times \text{Autonomy} \times \text{Feedback}$$

Whether a job with a high MPS will actually result in high individual motivation depends upon the characteristics of the jobholder. People with high growth needs—strong needs for achievement, self-actualization, and personal development—will be most motivated by jobs with high motivating potential. It is also possible for people who do not have high growth needs to find their growth needs stimulated by jobs with a high MPS. On the other hand, not all people react positively to challenging jobs, and the autonomy and challenge may result instead in anxiety and low performance.

When a person successfully accomplishes work that satisfies his or her needs, job satisfaction is experienced. This in turn contributes to the expectation that future performance will result in satisfaction, and high levels of motivation generally result. Satisfaction, however, can result from meeting other needs, either within or outside of the work place, that will not contribute to motivation or to job performance. For example, social needs may be satisfied in the work setting, but this may be unrelated to work performance or motivation. Thus high motivation resulting in effective work performance will result in satisfaction, but satisfaction in itself will not necessarily result in future high motivation or performance.

In summary, based upon analysis of work managers can design jobs and match them with individuals to optimize both the level of job performance and the direction of efforts toward organizational goals. This effort requires consideration of both work itself and working. However, it is not always possible to address work requirements through design of individual jobs. It is often necessary to consider coordination of the efforts of people responsible for interconnected elements of work. In such cases it is necessary to consider the design of work within organizational units, where several jobs combine to achieve organizational goals.

COORDINATING INTERCONNECTED WORK IN ORGANIZATIONAL UNITS

Interconnected elements of work are best placed within an individual job. The next best work design places the interconnected elements within a single organizational unit. This design allows for members to identify with the work of the unit and most easily to coordinate the interconnected elements within that single unit. How to achieve that coordination is the subject of this section. Additional aspects of coordination are considered in Chapter 7.

Coordination of work has been the subject of considerable research. Central to the research is the finding that organizational responses vary with the characteristics of the work performed. Duncan (19), who provided one of the first empirical studies of variation in coordination within work units, found that work units change their patterns of interaction in response to differing levels of task uncertainty. Building upon the theoretical work of March and Simon (20), Van de Ven et al. (12) found variations in patterns of coordination among units facing different levels of task uncertainty. Charns et al. (21) extended the findings of Van de Ven et al. and the theoretical writings of Mintzberg (22) to suggest that work groups use a combination of six approaches to coordination. They found that the use of these approaches is related to the effectiveness of patient care units, and Charns and Strayer (23) replicated these findings in a residential school for severely emotionally disturbed children. The six approaches fall into two categories: programming methods and feedback methods.

The set of programming approaches includes three ways of standardizing the performance of work. They are most effective when the work is well understood and programmable:

1. *Standardization of work processes* is the use of rules, regulations, schedules, plans, procedures, policies, and protocols to specify the *activities* to be performed.
2. *Standardization of skills* is the specification of the *training* or *skills* required to perform work. Often it is achieved through specification of minimum levels and types of education, certification as evidence of meeting minimum qualifications, or on-the-job training.
3. *Standardization of output* specifies the form of intermediate *outcomes* of work as they are passed from one job to another.

In situations of high uncertainty, programming approaches alone cannot provide the needed coordination. Exchange of information and feedback are needed. Feedback mechanisms, which facilitate the transfer of information in unfamiliar situations, include the following:

1. *Supervision* is the basis for coordination through an organization's hierarchy. It is the *exchange* of information between two people where one is responsible for the work of the other.

2. *Mutual adjustment* is the exchange of information about work performance between two people who are not in a hierarchical relationship.
3. *Group coordination* is the exchange of information among more than two people, such as through meetings, rounds, and conferences.

Feedback approaches to coordination are more time consuming and require more effort than programming approaches. However, they are needed in situations characterized by high levels of uncertainty.

Charns et al. (21) found that higher performing patient care units in a teaching hospital differ from lower performing units in their greater use of all six types of coordinating approaches. High-performing units utilize plans, rules, procedures, and protocols not as constraints and organizational red tape but as guidelines for routine work. Contrary to previous research findings, effective use of programming approaches actually allows staff—especially nurses—greater discretion in their work. In addition, when faced with unfamiliar situations, the higher performing units increase their use of feedback approaches to a greater extent than the lower performing ones.

It should be noted that, first, what is familiar to one person may not be familiar to another. For example, people with greater experience in a particular job will encounter fewer unfamiliar situations than people with less experience. The people with less experience therefore need to use feedback approaches to coordination to a greater extent than do highly experienced people. Second, the profile of coordinating approaches that can be used effectively depends upon the nature of the work of the unit. Greater advantage can be taken of programming approaches when the work of the unit is limited in scope and uncertainty. Finally, feedback approaches require trust and understanding among people, which requires consistency in working together. Such relationships are not often achieved in health care organizations. Physicians, nurses, and other health care providers in a hospital, ambulatory, or home care setting must coordinate their efforts. Nursing staff turnover and rotation, house staff rotation, and limited physician involvement in a unit or a remote care setting greatly hinder the development of such relationships and prevent full use of feedback approaches to coordination.

When coordination is not fully achieved, work performance is constrained. Thus the people who perform the work cannot attain the levels of achievement or obtain the sense of competence that satisfies their needs. Professionals often feel they are prevented from effectively carrying out their professional work by the ineffective way their organization functions. Where organizational factors hinder work accomplishment, people come to believe that hard work will not result in the desired outcome of good patient care. Using the expectancy model of motivation, the probability that effort will result in the desired outcome is low, and thus the motivation to work hard is reduced.

SUMMARY

Effective work design requires taking multiple perspectives based upon the analysis of work itself. In designing jobs, the work requirements should be matched to individual workers' needs. To the extent possible, interconnected elements of work should be combined into individual jobs that possess high levels of skill variety, task identity, task significance, autonomy, and feedback. The design of individual jobs must be done within a framework that considers other related jobs, including that of the supervisor.

The failures of job redesign too often have been caused by taking too narrow and restrictive a focus. Such an error can be avoided by taking a variety of approaches, including careful identification of the requirements and interconnections of the elements of work, which provide the basis for considering job design and coordination requirements.

APPLYING THE FRAMEWORK

The work design concepts provide a framework for analyzing the functioning of units 5B and 2-South (described at the beginning of the chapter) and determining options for change. The nursing staffs on both 5B and 2-South were previously organized on a functional basis, but implemented primary nursing about 3 years ago. With the functional organization, each nurse performed one or at most a few related functions—for example, administering medications, providing physical care, or taking vital signs—to a large number of patients. Generally, the most routine elements were performed by nurses' aides. This approach attempts to use the personnel efficiently and in line with their education. It appears quite rational, following the traditions of the scientific management and related approaches to work design.

In examining the work of patient care itself, however, it can be seen that the elements of work that make up the care for each patient are highly interconnected. Nursing work is highly interconnected with physicians' work, and under functional nursing the work elements performed by different nurses and aides also are highly interconnected. Prior to implementation of primary nursing, these interconnections were addressed on both units in a number of ways. First, both units utilized patient care protocols, although on 2-South they were used to a greater extent and were developed through greater involvement of the medical staff than on 5B. Both units also relied upon standardization of skills, reflected in hiring well-trained personnel and providing in-service education. Unit 5B, however, for several years had had a problem retaining nursing staff. Therefore many staff nurses had little experience, and until recently the unit relied on outside agency nurses to fill daily vacancies. Not only did the problem of inexperience hinder the performance of individual staff on 5B, but it hindered the unit's ability to use protocols and standardize skills to coordinate work. The unit had to rely heavily upon the personal methods of coordination—supervision and mutual adjustment. On both units the head nurse played a pivotal role in facilitating coordination, but on 5B she was continuously involved in personally working with inexperienced staff and did not develop other methods of coordination.

The nursing profession has advocated the arrangement of primary nursing as part of the effort to increase professionalism in nursing. Both units 5B and 2-South implemented this job design. In both cases the nursing service administration sought to provide more responsibility and broader professional roles for staff members. They expected that these benefits would outweigh the costs of using highly trained nurses for routine tasks. From a psychological perspective primary nursing inherently provides for greater skill variety, task identity, autonomy, and feedback than functional nursing. In this way it creates a job with greater motivating potential. It also places within individual jobs all of the interconnected elements of nursing work during the times that a patient's primary nurse is at work. These were important benefits to be gained in both 5B and 2-South.

The two units differed in their implementation of primary nursing, however. On 5B the administration considered that with primary nurses having total responsibility for their patients, the need for supervision would be reduced. Therefore, the head nurse's direct involvement with the unit could be reduced. Thus her responsibilities were expanded to cover several units. It was expected that more experienced and skilled nurses could assist others when needed. Since the professional development of new or more junior members of the staff was not formally the responsibility of anyone other than the head nurse, and she was physically removed from the unit, insufficient attention was given to this matter. The standardized approaches of coordination began to break down as the amount of training and orientation declined and new medical and nursing staff members were unfamiliar with the unit's procedures and protocols.

It was expected that primary nurses would coordinate their own work with other members of the nursing and medical staffs, when the primary nurse was off duty. The organizational arrangements hindered that coordination, however. Among nursing staff, coverage was arranged almost randomly, so that there did not develop a pattern of coverage among staff members that would encourage working relationships. In addition to hindering personal approaches to coordination among nurses, this arrangement made it difficult for a nurse providing care for another's patient to be involved or to identify with the patient. Interactions with house staff did not follow any consistent pattern, and each house officer had patients cared for by different primary nurses. Whereas before implementation of primary nursing many house officers depended upon the head nurse to function as the coordinating link between themselves and the staff nurses caring for their patients, under the new arrangement they had to seek out several different primary nurses. Usually they did not bother to do so.

Over time the trust between the nursing and medical staff members on the unit deteriorated. Medical staff blamed nursing for the poor functioning of the unit, and nursing did not see how they could improve the situation. Often the patients were caught between the two groups. Staff morale and productivity suffered. Although the intentions of nursing administration were good, inappropriate attention to the design of jobs and the organizational arrangements needed to address work interconnections resulted in jobs that were less efficient and motivating.

On 2-South nursing administration used the implementation of primary nursing to address difficulties in its coordination with medical staff. The internal organization of the nursing staff into three groups provided a basis for facilitating coordination both within the nursing staff and between nurses and physicians. The small size of each nursing group and the arrangement for associates to cover for primary nurses within the group allowed group members to identify with the group's patients. This contributed to the motivating potential of their jobs. Furthermore, the work interconnections among nurses were contained within each group. This facilitated the management of these interconnections and contributed to the development of the trust needed among nursing staff for effective mutual adjustment. Each group included a mix of experienced and less experienced nurses, and together with the head nurse the formally designated group leader had responsibility for staff development. Finally, by aligning teams of house staff with the nursing groups, an organizational basis for facilitating coordination was established.

The use of the assignment board further clarified responsibilities and contributed to the ease of locating staff members. As physicians and nurses worked together in a modified joint practice arrangement, trust between groups developed, adding to their ability to use mutual adjustment to coordinate their efforts. Both groups experienced a greater sense of accomplishment, contributing to their satisfaction and motivation. Because of the closeness and commitment of the personnel to other members of their group, they felt a sense of responsibility for the unit. Absenteeism was therefore low, and the more stable staffing in turn contributed to the unit's smooth functioning. It was not by chance that 2-South developed as it did. The nursing staff actively negotiated for the development of house staff teams and their alignment with the nursing groups. Furthermore, the head nurse considered house staff orientation to be a critical responsibility. Overall, 2-South organizationally addressed its work requirements more effectively than 5B, and its higher performance reflected that effectiveness.

As the examples demonstrate, several factors must be considered in designing productive work units consisting of inherently motivating and rewarding jobs. The basis for this design is analysis of the work itself. The content of individual jobs, the organization of work units, and the coordination of work both within and between units can be designed effectively only when the work requirements are understood. Just as the framework presented in this chapter can be used to analyze the jobs of health professionals on two different patient care units, it can be used to design work in other settings.

SUMMARY

In the evolving continuum of care which will characterize health care in the 1990s, coordination will become a paramount concern. Multiple levels of providers at multiple sites will have to develop work methods which will ensure safe, effective, and cost efficient care. The design of work will be more important than ever in the health care system.

The following guidelines are critical to assuring success.

MANAGERIAL GUIDELINES

1. Scientific management and engineering of jobs are concepts applied most effectively to work characterized by low inherent uncertainty. They focus primarily on work and do not consider aspects of working.
2. Psychological approaches, which focus more on working, can be applied most effectively to situations of high uncertainty.
3. Work should be designed so that the most highly interconnected elements are contained within individual jobs to the extent that is possible, given considerations of size, limitations imposed by technology, and separation of job elements in time and space. Interconnected work elements that cannot be self-contained within single jobs should to the extent possible be placed within single work groups.
4. To enhance motivation, individual jobs should be designed to provide opportunities to satisfy the needs of the person performing a given job. People with high growth needs are more highly motivated by jobs providing experienced meaningfulness, experienced responsibility, and knowledge of results.
5. Coordination of interconnected work elements that are not contained within a single job directly affects work performance. This coordination generally can be facilitated most effectively through a combination of programming (standardization) and feedback (personal) approaches.

DISCUSSION QUESTIONS

1. Under what conditions does a job with a high motivating potential lead to high job-holder motivation? To high satisfaction? To frustration?
2. What are the potential pitfalls in job redesign?
3. Give examples of highly motivated people who do not contribute greatly to organizational productivity.
4. What is the relationship among individual motivation and satisfaction and an organization's ability to coordinate work?
5. Give examples of situations in which dependable role performance is required in a job but effort above minimum levels is not. What happens when individuals in such jobs innovate? Give examples of jobs requiring cooperative behavior. What happens when people in such jobs are willing to give only dependable role performance?

SUGGESTED READINGS

Davis, L. E., & Taylor, J. C. (Eds.). *Design of jobs* (2nd ed.). Santa Monica, Cal.: Goodyear Publishing Co., 1979.
An edited volume of papers clarifying the technology and societal matrix that underlies the design of jobs. Provides an analysis of the relationships between the nature of the organization, its supporting social system, and the mode of job design appropriate to it.

Hackman, J. R., & Suttle, J. L. *Improving life at work: Behavioral science approaches to organizational change.* Santa Monica, Cal.: Goodyear Publishing Co., 1977.
This book is an outgrowth of a monograph series on strategies for improving the quality of work life. It is practical in orientation; there are chapters on career development, work design, reward systems, group and intergroup relations, managerial practices, and strategies for change.

Herzberg, F. *Work and the nature of man.* Cleveland: World Publishing, 1966.
A classic in its field. Extensive and well-documented treatment of individual motivation in the workplace.

O'Toole, J. (Ed.). *Work and the quality of life.* Cambridge, Mass.: MIT Press, 1974.
A series of 16 papers which were a followup to the seminal report Work in America. The papers cover such areas as work and health, job redesign, education and work, and federal work strategies. The main point of the papers is the close relationship between one's work and the quality of one's life in America.

REFERENCES

1. Taylor, F. W. *The principles of scientific management.* New York: Harper & Row, 1911.
2. Gilbreth, F. B. *Motion study.* New York: Van Nostrand, 1911.
3. Bureau of Health Manpower Education. *The utilization of manpower in ambulatory care: Development of a study methodology.* Report of a Cooperative Study, 1975.

4. Nelson, E., Jacobs, A., & Breer, D. A study of the validity of the task inventory method of job analysis. *Medical Care*, February, 1975, *13*(2), 104–113.

5. Braun, J. A., Howard, D. R., & Pondy, L. R. The physician's associate: A task analysis. *Physician's Associate*, 1972, *2*(3), 77–82.

6. Kane, R. & Jacoby, I. *Alterations in tasks in the physician's office as a result of adding a medex.* Paper presented at American Public Health Associates Meeting, San Francisco, California, November, 1973.

7. Drucker, P. F. *Management: Tasks, responsibilities, practices.* New York, Harper & Row, 1973.

8. Charns, M. P., & Schaefer, M. J. *Health care organizations: A model for management.* Englewood Cliffs, N.J.: Prentice-Hall, 1983.

9. Simon, H. A. *Administrative behavior* (3rd ed.). New York: Free Press, 1976.

10. Miller, E. J. Technology, territory and time: The internal differentiation of complex production systems. *Human Relations*, 1959, *12*(3), 243–272.

11. Galbraith, J. R. *Organization design.* Reading, Mass.: Addison-Wesley, 1977.

12. Van de Ven, A. H., Delbecq, A. L., & Koenig, R. Jr. Determinants of coordination modes within organizations. *American Sociological Review*, 1976, *41*, 322–338.

13. Thompson, J. D. *Organizations in action.* New York: McGraw-Hill, 1967.

14. McClelland, D. C. *The achievement motive* (2nd ed.). New York: Halsted Press, 1975.

15. Vroom, V. H. *Work and motivation.* New York: John Wiley & Sons, 1964.

16. Porter, L. W., & Lawler, E. E. III. *Managerial attitudes and performance.* Homewood, Ill: Irwin-Dorsey, 1968.

17. Hackman, J. R., Janson, R., Oldham, G. R., & Purdy, K. A new strategy for job enrichment. *California Management Review*, 1975, *17*(4).

18. Kotch, J. B., Burr, C., Toal, S., Brown, W., Abrantes, A., and Kaluzny, A. A performance-based management system to reduce prematurity and low birth weight. *Journal of Medical Systems*, 1986, *10*(4), 375–390.

19. Duncan, R. B. Multiple decision-making structures in adapting to environmental uncertainty: The impact on organizational effectiveness. *Human Relations*, 1973, *26*(3), 273–291.

20. March, J. G., & Simon, H. A. *Organizations.* New York: John Wiley & Sons, 1958.

21. Charns, M. P., Stoelwinder, J. U., Miller, R. A., & Schaefer, M. J. Coordination and patient unit effectiveness. Paper presented at the Academy of Management Annual Meetings, San Diego, August 1981.

22. Mintzberg, H. *The structuring of organizations.* Englewood Cliffs, N.J.: Prentice-Hall, 1979.

23. Charns, M. P., & Strayer, R. G. A socio-structural approach to organization development. Paper presented at the Academy of Management Annual Meetings, San Diego, August 1981.

CHAPTER 7

Coordination and Communication

Beaufort B. Longest, Jr.
James M. Klingensmith

MINI-CASE: SEARCH FOR A NEW PRESIDENT

The chairperson of the ad hoc Search Committee called the meeting to order at 7:30 P.M. She noted that the purpose of the meeting was to establish the criteria to be used in selecting a new president for Memorial Hospital. The committee, composed of members of the governing board, had been appointed upon the announcement by the present CEO that he had accepted another position.

Memorial Hospital is a prestigious, teaching hospital located in a large eastern city. The 600-bed institution is nationally prominent in organ transplantation and is the primary teaching hospital for the medical school located in the same city, but it is organizationally separate from the medical school. Memorial is considered by most members of the health field in its region to be the most influential "trend-setter" in the city. However, another large general hospital nearby has enjoyed very favorable response to its recent efforts at building a vertically integrated system.

One of the more aggressive members of the committee spoke first. "It is not at all clear to me what kind of person we ought to seek to be our next president. On the one hand, we need someone who can manage this institution; on the other hand, I'm very concerned that we appear to be isolated from the rest of the health care system, especially in comparison to our main competitor."

After considerable discussion, a consensus began to emerge that this concern was shared by all members of the committee. One member, an attorney, expressed his general agreement with the view widely expressed in the health care literature that over the next decade most health care services would be provided through a rather small number of highly integrated health care systems. Most committee members nodded their concurrence.

Another member, while expressing his concern about the "isolation" problem, pointed out how important it was to find a president who could manage the day-to-day operations of a major teaching hospital with all the complexities that entailed. He noted, "I'm not at all certain that any one person can be effective at managing the internal details of our hospital and its relationship to the rest of the world."

Sensing that this dichotomy was going to be troublesome to the committee, but recognizing that Memorial could only have one president, the chairperson asked the committee to begin listing the skills the next president should possess.

After a reflective pause, a member spoke. "Clearly, the person we select will have to be able to link together in an effective way all the various people and units that make up Memorial Hospital and, at the same time, link our hospital to other organizations and agencies."

The chairperson turned to the blackboard in the conference room and, condensing what had been said, wrote:

SKILLS NEEDED BY NEXT PRESIDENT:

1. Coordination ⟨ within the hospital
                   with other organizations

The meeting went on for another 2 hours. During that time, 15 skills were listed, but coordination remained at the top of the list.

The committee adjourned, satisfied that they knew what kind of person the next president should be.

INTRODUCTION

The establishment and use of effective coordination and communication mechanisms are vitally important tasks for managers of health care organizations. Both tasks are treated in this chapter because they are closely related, in combination representing the essential means through which managers link together the various people and units within their organizations and link their organizations to others. Because health care organizations have become increasingly complex internally and have established a wide variety of external relationships, the challenge of linkage has increased. If linkages are not effective, organizations may become fragmented, fractionated, and isolated, with concomitant declines in performance.

The central theme of this chapter is that health care organizations exhibit a great deal of interdependence among their various internal parts and external relationships. As a result, health care organizations traditionally have had an unusually high need for effective linkages. Coordination and communication strategies are important means through which managers establish and maintain these linkages.

INTERDEPENDENCE

Interdependence among the individuals and units within an organization or among organizations, while always present, varies with the structural complexity and goals of organizations. Thompson (1), for example, has identified three forms of interdependence: pooled, sequential, and reciprocal.

POOLED INTERDEPENDENCE

Pooled interdependence occurs when individuals and units are related but do not bear a close connection; they simply contribute separately in some way to the larger whole. For example, a group of geographically dispersed nursing homes owned by a single corporation may be viewed as linked in the sense that each contributes to the overall success of the corporation, but they have very little direct interdependence. Their activities are *pooled* to make the corporation more effective.

SEQUENTIAL INTERDEPENDENCE

Sequential interdependence occurs when individuals and units bear a close, but sequential, connection. For example, patients admitted to acute-care hospitals become the focal point for an extended chain of sequentially interdependent activities. The admitting office checks the patient in, schedules the patient for the operating room, notifies the dietary department of special needs, notifies the laboratory of the need for tests, and so on. Most of what is done until the patient is discharged occurs in a *sequential* manner.

RECIPROCAL INTERDEPENDENCE

Reciprocal interdependence occurs when individuals and units bear a close relationship and the interdependence goes in both directions. For example, a vertically integrated health care system with acute-care and long-term-care capacity exhibits reciprocal interdependence. The long-term-care beds are occupied by patients referred from the acute-care beds; the acute-care unit depends upon the long-term-care unit as a place to which to discharge certain patients. The acute-care unit suffers if the long-term-care unit cannot accept a patient. Conversely, the long-term-care unit suffers if patients are not discharged to it from the acute-unit. The interdependence between these units is *reciprocal*.

Bolman and Deal (2) have pointed out that the level of interdependence intensifies as its form moves from pooled to sequential to reciprocal. The higher the level of interdependence, the greater the need for managerial attention to effective linkages. Health care organizations generally exhibit very high levels of interdependence among their component parts, usually of the sequential or reciprocal forms. Thus the need for effective coordination and communication is usually very great in these organizations. The importance of effective communication in all organizations has been noted by Rakich et al. (3), in that if "communication is adequate, the work gets done more effectively and problems are solved more efficiently. In any organized effort, communication is essential for people to work together because it permits them to influence and react to one another." The same is true for coordination. Clearly, in highly interdependent health care organizations, coordination and communication are critical tasks for managers. These tasks are examined in depth below.

COORDINATION

Coordination, as a means of effectively linking together the various parts of an organization or of linking together organizations and dealing with interdependence, is one of the most important functions of management. Conceptually and historically, coordination has been defined as the conscious activity of assembling and synchronizing differentiated work efforts so that they function harmoniously to attain organization objectives (4). Some authors use the term "integration" for this concept. Lawrence and Lorsch (5) define integration as "the process of achieving unity of effort among the various subsystems in the accomplishment of the organization's tasks." Obviously, the two terms have similar meaning.

The definition provided above pertains to coordination within an organization; an *intraorganizational* perspective. Increasingly important today, with the elaboration of a wide variety of multi-institutional arrangements, is the issue of coordination among and between organizations; an *interorganizational* perspective (also see Chapter 10). While much of what is known about intraorganizational coordination applies to interorganizational coordination, there are basic differences, and these are examined later. It is important here, however, to extend the definition of coordination to encompass both inter- and intraorganizational situations. Thus *coordination is conscious activity aimed at achieving unity and harmony of effort in pursuit of shared objectives within an organization or among a set of organizations participating in a multi-institutional arrangement of some kind.*

INTRAORGANIZATIONAL MECHANISMS OF COORDINATION

The mechanisms of coordination (i.e., the activities managers use to achieve coordination*) are diverse; these mechanisms have different levels of success, depending upon the characteristics of specific situations. This contingency view of coordination is very important for the reader to keep in mind; clearly, no single coordinating mechanism is best for all situations.

The need for a contingency approach to coordination is even greater in health care organizations because of the predominance of professionals within these organizations. Scott (6) points out that because the activities of health professionals are seen as being complex, uncertain, and of great social importance, distinctive structural arrangements have evolved to support the autonomy of the professions. Scott identifies three types of such structural arrangements. The *autonomous arrangement* is present when an organization delegates to a professional group goal setting, implementation, and evaluation of performance, and the administration controls the support staff. Most health care organizations historically have had such an arrangement with their medical staffs. The *heteronomous arrangement* alternatively occurs when professionals are subordinated to the administrative structure with specific responsibilities delegated to various professional groups. Nursing and social service, for instance, traditionally have had such a relationship with hospitals. A third relationship, the *conjoint arrangement*, occurs when the profes-

---

*It should be noted that coordination is most usefully discussed in conjunction with control. Because control has traditionally received a great deal of attention in research on health care organizations, it is treated as a separate topic in Chapter 8. However, coordination mechanisms that are not backed up by control mechanisms quickly lose their effectiveness. Control provides the muscle that makes coordination mechanisms effective.

sionals and administration are equal in power. Although few examples of this form of structural arrangement currently exist, Scott notes that physician groups increasingly are moving toward the heteronomous and conjoint forms in response to various external pressures. Clearly, the type of structural arrangement affects the coordinating mechanisms employed.

In the same way that the manager's choice of coordination mechanism(s) is dependent on the structural arrangement with professionals, there are different levels of need for coordination within organizations. The activities required for organizational performance are separated through vertical and horizontal differentiation. Differentiation, in this context, is defined as "the state of segmentation of the organizational system into sub-systems, each of which tends to develop particular attributes in relation to the requirements posed by its relevant environment" (6). Vertical differentiation establishes the hierarchy and number of levels in the organization (7). Horizontal differentiation comes about to separate activities so that they may be performed more effectively and efficiently. This usually results in the formation of departments within the organization. For instance, in a hospital, horizontal differentiation accounts for radiology, pharmacy, and pathology. Vertical differentiation accounts for a CEO, a second level composed of vice presidents, a third level composed of department heads, and continuing on down. Once the organization's activities have been differentiated, they must be coordinated. Of course, the requirements of the environment and technical system involved very often determine the degree of coordination needed. In some organizations, it is possible to separate activities in such a way as to minimize the degree of coordination needed. In others, particularly those functionally departmentalized, such as most health care organizations, a high degree of coordination is essential. It is necessary to recognize the interaction between the need to specialize activities and requirements for coordination. The more differentiation of activities and specialization of labor, the greater the need for coordination.

As Rakich et al. (3), have noted, organizations establish several mechanisms to achieve coordination. Litterer suggests three primary means: through the hierarchy, the administrative system, and voluntary activities (8). In *hierarchical coordination*, the various activities are linked by placing them under a central authority. In a simple organization, this form of coordination might be sufficient. However, in complex health care organizations that have many levels and many specialized departments, hierarchical coordination becomes more difficult. Although the CEO is a focal point of authority, it would be impossible for one person to cope with all the coordinating problems that might arise in the hierarchy. Therefore, coordination through the hierarchical structure must be supplemented.

The *administrative system* provides a second mechanism for coordinating activities in Litterer's typology. "A great deal of coordinative effort in organizations is concerned with a horizontal flow of work of a routine nature. Administrative systems are formal procedures designed to carry out much of this routine coordinative work automatically" (8). Many work procedures, such as memoranda with routing slips, help coordinate efforts of different operating units. To the extent that these procedures can be programmed or routinized, it is not necessary to establish specific means for coordination. For nonroutine and nonprogrammable events, means such as committees may be required to provide integration.

A third type of coordination according to Litterer is through *voluntary action* when individuals or groups see a need for coordination, develop a method, and implement it (8). Much of the coordination may depend upon the willingness and ability of individuals or groups to voluntarily find ways to integrate their activities with other organizational participants.

Achieving voluntary coordination is one of the most important yet difficult problems for the manager. Voluntary coordination requires that individuals have sufficient knowledge of organizational objectives, adequate information concerning specific problems of coordination, and the motivation to do something. Fortunately, in health care organizations, voluntary coordination is often facilitated by the high degree of professionalism extant in many participants. Writing about hospitals (although their comments are equally applicable to all kinds of health care organizations), Georgopoulos and Mann (9) have said, "The hospital is dependent very greatly upon the motivations and voluntary, informal adjustments of its members for the attainment and maintenance of good coordination. Formal organizational plans, rules, regulations, and controls may ensure some minimum coordination, but of themselves are incapable of producing adequate coordination, for only a fraction of all the coordinative activities required in this organization can be programmed in advance." One of the primary forces ensuring voluntary coordination is the overall value system supportive of the patient's welfare. This fabric of shared values is developed through the training and professionalization of many participants in health care organizations.

Mintzberg (10) identifies five coordinating mechanisms. They are mutual adjustment, direct supervision, standardization of work processes, standardization of work outputs, and standardization of worker skills. Figure 7.1 illustrates these coordinating mechanisms. They can be summarized as:

- *Mutual adjustment*, which primarily provides coordination by informal communications. Similar to voluntary actions, the work is controlled and coordinated by those who perform the work (Figure 7.1a).
- Like hierarchical coordination, *direct supervision* occurs when one person takes responsibility for the work of others, including issuing them instructions and monitoring their actions (Figure 7.1b).
- *Standardization of work process* is an alternative coordinating mechanism that specifies or programs the contents of the work. Hospitals, for instance, attempt to standardize work processes whenever possible, such as inpatient admission and discharge procedures (Figure 7.1c).
- *Standardization of output* specifies the product or the expected performance, with the process to get there left to the doer.
- *Standardization of worker skills* occurs when neither the work nor its output can be specified and the resultant standardization occurs through the training of the doer. This form of standardization is that most frequently found in health care organizations where the complexity of the work often does not allow for the standardization of work processes or outputs.

The coordination mechanisms described above are not the only such mechanisms. Hage (11), for instance, describes four kinds of coordination mechanisms for health care organizations: programming, plans, customs, and feedback. In general, this framework builds on the early work of March and Simon (12), as modified by both Thompson (13) and Perrow (14). Each of the four mechanisms is unique, although, in a sense, they can be viewed as overlapping. These mechanisms are, with the exception of customs, similar to those of Van de Ven et al. (15).

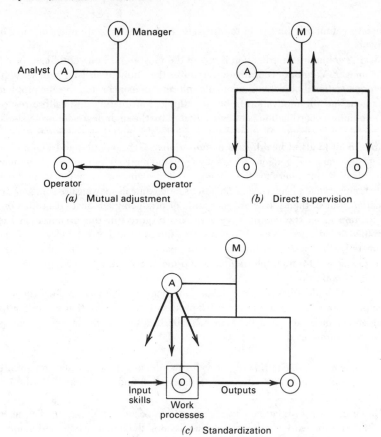

Figure 7.1. Mintzberg's five coordinating mechanisms. (From Henry Mintzberg, *Structure in Fives: Designing Effective Organizations*, © 1983, p. 5. Reprinted by permission of Prentice-Hall, Inc., Englewood Cliffs, New Jersey.)

An important mechanism in Hage's typology is *programming*. Organizations develop explicit rules and prescriptions, called programs, that define the job of each person in the organization, and the sequence of activities for all of the jobs within a department and for the organization as a whole. With programs, everyone can learn his or her job and execute it. The purpose of programming is to reduce the need for communication, except for questions about interpretation of a particular rule. The programming of an organization is accomplished with rules, manuals, job descriptions, personnel procedures, promotion policies, and so on. (This category is quite similar to Litterer's administrative system described above.) Health care organizations often rely very heavily on programming as a means of coordination.

Planning differs from programming in that a plan usually delineates a set of objectives that the organization hopes to achieve and the means by which it expects to achieve them. Planning and programming can, of course, be combined. Programs are the specific enactments of the means used to achieve the organization's planned objective(s). The usefulness of planning as an intraorganizational coordination mechanism can be seen in the need to think of planning in one unit of a health care organization as part of a larger whole (16). For example, the expansion plans of a health care organization must be taken into account in its nursing services' human resources planning. No departmental plan should be made that does not contribute to the objectives set out in the plans of the organization. It is the responsibility of senior management to ensure that all managers understand the objectives of the organization. It is the joint duty of all managers to determine whether their plans are compatible with all other plans in the organization. If this is done initially, coordination will be facilitated.

Customs also are a coordination mechanism. Many organizations rely upon the history and customs of the organization as coordination mechanisms. While programming is a rational attempt to spell out specific norms of human behavior in organizations, customs are norms developed over time that specify behavior of different participants in the social system. In this sense, customs may be more rational than programming rules because customs, based on a history of trial and error, represent a distillation of good practice, whereas programming can result from a manager's ideal sense rather than from lessons learned from reality. Customs can be an important coordinating mechanism; but in complex health care organizations they are not, in and of themselves, sufficient to achieve effective coordination.

Feedback, the fourth in Hage's typology of coordination mechanisms, occurs in both verbal and nonverbal forms. Indeed, machines are often designed with feedback mechanisms to improve performance. In coordination, verbal communications feedback indicates when the organization is not functioning well or when problems of conflict or inefficiency arise. Not all forms of communication represent feedback, but some, particularly those involving committees and horizontal communication, are likely to represent attempts on the part of the organization to coordinate through feedback.

Another approach to coordinating activities is through *committees.* Frequently, committees are made up of members from a number of departments or functional areas and are concerned with problems requiring coordination. Using committees for purposes of coordination is a well-established approach in health care organizations. Committees serve other purposes besides coordination; they may act in a service, advisory, informational, educational, or decision-making capacity. However, their chief purpose is coordination.

Additional means of coordination have developed in many organizations. Lawrence and Lorsch (5) studied six organizations operating in the chemical processing industry to determine how they achieve integration or coordination. These organizations use a technology that requires not only differentiated and specialized activities, but also a major degree of integration. The study analyzed how organizations achieve both substantial differentiation and tight integration when these forces seem contradictory. Results showed that successful organizations use *task forces, teams,* and *project offices* to achieve coordination. In the most successful organizations, Lawrence and Lorsch found the influence of *integrators* (people who seem to hold the key to successful integration) stems from professional competence rather than from formal position. They are successful integrators because of specialized knowledge and because they represent a central source of information in the organization. Although examples of effective integrators can be found among all health professionals, in most hospitals individual nurses, regardless of their formal position, often function as integrators, linking practicing physicians with the organization's formal administrative structure. These same individuals also often provide significant coordination among the hospital's various administrative units, particularly as they relate to the patient.

Project management (17) and its more advanced form, called *matrix organization* (see Chapter 9 for further discussion), are structural forms which can facilitate coordination within an organization. Project management is a structural means for coordinating a large amount of talent and resources for a given period on a specific project. The project team of various specialists is assembled under direction of the project manager, who is responsible for coordinating their efforts. A project team in a regional home health care program, for instance, could be utilized to plan for the organization's new automated telephone system. In more complex organizations, such as hospitals, Neuhauser (18) notes that: "The existence of coordination through departmentalization and the formal chain of command and simultaneously across departments (the patient care team) is called a matrix organization." Figure 7.2 schematically presents the hospital as a matrix organization. This coordination mechanism can be very important as health care organizations move toward a product-line management orientation.

Other structural forms have been recommended to help with problems of coordination.

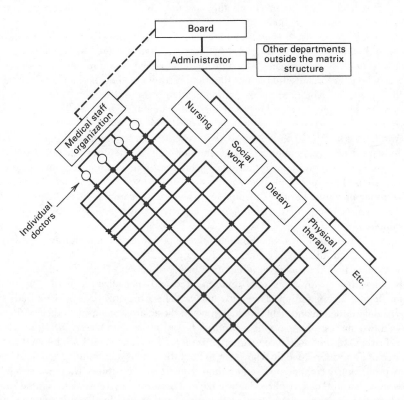

Figure 7.2. The hospital as a matrix organization; "x" indicates membership in both. (From Neuhauser, D. The hospital as a matrix organization. In A. R. Kovner, and D. Neuhauser (Eds.), *Health services management: Readings and commentary* (2nd ed.). Ann Arbor, MI: Health Administration Press, 1983, p. 256.)

Likert believes that one mechanism for achieving integration could be to have people serve as *"linking pins"* between various units in the organization (19). Horizontally, there are certain organizational participants who are members of two separate groups and who serve as coordinating agents between them. On the vertical axis, individuals serve as linking pins between their level and those above and below. Thus, through this system of linking pins, the coordination necessary to make the dynamic system operate effectively is achieved. This forms a multiple overlapping group structure in the organization. Likert (19) says:

> To perform the intended coordination well, a fundamental requirement must be met. The entire organization must consist of a multiple, overlapping group structure with every work group using group decision-making processes skillfully. This requirement applies to the functional, product, and service departments. An organization meeting this requirement will have an effective interaction–influence system through which the relevant communications flow readily, the required influence is exerted laterally, upward, and downward, and the motivational forces needed for coordination are created.
>
> SOURCE: R. Likert, *The Human Organization*, Copyright 1967, p. 156. Reprinted by permission of McGraw-Hill Book Company, New York, New York.

A relatively new mechanism for improved intraorganizational coordination is the *quality circle*. Originally developed in the United States, but brought to a high art in Japan, this mechanism is gaining considerable acceptance as a means of coordination, especially at the operational level. This mechanism features small-group, problem-oriented meetings in which employees focus on changes needed to improve morale, productivity, or quality (20). It is reported that quality circles enhance the quality of patient care and services, reduce errors, build an attitude of problem prevention, improve communications, and inspire more effective teamwork in health care organizations (21). This technique involves processes such as the nominal group process, multicriteria decision making, and critical incident examination. Quality circles require support from management in providing *(1)* approval for meetings during work hours, *(2)* training for circle leaders, *(3)* a responsive attitude toward proposals for improvement developed by circle members, and *(4)* incentives for achieving improvements.

SUMMARY OF INTRAORGANIZATIONAL COORDINATION MECHANISMS

As we have seen, there are a number of intraorganizational coordination mechanisms, including: administrative system, committees, customs, feedback, hierarchy, integrators, linking pins, matrix organization, plans, programming, project management through task forces or teams, standardization, quality circles, or voluntary action. Managers in health care organizations use various combinations of these mechanisms to achieve coordination; usually a number of them are used concurrently. Two basic dimensions help categorize the different types of health care organizations and explain the circumstances under which various coordination mechanisms might be used: scale of operations (small to large) and interdependence (pooled to sequential/reciprocal). Using this typology, Table 7.1 illustrates clusters of coordination mechanisms which might be most effective in various health care organizations.

TABLE 7.1. A Typology of Intraorganizational Coordination Mechanisms

Interdependence	Scale of Operations	
	Small	Large
Pooled	Customs	Administrative system
	Feedback	Direct supervision
	Mutual adjustments	Hierarchy
	Programming	Programming
	Voluntary activities	Matrix organization
Sequential/reciprocal	Administrative system	Integrators
	Feedback	Linking pins
	Programming	Plans
	Quality circles	Project management
		Standardization

INTERORGANIZATIONAL MECHANISMS OF COORDINATION

Interdependence is not limited to the situation *within* organizations. Increasingly, health care organizations experience interdependencies with other health care organizations (as in systems or other multi-institutional arrangements) or with other elements in their external environments, such as various levels of government, suppliers, third-party payors, and so on. These interdependencies may be pooled (a group of nursing homes under a single ownership), or sequential and reciprocal (a vertically integrated health care system). Whatever the form of interdependence, it requires management; that is, the focal organization must coordinate and communicate with other organizations or agencies with which it is interdependent.

TYPES OF INTERORGANIZATIONAL LINKAGES

The linkages (coordination and communication mechanisms) organizations use to manage their interdependencies with other organizations arise from the circumstances of a particular situation. As Pfeffer and Salanick (22) have noted, "When interdependence is problematic because it can lead to uncertain or unfavorable outcomes, the need to coordinate through social mechanisms is greatest, and this is particularly true when alternative ways of coping with interdependence are not available."

Thompson (23) has developed a categorization of these linkages: contracting, coopting, and coalescing. Starkweather and Cook (see Chapter 10) have added a fourth category, consumption. Each of these categories of linkage provide means through which interorganizational interdependencies can be managed.

Contracting

In a sense, this is the simplest form of linkage. It may entail nothing more than establishing an acceptable contract to purchase some needed item of supply or service or to provide defined services to a defined population as in an agreement with an HMO. At the more complex level, contracts permit a health care organization to establish stable and predictable (albeit interdependent) relationships with the federal government for reimbursement for Medicare patients, with state governments for reimbursement for Medicaid patients, and with commercial insurers for their subscribers. Contracts are, in essence, formal agreements, usually negotiated, which define parameters ɩf exchanges between two or more parties. Thus they are widely used as a mechanism of coordination in a great variety of interorganizational relationships.

Coopting

This form of linkage involves the absorption of leadership elements from other organizations into the focal organizations. In the health care industry this coordination mechanism often takes one of two forms: management contracts and the placing of representatives of interdependent organizations on the focal organization's governing body. Management contracts, labeled by Starkweather (24) as an example of coopting, permit one organization to supply day-to-day management to another by agreement. Management includes at least the CEO, who reports to the governing body of the managed organization and to the managing organization. This is in contrast to the practice prevalent in many health care organizations of using outside contractors to manage individual departments and programs such as housekeeping, food service, or respiratory therapy. The second coopting mechanism for achieving interorganizational coordination is by appointment of significant representatives from external organizations to positions in the focal organization, usually the governing body. As Pfeffer and Salanick (22) have noted, "Of all forms of interorganizational coordination, it is one of the most flexible and easiest to implement, two advantages that have made its use pervasive." For example, a hospital system, interested in access to capital, may find considerable advantage in placing an investment banker on its governing body. Similarly, an HMO may find it advantageous to place members of its medical group on its board.

Coalescing

This form of linkage, also known as coalition-building, is typified by joint ventures, wherein two or more organizations *partially* pool resources to pursue defined goals or create a new organization, sometimes called an "umbrella" organization, to span but not to replace those organizations forming it.

Starkweather (25) describes two important subtypes of the umbrella corporation in regard to hospitals:

> One is where only limited authorities are granted to the new corporation, but in these realms the umbrella corporation's authority is final. These arrangements often deal with planning or allocation of services among otherwise distinct hospitals. There is usually no central management or central fiscal control. In the other subtype the umbrella corporation's authority is more general and complete, usually exercised through unified management, policy, and fiscal control. This type is akin to the parent–subsidiary form found commonly in the business world. In this arrangement the participating hospitals are required to turn over all assets to the new corporation, and it in turn assumes their liabilities. New assets that are developed are typically owned by the umbrella corporation. Services which are combined in this arrangement include hospital support and administrative activities as well as professional services. In addition to these aspects of horizontal integration, the new cor-

poration may engage in vertical integration by developing or acquiring diagnostic clinics, group practices, home health services, extended care facilities, etc.

Joint ventures, increasingly common among health care organizations, "can be predicted by considerations of resource interdependence, competitive uncertainty, and conditions that make various forms of interdependence more or less problematic" (22). Shortell et al. (26) have examined primary care group practices sponsored jointly by hospitals and physicians and suggest that "hospitals and physicians are exploring new kinds of relationships through a variety of joint ventures. These range from highly formal activities such as hospital-sponsored group practices, health maintenance organizations sponsored by hospitals and their medical staffs, and preferred provider organizations (PPOs), to somewhat less formal arrangements involving leasing of space and equipment or providing ancillary services, computerized billing, financial analyses, and medical records services." Major health care networks, such as the Voluntary Hospitals of America and the American Health Care System, similarly are entering into separate joint ventures with major health insurance providers for the development of a range of new alternative delivery-system products.

A third coalescing mechanism for achieving interorganizational coordination, particularly prevalent in the health care industry, is in the form of trade associations. For example, the American Hospital Association has over 5,000 member organizations for which it conducts a political/lobbying activity. Similarly, there are regional and state hospital associations that base affiliation on a geographical or state community of interests. As states have become increasingly involved in regulatory and control processes, state hospital associations have undertaken important lobbying efforts. Associations serve other functions which help member organizations deal with their independencies; centralized information, research, and product definition are examples.

Consumption

An extreme organizational response to interdependence is to absorb or consume it, as in a merger or consolidation. Consolidation is a formal combination of two or more organizations into a single new legal entity that has an identity separate from any of the preexisting institutions. Merger is a formal combination of two or more institutions into a single new legal entity that has the identify of one of the preexisting organizations. Both forms of consumption as an interorganizational coordinating mechanism involve an essential restructuring of organizational interdependence. The restructuring can be in the form of vertical integration (a nursing home merges with a hospital—the hospital gains the ability to discharge patients to a less intensive level of care and the nursing home gains a source of referrals), horizontal expansion (two hospitals merge with a resulting larger capacity), or diversification (a hospital absorbs a retail pharmacy chain, gaining a new source of revenue).

COSTS OF INTERORGANIZATIONAL COORDINATION

Interorganizational coordination, necessary to manage interdependencies among organizations, is not achieved without costs. The obvious ones are time, personnel, and money needed to support the various forms of linkages described above. There also is the potential loss of some degree of autonomy. The less obvious, but very important, costs include what Porter (27) has termed the cost of compromise and of inflexibility. The cost of compromise arises when effectively coordinating across organizational boundaries requires that an activity be performed in a consistent way that may not be optimal for any of the participants in the interorganizational relationship. From the manager's perspective, the cost of compromise can be reduced if an activity is *designed* for sharing. For example, two merger participants may find that a new management information system designed to accommodate the needs of the new organization is better than applying that of either of the previously existing organizations or of simply linking together and "fixing" gaps in two separate management information systems.

The cost of inflexibility is not an ongoing cost of interorganizational coordination mechanisms but arises with the need for flexibility, usually in the form of potential difficulty in responding to a competitor's move or to a new market opportunity. It is simply that linkages developed to manage interorganizational interdependencies involve added complexity and, often, greater inflexibility.

Managers must weigh these costs of interorganizational coordination against the benefits to be gained in their decisions about interorganizational linkages.

MANAGERIAL GUIDELINES FOR EFFECTIVE COORDINATION

The development of effective coordination mechanisms is one of the most difficult tasks a manager faces. This activity is especially difficult in health care organizations owing to their extreme horizontal and vertical differentiation. It is even more difficult in circumstances involving coordination among organizations. To assist in this process we offer the following suggestions:

MANAGERIAL GUIDELINES

1. Health care managers should be aware of the relationship between functional specialization and coordination. Whereas the establishment of additional organizational units may improve the coordination within such units, efforts should also be made to establish coordinative mechanisms among all units within the organization.

2. Managers should recognize the need for developing overlapping forms of coordination within their organizations, including:

   a. Structural relationships, such as committees, project management teams, and quality circles.

   b. Administrative systems, such as planning, programming, and feedback processes.

   c. Organizational culture or customs.

3. In relating with other organizations, health care managers should choose from a variety of interorganizational mechanisms for coordination. In making their selection managers should carefully consider the relative benefits and costs inherent in such mechanisms as contracting, coopting, coalescing, and consumption.

COMMUNICATION*

As we noted in the introduction to this chapter, coordination and communication share the characteristic that both are important tasks for managers as they link together the various people and units in their organization. Similarly, both tasks arise out of the interdependence among individuals and units of an organization and the need to effectively manage the interdependence. As with coordination, communication becomes more important as interdependence moves from pooled to sequential to reciprocal forms. Communication, especially in the feedback form and in programming and plans, is an important coordination mechanism itself. Yet it fulfills other functions besides coordination. It can be a mechanism of control (see Chapter 8). It also can be used to infuse values and purposes into the organization as well as to encourage superior and peer support and motivation.

Communication, from the manager's perspective, has intraorganizational and interorganizational dimensions. Intraorganizational communication depends on formal establishment of channels and networks *within* the organization. Interorganizational communication occurs *between* organizations or between organizations and constituencies outside them, as in marketing efforts or attempts to influence (lobby) important political elements in an organization's external environment.

Both intra- and interorganizational communication can be defined as *the creation or exchange of understanding between sender and receiver(s)*. As Rakich et al. (3) have noted, this definition does not restrict communication to words alone; it includes all methods (verbal and nonverbal) through which meaning is conveyed to others. Even silence can convey meaning and must be considered part of communicating. A central component of this definition is "understanding." A sender will want the receiver to understand what was sent; this means the sender wants the receiver to interpret the message exactly as it is intended. Unfortunately, communication seldom results in complete understanding because there are so many environmental and personal barriers to effective communication. It is important for the manager to realize that information can be easily transmitted to others, but they may not necessarily understand it.

THE TECHNICAL MECHANISM OF COMMUNICATION

Figure 7.3 illustrates the basic mechanism of communication. The reader should note the feedback loop in this model. Where the interdependencies among individuals and units of an organization are of sequential and reciprocal forms, as is so often the case in health care organizations, the effectiveness of the feedback loop takes on special importance.

---

*This section draws heavily upon the treatment of communication in Rakich, J. S., Longest, B. B., Jr., and Darr, K. *Managing Health Services Organizations*, 2nd. ed. Philadelphia: W. B. Saunders Company, 1985, Chapter 12; and Longest, B. B., Jr. *Management Practices for the Health Professional*, 3rd ed. Reston, VA: Reston Publishing Company, 1984, pp. 158–167.

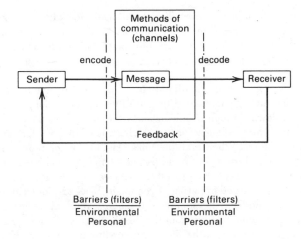

Figure 7.3. The basic mechanism of communication. (From Rakich, J. S., Longest, B. B., Jr., & Darr, K. *Managing health services organizations* (2nd ed.). Philadelphia, PA: W. B. Saunders Company, Copyright 1985, p. 376.)

BARRIERS TO COMMUNICATION

Other important elements of the model in Figure 7.3 are the barriers to effective communication. Environmental barriers are characteristic of the organization and work setting; personal barriers arise from the nature of individuals and their interaction with others. These environmental and personal barriers, typically present in any setting, can block, filter, or distort the message as it is encoded and sent, as well as when it is decoded and received.

Environmental Barriers

Two obvious environmental barriers are *competition for attention* and *time*. Multiple and simultaneous demands on the sender may cause the message content to be packaged inappropriately; such demands may also result in the message being filtered or distorted by the receiver. In such a situation, the receiver may hear the message without comprehending it because it is not getting complete attention—the receiver is not really "listening." Time may function as a barrier to effective communication by permitting the sender little opportunity to completely think through and structure the message that is to be conveyed, and by allowing the receiver too little time to fully discern its meaning.

Another set of environmental barriers that can filter, distort, or block a message consists of *managerial philosophy of the organization, multiplicity of hierarchical levels,* and *power–status relationships.* Managerial philosophy can often inhibit, as well as promote, effective communication. Viewing it in the negative sense, a manager not interested in promoting communication upward or disseminating information downward will, as a rule, establish procedural and organizational blockages. The requirement that all communication "flow through channels," inaccessibility of superiors, lack of interest in employees' frustrations, complaints, or feelings, and insufficient time allocated to receive information are symptoms of a managerial philosophy that retards communication flows. Furthermore, the lack of action with regard to complaints, ideas, and problems serves as a signal to those who wish to communicate upward and, as a result, discourages the free flow of information.

Multiple levels in an organization hierarchy, and especially among organizations in a multi-institutional arrangement, tend to cause message distortion. As the message is transmitted up or down through people at many levels, there is a likelihood that each person will interpret the message according to a personal frame of reference and vantage point in the organization. When multiple links exist in the communication chain, information will be filtered, dropped, or added, and emphasis will be rearranged as it is transmitted to other receivers. As a result, a message sent through many levels has a good chance of being distorted or perhaps even totally blocked. For example, very often a message sent from the CEO to employees through several layers of the organization is received in quite a different form than that originally sent. Or a report prepared for the CEO that is passed through the hierarchy possibly may not reach its destination because it sits on someone's desk and is, in essence, blocked.

Power–status relationships can also distort or inhibit transmission of a message. A discordant superior–subordinate relationship can dampen the flow and content of information. Furthermore, depending on past experiences, an employee may be inhibited about communicating for fear of reprisal, negative sanctions, or ridicule. For example, it is not unusual to find a situation in which, as a result of poor superior–subordinate rapport, the subordinate does not inform the superior that something is wrong or that a plan will not work.

Power–status communication barriers are particularly prevalent in health care organizations in which a number of professionals must interact. Status relationships among professionals create a complex situation. How often does the head nurse with 20 years of experience tell the resident a procedure or treatment might not be efficacious? How is the nurse's message encoded—bluntly or obliquely? Status and role conflicts, particularly among professionals, can serve as a major barrier to effective communication.

Finally, among environmental barriers, when messages require the use of *specific terminology* unfamiliar to the receiver and are *complex,* there may be a breakdown in communication. Most professionals have their own set of terminology. Those on the managerial side of the health care organization may use a substantially different set of terminology than those responsible for direct care. Terminology is important, since words mean specific things to those familiar with them and tend to minimize misunderstanding. However, interaction between participants who use different sets of terminology can result in ineffective communication. Similarly, when the complexity of the message is such that understanding must be precise, and when it is linked with terminology that may be unfamiliar to the receiver, there is a good chance that misunderstanding will occur.

Personal Barriers

In addition to environmental barriers, personal barriers also exist when people communicate with each other. When people encode and send messages or decode and receive them, they tend to do so according to their *frame of reference* and *beliefs,* and they consciously or unconsciously engage in *selective perception.* The sum of one's socioeconomic background and previous experiences can shape the manner in which one receives and interprets communication. For example, someone with a cultural background of "don't speak unless spoken to" and "never question elders" may be inhibited in communicating. Other people, who may be more naive, accept all communication at face value and do not filter out erroneous information or bragging. In contrast to this, aggressiveness and disseminating self-edifying information could result in the transmission of a message distorted for personal gain. Furthermore, unless one has had the same experiences as others, it is difficult to completely understand the meaning of their message. The wealthy may have a difficult time understanding hunger. Those who have never experienced pain or childbirth or witnessed death may not be able to truly comprehend them.

Closely related to one's frame of reference are beliefs, values, and prejudices. They can cause messages to be distorted or blocked in either transmission or reception. This occurs because people differ and their personalities and backgrounds differ; they have preconceived opinions and prejudices in a multitude of areas such as politics, ethics, religion, union or management perspective, sex, race, and life style. These biases, beliefs, and values filter and distort communication.

Selective perception is one of the most difficult personal barriers to overcome, both for the sender and the receiver. People tend to screen derogatory information and amplify words, actions, and meanings that flatter them. In other words, there is a tendency to screen out the "bad" in a message and retain the "good." Selective perception can be conscious or unconscious. When it is conscious, intentional distortion results. For example, supervisors with high turnover in their units may interpret that as a message and amplify the idea that the turnover is due to low wages, over which they have no control and, therefore, no responsibility or they may delete, diminish, or not admit that the real cause is supervisory style. Unfortunately, selective perception is part of human nature.

Other personal barriers to communication are *jealousy* and *fear*. We previously discussed fear as an environmental inhibitor to full and free communication flow. Jealousy, when coupled with selective perception, may result in conscious efforts to filter and distort incoming information, transmit misinformation, or both. For example, the manager with an extremely able assistant who makes the manager look good may tend to block or distort information that would reveal the situation to other sources. Furthermore, petty personality differences, the feeling of professional incompetence or inferiority, and sheer greed can lead to jealousy and communication distortion.

When people receive messages, there is a tendency for the receiver to *evaluate the source* (sender). Furthermore, conditions often exist in which there are incentives to *maintain the status quo;* both are personal barriers to communication. Evaluation of the source is frequently necessary in order to decide whether some of the message should be filtered out or discounted. Evaluation of the source can lead to bias on the parts of communicators. For example, a hostile union–management atmosphere may result in the employees ignoring messages from management, or managers may ignore messages from physicians with whom they frequently disagree. Source evaluation is important for coping with the barrage of communication; however, one must recognize that source evaluation carries with it the hazard that legitimate messages will not be received or understood.

The status quo barrier denotes a conscious effort by the sender or receiver to filter out information either in sending, receiving, or retransmitting that would upset the present situation. Basically, this implies transmitting information that the sender thinks the receiver wants to hear. Environmental conditions that promote "fear of sending bad news"—displeasure on the part of superiors, lack of candor in the organization, and insufficient confidence in the superior–subordinate relationship—foster erection of this barrier.

Three remaining personal barriers to communication are *semantics*, *symbols*, and *empathy*. We previously discussed terminology as an environmental barrier. Closely related to terminology is semantics. Since words have different meanings for people, care must be taken to communicate in easily understood language. The use of overly complex vocabulary and idioms can impede understanding a message.

In health care organizations, symbols are important and play a major role in communication. They can be characterized by physical things, pictures, and actions. For example, the use of different uniforms by personnel not only denotes status but also enables others to immediately evaluate the source. The nurse wears a white uniform, the nurse aide may wear a yellow uniform, and the doctor wears a long white coat. In this sense, physical symbols serve a functional purpose.

Pictures or visual representations are another type of symbol. They can be quite helpful in communicating, and greatly increase understanding. Think of how many words would be needed to explain the organization structure in lieu of a chart. Or imagine the difficulty of completely describing the message contained in a single radiology film so that it will be understood.

Finally, action is a symbol that can be used to communicate. A friendly smile or a pat on the back has meaning. A promotion or a pay increase conveys a great deal to the recipient and to others. Furthermore, lack of action can have symbolic meaning in messages. Davis (28) notes that:

> Failure to act is an important way of communication. The manager has communicated when he fails to compliment someone for a job well done or fails to take a promised action. Since we communicate both by action and lack of action, we communicate almost all the time at work, whether we intend to or not. Being at one's desk has meaning, but being away also has meaning.
>
> SOURCE: K. Davis, *Human Behavior at Work: Human Relations and Organizational Behavior*, Copyright 1972, p. 391. Reprinted by permission of McGraw-Hill Book Company, New York, New York.

Action can reinforce and can also be a barrier to communication. When the action is inconsistent with the words, contradictory messages are transmitted. For example, the superior who tells a subordinate, "I have confidence in your ability, your performance is excellent, and I want to expand your duties by delegating more to you" would not be consistent by going into a rage because of a small technical error. Or the receiver who says "I am listening" to the sender and then proceeds to look impatient or start to walk away would construct a powerful action barrier to effective communication.

A lack of empathy can impair communication. Empathy means being sensitive to the world of other people in the communication relationship. Being sensitive to the other person's frame of reference or emotional state can promote better understanding. Empathy can help the sender decide how to encode the message and help the receiver interpret its meaning. For example, a subordinate who empathizes with the superior may discount an angry message because the subordinate is aware that extreme pressure and frustration have created the superior's present state of mind. If the receiver of the message empathizes with the sender, it will be interpreted in a much different way. Similarly, a sender sensitive to the receiver can decide whether or not to communicate and how to encode the message.

Managing Barriers to Communication

Awareness that these barriers exist certainly contribute to minimizing their impact, as do positive efforts to eliminate them. The net effect is more effective communication between sender and receiver. Although the steps necessary to improve communication flows, decrease distortion and filtering, and eliminate blockages depend on particular circumstances, several general guidelines are suggested:

MANAGERIAL GUIDELINES

1. The receiver and the sender should ensure that adequate attention is given to the message and that time is devoted to really "listening" to what is being communicated. Equally important, a conscious effort by the sender and receiver to understand the other's frame of reference and beliefs helps promote effective communication.

2. A management philosophy that encourages communication flow should be helpful. In addition, the less the number of links (levels in the organization hierarchy) through which messages must pass, the less the opportunity for distortion.

3. Conscious efforts to tailor terminology so that it is understandable are important. Cautious use of symbols and reinforcing words with consistent action also significantly improve communication.

4. Finally, the use of multiple channels to reinforce complex messages certainly increases the likelihood that understanding will occur.

FLOW OF INTRAORGANIZATIONAL COMMUNICATIONS

Within health care organizations (intraorganizational), a variety of channels and networks for communicating typically exist. The study of communication networks has been extensive. Scott (29) defines communication networks as "a system of decision centers interconnected by communication channels." Figure 7.4 illustrates the most common communication networks. Bavelas and Barrett (30) have demonstrated the relationships between three types of networks and organizational performance. Their results, which appear in Table 7.2, suggest that the most appropriate network varies with and is contingent upon the objectives of the communication being undertaken.

Communication flows in organizations in downward, upward, or horizontal directions, each with its own uses and characteristics. Typically, downward flow is communication between manager and subordinates; upward communication operates through the same channels but in the opposite direction. Horizontal flow is usually manager to manager or worker to worker. We will examine the specific nature of each.

Downward Flow

Objectives of downward communication flow, according to Katz and Kahn (31) are to:

1. Give specific task directives about job instructions.
2. Give information about organizational procedures and practices.

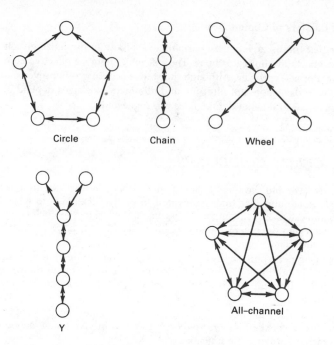

Figure 7.4. Common communication networks.

3. Provide information about the rationale of the job.
4. Tell subordinates about their performance.
5. Provide ideological information to facilitate the indoctrination of goals.

Downward communication flows through many channels. Most often it consists of information, verbal orders, or instructions from manager to subordinate on a one-to-one basis, but other channels include speeches to groups of employees or meetings. The myriad written methods such as handbooks, procedure manuals, newsletters, bulletin

TABLE 7.2. Sample of Results from Classic Network Studies

	Types of Networks		
	Circle	*Chain*	*Wheel*
Speed of performance	Slow	Fast	Fast
Accuracy	Poor	Good	Good
Emergence of leader	None	Marked	Very pronounced
Morale	Very good	Poor	Very poor
Flexibility to job change	Very fast	Slow	Slow

SOURCE: Bavelas, A., & Barrett, D. An experimental approach to organizational communication. *Personnel*, March 1951, *27*, 370. Reprinted, by permission of the publisher, from *Personnel*, March 1951 © 1951 American Management Association, New York. All rights reserved.

boards, and the ubiquitous memorandum are also channels of downward communication. Computerized information systems contribute substantially to downward flow in many health care organizations.

Upward Flow

Objectives of upward communication flow include providing managers with decision-making information, revelation of problem areas, data for performance evaluation, indicating the status of morale, and generally underscoring the thinking of subordinates in the organization. The upward flow becomes more important as organizational complexity and scale increase.

In addition to its direct usefulness to managers, the upward flow helps employees satisfy certain personal needs. It permits those in positions of lower authority to express opinions and perceptions to those in higher authority; as a result, they feel a stronger sense of participation. Of course, for upward communication to be effective, the fear of reprisal must be eliminated (32).

Several methods can be used for upward communication. The hierarchical structure is, of course, the main formal method used to communicate upward. However, Luthans (33) suggests the following supplementation:

1. *The grievance procedure.* Provided for in most collective bargaining agreements, the grievance procedure allows an employee to make an appeal upward beyond his immediate superior. It protects the individual from arbitrary action from his direct superior and encourages upward communication.

2. *The open-door policy.* Taken literally, this means that the superior's door is always open to subordinates. It is a continuous invitation for a subordinate to come in and talk about anything that is troubling him. Unfortunately, in practice the open-door policy is more fiction than fact. The boss may slap his subordinate on the back and say, "My door is always open to you," but in many cases both know the door is really closed. It is a case in which the adage that actions speak louder than words applies.

3. *Counseling, attitude questionnaires, and exit interviews.* The personnel department can greatly facilitate upward communication by conducting nondirective, confidential counseling sessions, periodically administering attitude questionnaires, and holding meaningful exit interviews for those who leave the organization. Much valuable information can be gained from these forms of upward communication.

4. *Participative techniques.* Participative-decision techniques can generate a great deal of upward communication. This may be accomplished by either informal involvement from subordinates or formal participation programs.

5. *The ombudsman.* A largely untried but potentially significant technique to enable management to obtain upward communication is the use of an ombudsman. The concept has been used primarily in Scandinavia to provide an outlet for persons who have been treated unfairly or in a depersonalized manner by large, bureaucratic government. It has more recently gained popularity in American state governments, military posts, and universities. (Health care organizations have applied this approach to improve communication between *patients* and the organization. If properly applied, it may very well work in the larger, more complex, and more depersonalized

health care organizations as they seek ways to improve upward communication flows from their employees.)*

Horizontal Flow

It is clearly recognized that effective downward and upward communication flows are not sufficient for effective organizational performance. In complex organizations, especially those subject to abrupt demands for action and reaction, there must also be an effective horizontal flow. Perhaps this is more true when care is being rendered to a specific patient by a variety of personnel from several different organizational units. Their actions must be coordinated in an atmosphere that often limits upward and downward communication flows in order to meet the needs of a specific patient. The concept of the hospital as a matrix organization, as described above as a coordination mechanism, illustrates this phenomenon.

The prevalence of committees in health care organizations can be attributed to the need for horizontal communication. Committees provide a mechanism for representatives of different organizational units to discuss common and potential problems face to face. Strict adherence to hierarchical communication flow would never permit this opportunity. As everyone who has been involved with committees realizes, there are some disadvantages to this form of horizontal communication. Committees tend to be time-consuming and expensive, and their decisions are often compromises that may represent an ineffectual solution. Nevertheless, it is important to note that committees are the main formal mechanism for horizontal communication flows in health care organizations.

Although horizontal communication flow has many positive uses (e.g., speed in an emergency or crisis situation), it presents the potential for causing problems. Hodgetts (34) has suggested two simple rules: obtain permission from the direct supervisor before undertaking the communication and inform the direct supervisor of any significant result of the cross-communication.

Informal Communication

Coexisting with formal communication flows is an informal communication flow. Sometimes this distinction is called "scheduled" and "unscheduled" (35). No matter what it is called, the informal flow of communication in organizations consists of channels and networks that result from the interpersonal relationships of organization participants.

Informal communication flows can be useful, if properly managed. When concerned with downward flow, the informal system tends to be much faster than the formal; for upward and horizontal flows, it is essential. In a health care organization, much of the coordination occurring between units does so through informal give-and-take information exchange. In the case of upward flow, informal communication can serve as a rich source of information about performance, ideas, feelings, and attitudes of people in the organization. Because of its potential usefulness, and its pervasiveness, managers should try to understand informal communication flows and use them to advantage.

---

* Source: F. Luthans, *Organizational Behavior: A Modern Behavioral Approach to Management*, Copyright 1973, p. 253. Reprinted by permission of McGraw-Hill Book Company, New York, New York.

SUMMARY OF INTRAORGANIZATIONAL COMMUNICATION FLOWS

In the case of intraorganizational communication, the degree of interdependence (pooled to sequential/reciprocal) coupled with the scale of operations (small to large) dictates the form of communication and the directions in which it flows to a large extent. For example, Table 7.3 illustrates a typology of communication patterns which can be developed under various mixes of interdependence and scale.

FLOW OF INTERORGANIZATIONAL COMMUNICATIONS

Health care organizations enter into a variety of linkages to manage their interdependencies. Similarly, they must develop communication flows with the organizations and agencies with which they share interdependencies. As Pfeffer and Salanick (22) have noted:

> Linkages arise when communication is most necessary between interdependent others. Linkages also serve as channels for persuasion and negotiation, and in these ways also stabilize interdependent relationships. By exchanging information about each other's activities, the organizations are in a position to plan more predictably. By obtaining commitments from each other, each organization develops certainty about the future course of exchange.
>
> SOURCE: Specified excerpt from *The External Control of Organizations: A Resource Dependence Perspective* by Jeffrey Pfeffer and Gerald R. Salancik. Copyright © 1978 by Jeffrey Pfeffer and Gerald R. Salancik. Reprinted by permission of Harper & Row, Publishers, Inc.

Effective interorganizational communication is complicated by the sheer number and variety of individuals and organizations with which communication is needed. If one considers a single organization and its relevant stakeholders—defined by Freeman (36) as "any group or individual who can affect or is affected by the achievement of an organization's purpose"—the communication demands can be enormous. Figure 7.5 illustrates this point. It is important to note in this stakeholder map that the arrows point

TABLE 7.3. A Typology of Communication Flows

	Scale of Operations	
Interdependence	Small	Large
Pooled	Few committees	Few committees
	Low-to-moderate volume of informal communication	Low volume of informal communication
	Multiple upward flows	Single upward flows
Sequential/reciprocal	Many committees	Many committees
	High volume of informal communication	Moderate volume of informal communication
	Upward and downward flows	Upward and some downward flows
	Few horizontal flows	
		Multiple horizontal flows

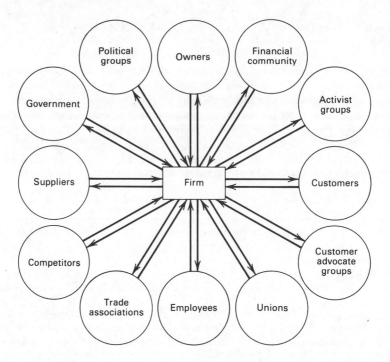

Figure 7.5. Stakeholder map of a very large organization. (From *Strategic Management: A Stakeholder Approach.* Copyright 1984 by R. Edward Freeman. Reprinted with permission from Ballinger Publishing Company.)

in both directions, suggesting that the focal organization is interested in stakeholders as well as the obvious interest (that is what makes them stakeholders) of the stakeholders in the focal organization. Managers in the interdependent organization must be concerned about communication flows to stakeholders *and* about flows from stakeholders. The reason for this concern is the interdependence of their organization with others. Managers cannot ignore interdependent others, nor can they be ignored by them.

Conceptually, the interdependencies can be managed in one of two ways: the focal organization can adapt itself to fit the requirements of interdependent others or it can alter the interdependent others so that they fit its capabilities. Obviously, in practice both occur and both are absolutely dependent upon effective communication. Unless what is expected from interdependent others is known and understood, effective adaptation cannot be made. Conversely, changing interdependent others requires effective communication. For example, as Kotler (37) has pointed out:

> Hospitals have to deal with several markets and publics, including patients, physicians, the general community, and volunteers and donors. A hospital needs to do research on these groups to learn their perceptions, needs, and preferences in order to prepare more effective services and communications. Newer types of health units, such as health maintenance organizations and neighborhood clinics, need to utilize marketing concepts to get established in communities and offer the services that are needed. Public health officials will find marketing analysis and planning of value in connection with appraising the health needs of

communities, improving the methods of delivering health-care services, raising money for health causes, and motivating people to more healthful behavior.

SOURCE: Kotler, P. *Marketing for Nonprofit Organizations*, Copyright 1975, p. 327. Reprinted by permission of Prentice-Hall, Inc., Englewood Cliffs, New Jersey.

Similarly, organizations can lobby or encourage associations to which they belong to lobby government to alter policies in favor of the focal organization. They can also lobby regulators to create more favorable environmental contexts. Lobbying is, at its heart, communication.

THE SPECIAL CASE OF COMMUNICATION AMONG UNITS OF SYSTEMS

Single health care organizations must be concerned with communication with the great variety of stakeholders relevant to them. Increasingly, health care organizations face an added challenge in the form of effective communication among organizations with which they share membership in a multiunit system. Systems of health care organizations have become prevalent through corporate restructuring (the creating of several related corporate entities to perform the various medical and nonmedical functions previously carried out by a single corporation—see Figure 7.6) and through active programs of merger

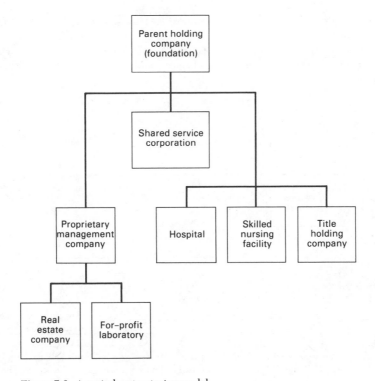

Figure 7.6. A typical restructuring model.

and consolidation within the health care industry. Figure 7.7 depicts a typical health care system developed in this way.

Achieving effective communication, and the more overarching task of effective coordination, across the various units of such systems is a demanding management task. Adapting Porter's (27) approach to achieving effective linkages among business units of a diversified corporation suggests several ways of managing the tasks of coordination and communication among units of a system:

- *Horizontal structure.* Organizational devices that cut across unit lines, such as partial centralization and interunit task forces or committees that facilitate communication.
- *Horizontal systems.* Management systems with a cross-unit dimension, in areas such as planning, control, incentives, capital budgeting, and management information systems.
- *Horizontal human resource practices.* Human resource practices that facilitate unit cooperation, such as cross-unit job rotation, management forums, and training.
- *Horizontal conflict resolution processes.* Management processes that resolve conflicts among units. Such processes can be usefully distinguished from horizontal structure and systems, and relate more to the style of managing an organization. The key is for senior management to install and operate a system that is fair in settling disputes among units.

Within such systems that have different boards for some or all of the units, effective communication is particularly important. The most effective mechanism in this situation may well be interlocking boards, because this provides the means through which a stable structure of coordinated activity and communication flow can be established and maintained.

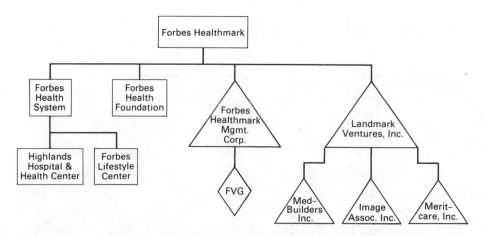

Figure 7.7. Forbes Healthmark Corporation organization chart. FVG-Forbes Vantage Group, Inc. (Courtesy, George H. Schmitt, President, Forbes Healthmark Corporation, Pittsburgh, PA.)

SUMMARY

This chapter has covered the coordination and communication mechanisms through which managers in health care organizations link together the various people and units within their organizations (intraorganizational coordination and communication) and link their organizations to others (interorganizational coordination and communication). These dual managerial tasks are vitally important in health care organizations; if these tasks are not carried out effectively, organizations may become fragmented, fractionated, and isolated, with resulting declines in performance.

Coordination is defined as *conscious activity aimed at achieving unity and harmony of effort in pursuit of shared objective within an organization or among a set of organizations participating in a multi-institutional arrangement of some kind.*

A number of mechanisms available to the manager to ensure effective intraorganizational coordination provide the manager with options that may be selected contingent upon particular needs and circumstances. These options include Litterer's hierarchy, administrative system, and voluntary activities as approaches to coordination. They also include Mintzberg's mutual adjustment, direct supervision, and standardization of work process, output, and worker skills. Other mechanisms include Hage's typology of programming, planning, customs, and feedback as well as committees, project management, matrix organization, integrators, linking pins, and quality circles.

Similarly, a number of mechanisms are available for addressing the need to manage interdependencies with other health care organizations or with other elements in the external environments of health care organizations. These interorganizational mechanisms of coordination include Thompson's contracting, coopting, and coalescing and Starkweather and Cook's addition to this typology, consumption.

Communication, whether it is intra- or interorganizational in nature, is defined as *the creation or exchange of understanding between sender and receiver(s).*

The technical mechanism of communication is described in Figure 7.3. Particular attention is given to means of overcoming environmental and personal barriers to effective communication.

Within health care organizations, intraorganizational communication flows in downward, upward, or horizontal directions, each with its own uses and characteristics. Coexisting with formal communication flows is an informal flow which consists of channels and networks that arise from the interpersonal relationships of organization participants.

As with interorganizational mechanisms of coordination, health care organizations must develop interorganizational communication flows with the organizations and agencies with which they share interdependencies. The need for effective interorganizational communication is especially acute among units of integrated systems.

DISCUSSION QUESTIONS

1. Distinguish between intra- and interorganizational coordination in health care organizations. What are the key mechanisms available to managers to achieve each type of coordination?
2. Define communication and draw a model of the basic technical process. How can managers overcome the barriers to effective communication?

3. You have just been appointed manager of a joint venture between the hospital where you work and some members of its medical staff to operate an ambulatory surgery facility. One of your initial concerns is the establishment of effective linkages to the hospital. Drawing upon the material in this chapter, develop your approach to this task and indicate the reasons for your plan.

4. Discuss the reasons for the location of the various intraorganizational coordination mechanisms as shown in Table 7.1. Do the same thing for the typology of communication shown in Table 7.3.

SUGGESTED READINGS

Hage, J. *Theories of organizations: Forms, processes and transformations.* New York: Wiley-Interscience, 1980.
A very advanced text, which synthesizes much of the literature on organization theory.

Mintzberg, H. *Structure in fives: Designing effective organizations.* Englewood Cliffs, NJ: Prentice-Hall, Inc., 1983.
A good overview of organization design, with considerable attention to ensuring effective coordination.

Pfeffer, J., & Salancik, G. R. *The external control of organizations.* New York: Harper & Row, 1978.
An excellent treatment of the interdependencies of organizations with managerial strategies for addressing them.

Van de Ven, A., Delbecq, A., & Koenig, R. Jr. Determinants of coordination modes within organizations. *American Sociological Review,* 1976, *41,* 322–338.
A highly readable and important study of work groups and effective means of coordination within them.

Weisbrod, M. R. Why organization development hasn't worked (so far) in medical centers. *Health Care Management Review,* 1976, *1,* 17–28.
A view of the interdependence among tasks in a health care delivery organization, and the implications for management and governance.

REFERENCES

1. Thompson, J. D. *Organizations in action.* New York: McGraw Hill, 1967.
2. Bolman, L. G., & Deal, T. E. *Modern approaches to understanding and managing organizations.* San Francisco: Jossey-Bass Publishers, 1984.
3. Rakich, J. S., Longest, B. B., Jr., & Darr, K. *Managing health services organizations* (2nd ed.). Philadelphia: W. B. Saunders Company, 1985, p. 370.
4. Haimann, T., & Scott, W. G. *Management in the modern organization,* 2nd ed. Boston: Houghton Mifflin Company, 1974, p. 126.
5. Lawrence, P. R., & Lorsch, J. W. Differentiation and integration in complex organizations. *Administrative Science Quarterly,* June 1967, *11*(3), 1–47.
6. Scott, W. R. Managing professional work: Three models of control for health organizations. *Health Services Research,* Fall 1982, *17*(3), 213–240.

7. Kast, F. E., & Rosenzweig, J. E. *Organization and management: A systems approach* (2nd ed.). New York: McGraw-Hill, 1974, p. 214.

8. Litterer, J. A. *The analysis of organizations.* New York: John Wiley & Sons, 1965, pp. 223–232.

9. Georgopoulos, B. S., & Mann, F. C. The hospital as an organization. *Hospital Administration*, Fall 1962, 57–58.

10. Mintzberg, H. *Structure in fives: Designing effective organizations.* Englewood Cliffs, NJ: Prentice-Hall, Inc., 1983.

11. Hage, J. *Theories of organizations: Forms, processes, and transformations.* New York: Wiley-Interscience, 1980. This section is adapted from Hage's treatment of this topic in the first edition of Shortell, S. M., & Kaluzny, A. D. *Health care management: A text in organization theory and behavior.* New York: John Wiley & Sons, 1983, pp. 241–243.

12. March, J., & Simon, H. *Organizations.* New York: John Wiley & Sons, 1958.

13. Thompson, J. *Organizations in action.* New York: McGraw-Hill, 1967.

14. Perrow, C. A framework for the comparative analysis of organization. *American Sociological Review*, 1967, *32*, 194–208.

15. Van de Ven, A., Delbecq, A., & Koenig, R., Jr. Determinants of coordination modes within organizations. *American Sociological Review*, 1976, *41*, 322–338.

16. Longest, B. B., Jr. *Management practices for the health professional* (3rd ed.). Reston, VA: Reston Publishing Company, 1984, pp. 58–74.

17. Cleland, D. I., & King, W. R. *Systems analysis and project management* (3rd ed.). New York: McGraw-Hill, 1983.

18. Neuhauser, D. The hospital as a matrix organization. In A. R. Kovner and D. Neuhauser (Eds.), *Health services management: Readings and commentary* (2nd ed.). Ann Arbor: Health Administration Press, 1983.

19. Likert, R. *The human organization.* New York: McGraw-Hill, 1967. pp. 156, 167.

20. Ingle, S., & Ingle, N. *Quality circles in service industries.* Englewood Cliffs, NJ: Prentice-Hall, Inc., 1983.

21. American Hospital Association. *Hospitals*, October 1, 1982, *50*(19), 72.

22. Pfeffer, J., & Salanick, G. R. *The external control of organizations: A resource dependence perspective.* New York: Harper & Row, 1978, pp. 146–147.

23. Thompson, J. D. *Organizations in action.* New York: McGraw-Hill, 1967.

24. Starkweather, D. B. *Hospital mergers in the making.* Ann Arbor, MI: Health Administration Press, 1981.

25. Starkweather, D. B. Trends and types of multi-hospital arrangements, Part I. Technical Assistance Memorandum, No. 56. San Francisco: Western Center for Health Planning, 1980.

26. Shortell, S. M., Wickizer, T. M., & Wheeler, J. R. C. *Hospital—Physician joint ventures.* Ann Arbor, MI: Health Administration Press, 1984, p. 327.

27. Porter, M. E. *Competitive advantage: Creating and sustaining superior performance.* New York: The Free Press, 1985.

28. Davis, K. *Human behavior at work: Human relations and organizational behavior.* New York: McGraw-Hill, 1972, p. 391.

29. Scott, W. G. *Organization theory.* Homewood, IL: Richard D. Irwin, Inc., 1967, p. 165.

30. Bavelas, A., & Barrett, D. An experimental approach to organizational communication. *Personnel,* March 1951, *27,* 370.

31. Katz, D., & Kahn, R. L. *The social psychology of organizations.* New York: John Wiley & Sons, 1966, p. 239.

32. Wendlinger, R. M. Improving upward communication. *Journal of Business Communication,* Summer 1974, *10,* 17.

33. Luthans, F. *Organizational behavior: A modern behavioral approach to management.* New York: McGraw-Hill, 1973, p. 253.

34. Hodgetts, R. M. *Modern human relations.* Hinsdale, IL: Dryden Press, 1980, p. 311; and Hodgetts, R. M., & Cascio, D. M. *Modern health care administration.* New York: Academic Press, 1983, p. 215.

35. Hage, J. *Communication and control: Cybernetics in health and welfare settings.* New York: Wiley-Interscience, 1974.

36. Freeman, R. E. *Strategic management: A stakeholder approach.* Boston, MA: Pitman Publishing, Inc., 1984, p. 53.

37. Kotler, P. *Marketing for nonprofit organizations.* Englewood Cliffs, NJ: Prentice-Hall, Inc., 1975, p. 327.

CHAPTER 8

Authority, Power, and Influence

Laura L. Morlock
Constance A. Nathanson
Jeffrey A. Alexander

The past decade has witnessed significant advances in technology, rapid changes in the legal and regulatory climate, increasing competition for resources and patients, and an unprecedented increase in the number of multi-institutional systems and other complex organizational arrangements. Health care institutions are the focus of simultaneous pressures for cost containment, enhanced accessibility, and better quality control. All of these factors have generated difficult and often contradictory demands that raise critical questions about the viability of traditional authority, power, and influence relationships within health care organizations.

The governing board, for example, has traditionally been responsible for the fiscal viability of the hospital, but the increasing role of third-party payers, as well as rate setting, planning, and other regulatory agencies, has eroded the governing board's autonomy and authority to make many fiscal decisions. In addition, although the governing board and hospital management are responsible for protecting the hospital's fiscal status, it is the medical staff who largely influences hospital costs through decisions on patient admissions, the ordering of diagnostic and therapeutic procedures, and the determination of length of stay. Similarly, although it is the medical staff that makes most of the critical decisions about patient care, a decade of court decisions has made it clear that it is trustees who bear the ultimate responsibility for the quality of care delivered within the institution. Clearly, recent developments have made inoperable the traditional distinctions between clinical and administrative influence domains (1). Rapid increases in the number and size of both multihospital arrangements and vertically integrated health care systems also have raised significant questions about how policy decisions are made and resources are allocated within these increasingly complex organizational networks.

Concern over authority and power relationships in health care organizations is not a recent phenomenon. It has been noted that George Washington, after a hospital inspection, reported that he had found "no principal director and no subordination among the surgeons" (2). This situation, he believed, led to disputes that would continue until the development of some more formalized system. At least until recently, many have argued that this criticism is still valid for a number of contemporary hospitals. The key to better performance, these analysts suggest, lies in the development of more successful formal mechanisms for joint decision making and conflict resolution among managers, trustees, and medical staff (3–9). This strategy requires, however, a sophisticated understanding of power relationships and influence systems within organizations, as well as a better awareness among managers of how authority and other types of power can be used constructively (10–16).

In this chapter we first consider the alternative types of power available to organizational participants, and then examine how various sources of power are converted into influence over organizational decisions and activities. Next we discuss in more detail the major groups with power and influence in health care institutions, as well as some of the major factors that are changing the distribution of power and patterns of influence among these groups. In addition, we summarize findings from comparative research studies that have examined the impact of variation in power and influence on the quality of services provided by health care organizations. In general we argue that owing to a variety of factors, governing boards and health care managers are becoming more influential in health services organizations, and that an increasingly important key to organizational viability will be the development of more successful methods of integrating formal authority and influence based on clinical expertise.

DEFINITIONS OF INFLUENCE, POWER, AND AUTHORITY

The terms "influence," "power," and "authority" have been used in a variety of ways within the literature on organizations and management. Although there are no universally agreed-upon definitions, the term *influence* has been used most often to indicate actions that, either directly or indirectly, cause a change in the behavior and/or attitudes of another individual or group.

Power has been defined traditionally as the ability (or potential) to exert influence. Max Weber (17), in a classic essay, described power as "the probability that one actor within a social relationship will be in a position to carry out his own will despite resistance, regardless of the basis on which this probability rests." To have power, in other words, is to be able to change the behavior or attitudes of other persons or groups.* But power may or may not be activated within any given situation, because converting power into influence usually requires the expenditure of time, energy, or other resources, and also may demand the utilization of interpersonal and/or political skills.‡

There are a number of well-recognized sources of power, or power bases, within organizations. One such source is *authority,* defined as legitimate or formally constituted power. Individuals or groups with authority are recognized as having the right, based

---

Control sometimes is used in a manner essentially synonymous with this definition of power, particularly in organizational studies modeled after the early work by Tannenbaum and his colleagues (18).

‡Some contemporary management theorists such as Mintzberg (19), Kanter (20) and McCall (21) believe that this distinction is largely of theoretical interest with little practical import, and utilize the two terms interchangeably. We have found the distinction useful, however, in trying to understand the influence of various groups over different types of decisions in comparative studies of health care organizations.

on their formal position, of exercising influence within certain limits. Organizational power bases are discussed in more detail in the following section.

SOURCES OF POWER

Power, as we have noted, may be a function of an individual's position within the formal organizational hierarchy. In addition, there are a number of other sources or bases of power, each of which may occur at least to some degree, at any level of the organization (19, 22). *Formal power,* or *authority,* is based on the acknowledgment that an individual or group has the legal or moral "right" to exert influence within established limits. It is also implied that others within the organization or system have the obligation to accept this form of power. Authority can be delegated. A hospital security guard, for example, may have the delegated authority to require even the chairman of the board of trustees to present an identification card before entering the building. There are two major perspectives on the origin of legitimate power or authority within organizations (23). The classical view is based on the belief that authority originates at some high level of the system and is then passed down to lower levels. The highest level of authority within this perspective may be God, the constitution or head of a nation-state, or the collective will of the people (24, 25). A second perspective on the origin of formal authority is the acceptance view, which argues that it is subordinates or other receivers of influence attempts who define such attempts as authoritative or illegitimate and who make decisions regarding compliance. Regardless of which perspective is adopted, it is often noted that most formal authority is accepted by organizational members if attempts to exert influence from this power base are perceived as falling within certain limits. These boundaries define what Chester Barnard (26) described as "zones of indifference" and what Herbert Simon (27) referred to as "areas of acceptance."

Control over a critical resource is a second type of power base. To serve as a source of power the resource must have three characteristics: (1) it must be essential to the functioning of the organization; (2) it must be in short supply, or concentrated in terms of the number of people who possess it; and (3) it must be nonsubstitutable. These three attributes make the resource critical and create organizational dependency on those individuals or groups who control its availability (19).

Expert power is based on a claim to special knowledge or skills that are critical to the organization. The primary power base of the hospital medical staff, for example, usually is perceived to be its possession of specialized knowledge and technical skills. More recently it has been recognized that the expertise required to deal effectively with the increasing financial and legal complexities of hospital management is itself a source of expert power (15, 28).

Charismatic or referent power is based on the ability to inspire in others the desire to identify with or imitate the influencer. The strength of referent power is a function of such factors as the amount of prestige and admiration conferred by others upon the individual or group. One frequently cited study of supervisory influence and work group performance in a manufacturing setting (29) found that referent power was the most effective, and formal power or authority the least effective, basis for affecting work group behavior. Referent power, however, may be the most difficult to delegate or transfer; thus systems of influence based on referent or charismatic power tend to be less stable over time than systems based on other power sources (17, 30).

Although these four power bases are likely to be the most important in health services organizations, there may be other sources of power as well. Mintzberg (19) argues that personal access, or control over access, to those who rely on the other bases of power should be viewed as an important source of power in its own right. In his view, access may be the result of close personal or professional relationships, or may derive from favors traded. In the latter case, power results not from the dependency of others, but rather from reciprocity—gaining power in one area by giving up power in another. Other frequently cited typologies of power (22, 31) regard the ability to offer rewards and the ability to apply negative sanctions as two separate sources of power. It also could be reasoned, however, that rewards and sanctions should be considered part of the conversion of power into influence: they are utilized formally by those with authority, and applied informally (i.e., outside the formal authority structure) by those who control critical resources, or who have expertise or referent power.

Within most health care organizations each of these power bases is at least potentially present in a manager's position. A specific degree of formal power, for example, usually accompanies a manager's job, and it shapes the hierarchical relationships within which other forms of power can be converted into influence. The structure of authority relationships is discussed in more detail in the next section.

We have emphasized, however, that these are potential sources of power only. Access to one or even all of them does not guarantee the ability to influence particular individuals or groups in specific ways. A manager may be widely respected and admired as an expert but still may be unable to influence his or her immediate staff to be more creative in their jobs or even to get to work on time (23). Thus the role of others in rejecting or accepting an influence attempt remains a key one.

This acceptance, as we have noted, is partly a function of the manager's political skill, which means, according to Mintzberg:

> . . . the ability to use the bases of power effectively—to convince those to whom one has access, to use one's resources, information, and technical skills to their fullest in bargaining, to exercise formal power with a sensitivity to the feelings of others, to know where to concentrate one's energies, to sense what is possible, to organize the necessary alliances. (19, p. 26)

Distinguishing among the different sources of power is also an important characteristic of managers who are successful at translating power into influence. One study that examined the use of power and organizational effectiveness concluded that effective managers are sensitive to the source of their power and are careful to keep their actions consistent with others' expectations. Successful managers, for example, did not try to influence actions in areas outside the field in which they were regarded as having expert power. The study also concluded that effective managers understand—at least intuitively—the costs, risks, and benefits of using each kind of power and are able to recognize which to draw on in different situations and with different people (1, 2, 8, 32).

The requirement that successful influence attempts usually involve not only political skill, but also the expenditure of time and energy, has at least two consequences. First, those who would be influential often must target their energies toward the issues most important to them and be willing to defer in other areas. Second, even those individuals without a significant power base can sometimes gain influence by investing considerable time in committee work and other aspects of the decision-making process. As a result, in many organizations influence becomes dispersed more widely than our discussion of power bases might indicate.

SYSTEMS OF INFLUENCE

In this section we examine the means through which power is converted into influence over decisions and activities. Following Mintzberg (19), we distinguish among four different systems of influence which operate simultaneously and are present to at least some degree in most organizations:

- The *system of authority*, including both personal and bureaucratic controls, in which individuals participate as "superiors" and "subordinates."
- The *system of ideology*, in which individuals participate as organizational "members."
- The *system of expertise*, in which participation is based on level of knowledge and skills critical to the organization.
- The *system of politics*, in which individuals and groups participate as "players" in one or more political games.

First, the major characteristics of each of these influence systems are discussed, followed by a consideration of how the systems may be interrelated in different types of organizations.

THE SYSTEM OF AUTHORITY

The authority system is the organization's formal structure of control over individual performance. Authority (also called legitimate or formal power) is a function of the location of a position within the hierarchical control structure. The underlying principle is that work involved in accomplishing an organization's mission usually must be divided into a series of tasks (the division of labor). These are assigned to specific positions which are then grouped together into various units. Coordination of activities is achieved through a formal hierarchy of positions—sometimes referred to as the "scalar chain of command"— with each position under the control of a higher one (17).

Types of Authority

Some management writers distinguish between two types of formal power—line authority and staff authority.* Line activities are those that are central to the achievement of organizational goals. *Line authority* denotes the right to require compliance from subordinates on the basis of one's position within the line or chain of command "that starts with the board of directors and extends down through the various levels in the hierarchy to the point where the basic activities of the organization are carried out" (23).

In contrast, the organizational staff members are those individuals or groups whose main functions are to provide service, advice, or counsel to the line or those who perform an auditing or monitoring function. *Staff authority* refers to relationships in which the occupant of one position can advise or counsel but not exercise direct command over another. Staff positions, in other words, have at their disposal expert power rather than the formal authority, reward, and coercive power available to line positions.

---

*Some management theorists, such as Fisch (33), Sayles (34), and Nossiter (35) believe that for many contemporary organizations the line/staff distinction has limited usefulness.

In practice, staff service and advisory roles may have considerable potential for informal reward and coercive power, because effective or timely performance often can either be provided or withheld (23). In addition, staff departments, particularly those responsible for audit or monitoring functions, may in reality have formal authority over line members within the limits of their staff functions.

This right to control the activities of other individuals or groups, but only as these activities relate to specific staff responsibilities, is usually called *functional authority*. Such authority may also be referred to as a "dotted line relationship," reflecting the custom of indicating such relationships on organizational charts with a dotted line in order to distinguish them from the solid lines depicting formal line authority.

Converting Authority Into Influence

Individuals with authority attempt to influence behavior through both personal and bureaucratic controls (19). Personal controls involve the direct supervision of subordinates by managers within the chain of authority. These personal controls may involve the giving of direct orders, the setting of decision premises, the reviewing of a subordinate's decisions, or the allocating of resources (e.g., approval of annual budgets) that set constraints on decisions and activities.

The bureaucratic control system includes the establishment of impersonal standards that guide decisions and activities of all organizational participants. Standards may be established for the content of work performed by formalizing job descriptions, rules, and regulations. Alternatively, standards may be set with respect to goals which must be achieved, allowing subordinates flexibility in determining how to accomplish desired outcomes (36). At least in theory, these personal and bureaucratic controls are reinforced by the organization's formal system of rewards and sanctions.

Designing the Authority Structure

Within classical management theory there are several guidelines for the establishment of authority relationships. One guideline, the *scalar principle*, states that there must be a clear line of authority running step by step from the highest to the lowest level of the organization. This clear line of authority indicates to whom each individual is accountable. The *unity of command* principle states that each individual in the organization should report to only one superior.

It is becoming increasingly common, however, for the structural design of organizations to violate these classical guidelines explicitly. Functional authority relationships often involve auditing or quality control functions that exist outside the framework of line responsibilities and authority. "Dual boss" arrangements are also present in matrix organizations (see Chapter 9). A matrix design usually includes two types of managers— directors of functional areas, such as medicine, nursing, and pediatrics, within a general hospital; and directors of project or program areas, such as emergency medicine, and primary care services. Both types of managers exercise authority over the same organizational members, with the functional managers primarily responsible for the maintenance and continued development of technical expertise and the program or project managers responsible for ensuring coordination and the timely delivery of services. The matrix organization is designed to include both a dual authority system and a balance of power between managers responsible for technical standards and those responsible for maintaining an adequate work flow (34, 37). Although a matrix design facilitates coordination across functional or disciplinary areas and rapid response to environmental changes, it has often been noted that its disadvantages stem largely from its explicit violation of the classical principle of unity of command (23). These disadvantages include ambiguity and conflict. There also may be additional costs resulting from the necessity for dual reporting systems.

The extent to which decision making authority should be centralized, or concentrated among a relatively few positions at the top of the administrative hierarchy, is also a critical issue in the design of the authority system. A large number of research studies have examined both the characteristics of organizations that have relatively more centralized or decentralized authority structures and the effects of degree of decentralization on employees. These studies have found that, in general, less hierarchical and more participatory authority structures tend to be found in organizations with greater task complexity and higher skill levels among employees (38). Several studies also have concluded that more decentralized organizations, which involve many participants in important decisions, tend to have employees with "less alienation from work, less dissatisfaction with work, greater satisfaction with supervision, increased performance . . . and greater communication frequency among co-workers at the same level in the organization" (39).

A number of management writers (23, 39, 40) have concluded, however, that many factors are likely to affect the desirability of decentralized decision making, including influences from the environment, particularly market characteristics and competitive pressures; size and growth rate of the organization; and other organizational characteristics, such as the costliness of given decisions, top management preferences, and the abilities of lower level participants. A review of organizational trends indicates that on balance decentralization probably increased during the period of great economic growth in American industry from the end of World War II to the early 1970s. Economic pressures during the 1970s, however, led many organizations to look for ways to avoid costly duplication of functions and probably encouraged greater recentralization of authority. However, higher education levels among organization members, increased desire for worker autonomy and participation, and a growing reluctance to simply accept established authority are all trends that, if they continue can be expected to exert greater pressures on top management for more decision-making authority at lower organizational levels (23).

The Organization as a "Rational Actor"

Viewing influence processes in organizations primarily in terms of the system of authority is characteristic of "rational actor" models of organizational behavior. Early organizational theorists and management writers in the classical tradition believed that the most efficient and effective organizations have a hierarchical structure based on legitimate authority (17). The management guidelines derived from their theories were based on the assumption that the components of an organization should be and can be "deliberately chosen for their necessary contribution to a goal, and the structures established . . . those deliberately intended to attain highest efficiency" in pursuit of that goal (41).

Some of the limitations of this approach are outlined in the discussion of "closed-system rational models" in Chapter 1. We would emphasize that although these assumptions may be valid for some organizations, there are many others in which the governing board and senior management are less able to express clear, unconflicting formal goals and objectives capable of being operationalized through the formal structure and control systems. This may be due to the nature of the organization's mission, the type of work performed, or a variety of other factors. In addition, in confining our attention to the system of authority, we lose sight of sources of power in the organization that form the basis for influencing behavior outside of the formal hierarchical structure. These influence systems are discussed in the following sections.

THE SYSTEM OF IDEOLOGY

The organization's ideology is a system of shared beliefs about the organization that make it unique or at least distinctive to its members. Typically the ideology (sometimes referred to as organizational culture) includes a shared sense of the organization's mission and history, as well as a set of established traditions, that invoke a sense of loyalty and "esprit de corps" among participants. Organizations that develop strong, well-established ideologies over time may evolve into "institutions"—they become valued for themselves in addition to the goods or services they provide (42, 43).

Individual identification with, or loyalty to, the organization may develop through a number of pathways: (1) through the natural attraction to the organization of individuals with compatible personal objectives; (2) as a result of selection procedures for new members; (3) through organizational attempts at socialization and indoctrination; and/ or (4) through the calculated cultivation of loyalty by individuals who want to succeed within the organization (19).

Individuals may identify with the organizational leadership (who may come to embody the organizational ideology), with the mission or goals, or with the organization itself (44). If primary loyalty is to the organization itself, participants may be likely to accept changes in goals, or even in the underlying mission, in order to insure organizational survival or growth (44).

The basis for influencing behavior within the system of ideology is the charismatic or referent power of current leadership, and/or the organization's founders or key leaders in the past. We would argue that this type of power also must underlie successful attempts to change key aspects of the ideological system, such as a major change in mission.

A strong system of ideology has a unifying and leveling effect on individuals who participate as organizational members. As Mintzberg (19) has noted, when individuals identify strongly with organizational goals, formal means of controlling behavior are less necessary. In addition, if everyone shares the same set of beliefs, there is the sense that anyone can participate in important decision making. Both of these tendencies in a strong system of ideology serve to weaken the need for a strong hierarchical system of authority.

THE SYSTEM OF EXPERTISE

An influence system based on expertise develops in organizations where work to be accomplished is complex enough that key participants must include technical experts or professionals who have received considerable training outside the work setting. Complex work, such as performing an operation or treating a cancer patient, cannot easily be understood or controlled by those who have not been trained to do it. In organizations such as hospitals, universities, or aerospace firms, where critical activities are performed by highly trained professionals, personal and bureaucratic controls available within the hierarchical control system are not sufficient to provide adequate work standards or to coordinate professional activities. At least in theory, work standards, rather than being imposed from without, are to a large extent internalized as the result of a long period of technical training and socialization into the canons of professional work.

The relatively routine activities of different professionals are coordinated to some degree by this standardization of skills (36). An oft-cited example is the surgeon who easily coordinates activities with the anesthesiologist during a long complex operation primarily because each knows what to expect of the other (45). When professionals must combine their expertise in nonroutine, innovative ways, they usually work in small groups—teams, task forces, or committees—where they coordinate activities informally (i.e., outside a formal chain of command) through more reciprocal influence processes which emphasize interpersonal consultation and mutual adjustment among colleagues.

The system of influence based on expertise is in many respects incompatible with the system of authority. As Mintzberg states:

> When an organization has to grant considerable discretion in the performance of its work to experts or professionals—whether they work autonomously or in small groups—and has to surrender power over their selection and training to professional institutions, its System of Authority is significantly weakened. In other words, power resides less in the formal systems of the administrators . . . and more in the informal bases of influence of the specialists—in expertise based on specialized knowledge and skills. (19, p. 165)

The amount of influence exercised by professionals is likely to be directly correlated with the degree to which their expertise is critical (i.e., essential, in short supply, and nonsubstitutable) to the organization. It must be noted, however, that expertise is unlikely to be a stable base of power for specific individuals and groups because what is critical to the organization is likely to change over time as environmental demands, technology, and other factors create new types of pressures.

The system of expertise, like the system of authority, serves to coordinate work activities in the organization. Unlike the systems of influence based on authority or ideology, in many respects it is not a unifying force. The essense of expertise is the differentiation of power based on specialized capability. Status hierarchies are created—between experts and nonexperts, among different kinds of experts according to the complexity of their specialty and the degree to which it is critical to the organization, and among experts in the same speciality according to their personal skills (19). Furthermore, as new professionals enter the organization and older ones age, these status hierarchies must undergo change. In addition, bodies of expertise often overlap, creating areas of conflict as professionals compete in those areas for influence over activities. These conflicts can be resolved through the authority system if it is strong. As we have noted, however, organizations with strong influence systems based on expertise have traditionally had weak authority structures. For this reason, conflicts often are played out through the system of political influence, to which we now turn.

THE SYSTEM OF POLITICS

The political system is the arena in which participants attempt to influence organizational decisions and activities in ways that are informal and illegitimate in the sense that they are sanctioned neither by formal authority, accepted ideology, or certified expertise (19). Mintzberg argues (19, pp. 173–174) that a system of influence based on politics arises when there are problems or gaps in the other three systems of influence and when there are important needs among organizational participants that are not fulfilled by these systems. The problems or gaps create areas of discretion in organizational activities, and participants with unsatisfied needs attempt to exploit that discretion. The system of politics that results may operate alongside the other influence systems, or it may displace parts of them.

Why Systems of Politics Arise

Frequently political systems of influence arise because of common problems in the system of authority. First, although one important function of the formal control system is to articulate and operationalize organizational goals in order to prioritize and direct activities, many goals are operationalized imperfectly, and some (e.g., quality of medical care and of the educational experience) are difficult to operationalize at all. In addition, most organizations have multiple goals, such as providing high-quality, accessible care and maintaining financial viability. But organizational participants are rarely provided with a means to weigh the importance of different goals in order to direct their activities. The ambiguity in how to operationalize and prioritize organizational objectives creates an arena for potential conflict among even the most dedicated, well-intentioned participants. Second, problems and gaps in the authority system arise because of the division of labor and the assignment of different tasks, and sometimes different organizational goals, to different units. The tendency is for each unit or subgroup to emphasize the importance of its own activities, and sometimes to treat its own tasks as ends in themselves. Group pressures may develop, and "we–they" relationships emerge. These types of organizational factors, as well as the unsatisfied intrinsic needs of participants, generate attempts to influence decisions and activities outside of formal and legitimate channels.

The Political Games

The political influence system has been described as a set of "games," each with its own structure and rules that are "played" outside of the legitimate influence systems. These games are structured in the sense that they have established positions, paths through which individuals gain access to positions, and rules that constrict the range of decisions and actions that are acceptable (19, 46). The most common games and the reasons they are played are listed in Table 8.1.

The *insurgency games* are usually played to resist authority, or as a means to effect or prevent change in the organization. Frequently they are played at the point where decisions made at upper levels of the authority hierarchy have to be implemented. They may be played by lower-level participants who attempt to circumvent, sabotage, or manipulate elements of the authority system. They often are played by managers who distort or limit the amount of information sent to superiors in the authority structure. They can be played subtly by individuals or small groups, or aggressively by a large number of participants willing to take unified, visible action.

The insurgency games are sometimes met by attempting to increase authority—that is, by tightening personal and bureaucratic controls and administering sanctions. They also may be countered in a retrospective or prospective fashion by the *counterinsurgency games*. The most frequent are limiting the amount of information available to subordinates, fostering competition among subordinates to maintain control, and various forms of cooptation.

TABLE 8.1. Common Political Games

Games to resist authority	The insurgency games
Games to counter the resistance to authority	The counterinsurgency games
Games to build power bases	The sponsorship game (with superiors)
	The alliance-building game (with peers)
	The empire-building game (with subordinates)
	The budgeting game (with resources)
	The expertise games (with knowledge and skills)
	The lording game (with authority)
Games to defeat rivals	The line versus staff game
	The rival camps game
Games to effect organizational change	The strategic candidates game
	The whistle-blowing game
	The young Turks games

SOURCE: Henry Mintzberg, *Power in and around organizations*, © 1983, p. 188. Reprinted by permission of Prentice-Hall, Inc., Englewood Cliffs, New Jersey.

There are a variety of political *games played to build power bases*. *Sponsorship games* have simple rules: "The individual attaches himself or herself to a rising star—or one already in place—and professes loyalty in return for a 'piece of the action' " (19). The *alliance-building game* is played by individuals or groups who negotiate with their peers implicit contracts of support for each other. The *empire-building game* is played by individuals to enlarge their power base by collecting subunits and/or loyal subordinates. Kanter, in her study *Men and Women of the Corporation,* found that individuals who wanted to have significant influence in the organization had to play at least one of these three games: "People without sponsors, without peer connections, or without promising subordinates remained in the situation of bureaucratic dependency." (20, p. 188)

Budgeting games are used to acquire more resources for the positions or units the individual already has under his or her control. They are the best known of the political games, probably because they are the most visible and have the most well-defined rules. With respect to operating budgets, a variety of strategies are used to gain the largest possible allocation (e.g., always requesting more than required in the knowledge that a given percentage will be cut in the final negotiations). In the case of capital budgets, typically methods are found to underestimate costs and overestimate benefits.

Professionals may play a variety of games in which their *expertise* is exploited as a political means of influence. These games are played offensively by emphasizing the uniqueness and importance of their skills and knowledge, and defensively by both limiting the access of others to their expertise and discouraging attempts on the part of managers and others to rationalize or routinize it (i.e., to disaggregate it into easily learned steps). The *lording games* involve the utilization of legitimate authority or certified expertise for illegitimate, usually personal, reasons.

Games to defeat rivals, such as the *line–staff* or *rival-camps games* are zero-sum struggles for control over organizational decisions, resources, and/or activities by weakening, or sometimes eliminating, competitors.

The *strategic-candidates game* is the most common of the *games played to effect organizational change.* An individual or group seeks a strategic change by promoting through the legitimate systems of influence its own project, proposal, or person as a "strategic candidate." The decision-making process involving strategic (nonroutine) decisions often is relatively unstructured, thus inviting political influence attempts. Furthermore, power within the organization frequently is redistributed during periods of strategic change, usually in favor of those who initially proposed and fought for it. Although "strategic candidates" in this game are promoted through the legitimate channels of influence, it is important to note that they are supported, at least in part, for nonlegitimate reasons (e.g., in order to defeat rivals or to facilitate empire building).

The *whistle-blowing game* usually is played by an individual at a relatively low level in the hierarchy of authority who questions the legitimacy of actions by superiors and appeals to powerful individuals outside the organization for support. In the *young Turks games* a small group, often with a significant power base, uses political means in attempts to effect fundamental changes in the organization's mission or in the systems of authority, expertise, or ideology.

The Organization As a Set of Political Games

Conceptualizing influence processes in organizations primarily in terms of the system of politics is characteristic of political or coalitional models of organizational behavior. These approaches reject the assumptions of either hierarchical control or decision making by consensus; instead they view organizations as struggles for power among individuals and groups with conflicting interests, in which victory is obtained by those who are able to mobilize resources most effectively.

The elements of the political or coalitional models of organizations have their roots in the early work of March and Simon (47), Cyert and March (48), Crozier (49), and Thompson (50). This view of organizations "emphasizes the differences in objectives and preferences of subunits and participants and seeks to describe the process by which conflicting preferences and beliefs are resolved" (51). Political models assume that organizations have multiple objectives, rather than one unitary goal toward which activities can be directed in the most efficient manner. The focus is on horizontal rather than vertical differentiation of power, with attention to the variety of ways in which subgroup power can be acquired and maintained, in addition to reliance on formal authority, accepted ideology, or technical expertise.

Although the political model of organizations is intuitively appealing, there are unresolved issues in much of the work based on this perspective. A major concern has been that the majority of organizations do have a formal hierarchy and codified rules and procedures; they are, by and large, bureaucratic in form. The relationship between the formal structure and internal political processes often is unclear in political models of organizational behavior. It could be argued, however, that the formal structure is likely to influence both how much and among whom political conflict occurs. Furthermore, hierarchical status within the formal structure may reflect the outcomes of past political struggles. Possible relationships among authority, political and other systems of influence are discussed in greater detail in the following section.

INTERRELATIONSHIPS AMONG THE INFLUENCE SYSTEMS

In this section we suggest that four major systems of influence based on authority, ideology, expertise, and politics are present to at least some degree in most organizations.

In the majority of organizations, we would argue, one or perhaps two of the systems are clearly dominant, while the other systems either coexist, serve to reinforce, or have an antagonistic relationship with the dominant system. We have noted that the system of politics, for example, tends to become well developed when there are ambiguities, gaps, or other problems in the other three influence systems and when important personal needs of at least some organizational participants are not being met. In this situation individuals become more motivated to participate as players in one or more political games. The political system may supplement or substitute for missing elements in the other systems—it may, for example, determine which of many potential objectives should be pursued at any given point in time, or decide how tasks will be divided, activities coordinated, or resources allocated. Alternatively, political games such as "strategic candidates" or "young Turks" exist in an antagonistic relationship to the other influence systems, and may become an important source of major change in the organization.

Most health services organizations must coordinate the activities of a diverse group of highly trained professionals. Traditionally, they have had strong influence systems based on expertise. As we have noted, influence based on authority or ideology tends to be relatively weak in these types of organizations, but politics often emerges as a powerful force for several reasons:

• First, there often is ambiguity in how to operationalize or prioritize organizational goals, particularly with respect to the curing, caring, and rehabilitation functions of health services organizations. In addition, because of the difficulties involved in measuring outcomes of professional performance, when goals are imposed on professionals by the managerial hierarchy, they often are easy to deflect.
• Among highly trained professionals, identification with the discipline and professional society may well be stronger than with the organization. When many types of professionals are present, intergroup conflict is likely as factions develop.
• Highly skilled professionals have a tendency to invert means and ends—to focus on maintenance and further development of their own skills rather than broader organizational objectives. Furthermore, although the skills themselves may be well defined, the situations to which they may be most appropriately applied often are not. This situation may lead to territorial disputes over patients, clients, and activities among the different disciplines and specialties.
• Professionals traditionally have been expected to give highest priority to the needs of their own individual patients or clients—an expectation likely to generate conflicts both with other professionals serving as patient or client advocates and with managers espousing organization-wide objectives.

The ambiguities and conflicts generated by strong expertise and weak authority systems are most likely to give rise to those political games in which peers compete with each other for the allocation of resources (19). Alliance and empire building, budgeting, rival camps, and strategic candidates games tend to be particularly important.

It is perhaps ironic that managers often can exercise considerable influence in these types of organizations—not by relying on the formal system of authority, but rather by their centrality in the organization and a willingness to engage in the political process. When conflict resolution emerges as a critical organizational function, managers may attain influence commensurate with their skills in mediation and negotiation (52).

POWER AND INFLUENCE IN HEALTH CARE ORGANIZATIONS

In this section we examine power and influence relationships in health care organizations, with particular emphasis on the general community hospital. Early descriptions of these relationships explained that "essentially, authority in the hospital is shared (not equally) by the board of trustees, the doctors, and the manager—the three centers of power in the organization, and, to some extent, also by the director of nursing" (53). A classic article on the top management triangle of governing body, manager, and medical staff argued that interrelationships arise out of:

> . . . the power relationships, the control relationships, and the alternatives available to each group in what can here best be seen as a negotiated relationship and one constantly subject to renegotiation. They stem out of the alternative means of leverage and the amount of power behind that leverage that is available to each party involved in the negotiation." (54, 55)

Traditionally, as we have noted in previous sections, health services organizations have had strong influence systems based on expertise and politics and relatively weak authority systems. Currently, however, a wide variety of factors is changing the balance of power and reshaping influence patterns within many health care institutions. Rapid changes in technology and in the legal and regulatory climate, the altered incentives provided by prospective reimbursement programs, increasing competition for patients, the growing trend toward multi-institutional arrangements—these factors among many others can be seen as affecting the differential ability of trustees, managers, and medical and nursing staff members to influence decision-making processes and activities within hospitals and other health care organizations.

In the following sections we discuss in more detail the major groups with power and influence in health care institutions, as well as some of the significant factors that are changing the distribution of power among these groups. In addition, we summarize findings from comparative studies that have examined the impact of variation in power and influence patterns on the quality of services provided by health care institutions. In general, we argue that owing to a variety of factors, governing boards and health care managers are becoming a more powerful force in health services organizations, and that an increasingly important key to organizational viability will be developing methods of integrating formal authority and the influence system based on clinical expertise.

GOVERNING BOARD

The governing body, or board of trustees, is a group of people authorized by law to maintain and operate the health care institution. Historically, the major role of trustees was to maintain or enhance the legitimacy and prestige of the institution within the community, as well as to attract resources to the institution from the surrounding environment. The heavy preponderance of bankers, lawyers, and businessmen on the governing boards of community hospitals (56, 57), for example, was considered an important prerequisite for successfully fulfilling these obligations. A study undertaken during the early 1970s (58) concluded that a hospital's ability to attract resources was indeed a function of its relation to the community and the size and composition of its governing board. More recently, however, it has become clear that this traditional external role has been eroded both by the increasing complexities of hospital financing and by the rapid escalation in regulatory requirements (59). Although the management literature continues to highlight the governing board's so-called boundary spanning function, emphasis is now placed on linkage activities with consumer groups and with regulatory agencies such as state rate-setting or review commissions (59, 60).

In the past the internal role and responsibilities of the hospital governing board were not clearly defined. In some hospitals the board of trustees played an active role in policy and program development, but in many other institutions the board performed largely ceremonial functions and either delegated or abdicated much authority for corporate decision making to the chief executive officer, the medical staff, or one or two very active board members (61). This situation was reflected in the management and research literature. Economic models of hospitals, for example, have typically viewed the organization as essentially a physician's cooperative (62) or have employed an exchange perspective in which the only relevant actors were managers and medical staff (63, 64). Most comparative studies of hospital decision making also have failed to examine the influence of trustees in relation to other groups within the institution (65–69).

Currently the board's internal role is described as a paradoxical one: on the one hand its internal decision-making authority, like its external functions, is viewed as subject to continual erosion by increased regulations, state budget review, health planning agencies, and the requirements of the Joint Commission on Accreditation of Hospitals (JCAH). The board's authority to set financial goals and policies, for example, is severely constrained by regulations imposed by third-party payers and, in an increasing number of areas, by state regulatory or review agencies established to contain health care costs.

At the same time, pressures from these groups, as well as over a decade of court decisions, have placed the hospital under increased public accountability and have thereby forced governing boards to become more active in many areas of decision making. The Darling case (70) and several other court decisions within the past decade have made it clear that the hospital corporation, and thereby the governing board, is fully responsible for the institution, including the quality of care it provides. These court decisions have involved costly judgments against hospitals and have made it clear that the customary practice of delegating monitoring activities to the medical staff is no longer a viable strategy for governing boards within the current legal climate. Similarly, the Sibley Hospital case (71) illustrated the problems that can arise when a board of trustees does not participate actively in corporate financial management. This case helped clarify the standards of conduct that directors of not-for-profit hospitals should meet with respect to financial and investment matters (61). These cases have made it clear that the governing board's ultimate responsibility for the institution cannot be delegated. In addition, during the 1970s the courts began to specify standards of conduct that individual board members should meet in order to fulfill their responsibilities and avoid liability (72, 73).

This stream of legal decisions, and such factors as increasing competition for patients and resources, has prompted observers such as Scott (74) to argue that governing boards must assume greater influence vis-a-vis hospital management and physicians in the decision-making process. Exactly how this should be accomplished, however, is not clear. There is, for example, no agreement in the management and governance literatures regarding how responsibilities should be divided between the governing board and hospital management. Umbdenstock (75, p. 12) advises that ". . . whereas the board is concerned primarily with whether or not the hospital will do something, the administrator is responsible for how it will be done once the board gives the go-ahead." In contrast, others (19, 76) argue that strategic decision making should be the prerogative of top management, with review by the governing board. Mott (77) in a recent book on hospital trusteeship views strategic planning, financing, quality assurance, and community relations as essential functions for hospital boards, while Kovner (76) argues that the latter two areas should be assumed by management. Furthermore, there is relatively little in the research literature that facilitates understanding and predicting the functions of governance in health care organizations, or that is helpful to governing bodies who are trying to clarify their role and improve their functioning.

These questions concerning what roles governing boards should perform, and how responsibilities should be allocated between governance and management are becoming even more complex as the health care industry moves rapidly toward multiple or tiered governance structures both in many multihospital systems and in independent hospitals that have corporately restructured. Currently one out of every three U.S. hospitals belongs to a multihospital system defined as two or more hospitals that are owned, leased, or managed by a single organization. Recent studies indicate that approximately 40% of these systems use a parent holding company governance approach in which there is a system-wide corporate governing board and separate governing boards for each member hospital (see Fig. 8.1). About one-fifth of the systems substitute advisory for governing boards at the local hospital level, while 23% of systems rely solely on one governing board at the system-wide level (78). A survey of these systems revealed that the system-wide governing board almost always has decision-making responsibility for certain types of issues including the transfer, pledging, and sale of assets, the purchase of assets greater than $100,000, the formation of new companies, changes in hospital by-laws, and the appointment of local board members when such boards are utilized. The allocation of decision-making responsibilities varies considerably, however, for other types of issues, including (1) hospital-level service additions and deletions, (2) operating and capital budgets, (3) decisions regarding medical staff privileges, (4) hospital-level long-range planning, (5) appointment of hospital chief executive officers (CEOs), and (6) hospital CEO performance evaluation. Responsibility for these types of decisions may reside with the local board, with the system-wide board, or with corporate management, or may be shared among two or all three of these groups (78).

Tiered governance arrangements also are becoming increasingly common among the approximately one-third of U.S. hospitals which have corporately restructured. In one approach to reorganization, the hospital becomes the parent corporation to a variety of subsidiaries (see Fig. 8.2). In the "holding company model," a corporate board is formed which owns the hospital and other subsidiaries, some or all of which may have separate boards. These legal arrangements have been formed for a variety of purposes, including protection of the not-for-profit hospital's tax-exempt status and reimbursement formulas from third-party payers while it diversifies into both not-for-profit and for-profit ventures (79).

Multiple board structures in both multihospital systems and corporately restructured independent hospitals are widely perceived to have a number of advantages: it is thought that tiered governance facilitates both horizontal and vertical expansion, while allowing a workable size for governing boards and perhaps avoiding the overworking and possible burnout of both board members and management (80). It is well recognized, however, that virtually all governance issues become more complex with multiple boards (81, 82). This added complexity may lead to problems in communication and coordination, higher levels of conflict, and confusion over lines of authority and the division of responsibilities.

In recognition of the potential problems created by the presence of multiple boards, JCAH issued revised standards in 1986 that require hospital bylaws to specify the re-

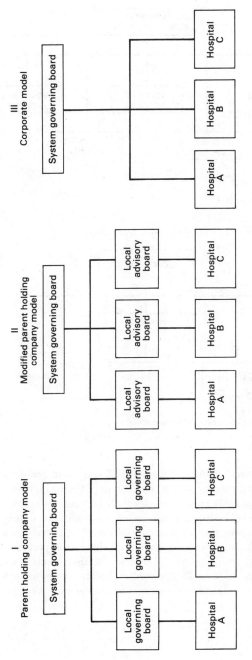

Figure 8.1. Governance models most often utilized by multihospital systems.

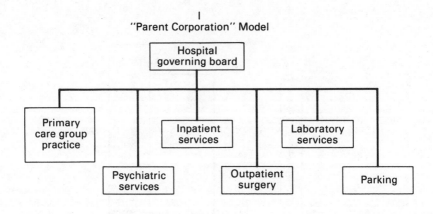

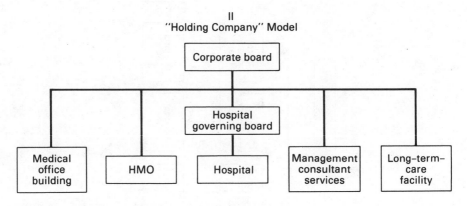

Figure 8.2. Models of hospital corporate reorganization.

lationship between responsibilities of the hospital governing board and any authority superior to the hospital governing body if one exists (83). There also must be a specification of authority and responsibilities for each level of the organization. In addition, there must be systematic and effective mechanisms for communication between the hospital's governing body, management, and medical staff, and the governing bodies and management of any health care delivery organizations that are corporately and functionally related to the hospital. Furthermore, if there are multiple levels of governance, there must be established mechanisms for the medical staff to communicate with all levels of governance involved in policy decisions affecting patient care services in the hospital.

MANAGEMENT

Responsibility for the implementation of institutional policies and for the management of hospital operations is delegated by the governing board to the CEO and through him or her to other members of the managerial staff. This staff includes a number of supervisory personnel who head departments and services in the functional areas of *(1)* business and finance; *(2)* support services, such as dietetics, housekeeping, building and grounds, personnel, security, purchasing, laundry, and medical records; *(3)* professional services, such as radiology, pathology, pharmacy, and out-patient services; and *(4)* nursing services. Managerial and medical staff influence are particularly likely to overlap in these latter two areas.

Historically, managers were viewed as providing the facilities for running the "hotel" aspects of the hospital, and their status was low in comparison to that of the medical staff. Within the past decade, however, many factors have at least potentially increased the relative power and influence of managers by increasing their overall responsibilities. These factors include the increased size and complexity of health care organizations, the trend toward horizontally integrated and vertically linked multi-institutional systems, the increasing need to coordinate activities within the institution as well as with government agencies and other organizations, and growing pressures to increase efficiency and reduce costs. Coupled with these trends has been a movement toward increased professionalization of health care managers. One indicator of this relatively recent development is the creation in many universities of specialized programs in health services management at the graduate level. There also is evidence of greater visibility and more activities of professional associations for health care managers.

These factors undoubtedly have served to increase the expert power of health care managers. Some of these trends also have strengthened the CEO's positional power, or formal authority. For example, during the 1970s, a large number of hospitals adopted a "corporate structure" in which the CEO and sometimes the chief of the medical staff and director of nursing were included as voting members of the governing board. Currently, in about half (49%) of all general acute-care hospitals the CEO not only serves on the board of trustees, but also is a member of the board executive committee (84). Such a position is likely to increase the CEO's formal participation in establishing policy alternatives for the institution, and may also increase his or her formal influence over the board as a whole.

Participation by the hospital in a multi-institutional system apparently also serves to increase the CEO's positional authority: the CEO is a member of the governing board executive committee in 70% of hospitals that are owned by a religious order or organization, in 84% of hospitals that are members of some other type of not-for-profit multi-institutional system, and in 66% of hospitals whose boards report to an investor-owned corporation.* In contrast, the CEO holds governing board executive committee membership in only 47% of autonomous general hospitals (85).

Some of these same factors, however, also have encouraged the development of more formal mechanisms of accountability between the CEO and the governing board. Currently, a majority of hospital boards (66%) conduct an annual performance review of the CEO, and 47% of boards that conduct such reviews use preestablished criteria (84). Although trustees of autonomous hospitals and boards whose hospitals are part of a multi-institutional system are equally likely to conduct annual performance reviews, governing boards of hospitals belonging to a system are significantly more likely (56% compared with 43%) to conduct such reviews according to preestablished criteria (85).

---

*An exception to this trend are hospitals whose boards report to a unit of state, county or local government. Only 38% of these hospitals have their CEOs on the governing board executive committee.

In summary, results from these studies, as well as other recent surveys (86), suggest that participation in a multi-institutional system is associated with greater standardization in the CEO's role, but also serves to increase the CEO's positional authority and formal influence over institutional decision making.

MEDICAL STAFF

The hospital medical staff includes those fully licensed physicians permitted by law and by the hospital to provide patient-care services independently within the scope of their clinical privileges. The JCAH has established as a basic principle of hospital organization that:

> "There is a single organized medical staff that has overall responsibility for the quality of the professional services provided by individuals with clinical privileges, as well as the responsibility of accounting therefor to the governing body." (83)

The medical staff is governed by a set of bylaws, rules, and regulations described by the JCAH as "a framework for self-governance of medical staff activities and accountability to the governing body" (83). This document (1) delineates the organizational structure of the medical staff; (2) specifies qualifications and procedures for admission to, as well as retention of, staff membership; (3) provides methods for the selection of medical staff officers and clinical department and service chairpersons, as well as an outline of their responsibilities; (4) specifies the composition and purposes of standing committees; and (5) specifies policies and procedures for a number of other medical staff functions.

The officers of the medical staff are usually the president (or chief of staff), the vice-president or president-elect, , the secretary-treasurer, and the immediate past president. According to JCAH guidelines, the responsibilities of the president or chief of the medical staff include serving as the presiding officer at medical staff meetings; chairing the medical staff executive committee and serving as an ex officio member of all other medical staff committees; enforcing medical staff bylaws, rules, and regulations; and acting as a spokesperson for the medical staff's external professional and public relations. As chairperson of the executive committee, the chief of staff represents the medical staff to the governing body and to the CEO. He or she may also serve on the governing board.

The only committee required by the JCAH is the executive committee, a group usually composed of the medical staff officers, departmental and service heads, and one or more members at large from the active medical staff. The JCAH guidelines recommend that the CEO also attend all meetings of this committee. Responsibilities of the executive committee include receiving and acting on reports and recommendations from other medical staff committees, clinical departments/services, and assigned activity groups. It also serves as the main structural link between the medical staff, the CEO, and the governing board.

Other standing medical staff committees usually include those concerned with credentials, medical audits, and utilization review, in addition to the joint conference committee, which serves as a liaison with the governing board. There also may be committees concerned with tissue review, infections, blood transfusions, pharmacy and therapeutics, medical education, and cost containment. A national survey in 1982 found that the average hospital had 14 medical staff committees, a significant increase over the average of 9 committees found a decade earlier (87). This increase was viewed as one indicator of the growing complexity of hospital medical staff organization.

The medical staff of a typical hospital, it often is emphasized, are not hospital employees. Although they have been authorized by the governing board to admit and care for patients, generally they are paid not by the hospital but rather by third-party payers or patients themselves. Further, while most physicians lack the authority that stems from formal positions within the organization, they are the only group with the legal authority to prescribe treatment, and they also possess expert power in the form of their specialized knowledge and technical skills. In addition, in our society high status and special qualities often are attributed to physicians, which may place substantial referent or charismatic power at the disposal of the medical staff.

In the past, management writers sometimes described the medical staff as "guests" of the institution and the hospital itself as a "doctor's workshop." These terms were used to describe a situation in which physicians utilized hospital facilities in order to treat their private patients and advance their professional interests but had relatively little involvement in and commitment to the institution itself. The physician's motivation to maximize the care and treatment for each of his or her patients was sometimes viewed as in conflict with a broader hospital perspective that emphasized both the organizational requirements of all patients, and the need for practice patterns that would enhance institutional viability. Furthermore, hospitals usually were viewed as dependent on physicians for patient admissions (a critical resource), and thus were in a weak position to exercise controls on medical staff behavior.

An alternate view is that prior to the institution of the Medicare Prospective Payment System (PPS) and more stringent utilization review by other third-party payers, there were in reality few conflicts between clinical choices and administrative decisions because the financial incentives were similar for both physicians and hospitals. For the most part, Medicare and other insurers reimbursed hospitals for whatever it cost to provide patient care. This supplied an incentive for managers to provide virtually any service or support requested by the medical staff. Glandon and Morrisey (88) argue that this situation facilitated the perception that medical staff members controlled the allocation of hospital resources.

At the same time, insurers paid physician charges on the basis of "usual, customary, and reasonable fees." Thus both physicians and managers had incentives to do everything that could be done for patients covered by third-party insurers, regardless of costs. Glandon and Morrisey (88) suggest that this similarity in incentive structures allowed the relationship between the hospital and a relatively independent voluntary medical staff to be a workable arrangement based on an implicit trade of access to hospital equipment and other resources for a steady flow of patients.

With the advent of PPS, however, hospitals are reimbursed a fixed amount for each category of Medicare patients, regardless of the amount or type of services provided. This system has fundamentally changed the financial incentives facing hospitals, but has left physician incentives unaffected. In addition to PPS, other factors, including state programs to limit hospital costs, employer concerns over health benefit expenditures, and the development of preferred provider organizations, place more pressures on hospitals than on medical staff members to limit resources spent on patient care. The resulting conflict in incentive structures, it is argued, will render unworkable the relatively independent arrangements that traditionally have formed the basis for relationships between hospitals and their medical staffs.

At the same time, several other trends have been interpreted as weakening the potential power of physicians by increasing their dependence on hospitals and/or by strengthening managerial controls. One such trend has been increased competition resulting from the rapid growth in the number of physicians. Increasing numbers of physicians desiring hospital privileges has placed hospitals in a stronger bargaining position, enabling them to demand greater institutional loyalty on the part of medical staff members (89). A recent study of the impact of physician competition on physician–hospital relationships found that the greater the number of physicians per capita, the more likely hospital-based physicians were to be salaried—a pattern suggesting that when physicians are relatively plentiful, hospitals have greater leverage in the negotiation process (90).

As a result of increases in the number of physicians, as well as other factors, the past decade has witnessed significant growth in salaried and other types of contractual relationships between physicians and hospitals. These relationships have become increasingly common not only for what traditionally have been the hospital-based specialties—radiology, anesthesiology, and pathology—but also in other areas, such as emergency departments and hospital-sponsored primary care services. Currently there are several types of contractual arrangements in use that determine methods of revenue and cost allocation between hospitals and physicians. Important methods of remuneration include a specified percentage of gross, or of net, departmental revenue; fee-for-service arrangements, in which patients are billed directly by the hospital-based physician or by the hospital and costs are allocated between the physician and the hospital according to pre-arranged terms; compensation based on salary; and some combination of the above. Such arrangements frequently differ for the chief and other members of a department.* Existence of these relationships is thought to increase physician dependence on and commitment to the institution (94).

There also has been a trend toward the formalization of medical staff administrative positions. While in 1973 only 4% of hospitals reported compensating any physicians for administrative activities in the hospital, by the mid-1980s, 41% of hospitals provided full- or part-time compensation to at least one physician for administrative duties (95). Chiefs of the medical staff and clinical department heads are becoming particularly likely to occupy full-time salaried positions. It often has been argued in the hospital management literature that incumbents of these positions are better able to influence physician behavior when they are salaried and appointed by management, rather than elected by members of the medical staff (96, 97).

Medical staff involvement in the policy and decision-making process of the hospital also has become increasingly formalized through representation on the board of governance. The JCAH now mandates a formal means for medical staff to participate in institutional policy making relevant both to patient care and hospital management (83), and the American Hospital Association (AHA) strongly endorses physician membership on hospital governing boards (98). By the mid-1980s, approximately three-quarters of the nation's hospitals had one or more physicians serving on their governing boards. In the average hospital, physicians occupied 22% of voting positions (95). Medical staff representation on the board is thought to be one important mechanism for conflict resolution between the hospital board, senior management, and the medical staff, as well as a method for fostering an institution-wide perspective among medical staff members.

We would argue that in general all of these trends have served to weaken the potential power of physicians in relationship to hospital management and governance, to strengthen the hospital's system of influence based on formal authority, and to better integrate the authority and expertise influence systems.

The extent to which these developments have occurred, however, varies significantly

---

*Types of contractual arrangements frequently used are discussed by Sattilaro (91), Berg (92), and Lathrop and Reynolds (93).

by hospital size, ownership, location, and whether it is freestanding or a member of a multi-institutional system (87, 90, 95, 99, 100, 101). Several recent studies have found that membership in a multihospital system has a particularly significant effect on hospital medical staff relationships. In general these findings suggest more integrated relationships between medical staff and management in system hospitals, and less medical staff involvement in institutional decision making with respect to either hospital-level or system-level governance (85, 100). There is variation in this pattern, however, by system ownership, with investor-owned systems having less medical staff involvement at the managerial level and more involvement at the hospital board level than other types of systems (90, 101).

NURSING STAFF

Traditionally physicians have had direct authority over hospital nurses with respect to the medical aspects of each patient's treatment. At the same time, the majority of nurses have been full-time members of the administrative organization, reporting within a hierarchical chain of command through a head nurse, nursing supervisor, and director of nursing to the hospital CEO. It has been argued that the nursing staff has more power and exercises more influence within the hospital than is indicated by the typical organization chart, because of their full-time association with the institution, their familiarity with established rules and procedures, their ability to develop informal relationships with other participants, and their close association with both patients and doctors (102).

Many writers have noted that at the level of individual patient care hospital nurses serve to integrate the "technical subsystem represented by the physician" (system of expertise) with the "coordinative subsystem represented by the administrative staff" (system of authority) (102). Suggestions have been made that this de facto arrangement should be formalized with the professional nurse as head of the patient-care team within a matrix organizational structure. The matrix authority would not confer upon the nurse the right to command; rather, "the nurse's authority would be derived from the legitimacy of the assignment, influence with the physician, and expertise" (103).

Several relatively recent trends have been viewed as having a significant impact on the potential power and influence of nursing within the hospital. One change during the past decade has been increasing emphasis in the education and training of nurses on professional and technical roles. The nursing profession, as well as nurses at the organizational level, has pressed for a reduction in the amount of time spent on clerical tasks and an increase in the percentage of time devoted to clinical work and direct patient-care functions. A related trend has been the development of more specialized nursing roles in such areas as intensive care, the cardiac unit, surgery, orthopedics, oncology, and psychiatry.

Some writers argue that the registered nurse is becoming a specialized professional, which is resulting in a decrease in the relatively high status differential between nurses and physicians (102). It is certainly clear that the nursing profession desires more participatory management (104, 105), greater equity in power relationships (106, 107), and more participation by nurses in hospital decision making with respect to programs and policies (108, 109). Several studies have indicated that nurses want influence in decisions about patient care, nursing department issues, and hospital governance and planning (110–112). A recent study of over 600 executive, middle, and first-line nursing managers in 24 general hospitals (113) concluded that nursing managers desired a greater participative role, and that their expectations for participation in hospital decision making were not being met, particularly in the areas of budgeting and planning. Study results suggested that the most important predictors of a nurse manager's participation in hospital decision making were one's preference for participation, committee membership, and position level. These predictors, in turn, were enhanced by the organizational variables of higher nursing membership on medical staff committees, hospital vice-presidential status for nursing directors, and a higher ratio of nurses to physicians in the hospital.

It has been argued that the cyclical shortages of nurses willing to work in hospitals is one symptom of the problems caused by the unwillingness of hospital groups with power to share their control of both resources and decision making (114). The National Commission on Nursing has concluded that organizational structures that do not accommodate nurses as professionals must be changed and recommends including the director of nursing or another nursing representative as a voting member of the governing board (115, 116). Although currently nursing representation on the board is present in only a very small minority of hospitals, it is important to note that JCAH now recommends in its accreditation manual that there be provisions for nursing department/service participation in policy decisions that affect patient care services in the hospital. In addition, if there are multiple levels of governance, JCAH recommends that there be established mechanisms for the nursing department/service to communicate with those levels of governance and management involved in policy decisions affecting patient care services (83).

POWER RELATIONSHIPS, INFLUENCE PATTERNS, AND ORGANIZATIONAL PERFORMANCE

Several studies have examined the impact on organizational performance of variation either in distribution of power or patterns of influence over decision making. Comparative studies of hospitals have investigated associations between the influence of various groups over hospital decision making and the quality of medical care within the institution. In addition, several studies have examined the effects on quality of services of high levels of physician autonomy in comparison to relatively tight professional or administrative control over practice behavior.

Influence Patterns and Quality of Medical Care

Five comparative studies (68, 69, 117–119) have examined relationships between characteristics of the hospital influence structure and indicators of the quality of medical services within the institution. A study (117) of 30 medium-sized community hospitals in Chicago assessed physician participation in hospital-wide activities by means of the following measures: a rating by the chief of the medical staff in each hospital of (1) the degree of influence exercised by physicians in hospital affairs, (2) degree of physician participation as voting members of the governing board, (3) and extent of physician involvement in joint conference committee activities. Quality of care was measured by an overall rating by a panel of five outside physician experts, the JCAH evaluation, and the hospital mortality rate adjusted for case severity (as measured by average length of stay). Contrary to expectations, the study found that physician influence as perceived by the chief of staff was associated with higher rather than lower severity-adjusted death rates. A positive relationship between physician participation as voting members of the governing board and involvement in joint conference committee activities, and the JCAH and expert panel's evaluations of quality of care was noted. These relationships between physician participation and quality of services were not strong enough to attain statistical significance, however.

Another study (68) examined the effects of management practices on hospital efficiency and quality of care in 42 general acute-care Massachusetts hospitals. Variables used to measure participation in decision making included (1) whether the hospital administrator was a voting member of the board of trustees, (2) the extent to which department heads believed they participated in hospital operating decisions (always or usually versus seldom or never), and (3) the degree to which a sample of physicians in each hospital perceived that they, in comparison to the hospital administrator, exercised influence in hospital operating decisions, such as the purchase of new equipment. Quality of care was measured by post-operative complication rates and medical–surgical death rates adjusted for case mix severity. An index of severity was constructed for each hospital by determining the percentage of non-Medicare patients within each of 38 selected diagnostic categories, weighted by a value indicating risk of death or complications for patients within each category, as determined by a physician panel. Analysis results indicated a significant association, after the introduction of controls, between greater participation of department heads in hospital operating decisions and a lower medical–surgical death rate (68).

A third recent comparative study examining characteristics of hospital influence structure and quality of care was conducted based on a national sample of 17 acute-care hospitals (69). On the assumption that professionals in organizations must be able to define and defend an arena of professional autonomy, the hospital decision-making process was conceptualized as involving decision arenas within the spheres of competence of administrators, nursing, and medical staff. Influence measures were constructed for each of these three groups with respect to within-domain influence as well as encroachment into the decision arenas of other groups. Influence was determined, following an approach developed by Tannenbaum (18), by requesting a set of informants in each hospital to rate, on a five-point scale, the amount of influence that would be exercised by the hospital administrator, the chief of surgery, the director of nursing services, and physicians as a group on each of a series of eight hypothetical decisions. Separate scores were developed based on ratings of influence over decisions within and outside each position or group's legitimate domain as defined by the investigators. Within-domain influence of the hospital administrator, for example, was determined by ratings of probable influence over a single hypothetical decision to purchase contract services (e.g., laundry), while encroachment of the administrator on the domain of the surgical department was measured by influence ratings for the hypothetical decisions to add a clinical service, add an ear-nose-throat specialty room in the operating suite, and terminate a major department head, such as the operating-suite nursing director.

Relationships were then examined between within- and outside-domain influence measures and quality of performance. The quality of surgical care was measured by mortality and morbidity experiences of a large sample of surgical patients, controlling for detailed information on characteristics of each patient's condition. A second measure of quality relied on the overall rate of in-hospital mortality adjusted for patient characteristics. The results indicated that among the various influence measures considered, the perceived ability of hospital administrators to influence decisions within their own domain was the factor most strongly and consistently related to better-quality surgical care (120). A more recent analysis (69) using the adjusted in-hospital mortality rate as an overall measure of quality also found only the within-domain influence of administrators significantly associated with the outcome measure. Contrary to the previous results, however, the pattern was reversed: after the introduction of relevant controls, within-domain administrator influence was related to higher adjusted mortality rates.

A fourth large comparative study (118) was recently conducted in 96 hospitals within the east north central region. As part of this study, relationships were examined between medical staff participation in hospital decision making and quality of care for two indicator conditions: acute myocardial infarction (AMI) and appendicitis. Mortality ratios were used to examine the quality of care for approximately 51,000 AMI patients across the 96 hospitals, and the percentage of normal tissue removed was used as an outcome measure for approximately 8,100 appendectomy patients. Both quality-of-care indicators were adjusted for differences in case mix severity and standardized against the experience of other hospitals in the sample.

Measures of physician participation in decision making included whether the president of the medical staff served on the hospital governing board, whether other medical staff officers were members of the board, and the number of physicians who served on the governing board executive committee. Other hospital and physician characteristics were used as control variables. Study results suggested that physician participation in decision making was the single most important variable associated with lower standardized mortality ratios for AMI patients. This variable was in fact more significant than either of the other predictors of good AMI outcomes, including the volume of AMI patients per internist and family practitioner and the presence or absence of a coronary care unit. The researchers conclude that, apparently, "simply having good people [e.g., well-trained, board-certified physicians] and having these people affiliate with 'good' hospitals [e.g., large, teaching-oriented hospitals] is not sufficient to guarantee superior results. Rather, the actual organization of the medical staff itself, as reflected partly by participation in hospital-wide decision-making bodies . . . appears to be most strongly associated with the quality of care provided" (118).

A fifth study (119) utilized data from 17 acute-care general hospitals within one metropolitan area to examine relationships between variations in decision-making patterns and hospital performance as measured by adjusted mortality rates. Approximately 21 personal interviews in each hospital were used to collect detailed information on how six specific decisions had been made during the past 3-year period. In each hospital, one specific decision was chosen for examination from each of six issue areas: the organization of hospital departments and personnel; major changes in allocation of the hospital budget; hospital-physician relations; the introduction or elimination of hospital programs and services; long-range planning; and problems, such as pressures from governmental or regulatory agencies, requiring relatively immediate action by the hospital.

Data from all the informants about all six decisions were utilized to construct influence scores for each of the following eight categories: chief executive officer; director of nursing and other nursing administrators; other non-nursing administrators, such as the chief financial officer; chairman of the board of trustees; other trustees; chief of the medical staff; medical department heads; and attending medical staff. Mortality and diagnostic data, as well as other patient characteristics, were available from hospital discharge abstracts as part of a state-wide data system.

Study results indicated that hospitals in which the chairman of the governing board was active and influential in hospital-wide decision making had better performance indicators. A reverse pattern existed for hospitals with influential chiefs of the medical staff. Strong relationships persisted after controls were introduced for other hospital characteristics associated with mortality rates, including case mix severity and proportion of patients with Medicaid and self-coverage. Analysis of additional data suggested that these relationships may be a function of tighter monitoring and control systems within hospitals whose governing boards are active and influential in decision making. In addition, this study found that trustee activity and influence was stronger in hospitals with a relatively greater number of physicians on the governing board. Physician membership on the board, however, was not directly associated with hospital performance as measured by case mix-adjusted mortality rates. Other board characteristics were found to be unrelated to the influence of trustees in decision making, including size of the board, limitations on the tenure of board members, and adoption by the hospital of a corporate structure.

Participation in Decision-Making and Organizational Performance

Several studies have examined the degree of association between centralization or decentralization of organizational decision making and employee attitudes and behaviors. As we have previously noted, recent studies in nonhealth settings have indicated that decentralization—defined as member participation in important organizational decision making—tends to generate less alienation and dissatisfaction with work, greater satisfaction with supervision, and higher levels of performance (39). Similar findings have been reported in recent studies of health-related settings, where high levels of participation in decision making contributed to greater job satisfaction among nurses in seven hospitals (121) and among staff physicians in four HMOs (122).

A concept similar in many respects to this definition of decentralization is the idea of high overall levels of staff control. The early work of Tannenbaum and his associates (18) suggests that the most effective organizations are those in which influence, or control, is judged to be high among all major groups within the organization. In a study of six outpatient clinics, Nathanson and Becker (123) assessed the degree of influence or control over clinic activities exercised by each of the following: physician-administrators, nonphysician administrators, clinic physicians, nurses, social workers, registrars, and nurse's aides. They concluded that coordination was facilitated in those clinics in which influence was relatively high among all groups. Furthermore, as a consequence of greater reciprocal influence and effective coordination, there was wider staff consensus and decreased conflict in clinics with relatively high levels of total staff control.

Effects of Controls Over Professional Behavior

There is a growing body of evidence that a strong degree of control exercised over practicing physicians at the departmental level is related to increased organizational effectiveness. Scott et al. (124), for example, developed a measure of strictness of requirements for gaining admission to membership on the surgical staffs of 17 hospitals. Their measure of strictness of control was based on the average length of the probationary period, whether the probationary period differed by specialty or was ever waived, and the number of review bodies that had to pass on any appointment. Strictness of control over admissions was significantly related to other indicators of strictness of staff regulation, such as the extensiveness of written procedures governing surgical privileges, but was not related to the qualifications of individual surgeons on the staff, as measured by proportion of surgeons with board certification, or to hospital size or teaching status.

Strictness of control over admissions (but not proportion of surgeons with board certification) was found to be strongly related to quality of surgical care, as measured by case-adjusted postoperative mortality and morbidity. Similarly, other studies (66, 68) have found that high levels of perceived medical staff autonomy (defined as the percentage of time free to decide what, where, when, and how clinical work is to be done) are related to lower levels of quality of care.

SUMMARY AND GUIDELINES FOR HEALTH CARE MANAGERS

In this chapter we have examined the alternative types of power commonly available to organizational participants, and have considered how various sources of power are converted into influence over organizational decisions and activities. Within most health care organizations each of the power bases—including formal authority, control over critical resources, expert power, and sometimes referent or charismatic power—is at least potentially present in a manager's position. The successful conversion of power into influence usually requires both the expenditure of time and energy and some degree of political skill.

In a discussion based on Mintzberg's analysis (19) we have suggested that four major systems of influence based on authority, ideology, expertise, and politics are present to at least some degree in most organizations, although one or two of the influence systems usually is/are dominant. Traditionally, health services organizations have had strong influence systems based on expertise and relatively weak systems based on formal authority or ideology. Politics often has emerged as a powerful force, at least partly owing to the ambiguities, gaps, and other problems inherent in organizations characterized by relatively weak authority and strong expertise. Political games such as alliance and empire building, budgeting, rival camps, and strategic candidates have tended to be particularly important.

A variety of recent developments—including the increasing complexity of health care organizations, changes in the legal and regulatory climates, greater pressures for cost containment, and increasing numbers of physicians—are likely to increase the formal authority available to managers and governing boards and decrease the potential power available to physicians. The system of politics may become a less potent force as formal systems of authority are strengthened. It will become increasingly important to develop more successful methods of integrating formal authority and influence based on clinical expertise.

Many of the trends we have discussed in this chapter suggest that power in health care organizations of the future may be more evenly distributed among managers, governing boards, and medical and nursing staffs. Although this could intensify political struggles among competing groups, the research literature suggests that relatively high levels of reciprocal influence can lead to better coordination and lower levels of conflict. Of central importance in bringing about such changes will be health care managers who are able to analyze the benefits and costs of different types of power and who can effectively integrate authority and expertise in institutional decision making.

MANAGERIAL GUIDELINES

1. In the majority of health care organizations, power is derived from multiple sources—formal authority, control over critical resources, expertise, and to a lesser extent, individual charisma. Effective health care managers must be able to distinguish among different types of power, be sensitive to the source of their own power, and be careful to keep their actions consistent with others' expectations.

2. Effective health care managers must understand the costs, risks, and benefits of using each type of power and must be able to recognize which to draw on in different situations and with different people.

3. Influence in health services organizations should be considered a finite, rather than an unlimited resource. Managers should direct their influence attempts toward those issues of highest priority or where the greatest benefits are likely to result, and be willing to defer in other areas.

4. The highly complex and professional nature of most health services organizations usually results in multiple power centers. Managers often can exercise considerable influence, not by relying on the formal system of authority, but rather by establishing themselves in a central position vis-a-vis other power holders, and being willing to engage in the political process.

5. The diffuse power arrangements and multiple goals of health services organizations may lead to recurring conflicts among individuals and groups. When conflict resolution emerges as a critical function, managers who have developed negotiation and mediation skills may attain considerable influence.

6. Cost containment pressures, greater physician supply, and other recent changes in health care have increased the power of managers vis-a-vis the medical staff, and have established greater incentives for managers to influence the behavior of individual physicians. Formal mechanisms that may be useful for integrating managerial and clinical activities include salaried full-time chiefs of staff, salaried physician managers as heads of clinical departments, and salaries or other contractual relationships with hospital-based physicians. Health care managers also should encourage and facilitate development by the medical staff of more formalized systems for the monitoring and evaluation of physician performance.

7. At the institutional level, research evidence suggests that hospital performance is enhanced by medical staff representation on the governing board, including membership on the board executive committee for the medical staff president.

8. Health services organizations increasingly are characterized by multiple levels of governance. In such institutions particular attention should be directed toward establishing formal mechanisms for coordination and communication among the different boards involved in patient care activities and the medical and nursing staffs.

DISCUSSION QUESTIONS

1. Why has organizational politics traditionally been an important factor in health services organizations?

2. What probable effects will recent changes in the legal and regulatory climate have on the distribution of power within the community hospital? What other trends are expected to affect the ability of different groups to influence hospital decision making?

3. What have recent studies concluded about the association between hospital influence patterns and quality of care?

4. Summarize the findings of recent studies regarding the relationship between centralization versus decentralization of decision making and organizational performance.

5. What are the possible consequences of the growing trend toward multi-institutional arrangements for power and influence relationships among health care managers, physicians, and governing boards?

SUGGESTED READINGS

Alexander, J.A., Morrisey, M.A., and Shortell, S.M. The effects of competition, regulation and corporatization on hospital–physician relationships. *Journal of Health and Social Behavior*, 1986, 27.

Examines alternative mechanisms whereby physicians are integrated into the management policy-making structure of the hospital and tests a number of hypotheses related to the conditions under which various forms of integration occur. Regulation and physician competition are found to result in more integrated hospital–physician relationships. The effects of corporatization are found to vary by type of ownership.

Flood, A.B., & Scott, W.R. Professional power and professional effectiveness. The power of the surgical staff and the quality of surgical care in hospitals. *Journal of Health and Social Behavior*, 1978, 19, 240–254.

Describes a large empirical study of the determinants of professional effectiveness, relating the power of the surgical organization in hospitals to the quality of surgical care delivered. Regression analysis revealed that the power of the surgical staff was not related to the quality of care; rather, greater power of the hospital administration was the factor most strongly associated with quality of surgical care.

Mintzberg, H. *Power in and around organizations.* Englewood Cliffs, N.J.: Prentice-Hall, 1983.

Provides a conceptual framework for understanding power and influence relationships in a variety of different types of organizations. A successful integration of the research literature based on alternative models of influence.

Prybil, L.D. The evolution of hospital governance. In S. Levy & T. McCarthy (Eds.), *Health Management for Tomorrow.* Philadelphia: J.B. Lippincott, 1980.

The hospital industry consumes about 40% of total spending for health care or about 4% of the total GNP. Those responsible for hospital governance and administration face an increasingly complex, difficult, and often contradictory set of demands. The changing role, structure, and function of hospital governing boards is described in this light. Likely future developments are proposed.

Shortell, S.M., Becker, S.W., & Neuhauser, D. The effects of management practices on hospital efficiency and quality of care. In S.M. Shortell and M. Brown (Eds.), *Organizational research in hospitals.* Chicago: Blue Cross Association, 1976.

Empirical study of 42 hospitals in regard to factors that influence hospital efficiency and quality of care. A significant percentage of variation was explained by variables under the manager's control. Further, the more efficiently managed hospitals (from a cost perspective) also appeared to provide higher-quality care.

Shortell, S.M., & LoGerfo, J.P. Hospital medical staff organization and quality of care: Results for myocardial infarction and appendectomy. *Medical Care*, 1981, *19*, (10), 1041–1056.

Examines the relationships among hospital structural characteristics, individual physician characteristics, medical staff organization, and quality of care for two conditions. Medical staff organization factors, particularly physician involvement in hospital-wide decision making, were positively associated with higher quality of care based on data from 96 hospitals in the east north central region.

REFERENCES

1. Shortell, S.M. The medical staff of the future: Replanting the garden. *Frontiers of Health Services Management*, 1985, *1*, 3–48.

2. Smith, H.L. Two lines of authority are one too many. *The Modern Hospital*, 1933, *84*, 59–64.

3. Guest, R.H. The role of the doctor in institutional management. In B.S. Georgopoulos (Ed.), *Organization research on health institutions*. Ann Arbor, Mich.: Institute for Social Research, 1972.

4. Kovner, A.R. The hospital administrator and organizational effectiveness. In B.S. Georgopoulos (Ed.), *Organization research on health institutions*. Ann Arbor, Mich.: Institute for Social Research, 1972.

5. American Hospital Association. *Digest of hospital cost containment programs and cost containment selected bibliography* (2nd ed.). Chicago: American Hospital Association, 1978.

6. Weeks, L.F. The administrator, the physician, the trustee: The triad in the management of today's hospital. *Inquiry*, 1977, *14*, 319–320.

7. Jacobs, M.O. Administrators, boards, physicians must help change health system. *Hospitals*, August 1, 1978, *52*, 78–80.

8. McMahon, J.A. Hospital-physician relations: Where do we go from here? *Trustee*, 1975, *28*, 25–26.

9. Petersen, L.P., Rogatz, P., & Meyers, D. Medical staff: Physicians seek new responses to mounting pressures. *Hospitals*, April 1, 1979, *53*, 147–152.

10. Kotter, J.P. *Power in management*. New York: AMACOM, 1979.

11. MacMillan, I.C. *Strategy formulation: Political concepts*. St. Paul: West, 1978.

12. Schein, V.E. Individual power and political behaviors in organizations: An inadequately explored reality. *Academy of Management Review*, 1977, *2*, 64–72.

13. Kanter, R.M. Power failure in management circuits. *Harvard Business Review*, 1979, *57*, 63–73.

14. Bacharach, S.B. *Power and politics in organizations*. San Francisco: Jossey-Bass, 1980.

15. Moore, T., & Wood, D. Power and the hospital executive. *Hospital and Health Services Administration*, 1979, *24*, 30–41.

16. Zaleznik, A., & DeVries, K. *Power and the corporate mind*. Boston: Houghton Mifflin, 1973.

17. Weber, M. *The theory of social and economic organization*. New York: Free Press, 1947.

18. Tannenbaum, A.S. *Control in organizations*. New York: McGraw-Hill, 1968.

19. Mintzberg, H. *Power in and around organizations*. Englewood Cliffs, N.J.: Prentice-Hall, 1983.

20. Kanter, R.M. *Men and women of the corporation*. New York: Basic Books, 1977.

21. McCall, M.W., Jr. Power, authority, and influence. In S. Kerr (Ed.), *Organizational behavior*. Columbus, Ohio: Grid, 1979.

22. French, J.R.P., & Raven, B.H. The bases of social power. In D. Cartwright (Ed.), *Studies in social power*. Ann Arbor, Mich.: University of Michigan Press, 1959.

23. Stoner, J.A.F. *Management* (2nd ed.). Englewood Cliffs, N.J.: Prentice-Hall, 1982.

24. O'Donnell, C. The source of managerial authority. *Political Science Quarterly*, 1952, 67, 573–588.

25. Bendix, R. *Kings or people: Power and the mandate to rule*. Berkeley: University of California Press, 1978.

26. Barnard, C. *The functions of the executive* (30th anniversary ed.). Cambridge, Mass.: Harvard University Press, 1968.

27. Simon, H.A. *Administrative behavior: A study of decision making processes in administrative organization*. New York: Macmillan, 1961.

28. Perrow, C. Goals and power structures: A historical case study. In E. Freidson (Ed.), *The hospital in modern society*. New York: Free Press, 1963.

29. Student, K.R. Supervisory influence and work group performance. *Journal of Applied Psychology*, 1968, 58, 188–194.

30. Kotter, J.P. Power, dependence and effective management. *Harvard Business Review*, 1977, 55(4), 135–136.

31. Etzioni, A. *Comparative analysis of complex organizations*. New York: Free Press, 1961.

32. Kotter, J.P. Power, success and organizational effectiveness. *Organizational Dynamics*, 1978, 3(3), 27–40.

33. Fisch, G.G. Line-Staff is obsolete. *Harvard Business Review*, 1961, 39(5), 67–79.

34. Sayles, L.R. Matrix management: The structure with a future. *Organizational Dynamics*, 1976, 5(2), 2–17.

35. Nossiter, V. A new approach toward resolving the line and staff dilemma. *Academy of Management Review*, 1979, 4(1), 103–106.

36. Mintzberg, H. *The structuring of organizations: A synthesis of the research*. Englewood Cliffs, N.J.: Prentice-Hall, 1979.

37. Galbraith, J.K. Matrix organization designs. *Business Horizons*, 1971, 14(1), 29–40.

38. Scott, W.R. Organizational structure. *Annual Review of Sociology*, 1975, 1, 1–20.

39. Cummings, L.L., & Berger, C.J. Organization structure: How does it influence attitudes and performance? *Organizational Dynamics*, 1976, 5(2), 34–49.

40. Webber, R.A. *Management: Basic elements of managing organizations*. Homewood, Ill.: Richard D. Irwin, 1979.

41. Thompson, J.D. *Organizations in action*. New York: McGraw-Hill, 1967.

42. Selznick, A. *Leadership in administration: A sociological interpretation*. New York: Harper & Row, 1957.

43. Perrow, C. *Complex organizations: A critical essay*. Glenview, Ill.: Scott, Foresman, 1972.

44. Simon, H.A. *Administrative behavior* (2nd ed.). New York: Macmillan, 1957.

45. Gosselin, R. A study of the interdependence of medical specialists in Quebec teaching hospitals. Ph.D. thesis, McGill University, 1978.

46. Allison, G.T. *Essence of decision: Explaining the Cuban missile crisis*. Boston: Little, Brown, 1971.

47. March, J.G., & Simon, H.A. *Organizations*. New York: John Wiley & Sons, 1958.

48. Cyert, R.M., & March, J.G. *A behavioral theory of the firm*. Englewood Cliffs, N.J.: Prentice-Hall, 1963.

49. Crozier, M. *The bureaucratic phenomenon*. Chicago: University of Chicago Press, 1964.

50. Thompson, J.D. *Organizations in action*. New York: McGraw-Hill, 1967.

51. Salancik, G.R., & Pfeffer, J. The bases and use of power in organizational decision making: The case of a university. *Administrative Science Quarterly*, 1974, *19*, 453–473.

52. Baldridge, J.V., Curtis, D.V., Ecker, G., & Riley, G. *Policy making and effective leadership*. San Francisco: Josey-Bass, 1978.

53. Georgopoulos, B.S., & Mann, F.C. *The community general hospital*. New York: Macmillan, 1967.

54. Gordon, P.J. The top management triangle in voluntary hospitals. I. *Journal of the Academy of Management*, 1961, *4*, 205.

55. Gordon, P.J. The top management triangle in voluntary hospitals. II. *Journal of the Academy of Management*, 1962, *5*, 66–75.

56. Kaufman, K., Shortell, S.M., Becker, S., & Neuhauser, D. The effects of board composition and structure on hospital performance. *Hospital and Health Services Administration*, 1979, *24*, 37–62.

57. Kovner, A.R. Hospital board members as policy makers: Role, priorities and qualifications. *Medical Care*, 1974, *12*, 971–982.

58. Pfeffer, J. Size, composition and function of hospital boards of directors: The study of organizational-environment linkages. Reprint 373, Institute of Industrial Relations, University of California, Berkeley, 1973.

59. Maryland Hospital Education Institute. *Hospital boardmanship for the 80's*. Lutherville, Md., 1979.

60. Umbdenstock, R.J. Goverance trustees are closing the gap between hospitals and consumers. *Hospitals*, April 1, 1979, 111–115.

61. Prybil, L.D. The evolution of hospital goverance. In S. Levey & T. McCarthy (Eds.), *Health management for tomorrow*. Philadelphia: J.B. Lippincott, 1980.

62. Pauly, M., & Redisch, M. The not-for-profit hospital as a physicians' cooperative. *The American Economic Review*, 1973, *63*, 87–99.

63. Harris, J.E. The internal organization of hospitals: Some economic implications. *The Bell Journal of Economics*, 1977, *8*, 467–482.

64. Jacobs, P. A survey of economic models of hospitals. *Inquiry*, 1974, *11*, 83–97.

65. Shortell, S.M. Hospital medical staff organization: Structure, process and outcome. *Hospital Administration*, 1974, *19*, 96–107.

66. Roemer, M.I., & Friedman, J.W. *Doctors in hospitals*. Baltimore: Johns Hopkins University Press, 1971.

67. Morse, E., Gordon, G., & Moch, M. Hospital costs and quality of care: An organizational perspective. *Milbank Memorial Fund Quarterly*, 1974, *52*, 315–346.

68. Shortell, S.M., Becker, S.W., & Neuhauser, D. The effects of management practices on hospital efficiency and quality of care. In S.M. Shortell & M. Brown (Eds.), *Organizational research in hospitals*. Chicago: Blue Cross Association, 1976.

69. Scott, W.R., Flood, A.B., & Ewy, W. Organizational determinants of services, quality and cost of care in hospitals. *Milbank Memorial Fund Quarterly*, 1979, *57*(2), 234–264.

70. Darling *vs.* Charleston Community Memorial Hospital, 33 Illinois, 2d. 236. 211 ME 2d. 253 (1965).

71. Stern *vs.* Lucy Webb Hayes National Training School for Deaconesses and Missionaries, 367 F. Supp. 536 (Washington, D.C., November 30, 1973): F. Supp. 1003 (Washington, D.C., 1974).

72. Mace, M. Standards of care for trustees. *Harvard Business Review*, 1976, *54*, 14–16, 21, 28, 148.

73. Bernstein, A. Judging hospital trustees. *Hospitals*, January 1, 1975, *49*, 83–84, 99.

74. Scott, W.R. Managing professional work: Three models of control for health organizations. *Health Services Research*, 1982, *17*, 213–240.

75. Umbdenstock, R.J. *So you're on the hospital board!* (2nd ed.). Chicago: American Hospital Publishing, 1983.

76. Kovner, A.R. Improving the effectiveness of hospital governing boards. *Frontiers of Health Services Management*, 1985, *2*, 4–33.

77. Mott, B.J.F. *Trusteeship and the future of community hospitals*. Chicago: American Hospital Publishing, 1984.

78. Morlock, L.L., & Alexander, J.A. Models of governance in multihospital systems: Implications for hospital and system-level decision-making. *Medical Care*, 1986, *24*, 1118–1135.

79. Starr, P. *The social transformation of American medicine*. New York: Basic Books, 1982.

80. Brasher, P. Corporate reorganization modules. Department of Health Systems Management Working Paper Series, School of Public Health and Tropical Medicine, Tulane University, 1984.

81. Mannisto, M.M. Multis' delicate balancing act: Corporate goals and local board autonomy. *Trustee*, 1984, *37*, 17.

82. Plant, J. Who's on first? Making the transition to a multiple-board structure. *Trustee*, 1985, *38*, 19.

83. AMH/86: *Accreditation manual for hospitals*. Chicago: Joint Commission on Accreditation of Hospitals, 1986.

84. Alexander, J., & Morlock, L. Multi-institutional arrangements: Relationships between governing boards and hospital chief executive officers. *Health Services Research*, 1985, *19*, 675–699.

85. Morlock, L.L., Alexander, J.A., & Hunter, H.M. Formal relationships among governing boards, CEOs, and medical staffs in independent and system hospitals. *Medical Care*, 1985, *23*, 1193–1213.

86. Weil, P., & Stam, L. Transitions in the hierarchy of authority in hospitals: Implications for the role of the chief executive officer. *Journal of Health and Social Behavior*, 1986, *27*, 179–192.

87. Noie, N.E., Shortell, S.M., & Morrisey, M.A. A survey of hospital medical staffs—Part I. *Hospitals*, 1983, *57*.

88. Glandon, G.L., & Morrisey, M.A. Redefining the hospital–physician relationship under prospective pricing. *Inquiry*, 1986, *23*, 166–175.

89. Shortell, S.M. Theory Z: Implications and relevance for health care management. *Health Care Management Review*, 1982, *7*, 7–21.

90. Alexander, J.A., Morrisey, M.A., & Shortell, S.M. Effects of competition, regulation and corporatization on hospital–physician relationships. *Journal of Health and Social Behavior*, 1986, *27*, 220–235.

91. Sattilaro, A. An open approach to contractual arrangements. *Hospital Medical Staff*, 1978, *7*, 1–7.

92. Berg, R.I. Contract defines provider-based physician payment methods. *Hospital Financial Management*, 1979, *33*(7), 16–23.

93. Lathrop, J.P., & Reynolds, J. Physician contracts—Have you thought of everything? *Hospital Financial Management*, 1979, *33*(11), 24–31.

94. Roemer, M.I., & Friedman, J.W. *Doctors in hospitals*. Baltimore: Johns Hopkins University Press, 1971.

95. Morrisey, M.A., & Brooks, D.C. Physician influence in hospitals: An update. *Hospitals*, 1985, *59*, 36–39.

96. Johnson, E. Medical staff liability. *Health Care Management Review*, 1978, *3*, 43–49.

97. Williams, K. The role of the medical director. *Hospital Programs*, June 1978, 50–57.

98. American Hospital Association. *Guidelines on physician participation in the governance of health care institutions*. Chicago: Author, February 1978.

99. Rehm, J.L., & Alexander, J.A. Governing board–medical staff relations in the 80's. *Trustee*, 1986, *39*, 24–27.

100. Shortell, S.M., Morrisey, M.A., & Conrad, D.A. Economic regulation and hospital behavior. The effects on medical staff organization and hospital–physician relationships. *Health Services Research*, 1985, *20*, 597–628.

101. Alexander, J.A., Morrisey, M.A., & Shortell, S.M. Physician participation in the administration and governance of system and freestanding hospitals: A comparison by type of ownership. In *For-profit enterprise in health care*. Washington, D.C.: Institute of Medicine, 1986, pp. 402–421.

102. Kast, F.E., & Rosenzweig, J.E. *Organization and management: A system and contingency approach*. New York: McGraw-Hill, 1979.

103. Johnson, G.V., & Tingey, S. Matrix organization: Blueprint of nursing care organization for the 80's. *Hospital and Health Services Administration*, 1976, *21*, 27–39.

104. Bopp, W., & Rosenthal, W. Participatory management. *American Journal of Nursing*, 1979, *79*, 670–672.

105. Kraus, S.I. The role of the nurse in the hospital setting of the 1980's. *World Hospitals*, 1979, *15*(2), 132–135.

106. Christman, L., & Kirkman, R.E. Nursing administrative action on the management team. *Nursing Digest*, 1978, *6*, 80–82.

107. Shiflett, N., & McFarland, D. Power and the nursing administrator. *Journal of Nursing Administration*, 1978, *8*(3), 19–23.

108. Aiken, L. Hospital changes urged to end nurse shortage. *American Nurse*, February 1981, 4.

109. Brown, B., Gebbie, K., & Moore, J. Affecting nursing goals in health care. *Nursing Administration Quarterly*, Spring, 1978, *3*, 17–31.

110. Godfrey, M. Job satisfaction—Or should that be dissatisfaction? *Nursing*, April–May 1978, 89–100.

111. Lebreton, P. Strategic factors in hospital nursing practice. *Nursing and Health Care*. 1980, *1*(4), 197.

112. Wandelt, M. *Conditions associated with registered nurse employment in Texas.* Austin: Center for Research, School of Nursing, University of Texas, 1980.

113. Stuart, G.W. Nursing participation in hospital decision-making. Ph.D. thesis, The Johns Hopkins University, 1985.

114. Kernaghan, S. The nurse shortage: How can we turn the exodus around? *Hospitals*, February 1, 1982, 53–56.

115. National Commission on Nursing. Nursing in transition. Models for successful organizational change. Chicago: The Hospital Research and Educational Trust, 1982.

116. Trustee Development Program. Issues in nursing. *Trustee*, September, 1980, 37–42.

117. Neuhauser, D. The relationship between administrative activities and hospital performance. Research Series No. 28, Center for Health Administration Studies, University of Chicago, 1971.

118. Shortell, S.M., & LoGerfo, J.P. Hospital medical staff organization and quality of care: Results for myocardial infarction and appendectomy. *Medical Care*, 1981, *14*(10), 1041–1056.

119. Morlock, L.L., Nathanson, C.A., Horn, S.D., & Schumacher, D.N. Organizational factors associated with quality of care in 17 general acute care hospitals. Paper presented at the annual meeting of the Association of University Programs in Health Administration, Toronto, May 7–9, 1979.

120. Flood, A.B., & Scott, W.R. Professional power and professional effectiveness: The power of the surgical staff and the quality of surgical care in hospitals. *Journal of Health and Social Behavior*, 1978, *19*, 240–254.

121. Price, J.L., & Mueller, C.W. A causal model of turnover for nurses. *Academy of Management Journal*, 1981, *24*, 543–565.

122. Barr, J.K., & Steinberg, M. Professional participation in organizational decision-making: Physicians in HMOs. *Journal of Community Health*, 1983, *8*, 160–173.

123. Nathanson, C.A., & Becker, M.H. Control structure and conflict in outpatient clinics. *Journal of Health and Social Behavior*, 1972, *13*, 251–262.

124. Scott, W.R., Forrest, W.H., & Brown, B.W. Hospital structure and postoperative mortality and morbidity. In S.M. Shortell and M. Brown (Eds.), *Organizational research in hospitals*. Chicago: Blue Cross Association, 1976.

PART FOUR

Renewing the Organization

*In a world that is rocking with change we need more
than anything else a high capacity for adjustment to
changed circumstances, a capacity for innovation. . . .
Some people have greatness thrust upon them. Very few
have excellence thrust upon them. They achieve it. . . .
All excellence involves discipline and tenacity of
purpose.*

John Gardner

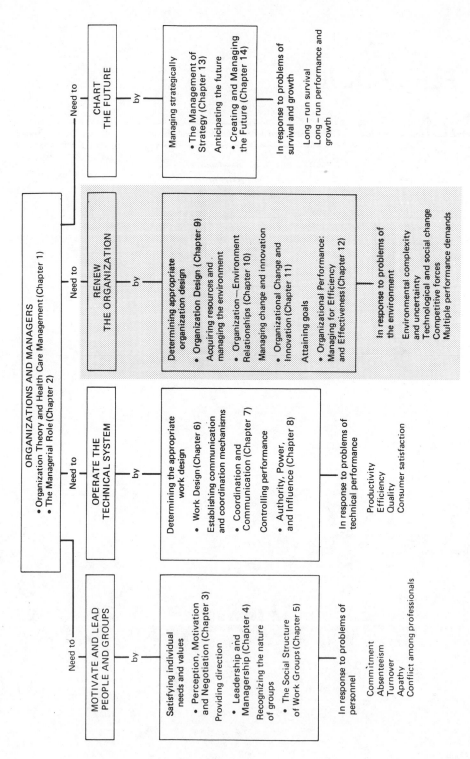

ORGANIZATIONS AND MANAGERS
• Organization Theory and Health Care Management (Chapter 1)
• The Managerial Role (Chapter 2)

Need to — MOTIVATE AND LEAD PEOPLE AND GROUPS

Need to — OPERATE THE TECHNICAL SYSTEM

Need to — RENEW THE ORGANIZATION

Need to — CHART THE FUTURE

MOTIVATE AND LEAD PEOPLE AND GROUPS

by

Satisfying individual needs and values
• Perception, Motivation and Negotiation (Chapter 3)

Providing direction
• Leadership and Managership (Chapter 4)

Recognizing the nature of groups
• The Social Structure of Work Groups (Chapter 5)

In response to problems of personnel

Commitment
Absenteeism
Turnover
Apathy
Conflict among professionals

OPERATE THE TECHNICAL SYSTEM

by

Determining the appropriate work design
• Work Design (Chapter 6)

Establishing communication and coordination mechanisms
• Coordination and Communication (Chapter 7)

Controlling performance
• Authority, Power, and Influence (Chapter 8)

In response to problems of technical performance

Productivity
Efficiency
Quality
Consumer satisfaction

RENEW THE ORGANIZATION

by

Determining appropriate organization design
• Organization Design (Chapter 9)

Acquiring resources and managing the environment
• Organization — Environment Relationships (Chapter 10)

Managing change and innovation
• Organizational Change and Innovation (Chapter 11)

Attaining goals
• Organizational Performance: Managing for Efficiency and Effectiveness (Chapter 12)

In response to problems of the environment

Environmental complexity and uncertainty
Technological and social change
Competitive forces
Multiple performance demands

CHART THE FUTURE

by

Managing strategically
• The Management of Strategy (Chapter 13)

Anticipating the future
• Creating and Managing the Future (Chapter 14)

In response to problems of survival and growth

Long – run survival
Long – run performance and growth

The nature of organizations. Framework for the text.

The open systems approach to management emphasizes the interaction between the organization and its environment. Increasingly, health care executives are becoming managers of environments as part of their overall leadership and managerial role. The four chapters in this section highlight the nature of this newly emerging role and present a number of ideas, insights, and examples for consideration.

Chapter 9, on organization design, focuses on the following questions:

- Which aspects of the organization can be deliberately designed? Which must be left to chance?
- What are the pros and cons of different kinds of designs, and what influences the choice of more effective rather than less effective designs?
- How can different designs take into account the organization's unique history, cultural context, and stage of development?
- What different designs should be used for new organizations versus established organizations?
- What suggestions can be made for organizations that are experiencing stress or are in various stages of decline?

Several mini-case studies are presented to illustrate a range of answers to the questions listed above.

Chapter 10, on organization-environment relationships, highlights the complexity of the manager's job in dealing with the external environment. The chapter focuses on the following questions:

- What are the major perspectives from which the manager can obtain understanding and insight on the nature of the organization's relationship to its environment?
- What is the nature of interorganizational relationships and how do these affect the manager's role?
- How much control do managers exert over the environment? How can the manager's influence be expanded?
- Are there examples of effective health care organization-environment relationships? What lessons can be learned from these experiences?

Chapter 11, on managing organizational change and innovation, presents a variety of ways of attaining and implementing change and innovation. Among the questions it addresses are the following:

- What are the major models by which the manager can gain perspective on the change and innovation process?
- Under what conditions are particular models more relevant than others?
- What different kinds of change should health care managers consider?
- What are the characteristics of the change and innovation process?
- What specific strategies exist for instituting and implementing different kinds of changes?
- Which changes prove more or less effective under what particular circumstances?

Chapter 12, on organizational performance, provides a comprehensive overview and analysis of performance issues that face health care managers and their organizations. Among the questions addressed are the following:

- What is performance? For example, what are the differences between the system resource, social support and maintenance, and goal-attainment approaches to performance?
- What problems are associated with measuring organizational effectiveness?
- What evidence exists that some organizations perform more effectively than others?
- What factors are most strongly associated with differences in performance?
- What tools, skills, and strategies exist by which managers can influence performance?

Upon completing these four chapters readers should be able to accomplish the following:

- Distinguish between the simple structure, machine bureaucracy, professional bureaucracy, divisional, and adhocracy types of organizational design and know under what circumstances each design is most likely to be effective.
- Understand the importance of the information-processing view of organization design.
- Understand the differences between functional, divisional, and mixed (matrix) structures in the design of health care organizations and the circumstances in which each is most likely to be effective.
- Take into account the organization's life cycle (new, mature, declining) in the choice of design.
- Distinguish different methods and strategies for implementing changes in organization design, including education and communication, participation and involvement, facilitation and support mechanisms, and negotiation and agreement.
- Distinguish between the natural selection/population ecology and resource dependence/exchange perspectives on organization-environment relationships.
- Understand how interorganizational relationships affect the internal functioning of the organization.
- Understand how technology affects the relationship between an organization and its environment.
- Identify at least four methods or strategies by which health care managers can influence their organization's environment.
- Define and distinguish between the rational, resource dependency, and population-ecology models of organizational change.
- Define and distinguish between technical change, adjustive change, and adaptive change.
- Define and distinguish various sources of change and innovation, including origination, adaptation, and borrowing.
- Identify various stages and characteristics of the change and innovation process; including the recognition stage, identification stage, implementation stage, and institutionalization.
- Distinguish between productivity, efficiency, and effectiveness and understand the relationship among these three concepts.
- Distinguish between the resource-acquisition, system-maintenance, and goal-attainment models of organizational effectiveness, enumerate the advantages and limitations of each approach, and understand their relationship to each other.

- Identify structural, process, and outcome measures of organizational performance and the advantages and limitations of each.
- Understand how environmental assessment, strategy formulation and policy development, implementation, organization design, and evaluation functions relate to the adaptive, boundary spanning, production, maintenance, and managerial subsystems of the organization for purposes of managing organizational performance.
- Identify at least four factors that appear to be consistently associated with better performance and identify what kinds of managerial actions are associated with each of these factors.

CHAPTER 9

Organization Design

Peggy Leatt
Stephen M. Shortell
John R. Kimberly

I was thinking of installing one of those automatic garage door openers over the weekend. The directions say, 'Make certain the garage door is square and straight and that the garage floor is level.' Directions always read like that. Is everything in your house straight, square, and level? If my house was straight, square, and level, I would never have to fix anything. What we all need is directions that tell us what to do when everything is crooked, off-center, and all screwed up."

Andy Rooney

This chapter offers some suggestions for what to do when your organization is crooked, off-center, or generally all screwed up. It also offers some suggestions for preventing organizational screw ups and crookedness. Paradoxically, suggestions are also made for designing in a certain degree of off-centeredness and crookedness to promote flexibility and adaptiveness to external changes. The emphasis is on assisting managers in developing high-performing health care organizations (see Chapter 12). The major approaches to organization design are reviewed and a number of case studies are used to illustrate the key strengths and weaknesses of each design and their specific applicability to health services organizations.

WHAT IS ORGANIZATION DESIGN?

Organization design is the arrangement or rearrangement of the structure of organizations to improve their effectiveness, efficiency, adaptability, and survival (1). Organization design refers to the way in which authority, responsibility, and information are combined within a particular organization. Design can influence performance: a design that fits the organization's mission and strategies can enhance performance; an inappropriate design may impede success.

This chapter provides ideas and examples to assist health services managers in designing their organizations to achieve the greatest effectiveness and efficiency (see Chapter 12).

WHAT IS A MANAGER'S ROLE IN ORGANIZATION DESIGN?

Management's primary task is to maintain and improve performance in the organization. In fact, management texts refer to organization design as one of management's most critical functions (2–3). Usually, the activities of design are seen as the responsibilities of senior management; however, the most successful designs appear to be those that have been built with input from a broad range of organizational members, including key external and internal stakeholders, and from persons at all levels within the orga-

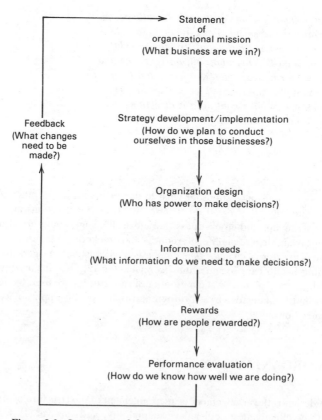

Figure 9.1. Organizational design in relation to other management activities.

nization. Outside consultants are sometimes brought in to provide technical advice on the range of designs that might be considered (4). Outside consultants are most useful in attempting to design rather large complex organizations, such as a large teaching hospital or a system of hospitals.

Often, organization design has been thought of as a "once and for all event" parallel to an architect or engineer designing and constructing a new building. In our view, when a new organization is formed a new design will be created; however, the redesign of the organization is an ongoing process where the design needs will change as the organization's needs change. The idea that designing organizations may be a recurring activity is most important for managers who may not only have responsibility for redesigning their organizations but also for ensuring that the design is implemented (5).

The design process is not carried out in isolation from other management activities. In fact, ideas about the type of design that might be appropriate should be derived from the organization's mission and strategic planning process (6–7). For example, if an organization, such as a hospital, decides to diversify its product lines and expand to new patient programs, it may be necessary to rearrange the division of labor within the organization. Alternatively, if a long-term-care facility decides to close down a geriatric day program, it may be necessary to regroup ongoing services within the organization.

Also, the way in which an organization is designed has considerable importance for the nature and content of the information system needed by the organization. Since an organization design specifies who has power to make which decisions, it also indicates which positions need what types of information and at what times. Organization design also has implications for how performance will be evaluated and especially for the degree to which the reward system of the organization matches achievement or performance. Finally, the knowledge gathered from performance indicators will be fed back to subsequently influence the organization's mission. The relationships of organizational design to these other management activities can be seen in Figure 9.1.

AT WHAT LEVELS MAY HEALTH SERVICES ORGANIZATIONS BE DESIGNED?

Several aspects of an organization can be redesigned or changed. For example, decisions can be made to change the overall size of the organization, the number and types of units or departments within, and how these units may be grouped. We can also decide to change the span of control of individual managers, reorganize tasks, specify rules and procedures in a formalized or standardized way, reallocate decision-making authority, alter communication channels, change mechanisms of control and reward, and determine how coordination will be achieved.

We typically think of design being achieved for a whole organization, such as a nursing home, a hospital, or a public health unit; however, design may take place for a particular group of departments, for an individual unit or department, or for a specific position (see Chapter 6). Mintzberg (8) has pointed out that the design of individual positions forms the basic building blocks on which the design of a whole organization is developed. On a wider scale than a single organization, we may also create a design for a network of organizations in a given community or for a system of organizations. These interlocking levels of design are illustrated in Figure 9.2.

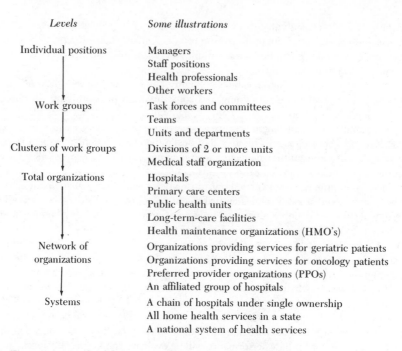

Levels	Some illustrations
Individual positions	Managers
	Staff positions
	Health professionals
	Other workers
Work groups	Task forces and committees
	Teams
	Units and departments
Clusters of work groups	Divisions of 2 or more units
	Medical staff organization
Total organizations	Hospitals
	Primary care centers
	Public health units
	Long-term-care facilities
	Health maintenance organizations (HMO's)
Network of organizations	Organizations providing services for geriatric patients
	Organizations providing services for oncology patients
	Preferred provider organizations (PPOs)
	An affiliated group of hospitals
Systems	A chain of hospitals under single ownership
	All home health services in a state
	A national system of health services

Figure 9.2. Levels of design in health services organizations.

DESIGNING A POSITION

In terms of designing individual positions in the organization, there may be hundreds to choose from, depending upon the organization's size and complexity. Often a new manager is hired into a hospital or other health services facility as an executive assistant to the President. If you were in this position, you would likely be excited about the possibilities and ask the President for a copy of your job description. The President, being amused, might inform you that your first task is to prepare a draft of your own position description for management's approval. It is, therefore, in your best interest to create a clear statement about your job which will minimize role ambiguity, conflict, and stress (9–12).

In designing an individual job or position for any level within an organization it is necessary to identify the breadth and scope of tasks that can be performed and the extent to which the work can be standardized. Both of these factors have implications for the skills and training that will be necessary for the persons filling the job (8). Some of the basic parameters that should be identified include: *(1)* the major responsibilities and roles inherent in the position; *(2)* to whom the position is accountable; *(3)* for whose work the position is accountable; and *(4)* the relationship of other peer positions to it. One technique which has been successfully used in clarifying responsibilities of individual positions is responsibility accounting. With this method the perceptions of members of the relevant role set are obtained to identify who is responsible for which decisions in the organization and who they believe should be responsible (13). Additional suggestions are discussed in Chapter 6.

DESIGNING A WORK GROUP

Often managers are placed in the position of creating a task force to complete a problem-solving exercise in a short time frame. For example, a nursing home manager may be interested in identifying approaches that could be used to implement and maintain a quality-assurance program. The manager should clarify the specific purpose of the work group, the time frame for completion of the problem solving, and the boundaries of the group's authority (14–15). Depending upon the complexity of the problem at hand, the manager should make decisions about the skills and knowledge necessary to complete the task. For example, to investigate quality-assurance programs, it may be appropriate to use a multidisciplinary approach (16) which could include a nurse, a physician, a physiotherapist, a social worker, a pharmacist, or other health workers. The appointment of a leader for the group is also a critical design decision (17–18). A similar design approach may be used for deciding upon more permanent work groups, such as departments or subunits (refer to Chapter 6).

DESIGNING A CLUSTER OF WORK GROUPS

In some circumstances it may be necessary to redesign a cluster of departments or units within an organization to form a division. One of the most important design decisions to be made in clustering work groups involves the most appropriate grouping of units to achieve coordination within the division. Grouping of units implies that the units will share a common manager, common resources, and common performance measures (8). To illustrate the various ways in which units may be grouped we use the example of the medical staff organization in a general hospital (19). Units may be grouped by *knowledge and skill*. For example, physicians may be grouped to form divisions by specialty and subspecialities (e.g., all medical specialities, all surgical specialities). Physicians may be grouped by *work process*, for instance, by placing the operating rooms, emergency departments, and radiology under the same management, where they have a common patient flow. Ambulatory-care clinic physicians may be grouped by *time* because they tend to hold clinics in the same time frame. Physicians may be grouped by commonality of *clients/patients*, for example, cardiovascular surgery and cardiology. Finally, physicians may be grouped because they are physically located *geographically close* in the same hospital. Mintzberg (8) points out that in large organizations such as hospitals, which employ many professionals, a number of these bases for grouping may be used simultaneously.

In addition to the decisions about grouping in designing a division, all the other variables mentioned for designing a work group must be considered.

DESIGNING A TOTAL ORGANIZATION

The parameters of design decisions for this level of analysis have already been mentioned and are the focus of much of the rest of the chapter; briefly, it may be emphasized that at this level, organization design usually involves deciding the degree of complexity, formalization, and decentralization of the structure and ensuring effective coordination of the tasks to achieve the organization's goals.

DESIGNING A NETWORK

A network of organizations comprises those organizations that exist in a particular community or environment, which may be loosely or closely connected to achieve a common purpose or serve a common clientele (20). An example is the network of health and social services that may exist in a community to provide services to geriatric patients. Types of organizations within the network may include an acute hospital, a psychiatric hospital, a nursing home, home health services, day-care services, meals on wheels, friendly visiting services, housing and transport services, and so on. The objective in the design of the network is to ensure coordination of services and smoothness of client flow between organizations to maximize effectiveness. At the network level the design process is relatively complex because it involves examining the nature of the relationships among the organizations in the network. Design decisions may include analyzing the interorganizational relationships in terms of deciding which organizations should have the most power, which resource transactions may take place, and how innovations will be diffused (21).

DESIGNING A SYSTEM

At the system level the design decisions are even more complex, depending upon the purpose(s) of the system and the heterogeneity of the programs provided. One of the most important factors to be analyzed at the system level is concerned with the degree of centralization and decentralization of decision making. For example, given a system of hospitals, which may include a chain of perhaps 60 acute general hospitals, it is essential to clarify which decisions will be made at the corporate level and which decisions will be made at the regional or individual hospital level (22–24). Where the majority of decisions are centered at the corporate office, the organization is said to be vertically centralized. In high-technology industries such as health care, greater vertical decentralization is expected because of the expertise at lower levels in the organization. As a general rule, decisions should be made at the lowest possible levels, especially when the majority of workers are professionals (25). Horizontal decentralization refers to the extent to which influence and decision making is shared laterally. In the example of the hospital chain, an important design factor may be deciding upon the extent to which individual hospitals can develop their own marketing plans separately from those developed by the corporate office.

THE EVOLUTION OF THE PRINCIPLES OF ORGANIZATION DESIGN

The possibility that organizations may adopt alternative organization designs has not always been an issue.

The major schools of thought and the main authors of the evolution of the principles of organization design are shown in Table 9.1. (Also see Chapter 1 for further discussion of major organizational paradigms.)

During the early 1900s the scientific management school considered only "one best way" to structure organizations, which was based on bureaucratic principles. Following

TABLE 9.1. Summary of the Evolution of the Principles of Organization Design

Major Schools of Thought	Principal Authors	Major Themes
Historical		
Scientific management (1920s)	F. W. Taylor	Management should be based on a scientific/data approach
Theory of bureaucracy (1920s)	M. Weber	Organizations should be structured by bureaucratic principles
Human relations (1930s)	E. Mayo (Hawthorne Studies)	Organizations should maximize potential for workers' growth and participation
Human resources (1950s–1960s)	R. Likert, W. McGregor	Both individual and organizational perspectives are important
Contingency		
More than one way to organize (1960s)	T. Burns and G. M. Stalker	Polar extremes of mechanistic and organic management systems were defined
Open systems (1960s)	D. Katz and R. L. Kahn	Applied general system theory to analyzing organizations
External environment (1960–1970s)	S. Terreberry	Organizations adapt to their environments
	P. Lawrence and J. Lorsch	Environmental complexity
Technology (1960–1970s)	J. Woodward J. D. Thompson C. Perrow	General importance of technology for organizational structure and processes Application to human service organizations defining technology in terms of routine-nonroutine tasks
Alternatives to Contingency		
Population ecology and natural selection model (1970s–1980s)	M. Hannan and J. Freeman H. Aldrich H. Aldrich, B. McKelvey, and D. Ulrich	Organizations are passive recipients of changes taking place in their environments
Strategic choice (1970s–1980s)	A. D. Chandler J. Child J. Pfeffer and G. R. Salanick	Top managers are proactive in assessing their environments, choosing a mix of technologies, and designing organizations to maximize effectiveness

this era, the human relations school outlined their "one best way," which suggested that individual employees should be the most important focus of organizations and that structure should maximize the potential for workers' growth and development and involvement in decision making.

As a departure from the "one best way" approach, Burns and Stalker (26) described two structural forms called mechanistic and organic management systems. Mechanistic management represented situations where the work in the organization was divided into specialized tasks, there was a clearly defined hierarchy, rules, and regulations, and decision making was centralized at the top. Organic management emphasized the importance of specialized knowledge. Problem solving was initiated at all levels in the organization. The location of authority was determined by concensus among workers and the leadership was flexible and adjustable.

THE IDEA OF CONTINGENCY

Organizational size is often cited as the single most important factor contributing to the degree of bureaucratization (27). However, as an outgrowth of the open-systems perspective on organizations of the 1960s (28–29), it was recognized that organizations are not closed systems and that the appropriateness of an organization design may be contingent upon a number of external contextual factors (30).

THE IMPORTANCE OF THE EXTERNAL ENVIRONMENT

Understanding the relationships between organizations and their environments has progressed rapidly since Terreberry (31) suggested that (1) organizational change is increasingly induced by external factors and (2) organizational adaptability is a result of key members making accommodations to changes in the environment. This perspective assumes that organizational performance is contingent upon a proper match between the environment and the design of the organization.

Environmental complexity as defined by Lawrence and Lorsch (32) assumes that both instabilities in the environment and the heterogeneity of components of the environment create uncertainties which result in different organizational designs. It has been assumed that environmental uncertainty affects the degree of formality of structure, the nature of interpersonal relationships, and the time orientation (short- vs. long-run) of employees. As uncertainty increases—that is, as environmental conditions become less stable—different organizational functions are affected in different ways. To cope and to maintain performance, organizations may divide into specialized subunits along functional lines. As a consequence, the subunits may develop varying priorities and have different time horizons. To ensure expected levels of effectiveness, managers must design a variety of mechanisms to achieve integration across subunits. Absence of such mechanisms may lead to conflict and diminished performance.

What design options are available to the manager faced with the consequences of increasing environmental uncertainty? Lawrence and Lorsch (32) advocate the creation of lateral relations, such as direct managerial contact across functions, interfunctional teams (either permanent or temporary), liasion roles, and integrating departments. Such design strategies have the ultimate effect of decentralizing decision making so that it takes place at the level of the organization where the necessary information exists. As we discuss later in this chapter, Stein and Kanter (33) have suggested a parallel organizational design as one mechanism for integrating persons from all levels in the organization in the decision-making process.

THE IMPORTANCE OF TECHNOLOGY

It has also been recognized that organizational design may be contingent upon the technology of the organization (29, 34). This approach suggests that organizational performance is contingent upon the congruence between the technology of the organization and its structure. Although the early work on technology and structure was conducted in industrial organizations, Perrow (35) recognized the importance of technology for human service organizations, especially hospitals (36). Technology was defined to include all activities or techniques necessary to change inputs or raw materials to outputs. In human service organizations, the raw materials are clients or patients, the techniques are treatments or services provided, and outputs are the clients or patients in their new form (37). Perrow described technology in terms of its degree of routineness. Two conditions were considered necessary for work to be routine: first, there are well established techniques which are sure to work; and second, these must be applied to essentially similar raw materials. Perrow (38) maintained that in human service organizations, such as health services organizations, the nature of the raw materials (patients or clients) is important, especially their variability, their instability, and the degree to which they are understood.

Specifically, Perrow (38) indicated that in many human service organizations where technology is more likely to be nonroutine, the structure will be less bureaucratized, there will be less programming of tasks, fewer rules and regulations, fewer levels in the hierarchy, greater coordination by feedback, greater decentralization in decision making, and a tendency to employ more professionals. Existing work on hospital nursing subunits by Leatt and Schneck (39) supports some of those ideas. In nursing units where technology was more complex (such as intensive care units), more professionals were employed and there was greater decentralization of decision making than in units where the technology was more routine (such as obstetrics or long-term care). Also, the characteristics of the technology appeared to account for considerable stress in nursing units, which in some instances could be modified by changes in structure and leadership style (40).

THE CONCEPT OF "FIT"

Since the introduction of systems analysis to organizations it has been recognized that organizations strive for a state of equilibrium or balance to survive (28, 41). An organization must maintain a favorable equilibrium not only with the external environment but specifically with its internal component parts. Contingency theory also recognizes the need for organizations to match organization designs to the various contingencies being faced in order to maximize performance. Recently, a number of writers (42–43) have emphasized a congruence perspective for organization design. Congruence suggests that the organization is most effective when its pieces fit together; this fit includes relationships among the organization's external environment, strategies, technologies, people, tasks, organization design, and informal arrangements.

ALTERNATIVES TO A CONTINGENCY APPROACH

Although organizational theorists have found the contingency model of organizations conceptually appealing, there has been little research demonstrating its validity, especially in health services organizations. A major limitation in contingency research has been that there have been few attempts to identify the combined effects of environment, technology, and size on organizational structures. Several authors have pointed out that any relationships between environment, technology, and structure may be coincidental and arbitrary, perhaps simply a product of the organization's myths, rituals, and traditions (44–45).

One alternative explanation of relationships between organizations and their environments has been provided by the population ecology or natural selection model (46–48). This approach focuses upon the birth, death, and dispersion of populations of organizations in specific environments over time.

Alternatively, the strategic choice perspective assumes that organizations are proactive, purposeful, and rational (49). This approach suggests that organizational design, rather than being a product of environmental/technological contingencies, is a result of strategic choices being made by top managers (50–52).

SYSTEMATIC ASSESSMENT BEFORE DESIGN

Earlier in the chapter, the need to carefully plan a change in organization design was stressed. The importance of matching a design with the organization's mission and strategies as well as obtaining participation from major stakeholders was emphasized. There are certain circumstances when health services managers will recognize that a design change may be necessary (5). For example:

1. *When the organization is experiencing severe problems.* Indicators of inadequate performance may be presented to the manager from external reviews such as accreditation processes, or from internal reviews such as financial statements and clinical audits. These problems may be identified at varying levels within the organization, for example, for a particular position, a workgroup, a department, or a total organization.

2. *When there is a change in the environment which directly influences internal policies.* In some circumstances there may be major changes in the environment, such as prospective payment for hospital services or capitation payment for all health services received by a given population. These changes may require a redesign and refocusing of key organizational groups.

3. *When new programs or product lines are targeted by the mission statement.* When an organization recognizes as high priority certain markets or product lines, an organization design change may be necessary to infuse resources into the new areas. Conversely, when old programs are to be dropped, new structural arrangements may be necessary.

4. *When there is a change in leadership.* New leadership may provide considerable opportunity to rethink the way in which the organization has been designed. New leadership tends to view the organization from a different perspective and may bring innovative ideas to the reorganization.

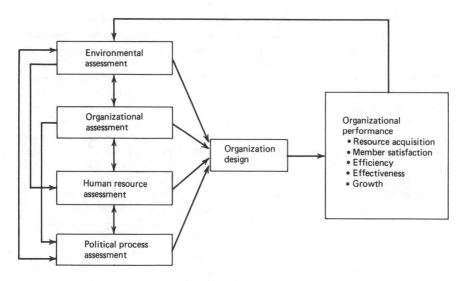

Figure 9.3. Overall framework for organization design considerations.

Once the potential requirement for a change in organization design has been identified, a systematic assessment of the organization is necessary. A number of models have been suggested as frameworks for categorizing the information needed for a thorough assessment (53–54). A model or conceptual framework is an essential tool to guide analysis and action. Most people who have been exposed to organizations have an implicit experience-based model; however, organizational theorists and researchers have now developed general models for thinking about organizations as total systems. The major factors that are essential to consider in an organizational assessment are shown in Figure 9.3.

These factors recognize that organizational design decisions should not be made in a vacuum; they need to be made in the context of a broad managerial framework, in which several factors are assessed simultaneously. The framework comprises *(1) environmental assessment* or assessment of the constraints and opportunities posed by the external environment, *(2) organization assessment* or systematic assessment of the strengths and weaknesses of the organization, *(3) human resource assessment* or consideration of the capabilities of employees and other participants in the organization, and *(4) political process assessment* or assessment of the internal political dynamics of the organization and how these may hinder or facilitate changes in organization design. By thinking broadly about organization design, health services managers may avoid mistakes such as failing to use the abilities of involved individuals in implementation, stumbling over political obstacles, or ignoring the wider environmental context of the organization at a given time.

SOME ALTERNATIVE ORGANIZATION DESIGNS

Recognizing that there is no one best way to design an organization, Mintzberg (8) has suggested five possible configurations. These five designs are based on a number of structural characteristics including job specialization, training needs, grouping and size of units, planning and control systems, horizontal linkages, and decentralization of decision making. The five designs—*simple structure, machine bureaucracy, professional bureaucracy, divisionalized form, and adhocracy*—are shown in Table 9.2.

The *simple structure* consists of a small unit with a few senior managers and a small group of workers. There are no specialized staff or technical support departments. Control is exercised by means of the CEO's direct supervision of workers. Information exchange is primarily informal, and there are few problems of coordination because of the small size of the organization. Within health services organizations this design option is most appropriate for such settings as a physician's practice, a physiotherapy clinic, or an independent nurse-practitioner's office. This design has the advantage of flexibility, but it is vulnerable to changes in key personnel such as the CEO.

A *machine bureaucracy*, as the name implies, is characterized by a highly formalized structure in which the emphasis is on work standardization. Decision making is centralized, and departments are grouped by function. This design option is appropriate for large, mature organizations that operate in stable environments. It is common among governmental hospitals, where the work is generally routine, repetitive, and stable.

Hospitals and universities are typical of *professional bureaucracies*. The key part of the organization is the operating core—in hospitals the patient-care units—and there is considerable decentralization in decision making to these areas. As the name implies, these organizations rely upon the skills of large numbers and varieties of professionals. The work is standardized by the skills of the individual professionals, which stem from their training and professional associations. Few first-line or middle managers are needed for supervision of work processes. This design option is appropriate in complex yet relatively stable environments and for perfecting techniques rather than inventing them.

The *divisionalized design* consists of a set of relatively independent organizations joined together by a cluster of central policies. The umbrella organization tends to be large, and each department or division is given considerable autonomy. There may be a high degree of decentralization in decision making; however, control of certain policy decisions may be retained centrally. A major advantage of the divisionalized structure is that decisions may be made within the semiautonomous units found in organizations that grow and become more complex, such as large hospital systems. While there are certain advantages to the divisional design, it is important to clarify the balance of power in terms of centralization/decentralization of decision making. One challenge with a divisionalized design is to achieve coordination within the organization across divisions.

The fifth type of design described by Mintzberg is the *adhocracy*. This design is considered appropriate for an organization that wishes to be innovative and therefore needs a fluid structure. Power continually shifts among teams of professionals and technical experts. A great deal of lateral communication and integration is necessary and coordination tends to be achieved through mutual adjustments among the teams. The adhocracy design can be costly, in that it creates role ambiguity for workers. This design may be most appropriate for a health services organization (such as an oncology unit) that focuses on research and whose main objective is to develop new techniques that can later be adopted by others on a more routine basis.

In an attempt to clarify how variations in organization design are important, even when providing the same kinds of services, Kaluzny and Konrad (55) illustrated Mintzberg's designs for primary-care services. Kaluzny and Konrad suggested that the simple structure is most appropriate for the conventional community-sponsored primary-care program where only a limited range of services is being offered and the organization is

TABLE 9.2. Mintzberg's Five Design Configurations

	Simple Structure	Machine Bureaucracy	Professional Bureaucracy	Divisionalized Form	Adhocracy
Key means of coordination	Direct supervision	Standardization of work	Standardization of skills	Standardization of outputs	Mutual adjustment
Key part of organization	Strategic apex	Technostructure	Operating core	Middle line	Support staff (with operatiang core in operating adhocracy)
Structural elements					
Specialization of jobs	Little specialization	Much horizontal and vertical specialization	Much horizontal specialization	Some horizontal and vertical specialization (between divisions and headquarters)	Much horizontal specialization
Training and indoctrination	Little training and indoctrination	Little training and indoctrination	Much training and indoctrination	Some training and indoctrination (of division managers)	Much training
Formalization of behavior—bureaucratic/organic	Little formalization—organic	Much formalization—bureaucratic	Little formalization—bureaucratic	Much formalization (within divisions)—bureaucratic	Little formalization—organic
Grouping	Usually functional	Usually functional	Functional and market	Market	Functional and market
Unit size	Wide	Wide at bottom, narrow elsewhere	Wide at bottom, narrow elsewhere	Wide at top	Narrow throughout
Planning and control systems	Little planning and control	Action planning	Little planning and control	Much performance control	Limited action planning (esp. in administrative adhocracy)
Liaison devices	Few liaison devices	Few liaison devices	Liaison devices in administration	Few liaison devices	Many liaison devices throughout
Decentralization	Centralization	Limited horizontal decentralization	Horizontal and vertical decentralization	Limited vertical decentralization	Selective decentralization

TABLE 9.2. Continued

	Simple Structure	Machine Bureaucracy	Professional Bureaucracy	Divisionalized Form	Adhocracy
Situational elements					
Age and size	Typically young and small	Typically old and large	Varies	Typically old and very large	Typically young (operating adhocracy)
Technical system	Simple, not regulating	Regulating but not automated, not very complex	Not regulating or complex	Divisible, otherwise like machine bureaucracy	Very complex, often automated (in administrative adhocracy), not regulating or complex (in operating adhocracy)
Environment	Simple and dynamic; sometimes hostile	Simple and stable	Complex and stable	Relatively simple and stable; diversified markets (esp. products and services)	Complex and dynamic; sometimes disparate (in administrative adhocracy)
Power	Chief executive control; often owner managed; not fashionable	Technocratic and external control; not fashionable	Professional operator control; fashionable	Middle-line control; fashionable (esp. in industry)	Expert control; very fashionable

SOURCE: Reprinted by permission of the Harvard Business Review. An exhibit from "Organizational Design: Fashion or Fit?" by Henry Mintzberg (January/February 1981). Copyright © 1981 by the President and Fellows of Harvard College; all rights reserved.

small. A machine bureaucracy may be more characteristic of primary health care services located within a government-funded department such as a public health unit. A professional bureaucracy may be appropriate for provider-sponsored primary care where the owners are the professionals (e.g., physicians). Finally, a divisionalized design may be illustrated by a primary-care program located within a general hospital setting. In this instance, the primary-care program is one division within the overall hospital design (56).

SOME DESIGNS FOR A VARIETY OF HEALTH SERVICES ORGANIZATIONS

What specific design options are available for health services managers, keeping in mind that the choices will depend on environmental demands, the organization's strategies, how activities can be grouped, and how decisions will be made?

Some examples of common designs seen in health services organizations are functional, divisional, matrix, and parallel.

FUNCTIONAL DESIGN

A functional design exists when labor is divided into departments specialized by functional area. An example is shown in Figure 9.4.

This kind of structure is typical of a nursing home, chronic-care facility, or small (less

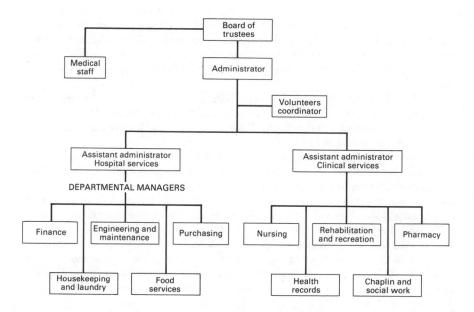

Figure 9.4. A functional design: nursing home or chronic-care facility.

than 100 beds) community general hospital. In Figure 9.4, the basic hospital services are separated from the clinical services. The actual number of functional departments (and departmental manager positions) depends upon the size of the organization. The functional design is most useful when the organization has only a few products or goals. From the management's viewpoint, the functional design enables decisions to be made on a centralized, hierarchical basis. Departmental managers are usually promoted from within the organization and have a depth of technical knowledge in the functional area.

The functional design is most appropriate when an organization is in a relatively simple, stable environment in which there are few changes taking place and there are a limited number of other organizations with which the organization has contact. Clearly, a functional design becomes unsuitable when an organization grows and begins to diversify its services, because interdepartmental coordination tends to be poor and decisions pile up at the top. If the environment becomes unstable, the functional design cannot cope because it does not have the facility to handle rapid information input or output and the response time is generally too slow.

DIVISIONAL DESIGN

The divisional design is often found in large academic medical centers that operate under conditions of high environmental uncertainty (exacerbated by relationships with the medical school), and high technological complexity because of intensive research activities. It is most appropriate for situations where clear divisions can be made within the organization and semiautonomous units can be created. Traditionally, in teaching hospitals the way of grouping units has been relatively clear cut; units have been grouped according to the accepted medical specialities, such as medicine, surgery, pediatrics, psychiatry, radiology, and pathology. More recently, hospitals are beginning to question the appropriateness of these traditional groupings and are moving toward defining product lines that cross traditional boundaries. Examples of "new" product lines are those organized around body organs (57), such as the heart (grouping cardiology and cardiovascular surgery) and the liver (grouping endocrinology, internal medicine, and surgery), or those grouped around services to specific target groups, such as the elderly or persons with cancer.

Divisionalization decentralizes decision making to the lowest level in the organization where the key expertise is available. Individual divisions have considerable autonomy for the clinical and financial operations. Each division has its own internal management structure, as illustrated in Figure 9.5.

The model illustrated in Figure 9.5 shows the physicians in charge of each clinical service as the person with direct authority over all divisional operations. Each division has a manager of nursing and/or patient services, a manager of administrative services, and a finance officer. These managers work as a team to direct the division's operations. The managers are also accountable to the vice-presidents of their disciplines.

In some hospitals, the manager of administrative services is given the authority of leader of the team at the divisional level. One advantage of placing the physician–manager as leader of the team is that the physicians within the division become more acutely aware of both the clinical and financial operations. In most instances, physicians who assume managerial responsibilities require some education in the principles of management (58).

This subunit structure enables the specialized units to handle relevant elements of

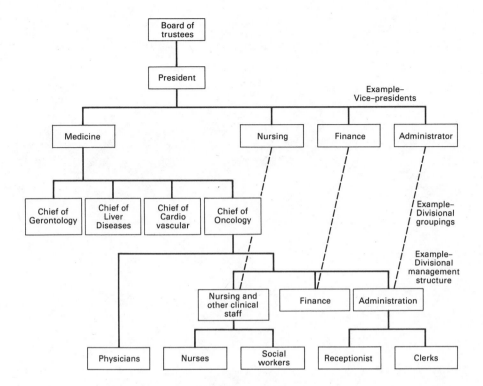

Figure 9.5. A divisional design: an academic medical center.

the environment directly, enhancing the organization's capacity to exchange information with the environment and to develop strategies tailored to the product lines. In many instances the divisions "purchase" central services from within the hospital and are provided incentives to operate their units cost effectively (59). At the same time the central service units are driven to operate efficiently, otherwise the divisions may choose to purchase services outside the hospital at a better rate.

Difficulties with the divisional design tend to occur in times of resource constraints, when priorities must be set at higher organizational levels. For example, a large teaching hospital may have difficulty arriving at a consensus about which patient programs should be given priority if divisional managers cannot see the perspective of the whole organization. In times of resource constraints, greater sharing of resources between divisions is required, and more effective horizontal integrating mechanisms need to be established (60).

MATRIX DESIGN

To overcome some of the problems of the functional and divisional designs, matrix or mixed designs have evolved to improve mechanisms of lateral coordination and infor-

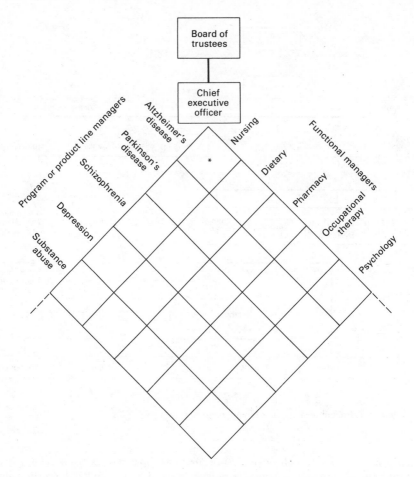

Figure 9.6. A matrix design: a psychiatric hospital. An individual worker in this example is part of the Alzheimer program as well as a member of the nursing department.

mation flow across the organization (61–62). An example matrix organization for a psychiatric hospital is provided in Figure 9.6.

The matrix organization, originally developed in the aerospace industry, is characterized by a dual authority system. There are usually functional and program (product line) managers, both reporting to a common superior and both exercising authority over workers within the matrix. Typically, a matrix organization is particularly useful in highly specialized technological areas that focus on innovation. The matrix design allows program managers to interact directly with the environment vis-a-vis technological developments. Usually, each program requires a multidisciplinary team approach; the matrix structure facilitates the coordination of the team and allows team members to contribute their special expertise.

The matrix design has some disadvantages that stem from the dual authority lines. Individual workers may find having two bosses to be untenable, since it creates conflicting expectations and ambiguity. The matrix design may also be expensive in that both functional and program managers may spend a considerable amount of time in meetings attempting to keep everyone informed of program activities. Additional costs may also be incurred because of the frequent requirement for dual accounting, budget, control, performance evaluation, and reward systems.

The use of the matrix design in health services organizations is becoming more common, particularly in organizations in which multidisciplinary approaches to patient care are being encouraged. Also, a program form of organization is being used in some health services organizations as a means of obtaining better control and accountability for program costs. This is especially true for health services organizations that are beginning to organize around product lines (as described in the divisional design), brought about by payment from third-party payers for specific groups of diagnoses.

To some degree, most health services organizations have many characteristics of a matrix organization, although their design may not be formally named as such. For example, multiple authority over patient care is clearly apparent in most hospitals. Most health professionals, such as nurses, psychologists, physiotherapists, pharmacists, occupational therapists, and social workers, have formal reporting relationships to their functional department, but are also accountable to physicians for the quality of care provided. Multidisciplinary teams, which facilitate lateral communication and coordination of work, are an essential feature of almost all health services organizations, including community health, long-term care, home care, and hospitals. Accordingly, many health services organizations may be moving toward a formal matrix structure.

PARALLEL DESIGN

A further example of a mixed design is a parallel structure, which has developed as a mechanism for promoting quality of working life in organizations (33). The bureaucratic or functional organization retains responsibility for routine activities in the organization, while the parallel structure is responsible for complex problem solving that requires participatory mechanisms. The parallel structure is a means of managing and responding to changing internal and external conditions. It also provides an opportunity for persons occupying positions at various hierarchical levels in the bureaucratic structure to participate in organizational decisions (14). It is on this basis that the parallel organization has potential for building a high quality of working life. Within the parallel organization a series of permanent committees are established with representation from all levels in the formal hierarchy as well as from all departments, depending upon the problem or task at hand. An example of a parallel structure for an acute general hospital is shown in Figure 9.7.

Advantages to individual staff members are perceived to include expansion of their power, opportunities to affect the organization's decisions, the feeling of being involved in organizational issues, and the potential for individual growth through broadening of the range of work activities. Advantages to the organization are potentially those of increased performance. Some possible disadvantages of the parallel structure are: *(1)* organization members may spend too much time in meetings, thus increasing costs of operations; *(2)* the parallel structure may begin to assume responsibilities for routine decisions, consequently overriding the bureaucratic structure; and *(3)* conflicts over perceived priorities and resource allocation may occur between the bureaucratic and parallel structures.

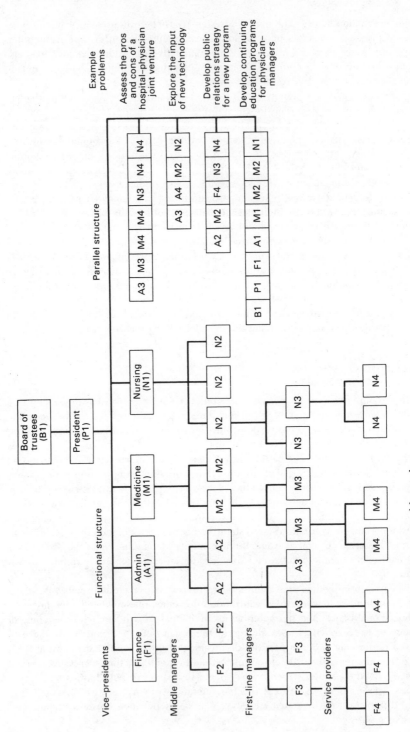

Figure 9.7. A parallel design: an acute general hospital.

WHAT WILL INFLUENCE DESIGN DECISIONS IN HEALTH SERVICES ORGANIZATIONS OF THE FUTURE?

Based on the previous sections, a number of suggestions can be made about particular factors, somewhat unique to health services organizations, which may influence design decisions. These factors are generic and are likely to vary in importance through time and in various geographic locations. These influences may be classified according to whether they originate from the environment, the organization itself, the human resources, or the political process (see Figure 9.3).

THE FUTURE ENVIRONMENT

The future environment for most health services organizations is predicted to be both complex and dynamic (see Chapter 14). A variety of pressures will be exerted externally which will by necessity influence design decisions. Some of the most important pressures will be:

- Increasing competition among health services organizations providing similar services in the same geographic location to maximize their market share.
- Increasing attempts by governments at all levels to regulate the quantity and quality of services provided.
- Changing systems of reimbursement to health services organizations to control costs.
- Expanding private sector involvement in health services and the continued growth of large multihospital systems.
- Changing demographic characteristics of the population being served with an increase in the proportion of elderly persons needing services.
- Greater sophistication of the general public and consumers of health services in terms of their demands on the system.
- Increasing involvement of trustees, physicians, and other health professionals in the strategic planning function of health services organizations.
- Increasing attempts by external professional associations and accrediting bodies to set standards for professional conduct in health services organizations.
- Increasing range of services being provided outside the traditional hospitals including ambulatory care programs, home care, long-term care, and so on.
- Rapidly developing medical technologies and proliferation of increasing specialized services.
- Increased information demands; development of real-time information-processing systems to relate to the external environment; and growth of artificial intelligence systems.

THE ORGANIZATION

Internal to most health services organizations are a series of structural and operating processes which provide opportunities or constraints on design decisions. For example:

- Increasing corporatization of the structure of health services organizations.
- Demands to monitor quality of care.
- Demands to control costs, operate efficiently, and increase productivity.
- Increasing need for comprehensive clinical and financial information systems.
- Fewer financial resources.
- Changing working relationships to create more situations with two or more boss systems.
- Increasing need to coordinate activities internally and to manage conflict creatively.

HUMAN RESOURCES

The particular characteristics of employees and other service providers available now or in the future may strongly affect the types of design decisions that may be made. For example:

- Many physicians who are important providers of service in health services organizations are not employees and, therefore, have considerable autonomy.
- Increasing attention by physicians to malpractice insurance.
- The number and variety of occupational groups in health services is continuously increasing.
- Most of the occupational groups perceive themselves to be professionals or are aspiring to full professional status.
- Increasing availability with a tendency toward oversupply of certain physician specialists.
- Increasing need for managers with professional training.
- Increasing invasion of health services organizations by a variety of unions.
- Closer scrutiny by unions as some health services organizations undergo retrenchment.
- Increasing need to educate middle managers in strategic management and in adopting a marketing orientation.
- The need for career planning and management development programs linked more closely to the organization's strategic plan.
- Escalating pressures to provide continuing education programs to health professionals.

POLITICAL PROCESS

Because of the uncertainty and ambiguities which may exist in health services organizations and the variety of professional groups involved, the informal network may be particularly active. Informal leaders may be especially helpful to managers in identifying how a change in organization design might be received. Informal leaders may be useful in communicating ideas about change to the grass-roots level in the organization or in repressing incorrect rumors that could damage the implementation process. Through the informal network, managers can identify which units or departments might be most or least receptive and attempt to involve key players in the redesign process. Additional suggestions are discussed in Chapter 11.

Although these factors are perhaps not comprehensive of all situations or applicable in all circumstances they are potentially important when considering a new organizational design. Most importantly, they emphasize the need for designs that are flexible; designs that can breathe and grow with the organization.

THE LIFE-CYCLE VIEW

Until now our discussion has focused on the importance of designing organizations in keeping with their environments, their information needs, their human resources, and their politics. However, environment, information needs, human resources, and politics all change. To a certain extent, organizations go through relatively predictable cycles that have different design implications. For example, Starkweather and Kisch (63) suggested four phases through which health services organizations pass. The first is the *search* phase, which is characterized by newness, innovation, and a sense of ascendency as the organization procures resources and seeks to establish its identity. The administrative structure of an organization in this phase is typically open and informal. The *success* phase is characterized by achievement in procuring patients, staff, and financial resources. The internal structure of the organization during this phase becomes somewhat more formalized to manage the usually larger scale of operation. The *bureaucratic* phase is characterized by a relatively rigid conformity to rules and procedures; the organization is isolated from its clients in that it receives little feedback from them. During this phase the organization may begin to decline because of its inability to respond to changes in the environment or to alter the environment to fit its needs. The *succession* phase is characterized by the development of new ways of providing services, often through the development of new units within the organization.

Kimberly and Miles (64) and Kimberly and Quinn (65) raise important questions about organization design issues associated with such stages of the life cycle. Given that managers wish to design organizations for optimal performance, it makes sense that different designs are more appropriate at different stages of an organization's development. For example, a simple structure might be appropriate for a new organization during its search phase. As the organization grows, achieves success, and perhaps diversifies, a different design, such as a machine or professional bureaucracy, may be appropriate. During periods of temporary or permanent decline, the organization may need to consider the appropriateness of an adhocracy or a parallel design to help generate new ideas and services. These issues are critically important for organizational viability. The following section provides two case studies of health services organizations in transition.

MINI-CASE: STAYWELL'S PRODUCT-LINE MANAGEMENT DESIGN

Staywell Memorial is a 400-bed, acute-care community hospital located in the midwestern section of the United States. Until recently it was organized along traditional, functional lines. However, with the growth of prospective payment plans and increased competition, the hospital found it necessary to better monitor its costs and market its programs on a service-by-service basis. As the vice-president for planning commented: "Managing a hospital these days on a functional department-by-department basis doesn't really capture the way in which services are provided and marketed to consumer groups."

As a result, the hospital is considering a product line management concept

(66). *Product line management* is defined as the placement of a person in charge of all aspects of a given product or group of products. The product line is a revenue and cost center and the person in charge is responsible for all budgetary and financial responsibilities associated with the product. The person is also responsible for coordinating all the functional resources (e.g., planning, marketing, human resources, etc.) required to successfully manage the product line. The hospital believes that product line management will provide important advantages by increasing operational efficiencies and enhancing market share. Operational efficiencies will be gained by analyzing cost and revenues across related product lines so that redundancies will be eliminated and synergies captured. Market share can be enhanced by targeting marketing strategies to the group of products and being able to promote these to different segments of the market as appropriate (e.g., the elderly, women, children, etc.).

The major challenges the hospital faces in implementing the new concept include: *(1)* educating the board, management, and medical staff to the change; *(2)* choosing criteria for grouping the products; and *(3)* selecting and training the product line managers. The hospital realizes that the change will require board and top management support and appropriate involvement and support of key medical staff and hospital-based physician leaders. The physicians must see it as a better way to manage resources, maintain or enhance quality, and increase patient flow.

While many criteria can be used for grouping products, the hospital plans to use the following: *(1)* similarity of technology, *(2)* similarity of markets, *(3)* similarity in the production process, *(4)* similarity in the distribution process, and *(5)* similarity in the use of human resources. By grouping products with these kinds of similarities, economies of scale and synergies ($2 + 1 = 5$ solutions) can be generated. Based on these criteria, the hospital is considering the following product line candidates: women's care, oncology, cardiology, rehabilitation, substance abuse, long-term care, and health promotion.

The selection and training of the product line managers is particularly important. Individuals must be identified who have good technical knowledge of the product line and good analytical and interpersonal skills. In particular, they must be innovative, feel comfortable with ambiguity and complexity, and be able to work with more than one manager. The latter is reflected in the hospital's planned organizational chart, shown in Figure 9.8. This chart shows a matrix organization in which the product line managers work with both the functional department heads and with the product line assistant vice president. Recognizing that many problems and issues cut across the product lines, the hospital also plans to establish a steering committee to deal with these issues. This committee, composed of both product line managers and functional department heads, will also be charged with reviewing the overall performance of the product lines, and recommending addition, deletion, or modification of existing product lines.

The hospital believes that the *key success factors* include the following:

- A strong management information system that links clinical, financial, and volume data by product.
- A strong budgeting/financial system that can disaggregate costs and revenues so that accountability can be appropriately assigned.
- Reward systems to encourage innovation and risk taking.
- Relevant clinical involvement of physicians, nurses, and other health professionals to deal with new technology, diagnosis and treatment patterns, quality, and patient convenience issues.

- A strong support staff, particularly in the areas of marketing, finance, and planning.
- The need to align authority and responsibility.
- The need for integrative mechanisms that cut across product lines; hence the development of the steering committee.
- The need for a concerted management development program that emphasizes *(1)* the ability to work with more than one manager, *(2)* communication skills, *(3)* conflict management skills, *(4)* computer literacy, and *(5)* creativity.

While the hospital has a well-developed plan for implementing the product line management concept, we would advise them to think ahead 3–5 years to the possible evolvement of a *market manager concept.* Product line management works best when many products go to relatively few markets. This is the situation which the hospital currently faces. But as markets grow and segment by geography, age, buyer groups, and preferences and tastes, the hospital may face a situation where the number of target markets is as large or larger than the number of products. In this case, it may be wiser to organize around markets and convert product line managers into market managers. This will require an increased emphasis on marketing skills and the need to differentiate the different products for different markets. Examples include the development of executive fitness programs for men versus women and the development of health promotion programs for young adults versus the elderly.

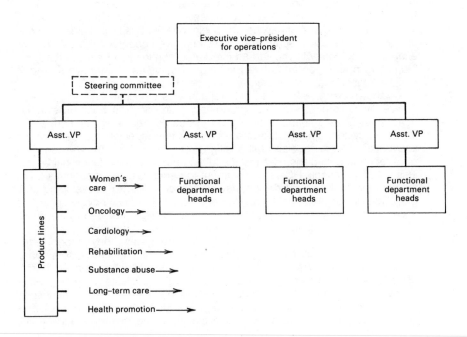

Figure 9.8. Product line manager design.

MINI-CASE: MACRO ORGANIZATIONAL DESIGN IN A MULTIUNIT HEALTH CARE COMPANY

Founded in 1968, the Hospital Corporation of America (HCA) owns or manages approximately 500 hospitals worldwide and is involved in a variety of alternative delivery system activities. A $6-billion company headquartered in Nashville, Tennessee, it has grown rapidly over the past 20 years. Rapid growth requires continual changes in organization. As one HCA executive expressed: "The organization design we choose is almost outdated the day we implement it."

In recent times, HCA's organization design has been based on three guiding principles. First, the design should fit and promote the company's strategic direction. In brief, structure follows strategy; form follows function. Second, the design should speed up and facilitate decision making. While the company has a long history of decentralized management, it has recognized the need to balance decentralization with structures that facilitate coordination across previously independent operations. This approach is necessary to respond more quickly to changing market conditions.

A third guiding principle recognizes the need to develop different structures and designs in different parts of the company. Different areas have different needs, demands, preferences, and circumstances. The organization should be designed to meet these varying needs. The overall design need not be internally consistent.

Design Follows Strategy

The overall strategic vision of HCA is to become a national health care company. A central part of this vision is to develop several regional health care systems through ownership and affiliations which join together hospitals, long-term care, ambulatory care, and insurance services in a given geographic area. This will enable the company to provide an integrated continuum of care to the community, to present an attractive package of services to employers, and to achieve managerial and service economies of scale.

As shown in Figure 9.9, their general acute-care hospitals are currently organized in two groups with each group having six divisions. Each division has a vice-president, a financial officer, a business development person, an information system specialist, and a reimbursement specialist. Except for the information system specialist, all positions report directly to the division vice-president with dotted-line relationships to the corporate office functional heads. This structure reflects HCA's commitment to decentralized management. But the company believes the design may not fit their strategy of developing geographically integrated health care systems, since there is no direct linkage to the alternative delivery system activities currently being developed by the health plans and the marketing and development divisions of the company.

As they develop the geographical health care system, they recognize the need to modify their current hospital divisional structure, at least in some parts of the country. One alternative is to develop regional health system vice-presidents in charge of owned hospitals that operate in "cluster markets," other hospitals in the larger area, managed hospitals in the areas, and out-of-hospital services such as home health and ambulatory surgery (see Figure 9.10). This type of structure will facilitate decision making along the entire service line

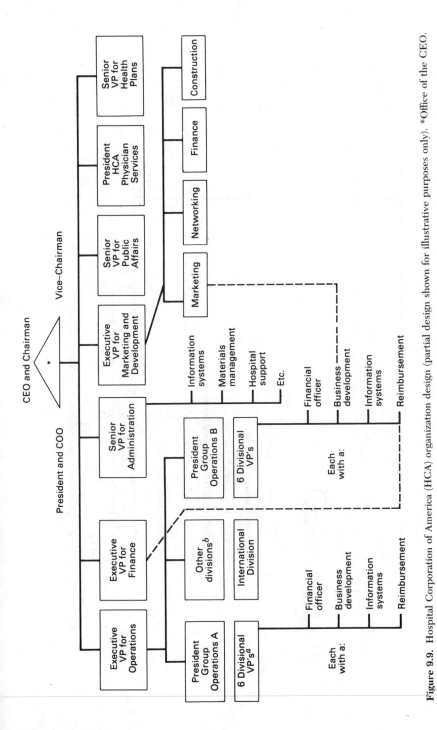

Figure 9.9. Hospital Corporation of America (HCA) organization design (partial design shown for illustrative purposes only). *Office of the CEO.

[a]Approximately 15 hospitals in each division. [b]Includes separate division for psychiatric hospitals, managed hospitals, and the international hospital division.

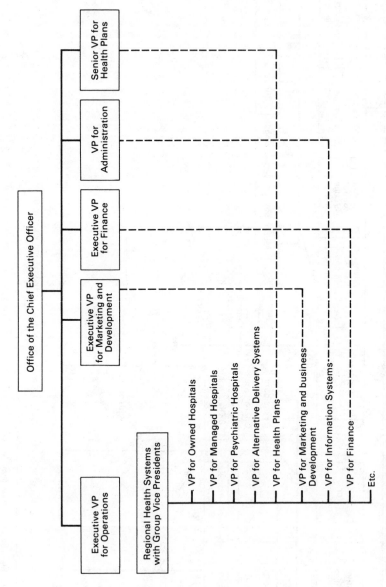

Figure 9.10. Hospital Corporation of America (HCA) transition design.

continuum and will help assure needed integration across the various delivery channels.

Current Design and Environment Constrain Strategy

While HCA recognizes that their organization structure must largely follow and be supportive of their new strategic directions, they are also aware that their strategic choices (see Chapter 13) are to some extent constrained by their current structure and environment. Three factors to note are: *(1)* the speed of change in the health care industry; *(2)* people's current skills, experiences, interests, and mindsets; *(3)* organization culture. The speed of change within the health care industry has caused the company to change some of its plans "on the dime." For example, when an early strategy to develop its own insurance company was met with formidable opposition by Blue Cross/Blue Shield plans in key markets, HCA quickly dropped the idea and switched to developing a business joint-venture relationship with Equitable Life Insurance Company. Such quick shifts in strategy often result in quick "jerks" in organization structure. For example, a newly created office of business development was dismantled and a separate division of health plans established along with a new division of marketing and development.

Also, HCA faces the constraint of matching people's skills, interests, and experience with the needs of the new strategy and demands of the new organization design. Sometimes, what seems to be the best match between design and strategy cannot be implemented because the right human resources are not available. In HCA's case this was true in developing marketing expertise to serve the new strategic directions.

In some cases the biggest constraint on the ability to implement a new strategic direction is the culture of the organization itself. This problem is particularly significant when the new direction differs greatly from what has gone on before. In HCA's case, this has involved going from a *hospital* company to a diversified health services company. Providing out-of-hospital and insurance services requires different technologies, resources, philosophies, and mindsets—in addition to different organization structures. It takes time for individuals who have previously been rewarded for managing efficient individual hospitals to effectively change to a system in which they will be rewarded for cooperating with and managing a continuum of health services both inside and outside the hospital. This involves fundamental changes in the organization's culture, values, and methods of behaving. While new organization designs can facilitate adoption of new cultures and values, time is also needed to prepare people for the changes; HCA recognized this need. The president and chief operating officer spent much of 1 year personally visiting hospital managers in the field explaining the importance of the new strategic direction and what would be needed on the part of everyone to succeed.

At the time of this writing, HCA's structure is in transition. More importantly, they realize that it will always be in transition. This is not only because of changes in strategy and the environment (see Chapter 10), but also because the people and culture of the organization are often not in sync with the strategy–environment demands. Thus organization design at any one point in time will seem incomplete and, over time, may appear somewhat fluid and even amorphous. The lesson of HCA, as one example of a major multiunit health care company, is the need to give *continuous attention* to the environment–strategy–design–people–culture interface.

DESIGN GUIDELINES FOR HEALTH SERVICES MANAGERS

Although it is not possible to predict all possible factors which should be taken into consideration in organization design decisions, we offer the following principles as guidelines.

MANAGERIAL GUIDELINES

Designing New Organizations

1. Development of a mission statement and strategic plan that fits the constraints and opportunities of the environment is essential to the development of a new organization.

2. At least minimal goal agreement among the major participants is essential.

3. A balance must be struck between organic and mechanistic structures and processes. Organic design features are important for developing and recognizing new ideas. At the same time, it is important to be sensitive to the need for some degree of structuring as the organization implements these ideas and begins to grow.

4. The roles of the major parties involved should be relatively clearly articulated.

5. The development of lateral relationships can be particularly useful in organizations characterized by a high percentage of professionals. Lateral relationships permit loyalty to one's profession at the same time they create a forum for sharing information on organizationally relevant role expectations and feedback on performance.

6. Skill development is particularly important in the early stages of an organization's growth, especially the development of interpersonal skills to facilitate communication.

7. The amount of autonomy granted to subunits depends on the degree of task interdependence, the autonomy needs of organizational participants, and the communication and related skills of the individuals involved. The role of the CEO is particularly important during the start-up period (55, 67).

Designing Established Organizations for Long-Term Growth and Stability

1. There is often a need to reassess the organization's mission and strategic plan in light of changes occurring as time passes.

2. As organizations consider issues related to long-term growth and stability, accountability becomes particularly important. It may be necessary to change the organization's design to make health professionals more accountable for their behavior, especially when there are pressures from the external environment to control costs. This may involve decentralized structures or the creation of lateral relationships.

3. Management/clinical information systems, reward systems, and evaluation systems that are consistent with the new designs must be created.

4. The compatibility between changes in job design, unit design, and overall organization design must be considered. For example, a shift to primary nursing may require different administrative support and different patterns of linkages with other departments (see Chapter 6).

Designing to Correct Organizational Decline

1. Most importantly, managers must recognize early signs of decline. They must guard against "perceptual insensitivity," the danger of seeing their behaviors as succeeding long after their effectiveness has waned.

2. Strategies used during the growth and stability phases will not work during the decline phase. The organization's mission and overall strategies should be reassessed and priorities reexamined. The organization must contemplate the following actions (68):

   a. Acquiring more resources from external sources rather than arguing over the limited resources at hand.

   b. Attempting to manipulate the environment.

   c. Identifying entrepreneurial personnel with creative ideas and giving them freedom of action.

   d. Adopting a more fluid organizational structure characterized by free communication, even if consensus is minimal.

   e. Deciding which projects should come first.

   f. Counteracting internal dissension and inefficiency by increasing participation, coordination, and trust.

3. As suggested above, forums should be established for making information accessible for problem solving. Task forces and parallel organizations may be necessary.

4. Where changes must be made, it is frequently better to drop entire units in the organization than to make across-the-board cuts. The latter weakens all aspects of the organization including its areas of strength. Reduction of services may have positive effects. These can provide opportunities for selective program development and creation of excellence in targeted areas.

SUMMARY

Throughout the chapter we have attempted to emphasize the critical importance of managers assuming a proactive role in organization design. The design tasks are too essential to be delegated completely to others inside or outside the organization. A team approach is necessary if a design is to be successfully implemented and to maximize organizational performance.

We have also emphasized that transitions for organizations almost inevitably involve changes in the organization's structure. The design of an organization flows most naturally following decisions to modify an organization's strategy whether the aim is to expand or contract services or simply to stay the same (69).

We have four concluding suggestions for health services managers when considering design changes (69).

1. *Keep things small.* Even though many of our health services organizations today are large and complex and consequently may have a tendency to become too bureaucratized, it is still possible to introduce a feeling of smallness in the organization. A skillful health services manager will be able to create

"pockets" of activity within the organization which will foster creativity. The organizational culture of smallness can be fostered through maximizing face to face communication within and among groups, by the creation of task forces and ad hoc groups to address special problems the organization may face (70–71).

2. *Keep things flexible.* Organizations, like individuals faced with uncertainty or ambiguity, have a tendency to become rigid and to hang on to often unimportant traditions. During periods of transition it is essential that an organization remains flexible, ready for action, and open to new ideas. We have already discussed the parallel design, a form of organizational structure that maximizes flexibility. This approach enables a health services manager to keep on top of things and to be prepared to act as necessary. All organizations are or should be in a constant state of redesign.

3. *Keep in tune.* During times of transition it is critical that health services managers continuously monitor events taking place within their organization as well as in the environment. It is important that health services managers develop a network of individuals with whom a relationship of trust can be established so that information on changes inside and outside the organization can quickly be obtained.

4. *Know what your organization can do well.* Part of keeping in tune involves a rather objective assessment of your own organization's strengths. Knowing what your organization can do well facilitates the strategic planning process to enable the organization to build upon its strengths. In health services organizations we are becoming increasingly aware that it is not essential, efficient, or effective for every health services organization to try to provide all services to all people. Accordingly, a successful health services manager will target the services the organization can provide at a level of excellence and match those with target groups in the market place.

DISCUSSION QUESTIONS

1. You have just been appointed Director of Ambulatory Care Programs in a major academic medical center in a large metropolitan area. The programs you have been made responsible for include emergency services, day surgery, a rape crisis center, doctors' outpatient clinics, and radiological and laboratory services. Each of these programs has a program manager, but there is no job description for these positions. How would you proceed to design the role of the program manager in relation to other positions in your department?

2. Take an organization you are familiar with (preferably one you have worked in) and reflect upon the potential problems in the design of the organization. What categories of information would you need to assess the appropriateness of the design of the organization?

3. As a manager of a nursing home in a small community with a large proportion of elderly persons you suspect there may be an opportunity to diversify and expand the services of your organization to include home health services, emergency services, and day care services. What alternative organizational designs might you consider both for the initial start-up phase as well as for the long run?

4. You have been given a job as an executive assistant in the corporate office of a large chain of hospitals which includes over 200 hospitals in 6 different states. The orga-

nization is going through a stage of developing its policies concerning the extent to which physicians in each of the hospitals can set standards for the practice of medicine in each facility independently from the corporate office. The president has asked you to draft a policy indicating which decisions should be centralized and which should be decentralized. What should the policy say?

5. Your organization, a 250-bed community general hospital, is located in the suburb of a large metropolitan area. Many young professional couples who work in the city have recently moved into the community because a new commuter train has been implemented which facilitates fast commuting. Many of these couples have young families. Traditionally the hospital has provided a wide range of services to all age groups. Discuss the potential of the organization to target the health needs of the new community groups and consider the implications any changes may have for the hospital's organization design.

SUGGESTED READINGS

Daft, R.L. *Organization theory and design* (2nd ed.). Minnesota: West Publishing Co., 1986.
The second edition of this book provides an up-to-date review of basic concepts of organizational theory and design. The discussion relates to general theory and design without application specifically to health services organizations. As such, it provides a good overview.

Hasenfeld, Y. *Human service organization.* Englewood Cliffs, NJ: Prentice Hall, 1983
Hasenfeld provides an excellent review of the key characteristics of human services organizations and their unique needs in designing structure and processes. The book is well grounded in theory and reviews empirical research that has examined goals, technology, structure, and processes in human service organizations.

Mintzberg, H. *Structuring in fives: Designing effective organizations.* Englewood Cliffs, NJ: Prentice Hall, 1983.
This book is written for managers, staff specialists, and consultants who have particular interests in designing effective organizations. The main parameters of design are discussed and Mintzberg's five designs are outlined in detail.

Zander, A. *The purpose of groups and organizations.* San Francisco, CA: Jossey-Bass, Publishers, 1985.
In this book a systematic account is provided of how groups develop within organizations, how decision-making roles are decided, and how groups evaluate their own performance.

REFERENCES

1. Kilman, R. *Social systems design.* New York: North-Hillard, 1977.
2. Stoner, J.A.F. *Management.* Englewood Cliffs, N.J.: Prentice Hall, 1978.
3. Hodge, B.J., & Anthony, W.P. *Organization theory* (2nd ed.). Boston, MA: Allyn and Bacon, Inc. 1984.
4. Nees, D.B., & Greiner, L.E. Seeing behind the look-alike management consultants. *Organizational Dynamics,* 1985, Winter, 68–79.

5. Kimberly, J.R. The anatomy of organizational design. *Journal of Management*, 1984, *10*(1), 109–126.

6. Jaeger, B.J. The concept of corporate planning. *Health Care Management Review*, 1982, Summer, *7*(3), 15–24.

7. Pearce, J.A. The company mission as a strategic tool. *Sloan Management Review*, 1982, Spring, *23*(3), 15–24.

8. Mintzberg, H. *Structuring in fives: Designing effective organizations.* Englewood Cliffs, NJ: Prentice-Hall, 1983.

9. Kotter, J.P. Power, success, and organizational effectiveness. *Organizational Dynamics*, 1978, *6*(3), 27–40.

10. Quick, J.C., Dalton, J.E., Nelson, D.L., & Quick, J.D. Health administration can be stressful . . . . but not necessarily distressful. *Hospital and Health Service*, 1985, Sept./Oct., 101–111.

11. Kovner, A.R. *Really trying: A career guide for the health services manager.* Washington, D.C.: AUPHA Press, 1984.

12. Wowk, P.I. Health care management: A letter to the President. *Hospital and Health Services Administration*, 1985, March/April, 35–45.

13. McCann, J.E., & Gilmore, T.N. Diagnosing organizational decision making through responsibility charting. *Sloan Management Review*, 1983, Winter, *24*(2), 3–15.

14. Kanter, R.M. Dilemmas of managing participation. *Organizational Dynamics*, 1983, Winter, 5–27.

15. Zandler, A. *The purposes of groups and organizations.* San Francisco, CA: Jossey-Bass Publishers, 1985.

16. Kaluzny, A.D. Design and management of disciplinary and interdisciplinary work groups in health service organization: Review and critique. *Medical Care Review*, 1985, *42*(1).

17. Bass, L.W. *Management by task forces.* Mt. Airy, MD: Tavistock, 1961.

18. Delbecq, A.L., & Gill, S.L. Justice as a prelude to teamwork in medical centres. *Health Care Management Review*, 1985, Winter, 45–51.

19. Shortell, S.M. The medical staff of the future: Replanting the garden. *Frontiers of Health Services Management*, 1985, Spring, *1*(3), 3–48.

20. Perrow, C. *Organizational analysis: A sociological view.* Belmont, CA: Wadsworth Publishing Co. Inc., 1970.

21. Aldrich, H.E., & Whetton, D.A. Organization-sets, action-sets, and networks: Making the most of simplicity. In P.C. Nystrom and W.H. Starbuck (Eds.). *Handbook of organizational design*, Vol. 1. London: Oxford University Press, 1981, 385–408.

22. Alexander, H.E., & Schroer, K.A. Governance in multihospital systems: An assessment of decision-making responsibility. *Hospital and Health Services Administration*, 1985, March–April, 9–20.

23. Provan, K. Interorganizational cooperation and decisionmaking autonomy in a consortium multihospital system. *Academy of Management Review*, 1984, 9, 494–504.

24. Alexander, J.A., & Fennell, M.L. Patterns of decision making in multihospital systems. *Journal of Health and Social Behavior*, 1986, *27*(March), 14–27.

25. Perrow, C. *Complex organizations: A Critical Essay.* Glenview, IL: Scott, Foresman and Co., 1972.

26. Burns, T., & Stalker, G.M. *The management of innovation*. London: Tavistock, 1961.

27. Child, J. Predicting and understanding organizational structure. *Administrative Science Quarterly*, 1973, *18*, 168–185.

28. Katz, D. and Kahn, R.L. *The social-psychology of organizations*. New York: John Wiley and Sons, 1966.

29. Thompson, J.D. *Organizations in action*. New York: McGraw-Hill, 1967.

30. Strasser, S. The effective application of contingency theory in health settings: Problems and recommended solutions. *Health Care Management Review*, 1983, Winter, 15–23.

31. Terreberry, S. The evolution of organization environments. *Administrative Science Quarterly*, 1968, *12*, 590–613.

32. Lawrence, P., & Lorsch, J. *The organization and its environment*. Cambridge, MA: Harvard University Press, 1967.

33. Stein, B.A., & Kanter, R.M. Building the parallel organization: Creating mechanisms for permanent quality of work life. *Journal of Applied Behavioural Science*, 1980, *16*, 371–286.

34. Woodward, J. *Industrial organizations*. London: Oxford University Press, 1965.

35. Perrow, C. A framework for comparative analysis of organizations. *American Sociological Review*, 1967, *32*, 194–208.

36. Perrow, C. Hospitals: Technology, structure, and goals. In J.G. March (Ed.). *Handbook of organizations*. New York: Rand McNally and Co., 1965, 910–971.

37. Hasenfeld, Y. *Human service organizations*. Englewood Cliffs, NJ: Prentice Hall, 1983.

38. Perrow, C. *Organizational analysis: A sociological view*. Belmont, CA: Wadsworth Publishing Co. Inc., 1970.

39. Leatt, P., & Schneck, R. Technology, size, and environment and structure. *Organization Studies*, 1982, *3*(3), 221–242.

40. Leatt, P., & Schneck, R. Sources and management of organization stress in nursing subunits in Canada. *Organization Studies*, 1985, *6*(1), 55–79.

41. Katz, D., & Kahn, R.L. *The social-psychology of organizations*. New York: John Wiley and Sons, 1966 and 1978.

42. Nadler, D.A., & Tushman, M.L. A model for diagnosing organizational behaviour. *Organizational Dynamics*, 1980, *8* (Autumn), 35–51.

43. Randolph, W.A., & Dess, G.G. The congruence perspective of organization design: A conceptual model and multivariate research approach. *Academy of Management Review*, 1984, *9* (1), 114–127.

44. Meyer, J., & Rowan, B. Institutionalized organizations: Formal structure as myth and ceremony. *American Journal of Sociology*, 1977, *83*, 340–363.

45. Starbuck, W.H. Congealing oil: Inventing ideologies to justify acting ideologies out. *Journal of Management Studies*, 1982, *19*, 3–27.

46. Hannan, M., & Freeman, J. The population ecology of organizations. *American Journal of Sociology*, 1977, *82*, 95–115.

47. Aldrich, H.E. *Organizations and environments*. Englewood Cliffs, NJ: Prentice Hall, 1979.

48. Aldrich, H.E., McKelvey, B., & Ulrich, D. Design strategy from the population perspective. *Journal of Management*, 1984, Spring.

49. Pfeffer, J. Organizations and organization theory. Research paper No. 597, Research Paper Series, Graduate School of Business, Stanford University, 1981.

50. Chandler, A.D. *Strategy and structure*. Cambridge, MA: M.I.T. Press, 1962.

51. Child, J. Organizational structure, environment, and performance: The role of strategic choice. *Sociology*, 1972, *6*, 2–22.

52. Pfeffer, J., & Salancik, G.R. *The external control of organizations: A resource dependency perspective*. New York: Harper & Row, 1978.

53. Van de Ven, A.H., & Ferry, D.L. *Measuring and assessing organizations*, New York: John Wiley and Sons, 1980.

54. Tichy, N.M. Diagnosis for complex health care delivery systems: A model and case study. *The Journal of Applied Behavioural Sciences*, 1978, *14*(3), 305–320.

55. Kaluzny, A.D., & Konrad, T.R. Organizational designs and the management of primary care services. In *Management of rural primary care concepts and cases*. Chicago, IL: HRET, 1982.

56. Shortell, S.M., Wheeler, T.M., & Wittinger, J.R.C. *Hospital–physician joint ventures*. Ann Arbor, MI: Health Administration Press, 1984.

57. Gosselin, R. Probing into task interdependencies: The case of physicians in a teaching hospital. *Journal of Management Studies*, 1985, *22*(5), 466–497.

58. Aluise, J.J., Boddewic, S.P., & McLaughlin, C.P. Organizational development in academic medicine: An educational approach. *Health Care Management Review*, 1985, Winter, 37–43.

59. Heyssel, R.M. et al. Decentralized management in a teaching hospital. *New England Journal of Medicine*, 1984, *310*(22), 1477–1480.

60. Phillips, R.L., Posner, B.C., & Walker, D.D. A strategy for interunit problem solving. *Health Care Management Review*, 1985, Winter, *10*(1), 53–59.

61. Kolodny, H.F. Evolution to a matrix organization. *Academy of Management Review*, 1979, *4*, 543–553.

62. Griener, L.E., & Schien, V.E. The paradox of managing a project-oriented matrix: Establishing coherence within chaos. *Sloan Management Review*, 1981, Winter, *22*(2), 17–22.

63. Starkweather, D., & Kisch, A. A model of the life cycle dynamics of health service organizations. In M. Arnold et al. (Eds.). *Administering health systems*. New York: Atherton Press, 1971.

64. Kimberly, J.R., & Miles, R.H. *The organization life cycle: Issues in the creation, transformation, and decline of organizations*. San Francisco, CA: Jossey-Bass, 1980.

65. Kimberly, J.R., & Quinn, R.E. *Managing organizational transitions*. Homewood, IL: Richard Irwin, 1984.

66. Fetter, R.B., & Freeman, J.L. Diagnosis related groups: Product line management within hospitals. *Academy of Management Review*, 1986, *11*(1), 41–54.

67. Harrison, R. Startup: The care and feeding of infant systems. *Organization Dynamics*, 1981, 5–28.

68. Hedberg, B.L.T., Nystrom, P.C., & Starbuck, W.H. Camping on seesaws: Prescriptions for self-designing organizations. *Administrative Science Quarterly*, 1976, *21*(1), 41–65.

69. Shortell, S.M., & Mickus, R. Standing firm on shaky ground. *Health Care Forum,* 1986, Jan./Feb., 55–58.

70. Hawley, J.A. Transforming organizations through vertical linking. *Organization Dynamics,* 1982, 68–80.

71. Burns, L.R. The structure and development of matrix management: Theory and evidence: Tuscon, AZ: Department of Management and Policy, College of Business and Public Administration, 1985.

CHAPTER 10

Organization–Environment Relations

David Starkweather
Karen S. Cook

The dominant view of organizations has shifted during the past two decades from a closed-systems perspective, with exclusive emphasis on the efficient internal structuring of organizational activities, to an open-systems perspective, which acknowledges the importance of the interface or optimum fit between the organization and its environment (see Chapter 1). This shift in perspective has brought increased attention to the management of organization–environment relations. As Scott (1) notes, "managers of today's organizations must devote as much time and energy to managing their environments as to managing their production systems." This chapter identifies important types of organization–environment relations and indicates how managers can broaden their spheres of influence and their effectiveness by means of successful management of external relations.

INCREASING ENVIRONMENTAL COMPLEXITY

This recent emphasis upon organization–environment relations stems from broad social changes which have occurred in "post-industrial society" (2) in which the production of manufactured goods gives way to tertiary activities such as public services and communications. Organizations are sensitive to new technologies, many of which become obsolete after short periods of time. There is ever-increasing complexity coupled with increased uncertainty. Jobs, tasks, and organizations are all highly interdependent.

The implications of these changes for managers are fundamental. Biller (3) believes that most existing organizations were designed to accomplish tasks and solve problems identified with the earlier industrial era—problems he calls "determinant." Whether or not these problems have been solved, they have now been replaced by new kinds of problems that Biller calls "swampy." Again, there is a shift in managerial focus from internal, closed systems to open-systems matters: environmental scanning, development of an external infrastructure, and organizational strategy. Further, the basis of organizational power has shifted. In the industrial era there was rational or legal power, derived from training and experience and based upon the position one held in an organizational hierarchy (4). In the post-industrial era this basis of power has been undercut by the authority of knowledge, rather than the authority of office. Information and expertise are now major sources of power, and decision making is based on and justified by the highest amount and quality of information. Thus managers of organizations use and exploit all possible kinds and sources of information, most notably those that stem from the environment.

MINI-CASE: A CASE STUDY: VALLEY HOSPITAL

We begin our analysis of organization–environment relations with a description of a hospital faced with environmental turbulence and uncertainty. The first part of this case deals with Valley Hospital during the decade of the1970s— a time in which it became the focus of increased public attention and pressures for accountability. This case is based on a real hospital; however, names and locations have been disguised.

The institution is a "typical" community hospital of 215 beds, located in a city with a population of 180,000. As a nonprofit hospital, it prides itself on service to the poor and has a long history of innovation in community-oriented services and outreach programs. Founded at the turn of the century by Dr. Hansen, it became a community hospital after he turned over his proprietary interests during the Depression. Valley Hospital is a multiracial organization. Another hospital in the city, Riverview, is of approximately equal size, but serves the higher socioeconomic populations of the community. Riverview's services are also more specialized, and in recent years it has become a regional referral hospital.

As recently as 1970 Valley operated as a closed-systems organization. Its board was controlled by descendants of the original Hansen family. The medical staff was relatively unorganized and related to administrators primarily on a one-to-one basis. The administrator, the son-in-law of Dr. Hansen, followed the style of his father-in-law, the former administrator for approximately 30 years. The hospital was run in a top-down manner, and the department heads were long-term employees with both job and personal loyalties to the Hansen family.

Starting in about 1970 the hospital came upon dramatically turbulent times. In the course of 10 years the organization was reoriented and restructured in a manner that recognized its open-systems context and the need to emphasize the management of its environmental relationships.

The first prominent external group that put pressure on the hospital was consumers. Consumer activism resulted in part because the hospital was located in a university town known for activism. The hospital was also located in a federally designated Model Cities zone, thus all federal projects had to be approved by the local board of the Model Cities agency. A group of university activists and black radicals from the community obtained control of this agency and demanded control of the hospital, in the form of a majority proportion of seats on its governing board, as a condition of the agency's approval of a $6-million federal grant needed to continue the hospital's psychiatric programs. City government informally backed this position, so the hospital had to negotiate with both the federal Model Cities agency and local government. The hospital refused to relinquish control, and the federal funds were vetoed not long after this.

During this time Valley was picketed by a well-organized group of para-plegics and quadriplegics who desired control over the hospital's special clinic for disabled persons. This was largely a news-media battle and was settled after an advisory board was established to provide disabled persons with input into hospital decision making concerning the clinic.

In connection with plans to replace approximately 125 of the hospital's 225 beds, community residents became upset about the prospects of a high-rise tower development, coupled with increased traffic, street noise, and parking congestion. The hospital found itself facing a well-organized neighborhood group that not only petitioned the hospital but also carried its concerns to the local city council. The hospital needed approval of the city council for con-struction of its replacement facilities, since zoning variances were involved.

In the middle of this process, another group surfaced demanding that the hospital abandon its practice of electroshock therapy. The group's appeals caused a 6-month delay in decision making by the city council. This involved Valley Hospital not only with a group of former patients and local city govern-ment, but also with state government, because the state legislature had recently passed a law restricting the use of electroshock therapy.

Furthermore, in the mid-1970s the nearby university began a new health sciences program, which included a school of medicine. This school was un-usual in that its students' clinical experiences would be obtained in community hospitals and clinics instead of university-owned facilities. Thus Valley found itself in need of new linkages and relationships with the medical school and the university.

Most of these dynamics had to do with the hospital's past, present, and future consumers. Another important set of elements in the environment con-sisted of people who supplied resources to the hospital: physicians, employees, unions, consultants, capital financiers, equipment suppliers, and financial reimbursers. For example, a group of black doctors organized as a caucus to demand a larger proportion of blacks in the employed ranks of the hospital and on the hospital board. They threatened to withdraw their patients if affirm-ative action practices were not accelerated. This coalition represented one of the first times black physicians acted politically as a subgroup.

Subsequently, the professional nurses in the hospital organized as a col-lective bargaining unit, signaling not only a massive increase in the percentage of employees under union contract, but also an expansion of organized bar-gaining units into the professional ranks. In response, Valley formed an as-sociation with six other hospitals to facilitate collective action among man-agements. Subsequently one of the six hospitals claimed an inability to withstand a strike in progress and petitioned the other five hospitals for financial aid. Valley Hospital's board decided to loan this hospital $200,000 to support the employers' federation and maintain the hospital's union negotiating position.

As the decade of the seventies closed, the hospital found itself using more consultants: marketing experts, lawyers, architects, general contractors, and strategic planners. These consultant groups were outsiders, each requiring special supervision and management. In particular, the hospital's legal fees skyrocketed. Valley's management finally concluded that it had to sever the hospital's traditional relationship with its law firm because of a conflict of interest stemming from the law firm's representation of Riverview's certificate-of-need request before the local health systems agency.

An interesting pattern emerged in most of these consulting arrangements: what started as an arms-length relationship with an independent contractor became over time an in-house specialty resulting in organizational expansion. Thus by the end of the decade Valley had acquired its own corporate legal staff, its own marketing staff, a construction manager to supervise architects and general contractors, and a well-developed strategic planning department.

Yet another set of resource-oriented specialists were those involved in borrowing approximately $20 million for hospital reconstruction. This involved another consulting group: a financial brokerage house. Since Valley was seeking guaranteed loan funds through a state mortgage insurance agency, hospital management had to establish direct and active relationships with a new office of state government. This required the appointment of a director of finance with capital and strategic financial skills relating to the external world (open system), in marked contrast to the bookkeeping skills (closed system) required of the former controller.

But near the end of the 1970s all of these resource-related relationships took second billing to a set of relationships with reimbursers, notably insurance companies and state government agencies that administered Medicaid funds. With Valley's high percentage of Medicaid patients, the hospital's existence was threatened. It had difficulty meeting its payrolls and making payments to suppliers. In 1978, Valley decided to shift from a passive to an aggressive strategy: it authorized its new lawyers to exhaust all administrative remedies and then file lawsuits against the state. Some of these suits were filed by Valley alone and others in conjunction with nearby hospitals. These lawsuits took time to reach trial, but most were successful. Relationships with state government had become very sensitive, since Valley was suing the state for failure to reimburse, while requesting a guaranteed loan of approximately $20 million.

Valley's relationship with Riverview Hospital also became more complex, evolving into a mixed pattern of collaboration and competition. In the fifties and sixties the two hospitals had made a trade-off agreement wherein Riverview would offer maternity and pediatric services, while Valley would offer psychiatric and emergency services and continue its rehabilitation services. Both hospitals would have general medical and surgical services, as well as certain medical and surgical specialties. In the mid-seventies the two hospitals agreed to sponsor jointly a health maintenance organization (HMO). A separate corporation was established as a joint venture owned by the two hospitals. By 1981 this HMO had obtained almost half a million dollars in developmental grants and had become operational. It was the product of a planning committee established in the mid-seventies by the two hospitals to review plans for new services, changes in bed allocations, and new construction.

The two hospitals also competed actively and bitterly. Since their service areas overlapped, there was increasing competition for doctors and patients. On two major issues there was open warfare. One involved Riverview's opening of a complete emergency service, despite what Valley claimed was an ironclad agreement to the contrary. Valley countered by opening an "Urgent Care Center" in a nearby community whose residents typically went to Riverview's emergency room. The other issue was a series of battles before the local health systems agency centering on efforts by Riverview to obtain certificates of need for additional surgical beds. This application was fought by Valley because it had just renovated its operating rooms and had idle surgical capacity both in its surgery suites and surgical wards.

A final set of significant environmental relationships were those between Valley and various regulatory groups: government and professional certification bodies. Direct relationships with four different levels of government were under constant management. At the local (city) level, planning commission approval for a $20-million renovation project was needed. In the late 1970s the city established a health care advisory board that potentially would establish significant new regulations affecting both Valley and Riverview. Then there was the local health systems agency (HSA) from which Valley needed certificates of need for its bed renovation project. After these were obtained, Valley continued its active relationship with the HSA in an attempt to influence the outcome of Riverview's requests.

At the county government level, contracts involving Valley's psychiatric program were continually under negotiation. Also, the county had passed a far-reaching affirmative action policy mandating the hospital to accomplish its building renovation project with at least 25% minority labor and subcontractor involvement. Valley's most crucial relationship was with state government, because of both Medicaid reimbursement and the hospital's application for a state-guaranteed loan. By 1980 the hospital was experiencing a $5-million shortfall in state reimbursement for indigent Medicaid patients. Relations with state licensure authorities focused on portions of the hospital's plant declared unusable as a result of new earthquake protection codes. Likewise, the Joint Commission on Accreditation of Hospitals had given Valley a 1-year probationary accreditation pending the hospital's immediate installation of fire sprinklers in one portion of the facility.

There are two ways to summarize Valley's involvement in an increasingly complex set of environmental relationships. One is to classify these relations in the manner developed by Dill (5). He identifies four aspects of the environment that "influence managerial autonomy:" (1) relations with customers, (2) relations with suppliers, (3) relations with competitors, and (4) relations with various regulatory groups. We have seen in this case examples of Valley's involvement in all four types of relations.

A second method is to classify Valley's responses by organizational level. At the trustee level, over the 10-year period the composition of the board changed almost entirely from one dominated by the founding family to one carefully designed to represent environmental linkages important to the hospital (6, 7). Developments in medical education, for example, necessitated the appointment of someone affiliated with the university. Local governmental relationships at the local level called for the appointment of two persons active in local government. Valley's legal strategy suggested the appointment of a retired judge and two attorneys to the board. Finally, the appointment of a person knowledgeable and active in state legislative activities as a hospital lobbyist was important for maintaining successful relations with state government.

At the management level there was a complete restructuring of top administration, with the appointment of the former administrator as an executive vice-president to manage primarily external relations, including active involvement with the health systems agency and local government. In recognition of the importance of finance, the former director of finance was appointed administrator of the hospital. Much of his time was spent in the state capital dealing with problems of reimbursement and capital financing. At middle levels of management and at the operations level, expansion and reorganization brought many new staff departments and specialists to Valley. These additions represented the acquisition of new boundary-spanning and environmental management skills obtained previously from outside consultants.

MODELS OF THE ORGANIZATION–ENVIRONMENT LINKAGE

Two general models developed to explain organization–environment relations are the natural selection model and the resource-dependence perspective. We briefly describe these frameworks, indicating how each conceptualizes the nature of an organization's relations to its environment, and discuss the applications of these models to health care management.

NATURAL SELECTION

The natural selection model, introduced briefly in Chapter 1, is also called the population ecology model because it takes an evolutionary view drawn from biology and argues that changing environmental circumstances "select out" certain institutions for survival. As conceptualized by Hannan and Freeman (8) and Aldrich (9), the natural selection model applies to the population of organizations rather than to any single organization, and deals with long-term rather than short-term structural changes. The first stage in the natural selection process is the appearance of variations between organizations, for whatever reasons, planned or unplanned. This is analogous to genetic mutation among biological forms. The second stage is the operation of consistent selection criteria that differentially choose some variations over others, or selectively eliminate certain ones. The last stage involves retention mechanisms for those variations or organizational forms that have been positively selected.

Scott (1) suggests that the natural selection perspective can be applied more readily to small organizations that are not in a position to affect or control their environments significantly. In this category Scott includes colleges, hospitals, and small businesses such as local newspapers and restaurants. By contrast, larger and more powerful organizations can influence and to some extent control their environments; it is thus difficult to argue that the environment selects these larger, more powerful organizations for survival. Galbraith's (10) widely read analysis of large corporations reveals their ability to create demand for their own products and to control their environment.

It is in economics, however, that the notion of the survival of the fittest has received the greatest amount of attention. This notion stems from microeconomic theory, which acknowledges the existence of competitive market forces that constrain organizational behavior. There is a sense of inevitability to these theories: their predictions specify that only firms with certain characteristics will achieve optimization in a competitive environment. One of the chief characteristics examined is size.

The survival principle advanced by Stigler (11) and Saving (12) and tested by Weiss (13) states that a particular size class of firms increases in relative importance over time because it has had advantages over smaller or larger firms whose size classes have declined in relative importance. Thus success is defined as market power or dominance (14), and optimal efficiency means that the firm has met any and all problems an entrepreneur faces, including strained labor relations, rapid innovation, and governmental regulation. This theory says nothing about social efficacy. Larger firms may survive through possession of monopoly power, undesirable labor practices, or discriminatory legislation. Small firms may survive because of their ability to exploit local labor markets or to circumvent the law.

Several studies of hospital closures and mergers support natural selection principles. One is Williams's study of hospital closures and mergers in New York City between 1960 and 1975 (15). Another is Kennedy's longitudinal study of 309 hospitals in three states (16). A third is Mullner and Anderson's study of all U.S. hospitals that combined between 1980 and 1985 (17). For the most part the hospitals that failed to survive were small institutions gripped by financial difficulties, specialty hospitals, government or investor owned hospitals, and those located in unfavorable environments.

Fennell (18) examined "clusters" of hospitals instead of individual institutions. Her study of the effects of environmental characteristics on these clusters is strongly in the vein of the population ecology perspective. She found that the proportion of cluster variation that was explained by supplier diversity variables involving the influence of physicians and managers was considerably larger ($R^2 = .54$) than the proportion explained by the patient diversity variables involving patient needs for hospital services ($R^2 = .38$).

> Apparently, hospitals can increase their range of services not because there is an actual need for a particular service or facility within the patient population, but because they will be defined as fit only if they can offer everything other hospitals in the area offer. This notion of fitness is not in accord with either market efficiency, or ecological fitness (p. 505).

We will discuss some explanations for this, namely that prestige exerts a strong influence as an important environmental resource.

The natural selection models like Fennell's, and particularly those stemming from economics, are most useful when the level of variation among firms is high and the life span of any one unit is relatively short (19). Clearly, different industries vary in these respects, and one industry will vary over time. Even so, this model shows that the environmental landscape is littered with organizations that have not survived (20). It is estimated that as many as half of all new small businesses fail within the first 2 years (21).

It has been speculated that firms in the health field, even though small, do not face this same level of risk, because they enjoy a degree of legitimacy in society. Some are government entities, which rarely go out of existence. Others are private organizations, such as small clinics, protected by various government or private grants. Still others enjoy special forms of community support designed to sustain them under poor economic conditions. Even so, many Office of Economic Opportunity-sponsored clinics failed in the late seventies, and many small HMOs failed in the early eighties.

However, numerous forms of modification falling short of complete organizational failure or demise take place. Particular structures or organizational behaviors are modified under the impact of environmental forces. These modifications, which fall short of the biological analog of survival of the fittest, are the subject of our next application of the basic natural selection model.

A Modification of the Natural Selection Model

The natural selection model in its original form applies only to populations or aggregates or organizations. The underlying concept is a simple one: environments differentially select organizations for survival on the basis of their environmental fit. Those organizations that, for whatever reason, have the appropriate structure for a particular environmental niche are selected over those that do not.

This feature of the model has led to criticism from a managerial point of view because the theory does not specify what can be done even at the population level to ensure organizational survival. The organization is thus a passive actor facing the inevitable outcome of environmentally determined pressures.

Aldrich and Pfeffer (19) believe that this model can be applied not just to the survival or failure of an entire organization, but also to the partial modification of structure and activities. Whereas organic evolution proceeds by a process of differential survival of entire organisms, social organizations can change through the adaptation of some aspects of their structure or conduct. Thus "modifying the ecological model is a necessary step toward recognizing the difference between organic and social evolution and toward making natural selection theory useful for organizational analysis" (19).

We thus have two branches of this school of thought. One argues that the environment leads to the selection of certain units for survival, and only in the long run can we note adaptation, as in biology. The other argues that the environment "inspires" some organizations to change, at least in part, and that these relatively short-term adaptations lead to higher survival rates than would otherwise be the case. The latter perspective includes a theory called "structural contingency" or "contingency theory" (see Chapters 1 and 9) (22). Both the "pure" and modified versions assume an optimal fit between the organization and its environment, but the structural contingency theory places emphasis upon managerial strategies designed to find the optimum fit through organizational adaptation rather than on change accomplished solely through differential rates of long-run survival.

The primary hypothesis is that organizations whose internal features can be arranged to best match the demands of their environments will adapt and thrive. It follows that (1) there is no one best way to organize (see Chapter 9), (2) different ways of organizing are not equally effective (23), and (3) the most effective way to organize depends upon the nature of the organization's environment (3).

Using the biological analogy, Starkweather and Kisch (24) present a life-cycle model of health care organizations and illustrate how many organizations pass through four stages: *search, success, bureaucracy,* and *succession.* The four stages are examined in the context of two broad categorizations of the environment borrowed from Evan (25): "input constituencies," relating to the variety of resources necessary for organizational survival and growth, and "output constituencies," relating to service objectives and client relationships. Starkweather and Kisch suggest that organizations typically position themselves differently during each of the four stages relative to these two sets of environmental elements: there is an increased orientation toward output constituencies during the search phase and an increased orientation toward input constituencies during the bureaucratic phase. The different characteristics of health care organizations engaged in each stage of development are discussed, including general features of their leadership characteristics. The Starkweather–Kisch model represents a blend of the two types of natural selection models. Their model focuses upon longer-term social evolution because it emphasizes the risk of failure (death of the organism), but it also includes elements of structural contingency theory because numerous examples are given of short-term and successful adaptation strategies. For example, they describe how larger, older, and more bureaucratized organizations may give rise, in the succession phase, to new enterprises with remarkably different organizational characteristics and new capacities for adaptation.

This life-cycle view fits the population ecology model. For instance, Stinchcombe (26) has suggested that organizations face a "liability of newness"—a heightened chance of organizational death when they are first formed because they are unable to secure sufficient environmental support. Carroll et al. (27) provide empirical support for this thesis. The third stage of the cycle, "bureaupathology," conforms to Hannan and Freeman's (28) proposition that structural inertia increases with organization age and size.

Veney and Khan (29) conducted a test of the structural contingency model using data from a representative sample of 480 short-term general nonfederal hospitals. The primary dependent variable was change, defined as any elaboration of or alteration in hospital services. The independent variables were divided into three classes: *(1)* characteristics of the environment; *(2)* characteristics of the organization; and *(3)* characteristics of the administration. Various causal models specifying the determinants of change were tested. The best-fitting model explained approximately 50% of the change variable. The environmental variables accounted for 30% of the variance, while the organizational variables, primarily size, accounted for 15%. Characteristics of the administration accounted for the remaining 5% of the variance. In short, Veney and Khan's research demonstrates clearly the role of environmental factors as a major cause of organizational change.

Lawrence and Lorsch (30), originators of contingency theory, found that the more varied the types of environments faced by a given organization, the more differentiated the organization's structure should be. However, the more differentiated the structure, the greater the effort that must be devoted to integrating the various parts of the organization. The most successful companies in their study were both highly differentiated and successfully integrated.

In a study of hospitals Baldwin (31) found that both integration and differentiation were related to organizational performance, with a stronger correlation obtaining between performance and differentiation. This led Baldwin to suggest that "improving integration when the proper state of differentiation has not been reached will not be as rewarding in terms of improved performance as increasing the degree of organizational differentiation."

Within the structural contingency perspective considerable attention has been given to the influence of technology on the ability of organizations to adapt to rapidly changing environments (32–35). Indeed, the pace of this change may best be detected and measured through changes in technology. An example is the impact of the computer age on the technology of radiographics. In previous environments the relationships between manufacturers and hospitals, and between hospitals and radiologists, were relatively standard. However the computer age ushered in an era of rapid change. New research and development became paramount, yielding products like magnetic nuclear resonators. New organizations have sprung up with new ideas and products that challenge the traditional companies and relationships. And the hospital–radiologist relationship is altered by corporate reorganizations and joint ventures that match the new technology and the new competitive environment. Thus the technological environment is a critical factor for organizations to take into account.

To summarize, we have the strict population ecology theory, using the analogy of organizations to biological species and their natural selection. Through long-run differential selection there are some organizations that are best fit to survive. And we have the modified view, structural contingency, which recognizes that organizations whose internal features can be arranged to match the features of the environment will adapt and thus survive. In comparing these two perspectives, Scott (1) concludes:

> Thus, we regard both points of view as valuable. However, we do take sides . . . to this extent: we believe that a single organization is capable of extensive structural change and elaboration over both shorter and longer time periods. In our opinion, some population [natural selection] ecologists have over-emphasized the structural rigidity or inertia present in organizations. . . . Although there are important analogies between biological and social forms, we side with the open-systems theorists in insisting that an important hallmark of organizations is their unusual capability for structural modification and elaboration.

The basic feature of the natural selection perspective is that the environment selects the most fit or optimal organizations. The organization is thus seen as relatively powerless to affect the selection process. But our review of some of the research on health care organizations suggests otherwise. Furthermore, from a managerial perspective it is difficult to accept so much organizational fatalism and inevitability.

Thus we move to the discussion of the second major model of organization—environment relationships, one that provides for more discretion on the part of managers.

THE RESOURCE-DEPENDENCE MODEL

The second major perspective on organization–environment relations views the organization as proactive rather than reactive, providing for a more active management role. An organization is capable of even altering the environment. The resource-dependence perspective assumes that organizations are seldom capable of internally generating all of the resources required to accomplish their tasks; therefore they must engage in transactions with elements in the environment that can supply these resources. Thus organizations of necessity engage in a complex set of interorganizational relations, some highly competitive and some more cooperative. As Thompson (36), Cook (37), and others have argued, organizations' positions in this network of interorganizational exchange relations determines the relative power and dependence of the organizations in the network (38). Those with greater access to alternative suppliers of their essential resources maintain power (39). A decrease in the availability of resources from alternate suppliers increases organizational dependence and thus reduces power, yielding "asymmetrical" relationships. Managing these power-dependence relations is an important task for managers and boundary-spanning personnel; thus strategic choice and the effectiveness of organizational strategy become important determinants of success.

An early, influential article by Levine and White (40) applied the concepts of resource dependency to the health field. They introduced the basic concepts of organizational domain and domain consensus. The domain of an organization consists of "the specific goals it wishes to pursue and the functions it undertakes in order to implement its goals." Their study of 22 health agencies indicates that a new organization will not survive unless it can carve out its own legitimate domain. In addition, this domain license must be continually renegotiated, given turbulent and increasingly uncertain environments.

Thompson (36) states that organizations seek to establish those relations that meet their critical contingencies with minimum cost to the organization in loss of autonomy and power.

> The organizatic.a that adopts a strategy of competition where cooperation is called for may lose all opportunity to realize its goals, or may finally turn to cooperation or coalition at a higher cost than would have been necessary originally. On the other hand an organization may lose part of its integrity and therefore some of its potentiality if it unnecessarily shares power in exchange for support. Hence, the establishment of the appropriate form of interaction with its environment can be a major organizational consideration in a complex society.

Williamson (41, 42) pursues this line of reasoning in terms of organizational transaction costs. Three types of transaction costs are: (1) negotiating costs of reaching an agreement; (2) monitoring costs to ensure compliance; and (3) enforcement costs if parties have to resort to judicial or other resolutions. In making strategy decisions organizations attempt to minimize transaction costs. Further, the characteristics of these transactions become central determinants of structure and strategy. In Williamson's view (43) markets fail to govern transactions efficiently when (1) markets are not competitive, (2) actors are self-interested and behave opportunistically, (3) there is uncertainty about the exchanges, and (4) there is bounded rationality or other limits on the organization's ability to process information. In these circumstances it is difficult to write contracts to specify properly the obligations of each party. Organizations in these markets will seek horizontal or vertical integration or other means of establishing hierarchies to minimize transaction costs. Thus many health care organizations have chosen to engage in horizontal or vertical integration instead of increasing the extent to which transactions are mediated by arms-length market relationships.

Cook et al. (44) and Morrisey et al. (45) applied Williamson's notions to the analysis of the development of multi-institutional hospital systems, and to changes in the nature of the contractual relations between hospitals and various physician specialists in response to regulation. Vertical integration may be undertaken to reduce the transaction costs surrounding frequent or recurrent negotiations over the terms of the exchange of critical resources, and to reduce the organization's dependence upon its environment (35). For example, hospitals construct their own medical office facilities to attract a ready supply of physicians, or two hospitals in the same community merge to restrict competition and thus maintain a position of power in the interorganizational exchange network.

Scott and Meyer (46) have recommended expanding the scope of relevant inter-organizational networks to include "sector analysis." Instead of viewing the set of interacting public service organizations as locally based, consisting of internal connections primarily, as did Levine and White, they point to the importance or even the dominance of vertical connections.

. . . contemporary socieities increasingly exhibit functionally differentiated sectors whose structures are vertically connected with lines stretching up to the central nation state. A variety of social changes in the world—economic integration and competition, expanded ideologies of justice and equality, improved systems of technical control—support a process of centralization, and of centralization under rather explicit organizational controls (p. 139).

As examples of the effects of sector environments, Scott and Meyer offer the following hypothesis (from a total of 19):

H: The more centralized, unified, and concentrated is the decision making within a sector, the smaller is the number of different organization forms within the sector and the greater the variance between them.

This seems to hold for the health care sector. At the height of federally centralized regulation in the early 1980s, there was a "match" of more multihospital systems with substantial variation between them. But with the deregulation of health care and the decline of federal centralization—both hallmarks of the Reagan administration—by the mid-1980s we see a great increase and proliferation of different organization forms, and a reduction in the rate of formation of nationally centralized corporations as compared to local or regional systems.

In the early open-systems model, relationships between an organization and its environment were seen as highly articulated and capable of close regulation, as in cybernetics. But later analysts saw these links as more loosely coupled (47). Cyert and March (48) proposed that key actors in an organization should not be viewed as fitting into any unitary hierarchy or set of stratified layers, but rather into loosely linked and continuously shifting coalitions. Pfeffer and Salancik (49) adopted this formulation and argued that a single organization can best be seen as a coalition of groups and interests, each attempting to obtain something from the collective by interacting with it, but each with its own set of preferences and objectives. Thus the organization is made up of subsystems that are themselves also part of other, larger systems—an arrangement that creates strong linkages across organizations and confounds any attempt to establish and maintain clear boundaries between them.

In many instances coalitions among organizations occupy a middle ground between free, uncertain markets and negotiated vertical or horizontal hierarchies (D'Aunno and Zuckerman, 50). The health care field has recently witnessed a number of coalition organizations, such as Voluntary Hospitals of America and American Health Systems. These associations do not stem from merger or consolidation of their members into national corporations. Rather they are "loosely coupled" networks that help member hospitals deal with critical environmental contingencies and resource needs. For example, the American Health Capital is a subsidiary of Voluntary Hospitals of America that arranges capital financing for members which might not otherwise qualify.

D'Aunno and Zuckerman (50) define coalitions as consisting of two or more organizations that voluntarily choose to work together toward stated objectives. There is no change in corporate ownership, though there is often a management to coordinate activities and organizations are free to withdraw. Coalitions are less costly in terms of autonomy and resources than other forms—joint ventures or mergers—for dealing with environmental uncertainty. Coalitions whose members are geographically dispersed but are similar in size, type of community, and the problems they face are attractive. Thus there is a coalition of approximately 40 university owned U.S. hospitals, and another embracing most public hospitals. Coalitions are enhanced if their members share ideology; shared norms help regulate transactions among members and contribute to the development of consensus and common purpose. The number of members is important: too many make it difficult or costly to develop or maintain the coalition. Finally, an organization will choose to join the coalition(s) that best fits its needs. D'Aunno and Zuckerman offer the example of the hospital that wishes to reduce its dependence on its current insurers; it will likely join a coalition that has developed alternate mechanisms to finance health services, such as an HMO.

Other forms of loose coupling are special-purpose joint ventures between physician groups and hospitals for the purpose of financing and operating new services such as magnetic resonance imaging, ambulatory surgery centers, or urgent care centers. Often these are temporary, since they change or disband at the end of the technology's product life cycle, or when equity has been returned to the original "couplers."

DIMENSIONS OF THE ENVIRONMENT

In this section we review various properties and elements of the environment that are important to a manager's formulation of successful strategies for adaptation.

THE ENVIRONMENT AS A SOURCE OF INTELLIGENCE

One view of the environment is as a primary source of critical information. If there is uncertainty, the organization needs to minimize information dependence. A turbulent environment must be closely monitored. Failure to detect critical changes in the industry or in general economic, political, demographic, or legal conditions will result in reduced effectiveness or poor performance and, in the extreme, organizational failure. This monitoring capability, Thompson suggests (36), is especially critical in sectors faced by rapid rates of product innovation and changing consumer demands.

Information-gathering and processing requirements increase with environmental uncertainty, which is influenced by the number of different organizations with which relationships must be established (49), the extent of similarity or difference among the organizations (5), and the extent to which there is coordinated action versus autonomous action among the relevant environmental entities (51). The Valley Hospital example indicates clearly the importance of these environmental elements.

THE ENVIRONMENT AS A SUPPLY OF CRITICAL RESOURCES

Managers must develop methods for increasing the organization's power to obtain necessary resources such as finance, capital, labor, goods, and services. At the same time, they must act to decrease dependence upon particular sources by maintaining alternatives, thus enhancing bargaining power. As Scott puts it, "the greater the scarcity of resources, the higher the degree of concentration, and the greater the degree of organization exhibited by entities within the environment, the greater the dependence of the [focal] organization" (1). Aldrich (9) refers to this dimension of the environment as the extent to which an organization's resources are "munificent" versus scarce and concentrated versus dispersed.

For example, at Valley Hospital the relevant entities in the environment became more numerous, heterogeneous, and complex, as well as more interconnected and less coordinated, all of which increased environmental uncertainty. Furthermore, as resources became more scarce the environment became harsher, and Valley's dependence upon its immediate environment increased. It became more dependent upon the local community not only for clients but also for financial and political support.

It is important to recognize that different components of any single organization confront quite different environments. Scott (1) states this well:

> Every organization is related to a number of different environments, and these environments may exhibit differing characteristics. And any attempt to determine *the* characteristics of *the* environment requires the . . . investigator to arrive at a summary judgment that may conceal a great deal of variance. (p. 170)

THE ENVIRONMENT IN RELATION TO TASKS

The task environment includes all aspects of the environment potentially relevant to goal setting and goal attainment (5). Dill reduces this broad definition to focus on four major sectors to which most organizations must relate: customers, suppliers, competitors, and regulators. Perrow (33) adds two more relevant to health care organizations: sources of new technologies and "the complex social and political context" of the community.

Organizations are created to perform special types of work. Thompson (36) defines these central tasks, including the necessary personnel, as the "core technology" of an organization. The organization works hard to protect and advance this core technology, and "under norms of rationality, it seeks to seal it off from environmental influences."

This concept reduces the relevant set of critical environmental relationships to the specific set of exchanges required to sustain the focal organization's core technology. This set of environmental relationships is often called the "organizational set" (25); or the set of interorganizational relations that must be managed effectively if the organization is to achieve its primary goals.

One way to view the changes at Valley Hospital during the 1970s is to list the organization set it developed: Model Cities, the neighborhood organization, the local government, the HSA, the nearby university, a group of black doctors on its medical staff, unions, other hospitals in the employer's association, the state bonding authority, the state Medicaid agency, and the county equal opportunity employment agency.

THE ENVIRONMENT AS A NETWORK OF EXCHANGE RELATIONS

The environment can also be conceptualized as a field (52) or network of interorganizational relations. Turk (53), among others, views communities, cities, states, and nations as complex sets of interdependent entities. Various perspectives have been developed to explain the formation and maintenance of interorganizational relationships. Perhaps the most prominent is the exchange approach, which is also the basis for the resource-dependence model.

Organizations enter into relations to obtain necessary resources, and the relations are governed by basic exchange principles (37, 54–57). In brief, these principles state that actors (either individual or corporate) seek exchanges that are mutually beneficial or rewarding. Actors are calculative, that is, they make assessments of both rewards and costs. This economic view of exchange relations, often criticized as overly calculative when applied to interpersonal relations, is highly applicable to the analysis of interorganizational relations, where the corporate entities have well-established mechanisms for monitoring rewards and costs.

Emerson (57) and Cook (58) extended this theory beyond the dyad to the analysis of organizational networks. Power and dependence are determined by an organization's location in a network of exchange relations. One organization's power over another is rooted in dependence on the resources it controls. This depends on two factors: (1) the importance one organization places on the resources another mediates (directly proportional); and (2) the availability of these resources outside of the relationship (inversely proportional).

There have been several applications of exchange theory in the health field. In the studies conducted by Levine and White (40, 59), exchanges among community health agencies were classified as referrals, resources, written and verbal communications, and joint activities. Levine and White found that different needs for local exchanges emerged depending upon the extent to which the focal organization had access to resources outside the community through linkages to national federations. They also found that the agencies in the two communities knew little about each other. They argued that without this knowledge the organizations could not maximize their exchange opportunities. They showed how this ignorance led to a lack of domain consensus and the existence of multiple competing sources of authority. Their suggestions for improving interorganizational cooperation were highly normative because they assumed that some form of cooperation was good, leaving out the possibility that competition is a useful mechanism for improving the quality of service and reducing costs.

THE ENVIRONMENT AS A SOURCE OF POWER

It is clear that communities have power networks, but there is debate over their nature. The study of community power has developed along two distinct lines, generally referred to as "elitist" and "pluralist" theories. The elitist tradition maintains that community life is dominated by a relatively small group of people with economic and political power. Members of this group initiate, direct, and resolve most key community issues. Citizen participation is relatively insignificant and is exercised through powerless voluntary associations that serve as vehicles for legitimizing the actions taken by elites. Hunter's (60) study of health planning in a small eastern city is strongly in this tradition. The powerful interests in the community studied by Hunter represented old-line families, business, political factions, and newspapers.

The pluralist view sees power as distributed among various community groups with dominance shifting according to issues, rather than residing within a single stable network.

Turk (53) has pointed out that both approaches miss the point: community power resides in a network of individuals who represent institutional influence rather than individual power. Weick (61) states that control is vested in relationships, not individuals. Access to needed community resources may depend on leaders' knowledge of and involvement with a community power network.

Elling (62) conducted a series of studies that show the relevance of this approach to the health field. In a study of 136 short-term general hospitals, Elling and Halebsky (63) found that local government hospitals received less support than did nongovernmental institutions. The difference was said to be a function of class control and use of hospitals: "sponsorship differentiates between organizations so as to associate them with elements in the community which have varying abilities to channel support. . . ."

A prime means of linking an organization to community power networks is through membership on boards of trustees. We noted in our case study of Valley Hospital how a number of trustees were added who could relate to specific segments of the hospital's environment and who had abilities to channel support.

Pfeffer (6) found in a random sample of 80 nonfinancial corporations that board size and composition were systematically related to the organization's requirements for coopting sectors of the environment. In a related study of 57 hospitals in a large midwestern state, Pfeffer (64) found that the size of boards of directors was related to the hospital's need for successful linkage with the environment as well as to the functions of the board. He concluded that "The hospital is likely to be more successful in attracting resources to the extent that its board is composed in such a way as to represent the social context in which the organization is embedded."

Elling and Lee (65) obtained similar results, and also showed that the distribution of these types of leaders varied across five different types of hospitals, demonstrating again the hypothesis both that (1) the availability of such persons differentially affects the success of the organization and that (2) an organization's choice of goals and clientele affects its ability to attract community support.

THE ENVIRONMENT AS A SOURCE OF PRESTIGE OR LEGITIMACY

Terreberry (66) stated that "an input called legitimacy is popular in sociological circles, but highly resistant to empirical specifications" (p. 591). She believes that this resource is more important to what have been called social institutions, which include most health care organizations, than to economic institutions. For social institutions, competition centers upon maximizing services rather than profits. If one institution expands or improves its service capacity, others feel challenged to match or surpass that performance. If this results in costs that seem excessive, efforts will be directed toward lowering costs through grants, subsidies, endowments, and related means. Social institutions operate under the control of elected or volunteer officials who do not seek or accept these positions because of economic rewards. The positions offer personal gratification, such as power, prestige, and achievement. To obtain these rewards it is necessary for institutions to create a record of accomplishment, including a reputation for meeting social needs, providing public service, expanding programs, responding to demands, and improving quality. It is these underlying motivations that create the drive for expansion and growth, which in turn generate more service than would result from the ordinary interplay of market forces. For example, operating a revenue-producing activity at a loss solely to avoid reducing the scope of operations is not considered acceptable business behavior, but social institutions do so with pride, particularly if they can claim that the public benefits. Thus in the end it is community approbation that the decision makers in social institutions often seek, and their judgments are influenced accordingly. The ability to anticipate community reaction and to persuade the public is an important determinant of success.

It follows that one way an organization may influence its dependency upon the environment is by acquiring legitimacy or prestige. This is done by creating and maintaining a favorable image. If its product is well regarded, an organization will more easily attract personnel, influence legislation, wield informal power, and ensure an adequate number of clients, donors, and investors. Perrow (67) draws a sharp distinction between "intrinsic" and "extrinsic" sources of legitimacy. With intrinsic sources, legitimacy rests upon the quality of goods or services produced, as judged by those capable of evaluating them. With extrinsic sources, prestige rests on the image of the product or service, irrespective of its essential quality.

In health care organizations the development of these indirect prestige indices relies on assertions regarding the reputation of personnel, state-of-the-art equipment, research projects, amounts of free or part-pay care given to patients, and teaching programs that contribute not only to medical education, but also to high-quality patient care.

Perrow goes on to identify organizational strains resulting from the subversion of goals that stem from efforts to promote prestige and legitimacy. Meyer and Rowan (68) note that organizations need "normative" as well as "technical" resources—a distinction that is similar to Perrow's "extrinsic" versus "intrinsic" reputations. Meyer and Rowan assert that some organizations are created and maintained by "rationalized beliefs" that often play a primary part, not a mere backstage legitimizing role. The beliefs are "rational" because they represent elaborate statements of rules and procedures to be followed in achieving certain ends. They are "myths" because they cannot be verified empirically, yet they are believed widely enough to become institutionalized. Organizations survive, then, through the stability provided by social legitimation or institutionalized myths. Meyer and Rowan believe that some organizations are dominated by their technical factors, others rely primarily on institutional resources. They classify health care organizations in the second category because they operate on myths about the sanctity of the medical profession, the furtherance of human-life functions of hospitals, and the necessity of maximum health care for all; these function to buffer health care organizations from the criterion of efficiency.

D'Aunno and Zuckerman (50) offer a further example from the health field. An institutional perspective on the emergence of coalitions argues that they have arisen not to help their organization members manage resource dependency or reduce transaction costs, but rather because joining them is both an expected and a legitimate response to environmental changes. It is "rational" to form coalitions, and managers who do not respond are violating norms implying that some response is necessary. So managers whose organizations join coalitions may be both responding to expectations and creating norms or expectations for other managers in the field. Perhaps the emergence of coalitions is most likely when both resource-dependence problems and normative pressures exist.

Although Meyer and Rowan assign no label of "good" or "bad" to this phenomenon, Illich (69, 70) is entirely critical. He regards the substitution of legitimacy-seeking processes for real outcomes as a delusion. He offers many examples: (1) pupils who confuse teaching with learning, grade advancement with education, or a diploma with competence; (2) medical treatment that is mistaken for health care; (3) social work regarded as an improvement of community life; (4) police protection that is associated with safety; and (5) work that is automatically taken for productivity. This criticism underscores the power and importance of social legitimacy as an organizational resource. The larger an organization becomes and the greater the role of media communication in society, the more important social prestige becomes.

This classification of environmental dimensions begs a fundamental question: at what point can boundaries be drawn between an organization and its environment in order to define a sphere of influence and activity? A widely accepted answer, offered by Churchman (71), asserts that anything over which an organization's decision makers have control is within the organization and anything over which they have no control is part of the environment. Pfeffer and Salancik state that "The organization ends where its discretion ends and others' begin" (49).

This distinction is important to the manager: when we refer to an organization "affecting its environment" and an executive "managing organization–environment relations," the effort is actually one of shifting elements that would otherwise be included in the environment to the sphere of managerial discretion. In the Valley case examples of this type of shift include: changes in board composition, acquisition of new management specialists, and efforts to redefine reimbursement laws.

MANAGING ORGANIZATION–ENVIRONMENT RELATIONS

Most of our generalizations can be restated in the form of guidelines for management practice. Inclusion of environment relations within the sphere of management discretion enhances the organizational power of executives. But this power is based less on closed-systems assumptions and the authority of office than on open-systems assumptions and the power of information. Environmental intelligence is a critical resource. It requires assessments of transactions and dependency costs, just as other important resources do. Since it is difficult to predict what kind of information will be required, managers need to develop intelligence-gathering networks which often include informal or formal coalitions. Thus management of coalition behavior is an important activity.

One important goal of management is to maximize the certainty of the organization's future. Under the assumptions of resource dependency, future assurance comes only from a proactive strategy toward the environment: managers must be agents of change. Maximizing future certainty has its price, however. Exchange theory measures this cost in terms of dependency. A manager must continually make tradeoffs between acquiring control over resources and making excessive commitments, particularly commitments that would constrain the organization's future discretion or yield that discretion to others. These parties may be without or within the organization. Here again we are dealing with coalitions: internal subpowers are also engaged in exchange relations and have mutual dependencies. These subpowers may have goals and linkages clearly in congruence with the focal organization, or their goals and linkages may be divergent. Thus an organization can become the captive of its own participants' external interests. We begin to see the implications of viewing and managing organizations as open systems.

If maintaining future discretion and warding off unnecessary dependencies are both desirable, a manager's preference will usually be for competitive rather than cooperative relations; this is the approach that preserves independence (36). But this oversimplifies. The organization–environment exchanges that must occur in order to absorb uncertainty vary for different core technologies and organizational parts. Lawrence and Lorsch (30) and Hunt (34) warn of the dangers that occur when managers think that an entire organization needs to be patterned in the same way. For example, joint ventures can occur between competitors or exchange partners. We noted that at Valley Hospital there was harsh competition with Riverview over emergency and surgical services while at the same time the two hospitals joint-ventured an HMO. Baldwin's research (31) suggested that hospital organizational differentiation is more important than integration. Clearly, mixed strategies are necessary.

STRATEGIC OPTIONS FOR MANAGERS

The strategies available for the management of organization/environment relations are numerous and varied. We start with options that assume maximum autonomy and discretion for the focal organization, and also assume that it is operating in a competitive mode vis-a-vis other organizations. We progress toward options that assume maximum interdependency with other organizations, even to the point of engulfment of the focal organization.

Scott (1) has indicated that all of these possibilities can be classified as either (1) "buffering" activities that concentrate on the central processes and structures of the organizations (the technical core) and seek to protect them from disturbances arising from the environment, or (2) "bridging" activities that forge connections between the focal organization and its exchange partners. Buffering strategies are derived from closed-systems theories, but in this instance environmental influences are recognized as important, in the manner of Thompson (36): managers recognize the forces that operate in the task environment, but seek to protect the technical core from them. The second category, bridging, is derived from open-systems theory: not only must an organization be internally restructured to match its environment (contingency theory), but it must be linked with other organizations to obtain essential resources.

Our classification has six categories: (1) environmental scanning and mapping; (2) changing internal procedures in order to buffer; (3) borrowing and incorporating skills that will strengthen an organization's capacity to adapt; (4) restructuring to match the environment; (5) changing the environment; and (6) redrawing organizational boundaries through linking.

Scanning and Mapping

How does a manager scan the environment to determine the proper strategies, establish the variety of needed relationships, and maintain the proper balances between decision-making discretion and resource dependency?

The process has been called "mapping" the environment. Bourgeois (72) divides this process into two phases: "domain definition" strategies and "domain navigation" strategies. Domain definition strategies are primary. They focus on opportunities in the general environment, and they should precede the secondary strategies of domain navigation. Domain definition strategies refer to an organization's choice of territory or changes in territory (i.e., markets). Strategies in this category have been called "entrepreneurial" (73); they consist of diversification into or exit from particular products or markets. Three examples from our case study are: (1) Valley Hospital's decision to develop an urgent care center (new product) in a new market (a community filled with private paying patients); (2) its decision to develop an HMO (new product) to challenge the domain of a large prepaid health plan in the area (market segmentation); and (3) its efforts to maintain older products and markets (domains) in emergency care and surgery services, developed by means of earlier exchange agreements with Riverview (domain consensus).

Domain navigation refers to secondary decisions within a particular product market or task environment that are made once the primary territory has been determined. This is the realm of structural contingency: the acquisition of expertise, and internal reorganization that is appropriate to the primary domain definition.

Continuing our Valley Hospital example, the domain navigation strategy concerning urgent care in a new community was one of corporate diversification, the strategy concerning a new HMO to compete with an established prepaid health plan was to form a joint venture with Riverview, and the strategy concerning the protection of prior products and markets was to influence regulators by invading the decision-making processes of the local health systems agency.

Bourgeois observes that business organizations generally focus more frequently on domain definition activities than on strategy implementation. By contrast, in the health care field, secondary aspects of domain navigation, with particular regard for organization structure and the kind of managerial expertise introduced, have occupied managers' attention a great deal, sometimes diverting them from first-order domain definition considerations. Many health care organizations are reluctant to face new market and new product issues. Only recently have health care managers considered marketing to be a valid strategy.

Evan (25) states that organization–environment relations can be made operative only by "descending to a lower level of aggregation" and examining the linkages observable in the role-set relationships of "boundary personnel." He identifies an important set of organizational actors whose ranks expand as environments become more turbulent and heterogeneous: executives, lawyers, purchasing agents, marketing specialists, personnel officers, and so on. We note at Valley Hospital the increased use of boundary spanners as its environment became more complex and as it targeted different segments of the environment: local government, financial reimbursers, the courts, and planning agencies.

Utterback's (74) review of studies about organizations' technological environments indicates that information on changes in technology is communicated primarily through a few individuals who are identified as "technical gatekeepers." These persons usually have a wide communication network, consisting of colleagues and technical readings, and are frequently chosen as informants or internal consultants.

The development of boundary spanners and gatekeepers introduces a management risk that Evan (25) calls their "normative reference group orientation." The risk is that outside commitments and connections come at the expense of organizational loyalty; this can impede goal attainment and in the extreme lead to organizational "engulfment" or demise. Starkweather (75) has described this process in connection with hospital mergers, where the survival of organizational subgroups through the establishment of new relationships with other hospitals takes primacy over the survival of their prior existing institution.

Perrow (76) documented the changes that occurred over time among three boundary-spanning groups. In the first era trustees controlled, because this group had access to both capital investments and community support or legitimation for the hospital—in this instance, a Jewish hospital dependent on Jewish philanthropy. In a second era the power shifted to physicians, because of the increasing complexity and importance of their skills and in response to the needs of the organization for funds to conduct medical research. In the third era the focus of power moved to the administration, because of the mounting complexity of hospital activities and the increasing need for contacts with the health agencies that had proliferated outside the medical center. But power during this third era was seen as a form of "multiple leadership" in which the hospital director was managing a coalition-type organization (77).

Changing Internal Procedures

This category of management technologies derives from Thompson's (36) now familiar assertion that, under norms of rationality organizations seek to seal off their core technologies from environmental influences. Many health care organizations contain some production-line aspects of technology. An example is a surgical suite. Scott (1) describes several buffering tactics. Through "coding," managers can classify resources and inputs before introducing them into the technical core. This aids in their proper handling and allows the exclusion of any that are inappropriate. Thus health care organizations carefully classify and code patients; it would certainly shut down the "production line" for an infected baby to be admitted to the newborn nursery. Yet organizations can overcode: they may screen and classify inputs so carefully that they fail to notice important environmental changes.

A manager can avoid this risk by another buffering tactic: "forecasting"—anticipating changes in input or output conditions and attempting to adapt to them, making short-term changes in operations by rescheduling personnel, hiring or laying off staff, and so on. There is an entire management science that applies operations research models such as queuing theory and simulation to this problem. Further, sensitivity analysis can determine when the costs of adaptation exceed the costs that would otherwise be incurred. Longer-range forecasting techniques such as statistical trend analysis and future scenario building are more appropriate to basic environmental changes. These usually lead to changes in internal structures and procedures rather than attempts to modify environmental inputs to fit the existing organization.

By "stockpiling" a manager stores critical resources so they can be introduced into the technical core at the right time. For example, float nurses may be employed in case the number of newborns increases. Operating room nurses may be stored in an on-call capacity if emergency surgeries must be performed in the middle of the night. By "leveling" or "smoothing," a manager undertakes a more active effort: to reduce environmentally induced fluctuations. For example, elective clinic visits are switched from peak to slack times.

Developing alternative suppliers of resources is another tactic that aids in preserving independence and avoiding dependency relationships. Valley Hospital developed a medical office building, partly to obtain a secure and loyal supply of physicians.

Growth is among the most common strategies, albeit a longer-term one. There are only two ways to grow, from within or by means of merger. The former is a strategy of independence. The latter may or may not be, depending on the controlling power of the focal organization. Growth achieves distinct advantages for an organization. Size brings stability, removing some of the risks small enterprises must undertake. Larger organizations are usually more widely diversified, leaving them less vulnerable to destructive forces at work in one localized segment. Status is associated with bigness, and is enhanced by growth. Finally, most communities cannot tolerate the collapse of very large institutions and will extend support to them that would not be forthcoming to smaller ones.

A strategy of diversification is based on the fact that organizations with dispersed resources are better off than ones highly dependent on a few (78). Strategies such as product differentiation and market segmentation can be viewed as attempts by managers to achieve a wider range of discretion (19), and maximizing discretion increases certainty about the future. Valley Hospital sponsored an HMO for this reason, and opened an urgent care center. Indeed, Valley's decision about the latter program was made in direct response to the realization that 40% of its inpatients were admitted from its emergency room—a condition of high dependence on a single source—and that Riverview's actions to open an emergency service threatened that source.

Borrowing and Incorporating

It is usually easier and faster for an organization to scan the environment and select successful innovations from other enterprises than to undertake the development process from within. After all, innovations that succeed have survived some sort of environmental test that others have not, so why take on the risk and cost of possible failure? This strategy assumes that *(1)* the focal organization has the capacity to scan, *(2)* information about others' practices can be obtained, and *(3)* the borrowing and lending units are similar enough in organization and environmental context they face to make diffusion sensible (79).

We have dealt with the first proviso in our discussion of boundary-spanning personnel. As for the second, information about other organizations' activities may not be readily available. A tactic in this instance is to hire personnel from the organization that has made the innovation or to hire personnel that are familiar with the kind of development to be borrowed. Indeed, the movement of personnel is a major avenue of new product and service diffusion among organizations (27). An example from our Valley Hospital case is the appointment as chief executive of the new HMO of a manager who had previously been in the top ranks of the large HMO with which Valley and Riverview had chosen to compete.

Acquisition of personnel with special information need not be limited to the arena of new product or service development. Employees can also be hired or otherwise incorporated simply for their connections. Thus companies that do defense contract work for the federal government often hire former military officers. This practice is common with firms in other regulated industries. In the health field, hospitals have hired executives of health systems agencies and have secured the consultant services of former government planning officials. At Valley Hospital, the new director of corporate planning had formerly been on the staff of the local health systems agency.

We have noted the same practice at the board of directors level: the use of board appointments to acquire strategic intelligence and connections to sensitive elements of the environment (64). At Valley Hospital individuals were appointed to the board specifically to advance the hospital's connections with local government and the nearby university. Other appointments were made to acquire intelligence about the legal environment, in support of Valley's strategy of lawsuits against the state government over Medicaid reimbursements, and the state political and policy making apparatus, with the hopes of influencing it.

' Two aspects of this strategy go beyond the realm of borrowing and incorporating. First, hiring people with connections is presumably done for the purpose of using those connections to alter regulations, flow of resources, and so on. This then is a positive and aggressive strategy of changing the environment by forming bridges to it, rather than simply buffering a technical core. Secondly, incorporating well-connected individuals introduces the possibility of cooptation: new outside influences could alter the goals and decisions of the focal organization. So a strategy to coopt another organization opens the focal enterprise to the possibility of the reverse. Valley Hospital faced this risk when it sought university connections: community hospitals have sometimes become dominated by medical schools and their teaching interests.

Restructuring to Match the Environment

This category of strategies clearly goes beyond those that seek to buffer and isolate the technical core. This strategy assumes that some sort of match is needed on the part of the organization to a changed environment. This is the realm of structural contingency.

Restructuring flows almost inevitably from the strategies we have outlined thus far: scanning, mapping, changing internal procedures, borrowing, and incorporating. These result in the addition of new organization members with skills different from those of members employed in the technical core, and they require the development of new specialized roles and departments. As we observed at Valley Hospital, most of these additions involved the creation of new staff departments at the managerial level, and secondarily some elaboration at the governance level. Open-systems theory says that increasing complexity of the environment is adapted to by increasing differentiation on the part of the organization. The organization that successfully adapts often carries this differentiation and elaboration beyond the incorporation of new managerial staff and governance changes; it restructures.

Restructuring often brings forth intentions of (1) tight lines and boxes that achieve clarity in roles, authorities, and responsibilities, (2) a rational pattern that can be applied uniformly throughout an organization, and (3) a structure that will survive for a relatively long period of time. Open-systems and contingency theories say that these are misguided intentions. Instead, structure should be seen as loose couplings with a variety of units differentiated externally and integrated internally through special bridging persons, with different designs to match different environments, and as patterns that will likely need changing frequently. To the extent that different organizational units are free to vary independently, they will provide a sensitive mechanism for detecting and responding to environmental variations. Further, if problems develop in one unit it can more readily be sealed off from the larger system. Allowing local units to adapt without requiring changes in the larger system reduces coordination costs for the organization as a whole and the need for large-scale changes that are inappropriate for other units and take too long to accomplish. Hage (80) and Hunt (34) concluded that organizations tend to drift toward over-routinization (overstructuring) and these circumstances require deliberate and positive management effort to resist such evolution when it compromises the flexibility and creativity of the organization.

Changing the Environment

Strategies that seek to alter the environment may be undertaken by individual organizations or through collective action. Individual action is more likely if the effect of some environmental features uniquely or especially on the focal organization; collective action is more likely when the environmentl feature is more pervasive. Which of these pathways to use can itself be an important tactical choice. For example, the management and board of Valley Hospital had a choice of undertaking legal action against the state as the sole plaintiff or of undertaking it through the state hospital association with numerous other hospitals. Valley's decision makers preferred individual action because they felt that Valley's situation was unique and thus a lawsuit would more likely prevail. Yet at the outset of one of Valley's several lawsuits, the hospital was at the same time pleading with the state government for a guaranteed loan for its hospital modernization project. Since the same department of state government was the target of the proposed lawsuit that held authority over the loan-guarantee decision, Valley officials decided to urge the state hospital association to take up the suit in behalf of Valley and numerous other hospitals. In short, Valley's efforts to change the environment were sometimes direct and sometimes indirect.

As our example suggests, creating connections to government becomes an important bridging strategy. Government helps determine the overall context of organizational activity by defining what actions will be supported by law. Government imposes on all organizations constraints and requirements to benefit the general society: taxes, requirements for insurance to cover employees' work-related injuries or retirement, industrial pollution controls, antitrust laws, and consumer protection regulations. Government places special constraints on certain organizations: airlines and banks have been highly regulated. Likewise, health care organizations are seen as enterprises involved in the public interest.

Numerous observers have concluded that the organizations that are regulated benefit from this attention: competition is reduced, prices are set at comfortable levels, and so forth. These advantages stem from efforts by regulated companies to alter their environments.

The development of multihospital systems has been seen as a strategy for private takeover of the government functions of franchising hospital beds and services. Cooney and Alexander (81) write:

> The advantage [of hospitals merged into multiunit corporations] rests in the fact that this domination, if it is realized, can provide the resources and power base for the system to play the role of a planning authority. . . . It can design the scope, quantity, quality, and distribution of services in such a fashion as to serve the community it dominates and avoid duplication of facilities by better utilizing hospital services.

If such a result comes to pass, it clearly secures greater resource control and reduces future uncertainty for the hospitals involved.

Finally, government influences certain organizations as a provider of resources: indirectly through tax breaks, directly through grants or as a buyer of services. For some organizations the relations with government are so numerous and important that the familiar distinction between private and public organizations seems invalid.

Not all efforts to manage task environments are as targeted or as pragmatic as these examples of hospital–government relations. Some are designed to secure resources as pervasive and elusive as public legitimacy and reputation. Recalling Meyer and Rowan's (68) focus on rational myths, this kind of activity is important "since an organization is little more than an embodiment of externally defined meanings" (1). It follows that the management of organization–environment relations should include efforts to create or modify these public meanings.

An example from our Valley Hospital case is the market research conducted by a consultant in the mid-1970s. It revealed that Valley had little identity or reputation in many segments of its service area, and if known was viewed as a government hospital for the poor rather than as a general community hospital. This impression was verified by prominent and wealthy citizens and corporation executives whom the hospital approached for donations; these persons declined to donate because Valley was "financed by the government—we're already contributing through taxes." Market research also indicated that patients without the ability to pay were self-referring to Valley because they assumed it was a county hospital.

It seemed clear to Valley's management that the hospital's embodiment of these rational myths had to be changed—both the hospital's character and the community's image. The new 150-bed patient-care wing was designed to attract more private paying patients through a changed mix of room accommodations, physical appointments, and new services. An employee education program was aimed at changing the myth that had become internalized. Management also developed an environmental strategy aimed both at the general public and at community influentials. The name of the hospital was changed to foster a new image: Valley Hospital and Health Center. A variety of new external publications were developed, including a newsprint mass mailer that emphasized personal health promotion and disease prevention. Valley's name and new services were displayed prominently on billboards. Community influentials were invited to special and regular hospital functions for reorientation. The fund development program was modified to schedule 2 years of information presentations about Valley to precede the hard sell.

The results were revealed in a replication of the marketing study 5 years later. The culture that legitimized the hospital had indeed been changed, and this was beginning to show in patient admission statistics.

Linking

A strategy of linking to other organizations creates new mutual dependencies recognizing the need for exchange relationships. These mutual dependencies may be balanced or imbalanced; in the latter case an organization can lose control over its future destiny, becoming engulfed.

The types of links that organizations develop to manage and monitor their interdependencies have been categorized by numerous theorists on a general continuum from cooperation to conflict. We will use and modify Thompson's (36) categorization of the various types of cooperation—contracting, coopting, and coalescing—to which we will add a fourth, consumption. "Contracts" are negotiated agreements for the exchange of

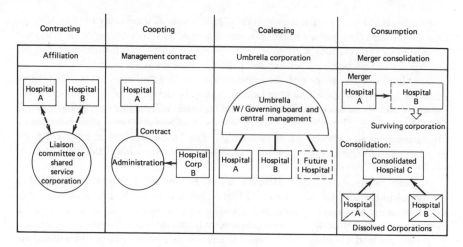

Figure 10.1. Corporate relationships: different types of hospital combinations. (From Starkweather, D.B., *Hospital mergers in the making.* Ann Arbor, Mich,.: Health Administration Press, 1981, p. 39.)

future performance. These rest either on faith and belief that each party will perform in order to maintain its reputation (79) or prestige, or on specific documents, such as binding legal agreements which third parties can evaluate and for which penalties can be assessed for failure to comply. In "coopting" one organization absorbs new elements into its leadership from another to avoid threats to its stability and to increase the certainty of support from the coopted organization. This act is more constraining and potentially more costly in terms of loss of autonomy than is contracting; it places an element previously in the organization's environment in a position to exert internal power and influence. "Coalescing" is a joint venture between two or more organizations wherein they act as one to achieve certain goals or activities. This not only provides the basis for conducting exchange, but also requires commitment to future joint decision making; thus it is even more constraining or potentially costly than the other forms of cooperation.

Starkweather (82) has demonstrated how the emerging forms of consortia, multihospital systems, and mergers among hospitals can be seen as a manifestation of Thompson's basic model. Specifically, in Starkweather's study "affiliation" is defined as an example of contracting, "management contracts" as an example of coopting, and "umbrella corporations" as an example of coalescing. Starkweather's fourth type of hospital combination—"merger consolidation"—goes beyond Thompson's three forms. In the case of "consumption," the price paid for reduction of uncertainty is surrender of decision-making autonomy: the organization loses its independent identity. Starkweather goes on to show the variations in the characteristics of these types of hospital combinations with respect to five different dimensions: organizational patterns, legal bonds, services, geography, and organizational impact. These characteristics are summarized in Figure 10.1 and Table 10.1.

TABLE 10.1. Characteristics of Different Hospital Combinations

Pluralism		Fusion		
	Affiliations	Management Contracts	Umbrella Corporations	Mergers/Consolidations
Organizational pattern	Voluntary subscription or joint development, usually involving a third party; trade-off agreements	Preserve prior ownerships; new management	Delegation of policy making to new agency; new ownership and financial development	Absorption of one or more prior entries; loss of prior identities and functions
Legal bonds	Implied agreements, contracts, and formal agreements with escape clauses	Contract, typically for several years	Transferred assets; prior corporate entities continue	Replacement agreements; prior entities abolished
Services combined	Support, logistic	Administrative, broadly defined	Administrative, professional services	Administrative, professional, direct patient care operations
Geography	Dispersed or local	Separate communities; often same region	Sometimes serve same population; often regionally organized	Often a common geographic population; physical integration often intended
Organizational impact	Minimal changes of tasks, jobs, rules	Reorganization of departments; new efficiency procedures	Substantial change—new functions, accomplished by planned intervention	Evolutionary, systemwide; involving new structures; change may be spontaneous, involving unpredictable consequences

SOURCE: Starkweather, D. B., *Hospital Mergers in the Making.* Ann Arbor, Mich., Health Administration Press, 1981, p. 39.

MINI-CASE: CASE STUDY—VALLEY HOSPITAL REVISITED

As a remarkable example of the linking strategy, we return to Valley Hospital and an extension of our case presentation to include the first half of the 1980s.

By 1982 it had become clear that the cost-shifting strategy was working against the goal of expanded private-pay patients: physicians and patients simply would not use Valley's services when its private rates were in excess of any other hospitals in the region. Furthermore, since for years Valley had been committing substantial funds toward charity care, it had not set aside sufficient funds for capital replacement. In 1980 it had completed rebuilding slightly more than half of the facility, but had done so with heavy borrowing that left it highly leveraged and with heavy debt service requirements. The outlook for acquiring funds for further needed capital replacements and equipment was dubious.

The Search for Links

In 1982, Valley began a domain definition and strategic planning process. The strategic plan stated that the hospital should commit itself to "active exploration of affiliation opportunities that could provide it with increased fiscal stability."

This occurred shortly before the state government undertook a major change in the method of reimbursement for Medicaid patients, which constituted approximately 40% of Valley's total volume. The state shifted from a "reasonable cost" basis of reimbursement to a per diem price negotiated with each hospital that chose to enter a bid for the care of Medicaid patients. Valley was not in a position to "sharpen its pencil" as much as other hospitals which could submit lower prices to the state because they had larger proportions of private-pay patients upon which to shift the differences between negotiated price and cost of hospital services. The result was that Valley did not obtain a Medicaid contract. The hospital suddenly had to reduce its employed staff of 1,000 full-time equivalents (FTEs) to 600 and its inpatient occupancy dropped to half its former level. Valley Hospital's very survival now was at stake.

Riverview easily won a Medicaid contract because its prior proportions of government-sponsored and private patients were almost the reverse of Valley's; thus it could submit a lower price to the state because of its larger base of private patients upon which to shift unrecovered costs. The resulting change in patient mixes made the two hospitals much more alike than they had been before.

Valley then revised its strategic plan concerning affiliation to incorporate nine criteria that would guide negotiations with other hospitals:

1. Ensure long-term access to capital.
2. Improve negotiating position with purchasers of care.
3. Spread risk through vertical and horizontal diversification.
4. Ensure ability to maintain and improve physical plant and equipment.
5. Improve flexibility and adaptability in face of continuous environmental change.
6. Maintain institutional identity/autonomy.
7. Increase political clout.
8. Ensure ability to serve current patient population.
9. Enhance community image.

The Two Alternative Link-ups

Following this strategy, Valley identified several potential affiliation partners and undertook negotiations. The options soon boiled down to two strong possibilities.

One was an affiliation with South Health, a nonprofit multihospital corporation 400 miles away. That corporation was anxious to expand its operations to the portion of the state in which Valley was located. South Health offered a variety of services in management and marketing, and its efficiencies and entrepreneurship in these areas would help Valley survive as an independent hospital. However, because of its distance, little could be joined in the way of clinical or professional services. Further, while South Health wanted Valley's board and medical staff to remain as autonomous units, it insisted on appointing all hospital board members and ultimate power over the board through the casting of a single controlling vote on any issue South Health felt was important. (This is a common provision in parent/subsidiary corporation arrangements, stemming from the need to control the subsidiary in order to meet debt payments and other financial obligations.) South Health offered to appoint two Valley board members to its board, a group that met quarterly to review the actions of an executive committee. Strangely, South Health did not offer capital financing availability to Valley, since it had yet to create a master indenture form of debt financing for its subsidiaries.

The other merger option was with Riverview Hospital. Although there had been a long history of animosity between these two institutions, by 1982 both board presidents were prominent civic leaders who enjoyed mutual respect and longstanding friendship. Negotiations started privately. The parties soon realized that the two institutions were quite alike because of the changes brought about by Medicaid contracting. Medical staff memberships overlapped substantially and the hospitals' services were complementary. The negotiations resulted in a plan for a consolidation in which a new corporation would be formed that would take over most important authorities from the two existing hospitals, but the separate corporations would not be abolished as operating entities.

This approximated a full merger in that (1) the trustees of the two boards would be the directors of the new corporation's board, (2) management would be unified and centralized, and (3) financial control would reside at the new corporation. Valley Hospital negotiated a 50% representation on the board of the new corporation. Only the two medical staffs would remain formally separate and autonomous, but soon the physician groups started a discussion of various forms of integration.

It was understood that the two hospitals would remain physically separate (1 mile) because neither institution's campus space could accommodate the other. Certain clinical and patient care services would be transferred from one hospital to the other and duplications would be eliminated. If, in the long run, hospital utilization continued to decline, the need for separate acute-care institutions would be questioned.

Comparing the two possibilities, Valley concluded that its survivability—the preservation of its mission, commitment to certain types of patients, multiracial hospital staff, and so on—was greater with Riverview than with South Health, for a number of reasons.

- The opportunities for operating gains were much more substantial where local proximity allowed the integration of clinical as well as management activities.

- The two hospitals together could negotiate better arrangements with governments and insurance companies for local health care delivery than they could separately.
- Valley would obtain much greater influence in the Riverview affiliation, with its 50% of board seats, than with token representation on the South Health board; indeed, this 50% would allow Valley to veto any decisions contrary to its interests.
- The operating gains inherent in a local integration meant that capital borrowing would be available in the future, where it might not be in the "long-distance" link.

On the basis of these (and other) factors, the Valley–Riverview merger was agreed to in 1984 and immediately implemented.

Some Lessons

It is possible for a hospital to merge and at the same time retain important elements of its operation, its staff, and its mission. The results of a merger will differ from one hospital subgroup to another; indeed, there is no such thing as a single or uniform result—rather, there is a set of various linkages that satisfy the resource dependencies of various organizational parts of the coalitions. These subgroups reacted   The second lesson from the Valley case is that the linkage would not have happened without careful assessment and management of organization–environment relations, vial Valley's strategic planning.

- Valley had systematically examined all the alternatives to merger and concluded that a hospital linkage of some sort was an essential part of its future.
- Valley's board and management advanced the general concept through the development of criteria to guide their actions and decisions.
- Valley aggressively pursued partners rather than waiting for "someone to come along," thus it was creating and altering its environment.
- Valley put together a negotiaion team that reflected the essential power of its coalition. Its team of key directors, managers, and doctors were able to bargain effectively in Valley's behalf when the chips were down.

None of these things happened casually or accidentally. They occurred because of Valley's commitment and capacities for aggressive strategic management.

MANAGEMENT SKILLS

Clearly, management based on the assumptions of open-systems theory calls for different orientations and skills than those needed for management under the assumptions of closed-systems theory. Some of these needed management skills are obvious and straightforward: *(1)* problem solving—finding the best way of getting something done; *(2)* communication—either directly (task-oriented) or indirectly (dealing with staff morale and motivation); and *(3)* value setting—attaching values to necessary choices and establishing an organization's culture and norms (83). A fourth activity is vital but dimly understood: the formation of order out of environmental chaos. This skill is closest to that of creativity. It is what Thompson (36) judges to be the most crucial managerial function—coalignment. It involves the discernment of hitherto unnoticed relationships or patterns in the complex environment of the organization, calculating their cause-and-effect relationships, and translating them into appropriate programs of action.

This is a good prescription for the management of organization–environment relations.

SUMMARY

Based on existing research and practice, the following guidelines are likely to help managers deal effectively with their environment:

MANAGERIAL GUIDELINES

1. Effective managers need to rigorously and systematically scan and assess the organization's environment.
2. Effective managers need to actively manage and act upon the organization's environment. This can be accomplished through increased resource acquisition, political activity, and coalition network building.
3. Negotiation skills will become increasingly important to managers in dealing effectively with their organization's environment.
4. Interorganizational strategies such as networking, coalition building, and system affiliation will be increasingly important for successful "environmental" management.

DISCUSSION QUESTIONS

1. Considering different types of health care organizations, identify ones that *(1)* failed through natural selection, *(2)* survived through natural selection, *(3)* failed despite efforts of structural contingency that recognized resource dependency, and *(4)* flourished through strategies of environmental adaptation. What distinguished the policy-making, managerial, and decision-making activities of these different organizations?

2. Contrast social organizations and business organizations with respect to their environments of importance and strategies of environmental influence and control. In what ways are they similar? In what ways are they different?

3. Thompson (36) emphasizes the importance to an organization of striking the appropriate relationship between dependence on other parties in order to obtain a crucial resource and the giving away of influence to parties outside the organization to reduce future uncertainty. Discuss ways in which a health cae manager can determine how to strike this balance properly.

4. Choose a health care organization you know and state how you would structure it along loosely coupled lines to advance the twin gols of environmental adaptation and organizational integration.

SUGGESTED READINGS

Biller, R. P. Some implications of adaptation for organizational and political development. In F. Marini (Ed.), *The new public administration?* San Francisco: Chandler Press, 1971.
Discusses different organizational and managerial behaviors vis-a-vis the post-industrial society, with particular reference to public-service agencies.

Meyer, J. W., & Scott, R. W. *Organization environment, ritual and rationality,* Beverly Hills: Sage, 1983.
Chapters 4 and 6 are specific to the health field.

Pfeffer, J., & Salancik, G. R. Organization design: The case for a coalition model of organizations. *Organizational Dynamics,* 1977, *6,* 15–29.
Expands on the coalition model of organizations, with applications to both internal management and organization–environment relations.

Pfeffer, J., & Salancik, G. R. *The external control of organizations.* New York: Harper & Row, 1978.
Best complete treatment of resource-dependence approach, including numerous managerial strategies.

REFERENCES

1. Scott, W. R. *Organizations: Rational, natural, and open systems.* Englewood Cliffs, N.J.: Prentice-Hall, 1981.

2. Bell, D. *The coming of the postindustrial society: A venture in social forcasting.* New York: Basic Books, 1973.

3. Biller, R. P. Some implications of adaptation for organizational and political development. In F. Marini (Ed.), *The new public administration?* San Francisco: Chandler Press, 1971.

4. Weber, M. *The theory of social and economic organizations.* A. H. Henderson and T. Parsons (Eds.). Glencoe, Ill.: Free Press, 1947.

5. Dill, W. R. Environment as an influence on managerial autonomy. *Administrative Science Quarterly,* 1958, *2,* 409–443.

6. Pfeffer, J. Size and composition of corporate boards of directors. *Administrative Science Quarterly,* 1972, *17,* 218–228.

7. Pfeffer, J. Size, composition, and function of hospital boards of directors: A study of organizational–environment linkage. *Administrative Science Quarterly,* 1973, *18,* 349–364.

8. Hannan, M. T., & Freeman, J. The population ecology of organizations. *American Journal of Sociology,* 1977, *82,* 929–964.

9. Aldrich, H. E. *Organizations and environments.* Englewood Cliffs, N.J.: Prentice-Hall, 1979.

10. Galbraith, J. K. *The new industrial state.* Boston: Houghton Mifflin, 1967.

11. Stigler, G. J. The economies of scale. *Journal of Law and Economics,* 1958, *1,* 54–71.

12. Saving, T. R. Estimation of optimal size of plant by the survivor technique. *Quarterly Journal of Economics,* 1961, *75,* 569–607.

13. Weiss, L. W. The survival technique and the extent of suboptimal capacity. *Journal of Political Economy*, 1964, *72*, 246–261.

14. Scherer, F. M. *Industrial market structure and economic performance*. Chicago: Rand McNally, 1970.

15. Williams, H. *Hospital closures and mergers, New York City, 1960–1975*. New York: Health and Hospital Planning Council of Southern New York, 1976.

16. Kennedy, L. Hospital closures and survivors: An analysis of operating characteristics and regulatory mechanisms in three states. *Health Services Research* (in process).

17. Mullner, R. M., & Anderson, R. M. A descriptive a ratio analysis of merged and consolidated hospitals States, 1980–1985 (unpublished manuscript), June 5, 1986.

18. Fennell, M. L. The effect of environmental characteristics on structure of hospital clusters. *Administrative Science Quarterly* 1980, *25*, 485–510.

19. Aldrich, H. E., & Pfeffer, J. Environments of organizations. *Annual Review of sociology*, 1976, *2*, 79–105.

20. Collins, N. R., & Preston, L. E. The size structure of the largest industrial firms, 1909–1958. *American Economic Review*, 1961, *51*, 986–1011.

21. Mayer, M. W., & Goldstein, S. *The first two years: Problems of small firm growth and survival*. Washington, D.C.: U.S. Government Printing Office, 1961.

22. Pennings, J. M. "The relevance of the structural-contingency model for organizational effectiveness. *Administrative Science Quarterly*, 1975, *20*, 393–410.

23. Galbraith, J. *Designing complex organizations*. Reading, Mass.: Addison-Wesley, 1973.

24. Starkweather, D. B., & Kisch, A. I. A model of the life cycle dynamics of health science organizations. In M. Arnold, L. V. Blankenskip, & J. M. Hess (Eds.), *Administering health systems*. Chicago: Aldine–Atherton Press, 1971.

25. Evan, W. M. The organization set: Toward a theory of interorganizational relations. In J. D. Thompson (Ed.), *Approaches to organizational design*. Pittsburgh: University of Pittsburgh Press, 1966.

26. Stinchcombe, A. L. Social structure and organizations. In J. G. March (Ed.), *Handbook of organizations*. Chicago: Rand McNally, 1965.

27. Carroll, G. R., Delacroix, J., and Goodstein, J. The political environment of organizations. To appear in *Organizational Behavior*, Vol. 10 B. H. Stan and L. Cummings, eds. JAI Press, 1987.

28. Hannan, M. T., and Freeman, J. *Disbanded rates of national labor unions, 1936–1985: Density, dependence and age*. Technical Report 86-6, Cornell University, 1986.

29. Veney, J. E., & Khan, J. Causal paths in elaboration of organizational structure: A case of hospital services. *Health Services Research*, 1973, *8*, 139–150.

30. Lawrence, P. R., & Lorsch, J. W. *Organization and environment: Managing differentiation and integration*. Homewood, Ill.: Richard D. Irwin, Inc., 1969.

31. Baldwin, E. L. An empirical study: The effect of organizational differentiation and integration on hospital performance. *Hospital Administration*, 1972, *17*, 52–71.

32. Woodward, J. *Management and technology*. London: Her Majesty's Stationery Office, 1958.

33. Perrow, C. *Organizational analysis: A sociological view*. Belmont, Calif.: Wadsworth, 1970.

34. Hunt, R. G. Technology and organization. *Academy of Management Journal*, 1970, *13*, 325–342.

35. Thompson, J. D., & Bates, F. L. Technology, organization, and administration. *Administrative Science Quarterly*, 1957, *2*, 325–342.

36. Thompson, J. D. *Organizations in action*. New York: McGraw-Hill, 1967.

37. Cook, K. S. Exchange and power in networks of interorganizational relations. *Sociological Quarterly*, 1977, *18*, 62–82.

38. Emerson, R. M. Power–dependence relations. *American Sociological Review*, 1962, *27*, 31–40.

39. Jacobs, D. Dependency and vulnerability: An exchange approach to the control of organizations. *Administrative Science Quarterly*, 1974, *19*, 45–59.

40. Levine, S., & White, P. E. Exchange as a conceptual framework for the study of interorganizational relationships. *Administrative Science Quarterly*, 1961, 5, 583–601.

41. Williamson, O. E. *Markets and hierarchies: Analysis and antitrust implications*. New York: Free Press, 1979.

42. Williamson, O. E. Transaction cost economics: The governance of contractual relations. *Journal of Law and Economics*, 1979, *22*, 233–261.

43. Williamson, O. E. The economics of organization: the cost approach. *American Journal of Sociology*, 1981, *87*, 548–577.

44. Cook, K. S., Shortell, S. M., Conrad, D., & Morrisey, M. A theory of organizational response to regulation: The case of hospitals. *Academy of Management Review*, 1983, *2*, 193–205.

45. Morrisey, M. A., Conrad, D. A., Shortell, S. M., & Cook, K. S. Hospital rate review: The state of the empirical knowledge. Unpublished technical report, American Hospital Association, Chicago, 1981.

46. Scott, R. W. and Meyer, J. W. The organization sectors. In J. W. Meyer and W. R. Scott (Eds.), *Environments: Ritual and Rationality*. Beverly Hills, Sage 1983.

47. Ashby, W. R. Principles of self-organizing systems. In W. Buckley (Ed.), *Modern systems research for the behavioral scientist*. Chicago: Aldine, 1968.

48. Cyert, R. M., & March, J. G. *A behavioral theory of the firm*. Englewood Cliffs, N.J.: Prentice-Hall, 1963.

49. Pfeffer, J., & Salancik, G. R. *The external control of organizations*. New York: Harper & Row, 1978.

50. D'Aunno, T. A. and Zuckerman, H. S. Organization integration of alternative perspectives. (Manuscript) 1985.

51. Jurkovich, R. A core typology of organizational environments. *Administrative Science Quarterly*, 1974, *19*, 380–394.

52. Warren, R. The interorganizational field as a focus of investigation. *Administrative Science Quarterly*, 1967, *12*, 396–419.

53. Turk, H. Comparative urban structure from an interorganizational perspective. *Administrative Science Quarterly*, 1973, *18*, 37–55.

54. Pfeffer, J. Beyond management and the worker: The institutional function of management. *Academy of Management Review*, 1976, *1*, 36–46.

55. Homans, G. C. *Social behavior, its elementary forms*, (2nd Ed.). New York: Harcourt Brace Jovanovich, 1974.

56. Blau, P. *Exchange and power in social life*. New York: John Wiley & Sons, 1964.

57. Emerson, R. M. Exchange networks, part II. In J. Berger, M. Zelditch, & B. Anderson (Eds.), *Sociological theories in process* (Vol. II). Boston: Houghton Mifflin, 1972.

58. Cook, K. S., & Emerson, R. M. Exchange networks and the analysis of complex organizations. In S. B. Bacharach & E. J. Lawler (Eds.), *Perspectives in organizational sociology: Theory and research* (Vol. III). Greenwich, Conn.: JAI, 1983.

59. Levine, S., White, P. E., & Paul, B. D. Community interorganizational problems in providing medical care and social services. *American Journal of Public Health*, 1963, *53*, 1183–1195.

60. Hunter, F. *Community power structure*. Chapel Hill: University of North Carolina Press, 1953.

61. Weick, K. E. Middle range theories of social systems. *Behavioral Science*, 1974, *19*, 357–367.

62. Elling, R. H. The hospital support game in urban center. In E. Freidson (Ed.), *The hospital in modern society*. New York: Free Press, 1963.

63. Elling, R. H., & Halebsky, S. Organizational differentiation and support: A conceptual framework. *Administrative Science Quarterly*, 1961, *6*, 185–209.

64. Pfeffer, J. Size, composition, and function of hospital boards of directors: A study of organizational–environment linkage. *Administrative Science Quarterly*, 1973, *18*, 349–364.

65. Elling, R. H., & Lee, O. J. Formal connections of community leadership to the health system. In E. G. Jaco (Ed.), *Patients, physicians and illness: A sourcebook in behavioral science and health* (2nd ed.). New York: Free Press, 1972.

66. Terreberry, S. The evolution of organizational environments. *Administrative Science Quarterly*, 1968, *12*, 590–613.

67. Perrow, C. Organization prestige: Some functions and dysfunctions. *American Journal of Sociology*, 1961, *66*, 335–341.

68. Meyer, J., & Rowan, B. Institutionalized organizations: Formal structure as myth and ceremony. In M. W. Meyer (Ed.), *Environments and organizations*. San Francisco: Jossey-Bass, 1978.

69. Illich, I. *Deschooling society*. New York: Harper & Row, 1972.

70. Illich, I. *Medical nemesis*. New York: Random House, 1976.

71. Churchman, C. W. *The systems approach*. New York: Delacorte Press, 1968.

72. Bourgeois, I. J. III. Strategy and environment: A conceptual integration. *Academy of Management Review*, 1980, *5*, 25–39.

73. Miles, R. E., Snow, C. C., & Pfeffer, J. Organization–environment: Concepts and issues. *Industrial relations*, 1974, *13*, 244–264.

74. Utterback, J. The process of technological innovation within the firm. *Academy of Management Journal*, 1971, *14*, 75–88.

75. Starkweather, D. B. *Hospital mergers in the making*. Ann Arbor: Health Administration Press, 1981.

76. Perrow, C. Goals and power structure: A historical case study. In E. Freidson (Ed.), *The hospital in modern society*. Glencoe, Ill.: Free Press, 1963.

77. Pfeffer, J., & Salancik, G. R. Organization design: The case for a coalition model of organizations. *Organizational Dynamics*, 1977, *6*, 15–29.

78. March, J. G., & Simon, H. A. *Organizations*. New York: John Wiley & Sons, 1958.

79. Macauley, S. Noncontractual relations in business. *American Sociological Review*, 1963, *28*, 55–67.

80. Hage, J. *Communication and organizational control: Cybernetics in health and welfare agencies*. New York: John Wiley & Sons, 1974.

81. Cooney, J. P., & Alexander, T. L. *Multihospital systems: An evaluation* (Part I). Health Sciences Research Center of the Hospital Research and Education Trust, and Northwestern University, Chicago, 1975.

82. Starkweather, D. Health facility mergers: Some conceptualizations. *Medical Care*, 1971, *9*, 468–478.

83. Whisler, T. L. *Information technology and organizational change*. Belmont, Calif.: Wadsworth, 1970.

CHAPTER 11

Organizational Change and Innovation

Arnold D. Kaluzny and
S. Robert Hernandez

Health care organizations face constant change. Their success or failure depends upon how well health service managers understand the change process, diagnose organizational problems, and present appropriate solutions.

Understanding of change and ability to affect the change process depends upon the particular model managers employ. While managers traditionally pride themselves on their pragmatic orientation, in reality each is using some model or perspective to identify and give meaning to the vast array of information and relationships that need to be considered in dealing with change. As described by Graham Allison (1), "what we see and judge to be important depends not only on the evidence but also on the 'conceptual lens' through which we look at the evidence."

Chapter 1 presented a number of organizational models which implicitly or explicitly influence our ability to understand and manage the change process; the rational model, the resource dependency model, and the organizational ecology model:

- The *rational model* assumes that organizational performance can be defined unambiguously and that change and innovation within the organization can be planned or systematically effected to enhance various aspects of performance.
- The *resource dependency model* considers the effects of environment on internal organizational processes and the manner in which the organization adapts to and manages its environment to facilitate change and innovation.
- The *organizational ecology model* views organizations and their change from an evolutionary perspective emphasizing the probabilistic rather than deterministic nature of change as the unfolding of larger events within the environment selects those organizational characteristics that best fit the environment (2).

Each model is discussed in terms of its definition, its critical variables, its view of organizational change, and strategies appropriate for affecting the change process within

379

or between organizations. Before presenting each of the models it is important to confront a number of recurring issues in the management of change and innovation within health care organizations. These are generic to each of the perspectives, and their relationships to the particular perspectives are discussed later in the chapter.

TYPES OF CHANGE

Health care executives are involved in various types of changes and innovation ranging from the introduction of new pieces of equipment or programs to redefinition of goals of the organization. Several distinctions are necessary. First, change must be differentiated from innovation. Change is a generic concept that deals with any modification in operations, structure, or ends of the organization. Innovation is more restricted and is defined as any idea, practice, or material artifact perceived to be new to a relevant unit of adoption—organization, work group, or individual (3). Thus all innovation is considered change—but not all change is innovation.

Second, since any change involves some modification of ends and means, managers need a framework by which to classify various types of change. To classify an almost endless array of activities, consider the means–end classification scheme in Table 11.1 (4, 5). *Technical change* refers to the internal modifications of ongoing structure and process in order to enhance organizational operations. *Transition* refers to the modification of goals and/or output of the organization, not modification in ongoing functional form of the organization. Finally, *transformation* refers to the modification of the internal structure and processes as well as change in goals and output. The characteristics of these three types of changes have significance for health care organizations.

TECHNICAL CHANGE

Technical change involves some modifications in the means by which the normal and usual activities of the organization are carried out. This may involve some innovative technology or some programmatic–structural alteration in the design of the organization to meet its designated objectives. Technical changes may vary in focus, cost, and impact, but they do not represent changes in the basic goals of the organization. For example, the decision of a hospital to require estrogen receptor assay tests may represent little cost beyond the laboratory fees and may have little impact on the overall organization. However, the decision by the hospital to implement computer-based information systems (6–8) or to install tomography, lithotripter, or angioplasty will have substantial financial

TABLE 11.1. Types of Organizational Change

Types	Means	Ends
Technical	Change	No change
Transition	No change	Change
Transformation	Change	Change

SOURCE: Adapted from Kaluzny, A. D., & Veney, J. E. Types of change and hospital planning strategies. *American Journal of Health Planning*, 1977, *1*, 13–19.

impacts. Moreover, such a decision will affect many hospital functions, placing new demands on available resources and reallocating power among the existing departments.

Structural programmatic changes are more difficult to define than technological changes, but they also focus on the manner in which work is conducted within the organization, rather than on any modification of the goals of the organization itself. For example, the introduction of service-unit management (9, 10) nurse midwifery services, childbirth preparation classes, prenatal contraceptive counseling (11), organizational development (12), or quality assurance programs as a managerial innovation (13) centers on the reallocation of tasks and changes in reporting relationships among individuals.

TRANSITION

Transition means change in organizational goals but not in the essential means of achieving these goals. The provision of nontherapeutic abortions and the sale of governmental or not-for-profit community hospitals to for-profit systems are examples of transition. In these situations the technology and basic structure (the organizational means) are already available within the institution; however, the intent is to apply these to achieve different objectives. These changes occur less frequently; however, when they occur they are associated with a great deal of stress and trauma since goals are usually identified with some powerful group within the organization.

TRANSFORMATION

Transformation is the most extreme form of change. Change occurs in the means the organization uses to reach its end, and also in the ends themselves. For example, hospitals replace traditional inpatient curative services with provision of preventive health care programs to various employer organizations. They also may diversify their operations to include the building and management of condominiums, office buildings, shopping centers, and retirement homes. Each of these activities involves substantial changes in organizational ends and means. Transformation occurs less frequently than other forms of change, but when it does, it involves a basic modification of overall organizational direction and reflects changes in the means by which organizations accomplish these modified ends.

LEVELS OF ANALYSIS

Not only are there different types of change, but change and innovation occur at different levels of analysis which managers can influence in different ways. Three levels of change are considered: (1) change internal to the operations of the organization, (2) change in the organizational structure vis-a-vis the environment, and (3) overall societal change involving populations of organizations. At the internal level and within the immediate purview of management, managers focus on the ongoing processes and interpersonal relationships affecting organizational change. Attention is given to new programs and technology as well as fairly short-term alterations in variables such as communications, organizational culture, coordination, and leadership. Interventions at the internal level target primarily individuals and work groups within the organization.

At the organizational level, change focuses on the basic design and structure of the organization vis-a-vis the larger environment. Attention concentrates on authority and power relationships and the placement of different work units relative to each other in the overall organization. Finally, at the population level attention shifts to external changes often beyond the control of management. Change in basic social values, demographic shifts and availability of resources fall into this category and profoundly affect the operation and survival of groups or populations of organizations.

Moreover, the various levels of analysis are interrelated in a complex manner. In fact the implementation of change at one level may be quite different than implementation at another level. At each level different factors and processes operate (14). For example, at the population level, attention focuses on a macro perspective involving an entire policy sector which includes both federal and local levels. The policy sector typically has tacit operating rules, established roles, routinized procedures, and reasonably stable conditions. At the organizational level implementation is at the discretion of a local delivery organization. Here implementation, greatly influenced by the characteristics of the implementing organization, can result in a considerable discrepancy between the adopted project and the implemented practice. Failure to account for these differences of both level and unit of analysis guarantees failure of the whole project.

SOURCES OF CHANGE

In addition to levels and types of change it is important to distinguish various sources of change. Three sources have been identified (15):

- Origination. Creation or invention of some solution to deal with a problem confronting an organization.
- Adaptation. Application of some prototype solution developed outside the total organization but modified to resolve some problem identified within the organization.
- Borrowing. Application of a solution developed in some other setting with little modification.

Origination occurs when no solution to a problem is found to operate elsewhere. Here the organization is required to recognize the problem and develop a first-time solution. While to date this has not been a major focus within health services, origination is likely to become more important as multi-institutional systems dominate the provision of health services and competition requires the development of entrepreneurial, (i.e., origination type) activity. Research on managerial entrepreneurs in nonhealth service settings suggests behavior that managers should avoid if they expect originations to resolve problems confronting the organization. The managers should be aware of the temptation to (16, p. 101):

- Regard any new idea from below with suspicion—because it's new, and because it's from below.

- Insist that people who need your approval to act first go through several other levels of management to get their signatures.
- Ask departments or individuals to challenge and criticize each other's proposals. (That saves you the job of deciding; you just pick the survivor.)
- Express your criticisms freely, and withhold your praise. (That keeps people on their toes.) Let them know they can be fired at any time.
- Treat identification of problems as signs of failure, to discourage people from letting you know when something in their area isn't working.
- Control everything carefully. Make sure people count anything that can be counted, frequently.
- Make decisions to reorganize or change policies in secret, and spring them on people unexpectedly. (That also keeps people on their toes.)
- Make sure that requests for information are fully justified, and make sure that it is not given out to managers freely. (You don't want data to fall into the wrong hands.)
- Assign to lower-level managers, in the name of delegation and participation, responsibility for figuring out how to cut back, lay off, move people around, or otherwise implement threatening decisions you have made. And get them to do it quickly.
- And above all, never forget that you, the higher-ups, already know everything important about this business.

Adaptation and borrowing are prevalent in health services and represent forms of diffusion, that is, the particular innovation, developed elsewhere, is modified to fit the particular characteristics of the implementing organization (adaptation)—or implemented with little modification (i.e., borrowing). The study of diffusion, particularly borrowing of medical technologies and factors that facilitate or impede diffusion, has received a great deal of attention in the health services literature. Studies of technology and program diffusion focus on either the organization or individuals as units of analysis. For example, among organizations attention has been given to the diffusion of technologies such as magnetic resonance imaging (MRI) and computer tomography (17), electronic fetal monitoring, voltimetric diffusion pumps, centralized energy management systems (18) as well as more programmatic innovations such as unit management (10) and intensive care units (19). Similarly diffusion of technology among individual physicians has included the use of steroid receptor assays in breast cancer and cervical cancer screening (20) as well as the effect of clinic evaluation on physician utilization of various technologies (21).

CHANGE AS A PROCESS VS. AN OUTCOME

Organizational change and innovation may be viewed as an outcome or as a process (22). As an outcome the focus is on attempting to determine an explanation of the occurrence of innovation or change as a dependent variable. Most of the research on change and innovation within health services has been of this type. For example, in analyzing innovation from this perspective one focuses on some quantifiable characteristic, such as the implementation of an innovation or the timing of implementation, and searches for factors that explain differences in quantitative levels or amounts.

Change or innovation as a process means that attention is on a series of events rather than on a set of relations among variables. The intent is not to explain variation in some dependent variable but to demonstrate how a particular event came about over a period of time because of the occurrence of certain prior events. The process is seen as a probabilistic series of events in which precursors are necessary but not necessarily sufficient conditions for the outcome. For example, in the study of diffusion, the existence of other organizations that have made the innovation is viewed as a precursor, considered a necessary but not sufficient condition for adoption. Thus a particular innovation may or may not be diffused from organizations possessing the innovation to those without the innovation.

TYPES OF ORGANIZATIONAL CHANGE STRATEGIES

The ability to implement various types of change derived from different sources and operating at different levels is a function of various techniques and strategies used by health care managers. In some situations the application appears almost random, while in others, it is largely determined by the personal orientation of the user independent of the situation. However, increasing attention is focusing on the application of change strategies and techniques to health service organizations within a systematic framework involving data collection, diagnosis, interpretation, selection of specific interventions to deal with diagnosed problems, and, finally, monitoring and feedback (23). Using this approach, several specific points require attention.

Successful change and innovation efforts require a precise definition of the level of analysis: individual, group, basic organizational structure, or environment. Failure to define clearly the level of analysis and match the strategy to the unit results in either little change or unanticipated change that may be dysfunctional to the organization (24). For example, the application of techniques appropriate to modifying individual or group-level activities will have little effect on basic structure.

The application of techniques within a particular level of analysis must also be in accordance with a designated set of variables. In essence, a contingency approach focuses change in accordance with specific types and sources of change and specific variables involved in that process (23, 25, 26). Later in the chapter specific strategies are presented relevant to the rational, resource dependency, and ecological models of change and innovation.

DISTINCTIVE CHARACTERISTICS OF HEALTH CARE THAT AFFECT ORGANIZATIONAL CHANGE AND INNOVATION

While organizational change is pervasive, health care has a number of distinctive characteristics that affect the process and the efficacy of various change strategies. These characteristics present a special challenge to health care managers attempting to understand the change process (27) and to apply various management strategies to facilitate the process (28–30).

NATURE OF THE TASK

The provision of health care is characterized by considerable uncertainty, vagueness, and ambiguity, making it difficult to set meaningful and measurable goals. Moreover, the technology is labor intensive and centers on high-status individuals within the organizations. These characteristics are confounded by the fact that health care organizations often deal with human beings who are struggling with problems of life and death.

These characteristics have significant implications for the various types of change. First, many structural changes are perceived as directly affecting high-status individuals providing professional services. These alterations, which affect the way individuals function in the delivery of services, are likely to encounter considerable resistance. Second, despite the recognition of uncertainty of technology, considerable emphasis within health care is given to the efficacy of any proposed change. Unfortunately, many structural and programmatic changes have no precedent and lack clinical or empirical evidence to support their efficacy.

INTERNAL RESOURCES

Critical factors affecting change are the personnel within the organization and their orientation to change. These personnel and their orientation are influenced by what is termed the "medical model," characterized by (1) the general edict that one should do no harm and (2) the authoritative role of the provider in the classic doctor–patient relationship. Unfortunately, many change strategies seriously challenge both of these assumptions. Change, by definition, implies risk taking, and many transitions and transformations are unproven. Changes viewed as taking on unnecessary risks meet considerable resistance.

Second, many change strategies are based on a model contrary to the classic doctor–patient relationship—demanding fairly active intervention on the part of the physician to diagnose and resolve a problem presented by the patient. In contrast, most change strategies operate from a different perspective. They attempt to work out problems in full consultation with the major actors within the organization. Thus the prevailing organizational change strategies tend not to meet the expectations of the medical model, and conflict with the values and expectations held by many health professionals within the organization, thereby undermining their credibility and generating resistance.

ORGANIZATIONAL STRUCTURE

The distribution of power within health care organizations makes it difficult to manage critical influence points. Many important actors are not even part of the formal organization. Moreover, even professionals who are part of the structure have little experience with collaborative problem solving and joint decision making. The dominant actors are trained to make decisions in an authoritative manner and are constantly confronted with situations that require authoritarian responses, making it difficult for them to adapt to more consultative approaches characterizing planned change efforts (29).

The interface of management and provider structures is critically important to understanding the change process and the application of change strategies in health care organizations. In many health care settings management structures may be embryonic and inadequate for overseeing provider service activities. Even when fully developed, management may have only tangential relationships with service provider activities, thereby limiting the manager's overall impact (26, 30).

VALUE ORIENTATION AND EXPECTATIONS

Health care organizations are imbued with the ideology of providing care to suffering individuals. Moreover, in many medically desperate situations, the prevailing norm is to act without regard to financial cost or liability. This orientation results in the adoption of many poorly understood, extremely costly technological innovations (31).

The ideology of providing care to suffering individuals has slowly transformed itself into a set of rules and expectations that cause hospitals and other health care organizations to be held to an ever-higher standard of performance. To meet this rising standard, health care organizations are becoming increasingly dependent upon the implementation of various technological innovations. Although many technologies are of questionable quality and reliability, they provide the basis for protecting the organization against liability. In fact, a hospital may buy complex equipment not to prevent specific injuries or damages, but to enable the hospital to cite the purchase of the equipment as exculpating the institution from any blame in a malpractice suit (32).

MODELS OF ORGANIZATIONAL CHANGE

Three models of organizational change have been suggested: rational, resource dependency, and organizational ecology. The major difference among the models centers on the organizational—environmental interface, highlighting different types of change and levels of analysis. The rational model, for example, dealing with all three types of changes, tends to focus on the internal characteristics of the organization. Moreover, when the environment is considered, the relationship is presented in a rather deterministic form. The resource dependency model emphasizes the interdependence between environment and the organization; moreover, the interrelationship, presented in a far less deterministic manner, emphasizes the manipulation of the environment to enhance organizational operations. Finally, the organizational ecology model focuses primarily on transitions and transformations, viewing organizations as the repository of environmental influences over which the organization and management have relatively little control.

A detailed presentation of each model is given below, including its major features, its approach to organizational change and innovation, and a presentation of strategies appropriate to each. While each is presented as a distinct model, they are not mutually exclusive. Taken together they present a comprehensive and interdependent view of organizational change and innovation.

RATIONAL MODEL

The rational model views organizational change and innovation as affected by various aspects of organization design that can be manipulated to enhance performance (see Chapters 10–12). This model primarily concerns the internal functioning of organizations and has a number of distinctive features.

Whether technical, transitional, or transformational, change is viewed as a process involving a number of stages. Several models are available (33–35); however, all models tend to emphasize four basic stages in the change process. The first stage is *recognition*, or diagnosis of a problem by organizational participants who perceive a gap between what the organization is currently doing and what it should or could be doing. The second phase occurs when decision makers *identify* a possible course of action to narrow the gap between action and desired performance. The third stages involves the actual *implementation* of this action within an organization. The final stage, *institutionalization*, is the acceptance of implemented change by relevant actors within the organization.

Two things are important to note. First, more problems are recognized than solutions are identified, and more solutions are identified than are finally implemented and institutionalized. Second, the process is not sequential. That is, identification may occur without recognition; in fact, implementation may occur without recognition or identification.

The source of change (i.e., origination, adaptation, or borrowing) has a great effect on the various stages of the change process (15). For example, when change is based on origination or adaptation, the identification stage is of primary importance. At this stage, considerable time and resources are expended as the organization attempts to generate a solution to a diagnosed problem or attempts to make appropriate modifications in a change that was developed as a prototype in some other organization. This process contrasts with change that is based on borrowing, in which the organization identifies the change as a solution to a diagnosed problem and moves directly to implementation.

The particular type of change has a set of attributes or characteristics that influences the various stages of the change process. Although understanding of specific attributes is in its early stages, these attributes include such things as technology complexity, compatibility with existing activities, cost, and overall effectiveness of what is proposed. Several major distinctions are important. First, it is important to distinguish between what Downs and Mohr (36) term the primary and secondary attributes of the proposed change. *Primary attributes* are those characteristics of the proposed change that exist without reference to the specific adopting organization. For example, a financially well-endowed hospital and an organization with no endowment might describe a particular type of change in the same way. *Secondary attributes*, on the other hand, are those characteristics of the change that are closely related to particular characteristics of the implementing organization. Thus the financially well-endowed hospital might classify a particular type of change as relatively inexpensive, whereas the organization with no endowment might classify the same change as prohibitively expensive.

Second, and particularly relevant to technological change (i.e., the change in organizational process but not ends), is the extent to which a change depends on a single configuration of physical elements ("hardware" versus "software"). As described by Pelz and Munson (15):

> MBO is an extremely soft innovation, having no machine boundedness; computer-aided medication scheduling system is significantly harder, and a word processor is an extremely hard innovation.

These distinctions affect the change process. For example, a programmatic innovation, such as *management by objective* (MBO), is more likely to experience continual revisions through the various stages of the change process than a hard technological change involving a lithotripter. The hardware–software distinction is also likely to affect appropriate change strategies. For example, where the change involves a soft technology, the possibility of revisions and modifications at various stages of the change process would benefit from a participatory change strategy. Through their involvement, individuals have an opportunity to make modifications, achieve a sense of ownership, and facilitate institutionalization. Conversely, hard technological innovations offer fewer opportunities for revisions and modifications throughout the various stages of the change process. Thus a more authoritarian or power-type strategy is appropriate during the implementation process.

Implementation of the innovation or change is not the same as institutionalization. In health care organizations many changes involve autonomous actors who have a secondary choice in whether the new program or technology is used after implementation by the organization (37). For example, the institutionalization of a hospice program requires both implementation (making the service available within or to the organization), and patient referrals to the program by physicians once the program is available. Many programs are implemented but later terminated because of a lack of patient referrals by physicians.

The change process and implementation of the various types of programs and activities are not totally random. There appears to be a predictable order that managers should follow as they attempt to implement programs (38). For example, certain innovations may be linked in such a way that implementation of one tends to facilitate implementation of another. For example, the implementation of insurance coverage of a treatment program for alcoholism facilitates the implementation of the treatment program itself (39). Similarly, implementation of a computerized medical record system is a prerequisite to the successful implementation of a quality assurance program (13). Armed with this information, managers might consider the overall sequence of implementation rather than simply implementing programs without providing the appropriate groundwork for subsequent implementation. In many cases the manager might first think about organizational redesign to provide the proper milieu for the implementation of various programmatic innovations that will significantly affect both the means and the goals of the organization.

The rational model of organizational change consists of three distinct perspectives, emphasizing particular determinates in the change process: behavioral factors, structural factors, and contingencies.

Behavioral Perspective

Using a behavioral perspective, managers seek to influence interpersonal relationships based upon a normative definition of the social psychological conditions required to facilitate change or innovation. These conditions include the nature of the culture, climate, and values within the organization, types of behaviors, quality of group interaction, and methods used for conflict resolution. For example, where culture, climate, and values are supportive, open, friendly, and responsive to organizational members, they provide an atmosphere conducive to increased productivity, risk-taking, and change. New technologies, activities, and programs within the organization can be nurtured under various cultural conditions (40). Similarly, managerial functions are critical to the performance of the organization. When managers and other key decision makers are knowledgeable about the operations of their organization with respect to other organizations in the community, they are capable of initiating appropriate action.

A number of studies have examined these issues and have identified specific behavioral factors associated with change and innovation including *(1)* the values of elites within the organization (41), *(2)* a positive attitude toward change by individuals directly involved in the change process (42), and *(3)* a knowledge among key decision makers about the operations of their organization vis-a-vis other organizations in the community (43, 44), as well as various sociodemographic characteristics of individuals involved in the change such as their local cosmopolitan orientation (45–47).

Interventions. Numerous interventions have been developed to affect basic organizational processes that facilitate change and innovation. Process interventions are designed to change managerial style, increase interpersonal sensitivity, and develop skills in communication and problem solving. An extensive review of 574 organizational development applications to public-sector organizations revealed that more than 80% were successful in improving the organizational processes that are the target of the intervention (48).

Survey feedback provides a mechanism for systematically gathering data on the ongoing social psychological conditions of the organization and confronting work groups with the findings. Data usually deal with intergroup relations, communication, supervision, employee satisfaction, employee attitudes (49, 50), and, with more recent efforts, organizational culture (51, 52). This information is usually gathered using questionnaire surveys of employees, but interview data also can be used. Results are fed back to individual work groups, starting at the top and moving down through the organization. Each group discusses survey results by analyzing potential problems, identifying possible causes, and agreeing upon solutions.

For effective results, three conditions must be met (53). First, discussion of findings must occur in a factual, task-oriented atmosphere. Second, each group must have the freedom to consider implications of findings at its own level. Upper-level management should handle general problems while problems affecting the work group should be handled at the source of the problem. Finally, reports of outcomes must be sent up the organizational hierarchy.

The assumption underlying these conditions is that management cannot directly influence the processes that exist within the organization (54). Individuals and groups must be given the opportunity to see how their units compare with other units of the organization or how their current operations compare with desired expectations, thus understanding their own problems and initiating corrective action themselves.

Because health care requires coordination of many disciplines and complex tasks, conflict can arise within groups delivering or managing delivery of services. *Team development* strategies attempt to remove barriers to group effectiveness, develop self-sufficiency in managing group process, and facilitate the change process. These interventions differ from survey feedback techniques in that team development places greater emphasis upon the changing and refreezing stages of the change process and the importance of external consultation (55).

External consultants are usually involved in all stages of this intervention strategy. Interventions begin with data gathering on leadership behavior, interpersonal processes, roles, trust, communication, decision making, task problems, and barriers to effective group functioning. After data are gathered, meetings are held during which problems are categorized and prioritized, selected problem areas are discussed, and action plans for change are developed.

The assumption underlying team development is that groups can solve their own problems if a catalyst is available to facilitate the process. Development activities require group participation, self-examination, problem confrontation, and goal setting.

A management tool receiving increased attention in health services is *quality circles*. Quality circles are small groups of employees from the same area who work on a range of problems to increase their productivity and quality. The first-line supervisor, who is usually the team leader, receives special training in group dynamics and problem solving. Management supports quality circles by allowing team meetings on company time, training leaders, and responding to team proposals.

The technique relies upon a number of processes, such as the nominal group technique, multicriteria decision making, and critical incident technique, to identify and solve problems. Work groups also receive information on outcomes, such as productivity data and quality control information. Results of meetings are recorded and reports are sent up the organizational hierarchy.

The use of quality circles is based on the assumption that those closest to problems should be responsible for the identification of issues and solutions. The approach also assumes that the use of group problem-solving techniques, combined with data and reporting responsibilities, will lead to changes that result in increased internal operating efficiencies. The circles have generally received favorable review from implementing health service organizations and have helped solve such problems as excessive overtime among operating room personnel and excessive nursing turnover. While an AHA survey estimates that about 200 member hospitals are experimenting with such programs, there are as yet almost no hard empirical data on their effectiveness (56).

The health services industry is experiencing rapid technological change in the provision of care. Changes require that personnel involved in service delivery stay abreast of innovations so that their organization can offer up-to-date services. It is assumed that participation in *continuing education* programs will provide health service personnel with the knowledge required to keep themselves and their organizations aware of new technology and service delivery programs. Change is assumed to be caused by the increased knowledge, awareness, and subsequent perception of a performance gap that results from continuing education activities.

However, continuing education programs for physicians have demonstrated no consistent association with quality of performance (57), unless the program directly involves clinical leaders and face-to-face contact on data feedback based on individual physician performance (58). A lack of association between continuing education programs and performance may occur for several reasons. First, participation in continuing education is mandatory in many states for most licensed health professionals. Professionals may attend continuing education programs without expecting substantive new knowledge to be gained from participation. Second, information acquired through these programs may not pertain to what the individual or organization is doing. Therefore, a stimulus for problem identification and corrective action does not exist.

If an organization faces an immediate threat or a need for rapid action, a *confrontation meeting* can provide direction in a much shorter time period than survey feedback. This technique brings together a large segment of the organization for problem identification and action planning (59). Up to 60 people may be involved. They are divided into small groups, each of which includes individuals from different organizational units. Supervisors are not placed in the same group with their own subordinates.

Each group lists organizational problems that require attention. These problem lists are reported to the larger group of participants, which combines the problems into categories with help from an external consultant. Next, new groups are formed along expert and functional lines in accordance with problem categories. The new groups select items to discuss and identify action steps to be initiated. Results are reported to the larger group.

Confrontation meetings provide rapid diagnosis, increase influence and commitment of lower-level personnel in problem identification and problem solving, reduce bureaucratic barriers in decision making, and improve decisions by having those with information solve problems. These meetings require a climate of openness for problems to be confronted by the organization.

Sensitivity training is designed to provide individuals with new experiences and data that disconfirm their perceptions of themselves and their environment. This training occurs in small unstructured groups that facilitate learning by nonevaluative feedback received by each individual from other group members. Feedback creates anxiety and tension, which causes the individual to unfreeze and eventually adopt alternative values, attitudes, and behaviors. These activities occur in the presence of a trainer who functions as a resource person and facilitator rather than as a formal leader.

This technique is intended to increase sensitivity, facilitate open communications, and encourage flexible role behaviors by individual organizational members. Sensitivity training conducted in groups that value personal risk taking and collaborative discussions is assumed to reduce defensiveness and resistance to self- and group examination. This examination leads to consideration of new attitudes and behaviors that may eventually be adopted.

Change and innovation also occurs through a better understanding of the personal, interpersonal, and group processes within the organization. *Process consultation* (60) involves an outside consultant helping a client to perceive, understand, and act upon process events that are occurring. Solutions can be developed to enhance the performance of the organization and can facilitate the overall change process. This technique focuses upon communications, role and function of group members, group problem solving and decision making, group norms, and the use of leadership and authority. The strategy, however, has limited effectiveness where individuals and/or groups are involved with high levels of conflict involving disputes over major unresolved issues (61).

Structural Perspective

The structural perspective views the structure of organizations as the primary factor involved in organizational innovation and change. Using this perspective managers seek to arrange or design (see Chapter 9) the basic activities, roles, and positions of the organization or groups within the organization to facilitate innovation and change. Here attention is given to the basic characteristics of these components and their relationships in terms of power, influence, and control. Structure vis-a-vis innovation and change is usually characterized in terms of such variables as complexity, centralization, stratification, and formalization.

Existing studies and reviews suggest specific relationships between various structural characteristics and change and innovation including *(1)* decentralized decision making (43, 58, 62), *(2)* organizational complexity (63, 64), *(3)* rules compatible with characteristics of the innovation (18), and *(4)* multiple decision systems and coalitions of hospital-based physicians, trustees, and administrators (65–67).

Interventions. Structural interventions assume that many of the behavioral process problems identified by the organization are symptoms of underlying structural issues.

Based on this assumption, strategies are focused on modifying existing structures or on creating new structures to facilitate the change process. As described by Plovnick (68):

> Structural interventional strategies do not differ from procedural interventional strategies in their basic principles or values as much as in their diagnostic focus. . . . The differences between structural and process approaches begin in the issues identified as underlying organizational problems and become manifest in the kinds of action plans that evolve to address these issues.

Successful change and innovation within an organization require that *specific roles* be designated to facilitate the change process. Organizations require the designation of an idea generator, a sponsor, and an orchestrator (69). The idea generator recognizes a problem and develops a response to solve it. This individual may come from any level in the organization, but acting as an individual, he or she lacks the resources or authority to develop and implement the changes. This situation creates the need for a sponsor to carry the idea through to implementation. Sponsors are usually middle managers who can take the idea and fund the increasingly disruptive and expensive development and testing efforts that it requires. Yet a third role is required to manage the political struggle that occurs with the organization against those that have authority and control of resources. The orchestrator, usually the CEO, must protect idea people and provide the opportunity for change. This role is critical because new ideas often conflict with established programs within the organization. Health care organizations must recognize the various roles required for change. Ideas that arise within the organization must receive support from the management structure for implementation to occur.

Task analysis focuses on the redesign of tasks within the organization to facilitate change and improve performance. Division of work into simple, specialized jobs was first suggested by the scientific management school to increase internal efficiency. This specialization allowed tasks to be differentiated, resulting in greater organizational control over individual behavior, selection of less skilled workers, and routinization of work flow to improve coordination.

However, routine jobs that require few skills and provide no challenge because of extreme specialization can lead to dissatisfaction, turnover and absenteeism, reduced motivation, and low-quality performance. Jobs may be redesigned by job enlargement (adding more activities) or job enrichment (adding more responsibility to the job) (70). The effect of job redesign to facilitate change has had mixed results; in some settings having a positive relationship to change and in other settings having little or no effect (71). These and related issues of work design are discussed in Chapter 6.

Information systems that provide data on performance within a system can serve two purposes: to measure and to motivate (70, 72). Both purposes can result in change, but through different methods. Information systems can be used to measure the performance within a unit and to signal when predetermined standards are not obtained. If management has formal authority over the unit, corrective action can be initiated. In health care settings actions may include temporarily closing selected hospital beds when occupancy rates fall below a desired level. This approach is most frequently seen in large hospital systems or governmental health service organizations that use management by objectives (MBO) to identify outcomes desired by those in charge of the organization.

However, managers of health care organizations frequently do not have formal control over health professionals who practice within the institution. In such cases, performance data can facilitate the change process by motivating individuals to initiate corrective action and by directing them toward changes that should be initiated (72). Use of information systems appears to be most successful in instituting change when data are presented face-to-face by a respected member of the professional community, when it is individualized for the physician, and when it represents current activity (58).

Integrative mechanisms are special liaison contacts between individuals and units within health care organizations that can be incorporated into the formal structure of the organization. These mechanisms can improve the flow of internal information, identify operational problems, aid in selection of solutions to problems, and facilitate changes. Available mechanisms include liaison positions, task forces and standing committees, integrating managers, and matrix structures (70). These and related mechanisms are discussed in Chapters 7 and 9.

Sociometric networks focus on the location of individuals in the social network and selecting individuals (i.e., those that influence others in the network) for specific training in a particular innovation. The approach builds on the growing evidence that individuals— particularly professionals—rely heavily on the experience and opinion of other professionals (8) and the recognition that leaders within the network are apt to be earlier adopters of the innovation. The approach has been successfully used in attempting to change the utilization of diagnostic procedures and patient care in three community hospitals (73). Currently it is being evaluated in an attempt to increase physician utilization of hospital information systems (74).

Responsibility charting is a technique that identifies decision making patterns among a set of actors—individuals, units, departments, or divisions within the organization (75). Attention is given to identifying decision areas, actors, and the type of participation in the decision area. The approach provides an opportunity to compare responses of a specific participant about that person's own role in a decision with the response of one or more participants about the same participant role, compare responses across all actors on a specific decision, examine responses of each actor across a set of decisions and compare actual decision patterns with desired activity. The technique is best used in combination with process type change strategies.

Contingency Perspective

Managing change and innovation within a rational model requires that managers account for the context affecting both structural and process factors. Which set of factors and their particular relationship to innovation and change will vary, depending upon the nature of the tasks being performed (76), the type of change or innovation being considered and its attributes (11, 45, 67, 77–79), the type of organization initiating change (46), and/or the stage of the change or innovation process (26, 80–84).

A number of contingency frameworks attempt to integrate the behavioral and/or structural factors that can be applied to different types of organizational change and innovation.

Contingency Models Applied to Technical and Transition Change. Scheirer (84) presents a model of program implementation as one phase in the overall innovation process and the effects of various levels of the organization on that process. As diagrammed in Figure 11.1, implementation is conceptualized itself as a five-stage process, although the stages may overlap in time and each stage is affected by macro level, intermediate level, or individual factors. The initial stage, the decision to adopt some innovative program, is affected primarily by *macro level* factors such as environmental pressures, interest of organizational participants, and the normal organizational control processes.

Once a decision has been made, three overlapping stages follow: assembling resources,

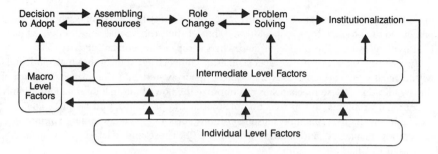

Figure 11.1 Stages of program implementation and level of analysis (schematic). (From Scheirer, M.A. *Program implementation: The organizational context.* Copyright © 1981 by Sage Publications, Inc. Reprinted by permission by Sage Publications, Inc.)

role change, and problem solving. Assembling resources includes securing funds and physical facilities for the new program, hiring new personnel, and reassigning existing personnel. Role change focuses on the actual behavior of the implementing staff members and the fit between new behavior and the expectations of existing personnel as well as ongoing work routines. Problem solving is the further modification of resources and roles required before final institutionalization of the change. Intermediate level factors such as supervisory expectations, information channels, work group norms, and standard operating procedures are likely to influence this stage of the process. Moreover, individual level factors such as behavioral skills, incentives, beliefs, and attitudes are presented as background variables affecting macro and intermediate level factors.

The final stage of this integrative model is institutionalization—or the acceptance of the innovation into the ongoing operations of the organization. Institutionalization is contingent on the successful completion of the prior stages. Where institutionalization completes the change process, the organization is able to return to an equilibrium point.

Duncan (85) presents a model in which innovation has two primary stages: initiation and implementation. The value of structural factors depends on the particular stage of the innovation process. The initiation stage is facilitated by structural characteristics such as high complexity, low formalization, and low centralization. The implementation stage is facilitated by lower complexity, higher formalization, and higher centralization. Process variables (such as effective interpersonal relationships and conflict resolution capabilities) are viewed as key factors in the organization's ability to differentiate its degree of complexity, formalization, and centralization in the initiation and implementation stages of innovation.

Kaluzny et al. (26) present a contingent relationship between the stages of the innovation process and the characteristics of the organization and attributes of the innovation (Fig. 11.2). Unlike the model of Duncan (85), however, characteristics of organizational personnel are included as primary predictors during the early and late stages of organizational innovation. Structure and process characteristics are important primarily during the implementation stage since the organization itself is the implementing unit. However, problem recognition, identification, and institutionalization of an innovation are actions involving individuals and thus are a primary function of the characteristics of personnel, not of the structure-process of the organization.

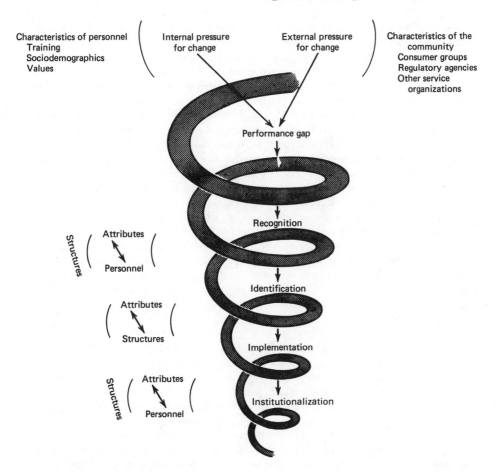

Characteristics of personnel
Training
Sociodemographics
Values

Internal pressure
for change

External pressure
for change

Characteristics of the
community
Consumer groups
Regulatory agencies
Other service
organizations

Performance gap

Recognition

Identification

Implementation

Institutionalization

Structures (Attributes ↔ Personnel (

(Attributes ↔ Structures (

Structures (Attributes ↔ Personnel (

Figure 11.2 Factors influencing the change process. (Reprinted with permission from Arnold D. Kaluzny: Change in health care settings. In P. Trohanis (Ed.), *Ideas in change*. Technical Assistance Development System, Frank Porter Graham Child Development Center, University of North Carolina at Chapel Hill, Chapel Hill, N.C., 1981.)

Second, the attributes of the innovation itself have significance at various stages of the innovation process. Attributes such as cost, risk, uncertainty, and communicability can be classified according to the particular stage at which their influence is most likely to be felt. For example, attributes such as communicability are likely to be most important at the initiation stage of the process. At the implementation stage such attributes as the perceived impact of innovation on interpersonal relationships within the organization become critical.

Third, the type of organizational characteristics that are important is contingent on the attributes of the innovation. Innovations that are easily congruent with the ongoing activities of the organization or compatible with the characteristics of organizational personnel will be implemented independent of particular structure and process characteristics. But innovations that are high in cost and have pervasive consequences throughout the organization require structural and process characteristics to accommodate and facilitate them. Where such structures and processes exist, the innovation can be more easily implemented. Implementation, however, does not mean adoption in the organization. There are many instances in which technology or programs are implemented but never institutionalized or used. Within the contingency model the degree of institutionalization is dependent on the characteristics of the innovation. When the innovation involves risk and disruption to ongoing tasks, the model suggests that acceptance is more likely to occur where individuals are involved in the decision to implement. Low-risk nondisruptive innovations do not require such high individual participation.

Daft (86, 87) presents another contingency type model which emphasizes the type of innovation—technical vs. administrative—and the structural characteristics required to implement each type of innovation. According to this model (78, 87), technical type innovations, such as those concerned with the production of services, will be facilitated by high levels of employee professionalism, decentralization of decision making, and low formalization of rules and regulations. Administrative innovations—those that concern the process of work within the organization—are facilitated by lower levels of employee professionalism, high levels of centralized decision making, and formalized rules and regulations. Which structure dominates depends upon the goals and environmental issues confronting the organization.

Contingency Models Applied to Transformations. A contingency model is equally applicable to the analysis of transformations. From this perspective, the organization is viewed as a complex set of interacting components which must be considered in some sequence in order to successfully affect change.

Kilmann (88) presents a holographic view of the organization with all its complexity. The organization is defined as an open system, composed of the environment, the organization itself, the manager, the work group, and a set of underlying cultural assumptions. For change to occur, it is necessary to address all the components in a sequential-integrated program of planned change-termed tracks. Five tracks are presented: cultural, management, team-building, strategic-structure, and reward system. The change program begins with the cultural track in order to enhance trust and openness to adaptation of innovation. The cultural track attempts to provide the necessary conditions to assure the success of subsequent interventions. The cultural track is followed by the managerial track. Here the focus is on augmenting ways of coping with complex problems and hidden assumptions. This stage is followed by team-building activities which help members identify and solve their most complex problems. The team-building track is followed by the strategy-structure track, which aligns all the organizational structures and resources with strategic directions of the organization. The final track involves rewards, setting up a system to measure performance objectively and link rewards to such performance.

The guiding principle of this view of innovation and change is the integration and sequencing of the tracks. The approach provides an opportunity to change what is the easiest and best to accomplish early and thus set the conditions for change efforts later in the process. The implementation of the tracks is presented in several stages including: *(1)* initiating the programs, *(2)* diagnosing the problem, *(3)* scheduling the tracks, *(4)* implementation, and *(5)* evaluation. Attention is given to the sequence of stages and the fact that sufficient time must be devoted to each stage to complete its activities before proceeding to the next stage.

Tichy (89) views organizational phases or cycles not as a logical predicted sequence based on some underlying maturational process but rather as three interrelated cycles that require the organization to make changes over time. Changes are made to deal with political, technological, and cultural uncertainty. *Political uncertainty* refers to the power to allocate rewards and decide on the goals of the organization. *Technical uncertainty* refers to uncertainty over production issues. Finally, *cultural uncertainty* refers to differences among organizational members with regard to values and ideologies.

Different issues dominate at different times, and because of the interrelated nature of the cycles, change in one cycle may affect or require changes in one or more of the other cycles. For example, a major technological adjustment often triggers political realignment within the organization, which in turn alters basic values and norms to fit the changed technology and political operations.

The concept of interrelated cycles in the change process has important implications for the use of change strategies. First, strategies must be appropriate to the particular cycle one is trying to affect. As described by Tichy (89):

> Successful managers of change will at times be political builders of coalitions, power brokers, and influence manipulators coping with the political cycle. At other times they will be solving problems rationally or relying on scientific data and principles to cope with the technical style. Or they may be active as molders of values and ideals.

Secondly, the application of strategies must be particularly sensitive to the particular time phase of the cycle. While they are obviously interrelated, each cycle might be tracked at a different speed, thereby focusing attention on that one cycle which requires specific intervention.

Interventions. The application of change strategies will vary as a function of the task being performed, the types of innovations being considered, and the stage of the innovation process. For example, organizational change strategies associated with improved efficiency in delivery of health services in a group of hospitals vary between medical and surgical units (76). Action systems changes that emphasize management control systems and that focus upon formal organizational structures and hierarchical controls are appropriate when simple tasks requiring relatively little information processing among health professionals are performed (such as surgery). Conversely, understanding system changes that emphasize informal relations and interpersonal psychological characteristics are appropriate when complex tasks are being performed and internal controls are possessed by health professionals (such as medicine).

Similarly, technical innovations within the operating core of health service organizations are encouraged by low formalization, decentralization, and high complexity (78). Managers who desire these types of innovations should use behavioral strategies such as quality circles or survey feedback to assist health professionals in problem identification and solution generation. The readiness for change could be facilitated by other interventions, such as team development or process consultation.

Administrative innovations are initiated under conditions of high formalization, centralization, and low complexity. If the organization desires these types of innovations, structural strategies should be used. For example, since administrative changes require specific roles, mechanisms must be established to facilitate the innovation process. Support staff, such as strategic planners, operations researchers, and marketers should be used to develop detailed plans. Top management also must be responsible for sponsoring and pushing administrative innovations.

Change strategies appropriate to transformations are similar to those applied to technical and transition types of change. However, their application varies depending upon the stage or cycle in which the organization is operating. For example, behavioral changes such as confrontation meetings would be beneficial for organizational change and development as the organization enters a crisis stage. This strategy would facilitate the solution of problems and allow development to the next stage of evolutionary growth. The succeeding period of tranquil growth still would require adaptive behaviors. Subsequent stages would benefit from structural design, strategies such as integrative mechanisms, or management information systems for problem identification and solution.

The following mini-case underscores both the importance and the complexity of initiating change within organizations using the contingency approach. Issues concerning the type of deliberation that should precede major organizational change are contained within the description that follows.

MINI-CASE

Memorial Hospital was established in 1953 as a nonprofit, acute-care community hospital. Licensed for 700 beds but currently operating only 550 beds because of decrease in demand for services, the hospital has a primary service area in the high-income suburbs of a large city. Memorial faces intense competition for market share from a recently constructed investor-owned hospital. This new facility has aggressively pursued a strategy of identifying market segments within the suburban communities and then packaging services to meet demands from these markets. In several instances, this approach has allowed the investor-owned hospital to develop unique products for a ready market.

In response to competitive pressures Memorial has considered initiation of product line management within the hospital. Management believes that this approach will allow the organization to respond more rapidly to new ventures developed by the investor-owned hospital. In their view, the product or "service" manager will be given specific responsibilities for a related group of services provided by the hospital. The managers will establish objectives for the services, develop marketing plans, determine financial needs for the services, establish quality care and review standards, and monitor day-to-day operations of service delivery.

The structure required for the product line approach is in sharp contrast to the current functional design of the organization. The new structure will group services provided by the institution into major diagnostic categories comparable to those used by the Medicare prospective system. A product manager will be identified for each of the 15–20 groupings used by the hospital. The manager will not be given direct control over all the individuals involved in delivery of services for the grouping. Rather, the hospital will build a matrix structure with product managers to establish objectives and plans for their services and then negotiate with other internal units for necessary supplies, manpower, and other essentials.

To assure the successful implementation of the product manager plan and the overall matrix structure, the executive vice president in charge of operations has taken a number of steps. First, the product manager is identified for the service units that have the most visible performance gap. Second, within these units special efforts are made to provide process consultation to facilitate the group problem-solving capacity. Finally, efforts are being made to monitor overall performance of the units and to chart patterns of decision making within these units.

RESOURCE DEPENDENCY

The resource dependency model views organizations as embedded in a larger social system that supplies needed resources. To acquire these resources the organization must enter into transactions with its environment, creating interdependency. From this perspective the critical issue is not the utilization of resources within the organization per se but the problems of acquiring these resources from the environment (90). Thus the nature of the organization's environment is closely linked to the basic operations and structure of the organization and the type of change involved.

As with the rational perspective the emphasis is given to a series of stages—but greater stress is given to the political/power process ongoing within the organization and the ability of the organization to influence its environment. Attention is given to the organization's "stakeholders," that is, individual actors, parties, and/or organizational groups and institutions that have bearing on the policy and actions of the organization and their perceptions of the urgency and feasibility of taking action (91).

One of the unique contributions of this perspective to understanding organizational change and innovation is its view of managerial succession—the removal and selection of managers as a result of the nature and context of the organization's environment. From this perspective managers are unable to unilaterally design organizational structure and process; rather, their very existence is seen to be affected by the uncertainty, contingencies, and interdependencies of the environment. Specifically, the nature of the organization's environment affects the distribution of power and control within the organization. The distribution of power and control in turn affects the tenure and selection of organizational managers and the resultant policies and structures of the organization. Managers, as they direct organizational activities, affect policies and structure. As these activities meet the critical contingencies of the environment, managerial selection and retention by the organization is determined (92).

The relationship of the manager to the environment is further affected by the symbolic nature of the managerial role (93). This role is particularly critical when it is necessary for the organization to change in order to meet changes in environmental demands. As described by Pfeffer and Salancik (90):

> In creating the symbolic role of the manager, the organization also creates a mechanism for dealing with external demands. When external demands cannot be met because of constraints on the organization, the administrator can be removed. Replacing the leader, who has come to symbolize the organization to the various interest groups, may be sufficient to relieve pressures on the organization. As long as all believe that the administrator actually affects the organization, then replacement signals a change taken in response to external demands. The change communicates an intent to comply, and this intent may be as useful as actual compliance for satisfying external organizations.
>
> Changing administrators offers a way of altering appearances, thereby removing external pressure, without losing much discretion. If the manager has little effect on organizational outcomes, his or her replacement will not change much, particularly if a person with similar views is chosen as the replacement. The manager is, therefore a convenient target for external influences, and provides the organization with a relatively simple way of responding to external demands.
>
> (SOURCE: *The External Control of Organizations*, Pfeffer, J., and Salancik, G. R., © 1978, p. 264. Harper & Row, Publishers, Inc.)

Interventions. The resource dependency perspective outlines two specific types of responses to the environment. The first presents the organization simply responding to changes to fit environmental requirements. This process involves technical, transition, and transformation changes. The mechanisms and strategies for dealing with these types of responses were discussed in the section on the rational perspective toward organizational change.

A second type of change response, unique to this perspective, is the organization's attempt to alter the environment or to enact an environment that fits existing organizational capabilities. A number of strategies are available.

Buffering refers to the ability of the organization to develop sufficient inventories of required resources to permit it to operate when supplies are scarce. This may occur in several ways and involve various resources required by the organization. For example, the development of hospital-sponsored primary-care group practice while improving access of care within the community also increases the hospital's market share of inpatient admissions, increases revenue for laboratory and radiology services, and facilitates physician recruitment and retention (94).

Market differentiation refers to the ability of the organization to segment the potential market into homogeneous subunits. The extent that these subunits are recognized by other organizations within the environment results in domain consensus (95). Such recognition by other organizations in the environment limits competition.

One of the immediate effects of segmentation is that it limits the extent to which organizations are able to provide a full array of comprehensive, continuous health services. Thus, although the approach may ensure a stable environment and thereby minimize the need for change within the focal organization as the environment changes, the success of organizations in differentiating markets creates the chronic problem of coordinating services provided by various organizations within the health service system.

Diversification concerns development of new products or markets that reduce an organization's dependence upon one element of its environment. A medical group that receives its patients almost exclusively from one major employer or industry will experience severe problems if that purchaser reduces expenditures for medical services. Development of diverse markets for its services reduces the trauma the group experiences from major expenditure changes by the purchaser. Similarly, a multihospital system may diversify its investment portfolio by entering product lines not associated with health services delivery. Diversification facilitates the channeling of organizational resources into alternative investment opportunities, should major shifts occur in reimbursement for health services.

A danger arises from diversification when the new products or markets differ radically from those the organization has previously known. Management may be unable to function effectively if it employs technology and expertise that is not appropriate for the new endeavor.

Vertical integration describes the organization's acquisition of other organizations critical to its input–output exchange. Acquisition may focus on the control of funds, supplies, patients, or the distribution of products. In the case of health services, vertical integration is illustrated by hospitals acquiring health maintenance organizations to facilitate the flow of patients into hospitals or acquiring long-term care facilities or rehabilitation facilities to receive discharged patients.

This strategy may be classified as facilitative in that it makes the operation of the organization easier. When the organization dominates other organizations involved in the input–output exchange, the acquisition may involve sanctions and thus be considered to be coercive.

Horizontal integration is the combining of similar organizations into a larger organization unit. The strategy, which may be either facilitative or coercive in nature, has as its primary objective enhancement of the organization's role in affecting its environment: enhancing its market power. In health services the approach is best illustrated by the development of multi-institutional hospital systems. Chapter 10 discusses the determinants and effectiveness of this approach at the organizational and health system level.

Antitrust activity is the organization's initiation of legal action to affect the state of the environment that the organization feels is harmful to ongoing operations. To date, this option is rarely used within the health services areas; however, with the development of multihospital systems, the initiation of legal activities by single facilities against multi-institutional systems and among multi-institutional systems is likely to increase.

Cooptation involves the inclusion of critical and perhaps hostile actors from the environment into the activities of the focal organization. Outside individuals are appointed to governing or advisory boards on the assumption that participation by individuals in the activities of the focal organization improves the probability that participants will accept the position of the focal organization or at least facilitate the flow of resources to that organization. Analysis suggests that cooptation is an effective strategy (96).

Regulation is the development of rules and regulations that affect the existing operations of the organization. In health services individual organizations are usually members of the association that protects their interests. Paul Feldstein (97) has attempted to document the role of various types of health provider associations and their demand for health legislation favoring policies that *(1)* increase the demand for services of health professionals and organizations and reimbursement for the services as a price-discriminating monopolization (i.e., providers are able to charge different purchasers different prices for their services based on each purchaser's willingness and ability to pay); *(2)* lower the price of comparable provider inputs; and *(3)* increase the price of substitutes for their services and restrict additions to the supply of health professions and organizations represented by the professional association.

Coalitions and networks consist of two or more independent organizations that voluntarily choose to work together to achieve some stated objective. They provide a mechanism for affecting the environment—specifically to alter or lessen the dependence on other organizations—particularly if it supplies valued resources or makes unreasonable demands on the organization. This is highly facilitative strategy, and is less costly in terms of autonomy and organizational resources (98).

The following mini-case demonstrates the approach taken by a group of hospitals to develop a collaborative relationship for a specific activity, even when they compete in other arenas. It illustrates a response to a competitive advantage they perceived to exist for their organizations.

MINI-CASE

Memphis, Tennessee has become a major distribution center for the United States because of its central location and its abundance of water, rail, and highway arteries available for transportation of goods and produce. Air service for the city has expanded in recent years with a major airline using the city as a hub for services. The distribution center and headquarters for Federal Express overnight delivery services are in Memphis. All packages collected across the country are routed to Memphis. Sorting takes place in a major terminal adjacent to the airport and return delivery flights are scheduled to guarantee overnight delivery to major cities in the United States.

Recognizing the unique opportunity presented by their geographic location and the Federal Express delivery service, three Memphis hospitals began a joint venture to provide nationwide laboratory services. The three hospital systems—Baptist Memorial Hospital, Methodist Health Systems, and Le Bonheur Children's Medical Center—established Medical Express to provide testing services for hospitals in other communities. Specimens may leave a city such as Houston as late as 7 P.M., arrive at the Memphis laboratory by 2:30 A.M. the following day, and test results can be forwarded to Houston by noon to 1 P.M. Some tests, such as Anti-ENA, may require 3 days for results to be obtained from regional laboratories. Medical Express can provide results in 48 hours and reduce turnaround time by several days for many esoteric tests currently provided only by regional laboratories. The three hospital systems are currently considering developing a superlaboratory to compete on a regional basis for less esoteric services.

ORGANIZATIONAL ECOLOGY

The organizational ecology model views change from an evolutionary natural-selection perspective. Unlike previous models change does not necessarily imply movement toward a more effective or efficient organization, but simply change over time.

The ecology perspective distinguishes two basic levels of analysis: organizational and population (2). From the organizational level the focus is on the study of demographic events and probabilistic processes across individual organizations. Illustrations of various ecological approaches are presented below.

The *garbage can* (99) model emphasizes the uncertainty of change. Unlike the contingency or resource dependency models in which individuals/organizations have an ordered preference in which change and/or innovations are selected, in the garbage can model change is a function of an unending stream of problems and solutions, and the particular change and/or innovation which occurs does not follow any ordered sequence, but simply develops as an outcome of several independent streams of events. As described by March and Olsen (100), "the central idea of garbage can models is the substitution of a temporal order for a consequential order." This particular view has important implications for innovation within organizations.

> We can understand the frequency of innovation adoption by tracing the stream of problems, solutions, and decision expectations that flow into and through organizations. Thus an organizational environment or structure that generates a rapid flow of solutions and problems, and the presence of participants that connect solutions to problems and make innovation proposals will cause innovation adoption to be high (86).

The *life cycle* model represents a long-term time perspective focusing on creation, growth, and decline of an organization (101). Empirical studies of creation in health services include the development of sheltered workshops for handicapped (102) and the creation of a new medical school (103). Most of the studies examine the patterns over time and relate variation of patterns to characteristics of the environment, such as the availability of resources, political uncertainty, and organizational density (2).

The growth and decline phases of the cycle have been traditionally in the realm of organizational development and more recently in that of organizational strategy (see

Chapter 13). The emphasis is on analysis of idiosyncratic purposeful behavior on the part of incumbents within the organization. When growth and decline, however, are viewed from an organizational ecology perspective, emphasis is given to the significance of environmental forces as opposed to managerial action.

Organizational death and mortality have received increasing attention in health services (104). For example, early studies of medical groups indicate that 25% of medical groups operating in 1969 were disbanded by 1975 (105, 106). As with growth and decline the ecological perspective argues that failure is frequently due to causes external to the organization. As suggested by Carroll:

> From the policy perspective, this position is radical, if not blasphemous, for it implies that business failure (and by implication, success) often cannot be controlled by managerial initiative (2, p. 84).

From the population level, the perspective portrays organizations as shaped by a natural selection process. The process is a function of the nature and distribution of resources in the environment and results in a series of unfolding processes with environmental factors selecting those organizations or organizational characteristics that best fit the environment. As with the previous level, the model presents a perspective on organizational change that focuses on long-term transformations, but here attention is on a population of organizations rather than on the specific experience of a single organizational unit.

Changes in organizational form are perceived as not adaptive but rather "inertial," owing to internal and external structural processes and constraints. Consequently, structural inertia represents a kind of paradox, not only giving organizational forms stability, accountability, and reliability (107), but also inhibiting and limiting their ability to change as environmental demands intensify and the natural selection process ensues. The theory of natural selection rests on the assumption of a struggle for existence within and between organizational forms for finite resources in the environment. The theory involves three related processes: variation, selection, and retention.

Variation represents the emergence of diversity within or between competing organizational forms, a diversity that differentiates them and enables environmental forces to reward their differentiation. The model is indifferent to the source of variation (e.g., planned vs. unplanned), since variation is important only to the extent that it provides raw materials for the selection process. However, variation is usually viewed more as a consequence of change than of managerial purpose.

> While there are some occasions in which 'strategic choice' may be exercised, there are usually severe limits to decision makers' autonomy. Many opportunities are closed to organizations because of economic and legal barriers to their entry; most organizations are not powerful enough to influence their environment and perceptual distortions and allusions bias most decisions. Error, chance, luck and conflict are more likely sources of variation. . . . (108).

The introduction of variation enables the selection process to occur as the environment, employing implicit or explicit criteria, favors some variations over others or selectively eliminates some variations completely. The model suggests that as selection criteria become explicit in retrospective analyses, organizational forms that survive are the residue of prior selection processes. Fitness as evidenced by survival has been interpreted by some, in a behavioral sense, as variation which has found reinforcement somewhere in the environment, even without cognition (109). Thus how well organizations compete reflects their relative rather than absolute superiority in acquiring resources in the struggle for survival.

Retention is the final process of natural selection. For organizations that have found environmentally induced survival paths, preservation and reproducibility are key challenges. The process is analogous to the gene system in organic evolution, but is more practically perceived as a system in which organizations effectively continue to follow a course proven to assure a fit with their environment.

The emergence of multi-institutional systems as a new organizational form is an excellent example of an evolutionary change which population ecology attempts to explain as resulting from the natural selection processes. The change began as a variation in the traditional single-unit hospital organizational form; in some sense the trend toward combining units was externally induced or at least originated outside the health system. Over time multi-institutional systems have developed to the point where systems seem a generally more fit form for the current hospital service environment. As systems incorporate management techniques, they transform confederations of individual facilities into diversified health care corporations, with multiple products produced in geographically dispersed units. The model suggests that from a retrospective view, an environment has emerged favoring health care institutions designed to provide health services as an economic good in the marketplace.

Other changes in type and form of health care organization illustrate the dynamic process of the population ecology model in which new organizational forms are favored if they enter into or emerge from environmental niches where they obtain a relative advantage over existing forms. For example, the development of self-help, self-care groups provides an organizational form to meet needs and demands traditionally ignored by existing health care facilities and providers. Also, in recent years ambulatory surgical centers are springing up to claim a niche for less costly and more convenient outpatient surgery. Differentiated from individual physicians and hospital inpatient surgical units, the new centers compete for certain resources (patients who value near-instant availability and accessibility of a limited range of services). Whether the centers survive the selection and retention processes and develop reproducibility of form is an interesting and important empirical question.

Similarly, linking-pin organizations can develop (110); business coalitions linking private-sector firms concerned with the increasing cost of care with health care provider organizations. A number of different types of coalitions are emerging (111) as the adaptive advantages of such organizations find rewards in environmental conditions. The development and survival of coalitions depends on the broad appeal of the coalition in an era of mounting scarcity of societal resources available for providing health care—not on its contribution to member organizations from the industrial/health care sectors.

Interventions

In the rational model intervention strategies focus on the organization's internal operations, while the resource dependency model emphasizes strategies with which organizational managers attempt to manipulate the environment. The organizational ecology model offers a more dynamic and probabilistic perspective than the other two models. Its approach is critical to managers' understanding of organizational change as well as their own behavior relevant to the change process. From this perspective, the manager role is presented as a searcher for environmentally induced survival paths (112) and as a source of variation or diversity. Experimentation and diversity generation are viable strategies for the manager who must assess the variation selected by the environment. Consequently, the ecological model tends to place organizations and organizational change into perspective with larger events that unfold in the environment within which the organization functions. This model can sensitize managers to persistently scan the environment to identify emergent trends that indicate the success of new and different organizational forms. In a predictive sense, population ecology suggests that relentless pressures of turbulent environments are likely to produce environmental transformations—births and deaths at an increasingly higher rate.

While environmental assessment and experimentation are possible strategies, the ecological approach nevertheless makes explicit that organizational variation, and particularly the eventual form that is successful, is not a direct function of managerial control. While managers may generate variations—some of which are selected favorably—the eventual organizational form develops as an accumulation of selected variation. In a sense managers are like downhill skiers "out of control."

Anyone who follows the sport will remember the fantastic run of Franz Klammer in the Men's Downhill in the 1976 Winter Olympics. In ski language he was "out of control" for the entire run. He seemed on the verge of falling from start to breathtaking finish, yet winning the Olympic Gold Medal, and changing the philosophy of downhill racing in one afternoon. Until Klammer's run the prevailing thinking about downhill racers was that the winner would be the skier in best condition, with the best technique, and the least danger of losing control. Now racers believe that the winner must ski out of control, hoping to avoid a fall by lucky recoveries. In 1976 Klammer was the only one (of the truly world-class skiers) who skied out of control. Since every other top skier was trying to ski just short of losing control, Klammer won easily. Now all the top skiers, perhaps fifteen or twenty, are skiing out of control. On any given day natural selection stemming from factors beyond the skier's control largely determines who wins. During any run racers meet many blind variations in the form of ruts, bumps, mistakes, and so forth, all beyond the control of the skier at high speed. The skier who takes the most risk and makes the most miraculous recoveries wins. The skier who skis in control has control which guarantees only one thing—losing. Since many good skiers ski o ' of control, the odds are excellent that one of them will always take enough risk and manage   ough miraculous recoveries to beat the under-control skier (Paraphrased 113, pp. 447–448).

Managers have to take risks in an uncertain environment even though it is impossible to know which variations will lead to an effective organizational form. Yet this forced choice must not be interpreted as being totally deterministic.

If managers did not perform up to the best of their ability, which includes learning appropriate areas of competence and acting with purposefulness (even though it is myopic) in pursuing what appear to be the best strategies, they will be guaranteed one thing—some other competitor will be selected instead. Managers have to be purposeful, highly talented, hard-working, and all of those other good things associated with nonalienated, useful people just to avoid being selected against. Managers who feel alienated, useless, and lacking in purpose will end up losers just like downhill skiers who, thinking the race is won only by luck, give up practicing and working to stay at the very peak of their competence (113, pp. 448–449).

Finally, the model suggests caution in our growing tendency to "over-manage"—particularly under conditions of uncertainty—that is, to assign questionable probabilities in an uncertain environment and proceed to design and control organizational activities as though the future had a real probability. Effective organizations require sufficient internal variance to accommodate external uncertainty. As described by one consultant:

> What may be radically wrong with many clients' strategic processes is that they are *too* organized. By the time they have defined what they mean by mission, goal, strategy, objective, plan, business unit, and the like, they may have so narrowly defined the boundaries as to proscribe experimentation (112:123).

The following mini-case provides an example of what can occur when organizations proceed toward major change while ignoring important environmental elements.

MINI-CASE

Greenfield Hospital is a 150-bed county hospital opened in 1957 to provide services to Edgeton, the county seat with a total population of 800,000 in the community and surrounding rural area. The hospital executive director, Mr. Barnes, and chief of nursing services, Wanda Ogelthorpe, have enjoyed the strong support of the Board of Commissioners since their appointment when Greenfield started operations. Both individuals have been active in their national professional associations and both have completed a series of continuing management education courses to keep them in step with developments in the hospital field. As a result Greenfield and its management personnel have won a number of prestigious awards for outstanding achievement.

Over the past 30 years Mr. Barnes and Ms. Ogelthorpe have implemented many administrative improvements including management by objectives, primary nursing, product management, and marketing campaigns, and they have invested in various medical innovations appropriate to providing quality service in this rural community. With enthusiastic support of community leaders and civic groups they have established a hospice program and expanded home health, family planning, and physical therapy programs. Computer software has allowed them to improve financial management and reduce clerical personnel.

However, rising malpractice insurance costs have forced many older physicians, particularly surgeons and obstetricians, to close their practice. As the hospital's surgical and obstetrical patient population declines, management has been forced to close a 50-bed wing within the hospital. Completion of a new interstate highway has cut travel time to the university hospital in the state capital 50 miles away and inauguration of a medical helicopter service by the university hospital has further cut into Greenfield's emergency service population. All the really serious cases are now routinely airlifted to the metropolitan hospital. Higher pay scales and urban amenities have made Greenfield's staffing problems acute. Perhaps most serious is Greenfield's imminent problems in the scheduled retirement of Barnes and Ogelthorpe. Although search committees have been hard at work trying to find replacements, no satisfactory candidates have been found for these two positions, which will be unfilled following the hospital's 30th anniversary celebration early in 1987.

The board is currently considering purchase offers from a national hospital corporation planning to turn the facility into a drug and alcohol rehabilitation unit and another from a large nursing home chain to convert this into a long-term facility. Several local physician groups are also developing plans for same-day surgical centers, group practice centers, and other options. Meanwhile a number of community groups are organizing for action to keep the hospital in the community—reorganize—raise money—do anything possible to avoid loss of their community hospital.

Greenfield faces a most uncertain future.

SUMMARY

The management of change and innovation requires an understanding of the basic design of health care organizations, the change process, the various change methodologies appropriate to the design of organizations, and the particular change process ongoing within these organizations (23). The understanding of each and the guidelines for action are suggested by various organizational models. Table 11.2 provides an overview of the three models, the focus of the change activity, an outline of strategies, and the time frame associated with each.

TABLE 11.2. Types of Models, Units of Analysis, Types of Strategies, and Time Frames

Model	Unit of Analysis	Type of Strategy	Time Frame
Rational	Organization	Survey feedback	Short-term
		Team development	
		Quality circles	
		Continuing education	
		Confrontation meetings	
		Sensitivity training	
		Process consultation	
		Role specification	
		Task analysis	
		Management information systems	
		Integrating mechanisms	
		Collateral organization	
		Sociometric networks	
		Responsibility charting	
Resource dependence	Organization to environment	Buffering	Intermediate
		Market differentiation	
		Diversification	
		Vertical integration	
		Horizontal integration	
		Antitrust	
		Cooptation	
		Regulation	
		Coalitions	
Ecological	Environment to organization	Environmental assessment	Long-term
		Experimentation/diversity	

Guidelines for the management of change and innovation in health service organizations are presented in two groups—those that deal with underlying assumptions of the change process and those that concern management of the change process.

MANAGERIAL GUIDELINES

Assumption-Based Guidelines

1. *Be clear about the type of change involved.* Change is not an undifferentiated phenomenon. Each type of change has a specific set of attributes that need explicit attention from the health services manager. Moreover, these attributes interact with organizational characteristics to confound the change process. Thus, what may intuitively appear obvious, or at least similar to previous situations, may in reality be quite different and require caution because unanticipated consequences may develop.

2. *Be conscious of the latent consequences of change at each level. Consider these latent consequences not as problems but as opportunities.* While managers need to be specific about the particular type of change involved, they must also recognize that one type of change may lead to other types having their own anticipated and unanticipated consequences. For example, Hage (114) found that the introduction of medical educators within a community hospital resulted in the expansion and enhancement of managerial activity within the overall operations of the organization. This analysis illustrates that planned change (i.e., the introduction of directors of medical education) results in subsequent alterations in the basic power distribution within the organization.

3. *Do not assume that the environment is a constant, not to be considered a level of analysis subject to intervention.* Managers traditionally have taken a fairly parochial view of the change process. As a result, organizations are often considered the sole focus of change. Attempting to manage the interdependencies within the environment to enhance the operations of the organization may be a more viable strategy. Attention needs to be given to the context within which organizations operate. Enacting environments more compatible with existing organizational operations thus requires less change in the organization to enhance its overall performance.

4. *Consider intraorganizational change as a process involving a number of different stages.* Organizational change is a process involving a set of distinct stages. Managerial attention needs to be given to clearly identifying the stages at which a particular type of change is currently located and to designing interventions that will facilitate or impede the process—depending on the objectives of management vis-a-vis that particular change activity.

5. *Recognize that the change process involves several levels of analysis.* Organizational change and innovation occur at different levels within the organization. While we usually consider change and innovation as involving the entire organization, they in fact take place at various levels such as work groups, departments, or within individual roles. Attention should be given to clearly designating the level of the organization involved and to not confusing individual change with modifications in organizational variables.

6. *Be aware that organizations are subject to large changes in the environment which managerial action can do little to affect.* Managers need to be cognizant of their own limitations. Not all problems are tractable and managers have

only a limited amount of personal and organizational resources at their disposal. Attention should be given to those situations that are tractable, rather than taking the position that resources are infinite and that all are applicable to facilitating or impeding the change process. Failure to make this distinction results at best in an inefficient use of limited resources and, more tragically, the "burnout" of managerial personnel.

7. *Be conscious of time dimensions involved in change.* Time, a difficult concept to understand, is particularly deceptive in an organizational setting. Shifting personnel and priorities contribute to the tendency to underestimate the amount of time involved in any change process (115). This tendency is particularly evident in transitions and transformations. For example, what may be expected to take 6 months may take 12–18 months, or may never be completed.

Management-Based Guidelines

1. *Follow a sequence of specific steps in managing change and innovation.* These steps involve:

    a. Organizational diagnosis depends on systematic measurement of the current state of the organization, focusing on critical variables prescribed by the particular model that is used to assess the organization.

    b. Data from the assessment are compared against some type of management model that prescribes the basis for interpretation.

    c. Select intervention strategies; that is, select specific techniques that will affect organizational variables considered to require modification.

    d. Monitoring and follow-up, that is, continual assessment to determine that *(1)* intervention has had the desired effects and *(2)* further changes are not required.

    While these steps seem quite simple, the critical problem facing managers is their tendency to move quickly from organizational diagnosis to interventions. In many situations, administrators have solutions in search of problems as opposed to systematic selection of strategies to resolve specifically diagnosed problems. A further explication of each of these statements is given below.

2. *Organization diagnosis should be as objective as possible and based on longitudinal assessment.*

    Managers have a propensity for action and have little patience with long-term assessment. Yet the use of objective indicators followed over time provides the basis for systematically diagnosing critical problems facing the organization and thereby guiding change efforts. Specifically, longitudinal assessment provides the basis for differentiating the type of change that is required and the stages of the change process ongoing within the organization. It also allows development of a better understanding of major factors which may facilitate or impede the change process.

3. *Change interventions should be matched with variables of interest and appropriate levels of analysis.*

    Given an organizational diagnosis, it is important that managers assure the appropriate match of strategies to variables in appropriate levels of analysis. As indicated in previous sections, specific techniques are associated with specific types of variables. Failure to consider these relationships results in unrealistic expectations about the interventions.

4. *Monitoring and follow-up should be an ongoing activity within the organization to provide a basis for organizational diagnosis over time.*

> While data to support the efficacy of many forms of change interventions are limited, the increasing use of interventions provides an opportunity for managers to document their efficacy under various considerations. Documentation may involve individual case studies or more elaborate quasi-experimental designs. Yet whether case studies or experiments are used, monitoring and follow-up are critical to more effective use of change interventions.

DISCUSSION QUESTIONS

1. Select a particular change and/or innovation in health care delivery with which you are familiar and analyze it using the perspectives of the rational model, the resource dependency model, and the organizational ecology model. Using each particular model what factors influence the process of change and/or innovation? What assumptions are applied by the use of one model rather than another? What strategies are suggested for managers by the selection of each model?

2. As the associate vice-president for operations of a large university teaching hospital you have been assigned the responsibility of managing the implementation of a primary care nursing program within your organization. As you know, this program is a system for the delivery of nursing care where each patient is assigned to a registered nurse who is responsible for the quality of care delivered to that patient 24 hours a day, 7 days a week. What strategies might you consider to assure the successful implementation and eventual institutionalization of this program?

3. What arguments can be made to support or refute the statement that "the worst feature of the American health care system is its resistance to change"?

SUGGESTED READINGS

Eisenberg, J. M. *Doctors decision and cost of medical care: The reasons for doctors practice patterns and ways to change them.* Ann Arbor, MI: Health Administration Press, 1986.
An excellent review of factors affecting physician decision-making patterns and programs designed to change these patterns.

Goodman, P. S., & Associates. *Change in organizations: New perspectives on theory research and practice.* San Francisco, CA: Jossey-Bass, 1982.
Provides a review and insightful analysis of the state-of-the-art of both research and theory as it relates to organizational change. While focusing primarily on industrial organizations it is particularly relevant to health care managers and their involvement in organizational change and innovation.

Institute of Medicine. *Assessing medical technologies.* Washington, D.C.: National Academy Press, 1985.
A compilation of papers that focus on the assessment and diffusion of biomedical technology. Provides an up-to-date review of technology and their impact on health service delivery and financing.

Jaeger, J., Kaluzny, A., & Magruder-Habib, K. (Eds.). *Cases in multi-institutional systems management.* Owens Mill, MD.: Rynd Communications, National Health Publishing, 1987.
A compilation of cases involving owned, horizontally and vertically integrated arrangements as well as managed horizontally and vertically integrated arrangements. The book presents a theoretical perspective for the assessment of transformation, a series of propositions, and corollaries in an attempt to assess the extent to which cases provide supporting evidence.

Kimberly, J. R. Managerial innovation. In P. C. Nystrom & W. H. Starbuck (Eds.), *Handbook of organizational design.* Walton Street, Oxford: Oxford University Press, 1981, 84–85.
An excellent review of one particular type of organizational change. It provides an exhaustive review of available literature on innovation and provides a good discussion on topics not usually considered such as utilization, exnovation, and invention.

Margulies, N., & Adams, J. (Eds.).
Organizational development in health care organizations. Reading, MA: Addison-Wesley, 1982.
An excellent compilation of organizational development theory and practical applications in health care organizations. Provides a realistic assessment of organizational development potential and limitations.

REFERENCES

1. Allison, G. *Essence of decision: Explaining the Cuban missile crisis.* Boston, MA: Little, Brown, 1971.

2. Carroll, G. R. Organizational ecology. *Annual Review of Sociology,* 1984, *10,* 71–93.

3. Rogers, E. M. *Diffusion of innovations.* New York: The Free Press, 1983.

4. Kaluzny, A. D., & Veney, J. E. Types of change and hospital planning strategies. *American Journal of Health Planning,* 1977, *1,* 13–19.

5. Hernes, G. Structural change in social processes. *American Journal of Sociology,* 1976, *82*(3), 513–547.

6. Dowling, A. F. A measure of computer-based information system success. Cleveland: Unpublished paper, Health Systems Management Center, Case Western Reserve University, 1984.

7. Counte, M. A., Kjerulff, K. H., Salloway, J. C., & Campbell, B. C. Implementing computerization in hospitals: A case study of the behavioral and attitudinal impacts of a medical information system. *Journal of Organizational Behavioral Management,* 1984, *6*(3), 109–122.

8. Anderson, J. G., & Jay, S. J. Computers and clinical judgment: The role of physician networks. *Social Science and Medicine,* 1985, *20*(1), 969–979.

9. Munson, F. C. Crisis points in unit management programs. In G. F. Wieland (Ed.), *Improving health care management: Organization development and organization change.* Ann Arbor, Mich.: Health Administration Press, School of Public Health, University of Michigan, 1981, 197–208.

10. Burns, L. R. The diffusion of unit management among U.S. hospitals. *Hospital and Health Services Administration*, 1982, 27(2), 43–57.

11. Nathanson, C. A., & Morlock, L. L. Control structures, values, and innovation: A comparative study of hospitals. *Journal of Health and Social Behavior*, 1980, 21(4), 315–333.

12. Tornatzky, L. G., Fergus, E., Avellar, J., Fairweather, G., & Fleisher, M. *Innovation and social process: A natural experiment in implementing social technology*. New York: Pergamon Press, 1980.

13. Kaluzny, A. D. Quality assurance as a managerial innovation: A research perspective. *Health Services Research*, 1982, 17(3), 253–268.

14. Berman, P. The study of macro and micro implementation. *Public Policy*, 1978, 26(2), 157–184.

15. Pelz, D. C., & Munson, F. C. A framework for organizational innovating. Paper presented at the Academy of Management Annual Meeting, 1980.

16. Kanter, R. M. *The change masters: Innovations for productivity in the American corporation*. New York: Simon & Schuster, 1983.

17. Hillman, A. L., & Schwartz, J. S. The adoption and diffusion of CT and MRI in the United States: A comparative analysis. *Medical Care*, 1985, 23(11), 1283–1294.

18. Romeo, A., Wagner, J., & Lee, R. Prospective reimbursement and the diffusion of new technologies in hospitals. *Journal of Health Economics*, 1984, 3, 1–24.

19. Russell, L. B. Technology in hospitals, medical advances, and their diffusion. Washington, D.C.: The Brookings Institute, 1979.

20. Kanouse, D. E., Brook, R. H., Winkler, J. D., Kosecoff, J., Berry, S. H., Carter, G. M., Kahan, J. P., McCloskey, L., Rogers, W. H., Winslow, C. M., Fink, A., & Meredith, L. *Changing medical practice through technical assessment: An evaluation of the NIH consensus development program*. Report prepared for the National Institutes of Health, Contract #N01-OD-2-2128. Rand Corporation, Santa Monica, CA, December 1986.

21. Feinberg, H. Effects of clinical evaluation on the diffusion of medical technology. In *Assessing medical technologies: Report of a study*. Washington, D.C.: Institute of Medicine, National Academy Press, 1985.

22. Mohr, L. B. *Explaining organizational behavior: The limits and possibilities of theory and research*. San Francisco: Jossey-Bass, 1982.

23. Tichy, N. M., & Beckhard, R. Organizational development for health care organizations. In N. Margulies, & J. Adams (Eds.), *Organizational development in health care organizations*. Reading, Mass.: Addison-Wesley, 1982, 25–72.

24. Katz, D., & Kahn, R. L. *The social psychology of organizations* (2nd ed.). New York: Wiley, 1978.

25. Wieland, G. F. (Ed.). *Improving health care management. Section IV: A contingency approach to organizational change*. Ann Arbor, Mich.: Health Administration Press, 1981, 395–474.

26. Kaluzny, A. D., Warner, D. M., Warren, D. G., & Zelman, W. N. *Management of Health Services*. Englewood Cliffs, N.J.: Prentice-Hall, 1982.

27. Kimberly, J. R. Managerial innovations and health policy: Theoretical perspectives and research implications. *Journal of Health Policy, Politics and Law*, 1982, 6, 637–652.

28. Rubin, I., Plovnick, M. S., & Fry, R. Initiating planned change in health care systems. *Journal of Applied Behavioral Science*, 1974, *10*, 107–124.

29. Weisbrod, M. R. Why organization development hasn't worked (so far) in medical centers. *Health Care Management Review*, 1976, *1*, 17–28.

30. Nadler, D. A., & Tichy, N. M. The limitations of traditional interventional techniques in health care organizations. In N. Margulies and J. Adams (Eds.), *Organizational development in health care organizations*. Reading, Mass.: Addison-Wesley, 1981, 359–378.

31. Warner, K. E. A "desperation-reaction" model of medical diffusion. *Health Services Research*, 1975, *10*, 369–383.

32. McNeil, K., & Minihan, E. Medical technology regulation and organizational change in hospitals. *Administrative Science Quarterly*, 1977, *22*, 475–490.

33. Zaltman, G., Duncan, R., & Holbek, J. *Innovations and organizations*. New York: Wiley-Interscience, 1973.

34. McKinlay, J. B. From "promising report" to "standard procedure": Seven stages in the career of a medical innovation. *Health and Society: Milbank Memorial Fund Quarterly*, 1981, *59*, 374–411.

35. Scheirer, M. A. Approaches to the study of implementation. *IEEE Transactions on Engineering Management*, 1983, *30*(2), 76–82.

36. Downs, G. W., & Mohr, L. B. Conceptual issues in the study of innovation. *Administrative Science Quarterly*, 1976, *21*, 700–714.

37. Rogers, E. M., & Shoemaker, F. F. *Communication of innovations: A cross-cultural approach*, 2nd ed. New York: The Free Press, 1971.

38. Kaluzny, A. D., Veney, J. E., Gentry, J. T., & Sprague, J. B. Scalability of health services: An empirical test. *Health Services Research*, 1971, *6*, 214–223.

39. Fennel, M. L. The effects of environmental characteristics on the structure of hospital clusters. *Administrative Science Quarterly*, 1980, *25*(3), 485–510.

40. Van Maanen, J., & Barley, S. F. Cultural organization: Fragments of a theory. In P. J. Frost, Moore, L. F., Louis, M. R., Lundberg, C. C., and Martin, J. (Eds.), *Organizational culture*. Beverly Hills, Calif.: Sage Publications, 1985.

41. Hage, J., & Dewar, R. Elite values versus organizational structure in predicting innovation. *Administrative Science Quarterly*, 1973, *18*, 279–290.

42. Kjerulff, K. H., Counte, M. A., Salloway, J. C., & Campbell, B. C. Measuring adaptation to medical technology. *Hospital and Health Services Administration*, 1983, *28*(1), 30–40.

43. Morse, E. V., Gordon, G., & Moch, M. K. Hospital costs and quality of care: An organizational perspective. *Health and Society: Milbank Memorial Fund Quarterly*, 1974, *52*, 315–346.

44. Becker, S. W., & Neuhauser, D. *The efficient organization*. New York: Elsevier, 1975.

45. Becker, M. Sociometric location and innovativeness: Reformation and extension of the diffuse model. *American Sociological Review*, 1970, *35*, 267–283.

46. Kaluzny, A. D., Veney, J. E., & Gentry, J. T. Innovation of health services: A comparative study of hospitals and health departments. *Health and Society: Milbank Memorial Fund Quarterly*, 1974, *52*, 51–82.

47. Mohr, L. B. Determinants of innovation in organizations. *American Political Science Review*, 1969, *63*, 111–126.

48. Golembiewski, R. T., Proehl, C. W., & Sink, D. Success of OD applications in the public sector: Toting up the score for a decade, more or less. *Public Administration Review*, 1981, *41*, 679–682.

49. Van de Ven, A., & Ferry, D. *Measuring and assessing organizations*. New York: Wiley-Interscience, 1980.

50. Seashore, S., Lawler III, E., Mirvis, P., & Cammann, C. *Assessing organizational change: A guide to methods, measures, and practices*. New York: Wiley, 1983.

51. Lundberg, C. C. On the feasibility of cultural intervention in organization. In P. J. Frost et al. (Eds.), *Organizational culture*. Beverly Hills, Calif.: Sage Publications, 1985.

52. Mirvis, P. H. Managing research while reaching managers. In P. J. Frost, Moore, L. F., Louis, M. R., Lundberg, C. C., & Martin, J. (Eds.), *Organizational culture*. Beverly Hills, Calif.: Sage Publications, 1985.

53. Katz, D., & Kahn, R. L. *The social psychology of organizations*. New York: Wiley, 1966.

54. Bowers, D. G., & Franklin, J. L. *Survey-guided development I: Data-based organizational change*. La Jolla, Calif.: University Associates, 1977.

55. Beer, M. The technology of organization development. In M. Dunnette (Ed.), *Handbook of industrial and organizational psychology*. Chicago: Rand McNally, 1976.

56. McKinney, M. M. The newest miracle drug: Quality circles in hospitals. *Hospital and Health Services Administration*, 1984, *29*(5) 74–87.

57. Palmer, R. H., & Reilly, M. C. Individual and institutional variables which may serve as indicators of quality of medical care. *Medical Care*, 1979, *17*, 693–717.

58. Eisenberg, J. M. Physician utilization: The state of research about physician practice patterns. *Medical Care*, 1985, *3*(5), 461–483.

59. Beckhard, R. The confrontation meeting. *Harvard Business Review*, 1967, *45*, 149–155.

60. Schein, E. H. *Process consultation: Its role in organization development*. Reading, Mass.: Addison-Wesley, 1969.

61. Lewicki, R. J., & Litterer, J. A. *Negotiation*. Homewood, Ill.: Richard D. Irwin, Inc., 1985.

62. Hage, J., & Aiken, M. Program change and organizational properties: A comparative analysis. *American Journal of Sociology*, 1967, *72*, 503–519.

63. Kimberly, J. R. Hospital adoption of innovation: The role of integration into external informational environments. *Journal of Health and Social Behavior*, 1978, *19*, 361–373.

64. Moch, M., & Morse, E. Size, centralization, and organizational adoptions of innovations. *American Sociological Review*, 1978, *42*, 716–725.

65. Greer, A. L. Medical technology and professional dominance theory. *Social Science and Medicine*, 1984, *18*(10), 809–817.

66. Greer, A. L. Adoption of medical technology: The hospitals three decision systems. *The International Journal of Technology Assessment in Health Care*, 1985, *1*(3), 669–680.

67. Greer, A. L. Medical conservatism and technological acquisitiveness: The paradox of hospital technology adoptions. *Research in the Sociology of Health Care,* Greenwich, Connecticut. JAI Press, Inc., 1986, *4,* 185–235.

68. Plovnick, M. S. Structural interventions for health care systems organizational development. In N. Margulies, & J. Adams (Eds.), *Organizational development in health care organizations.* Reading, Mass.: Addison-Wesley, 1982, 235–253.

69. Galbraith, J. R. Designing the innovating organization. *Organizational Dynamics,* 1982, *10,* 5–25.

70. Mintzberg, H. *The structuring of organizations: A synthesis of the research.* Englewood Cliffs, N.J.: Prentice-Hall, 1979.

71. Goodman, P. S., & Kurke, L. B. Studies of change in organizations: A status report. In P. S. Goodman & Associates (Ed.), *Change in organizations: New perspectives on theory, research, and practice.* San Francisco: Jossey-Bass, 1982, 1–46.

72. Nadler, D. A. *Feedback and organization development: Using data-based methods.* Reading, Mass.: Addison-Wesley, 1977.

73. Payne, B., Lyons, T. F., Neuhaus, E., Kolton, M. & Dwarskius, L. Methods of evaluating and improving ambulatory medical care. *Health Services Research,* 1984, *19*(2), 219–245.

74. Anderson, J. Comparative networks and physician use of a HIS. Proposal funded by the NCHSR/TA, 1985.

75. McCann, J., & Gilmore, T. Diagnosing organizational decision making through responsibility charting. *Sloan Management Review,* 1983, *24*(2), 3–15.

76. Wieland, G. F., & Bradford, A. An evaluation of the hospital internal communications (HIC) project. In G. F. Wieland (Ed.), *Improving health care management: Organizational development and organizational change.* Ann Arbor, Mich.: Health Administration Press, 1980, 425–449.

77. Meyer, A. D. Adapting to environmental jolts. *Administrative Science Quarterly,* 1982, *27,* 515–537.

78. Daft, R., & Becker, S. *The innovative organization: Innovation adoption in school organizations.* New York: Elsevier, 1978.

79. Kimberly, J. R., & Evanisko, M. J. Organizational innovation: The influence of individual, organizational and contextual factors on hospital adoption of technological and administrative innovations. *Academy of Management Journal,* 1981, *24*(4), 689–713.

80. Hernandez, S. R., & Kaluzny, A. D. Determinants of program innovation: The first stage of the innovation process. Paper presented at the American Sociological Association Annual Meeting, 1980.

81. Kaluzny, A. D. Change in health care settings. In P. Trohanis (Ed.), *Ideas in change.* Chapel Hill: Technical Assistance Development System, Frank Porter Graham Child Development Center, University of North Carolina, 1981, 43–65.

82. Aiken, M., & Bacharach, S. B. Organizational structure, work process, and proposal making in administrative bureaucracies. *Academy of Management Journal,* 1980, *23,* 631–652.

83. Nutt, P. C. Tactics of implementation. *Academy of Management Journal,* 1986, *29*(2), 230–261.

84. Scheirer, M. A. *Program implementation: The organizational context.* Beverly Hills: Sage, 1981.

85. Duncan, R. The ambidextrous organization: Designing dual structures for innovation. In R. H. Kilmann, L. R. Pondy, & D. P. Slevin (Eds.), *The management of organization design.* New York: Elsevier North-Holland, 1976, *1*, 167–188.

86. Daft, R. L. Bureaucratic versus non-bureaucratic structure and process of innovation and change. *Research in the sociology of organizations,* 1982, 1, Greenwich, Connecticut. JAI Press, Inc.

87. Daft, R. L. A dual-core model of organizational innovation. *Academy of Management Journal,* 1978, *21,* 193–210.

88. Kilmann, R. H. *Beyond the quick fix: Managing five tracks to organizational success.* San Francisco: Jossey-Bass, 1984.

89. Tichy, N. M. Organizational cycles and change management in health care organizations. In N. Margulies, & J. Adams (Eds.), *Organizational development in health care organizations.* Reading, Mass.: Addison-Wesley, 1982, 169–192.

90. Pfeffer, J., & Salancik, G. R. *The external control of organizations: A resource dependence perspective.* New York: Harper & Row, 1978.

91. Dutton, J., & Duncan, R. The creation of momentum for change through the process of strategic issue diagnosis. *Strategic Management Journal,* 1986.

92. Pfeffer, J., & Salancik, G. R. Organizational context and the characteristics and tenure of hospital administrators. *Academy of Management Journal,* 1977, *20,* 74–88.

93. Mintzberg, H. *The nature of managerial work.* New York: Harper & Row, 1973.

94. Shortell, S. M., Wickizer, T. M., & Wheeler, J. R. C. *Hospital–physician joint ventures: Results and lessons from a national demonstration in primary care.* Ann Arbor, Mich.: Health Administration Press, 1984.

95. Thompson, J. D. *Organizations in action.* New York: McGraw-Hill, 1967.

96. Greer, S. Citizens' voluntary governing boards: Waiting for the quorum. *Public Policy,* 1982, *14,* 165–178.

97. Feldstein, P. J. *Health associations and the demand for legislation: The political economy of health.* Cambridge, Mass.: Ballinger, 1977.

98. D'Aunno, T., & Zuckerman, H. "A Life-cycle model of organizational federations-A case of hospitals", *Academy of Management Review,* July 1987 (in press).

99. Cohen, M. D., March, J. G., & Olsen, J. P. A garbage can model of organizational choice. *Administrative Science Quarterly,* 1972, *17,* 1–25.

100. March, J. G., & Olsen, J. P. Garbage can models of decision making in organizations. In J. G. March, & R. Weissinger-Baylon (Eds.), *Ambiguity and command: Organizational perspectives on military decision-making.* Boston: Pitman Publishing, Inc., 1986.

101. Kimberly, J. R. The life cycle analogy and the study of organizations: Introduction. In J. R. Kimberly, R. H. Miles, & Associates (Eds.), *The organizational life cycle: Issues in creation, transformation, and decline of organizations.* San Francisco: Jossey-Bass, 1980.

102. Kimberly, J. R. Environmental constraints and organizational structures: A comparative analysis of rehabilitation organizations. *Administrative Science Quarterly,* 1975, *20*(1), 1–9.

103. Kimberly, J. R. Issues in the creation of organizations: Initiation, innovation, and institutionalization. *Academy of Management Journal*, 1979, *22*(3), 437–457.

104. Hernandez, S. R., & Kaluzny, A. D. Hospital closure: A review of current and proposed research. *Health Services Research*, 1982, *18*(3), 419–436.

105. Goodman, L. J., Bennett, E. H., & Odem, R. J. Group medical practice in U.S. American Medical Association, 1976.

106. Freshnock, L. J., & Goodman, L. J. Medical group practice in the United States: Patterns of survival between 1969 and 1975. *Journal of Health and Social Behavior*, 1979, *20*(4), 352–362.

107. Hannan, M. T., & Freeman, J. Structural inertia and organizational change. *American Sociological Review*, 1984, *82*, 929–964.

108. Aldrich, H. E. *Organizations and environments*. Englewood Cliffs, N.J.: Prentice-Hall, 1979.

109. Langton, J. Darwinism and the behavioral theory of sociocultural evolution: An analysis. *American Journal of Sociology*, 1979, *85*, 288–309.

110. Aldrich, H. E., & Whetten, D. Organizational-sets, action-sets and networks: Making the most of simplicity. In P. Nystrom and W. Starbuck (Eds.), *Handbook of organizational design*. New York: Oxford University Press, 1981, 285–408.

111. McNerney, W. J. Health care coalitions: New substance or more cosmetics? The 1982 Michael M. Davis Lecture. Chicago: Center for Health Administration Studies, Graduate School of Business, University of Chicago, 1982.

112. McKelvey, B., & Aldrich, H. E. "Applied Population Science" *Administrative Science Quarterly*, 28, 1 (March, 1983), 101–28.

113. McKelvey, B. *Organizational systematics: Taxonomy, evolution, classification*. Berkeley: University of California Press, 1982.

114. Hage, J. *Communication and organizational control. Cybernetics in health and welfare settings*. New York: Wiley-Interscience, 1974.

115. Pressman, J. L., & Wildavsky, A. *Implementation*. Berkeley: University of California Press, 1973.

CHAPTER 12

Organizational Performance: Managing for Efficiency and Effectiveness

W. Richard Scott
Stephen M. Shortell

*A chief executive officer was heard commenting to a
colleague that "Managers make better lovers because they
are constantly assessing their performance to improve it."
To which the colleague replied "Being aware of a problem
and being able to do something about it are two quite
different things."*

Managerial awareness and ability are the cornerstones of a high-performing organization.
In health care, the demands for high performance are increasing. This is reflected not
only in the cost containment incentives of prospective payment arrangements, but also
in the increased competition among providers:

> When the dominant themes become market share, pricing policies, marginal costs, and
> performance, and when seminars and conferences highlight these subjects, hospitals will
> have completed the journey from social and religious agencies and joined the mainstream
> of American industry. (1)

Because they operate in an environment of constrained resources, there are incentives
for health care organizations to improve productivity and quality and to expand their
share of the market in serving their communities. Increasingly, this has meant having

to trade off some programs, services, and markets for others. For example, a hospital may agree to give up its maternity services in order to expand its medical/surgical services or may share high-technology resources with another hospital in order to concentrate more effort in expanding its ambulatory care programs. Such tradeoffs have meant that chief executive officers (CEOs) of health care organizations have had to manage their organizations in relation to other organizations, in addition to considering the performance of individual subunits.

Another set of internal pressures comes from the concerns of committed health professionals—managers, nurses, physicians and others—to improve professional practice by using their knowledge, skills, and technology to the best of their abilities. This force is often neglected when considering the other, perhaps more visible, concerns.

As described in previous chapters, the presence of large numbers of professional workers with their relatively great autonomy and power, is one of the features that distinguishes health care systems from other types of organizations. Hospitals are known to vary in the extent to which the medical staff exercises control over individual physicians (2, 3), and in the extent to which health care managers are able to effectively influence the medical staff and other types of professional providers. Clearly, a major challenge to the health care executive is to put together an organization that maximizes coordinated professional competence in the service of patient care.

More than anyone else, the manager is responsible for the performance of the organization. In a real sense, all of the preceding chapters are building blocks for assisting the manager to improve organizational performance. This approach builds on the contingency/open-systems framework employed throughout this book. As outlined in Chapters 1 and 2, the manager's role includes environmental assessment, strategy formulation, policy development, organization design, implementation, and evaluation. Organizational performance is affected by how well managers perform these activities. These activities can be linked to the five basic subsystems of an organization identified by Katz and Kahn (4). These subsystems are:

1. *Adaptive subsystem,* which senses and interprets the environment for the organization.
2. *Boundary-spanning subsystem,* which secures resources and disposes of outputs.
3. *Production subsystem,* which produces the goods or services.
4. *Maintenance subsystem,* which maintains human and capital resources and promotes internal stability.
5. *Managerial subsystem,* which coordinates and controls relationships within the organization and between the organization and its environment.

Figure 12.1 shows this linkage. The environmental-assessment function is primarily associated with the adaptive subsystem; the strategy formulation and policy development functions with the boundary spanning subsystem; the implementation function with the production subsystem; the organization design function with the maintenance subsystem; and both the organization design and evaluation functions are primarily associated with the managerial subsystems.

Figure 12.1 emphasizes the manager's role, particularly that of the CEO, in guiding and overseeing all of the subsystems of the organization, not just the maintenance or managerial subsystems, which have been traditionally emphasized in health administration. Thus the manager can improve performance not only through the design of organizational structure, process, and control systems but also through environmental

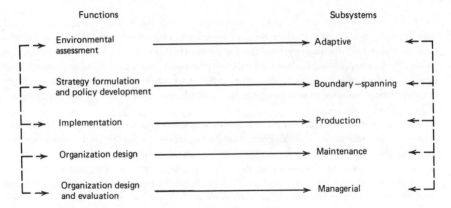

Figure 12.1. Organizational functions and subsystems for improving performance.

assessment, strategy formulation, and policy development activities. As noted in Chapter 4, these are part of the leadership functions of the manager. And as noted in Chapter 9, organization design initiatives must necessarily follow from the above activities. Further, the performance of health care organizations in the future may increasingly depend on the ability of health care managers to enact their environment rather than passively react to external changes (5). As discussed in Chapter 10, this will require not only more sensitive environmental assessment methods but also more creative ways of imagining the organization's future.

Health care managers face many performance issues. Some of these involve productivity, some involve efficiency, and some involve effectiveness. Because these terms are often ill-defined and sometimes used interchangeably, it is important to define them for present purposes. Because of the variety of dimensions of performance involved, it is useful to consider a performance profile approach that explicitly recognizes that there is no single criterion of organizational success. A productive or efficient organization is not necessarily effective; and vice versa.

Efficiency and productivity are closely related terms. *Efficiency* is defined as the cost per unit of output. An example is cost per admission. *Productivity* is defined as the ratio of outputs to inputs. An example of a productivity measure in the health care area is number of patient visits (adjusted for case mix) per full-time equivalent provider hours. A difficulty in all attempts to measure efficiency and productivity in health care organizations is the problem of measuring outputs. These problems will be considered throughout this chapter.

By *effectiveness* is meant the degree to which goals and objectives are successfully met. These may range from subobjectives, such as successfully recruiting a coordinator for the hospital's quality assurance program, to intermediate level objectives, such as improving the practice patterns of cardiologists in the treatment of acute myocardial infarction, to ultimate objectives, such as a reduction in the mortality rate for acute myocardial infarction cases. It should be noted that two health care organizations may be equally effective but one may be more or less efficient and/or productive than the other. In recent years, increased attention has been given to assessing the cost effectiveness of various health care programs. *Cost effectiveness* is a composite measure that takes into account both cost and degree of goal attainment. These issues are particularly difficult because of the problems associated with the measurement of productivity, efficiency, and effectiveness at the organizational level. Most health care organizations produce many different outputs and have different ways of accounting for inputs and outputs in attaching costs and prices to different departments. This creates a problem of developing an aggregate performance measure for the organization as a whole (6, 7).

These issues are also complicated because of the problems associated with defining and measuring organizational goals. As Scott (8) notes, assessing organizational effectiveness largely depends on the kinds of goals organizations adopt and their reasons for doing so. Goals serve many purposes. They may *(1)* motivate organization members to higher performance, *(2)* act as criteria for evaluating performance, *(3)* legitimize organizational activities, and *(4)* indicate to external agencies what the organization is about. The same stated goals may be used differently in different situations to serve any or all the above functions. Alternatively, different goals may be developed to serve different purposes. Finally, there is always the problem expressed best by the dictum: "When we're not near the goals we love, we love the goals we're near."

The following section examines the major approaches to assessing organizational performance, particularly in regard to effectiveness. This is followed by a review of the organizational literature, focusing particularly on studies of health care organizations. The chapter concludes with a discussion of high-performing health care organizations. Managerial guidelines are provided throughout the chapter.

APPROACHES TO CONCEPTUALIZING AND ASSESSING EFFECTIVENESS

Defining and assessing organizational performance is neither simple nor straightforward. A systematic consideration of the factors that contribute to this complexity may help to clarify the issues. Two classes of factors—conceptual and measurement—will be considered. Both are important, but the conceptual issues are more so. As Kanter (9) comments, "The most interesting questions in this area are not technical, they are conceptual: not *how* to measure effectiveness or productivity, but *what* to measure." One might add that *why* organizational performance is being measured is also important. For example, measures may differ depending upon whether their purpose is to satisfy external regulatory groups or to take internal corrective action. These conceptual issues are difficult because they are linked to central controversies regarding the purpose and nature of organizations.

CONCEPTUAL ISSUES

Nature of Organizations

Of the many factors that affect one's conception of organizational performance, none is more important than the view adopted of the fundamental nature of organizations. If organizations are conceived primarily as rationally designed instruments for the attainment of specific goals, then performance measures are likely to focus on goal attainment (10, 11). In this mechanistic view interest is centered on the production of goods and services for external consumption; thus emphasis is placed on measures of productivity and efficiency.

Alternatively, organizations can be viewed as collectivities capable of pursuing specific goals but primarily oriented toward their own survival—toward system maintenance (10, 11). In this more organic perspective, attention is diverted from output to support goals, such as members' satisfaction or morale or, more generally, the survival of the organization.

A third closely related perspective views organizations as open systems that are highly interdependent with their environments and engaged in system-elaborating as well as system-maintenance activities (12). Because system growth and elaboration is directly dependent on the organization's bargaining position with the environment, this approach stresses the importance of resource acquisition to organizational effectiveness (13). In addition to direct measures of the organization's ability to acquire scarce and valued resources—for example, through the fund-raising activities of volunteers and the choice of well-connected persons to serve on boards of trustees—this view also seeks evidence of an organization's capacity to adapt to changing environmental demands—for example, through the creation of organizational slack (uncommitted resources).

These different views of organizations are divergent; they emphasize different and somewhat conflicting features of an organizational system. To stress efficiency in the attainment of specific goals may not always be consistent with participants' satisfaction. Bales (14) and his associates have long emphasized the tensions that may arise between the task performance and the socioemotional requirements of a social system. And in a time of rapid environmental change, the organization that is well-suited to deal with today's demands may by that very fact be ill-equipped to handle tomorrow's challenges. Weick (15) notes that organizational features that preserve adaptability "look ugly and wasteful" in the present context but can prove invaluable when conditions change.

Domain of Activity

Once a general framework or model has been selected to guide the investigation, it is necessary to determine which particular functions or activities will be evaluated. Most complex organizations are multipurpose systems, serving a variety of aims and objectives. Modern hospitals, for example, not only provide a variety of types of patient care, including broad categories of services such as outpatient, inpatient, and emergency care, but many also pursue educational goals (e.g., residency training), research goals, and preventive and community service goals. Departmental and work-group subdivisions often reflect—and protect—these differentiated purposes, with different subgroups and types of personnel performing quite divergent tasks and pursuing quite distinct objectives. In some cases, these goals and the activities of the various groups are highly interdependent—in either negative or positive ways. Training objectives sometimes conflict with patient care interests and sometimes support and complement them. In other cases, the goals and activities may be quite independent: the preventive work of the public health unit may be largely unaffected by the acute services provided by the cardiac care unit. Thus the same organization may perform extremely well on one set of activities but relatively poorly on another. No organization is equally effective with respect to all the objectives it pursues.

Levels of Analysis

A third critical factor influencing conceptions of organizational performance is the level of analysis selected to guide the assessment. An important insight gained from open-systems theory is that all complex systems tend to be nested units: systems within systems. Thus a hospital is composed of departments, and the departments are composed of work units, while the hospital as a whole is part of one or more larger systems, such as a multiunit hospital or regional health system. The boundaries that separate these levels are seldom clear and are often rather arbitrary. Further, many of these boundaries are not organized in neat concentric circles but frequently overlap and cross-cut one another. Individuals in modern societies are not completely contained within any single organization but instead are partially involved in several, and professional occupations and union organizations cross organizational boundaries in complex and unexpected ways.

Although there are obviously various possibilities, it is conventional to identify at least three system levels: (1) the organization itself: for example, a hospital or an HMO; (2) a larger socially defined unit that contains the organization: for example, a community or a health services region; and (3) subunits contained within the organization: for example, individual departments or practitioners. Most analyses of organizational performance focus on one or more of these three levels. The critical point, however, is that one should be as clear as possible about what level of analysis is selected.

An additional consideration renders level-of-analysis issues sticky. System performance at any given level may not be analyzable as a simple aggregation of system performance at lower levels. Indeed, this is one of the principal features of any system: its performance is determined as much (if not more) by the arrangement of its parts—their relations and interactions—as by the performance of the individual components. A number of highly qualified physicians do not necessarily add up to a high-quality medical staff. Rather, how the staff members are deployed—by level of privileges and types of service—how their work is monitored and information fed back to allow improvement, the arrangements for continuing education—these and similar factors may be more decisive for many aspects of medical effectiveness.

One must be careful not to confuse level of analysis with the issue of whose interests are reflected in the determination of assessment criteria. Thus it is possible to focus on the performance of the hospital as a complex system but to assess this performance from the standpoint of the interest of the larger community. Whose interests are served in assessing effectiveness is best treated as a separate topic, a fourth factor that affects one's view of organizational performance.

Varying Constituencies

Early models of organizations stressed an entrepreneurial or, somewhat later, a managerial view. These conceptions emphasized the legitimacy of the interests of the owners or their agents, stressing profitability as the primary standard of performance. It was not long before such analysts as Berle and Means (16) and Burnham (17) began to perceive that the interests of owners (increasingly, stockholders) and managers could diverge, as could those of other classes of participants. Indeed, the history of organizations over recent decades is partly a story of the recognition and increasing legitimation of the varying interests of their multiple constituencies; stockholders, managers of diverse types, various categories of workers, clients or customers, and other interested or affected publics and their advocates.

This emerging view of organizations is best expressed in the coalition model of organizations formulated by Cyert and March (18). According to this model, organizations are usefully viewed as shifting coalitions of interest groups, some internal, others external to the organization, that are constantly engaged in negotiating and renegotiating the conditions of their participation. Of course, not all interests are equally powerful: in most organizations one can detect the presence of a dominant coalition whose interests carry more weight than others. But it is still important to note that in most organizations power is more widely dispersed today than in the past, and more diverse constituencies are perceived to be legitimate stakeholders in the enterprise.

Research by Friedlander and Pickle (19) supports the expectation that the interests of varying constituency groups may exhibit low convergence. Effectiveness criteria assumed to be important to several types of interested parties—owners, employees, customers, suppliers, creditors, community members, and governmental officials—were assessed across 97 small business organizations. Performance scores, as measured by these multiple criteria, revealed a pattern of low and often negative correlations: to do well on a criterion favored by one constituency was to do poorly on a criterion favored by another. Friedlander and Pickle conclude that "organizations find it difficult to fulfill simultaneously the variety of demands made upon them."

Time Considerations

Time enters into the assessment of organizational performance in at least two different ways. First, any given performance takes place within and produces its effects over some specific time frame. The point at which the performance is assessed may greatly influence the judgment reached. Steers (20) provides an illustration:

> If current production, a short-run effectiveness criterion, is maximized at the expense of research and development investments in future products, an organization may ultimately find itself with an outmoded product and threatened for its very survival, a long-run criterion.

Of course, even more compelling evidence can be adduced for the importance of this factor in health care organizations, since health is such a time-dependent phenomenon. Scott et al. (21) report that results of their studies of the quality of surgical care in hospitals were substantially affected by whether patients' conditions were assessed at 7 days or at 40 days after surgery.

Second, the organization itself and all of its subunits exist in time and are subject to changes that are a function of development over time. Interest is increasing in organizational life cycles (22), and simulation studies by Cameron and Whetton (23) suggest that effectiveness criteria vary according to stage of development. These researchers propose that earlier stages place stress on such factors as creativity and the mobilization of resources; later stages emphasize commitment and cohesion among members; still later, formal processes of control and efficiency concerns come to the fore; and finally, structural elaboration, decentralization, and flexibility receive emphasis. Life-cycle effects on performance criteria appear to be a fruitful new area of inquiry.

To summarize, a number of factors have been identified that have clear relevance to the evaluation of organizational performance. Views of the nature of organizations, activity domain, level of analysis, constituency groups, and time frames are sufficiently varied that one may expect to find little consensus in the selection of criteria employed to evaluate organizational effectiveness. This expectation is borne out by a substantial body of empirical research. Reviews by Price (24) Steers (20) and Campbell (25) all record lengthy lists of varying criteria that have been employed in past studies and conclude that there is little agreement among investigators or participants as to how effectiveness is to be conceptualized.

Moreover, surveys of studies that employed multiple measures of effectiveness report that the correlations among them are typically low and sometimes negative. Organizations performing well according to one effectiveness measure (e.g., an adjusted mortality-rate index) often fail to perform well on others (e.g., patient or employee satisfaction).

A Synthetic Model

Given the many approaches and choices, it is not possible to reconcile all simultaneously, but Zammuto (26) has outlined an interesting synthetic model, many of whose features are well adapted to analyzing the effectiveness of health care systems. He explicitly embraces an open-system model. Advocating what he terms an "evolutionary framework," he insists that "organizational performance be evaluated within the context of the environment in which it occurs" (p. 75). Recognizing that all organizations relate to a variety of constituencies, Zammuto proposes that the preferences of such groups play two important roles in the pattern of evolution: (1) denoting the preferred direction of change and (2) putting pressure on the system to change. Moreover,

> Unlike in other models, no single constituent perspective is raised to a position above those of other constituencies. This is not to say that all the constituencies have a legitimate stake in the functioning of an organization but none has a predominant set of interests, although it may be more important to satisfy one constituency at one point in time than others. Social legitimacy and the continued participation of the constituencies depends on satisfaction of their preferences over time (pp. 82–83).

Note also that the model emphasizes not only multiple constituencies but also the impact of time: constituencies come and go, wax and wane, and change their preferences.

> Effectiveness stems from the ability of an organization to satisfy changing preferences of its constituencies over time (p. 82).

Zamutto summarizes the advantages of his effectiveness model over previous attempts as follows:

> It specifies that organizational performance needs to be responsive to constituent demands. Second, it states that effectiveness stems from innovative performance which expands [the technical and institutional environment within which the organization operates] allowing organizations to satisfy changing constituent preferences. Third, "nest fouling" behavior is ineffective because the organization cannot survive apart from its environment since it is part of that environment. The organization which "wins" over its environment is, in the long run, "winning" over itself because it is destroying its niche (pp. 78–79).

Zamutto illustrates the utility of his model by applying it to the evaluation of the effectiveness of the physician extender training program.

MEASUREMENT ISSUES

Having described some of the critical conceptual issues confronted by those who determine how effectiveness is to be defined, we now examine problems relating to the measurement of performance. This brief review will not attempt to address the many technical and statistical issues that develop in any measurement process, but will focus on several concerns that arise particularly in the context of assessing performance, whether that of an individual, a subunit, or an organization. Whenever a performance is to be evaluated, several processes must be carried out: *(1)* properties or dimensions of the work must be identified, *(2)* standards must be established, *(3)* indicators of performance values must be selected and samples must be drawn, and *(4)* comparisons must be made between sampled performance values and standards (27). Finally, virtually all attempts to evaluate are reactive; the act of measuring the performance itself affects the performance. Each of these processes or problems will be discussed in turn, although some require only brief comment.

Selecting Properties

Performance is not evaluated—only selected properties of performance, for example, speed or accuracy or quality. Many of the difficulties encountered in the identification of performance properties have already been considered, since the bulk of them pertain to the issue of deciding what is to be evaluated. Still, choice of criteria, or level of analysis, and of time frame having been made, many more specific decisions remain before effectiveness can be assessed. Of course, performances themselves vary greatly in complexity, just as performance appraisal systems vary in terms of how comprehensive, elaborate, and systematic they attempt to be. Some conception of the detail and complexity reached by some performance appraisal systems is to be found in the protocols developed to evaluate selected aspects of the work of nurses and physicians (28, 29).

Setting Standards

Relatively little is known about the important issue of how standards used in the appraisal of performance are set. Thompson (30) has proposed that different types of standards exist to assess performance, depending on whether clear goals have been established and whether a known technology exists for pursuing them. If goals are clear and the means exist to achieve them, then efficiency standards may be set. Such standards support the assessment not only of whether the goal was attained but also with what degree of efficiency. When goal conceptions are clear but technologies are weak, then evaluators must settle for instrumental standards, which focus primarily on whether the goal has been achieved; less stress can be placed on efficiency in the use of resources. Finally, when goals are vague evaluators are likely to utilize social tests, looking to comparable systems to determine not only how well their own system is performing but also to ascertain what is meant by "well."

It appears that most organizations use some combinations of their own past experience plus knowledge of the performance of systems regarded as similar as a basis for setting standards. When new appraisal systems are set in place, the standards adopted often seem to be statistically determined norms based on the mean or modal level of performance. Such is the case with the standards regarding length of stay for patients within a given diagnostic grouping associated with the DRG prospective reimbursement system for Medicare and Medicaid patients. Professionals tend to resist the development of standards based on aggregate experience, emphasizing the unique characteristics of clients requiring a case-by-case approach (31). The DRG system recognizes the legitimacy of these concerns and includes provisions for granting exceptions; however, physicians correctly perceive that their discretion regarding patient care has been reduced. Many have resisted its adoption and some have acted to subvert it by misclassifying patients into more severe diagnostic categories justifying longer lengths of stay.

These strategies and conflicts should serve to remind us that assessments of organizational effectiveness are never purely descriptive or objective in character. The selection of properties and standards are decisions based on more or less explicitly formulated normative or prescriptive assumptions. Performance evaluation is, therefore, never an objective, value-free process, and there are no purely empirical procedures for arriving at criteria on which to base performance evaluations.

Selecting Indicators

Performance assessment requires that evidence be collected on which evaluations can be based. Indicators refer to the type of evidence employed. Donabedian (32) has usefully distinguished among three classes of indicators: structural, process, and outcome measures.

Structural Measures. Structural indicators are based on assessments of organizational features or participants' characteristics that are presumed to have an impact on organizational performance. They measure an organization's potential or capacity for effective work. Examples of such measures for hospitals would be the number and types of specialized equipment, such as CT scanners, the presence of an intensive-care unit, and the proportion of the medical staff that is board-certified. Most accreditation and certification reviews place great emphasis on structural measures of performance.

Process Measures. Process measures are based on evidence relating to the performer's activities in carrying on work. It is possible to assess either performance quality or quantity: either how accurately or how rapidly the procedures are performed. A second order of process measures frequently utilized in medical care settings is not focused directly on the quality of the work performed but on activities performed to improve or review quality, such as autopsy rates. Process measures also exist to assess the nonclinical aspects of performance. Examples in the financial area include liquidity ratios, such as the ratio of current assets to current liability, and activity ratios, such as the ratio of total operating revenue to total assets (33).

Outcome Measures. Outcome measures are based on evidence gathered from the objects on which the work is performed. Assessments are made to determine whether changes have occurred in their characteristics that can be attributed to the work performed upon them. Thus, for medical care systems, changes in the patient's health status are assessed; and for training institutions, changes in the student's knowledge or skills or attitudes may be examined. In the financial area, outcome might be measured by the operating margin (ratio of operating income to operating revenue) or the return on assets (33). Some examples of structure, process, and outcome measures in the financial, quality of care, and personnel areas are presented in Table 12.1.

It is important to recognize that each of these types of indicators is imperfect— subject to bias and misinterpretation. Process measures focus on energy and effort expended but neglect effects achieved. Moreover, measures based on process alone can only compare performance values with some specified standard; they cannot themselves assess the appropriateness of the standards employed. If process measures are once removed from effects, then structural indicators are twice removed, since they do not

TABLE 12.1. Examples of Selected Performance Measures in Selected Areas

	Financial Performance	Quality-of-Care Performance	Personnel Recruitment and Retention
Structure	Use of accrual accounting Education and qualifications of financial and accounting staff Existence of an organization-wide cost-containment committee Presence of a program planning and budgeting system	Percentage of board-certified active staff physicians JCAH accreditation Number of residency approvals	Education and qualifications of personnel office staff Existence of an up-to-date wage and salary administration system Existence of a position control system
Process	Examination of budget variances Ratio of current assets to current liabilities Ratio of net accounts receivable to average daily operating revenue	Medication error rates Postsurgical infection rates Percentage of indicated procedures performed for specific diagnoses	Quality of education and training programs Job satisfaction survey assessments Organization climate assessment
Outcome	Ratio of operating income to operating revenue Ratio of long-term debt to fixed assets Ratio of operating income plus interest to total assets Market share	Standardized case-severity adjusted mortality rates Standardized case-severity adjusted morbidity rates	Employee turnover Employee absenteeism Cost per applicant recruited

assess work performed or effort expended but only the organization's capacity for work. Presumed competencies may in practice turn out to be ineffectual, and existing capacities may on specific occasions be unemployed or underemployed. Outcome measures have the advantage of focusing attention on changes produced and results achieved. Their drawbacks are that they do not in themselves provide evidence that can connect observed outcomes to the effects of performance. Particularly in arenas such as medical care, it is common for poor outcomes to occur in spite of superior performance, and vice versa: causal factors that are beyond the control of the performer are at work. And at a more general organizational level, a high proportion of good outcomes—patient recoveries, student achievements, profitability—may be more a function of selection procedures than of transformation powers.

Associations are likely to exist between these classes of indicators and broadly defined categories of constituencies in organizations (8). It is expected that administrators and managers will prefer to employ structural measures of effectiveness, since these are the types of indicators over which they have most control. Similarly, performers are likely to emphasize process measures, because these values are more under their control. By contrast, clients and representatives of the various external publics may be expected to focus attention on outcomes; never mind capacity or effort, what results were actually achieved? Patients, for example, are much more likely to be concerned about remission of symptoms and restoration of function than about the technical correctness of the procedures employed or the formal qualifications of personnel. Managers are well advised to take account of the limitations of each class of performance indicator as well as to understand the proclivities of the various constituency groups—including their own—that has a stake in the functioning of their organization. Only such awareness will enable them to correct for these biases and take into account the conflicting interests of the several parties involved.

Comparing Performances to Standards

Comparing observed performance values with established standards is also seldom a simple mechanical process, but one requiring experience and judgment. It is to accommodate these skills that the appraisal function is typically assigned to a supervisor—a person selected on the basis of seniority or merit and located close to the work site. Experience and proximity allow these individuals to detect nuances in performers' activities and to take into account special circumstances that affect performance values and their associated outcomes. Many of the complaints and problems associated with supervisor–worker relations may be attributed to disagreements over performance appraisal and may signify both the complexities and the sensitivities associated with this process.

Reactivity

All attempts to evaluate a performance may be expected to have effects on that performance. The setting of standards, the selection of indicators, the sampling of performance, and the comparison of performances with standards all affect the performance itself. The primary purpose of any evaluation system is to exert influence on the performances of participants—if not the performance immediately under review, then subsequent ones. But equally important and less obvious are the unintended effects of performance evaluation. These biasing or diverting effects occur because it is often difficult or overly costly to devise evaluation systems and indicators that accurately reflect the complexity of desired outcomes to which the performance is addressed. Thus although examinations are developed to test learning, their repeated use is likely to influence what is taught or, more importantly, what is learned. And if diagnostic thoroughness is signified by the number of laboratory tests ordered, then the number of tests ordered may far exceed the number required by the patient's medical condition. In particular, hard measures—measures that are specific, capable of being quantified, and easy to observe—tend to drive out soft measures.

Considering all of these conceptual and measurement problems, it is not difficult to understand why Haberstroh (34), in a review of performance evaluation systems in organizations, draws two major conclusions: "First, performance reporting is omnipresent and necessarily so. Second, almost every instance of performance reporting has something wrong with it." Evaluation systems are the principal devices managers have for attempting to influence and improve the performance of their organizations. It is important for managers to become aware of the limitations of any particular system.

MANAGING FOR HIGH PERFORMANCE IN HEALTH CARE ORGANIZATIONS

The problems in conceptualizing and measuring performance, which occur in all organizations, are particularly challenging for health care organizations. This is because, as noted in Chapter 1, "the product" of health care organizations is frequently difficult to define and measure. In addition, many of the activities that influence the performance of health care organizations are not directly controllable by managers but, rather, are under the direction of physicians and other health care professionals. Add to this the environmental forces of inflation, regulation, competition, new technology, and changing consumer preferences and it's no wonder that some have referred to the health care executive's job as attempting to steer a wayward bus down a hill in which physicians control the brakes and other groups (trustees, third party payers, etc.) have their foot on the accelerator. Thus it is tempting to wave the white flag and conclude that there is relatively little that managers can do to define, measure, or influence performance. Nothing could be further from the truth.

It is precisely because the task of defining, measuring, and influencing performance is so difficult that management can play a key role. As discussed in Chapter 4, defining the organization's core values and reasons for being and translating these into operational reality lies at the heart of transformational leadership. Transformational leaders think about performance in terms of controllable and noncontrollable factors and constantly work to convert uncontrollable factors into factors that can be controlled. Figure 12.2 provides a continuum of such factors.

As shown, events such as natural disasters, international relations, and national economic policy are relatively uncontrollable by health care executives. In contrast, issues concerning the organization's mission/culture, labor mix, standards and policies, and organization design are, for the most part, directly controllable by executives. In between are factors involving intermediate degrees of control. These include issues of system consolidation, growth, and third-party payment trends on the one hand, and external regulation, competition, and new technological developments on the other. A major point of Figure 12.2 is that more effective managers not only focus on variables on the

Relatively uncontrollable →————————————→ Relatively controllable

Natural disasters
International relations
National economic policy (e.g., inflation, unemployment)
Population demographics (e.g., changing age mix of the population)
Stock market

External regulation and accreditation
New technological developments
Competition
Physician surplus
New legal developments
Societal preferences and tastes

Health care system
Consolidation
System growth
Organization size
Ownership status
Third-party payment trends
Medical staff organization and characteristics

Organization's mission/culture
Labor mix
Wage and salary administration
Human resource development
Capital investment strategy
Financial goals
New product/new market development
Marketing plans
Vertical and horizontal integration (acquisitions, alternative delivery system development)
Patient care policies and practices
Problem—identification and management
Organization design (coordination, centralization of decision making, etc.)
Conflict management practices

Figure 12.2. A continuum of factors that can be controlled by managers.

far right-hand side of the page that are most directly controllable, but also attempt to extend their influence over factors moving to the left, involving health industry trends and external regulatory, competitive, technological, and legal forces. They do this by refusing to accept these forces as givens and instead viewing them as opportunities for expanding their organization's mission and potential effectiveness. For example, many health care companies have developed, on their own or in joint ventures with insurance companies, the ability to provide health insurance services and other third-party financing which can channel more patients into their delivery system. Many hospitals have intentionally changed their size by reducing their inpatient bed capacity and converting formerly unused capacity to long-term care beds or outpatient programs. Other organizations have gained control over new technological developments through linkages with medical schools and research centers and through investment in biomedical and biological product companies. In similar fashion, these organizations are proactive in shaping consumer preferences and tastes through market research and new product development strategies rather than merely reacting to changes in consumer preferences. Indeed, some of the international health care companies are increasingly involved in foreign relations and national economic policy development because of the immediacy of these issues to their overseas health care interests. These attempts to broaden the influence base involve macropolitical strategies of networking, coalition-building, and joint venturing (see Chapters 7 and 10 for related discussions). They involve actively managing the environment and not merely managing one's own organization. As expressed by the executive of one multihospital system: "We work hard to create problems for others. Others don't create problems for us."

Thinking of effectiveness, in part, as a process that involves creating problems for others recognizes that effectiveness is as much a *process* as an end in itself. It is the way in which an organization relates itself to its various internal and external stakeholders or constituent groups (26, 35). Internal stakeholders include employees, physicians, and boards of directors. External stakeholders include suppliers, regulatory groups, competitors, third-party payers, and community groups. Some constituents, such as patients, serve as both internal and external stakeholders. Physicians, while viewed primarily as internal stakeholders, can also be considered as external stakeholders, depending on the degree to which particular physicians identify with a given health care organization. These stakeholders have different desires and needs to be met by the organization. They want the organization to "score points" on different things. They have varying expectations and criteria for effectiveness. Most employees want meaningful work, opportunity for growth, and a reasonable degree of job security. Physicians want up-to-date technology and support services and an environment in which they are free to practice medicine as they were trained. Third-party payers expect care to be provided in the most cost/ effective manner possible. Patients will have varying expectations depending on the severity of their illness, their education, and their financial resources. Regulators will be concerned with the organization's ability to contain costs. Suppliers of capital will focus on the institution's "bottom line." Given this disparate set of demands and expectations, it is not possible for a given organization to be seen as equally effective by all of its stakeholders or constituent groups at a given point in time. Priorities must be set and tradeoffs must be made. Nonetheless, all stakeholders would agree that the organization needs to obtain necessary resources (people, money, legitimacy) for its continued existence; to coordinate, manage, and integrate these resources in providing desired services and products; and to achieve a reasonable degree of goal attainment in those areas that are deemed most important. Thus the discussion and guidelines that follow are organized around the issues of resource acquisition, integration and system maintenance, and goal attainment.

RESOURCE ACQUISITION

The way in which hospitals and other health care organizations obtain resources has changed radically in the past 10 years. Philanthropy has declined to the point where it is no longer a major source of support and much greater emphasis is given to the debt and, for investor-owned organizations, equity markets. As a result, it has become increasingly important for health care organizations to have positive operating margins and strong balance sheets regardless of whether they are investor owned or not-for-profit. In addition, with more restrictive inpatient prospective payment policies, hospitals need to develop new revenue sources involving diversification into ambulatory surgery, satellite clinics, home health care, diagnostic imaging, ambulatory alcoholism and psychiatric care, health promotion, sports medicine, and related ventures (36). At the same time, mergers, consolidations, affiliations, and opportunities to join multihospital systems have enabled many hospitals to obtain resources otherwise not available (37).

The forces listed above have meant a different role for the institution's board of directors in the resource acquisition process. Previously, effective hospitals selected board members for their ability to provide and maintain rapport with community groups as a linkage to philanthrophic sources (38); today's boards require greater experience and expertise in marketing, finance, risk taking, and entrepreneurship. There remain important links to the external environment, but the linkage is now based on expertise and experience in helping hospitals make the transition from acute-care inpatient institutions to more diversified health care organizations operating in more competitive markets. The emphasis shifts from being the "stewards of the hospital's assets" to an active builder of a more diversified resource base. This is a particular challenge for rural, inner-city, public (39), and many university teaching hospitals (40), each of which faces different resource acquisition issues owing to low occupancy and financial instability (e.g., many rural hospitals), a high percentage of Medicaid and medically indigent patients (e.g., many inner-city and public hospitals), and diminished revenues from state governments coupled with increased competition from surrounding community hospitals (e.g., many state medical school affiliated teaching hospitals).

The issue of resource acquisition is particularly important in competitive environments. Studies indicate that in such environments hospitals with boards that are more entrepreneurially oriented tend to be more successful in obtaining needed resources (money, patients, and staff) than boards that are not so oriented (41). It has also been shown that in any environment, whether competitive or noncompetitive, effectiveness in obtaining resources is increased when there is greater *congruence* of interests between the CEO and the board chairperson (41).

A second important resource-acquisition issue involves the ability to recruit and retain physicians, nurses, and related professional staff, which, in turn, can help attract patients. The existing physician surplus enables hospitals, HMOs, and other health care organizations to have greater choice and leverage in physician recruitment. But these organizations need to develop carefully focused strategies to recruit the *best* physicians in specific specialties in order to develop and sustain a long-run competitive advantage. A hospital that recruits an outstanding cardiologist may have an immediate edge over a competitor, but this advantage is likely to be short lived. As a second step, the hospital may need to further differentiate its product; perhaps by adding specialists in electro-physiology and angioplasty. This, too, will be met by a competitive response such that the focal hospital will have to develop still further ways of sustaining its competitive edge. Thus resource acquisition will need to be more carefully targeted than in the past to conform with specialized market niches which receive high priority in the organization's overall strategic plan (see Chapter 13).

Failure of a given organization to attract sufficient resources on its own may result in corporate reorganization, consolidation, merger, affiliation membership, or multi-hospital system membership. With the exception of internal corporate reorganization, all of these represent to varying degrees a networking strategy designed to attract capital, strengthen political clout, and create economies of scale. Examples include hospitals that create for-profit subsidiary corporations and foundations designed to attract capital and additional revenue sources plus better protect market assets; teaching hospitals that have consolidated and share certain common programs and resources; hospitals in geographic proximity that have merged to better utilize assets; other hospitals that have affiliated with such organizations as the Voluntary Hospitals of America (VHA) to gain group-purchasing discounts and access to new capital opportunities; and hospitals that have been acquired by systems to gain greater management expertise and the financial and political support which systems can offer. Failure of a given organization to suc-cessfully negotiate such relationships may result in closure. In the past, hospital closures appeared to have been primarily associated with a combination of hostile environmental forces (e.g., poor third-party reimbursement and a high medically indigent population) and poor management practices, particularly in regard to financial management and staffing (42). In the future, closures will be due increasingly to the inability of executives to effectively network relationships that will give them a broader resource base.

The main guidelines that follow from this discussion are highlighted below.

MANAGERIAL GUIDELINES

1. Boards of directors need to adopt more corporate forms of organization with emphasis given to strategic planning, entrepreneurial, and risk-taking activities.
2. Linkages must be formed with new types of stakeholders, including employers, business coalitions, and special-interest consumer groups.
3. Executives need to make more use of macropolitical strategies involving the negotiation of network relationships which will form larger resource pools.
4. The effective health care organization needs to become more proactive in managing its environment in order to compete more effectively.
5. The organization needs to become adept at developing specialized market niches and initiating product/services for targeted market segments where sufficient resources exist to gain a distinctive long-run competitive advantage.
6. In order to be effective in the long run, organizations need to learn how to continuously differentiate their product/service relative to competitors.

Some measures of the effectiveness of organizations to acquire resources are summarized in Table 12.2.

TABLE 12.2. Resource Acquisition Measures

Bond Ratings—Moody's, Standard and Poors

Ability to raise capital (debt and equity markets)

Percent growth in federal, state, and local grant support for teaching and research

Growth of shared-service arrangements

Growth of affiliation and network arrangements

Percent growth in active staff physicians

Percent desired physicians attracted to staff

Percent desired RNs and other health professionals attracted to staff

INTEGRATION AND SYSTEM MAINTENANCE

Once necessary resources are obtained, a key factor in an organization's success is its ability to marshall resources to achieve goals. This involves issues of motivation (see Chapter 3), leadership (see Chapter 4), communication and coordination (Chapter 7), and conflict resolution (Chapter 9). It is also important to recognize that in human service fields such as health care, job satisfaction and personal and professional growth are important outcomes and effectiveness indicators in their own right.

A number of studies have examined these issues (43–50). Because of the high percentage of professionals involved, and their diversity, it is particularly important that health care executives assess the varying professional needs of each group. Physicians, in particular, have high need for achievement and autonomy. Other groups have less highly developed claims to autonomy, but desire organizational settings in which they can practice their full range of professional skills. Job autonomy, for example, is associated with less conflict, increased job satisfaction, and greater client satisfaction (45).

Almost all professionals have high standards of excellence and therefore organizations and managers that emphasize high performance expectations and provide the necessary support for obtaining excellence are likely to be more effective (47). Achieving such standards is a function of both specification of rules and procedures (43, 50) as well as informal communication and use of ad hoc task forces which involve relevant groups (43). Rules and procedures help to define and handle many problems, but because of the complexity and uncertainty of much professional work, informal and ad hoc mechanisms must also be used to deal with nonroutine problems. Examples include emergency cases, patients with multiple diagnoses, elderly patients with chronic-care needs that cut across many specialties and even organizations, and patients with illnesses involving complicated moral, legal, and economic/ethical issues.

Involving professionals in the development of standards, norms, rules, policies, and practices is essential. Studies indicate that such involvement is associated with greater professional satisfaction and can play an important role in staff retention (46, 48). Increasingly, professionals want to be involved, not only in deciding what will have an immediate impact on their work, but also in some of the larger organizational issues that may affect their future practice. Examples include the organization's relationship with third-party payers, regulators, and competitors. Thus there exists growing physician involvement in management and governance issues (51–53) and new forms of joint venture relationships (also see Chapter 9).

In sum, existing studies suggest that coordinated professional work and system in-

TABLE 12.3. Integration and System Maintenance Measures

Turnover

Absenteeism

Work stoppages

Organization climate and culture surveys (with particular attention given to communication, coordination, decision-making, and conflict-management issues)

Grievances

Promotion opportunities

Salary and fringe-benefit comparison with competitors

tegration is facilitated by high standards and clear expectations, specified rules and procedures combined with job autonomy, flexibility in coordinating work, and a high degree of professional involvement in decision making. These practices place a premium on the manager's interpersonal, communication and coordination (see Chapter 7), and organization design skills (see Chapter 9). As will be seen, they also appear to be related to goal attainment. Some specific managerial guidelines are highlighted below and specific measures of integration and system maintenance are summarized in Table 12.3.

MANAGERIAL GUIDELINES

1. Professionals working in health care organizations are largely self-motivated. Thus setting high standards consistent with professional norms of excellence promotes effectiveness.

2. Any organization requires rules and procedures. In health care organizations the rules and procedures must be based as much on professional needs, values, and aspirations as on the needs, values, and aspirations of the organization.

3. The professional's need for autonomy must be kept paramount in all organization design decisions.

4. The special needs of professional work demand that flexible mechanisms be used to coordinate such activity.

5. Professionals want to participate in decisions that will affect the professional nature of their work.

6. Increasingly, professionals want to participate in larger issues that will affect the nature of their work in years to come.

GOAL ATTAINMENT

Attempting to measure an organization's performance by the degree to which it has achieved its goals is a complex task. As previously noted, goals are often stated in vague terms, are not always easily measured, and vary at different points in time and in the degree in which they are shared by organizational members. In addition, the goals an organization has for itself may not be the same as those held by outside stakeholders and society at large. Nonetheless, all organizations must achieve some degree of goal attainment to maintain their legitimacy, their ability to attain resources, and to survive over time. Due to external pressures, health care organizations have given increased attention to goals involving productivity, efficiency, and effectiveness. The primary findings related to these issues are summarized below.

Productivity and Efficiency

As noted, productivity is defined as the ratio of outputs to inputs and efficiency as the cost per unit of output. Given cost-containment pressures, all health care organizations face the challenge of becoming more productive and efficient. Existing studies suggest that the factors associated with increased productivity and efficiency include: (1) setting high standards and goals (54, 55), (2) providing information and feedback (56), (3) interdepartmental coordination and resource sharing (54, 57), (4) compensation systems (58, 59), (5) physician involvement in decision making and governance (51, 54), (6) efficient staffing and concentration of work activity (54, 60–63), (7) active governing boards that deal with environmental pressures (40), and (8) ownership (64–66). Setting high standards for cost containment motivates organizational members, particularly when the compensation systems reinforce attainment of the productivity and efficiency standards. Productivity-based compensation incentives include sharing cost savings resulting from employee suggestions as well as year-end bonuses based on staying within budgets or generating net profits beyond expectations.

Obtaining useful information and feedback is critical to the manager's ability to take corrective action. Most health care organizations have invested heavily in improved management information systems. These systems enable the organization to assess the true cost and integrate financial and accounting data with clinical data on a diagnosis-by-diagnosis basis. This has allowed organizations to assess the productivity, efficiency, and profitability of specific service lines and, therefore, compete more effectively.

Most health care organizations are complex and interdependent and therefore require considerable coordination across specialized departments and functions. These include both scheduled and unscheduled meetings. In addition, many health care organizations have found economies in learning to share resources across departments and functions, including shared staffing arrangements and in some cases consolidation of departments. Examples include hospitals that have combined dietary, housekeeping, and maintenance departments or physical, occupational, and recreational therapy departments.

Performance-based compensation systems have been noted above (67). In addition, placing a greater number of physicians on salaried arrangements appears to be associated with lower costs (58). Salaried arrangements increase both the incentives for physicians to reduce costs and their involvement in the well being of the organization as a whole. At the same time, it may be necessary to supplement physician salary arrangements with some type of risk/reward relationship involving incentives for increasing productivity and revenues by containing costs. Such arrangements are often found in HMOs (59).

Professional involvement in decision making and governance provides management with important input to make difficult tradeoff decisions involving productivity, cost containment, access, and quality of care. In addition, involving such key professionals helps pave the way for smoother implementation of important decisions given that physicians, nurses, and other health professionals are frequently involved in implementing those decisions.

Paying close attention to staffing ratios and how work is organized has an obvious bearing on productivity and efficiency issues. Among other things, studies indicate that the greater the degree to which surgical work is concentrated among a smaller number of surgeons, the lower the cost (58, 59) and the length of stay (60).

Governing boards that are aware of the environmental pressures for cost containment are better able to hold management accountable for improving productivity and efficiency. This is particularly true when the board needs to make strategic decisions involving possible tradeoffs between productivity and efficiency on the one hand and access to services and quality on the other.

A number of studies have indicated that prior to the introduction of Medicare prospective payment in late 1983, investor-owned hospitals on average were somewhat more costly than voluntary hospitals (64–66). This is primarily due to higher mark-up of prices, newer physical plants, and to some extent the cost associated with corporate office overhead. However, investor-owned hospitals tend to be more productive in using fewer FTE personnel per unit of output. More recent work suggests that productivity and efficiency differences are due less to ownership form per se and more to the underlying strategies pursued by the organizations involved as well as the type of management practices used (68).

The discussion above and related work suggest the following managerial guidelines for improving productivity and efficiency (69).

MANAGERIAL GUIDELINES

1. Develop accurate, timely, and useful management information systems. Remember that all data is not useful information.
2. Concentrate productivity improvement programs in large departments where big payoffs will result.
3. Consider streamlining and consolidating departments and functions.
4. Develop scheduling systems consistent with professional values. Focus on areas where quality can be maintained or even enhanced through better scheduling of staff and support resources.
5. Cross-train staff to gain greater flexibility.
6. Develop productivity-based incentives based on work activities under the control of organizational members.
7. Set high standards by establishing "best practices" in one's own organization as well as using comparisons from competitors and industry leaders.
8. Involve organizational members, particularly professionals, in the development, implementation, and monitoring of productivity/efficiency initiatives.
9. Focus energy on working smarter, not necessarily harder.

Some specific measures of productivity, efficiency, and overall financial viability are shown in Table 12.4.

Effectiveness

Effectiveness is defined as attainment of the organization's major goals. To the extent that organizations succeed in being productive and efficient, they may be said to be effective in regard to those goals. However, productivity and efficiency for most orga-

TABLE 12.4. Productivity, Efficiency, and Financial Viability Measures

Productivity

Patient days per FTE
Admissions per FTE
Ancillary service units per FTE
Physician visits per FTE

Efficiency

Cost per patient
Cost per admission
Cost per ancillary unit of output
Cost per physician visit

Financial Viability

Profit margin
Cash flow ratios
Current assets/current liabilities
Days in accounts receivable
Market share
Debt/equity ratio
Bond ratings
Return on assets or net equity

---

nizations are means to the attainment of more outcome-oriented financial and service objectives. While financial viability measures are noted in Table 12.4, an important dimension of effectiveness for health care organizations is the quality of services delivered. This is because the price/quality relationship is becoming increasingly important to purchasers of health care services. Because there are limits to the ability to contain costs and vary prices, health care organizations increasingly have to differentiate themselves based on the quality of care delivered.

Measuring quality is difficult. Donabedian (32) defined the basic parameters in terms of structure, process, and outcome measures. With respect to the quality of medical care, structure involves assessing whether facilities, equipment, staff qualifications, and related variables meet established standards. The process approach involves assessing whether what is done to the patient in regard to diagnosis and treatment meets acceptable professional standards. Outcomes refer to the functional health status of the patient. The relationships among structure, process, and outcome measures are complicated. Much work remains to be done to identify those structural and process criteria that are most strongly associated with positive outcomes of care. The structural and process measures are important because they are factors over which health care executives and professionals have the most control. Brook and Lohr (70) stated the challenge as follows: "What is needed might be characterized as an epidemiology of effectiveness: some way of routinely collecting information that describes the outcomes of tests, procedures, drugs, and other services as they are customarily used in everyday practice" (p. 713).

It is also important to distinguish "objective" measures of quality from people's perceptions. For example, a given home health agency may have the highest possible accreditation rating, and best patient functional health status outcomes ("objective" measures), but be perceived by the community as relatively low quality, perhaps owing to problems of convenience and access to services or an occasional "war story" of poor care. In the same vein, it is important to recognize that the public's perception of quality may differ from those of physicians and caregivers. For example, the public may give greater weight to access, convenience, comfort, and interpersonal relationships while the professional caregiver places greater emphasis on technical skill. In part, this is due to the public's relative inability to evaluate technical expertise. As a result, they use other criteria as proxy measures or *assume technical quality* as a given and then make choices based on the nontechnical criteria discussed above. Despite the difficulties involved, a number of studies have shed some light on the relationship between managerial/ organizational practices and various measures of quality. These studies suggest that the following factor's are generally associated with higher quality of care: *(1)* quality of professional staff (43, 71, 72), *(2)* high standards (73–75), *(3)* concentrated output (60, 74, 76–78), *(4)* more formally organized professional staffs with well-defined coordination and conflict management processes (43, 50, 78, 79), *(5)* participative organization cultures emphasizing team approaches (56, 78, 80–82), *(6)* timely and accurate performance feedback (56, 83, 84), and *(7)* active management of environmental forces (40, 85). These findings are based on a study of community hospitals, teaching hospitals, psychiatric hospitals, free-standing hospitals as well as those belonging to systems, emergency rooms, and health maintenance organizations. There is no evidence to date suggesting that ownership form itself (for example investor-owned vs. not-for-profit) is related to differences in quality of care (64, 86, 87).

In regard to the quality of professional staff, key factors are recruitment, retention, and having people work within their professional abilities (72, 73). This involves concentrating the work of professionals in such a fashion that greater experience produces better patient-care outcomes over time. As noted, several studies have found higher volume of patients treated by both institutions and individual physicians to be associated with more positive patient-care outcomes (60, 76–78).

Setting high standards is compatible with professional values. A key factor involves strict admission requirements (73) and exerting strong control in enforcing standards (74, 75). More tightly organized professional staffs assist in this process by providing regular forums for problem management and conflict resolution (78, 79).

A participative organizational culture emphasizing team approaches is particularly important when the environment is changing rapidly (81). An ongoing team approach allows ideas to be communicated and discussed quickly by the professionals that will be most affected by the changes involved. A team approach also enhances the ability of executives to influence decisions (74). Overall, a participative culture helps to develop good work habits on the part of all involved and reinforces appropriate peer group pressure. Further, teams generally do a better job of solving complex problems than individuals (81).

Timely and accurate feedback raises the visibility of behavior in the organization such that accountability requirements are met and deviation from performance standards is assessed (56, 83, 84). A good clinical/financial management information system enables corrective action to be taken more quickly.

Finally, more active management of the external environment enables the organization to educate external groups (e.g., licensing and accreditation bodies, regulatory groups, third-party payers) about quality objectives and practices and the associated challenges involved. For example, university teaching hospitals, which have established their own hospital-specific governing boards separate from the university governing board, have been better able to negotiate with relevant external groups and communicate their mission and objectives more clearly (40).

Given what is known to date, the following managerial guidelines may be offered for maintaining and improving quality of care.

MANAGERIAL GUIDELINES

1. Establish high standards that appeal to professional standards. Link professional values and goals to those of the organization.
2. Develop systems that provide relevant, timely, and accurate information for purposes of taking corrective action in establishing even higher standards.
3. Develop a participative organizational culture built around teams that encourages input from professionals at all levels of the organization.
4. Develop reward systems that reinforce participation and high performance.
5. Develop organizational structures that promote communication, coordination, and conflict management.
6. Design work such that it makes the best use of professional's experience and expertise.
7. Actively manage the external environment to recruit the best available talent, to influence stakeholders that are concerned with quality, and to look for opportunities to improve quality.

Some examples of quality-of-care measures are presented in Table 12.5.

MANAGING TRADEOFFS

Many observers believe that there are inherent tradeoffs between efficiency and effectiveness; between containing costs and providing high-quality care. It is felt that attempts to become more efficient and productive will be made at the expense of quality. For

TABLE 12.5. Goal Attainment—Quality of Care Measures

Structure

JCAH accreditation
Staffing ratios
Staff qualifications
Compliance with licensure bodies

Process

Compliance with professionally defined standards of care
Compliance with defined treatment protocals
Medication errors
Critical incident reports

Outcomes

Severity adjusted disease-specific mortality rates
Severity adjusted disease-specific functional health status
Patient satisfaction

example, patients may be discharged too soon; they may receive fewer services; the quality of the services they receive may be reduced; and hospitals may not keep up with the latest technology advances to provide state-of-the-art care. All of these behaviors may indeed erode the quality of care provided as perceived by one group or another.

But a contrasting view may also be taken. Specifically, it is possible that attempts to become more productive and efficient may be associated with *improvements* in quality. For example, productivity improvements that reduce length of stay may facilitate patient discharge to more appropriate outpatient settings or home environments, which may facilitate the healing process and reduce patients' susceptibility to hospital-acquired infections and illnesses. Fewer tests and procedures reduces the risk of possible side effects and mistakes. It also requires that caregivers be better diagnosticians and provide more focused treatment. Given the lack of evidence supporting strong relationships between process and outcomes of care, it is uncertain how changes in the process of care may effect outcomes; although it is recognized that there are thresholds beyond which outcomes may not improve and may, indeed, even deteriorate. Reductions in the quality of inputs involving patient-care amenities may reduce patient satisfaction but are not likely to affect mortality or functional health status measures. Finally, the fact that not all hospitals will be able to have state-of-the-art technology may actually improve quality by channeling patients to selected high-tech hospitals where more qualified professionals exist to use the technology appropriately and where sufficient volume of cases exist to promote better patient outcomes (76–78).

Which of the scenarios described above is most likely to occur depends on a number of key variables. It would appear that the greatest potential for diminished quality exists in health care organizations that are financially stressed, serve a relatively high percentage of uninsured patients, operate in highly competitive markets, have difficulty recruiting highly qualified staff, and serve a patient population in which there is inadequate home and social support networks.

Existing studies, for the most part, suggest no tradeoffs between efficiency and effectiveness; in fact, cost containment appears to be associated with higher quality of care (56, 57, 88–93). The common thread underlying these results is effective management. In brief, these organizations have developed management and organization practices involving several of the guidelines discussed in this chapter. For example, several Rochester area hospitals identified patients who could be tube-fed rather than IV-fed. This resulted in a significant cost reduction while improving patient treatment (92). A study of the nursing home industry in New York State revealed that labor-intensive aspects of care involving the quality of nursing and rehabilitation services did not increase costs, perhaps because of careful screening of nurses (which reduces turnover), better staff training, and better coordination (93). However, capital-intensive aspects of patient-care quality were associated with higher costs, which is consistent with some hospital studies as well (91, 94).

Existing knowledge regarding the tradeoff issue must be viewed with caution. First, it is important to note that almost all of the studies have been done prior to the widespread introduction of Medicare prospective payment and related incentive reimbursement arrangements. Thus health organizations were not feeling the pressure to contain cost to the degree they are today. Second, all the studies have been cross-sectional at a single point in time, and thus have not been able to assess the issue of whether a strategy to cut costs at time T_1 actually results in a change in quality at time T_2. Third, all studies have struggled with the problem of developing valid measures of quality which adequately take into account the case-mix severity of patients. While great strides have been made, considerably more work needs to be done. Finally, it is important to remember that high cost does not necessarily mean inefficient management, but may simply reflect management's desire to provide more amenities to patients and staff, resulting in higher patient and staff satisfaction. More recently, however, the margins for such behavior are being reduced.

It is clear that the tradeoff issue will not go away. It places health care managers squarely in the center of the tension between those who view health care primarily as an economic good and those who view it primarily as a social good. We end the chapter by considering future management and organizational practices that appear to be associated with truly high-performing health care organizations. These are organizations that recognize the inherent tensions involved and see them as opportunities for greater achievement. They are high performing in the sense of enjoying outstanding reputations in their communities for high-quality cost-effective patient care, financial integrity, and innovative approaches to service delivery.

MANAGING FOR HIGH PERFORMANCE IN THE 1990s

High-performing health care organizations are both aware and able to act on the basis of their awareness. Truly high-performing health care organizations have both the ability and willingness to be outstanding (55). Some organizations have the desire, but not all of the ability required. They require additional talent and staff development to move out of the ranks of the mediocre. Other organizations have the ability but lack the willingness. They lack strategic vision of what they can become. They are underachievers. Still others lack both the willingness and ability. Without a radical transformation, their chances of survival are minimal.

A synthesis of existing research and observations suggest 10 characteristics of high-performing health care organizations. Some of these are better documented than others. Nonetheless, they provide suggestive insights into what differentiates truly high-performing organizations from others.

MANAGERIAL GUIDELINES: CHARACTERISTICS OF HIGH-PERFORMING HEALTH CARE ORGANIZATIONS*

1. Stretch themselves—set high standards.
2. Maximize learning.
3. Take risks.
4. Exhibit transformational leadership.
5. Bias for action.
6. Create a chemistry among top management teams.
7. Manage uncertainty and ambiguity.
8. Are loosely coordinated.
9. Have a strong culture.
10. Are spiritual—provide meaning to themselves and others.

---

*Source: Adapted from S. M. Shortell, High performing health care organizations: Guidelines for the pursuit of excellence. *Hospital and Health Services Administration*, July–August 1985, pp. 7–35.

Of the 10 factors, the first four involving stretching, learning, risk taking, and leadership appear particularly important.

STRETCHING

High-performing health care organizations set very high standards. They are constantly raising the high-jump bar. An example is provided by one multihospital system in which it is corporate policy to "give people responsibilities which they can't possibly fulfill." This is intentionally done to stretch people to their fullest capability and is an integral part of the organization's human resource planning. To prevent burnout and undue frustration, the organization has a strong management development program tied to its strategic plan. In addition, "stretching" is a core value of the organization's culture and people's efforts are reinforced and supported.

In addition to setting high standards, stretching is facilitated by the development of overarching goals which can be bought into by individual divisions and departments. For example, one HMO's goal of emphasizing consumer convenience was translated into the appointment/reception department's objective to reduce appointment and visit waiting times to a minimum. Toward this end, they worked for months to develop a computerized appointment and scheduling system which significantly reduced both appointment and visit waiting times. The system enabled one staff member on each shift to "work" the reception area answering patient's questions, providing information, and playing with children. As one patient commented, "I've never seen such personal attention in a waiting room."

In their commitment to high standards and overarching goals, high-performing health care organizations emphasize management development. Executives are trained to resist always being the hero or orchestrator of solutions, and, instead, to use every problem-solving situation as an opportunity to develop one's subordinates (95). Performance appraisal and reward systems are established to reinforce such behavior. As subordinates' skill levels increase along with their confidence and commitment to the organization, the organization is rewarded by having available a richer array of management skills than any single leader can alone possess.

MAXIMIZING LEARNING

The winning health care organizations of the 1990s will be those that learn quickly, learn accurately, and have the ability to put their learning to use. They are both proactive (i.e., plan ahead) and enactive (learning by doing) in their approaches. They engage in wide searches, conduct experiments to facilitate learning, have market-driven information systems, and create redundancies that emphasize effectiveness over efficiency.

High-performing health care organizations search their environments for opportunities and hidden threats. This involves what Argyris calls "double loop" learning (96), which goes beyond existing organizational practices and policies to question the underlying causes of present behavior and to imagine future behaviors in response to changing environmental circumstances. An example is provided by a west coast hospital which recognized the need for an upgraded physician referral service. Instead of simply looking at examples in their immediate area, they set as their goal to learn about the best system in the country. Their search led to the discovery of a system in an eastern hospital which enabled patients who phoned in to communicate with a specific physician and lock in the appointment at the time of the call.

Because learning is a core value for high-performing health care organizations, they are continually conducting experiments. They will undertake new initiatives based not only on the likelihood of success, but on the amount of learning that can be derived. An HMO in the early 1980s experimented with providing coverage to retirees. It was not particularly successful at the time, but what was learned from the experience enabled the HMO to be among the first to successfully participate in a federally funded HMO-waiver experiment to provide care to Medicare beneficiaries. Another example is represented by the hospital that undertook a home health care program that failed, but from which so much was learned that 2 years later a joint venture with another organization enabled the hospital to be the market leader of home health services in its area.

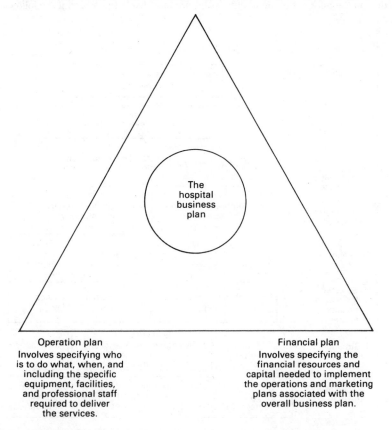

Marketing plan
Involves specifying particular products/services for specific market segments; packaging the product or service; determining the most appropriate distribution channels; establishing pricing policies; and determining the advertising and promotion policies.

The hospital business plan

Operation plan
Involves specifying who is to do what, when, and including the specific equipment, facilities, and professional staff required to deliver the services.

Financial plan
Involves specifying the financial resources and capital needed to implement the operations and marketing plans associated with the overall business plan.

Figure 12.3. The relationships among a hospital's business, marketing, financial, and operations plans. (Adapted from *Managing hospital marketing at AMI*, American Medical International, Beverly Hills, CA, June 1984. From work done by Carter, Achenbaum and Associates for AMI.)

Market-Driven Information Systems

As health care has become more price and consumer competitive, organizations need ways of linking information about consumer wants and needs with the fiscal and human resources of the organization designed to meet those demands and needs. Market-driven information systems must be based on the organization's overall strategic plan (Chapter 13) and associated market plans. Figure 12.3 shows the relationships among a hospital's overall business plan, marketing plan, financial plan, and operations plan. Figure 12.4 provides an example of the key components of a marketing plan and Figure 12.5 a summary of functional marketing strategies for each marketing function. Each of these suggests the underlying market, financial, and operational information required. As such data and information are collected and analyzed by staff specialists or selected consultants, it is most important that they also be analyzed and *used* by line managers. Marketing is essentially a line management function, not a staff function. Thus the information needs to be "pushed down" in the organization to the physicians, nurses, and other health professionals who are closest to patients and therefore can most readily act on the information.

In acting on the information, marketing plans are most likely to succeed if the following criteria are met (97):

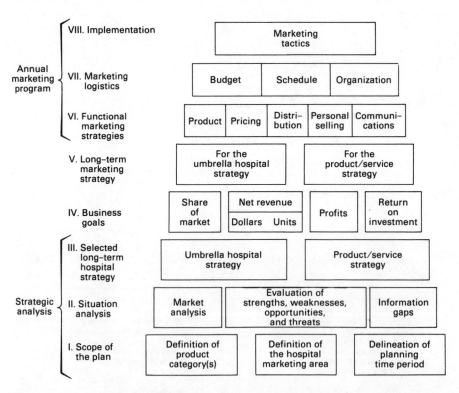

Figure 12.4. The building blocks of a hospital marketing plan. (From *Managing hospital marketing at AMI,* American Medical International, Beverly Hills, CA, June 1984. From work done by Carter, Achenbaum and Associates for AMI.)

For: _____
(Product/Service Strategy)

Marketing Function	*Marketing Strategy*
Product/Service	_____
	_____
	_____
Pricing	_____
	_____
	_____
Distribution	_____
	_____
	_____
Direct selling Industry relations	_____
	_____
	_____
Direct selling Physician relations	_____
	_____
	_____
Direct selling Community relations	_____
	_____
	_____
Indirect selling Advertising	_____
	_____
	_____
Indirect selling Publicity	_____
	_____

SOURCE: *Managing Hospital Marketing at AMI*, American Medical International, Beverly Hills, CA, June, 1984. From work done by Carter, Achenbaum and Associates for AMI.

Figure 12.5. Summary of functional marketing strategies. (From *Managing hospital marketing at AMI*, American Medical International, Beverly Hills, CA, June 1984. From work done by Carter, Achenbaum and Associates for AMI.)

1. The marketing plan is concerned with future behavior not the past. Incentives, reasons, and guides need to be offered for how and why people should behave now and in the future.
2. The plan should be based on enough relevant facts.
3. Top management should be actively involved in the planning process.
4. The plans must be complete. One cannot anticipate the future without a thorough situation analysis. One cannot set strategies without anticipating the future. One cannot establish relevant financial goals without establishing marketing strategies associated with those goals. All components are necessary.
5. Plans must be internally consistent. Goals, strategies, and tactics must be related to each other.
6. There must be adequate evaluation and feedback in the planning system. It is a dynamic process. Plans must be constantly updated and improved.

Redundancy—Effectiveness Over Efficiency

Existing analysis suggests that some amount of redundancy (i.e., inefficiency) appears to be associated with higher performance (98, 99). This is because redundancy facilitates learning, particularly when undertaking programs that are new and different from what the organization has done before. For example, in undertaking ambulatory-care joint ventures with physicians, successful hospitals were found to use both hospital and clinic personnel policies, purchasing policies, budgeting practices, and information systems. While not efficient, it enabled each hospital to learn more quickly about what systems worked best. In the long run, it was a more effective strategy than those that decided on a "one best way" approach that offered little opportunity for "learning by doing."

RISK TAKING

Nothing ventured, nothing gained. Analysis should not lead to paralysis. Sometimes, it is better to "ready, fire, aim." It is also better to be roughly right than precisely wrong! High-performing health care organizations believe in the above. Risk taking is one of the major ways these organizations learn. They are concerned only if they fail to learn from their mistakes.

Unlike studies in other industries (100) they do *not* necessarily "stick to their knitting"—that is, do things they know and do well. Instead, they recognize that the health care industry has undergone so much change that for organizations to operate as they have in the past begs mediocrity and failure. They recognize the need to develop new programs and services outside of their traditional areas of expertise and experience. They recognize the need to become something other than they have been. If they do not have the necessary expertise or experience, it can be purchased or developed, either internally or through networking with other organizations.

While recognizing the need to take risks, these organizations distinguish between prudent and foolish risk taking. They attempt to reduce uncertainty and maximize the probability of a positive outcome through careful analysis of their environment, their competition, their strengths and weaknesses, and the development of strategies that will enable them to sustain a long-run competitive advantage (see Chapter 13). They also involve a wide network of individuals (trustees, physicians, department directors) in the strategic planning/management process. This facilitates consideration of multiple perspectives, incorporation of additional knowledge and information, and, most importantly, support for projects that involve a high degree of risk. It also helps to instill a risk-taking culture, perhaps best captured by the words of Walter Wriston, ex-president of CitiCorps Bank in New York, who frequently told his employees: "When I make a mistake, the first thing I try to do is go back out and make an even bigger one. If you're not making mistakes, you're not learning."

TRANSFORMATIONAL LEADERSHIP

The effects of leadership are most pronounced in difficult times. In benign environments, most organizations do relatively well and there is relatively little performance differentiation among them. But in times of great change and uncertainty, truly outstanding organizations are revealed and a primary reason is often the presence of "transformational leadership" (101) (see Chapter 4). This involves spending a great deal of time on developing, communicating, and role-modeling the new strategic vision required to be successful. It involves showing how the organizational changes needed will help to promote the personal and professional growth of those involved. It involves assisting people in making career transitions. It involves paying attention to meanings and symbols. It involves helping people let go of the past, while showing new ways for success in the future.

The HCA executive mentioned in the mini-case study in Chapter 10 who spent the better part of a year talking personally with managers in local communities, explaining the need for structural changes, represents an example. Another example is provided by the CEO who spent nearly 2 years educating his medical staff about PPOs/HMOs and other alternative delivery systems. By carefully monitoring the timing and pacing of change, he was gradually able to get the staff to give up old practice patterns and become more comfortable with newer organizational arrangements for providing care. A third example is highlighted in the scenario below.

MINI-CASE

The chief operating officer of a 500-bed teaching hospital was about to attend a key meeting to close a 12-hospital joint group purchasing venture. Just before leaving for the meeting, she received a last minute phone call from a young physician on her staff. The physician indicated that he had some important things on his mind. Could she spend some time with him? Torn between the important meeting and the young physician's needs, the COO told the physician "Of course I have time. Let's discuss the situation right now." She then instructed her secretary to call the meeting site to let them know she would be late.

The physician wanted to discuss new compensation arrangements involving himself and several colleagues in the hospital-sponsored ambulatory care center. While the issue was clearly important to the hospital, it could have waited. When the COO was asked why she had not arranged a more suitable time to meet with the physician, she replied that it would have been the wrong thing to do. She said, "All of us are trying to develop better relationships with our physicians, become more psychologically and physically accessible to them."

It did not matter that this physician was not one of the established members of the medical staff or an office holder. In fact, the COO felt it was all the more important to spend time with him because he represented the leadership of the future. He was one of the younger physicians whom the hospital had targeted for a future leadership role and she considered this suddenly requested meeting an important opportunity to invest in him.

At the conclusion of the meeting, she let him know she was a half-hour late for a meeting to close a potentially multimillion dollar group purchasing venture involving hospitals throughout three states, but that she felt his concerns deserved immediate attention. She then suggested a series of subsequent meetings with him and his colleagues to discuss further the points raised. The hospital has subsequently developed several highly successful joint ventures with their physicians and has earned a reputation for maintaining an excellent relationship with its medical staff.

Under the circumstances, most managers would not have seen the physician. They would have indicated the meeting conflict, and arranged an appointment for another time. The COO in question saw it as a golden opportunity to express a key value of the organization—to be available and responsive to its medical staff. Putting the physician off would not have been exhibiting one of the hospital's key values. This is the essence of transformational leadership: making decisions according to values which have meaning for people. The group purchasing joint venture meeting, while important, was yesterday's business. The young physician was the hospital's future.*

---

*Adapted from S. M. Shortell, The high performing health care organization: Guidelines for the pursuit of excellence. *Hospital and Health Services Administration,* July–August, 1985, pp. 17–18.

While most examples of transformational leadership involve people at the top of the organization, outstanding organizations try to instill such qualities in key individuals throughout the organization. A culture develops in which members show a high degree of responsibility for each other and give and take meaning from each other.

SUMMARY

A number of guidelines for improving the performance of health care organizations have been offered throughout the chapter. It is also important to recognize that improving the performance of individual health care organizations is not the same as improving the overall ability of health care systems and communities to deliver cost-effective services. Nonetheless, as the delivery of health care becomes more consolidated both horizontally and vertically (see Chapters 10, 13, and 14) improvements in individual organizational performance are likely to have ripple effects. Conversely, failure to improve performance will have pervasive negative effects throughout the system. Thus a major challenge for health care managers in the future lies not only in improving individual organizational performance, but in improving the performance of networks, coalitions, affiliations, and systems. In the process, it will be important to remember that there is something wrong with every available measure of performance. Thus effective managers will use many indicators to assess individual, group, organizational, and network performance.

DISCUSSION QUESTIONS

1. Using a health care organization that you know well, provide three examples each of possible structural, process, and outcome measures of effectiveness. Would you expect these measures to be highly associated? Why or why not?

2. Consider a community hospital, a teaching hospital, and a health maintenance organization and for each list the major constituency groups (both internal and external). Indicate what kinds of effectiveness criteria each group would be most likely to promote.

3. It is often alleged that our health care organizations are largely unmanageable because physicians exert influence over approximately 80% of expenditures, particularly in hospitals. State whether you agree or disagree with this viewpoint and justify your opinion.

4. You are the manager of a 50-bed rural hospital with a 35% bed occupancy rate and a provisional 1-year accreditation by the Joint Commission on Accreditation of Hospitals. However, you have just received a $1-million grant from a private foundation to develop innovative strategies to improve the performance of rural hospitals. Drawing on the material in this chapter and other chapters of the text plus your own experience, develop a plan for improving your hospital's performance. How would you spend the money? In what areas or with what kinds of programs would you gain the greatest benefits? Be specific and justify your plan.

SUGGESTED READINGS

Bennett, A. C. *Improving management performance in health care institutions: A total systems approach.* Chicago: American Hospital Association, 1978.
Provides a practical, systematic approach to improving managerial performance. Chapter 7, on the making of an effective manager, is of particular interest. Each chapter concludes with a useful list of questions the manager should ask.

Cameron, K. S., & Whetton, D. A. (Eds.). *Organizational effectiveness: A comparison of multiple models.* New York: Academic Press, 1983.
A collection of essays in which social scientists from a variety of disciplinary perspectives are asked to address the same set of theoretical, research and practical issues as they comment on organizational effectiveness from their own vantage point.

Clifford, D. K., & Cavanaugh, R. E. *The winning performance: How America's high-growth midsize companies succeed.* Toronto: Bantam Books, 1985.
Provides insights on the structures and practices of highly successful midsize companies. Many of the findings contradict the conventional wisdom of how to succeed. Particularly strong on suggestions for fostering successful entrepreneurship.

Flood, A. B., & Scott, W. R. *Hospital structure and performance.* Baltimore, MD: Johns Hopkins University Press, 1987.
This book provides a comprehensive description of a program of research conducted by the Stanford Center for Health Care Research, Stanford University, examining the relation between the structural characteristics of hospitals and the quality and cost of care experienced by patients.

Kilman, R. H. *Beyond the quick fix.* San Francisco: Jossey-Bass, 1984.
Presents a systematic approach for improving organizational performance. Major components include paying attention to culture, developing management skills, team-building, integrating strategy and structure and developing appropriate reward systems.

Luft, H. *Health maintenance organizations: Dimensions of performance.* New York: John Wiley & Sons, 1981.
Provides a rigorous, systematic, and comprehensive assessment of the performance of HMOs. Chapter 14, on organizational and environmental factors in HMO performance, is of particular relevance.

Nash, M. *Managing organizational performance.* San Francisco: Jossey-Bass, 1983.
A practical guide to planning, measuring, and controlling performance at corporate department, group, and individual levels. Addresses performance issues for both for-profit and not-for-profit organizations.

Peters, T. J., & Waterman, R. H. *In search of excellence.* New York: 1982.
A study by McKinsey and Company consultants of some of America's leading companies. Identifies eight basic correlates of excellence including the willingness to experiment, to take risks, and to manage ambiguity and paradox.

Zammuto, R. F. *Assessing organizational effectiveness.* Albany: State University of New York, 1982.
An interesting attempt to devise a more comprehensive schema for conceptualizing the effectiveness of organizations. Drawing heavily on open-systems theory, the author develops his conceptual model of effectiveness and then illustrates its utility by applying it to assess the effectiveness of the U.S. automobile industry in the 1970s and the physician extender training programs.

REFERENCES

1. Johnson, R. L. The managers and the medical staff: Changing the behavior of the physician: A management perspective. Proceedings of the 21st Annual Symposium on Hospital Affairs, the Graduate Program in Hospital Administration and the Center for Health Administration Studies, Graduate School of Business, University of Chicago, June 1979.

2. Shortell, S. M., & LoGerfo, J. P. Hospital medical staff organization and quality of care: Results for myocardial infarction and appendectomy. *Medical Care*, 1981, *19*, 1041–1055.

3. Flood, A. B., & Scott, W. R. *Hospital structure and performance.* Baltimore: Johns Hopkins Press, 1987.

4. Katz, D., & Kahn, R. *The social psychology of organizations.* New York: John Wiley & Sons, 2nd ed., 1978.

5. Weick, K. E. Enactment processes in organizations. In B. M. Staw & G. R. Salancik (Eds.), *New directions in organizations and organizational behavior.* Chicago: St. Claire Press, 1977.

6. Johnson, E. A. Thinking conceptually about hospital efficiency. *Hospital and Health Services Administration*, 1981, *26*, 12–26.

7. Ruchlin, H. S. The quest for greater hospital productivity: Problems and issues. *Hospital and Health Services Administration*, 1981, *26*, 27–41.

8. Scott, W. R. Effectiveness of organizational effectiveness studies. In P. S. Goodman & J. M. Pennings (Eds.), *New perspectives on organizational effectiveness*. San Francisco: Jossey-Bass, 1977.

9. Kanter, R. M. Organizational performance: Recent developments in measurement. *Annual Review of Sociology*, 1981, 7, 321.

10. Gouldner, A. W. Organizational analysis. In R. K. Merton, L. Broom, & L. S. Cottrell, Jr. (Eds.), *Sociology today*. New York: Basic Books, 1959.

11. Etzioni, A. Two approaches to organizational analysis. A critique and a suggestion. *Administrative Science Quarterly*, 1960, 5, 257–278.

12. Buckley, W. *Sociology and modern systems theory*. Englewood Cliffs, N.J.: Prentice-Hall, 1967.

13. Yuchtman, E., & Seashore, S. E. A system resource approach to organizational effectiveness. *American Sociological Review*, 1967, 32, 891–903.

14. Bales, R. F. The equilibrium problem in small groups. In T. Parsons, R. F. Bales, & E. A. Shils (Eds.), *Working papers in the theory of action*. Glencoe, Ill.: Free Press, 1953.

15. Weick, K. E. Re-punctuating the problem. In P. S. Goodman & J. M. Pennings (Eds.), *New perspectives on organizational effectiveness*. San Francisco: Jossey-Bass, 1977.

16. Berle, A. A., & Means, G. C. *The modern corporation and private property*. New York: Macmillan, 1932.

17. Burnham, J. *The managerial revolution*. New York: John Day, 1941.

18. Cyert, R. M., & March, J. G. *A behavioral theory of the firm*. Englewood Cliffs, N.J.: Prentice-Hall, 1966.

19. Friedlander, F., & Pickle, H. Components of effectiveness in small organizations. *Administrative Science Quarterly*, 1968, 13, 289–304.

20. Steers, R. M. Problems in the measurement of organizational effectiveness. *Administrative Science Quarterly*, 1975, 20, 546.

21. Scott, W. R., Flood, A. B., Ewy, W., & Forrest, W. H. Jr. Organizational effectiveness and the quality of surgical care in hospitals. In M. W. Meyer (Ed.). *Environments and organizations*. San Francisco: Jossey-Bass, 1978.

22. Kimberly, J. R., Miles, R. H. (Eds.). *The organizational life cycle*. San Francisco: Jossey-Bass, 1980.

23. Cameron, K., & Whetten, D. A. Perceptions of organizational effectiveness across organizational life cycles. *Administrative Science Quarterly*, 1981, 26, 525–544.

24. Price, J. L. *Organizational effectiveness*. Homewood, Ill.: Richard D. Irwin, 1968.

25. Campbell, J. P. On the nature of organizational effectiveness. In P. S. Goodman & J. M. Pennings (Eds.), *New perspectives on organizational effectiveness*. San Francisco: Jossey-Bass, 1977.

26. Zammuto, R. F. *Assessing organizational effectiveness*. Albany: State University of New York Press, 1982.

27. Dornbusch, S. M., & Scott, W. R. (with the assistance of Busching, B. C., & Laing, J. D.). *Evaluation and the exercise of authority*. San Francisco: Jossey-Bass, 1975.

28. Payne, B. C. *Hospital utilization review manual*. Ann Arbor: University of Michigan Press, 1966.

29. Phaneuf, M. C. *The nursing audit: Profile for excellence*. New York: Appleton-Century-Crofts, 1972.

30. Thompson, J. D. *Organizations in action*. New York: McGraw-Hill, 1967.

31. Freidson, E. *Profession of medicine*. New York: Dodd, Mead, 1970.

32. Donabedian, A. Evaluating the quality of medical care. *Milbank Memorial Fund Quarterly*, 1966, *44*, Part 2, 166–206.

33. Cleverly, W. O. Financial ratios: Summary indicators for management decision making. *Hospital and Health Services Administration*, 1981, *26*, 26–47.

34. Haberstroh, C. J. Organization design and systems analysis. In J. G. March (Ed.), *Handbook of organizations*. Chicago: Rand McNally, 1965, 1182.

35. Gaertner, G. H., & Ramnarayan, S. Organizational effectiveness: An alternative perspective. *Academy of Management Review*, January, 1983, *8*, 97–107.

36. Shortell, S. M., Morrison, E. M., Hughes, S. L., Friedman, B. S., & Vitek, J. L. Diversification of health care services: The effects of ownership, environment, and strategy. In L. Rossiter & R. Schechter (Eds.), *Advances in Health Economics and Health Services Research*. San Francisco, JAI Press, 1986.

37. Ermann, D., & Gable, J. Multi-hospital systems: Issues and empirical findings. *Health Affairs*, Spring 1984, 50–64.

38. Pfeffer, J. Size, composition, and function of hospital boards of directors: A study of organization–environment linkage. *Administrative Science Quarterly*, 1973, *18*, 349–364.

39. Elling, R., & Halebsky, S. Organizational differentiation and support. *Administrative Science Quarterly*, 1961, *6*, 185–209.

40. Choi, T., Allison, R. F., & Munson, F. *Governance and management of university hospitals: External forces and internal processes*. Ann Arbor, MI: Health Administration Press, 1986.

41. Barrett, D., & Windham, S. R. Hospital boards and adaptability to competitive environments. *Health Care Management Review*, Fall 1984, 11–20.

42. Hernandez, S. R., & Kaluzny, A. D. Hospital closures: A review of current and proposed research. *Health Services Research*, Fall 1983, *18*, 419–436.

43. Georgopoulos, B. S., & Mann, F. C. *The community general hospital*. New York: Macmillan 1962.

44. Weisman, C. S. Determinants of hospital staff nurse turnover. *Medical Care*, 1981, *19*, 431–443.

45. Weisman, C. S., & Nathanson, C. A. Professional satisfaction and client outcomes: A comparative organizational analysis. *Medical Care*, October 1985, *23*, 1179–1192.

46. Price, J. L., & Mueller, C. W. A causal model of turnover for nurses. *Academy of Management Journal*, 1981, *24*, 543–565.

47. Hetherington, R., Soroko, S., & Bidle, I. Quality assurance and organizational effectiveness in hospitals. National Center for Health Services Research, Division of Intramural Research, Hyattsville, Md., *17*, No. 2, Summer 1982, 185–201.

48. Barr, J. K., & Steinberg, M. Professional participation in organizational decision making: Physicians in HMOs. *Journal of Community Health*, Spring, 1983, *8*, 3, 160–173.

49. Hernandez, S. R., & Kaluzny, A. D. A causal model of selective social psychological processes affecting work groups in health service organizations. *Proceedings of the Academy of Management*, San Diego, California, 1981.

50. Argote, L. Input uncertainty and organizational coordination in hospital emergency units. *Administrative Science Quarterly*, 1982, 27, 420–434.

51. Shortell, S. M. Physician involvement in hospital decision-making. In B. Gray (Ed.), *The new health care for profit: Doctors and hospitals in a competitive environment*. Washington, D.C.: National Academy Press, Institute of Medicine, 1983, pp. 73–102.

52. Shortell, S. M., Morrisey, M. A., & Conrad, D. Economic regulation and hospital behavior: The effects on medical staff organization and hospital–physician relationships. *Health Services Research*, December 1985, 20, 597–627.

53. Alexander, J. A., Morrisey, M. A., & Shortell, S. M. The effects of competition regulation and corporatization on hospital–physician relationships. *Journal of Health and Social Behavior*, September 1986, 27, 220–235.

54. Schulz, R. I., Greenley, J. R., & Peterson, R. W. Differences in the direct cost of public and private acute in-patient psychiatric services. *Inquiry*, Winter 1984, 21, 380–393.

55. Shortell, S. M. High performing health care organizations: Guidelines for the pursuit of excellence. *Hospital and Health Services Administration*, July–August 1985, 30, 7–35.

56. Neuhauser, D. *The relationship between administrative activities and hospital performance*, Chicago, Center for Health Administration Studies, University of Chicago, Research Series 28, 1971.

57. Shortell, S. M., Becker, S. W., & Neuhauser, D. The effects of management practices on hospital efficiency and quality of care. In S. M. Shortell & M. Brown (Eds.), *Organizational research and hospitals*. Chicago: Blue Cross Association, 1976.

58. Sloan, F., & Becker, E. Internal organization of hospitals and hospital costs. *Inquiry*, 1981, 18, 224–240.

59. Luft, H. *Health maintenance organizations: Dimensions of performance*. New York: John Wiley & Sons, 1981.

60. Pauly, M. Medical staff characteristics and hospital costs. *Journal of Human Resources*, 1978, 13 (Supplement), 78–111.

61. Garg, M. L., Mulligan, J. L., Gliebe, W. A., et al. Physicians specialty, quality and cost of in-patient care. *Social Science and Medicine*, 1979, 13C, 187–190.

62. Sherman, H. D. Hospital efficiency measurement and evaluation: Empirical test of a new technique. *Medical Care*, October 1984, 22, 922–938.

63. Alexander, J. A., & Rundall, T. G. Public hospitals under contract management: An assessment of operating performance. *Medical Care*, March 1985, 23, 209–219.

64. Institute of Medicine. *For profit enterprise in health care*. Washington, D.C.: National Academy Press, 1986.

65. Levitz, G. S., & Brooke, P. P. Independent versus system-affiliated hospitals: A comparative analysis of financial performance, cost, and productivity. *Health Services Research*, August 1985, 20, 315–339.

66. Coyne, J. S. Hospital performance in multi-hospital systems: A comparative study of system and independent hospitals. *Health Services Research*, Winter 1982, 17, 303–329.

67. Nash, M. *Managing organizational performance*. San Francisco: Jossey-Bass, 1983.

68. Friedman, B. S., & Shortell, S. M. The financial performance of multi-hospital system hospitals: Re-examining the evidence. Working paper, Center for Health Services and Policy Research, Northwestern University, August 1986.

69. Eastaugh, S. R. Improving hospital productivity under PPS: Managing cost reductions. *Hospital and Health Services Administration.* July/August 1985, *30*, 97–111.

70. Brooke, R. H., & Lohr, K. N. Efficacy, effectiveness, variations and quality. *Medical Care*, 1985, *23*, 710–722.

71. Rhee, S. O., Luke, R. D., Lyons, T. F., & Payne, B. C. Domain of practice and the quality of physician performance. *Medical Care*, January 1981, *19*, 14–23.

72. Payne, B. C., Lyons, T. F., & Neuhaus, E. Relationships of physician characteristics to performance quality and improvement. *Health Services Research*, August 1984, *19*, 307–332.

73. Rhee, S. O. Relative importance of physician's personal and situational characteristics for the quality of patient care. *Journal of Health and Social Behavior*, March 1977, *18*, 10–15.

74. Flood, A., & Scott, W. R. Professional power and professional effectiveness: The power of the surgical staff and the quality of surgical care in hospitals. *Journal of Health and Social Behavior*, 1978, *19*, 240–254.

75. Rhee, S. O., Luke, R. D., & Culverwell, M. B. Influence of client/colleague dependence on physician performance in patient care. *Medical Care*, August 1980, *18*, 829–841.

76. Flood, A. B., Scott, W. R., & Ewy, W. Does practice make perfect? Part I: The relationship between hospital volume and outcomes for select diagnostic categories. *Medical Care*, February 1984, *22*, 98–114.

77. Luft, H. S. The relation between surgical volume and mortality: An exploration of causal factors and alternative models. *Medical Care*, September 1980, *18*, 940–959.

78. Shortell, S. M., & LoGerfo, J. P. Hospital medical staff organization and quality of care: Results for myocardial infarction and appendectomy. *Medical Care*, October 1981, *19*, 1041–1055.

79. Roemer, M. I., & Friedman, J. W. *Doctors in hospitals; Medical staff organization and hospital performance.* Baltimore: Johns Hopkins University Press, 1971.

80. Holland, T. P., Konick, A., Buffum, W., et al. Institutional structure and resident outcomes. *Journal of Health and Social Behavior*, 1981, *22*, 433–444.

81. Denison, D. R. Bringing corporate culture to the bottom line. *Organizational Dynamics*, 1985, 5–22.

82. Mark, B. Task and structural correlates of organizational effectiveness in private psychiatric hospitals. *Health Services Research*, June 1985, *20*, 199–224.

83. Morlock, L., Nathanson, C., Horn, S., & Schumacher, D. Organizational factors associated with the quality of care in seventeen general acute hospitals. Paper presented at the annual meeting of the Association of University Programs and Health Administration, Toronto, 1979.

84. Morrow, P. C. Explorations in macrocommunication behavior: The effects of organizational feedback on organizational effectiveness. *Journal of Management Studies*, 1982, *19*, 438–446.

85. Mosely, S. K., & Grimes, R. M. The organization of effective hospitals. *Healthcare Management Review*, Summer 1976, *1*, 13–23.

86. Gaumer, G. Medicare patient outcomes and hospital organizational mission. *For profit enterprise in health care*. Washington, D.C.: Institute of Medicine, National Academy Press, 1986, pp. 354–374.

87. Shortell, S. M., Hughes, E., & Tibbits, H. The effects of ownership, financial constraints, and market competition on patient care outcomes. Working paper, Center for Health Services and Policy Research, Northwestern University, 1987.

88. Longest, B. B. An empirical analysis of the quality/cost relationship. *Hospital and Health Services Administration*, 1978, *23*, 20–35.

89. Schulz, R., Greenley, J. R., & Peterson, R. W. Management cost and quality in hospitals. *Medical Care*, September, 1983, *21*, 911–928.

90. Morse, E. V., Gordon, G., and Moch, M. Hospital costs and quality of care: An organizational perspective. *Millbank Memorial Fund Quarterly*, 1974, *52*, 315–345.

91. Scott, W. R., & Flood, A. B. Costs and quality of hospital care: A review of the literature. *Medical Care Review*, Winter 1984, 213–261.

92. Clinical services improved. *Human-size hospital economics*, AMI, Inc., July/August 1982, 4.

93. Ullmann, S. G. Differential effects of quality characteristics on long-term health care facility costs. *Inquiry*, 1986.

94. Flood, A. B., Ewy, W., Scott, W. R., Forrest, W. H., Jr., & Brown, B. W., Jr. The relationship between intensity and duration of medical services and outcomes for hospitalized patients. *Medical Care*, 1979, *17*, 1088–1102.

95. Bradford, D. L., and Cohen, A. R. *Managing for excellence*. New York: John Wiley & Sons, 1984.

96. Argyris, C. *Reasoning, learning, and action*. San Francisco: Jossey-Bass, 1982.

97. *Managing hospital marketing at AMI*. Beverly Hills, CA: American Medical International, June 1984.

98. Landau, M. On the concept of a self-correcting organization. *Public Administration Review*, 1973, *33*, 533–542.

99. Shortell, S. M., Wickizer, T. M., and Wheeler, J. R. C., Jr. *Hospital–physician joint ventures: Results and lessons from a national demonstration in primary care*. Ann Arbor, MI: Health Administration Press, 1984.

100. Peters, T. K., & Waterman, R. A., Jr. *In search of excellence*. New York: Harper & Row, 1982.

101. Burns, J. M. *Leadership*. New York: Harper & Row, 1978.

PART FIVE

Charting the Future

Some problems are so difficult they can't be solved in a million years unless someone thinks about them for five minutes.

H. L. Mencken

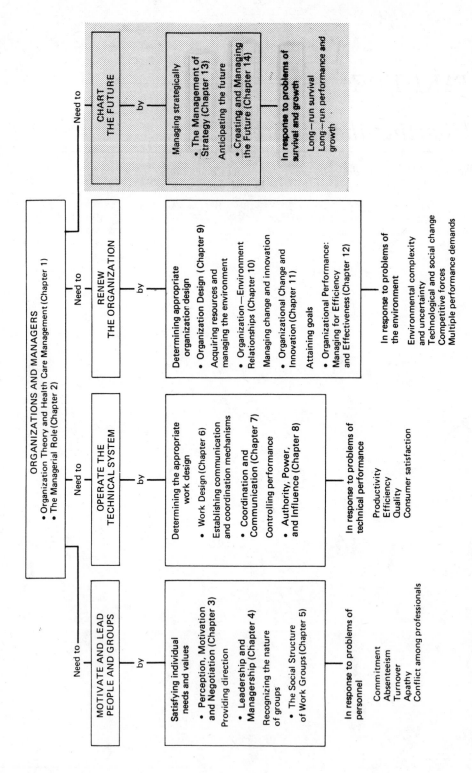

The nature of organizations: Framework for the text.

An important part of renewing the organization, which was the subject of the previous section, lies in the ability to chart the future. The two chapters in this section highlight a number of future trends that will influence the health care field and develop some new ideas related to managing strategically.

Chapter 13, The Management of Strategy, focuses on the following questions:

- What is strategic management and how does it differ from other forms of management?
- What are the major dimensions of strategy and of strategic management?
- What are the major steps in strategic decision making?
- What strategic models are available for dealing with different stages of growth? Are some models more appropriate than others? Under what circumstances?

Chapter 14, Creating and Managing the Future, highlights the following questions:

- What larger societal forces are shaping the health care system?
- How are the changing roles of physicians and nurses likely to influence the delivery of health care?
- How is the manager's role affected by changes within society and within the system itself?
- What factors are associated with the changing roles of women and minorities in health care management?

Upon completing these two chapters; readers should be able to accomplish the following:

- Define and distinguish strategic management from other forms of management.
- Identify, define, and give an example of each of the elements of strategy: external focus, long-term focus, important decisions, and so on.
- Be knowledgeable about the levels and steps of strategic decision making.
- Compare and contrast two strategic orientations: growth and action.
- Identify the major trends that are likely to shape the delivery of health services in the 1990s and beyond.
- Identify the ways in which health care managers can facilitate social experimentation, evaluation, and organizational research.
- Identify the effects of the changing roles of physicians and nurses on the provision of cost-effective health services.
- Identify the major opportunities and constraints faced by women and members of minority groups interested in pursuing health management careers.
- Suggest three ways in which the manager's role may change as a result of future trends and forces.

CHAPTER 13

The Management of Strategy*

Roice D. Luke
James W. Begun

Strategy is a concept that is not only of recent origin in the health care field (1,2), but has a relatively short history of development in the business management literature (3). The growing importance of strategy is driven largely by accelerated levels of threat and uncertainty in the external environment and by the expanding size and complexity of organizations of all types (4).

Strategy as a driving force for organizational change emerged in the language of health care in the 1970s. Rapid increases in the costs of care, catalyzed by funding provided through Medicare and Medicaid programs and widespread private insurance coverage, stimulated a series of responses that are still unfolding. Among the many responses is an almost paradigm shift in the industry from a structure that was fragmented, primarily community-service oriented, and relatively docile to one that is increasingly concentrated, business-oriented, and rivalrous.

Such developments have stimulated interest on the part of health executives in the management of strategy as an aid to achieving organizational survival. In the process of adopting a strategic orientation to their work, it has become clear that managers must have knowledge of both the content and processes of strategic decision making. Unfortunately, the weight of the literature concentrates on the processes for managing strategy rather than on the content of strategy (5,6). This is understandable, in view of the relative newness of both the literature and the application of strategic decision making processes within organizations.

The imbalance between process and content may even be greater in health care than it is in other industries. Recent and rapid environmental changes in health care essentially

*Preparation of this chapter was supported in part by a grant on graduate curriculum development in multi-institutional health systems, funded by the W. K. Kellogg Foundation and coordinated by the Hospital Research and Educational Trust of the American Hospital Association and the Association of University Programs in Health Administration.

463

caught off guard an industry in which strategy and its management had historically received little attention. Few models were available to guide the strategic development of hospitals and other types of health care organizations. Despite the lack of models, such organizations have moved quickly to implement strategic planning processes within their organizations, which may account for the pattern also observed in the health care field of emphasizing process over content.

In this chapter we first provide a general overview of the process for managing strategic decision making. The balance of the chapter then concentrates on the content of strategic decisions and the range of strategic orientations which health care organizations may adopt.

THE PROCESS OF MANAGING STRATEGY

What is strategic management and how does it differ from other forms of management? Are there unique managerial processes and techniques that must be learned by health care executives who wish to manage strategy? And where in the organization does responsibility for managing strategy reside? These are the kinds of questions that must first be addressed if the concepts of strategy are to be fully understood and implemented in health care organizations.

The formulation and implementation of strategy within an organization is the task of what has come to be known as *strategic management*. Other terms that have been used over the years include long-range planning, business policy, strategic planning, and corporate strategy (7–12). Although the definitions of strategic management are almost as numerous as the definitions of strategy itself, there is a high degree of consistency among them. The following are typical definitions:

> Strategic management is the process of managing the pursuit of organizational mission while managing the relationship of the organization to its environment (13, p. 3).

> Strategic management is a process that deals with the entrepreneurial work of the organization, with organizational renewal and growth, and more particularly, with developing and utilizing the strategy which is to guide the organization's operations (14, p. 11).

In these definitions, as in most (15,16), strategic management primarily involves the managerial processes required of top executives to orient their organizations to the environment—the role of strategy.

What distinguishes strategic management from other forms of management? We suggest that it is the challenge of dealing with the uniqueness of strategic decisions themselves. As pointed out by Luke and Kurowski (2), strategic decisions contain many common characteristics, including in particular:

- Have an external focus.
- Involve long-term organizational issues.
- Are important, or "nontrivial."
- Provide directionality for an organization, enabling it to accomplish its purposes.
- Have the effect of integrating an organization's departments and functions.
- Are focused at the system level (either at the corporate or individual business unit) rather than at the subunit level.

- Often emerge in an evolutionary or incremental fashion.
- Often evolve through predictable stages of growth (or decline).

Because of the unique content of strategic decisions, they often require distinctive design, implementation, and managerial processes.

LEVELS OF STRATEGIC DECISION MAKING

It is important to point out that the function of strategic management spans many levels within organizations. At the heart of strategy is the *key idea* of a firm, the core concept around which an organization assures its "formation, renewal, and survival" (14). In other words, the key idea embraces the central and often unique thought or thoughts that guide an organization as it faces the many competitive challenges and other threats in its environment.

Among the many purposes of such ideas, perhaps the most important is their role in formulating a distinctive position an organization might take relative to its rivals. The key ideas thus elaborate upon the essential adaptive responses an organization perceives will give it *competitive advantage* over other firms (17). For example, one firm achieves competitive advantage over another by getting into new markets early, expanding market share quickly, and, through advantages derived from learning and sheer economies of scale, earning profits where others might have failed (e.g., in health care, an advantage that might accrue to a large multihospital system). Another might achieve its advantage by diversifying and providing a solid financial base to support innovations in whatever market in which it may become involved (e.g., some of the large for-profit insurance firms that are now active in the health care field). And still another might achieve advantage because of its local market knowledge and contacts, which allow it to secure and maintain essential interorganizational relationships with either or both buyers and sellers (e.g., state-wide or regional networks of major hospitals that have entered into the health insurance business). The key to understanding organizational adaptation is thus to grasp the general concepts that organizations perceive will place them in competitively advantageous positions relative to rivals.

The key ideas themselves do not necessarily derive from complicated plans of action or fully formalized conceptualizations of a firm's pathway to success (18). Often, in fact, they reside apart from formal concepts and plans of action, in the minds of leaders of organizations and only emerge informally, incrementally, or unexpectedly, as guiding frameworks for action and growth (19). They thus often represent a perspective on a firm's future that is as much the product of insight as of formal analytic thinking (20).

Many terms have been coined to capture strategic content as it is more formally defined at various levels within organizations, ranging from mission statements to specific tactics for implementation. The highest (most general) level at which the content of strategy is formally specified is in an organization's *mission statement*. Such a statement serves many purposes, of which some of the most important are:

> Many organizations define the basic reason for their existence in terms of a mission statement. Such a definition can provide the basic philosophy of what the firm is all about. It usually emanates from the entrepreneur who founded the firm or from major strategists in the firm's development over time. The mission can be seen as a link between performing some social function and more specific targets or objectives of the organization. Thus the mission can be used to legitimize the organization.

When the mission of a business is carefully defined, it provides a statement to insiders and outsiders of what the company stands for—its image and character (21, p. 51).

The mission statement serves also to provide a general framework within which an organization establishes general policies and objectives, which themselves provide guidance to those who would choose and implement an organization's strategies. The implementation and control of all of these elements of an organization's strategy is, of course, the task of strategic management.

Strategies themselves also are specified at many levels within an organization. Such levels are commonly conceived to fit within a broad strategic framework, similar to but more comprehensive than the notion of the key idea, which some have referred to as the *master strategy* (14) or *grand strategies* (21,22) of a firm. This broad strategy, which may or may not be explicitly stated, serves as an umbrella for a hierarchy of other strategies that provide direction at various levels within an organization:

> The grand strategy is that combination of basic action strategies, such as concentration, growth, conglomerate diversification, etc.; and marketing strategies; and for very large firms, portfolio techniques that define the driving force of the organization—that central character attribute to which all else should adhere (13, p. 5).

Schendel and Hofer (14) suggest that such overall strategies—in their case, the master strategy—should encompass a four-level hierarchy of strategies, which includes:

- *Enterprise strategy:* ". . . attempts to integrate the firm with its broader noncontrollable environment, not in terms of product/market matches in a narrower economic sense, but in the sense of the overall role that business, as one of society's important institutions, should play in the everyday affairs of society." For health care organizations, such strategy would include the degree to which community service is a goal of the organization.
- *Corporate strategy:* ". . . addresses the question, 'What business(es) should we be in?' It also focuses on the ways that the different businesses a firm chooses to compete in should be integrated into an effective portfolio." This is a question confronting multi-institutional health care organizations as they expand into nonhospital and non-health care businesses.
- *Business strategy:* ". . . deals with the question, 'How should a firm compete in a given business?' That is, how should it position itself among its rivals in order to reach its goals?" Such decisions for health care organizations increasingly involve marketing and pricing strategies.
- *Functional area strategies:* ". . . address two issues. First they are intended to integrate the various subfunctional activities in the firm. Second, they are designed to relate the various functional area policies with changes in the . . . . environments." The latter issue addresses the fact that individual functional areas in the firm face different environments. Strategies to introduce efficiency into the production process in a hospital, for example, may effectively be applied to purchasing decisions but not to nurse staffing.

STEPS OF STRATEGIC DECISION MAKING

Strategic management, as we have stated, can be viewed as the process of making decisions about strategies, whether those strategies are at the enterprise, corporate, busi-

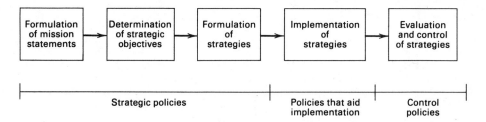

Figure 13.1. Strategic management process. (Adapted from *Strategy: Formulation, implementation and control* by Higgins, J. M. Copyright © 1985 CBS College Publishing. Reprinted with permission of Holt, Rinehart & Winston.)

ness, or functional area levels. Steps in the strategic management process are commonly laid out in models such as those illustrated in Figures 13.1 and 13.2. Figure 13.1 depicts the strategic management process as consisting of *formulation* of an organizational mission, strategic objectives, and master strategy; *implementation* of strategies; and *evaluation/control* of strategies. The process of formulating a master strategy is specified in greater detail in Figure 13.2. These models and, in fact, most such models, are built around four main decision-making steps. As identified by Glueck and Jauch (21, p. 7), these are:

- *Analysis and diagnosis:* "Determining environmental problems and opportunities and internal strengths and weaknesses. This involves recognizing problems and/or opportunities and assessing information needs to solve the problems and heuristics for evaluating the information."
- *Choice:* "Generating alternative solutions to the problem, assessing them, and choosing the best one."
- *Implementation:* "Making the strategy work by building the structure to support the strategy and developing appropriate plans and policies."
- *Evaluation:* "Through feedback, determining whether the strategy is working and taking steps to make it work."

While Figures 13.1 and 13.2 portray the decision-making steps as occurring in a neat chronological sequence, in reality this rarely occurs. Steps may be skipped, or completion of a later step may cause reformulation of an earlier one. The rational strategic planning model serves as a useful guide, however, for formal planning processes.

The analysis and diagnosis stage of the strategic management process has received considerable attention. A common method of analyzing and diagnosing strategic issues and alternative strategies generally begins with SWOT (Strengths, Weaknesses, Opportunities, Threats) analyses. Strengths are the internal abilities and activities that give the organization an advantage in achieving an objective, and these could be specific for functional areas, business units, or the organization as a whole. Examples of strengths are the ability to produce at a lower cost than competitors, the existence of a good reputation for high quality, or possession of the latest technological advances in production processes. Weaknesses, the opposite of strengths, might be reflected in a shortage of capital, an aging medical staff in a hospital, or an outdated physical plant. Higgins (13) argues that weaknesses are typically found in the marketing area at the individual business level (e.g., a shrinking target market) and in a lack of balance and synergy among com-

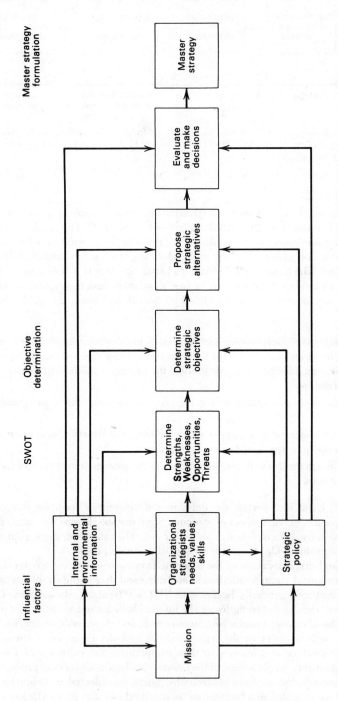

Figure 13.2. Master strategy formulation. (Adapted from *Strategy: Formulation, implementation and control* by Higgins, J. M. Copyright © 1985 CBS Publishing. Reprinted with permission of Holt, Rinehart & Winston.)

Labels within figure:

Master strategy formulation

Objective determination

SWOT

Influential factors

Master strategy

Evaluate and make decisions

Propose strategic alternatives

Determine strategic objectives

Determine Strengths, Weaknesses, Opportunities, Threats

Internal and environmental information

Organizational strategists needs, values, skills

Strategic policy

Mission

ponent businesses at the corporate level (e.g., conflict between hospitals and long-term care components in a multi-institutional health system).

Ideally, information about strengths and weaknesses is collected through systematic internal capability analysis, using data from a wide variety of sources and drawing upon multiple perspectives. Higgins (13), for instance, recommends that information about strengths and weaknesses be collected with respect to all of the following:

- Functional areas, such as marketing, finance, information systems, and human resources.
- Management values and capabilities.
- Performance of management functions.
- Performance of management systems.
- Stockholder orientations.
- Employee perspectives.

Opportunities are favorable events and circumstances external to the organization from which the organization can benefit. At the corporate level of a multihospital system, for example, opportunities for purchasing hospitals may be identified. Financial problems at one hospital may represent an opportunity for a competing hospital to move into its competitor's market area. Threats are external factors that interfere or might interfere with the achievement of organizational goals. Threats can come from competing organizations, demographic changes, societal pressures, or legal and regulatory changes. Many external factors, such as the implementation of the DRG reimbursement system, may be evaluated as threats by some organizations and as opportunities by others. Societal sectors in which organizational opportunities and threats may arise are (23):

- Government
- Technology
- Market (customers)
- Industry, including competitors
- Financial resources
- Raw materials
- Human resources
- Societal and cultural conditions
- Economic conditions

Each of the nine sectors can be scanned and analyzed by an organization's managers. Health care organizations have become particularly cognizant of the need to monitor (and influence) changes in governmental policies (e.g., Medicare and Medicaid reimbursement) and changes within the industry in regard to competitors and substitutes for their services (e.g., emergi-centers for hospital emergency rooms). Also, growing attention to market forces is a reality for almost all health care organizations today.

Many general business organizations, in reaction to accelerating rates of change in their environments, have developed specialized organizational units to compile and relay information about opportunities and threats to strategic decision makers. These units typically are referred to as environmental scanning or environmental assessment units

(24,25). Environmental scanning is increasingly being formalized and institutionalized within large organizations. Environmental scanning involves the collection of information from a variety of sources, forecasting of future changes, and forecasting of the impact of those changes on the organization. Forecasting techniques in use include, most commonly, trend extrapolation, statistical modeling (e.g., regression analysis), brainstorming, scenario development, and, less commonly, simulation, trend-impact analysis, and expert opinion/Delphi groups (24). While such methods often are rudimentary, improvement in the technologies of forecasting can be expected as organizations become more involved in environmental scanning and more dependent on its accuracy.

As the environmental changes in the health care field continue to grow, it can be expected that health care organizations will accelerate their involvement in the task of environmental analysis. While larger firms will have the resources to perform this task more comprehensively, even small health care organizations have ready access to environmental analysis information provided by professional associations, such as the American Hospital Association, or by private information services (26).

Proposing strategic alternatives may in some ways appear to be the easiest of all the steps identified in Figure 13.2. Almost all members of an organization will have some idea about prospective products or markets that they think should be given priority. On the other hand, few will understand the organization as a whole, how it is positioned relative to its rivals, what its history of development has been, or where it is headed in the long term. Many will not grasp how the totality of business ventures entered into by the organization fit together to constitute a coherent strategy for survival. The primary challenge of the health care executive is to conceptualize this broader strategic frame. This is where strategic "vision" enters into the decision-making process. It is an ingredient that comes more from an understanding of the general concepts of strategy and the logic of positioning of an organization within its markets and broader environment than it does from the formal techniques of strategic decision making.

Decisions about strategy, to the extent that they are formalized, involve the comparison of alternatives and selection of the best one based upon such techniques as cost–benefit analysis, portfolio analysis, and forecasting. Basically, all such techniques encourage organizations to think carefully about how strategic changes will affect their competitive positions (1). The choice process, however, is constrained by a litany of factors which make the process much less objective or rational than one might expect, such as:

• Objectives and goals are fuzzy and are not agreed upon.
• Managers are unaware of the full range of problems and strategic options.
• Managers often make choices based upon rules of thumb, historical precedent, or satisficing rather than maximizing criteria.
• Social and political relationships among decision makers affect the choice process.

Once choices about strategies are made, they must be implemented and evaluated. The most brilliant strategy is obviously of little value if it never reaches the stage of implementation. To achieve the latter, attention must be paid to the impact of strategic decisions on organizational structures and processes. Organizational structures appropriate for one strategy may be counterproductive for pursuing a different strategy. At the corporate level, for example, a strategy of firm growth may require greater decentralization of decision making, given the complexity and diversity of business activities in which it is involved. In the health care arena, expansion into different market areas may similarly require decentralization due to the local and unpredictable nature of much of health care delivery. Decentralization, in turn, may create the need for new integrating processes, such as temporary task forces, integrating roles and departments, more resources devoted to management information systems, or more goal setting and planning (27).

A major challenge facing health care executives, therefore, is to achieve an ideal or, at least, a workable fit between strategy and organizational structure (28). To do otherwise risks creating weakness in the implementation of an otherwise winning strategy. As Shortell et al. (1) argue, the degree of fit or match between the health care organization's strategies and its structure is more critical in highly competitive markets. It is likely, therefore, that health care organizations will devote more attention to assuring that strategy implementation is facilitated by needed structural change.

Successful implementation requires that precise objectives be stipulated for strategies, intermediate and short-term plans and budgets be derived, and plans for evaluation and feedback of results be structured within the planning sequence. Communication, leadership, and motivation of organizational members also are critical to successful implementation of strategic plans. Evaluation of the success of strategies is important, with revisions being made in accordance with feedback. Performance indicators such as financial ratios, return on investment, and increase in stakeholder value should be closely monitored in concert with implementation of new strategies. A host of traditional managerial tools, such as MBO (Management by Objective), PERT (Program Evaluation Review Technique), CPM (Critical Path Method), and Gantt Charts, also exist to facilitate the implementation and evaluation phases of strategic decision making.

The prototypical process of making decisions about strategy, while closely paralleling the rational model for making decisions, presents unique challenges to the health care executive. Some of these result from the unique role of physicians and the nature of the hospital medical staff (see Chapter 8). All involve decisions that are both complex and critical to the survival of the organization. Thus no matter how well one masters the logical processes of decision making, success in the strategy arena will significantly depend upon how well one grasps the content of the strategies being considered and how alternative strategies affect the organization's probable pattern of development over time. It is to this dimension—the content—of strategic management that we now turn our attention.

THE CONTENT OF STRATEGY

A number of conceptualizations or typologies of strategy are available in the literature (e.g., 3,29–31). The diversity of terms used to classify strategies is attributable to many factors, including the newness of the field, the many disciplines involved, as well as the great number of determinants that may constrain and dictate the available set of strategic alternatives (3,13,17). Despite the diversity, however, we suggest that most typologies of strategy, at least those that specifically address content, generally reflect two dimensions of strategy: (1) the key concept underlying a firm's approach to growth and (2) a firm's pattern of adapting to changing environments. Since these represent, in effect, important ways in which firms "orient" themselves to assure competitive advantage and therefore survival within their environments, we refer to them throughout the remainder of the chapter as *strategic orientations*.

The first orientation is concerned with the primary pathway along which a firm chooses to grow, which we label *growth orientation*. While growth can be achieved through a variety of approaches, in general it can only be accomplished in two ways: *(1)* by modifying the scale or level of production of existing business activities (e.g., expanding a hospital wing or new hospital acquisitions), or *(2)* by modifying the scope and diversity of business activities (e.g., a hospital investing in the long-term-care business). From a strategic viewpoint, each of these represents very different approaches to growth, a point that developed in greater detail below.

It should be noted that a firm's growth orientation need not necessarily be expansive but could, instead, lead to contraction. There are those who suggest that the broadest conceptualization of growth strategies should indeed include their *directionality* as well as other dimensions. Glueck and Jauch (21), for example, conceptualize the major growth alternatives as stability, expansion, retrenchment, and combinations (of the other three). Obviously, expansion and contraction represent radically different strategic alternatives. Contraction is a strategy most likely chosen either as a temporary response (turnaround) to short-term difficulties (e.g., a temporary drop in a hospital's occupancy rate) or as a more permanent response to long-run declines in the market for a firm's products or in its industry (e.g., a health care system closing one of its hospitals acquired prior to recent changes in reimbursement systems and market structures) (31–34). In the health care industry, examples of firm contraction exist both at the system level, in the form of divestiture of hospitals by large firms, and at the individual business unit level, in the form of personnel cutbacks or the dropping of certain services. By comparison to expansion, contraction is not only less desirable from a management perspective (it implies failure, threatens loss of jobs, etc.), but is, as a consequence, much less often pursued. For these reasons, while contraction strategies remain important in selected circumstances, we choose in this chapter to concentrate on the expansive growth alternatives.

The second orientation focuses on a firm's pattern of reaction to its environment, which we label *action orientation*. This pattern refers essentially to a firm's aggressiveness or willingness to assume risk in pursuing its chosen growth strategy. Since the intensity with which a firm pursues growth could conceivably be altered at any time, such an orientation could range from short- to long-term responses. Very short-term responses, such as aggressive advertising of a new wellness program, would likely fall into the category of tactics, and the longer-term responses, such as rapid movement of a hospital chain into the insurance/HMO business, would fall into the category of strategies.

The two strategic orientations are summarized in Figure 13.3. As indicated, we suggest that each contains two overall choices—size expansion or diversity expansion for growth and level of activity for action. Additionally, Figure 13.3 expresses as an element of growth the directionality dimension of expansion/contraction mentioned earlier. This latter dimension, for the reasons mentioned above, is not developed further in this chapter. Also, given the relatively greater complexity and diversity of growth alternatives compared with action alternatives, we give considerably more attention in this chapter to growth orientations.

GROWTH ORIENTATION

Growth appears to be a universal objective of most vital organizations. While there is some debate about the virtues of growth in terms of possible consequences for society

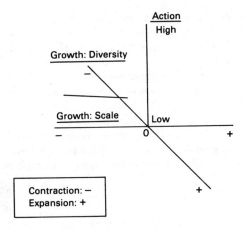

Figure 13.3. Typologies of strategy: growth and action orientations.

and/or the industry as a whole, there are many who argue that firms that consciously pursue some form of growth (whether or not growth actually occurs) will, because of the versatility, innovativeness, and readiness for change thus acquired, more likely detect early on important shifts in markets, the tactics of rivals, and structural shifts and other changes in their industries and environments (15,20,35). Of course, premature reactions to environmental change may be an unexpected and undesirable side effect (17).

Stages of Growth*

The importance of the size/diversity alternative mentioned earlier can perhaps best be illustrated by examining the stages through which firms tend to grow over time. As discussed below, significant shifts in strategy occur when a firm evolves from one that produces a single or dominant product or engages in a single market to one that produces multiple products and/or extends into multiple markets.

The study of firm growth over time has led to the suggestion that firms may pass through predictable stages as they grow and enter into new business activities. Haire (36), for example, suggested that growth is highly quantifiable and predictable, so much so that the analogy of biological growth in organisms may help to explain the growth of complex organizations. Chandler (37), however, was among the first to recognize the general stages through which organizations may be expected to grow. In the process of analyzing the emergence of corporate America in pre- and post-1900 periods, he identified four stages through which American firms appeared to develop: *(1)* expansion of volume through vertical and horizontal consolidations; *(2)* geographic growth, including overseas expansion; *(3)* product-line expansion through vertical integration and other forms of product development; and *(4)* new product development through diversification.

Others have attempted to build upon Chandler's analysis in an effort to formalize the staging concepts and to improve on the comprehensiveness and detail of the resulting classification schemes. Scott (38), for example, both simplified Chandler's categories and

---

*Some of the material in this section is taken directly or adapted from Luke and Kurowski (2), pp. 471–479.

identified one additional stage of growth through which organizations often pass in their early phases of development. He suggested that many organizations have much simpler beginnings than was implied in the Chandler analysis. They often begin as "one-person shows," marketing only a single product, and then grow sequentially through volume expansion, product-line development, and diversification. Each stage, Scott suggested, involves unique organizational structures and managerial styles. The stages thus are not only distinctive in strategic and organizational terms, but represent differentiated organizational forms through which many organizations pass.

Among the authors who have made important refinements to and extensions of Chandler's original stages s of growth, Leontiades (39) has provided perhaps the most useful conceptualization. He, like others, followed the Chandler example and kept the number of stages to four:

I.   Single-business stage
     Small business
     Dominant business

II. Multibusiness stage
     Related business
     Unrelated business

The key to this model is Leontiades' major division between single and multibusiness entities. It is along this juncture, he suggested, that major shifts occur within organizations in the overriding approach to growth, organizational structural arrangements, managerial styles, and so on. In this case, differences in strategy are clear: single-business organizations expand by increasing *size*, and multibusiness organizations expand by increasing the *diversity* and complexity of product offerings. We suggest again that almost all of the other growth-related typologies are simply derivatives of these two alternative pathways to growth.

Size/Diversity in Strategy. Interestingly, the size/diversity distinction has emerged at a number of other points in the business policy literature. The distinction between corporate and business-unit level strategies emphasized the same underlying logic for strategic development. Strategy at the business level, even within a conglomerate organizational form, generally focuses on single business activities. Growth at this level is thus dictated by a concern for volume or size expansion within single product or market configurations. At the corporate level, the primary strategy question is which business or set of businesses an organization should be in. The diversity of business involvements thus becomes the primary strategic variable to be manipulated and considered at the corporate level.

The strategic significance of the size/diversity distinction was also recognized, at least implicitly, in Ansoff's (7) useful product/market paradigm. Growth, he suggested, can be accomplished by expanding either or both product lines or markets in which the existing products are marketed. As illustrated in Figure 13.4, these two directions for development reveal four general strategic objectives: *(1)* market penetration—"growth . . . through the increase of market share in the present product-markets;" *(2)* market

Product

Mission Target	Present	New
Present	Market penetration	Product development
New	Market development	Diversification

Figure 13.4. Ansoff's product/market strategies for growth. (Adapted from Ansoff, H. I. *Corporate strategy: An analytic approach to business policy for growth and expansion.* New York: McGraw-Hill, 1965, p. 109.)

development—"new missions [markets] are sought for the firm's products;" *(3)* product development—"products [are created] to replace [or to add to] current ones;" and *(4)* diversification—"both products and missions [markets] are new to the firm." *Market penetration* is represented by a hospital's attempt to increase some of its inpatient utilization by appealing to a growing population of families living within its service area. *Market development* is represented by an inner-city hospital that initiates a small acquisition program in order to capture the expanding demand for hospital services within suburban areas and in small neighboring towns. An example of *product development* is a large hospital system that implements a plan to expand its contractual linkages with physician groups, home health services, and other providers and service groupings in order to create a system of services around which an HMO could be built. Finally, *diversification* is represented by a large multihospital system acquiring a small hotel chain (concentric diversification—expansion into business with similar strategies, production processes, marketing channels, or customers) and buying out a manufacturer of tennis rackets (conglomerate diversification—expansion into product or service areas unrelated to the activities of the existing firm).

The first three alternatives, Ansoff (7) pointed out, draw upon the "common threads" (product characteristics, technology, similarity of consumer need, etc.) that often link the new activities to "core characteristics" of a firm's current activities (7). That is, they build upon the existing capabilities and activities of a business. The last alternative, diversification, on the other hand, places a firm into business areas that are less well charted given its previous economic experience. In effect, Ansoff suggested that there are really two generic strategic alternatives—growth through product or market expansion (growth through size expansion) and growth through diversification (growth through diversity expansion).

Uncertainty and Growth. The stages of growth typologies are concerned with the following general questions: *(1)* what are the stages through which organizations evolve as they become larger and larger? and *(2)* what is the economic logic that, in general, dictates the sequencing of such growth? Imbedded in the stages concept are the essential logical threads that guide the growth of organizations. The underlying rationale for the stages-of-growth concept, unfortunately, is rarely made explicit, though a basic principle for development clearly emerges in the literature: marginal growth will occur in those areas in which there is the least uncertainty. This same principle is captured in Ansoff's

(7) "common threads;" Drucker's (40) metaphoric advice, "Shoemaker, stick to your last;" and Carman and Langeard's (41) suggestion that minimizing risk determines the pathways along which the service industries are expected to develop.

The learning-curve concept found so often in marketing textbooks also builds upon the concept of uncertainty. According to the reasoning behind the curve, the average cost of producing new products declines rapidly as one gains experience with their production. The extension of this concept to growth strategy is that an organization will generally expand in areas in which its experience and capabilities give it comparative advantage.

Many other factors, of course, govern the growth decisions of firms, such as economies of scale, access to capital markets, managerial aspirations, and perceptions of high growth potential. The need to minimize uncertainty and risk, however, seems to be a major influence on the general evolutionary pattern of organizational development. Further, the literature suggests that the least uncertainty is found in size expansion strategies and the greatest in those strategies that emphasize product and business diversity. To the extent that these points are valid, a general pattern of organizational growth, representing stages of increasing uncertainty, can be summarized as follows: organizations will grow first by volume expansion—increased size and geographic expansion—then by product line development, and last by diversification into related and unrelated products.

Integration of Ansoff and Leontiades Frameworks. The parallels between Ansoff's paradigm and Leontiades' major stages should now be apparent. Figure 13.5 combines the Ansoff and Leontiades frameworks. When a small single-business firm is expanding along the common threads of its existing business, it can be expected to rely most extensively on market-expansion strategies. As it becomes larger and develops greater corporate strength, it is able to take on strategies involving greater uncertainty, the market- and product-expansion strategies. It then moves toward the dominant business form, which is an organization that retains its identify with its primary product, but through product and market development increases its product mix in areas related to

Leontiades Stages	Ansoff Strategies			
	Market Penetration	Market Development	Product Development	Diversification
Single business Small business	X	X		
Dominant business		X	X	
Multibusiness Related business		X	X	X
Unrelated business				X

Figure 13.5. Interrelationships between Ansoff and Leontiades frameworks. (Adapted from Luke, R. D., & Kurowski, B. Strategic management. In S. M. Shortell and A. D. Kaluzny (Eds.), *Health care management: A text in organization theory and behavior.* New York: John Wiley & Sons, 1983, p. 476.)

its primary product. At some point in its growth cycle, the organization shifts into areas involving even greater uncertainty and begins to diversify into major new product and market areas. This takes the organization into the second major organizational form identified by Leontiades, the multibusiness stage of growth.

The business growth model quite obviously cannot be expected to predict the pattern of growth for all organizations. The model does, however, identify a generic and logical pathway that many organizations are likely to follow, even if they diverge along the way from the projected stages of growth.

Size Expansion

A number of conceptualizations focus on expanding markets for existing products rather than on diversifying the scope of business activities. Much of the marketing literature, for example, falls into this category, as the marketing function in organizations is primarily tactical rather than strategic *per se* and thus focused on strengthening the competitive position of firms within their existing product and market areas. We illustrate the concept of scale expansion by examining some of the important conceptualizations found in the literature.

Porter's Generic Strategies (Scale Advantages Through Market Penetration Tactics). Somewhat related to Ansoff's paradigm are Porter's (17) generic strategies for growth, which he identified as distinctive approaches a firm might take to achieve "competitive advantage" over its rivals. As pointed out by Porter (17, p. 14), there are two major approaches to achieving competitive advantage:

- *Low cost position:* "The sources of cost advantage are varied and depend on the structure of the industry. They may include the pursuit of economies of scale, proprietary technology, preferential access to raw materials, and other factors . . ."
- *Differentiation:* ". . . requires that a firm choose attributes in which to differentiate itself that are different from its rivals. A firm must truly be unique at something or be perceived as unique if it is to expect a premium price. In contrast to cost leadership, however, there can be more than one successful differentiation strategy in an industry if there are a number of attributes that are widely valued by buyers."

When combined with the scope—narrow (few) or broad (many) market segments—of a chosen strategy, the two primary strategies expand to four. These are illustrated in Figure 13.6. At first glance, these may appear to refer to yet another dimension of strategy, heretofore not identified. However, since they refer to approaches a firm might take to compete, given its particular product mix, they represent specific strategies a firm might pursue, in Ansoff's terms, to achieve market penetration (see Figure 13.4). These strategies are thus more applicable to individual business units within firms than they are to managing diversity within a diversified firm. They thus constitute approaches that individual business units might utilize to achieve competitive advantage within their own individual industries and markets. As such, they represent substrategies for expanding the size of existing operations.

Horizontal Expansion (Scale Advantages Through Geographical Expansion). There are basically only two ways in which the scale of business activity can be increased—by expanding either the volume sold through existing facilities or the locations and numbers

Competitive Advantage

Competitive
Scope

	Lower Cost	Differentiation
Broad Target	Cost leadership	Differentiation
Narrow Target	Cost focus	Differentiation focus

Figure 13.6. Porter's generic strategies. (Reprinted with permission of The Free Press, a Division of Macmillan, Inc. from *Competitive advantage: creating and sustaining superior performance* by Michael E. Porter. Copyright © 1985 by Michael E. Porter.)

of facilities themselves. The former approach is often achieved through market penetration and the latter through what is referred to as horizontal expansion. (Horizontal expansion is easily confused with other uses of the term "horizontal," e.g., as a concept in organization structure or as a form of strategic diversification through entry into related, synergistic product areas—the latter is discussed below.)

During the past 15 or more years, these alternative pathways to scale expansion have become particularly important in the hospital and other health care industries. Many hospitals, for example, have actively pursued scale expansion strategies to improve their competitive advantage in an increasingly cost-conscious environment. In so doing, they have had to choose from among a number of approaches to achieving larger scale, including combining into consortia (thus capturing some of the advantages of large-scale organizations, e.g., purchasing economies and shared corporate staff support), expanding existing facilities and local market penetration, acquiring/building facilities near the existing facility (largely to achieve local market dominance), or acquiring/building facilities in more distant market(s). The economic, regulatory, and strategic advantages associated with such choices are not only significant, but have changed in their relative importance over the past decade or more and are likely to change still further as the structures of the industry and its environment continue to evolve.

The choice from among these two alternatives depends significantly upon perceived tradeoffs between the advantages of facility size and/or multifacility consolidation and the costs of larger organizational control, burdensome bureaucratization, and perceived differentiation among facilities (42). In the hospital industry, which itself is relatively fragmented (the top four hospital firms in 1985 controlled only about 8% of the total national market share, while industries are often defined to be fragmented when the share is less than 40%), services have essentially been delivered at the local level by independent, often highly differentiated facilities.

Prior to the late 1970s, some limited advantages of facility scale had been observed in the industry and the advantages of multifacility organizations were undetermined. With the rise of the increasingly cost-conscious and economically powerful corporate "consumer," however, the potential advantages of larger scale organizations, at least multipoint organizations, have taken on greater significance. Realization of this stimulated a pattern of consolidation, at first, among hospitals and other delivery organizations and, more recently, among integrated health systems in which insurance and delivery organizations are combining to deliver packages of services to corporate and public clients.*

Diversity Expansion

The pursuit of diversity as a strategy can only be justified if, by combining different kinds of business activities, a net gain in competitive advantage is achieved through collective action over what might be achieved were each activity carried out independently. While there are many advantages and disadvantages that are the potential of collective action, such are primarily found in the financial, market, and administrative areas of organizational activity. For example, the combination of a business located in a stagnant or declining industry, in which there is little opportunity for growth, with one located in a high-growth industry, could facilitate the funneling of funds from the former to the latter to support needed growth. Alternatively, the combination of two businesses that share complementary technological expertise, could produce needed advantages in the respective markets of each. Or improvements in the organizational structures linking two or more businesses could, in the process, improve the performance of each.

Much attention has been given to conceptualizing the various combinational forms commonly referred to as *diversification* strategies (30,37,43). Figure 13.7 presents Ansoff's (7) conceptualization of various diversity strategies that firms might undertake. The number and variety of such strategies, however, are many and the number becomes even greater if the advantages of diversity for service firms are considered. A simplifying framework in which diversity alternatives might be summarized is thus needed.

All identified advantages attributable to the diversity strategy, we suggest, fall within two dimensions—the *direction* and *level* of firm *interrelatedness*. These are presented in Figure 13.8 along with a general typology of diversity strategies. As can be seen, two directions of interrelatedness are indicated, along and across chains of production, and two levels of interrelatedness, high and low. (The latter dimension encompasses all forms of interrelatedness discussed by Ansoff, including technological, customers, organizational, and functional). Within the cells of the typology are three general forms of diversity strategy pursued by firms: vertical integration, horizontal integration, and portfolio management. These three not only represent major forms of diversity strategy, but can be considered to be inclusive of most if not all diversifications. We therefore discuss briefly each of the three strategies.

Portfolio Management (Synergy Through Financial Interdependencies). This approach to strategy emphasizes financial balance among particular businesses within a diversified firm (44,45). It requires no assumption of interrelatedness, except with respect to the financial interconnectedness among business activities. For this reason, Porter (17) suggests that this pattern of strategy differs little from the management of a mutual fund. It is not our purpose here to discuss in detail portfolio management or its associated analytic techniques. Rather, it is to place this approach to strategy in the context of the broader range of strategies available to firms.

---

*Note the parallels between these patterns and those observed by Chandler, Leontiades, and others for firms in other industries—see the stages of growth concept discussed above.

| | New Products | |
New Functions	Related Technology	Unrelated Technology
Firm is its own customer	Vertical integration	
Same type of product	Horizontal integration	
Similar type of product	Marketing and technology-related concentric diversification	Marketing-related concentric diversification
New type of product	Technology-related concentric diversification	Conglomerate diversification

Figure 13.7. Ansoff's matrix of diversification options. (Adapted from Ansoff, H. I., *Corporate strategy: An analytic approach to business policy for growth and expansion.* New York: McGraw-Hill, 1965, p. 109.)

A primary objective of the portfolio approach is to achieve a desirable financial balance among a firm's portfolio of businesses. Typically, such balance is defined in terms of either *(1)* the structure of internal capital reallocations within a portfolio, in which, for example, cash is drawn out of established firms [e.g., those residing within mature industries ("cash cows") and invested in new business prospects ("question marks") or rapidly growing businesses ("stars" or "winners")], or *(2)* the types and levels of risk associated with a firm's businesses (44).

This approach to strategy, which has been widely adopted by large firms over the past half century (46), is not as generally pursued by firms in the health care field. Health care firms are for the most part single industry firms and thus have had little need for the portfolio approach to strategy. To the extent that they in time combine with other larger firms located outside of health care delivery (i.e., in the supply business, insurance, or other related business activities), however, they may become involved in strategic behaviors associated with portfolio management.

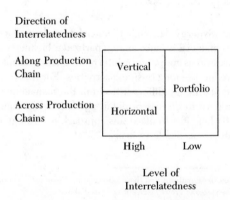

Figure 13.8. General diversification typology.

Horizontal Integration (Synergy Through Market and Organizational Interconnectedness). An alternative to relying solely on financial interdependencies is to achieve synergies by combining business activities in order to capture various market and/or organizational advantages. Porter (17) suggests that this purpose for combining is superior to the portfolio approach, and, in fact, "provides the only convincing rationale for the existence of diversified firms. . . ."

There are many possible interrelationships among firms. Porter (17), for example, identified the following three general categories: (1) tangible (advantages due to commonalities in buyers, rivals, technologies, etc.); (2) intangible (advantages attributable to sharing "generic skills" such as management knowledge, distribution technologies, technical production knowledge, etc.); and (3) competitive interrelationships (advantages attributable to competing with key rivals in more than one industry). The advantages that may accrue to horizontal integration within the health care field may be extensive, particularly across different types of business activities within the industry itself. Through horizontal integration, the extensive managerial talent and experience enjoyed by the hospital industry, for example, could be put to effective use in other, less well-developed sectors within the health care field (e.g., long-term care, wellness care). In addition, experience with multidisciplinary service production could prove an advantage for health care firms were they to pursue service-related businesses outside the health care industry.

The horizontal integration and portfolio management approaches to diversity expansion do share some similarities; some of the portfolio analytic techniques, for instance, are applicable to both forms of diversity expansion. Their primary difference is in their respective rationales for combining—financial interdependencies in the case of the portfolio management approach versus forms of organizational synergy in the case of horizontal integration. In general, horizontal integration requires more comprehensive analysis to determine the value of entering into new business ventures, for example, studying the advantages of sharing distribution channels and of the synergy between organizational management styles, human resource policies, and employee qualifications.

Vertical Integration (Synergy Through Control Within the Production Chain). A firm that expands its business activities along the production chain of one or more of its products engages, by so doing, in vertical integration. Such a firm chooses to avoid the market as a mechanism for either acquiring needed inputs or selling its products, depending upon whether the move is upstream (toward sellers) or downstream (toward buyers).

There are a number of reasons why a firm would choose a vertical integration strategy, including capturing production efficiencies through integration along the production chain, protecting needed supply or potential demand, raising entry barriers for potential rivals, and reducing the costs of bargaining/shopping. The potential costs of vertical integration, unfortunately, are also substantial, which, as a result, have limited the degree to which this popular strategy has been adopted in practice. Some costs of vertical integration include increased risk due to extended participation in a single production chain, reduced flexibility in selecting suppliers or potential consumers, reduced ability to adopt innovations, and greater strategic inflexibility (42).

This strategy has always been a part of the health care field, especially because of the significant interdependencies that exist in patient care between the many health care providers and levels of care (e.g., between ambulatory and acute-care providers). Historically, however, vertical integration has been quite restricted and where it has occurred, it has often been achieved through informal arrangements. Principally, vertical integration has occurred within health care in three areas: *(1)* between providers of service (e.g., by establishing physician offices on or near hospital campuses or entering into the emergency services business); *(2)* between providers of service and suppliers of inputs to care (e.g., hospitals developing hospital-based nursing schools); and *(3)* between providers and buyers of service (e.g., a hospital becoming a component of a health maintenance organization or a physician group contracting with an industrial firm to provide occupational services).

With the significant changes that have been occurring in the health care field, this strategy has increased significantly in its importance. At this stage in the development of the field, vertical integration may well be the single most important strategy being pursued by health care firms. Motivated by the increasing cost consciousness of the purchasers of insurance, insurance firms and providers of health care are recognizing the advantages of vertical integration as a strategy not only for bringing the costs of health care under control (as might be achieved through the use of either bureaucratic mechanisms or financing incentives), but for putting together the variety of insurance/ system packages (e.g., PPOs, indemnity programs, and HMOs) that are needed to meet the demands of the consumers of health insurance.

Vertical integration could actually be treated as a mere variant of the horizontal integration strategy discussed earlier, the only distinction being that interbusiness synergies for the former are achieved along rather than across production chains. We choose in this chapter to retain the distinction, not only because it is traditional to do so, but because of its particular importance as a strategy in the health care field. It should also be pointed out that many of the examples often cited for vertical integration are actually examples of horizontal integration. Acquisition by a hospital of a long-term care facility, an example typically provided of vertical integration, would only represent a vertical strategy if the acquisition were primarily motivated by a desire to have available a backup facility to which recovering patients could be referred (i.e., the long-term care facility would serve as a subacute-care facility) or if the long-term care facility were to provide a ready source of acute-care referrals. Many acquisitions of long-term care facilities by acute-care organizations, however, are actually made to achieve a more comprehensive service system, to achieve a presence in the care of the aged, or as an investment in a related product area—all of which fall within the purview of a horizontal integration strategy.

Finally, it is interesting to note that the trend toward "unbundling" so often noted in the health care field may actually be an example of reverse vertical integration. In this case, the costs of multiservice integration (particularly the provision of such services within a common facility) are perceived to be too great, thus providing the rationale for delivering some services apart from the facility or acquiring services through the market from outside vendors.

ACTION ORIENTATIONS

Each of the approaches discussed above to classifying strategy focuses on the primary pathways being pursued by firms in their quest for growth and competitive advantage. Each also recognizes the simple fact that growth can only be achieved by either increasing the size or diversity of business activities. An alternative approach to classifying strategy is to characterize the action patterns adopted by firms as they adapt to their environments. From this perspective, firms are seen as having distinctive styles of behavior, which can be differentiated according to such dimensions as their degree of aggressiveness in pursuing, say, market share or their relative preferences for innovation and/or efficiency objectives.

Such styles of behavior can vary regardless of the growth strategy selected by a firm, and they can have an important impact on the overall success with which that strategy is achieved. As a short-term concept, increased aggressiveness is sometimes used to preempt or ward off actions anticipated by firm rivals (47). Preemption may be essential for a firm not only to initiate successfully its desired growth strategy, but to hold its position in the market place once its strategy has been implemented. While the timing of the preemptive moves may produce improved competitive advantage, premature moves could produce strategic vulnerability.

That firms differ behaviorally in the marketplace according to their style of competition is obvious. What is not yet clear is whether or not such styles are enduring, that is, whether or not they reflect a "personality trait" or even an explicit strategy of an organization. There are those who suggest that such patterns of response carry over from year to year and may even have their roots in the very beginnings of an organization. Pfeffer (48, pp. 184–185) has argued, for example, that:

> Variation across organizations comes about primarily at the time organizations are founded. Stinchcombe (49) has made the argument most strongly that organizational structures persist over time. Different organizations founded at different times match the context of the time of their founding. But this initial context "imprints" the organizations, so that at some later point in time, rather than seeing organizations that are essentially similar because they have adapted to the current conditions, the initial differences will remain.

Evidence that such patterns may have some permanence in the strategic behaviors of organization is presented in the Miles and Cameron (29) study of firms in the tobacco i.:dustry.

Miles and Snow Typology

Perhaps the most extensive typology of strategic style developed thus far is that of Miles and Snow (50). They not only identify and observe empirically four distinct styles of strategic behavior, but argue that these often typify the behavior of firms for extended periods of time. In their study of the tobacco industry, for example, Miles and Cameron (29) observed that major tobacco firms tended to fall consistently into one of the four models of strategic behavior identified by Miles and Snow, even when the firms' overall strategies for growth may have changed significantly. When the firms shifted heavily into diversification or even international expansion strategies, for example, they appeared to do so with the same relative aggressiveness and risk-taking tendencies that characterized their earlier strategic behaviors.

The four patterns observed by Miles and Snow (50) are:

- *Defender*—seeks to maintain stability, control, and efficiency, defending current market niche (e.g., a single, locally-owned nursing home might be likely to operate in this pattern).
- *Prospector*—seeks to be flexible, pursuing new product and market opportunities and stressing innovation (e.g., a growing, financially secure multi-institutional health system

might well adopt a prospector action orientation, for instance, by becoming the first health care provider to offer its own health insurance product in a market area).

- *Analyzer*—seeks to combine control and flexibility, pursuing new opportunities after thorough analysis (e.g., growing health organizations unwilling or unable to take big risks might take the analyzer route, for example, by waiting until they observe and evaluate the activities of "first-mover" or prospector hospital systems).
- *Reactor*—has no consistent pattern, adjusting to the environment in an inconsistent and unstable pattern (e.g., a multihospital system which expands through purchasing hospitals one year, then contracts by divesting hospitals soon thereafter, then experiments with HMO businesses).

These four patterns represent differing degrees of aggressiveness and risk-taking as well as the degree to which a firm's chosen strategic actions are carried out either consciously or systematically (e.g., the prospector versus the reactor—both may represent aggressive, but not equally planned behaviors). They may thus prove useful in differentiating the strategic actions of organizations in the health care industry, given the newness of strategic behavior to the field and the overall pressures of change within the industry.

Entrepreneurialism

Another perspective of action orientations is found in the rapidly growing literature on entrepreneurialism. While its focus is at times on the individual as entrepreneur and at other times on the firm itself (51), the essential conceptual thread that underpins this particular dimension of strategy is the psychology of risk-taking behavior. More broadly, as pointed out by Long (52), this literature may be characterized by three basic themes: (1) willingness to assume uncertainty and risk, (2) the presence of managerial skills essential to achieve desired performance, and (3) an attitude of "creative opportunism."

An innovative twist on the concept of entrepreneurialism is found in Pinchot's (53) concept of intrapreneurialism. The intrapreneur, according to Pinchot, is one who expresses an entrepreneurial orientation while functioning as an employee (as against owner) of an organization. The innovative behaviors of such individuals are both sanctioned and, perhaps, funded by the larger organizational entity. Intrapreneurialism offers great potential for health care organizations. Not only do they enjoy enormous depth in professional talent, but they are engaged in a great diversity of complex service offerings. There thus resides in many health care organizations many fields of untapped opportunity for creative employee intrapreneurs to initiate new business ventures within their organizations.

An entrepreneurial perspective on the part of an organization may appear either as a generalized pattern of behavior, as discussed earlier, or as a transitional pattern of behavior that may occur at critical moments in the history of an organization, such as at the time it passes from one major stage of growth to another (54). The latter is seen as an essential adaptive response, that, though it may not persist in time may recur throughout the history of an organization:

> It seems most reasonable to expect entrepreneurial behavior in "bursts" which involve the re-creation of the enterprise but which cannot be sustained continuously, since they absorb energy and profits and must be balanced by energy building and profit-making periods (55, p. 5).

In sum, the concept of entrepreneurialism is particularly important to the health care field at this time, given the pace with which health care organizations are entering new business ventures and innovative organizational realignments. The need to take risks is seen to be critical to the long-run survival of many health care organizations (see Chapter 12). However, whether rapid movement into new business ventures will prove successful will likely depend upon the degree to which a well-thought-out growth strategy has been produced. Risk taking is only successful if the idea being advanced is right!

SUMMARY

In this chapter, we reviewed the process of strategic decision making, summarized major dimensions of strategy, and organized the major dimensions within two general strategic orientations. We stressed that no matter how carefully one carries out the logical processes of strategic decision making, success depends largely upon whether the key idea chosen to guide strategic behavior is consistent with the position of the organization in its markets and environment. It is clearly essential that future health care executives have the conceptual tools to think strategically. This is especially true now that the health care field is undergoing such radical restructuring. Two primary orientations to the external environment were identified—first, the general pathway a firm chooses to follow in pursuing growth, labeled growth orientation, and second, the intensity or aggressiveness with which that pattern of growth is pursued, action orientation. These two typologies capture broad patterns of strategic behavior in which most organizations engage as they react to an uncertain and threatening environment.

With respect to growth orientation, two general approaches to growth were identified—size and diversity expansion. Each of these represents a major alternative for how firms might approach growth and, more directly, achieve competitive advantage over rivals. Within each of these pathways to growth are, of course, a number of additional approaches to strategy, examples of which were also discussed. Action orientations, by comparison to growth orientations, are less well developed in the literature. To illustrate this approach to strategy, we therefore focused on the specific work of Miles and Snow (50) and on the concept of entrepreneurialism.

When considering the many approaches and combinations of strategic behaviors available to health care organizations, one must wonder if there exist among them some few that are more likely to be successful than are others. One could argue that in the long term it does not particularly matter, since most organizations will follow fairly predictable patterns of growth (as identified by those who have studied stages of organizational growth in other industries). On the other hand, within those very general stages, there exists a myriad of options and variations that could be pursued in the process of achieving competitive advantage. Further, the determinants of success within those stages are numerous, such that strategy has been conceptualized as a contingency approach to decision making (56).

We have already seen a number of themes being played out in the health care field that give some hints as to which strategic approaches might prove more or less successful (57). The early emphasis on marketing tactics to improve market penetration and product development, so prevalent in the late 1970s, gave way to a widespread assumption in the early 1980s that horizontal expansion into large multiunit systems (particularly in the hospital industry) would provide the winning edge. However, with the steady slowing in the demand for hospital acute care, the horizontal expansion strategy lost some of it momentum (at least temporarily), and in its place health care delivery organizations began combining local diversity strategies with vertical integration, in which delivery organizations and insurance companies were becoming more closely tied or the delivery organizations themselves entered into the insurance business (by forming local HMOs). Now there appears to be some weakness in the latter strategy as health organizations are learning that diversification strategies often require new areas of expertise and unexpectedly large amounts of capital to be successful. On the other hand, large, horizontally expanded and diversified insurance companies are learning that health care is a very complicated and local phenomena, thus making entry into the health insurance/HMO business more challenging than first thought.

The business of health care is indeed distinctive. For health care executives to succeed in this ever-changing environment, they must have a clear grasp of those essential strategic concepts that lead down the pathway to growth. No amount of care in following the formal steps in decision making will prove successful if the executives making these decisions do not fully understand the elements of strategy itself. To be sure, following those steps will be helpful. But the prize is likely to go to those who think creatively and strategically.

MANAGERIAL GUIDELINES

Some key managerial guidelines to assess in this effort are highlighted below:

Process Guidelines

1. Strategic management affects all levels of the organization, not just the top executive level. As such, it involves a philosophy or way of managing people and tasks throughout the organization.
2. Effective strategic management combines rational, analytical planning techniques and tools with managerial insight, intuition, and creativity.
3. Successful strategic managers need to develop the ability to distinguish between those issues and decisions that are truly strategic and those that are operational.
4. Top executives need to conceptualize the broader strategic environment in which the organization exists. This is at the cornerstone of developing effective strategic vision.

Strategic Content

1. Effective executives will recognize that successful strategies need to both look outward and inward at the same time. That is, the strategy needs to effectively match or fit the organization with its markets and its environment, but also, needs to take into account the organization's existing human resources, organizational structure, and decision-making and political processes.
2. The success of diversification strategies (new market development and new product development) depends on the degree to which they create synergy for accomplishment of the organization's mission.
3. Health care organizations will increasingly need to take risks, but the likely success of such risk-taking behavior will depend largely on the extent to which a well-thought out growth strategy is pursued.

4. The heart of strategic management is the establishment of a sustainable competitive advantage over one's competitors. One can obtain a sustainable competitive advantage through many means, including (1) early entry, (2) raising entry barriers for others, (3) building volume and experience quickly, (4) achieving superior access to resources, (5) achieving superior access to customers, (6) technological innovation, and (7) constant differentiation of products and services.

DISCUSSION QUESTIONS

1. Discuss the concept of strategy. How do strategic decisions differ from other types of decisions executives must make?
2. Distinguish between horizontal expansion, vertical integration, horizontal integration, and portfolio management. Discuss the importance and place of each in the changing health care industry. Discuss the organizational implications of each as applied to health care organizations. What adjustments in an organization's structure are likely to be needed to assure successful implementation of each strategy? How will the organization's culture need to be adjusted to facilitate the pursuit of each approach to strategy?
3. Assume that you are the chief executive officer of a large urban hospital that is struggling for its survival in the face of increasing local competition in both the hospital and insurance industries. Discuss the relative advantages and disadvantages you might encounter were you to combine a prospector orientation with a local diversification expansion strategy. What role should the medical staff play in deciding which strategy to pursue? How should they be involved in the implementation phase? How do you as the leader of the organization facilitate their involvement? What role should other actors in the organization play in this decision? What are some of the alternative strategies such hospitals might reasonably pursue? How are the strategic alternatives facing large urban hospitals likely to differ from those encountered by smaller suburban hospitals?
4. What are the implications of growing insurance competition for the kinds of strategies hospitals are likely to pursue? How will that competition affect the ambulatory care sector? Long-term care?
5. The insurance industry is becoming a major force for change in the health care industry and as a result must be understood by future health executives. Using the typologies presented in this chapter, classify the major types of firms active in the health insurance business. Discuss some of the advantages and disadvantages likely to accrue to each type.

SUGGESTED READINGS

Alexander, J. A., Lewis, B. L., & Morrisey, M. A. Acquisition strategies of multihospital systems. *Health Affairs*, 1985, *4*, 49–66.
   Study of seven multihospital systems which finds that the systems plan to move away

from traditional inpatient services and to develop nontraditional services such as insurance, health maintenance organizations, and preferred provider organizations. The systems, regardless of ownership type, move cautiously in their strategies of acquisition of new services.

Lawrence, P. R., & Dyer, D. *Renewing American Industry.* New York: Free Press, 1983.
An overview of how U.S. firms in several industries have adapted to changes, based on the framework that firms must engage in the "readaptive" process of becoming efficient and innovative. Discusses the evolution of the hospital industry and the relationship between external conditions and organizational forms. Uses the classic Lawrence and Dyer two-dimension model, basing the analyses on resource scarcity and information complexity.

Leontiades, M. *Strategies for diversification and change.* Boston: Little, Brown and Co., 1980.
Elaborates the work of Chandler and subsequent "stages of corporate growth" theorists. Links two fields of research by developing an organizational change model, called the matrix model, which incorporates a firm's management style with its stage of growth. This model allows one to capture the more "dynamic" dimension of a firm's strategy for change.

Meyer, A. D. Adapting to environmental jolts. *Administrative Science Quarterly,* 1982, 27, 515–537.
A natural experiment which examines hospitals' adaptations to a sudden and unprecedented event. Adaptive responses are analyzed in the context of each hospital's preexisting strategies, structures, ideologies, and slack resources. Ideological and strategic variables were the best predictors of how organizations responded to the "jolts."

Miles, R. E., & Snow, C. C. *Organizational strategy, structure, and process.* New York: McGraw-Hill, 1978.
Classic work which develops the strategic typologies of organizations adapting to their environments: Defenders, Prospectors, Analyzers, and Reactors. Applications of the strategic typology to specific cases.

Porter, M. *Competitive strategy: Techniques for analyzing industries and competitors.* New York: Free Press, 1980.
Using the industrial organizational economics research literature, discusses applications to the analysis of corporate strategy. Presents techniques to analyze the behavior of businesses and competitors.

Porter, M. *Competitive advantage: Creating and sustaining superior performance.* New York: Free Press, 1985.
Surveys techniques and action steps necessary to implement competitive strategy in order to gain competitive advantage over other firms.

Shortell, S. M., Morrison, E. M., & Robbins, S. Strategy making in health care organizations: A framework and agenda for research. *Medical Care Review,* 1985, 42, 219–266.
Comprehensive article in which key concepts and approaches to strategic management are applied to the health care field. Derives important hypotheses that need testing now that strategic management is emerging as a central management tool of the health executive.

REFERENCES

1. Shortell, S. M., Morrison, E. M., & Robbins, S. Strategy making in health care organizations: A framework and agenda for research. *Medical Care Review*, 1985, *42*, 219–266.

2. Luke, R. D., & Kurowski, B. Strategic management. In S. M. Shortell and A. D. Kaluzny (Eds.), *Health care management: A text in organization theory and behavior.* New York: Wiley, 1983.

3. Hofer, C. W. Turnaround Strategies. In W. F. Glueck (Ed.), *Strategic Management and Business Policy.* New York: McGraw-Hill, 1980.

4. Ansoff, H. I. Planned management of turbulent change. In L. R. Bittel (Ed.), *Encyclopedia of professional management.* New York: McGraw-Hill, 1978.

5. Hofer, C. W. *Conceptual constructs for formulating corporate and business strategies.* Boston: Intercollegiate Case Clearing House, #9-378-754, 1977.

6. Pitts, M. W., & Wood, D. R. A review and critique of the strategic management literature on not-for-profit community hospitals. *Health Care Strategic Management*, 1985, *3*, 4–12.

7. Ansoff, H. I. *Corporate strategy: An analytic approach to business policy for growth and expansion.* New York: McGraw-Hill, 1965.

8. Argenti, J. *Systematic corporate planning.* New York: Wiley, 1974.

9. King, W. R., & Cleland, D. I. *Strategic planning and policy.* New York: Van Nostrand Reinhold, 1978.

10. Steiner, G. A. *Strategic planning: What every manager should know.* New York: Free Press, 1979.

11. Andrews, K. R. *The concept of corporate strategy* (rev. ed.). Homewood, Ill.: Irwin, 1980.

12. Glueck, W. F. *Strategic management and business policy.* New York: McGraw-Hill, 1980.

13. Higgins, J. M. *Strategy: Formulation, implementation, and control.* Chicago: Dryden Press, 1985.

14. Schendel, D. E., & Hofer, C. W. *Strategic management: A new view of business policy and planning.* New York: McGraw-Hill, 1979.

15. Ansoff, H. I. The changing shape of the strategic problem. In D. E. Schendel and C. W. Hofer (Eds.), *Strategic management: A new view of business policy and planning.* New York: McGraw-Hill, 1979.

16. Leontiades, M. The confusing words of business policy. *Academy of Management Review*, 1982, *7*, 45–48.

17. Porter, M. E. *Competitive advantage: Creating and sustaining superior performance.* New York: Free Press, 1985.

18. Mintzberg, H. Of strategies, deliberate and emergent. *Strategic Management Journal*, 1985, *6*, 257–272.

19. Quinn, J. B. *Strategies for change: Logical incrementalism.* Homewood, Ill.: Irwin, 1980.

20. Hickman, C. R., & Silva, M. A. *Creating excellence.* New York: New American Library, 1984.

21. Glueck, W. F., & Jauch, L. R. *Business policy and strategic management*. New York: McGraw-Hill, 1984.

22. Pearce, J. A., II. Selecting among alternative grand strategies. *California Management Review*, 1982, Spring, 23–31.

23. Daft, R. L. *Organization theory and design* (2nd ed.). St. Paul, Minn.: West, 1986.

24. Klein, H. E., & Linneman, R. E. Environmental assessment: An international study of corporate practice. *Journal of Business Strategy*, 1984, 5, 66–75.

25. Lenz, R. T., & Engledow, J. L. Environmental analysis units and strategic decision-making: A field study of selected "leading-edge" corporations. *Strategic Management Journal*, 1986, 7, 69–89.

26. Sheldon, A., & Windham, S. *Competitive strategy for health care organizations*. Homewood, Ill.: Dow Jones-Irwin, 1984.

27. Galbraith, J. R., & Kazanjian, R. K. *Strategy implementation: Structure, systems and process* (2nd ed.). St. Paul, Minn.: West, 1986.

28. Kimberly, J. R., & Zajac, E. J. Strategic adaptation in health care organizations: Implications for theory and research. *Medical Care Review*, 1985, 42, 267–302.

29. Miles, R., & Cameron, K. *Coffin nails*. Englewood Cliffs, N.J.: Prentice Hall, 1982.

30. Rumelt, R. P. *Strategy, structure, and economic performance of the Fortune "500."* Boston: Harvard University Press, 1974.

31. Kotler, P. *Marketing management: Analysis, planning and control* (3rd ed.). Englewood Cliffs, N.J.: Prentice-Hall, 1976.

32. Hofer, C. W. Turnaround strategies. In W. F. Glueck (Ed.). *Strategic management and business policy*. New York: McGraw-Hill, 1980.

33. Harrigan, K. A., & Porter, M. E. A framework for looking at endgame strategies. *Proceedings of the Academy of Management*, 1978.

34. Harrigan, K. A. Strategy formulation in declining industries. *Academy of Management Review*, 1980, 5, 599–604.

35. Lawrence, P. R., & Dyer, D. *Renewing American industry*. New York: Free Press, 1983.

36. Haire, M. Biological models and empirical histories of the growth of organizations. In M. Haire (Ed.), *Modern organization theory: A symposium of the Foundation for Research on Human Behavior*. New York: Wiley, 1959.

37. Chandler, A. D. *Strategy and structure*. Cambridge, Mass.: The MIT Press, 1962.

38. Scott, B. R. *Stages of corporate development*. Boston: Intercollegiate Case Clearinghouse, #9-371-294, BP998, 1971.

39. Leontiades, M. *Strategies for diversification and change*. Boston: Little, Brown, 1980.

40. Drucker, P. F. *Management: Tasks, responsibilities, practices*. New York: Harper and Row, 1974.

41. Carman, J. M., & Langeard, E. Growth Strategies for Service Firms. *Strategic Management Journal*, 1980, 1, 7–22.

42. Porter, M. E. *Competitive strategy: Techniques for analyzing industries and competitors*. New York: Free Press, 1980.

43. Wolf, B. Industrial diversification and internationalization: Some empirical behavior. *Journal of Industrial Economics*, 1977, 26, 177–191.

44. Wind, Y., & Mahajan, V. Designing product and business portfolios. *Harvard Business Review*, 1981, *59*, 155–165.

45. Coate, M. B. Pitfalls in portfolio planning. *Long Range Planning*, 1983, June, 47–56.

46. Haspeslagh, P. A survey of U.S. companies shows how effective portfolio planning could be but often isn't. *Harvard Business Review*, 1982, Jan.–Feb., 58–73.

47. MacMillan, I. C. Preemptive strategies. *Journal of Business Strategy*, 1983, *3*, 16–22.

48. Pfeffer, J. *Organizations and organization theory*. Marshfield, Mass.: Pitman, 1982.

49. Stinchcombe, A. L. Social structure and organizations. In J. G. March (Ed.), *Handbook of organizations*. Chicago: Rand McNally, 1965.

50. Miles, R. E., & Snow, C. C. *Organizational strategy, structure, and process*. New York: McGraw-Hill, 1978.

51. Smith, N. R., & Miner, J. B. Type of entrepreneur, type of firm, and managerial motivation: Implications for organizational life cycle theory. *Strategic Management Journal*, 1983, *4*, 325–340.

52. Long, W. The meaning of entrepreneurship. *American Journal of Small Business*, 1983, *8*, 47–56.

53. Pinchot, G., III. *Intrapreneuring*. New York: Harper and Row, 1985.

54. Greiner, L. E. Evolution and revolution as organizations grow. *Harvard Business Review*, 1972, *50*, 37–46.

55. Murray, J. A. A concept of entrepreneurial strategy. *Strategic Management Journal*, 1984, *5*, 1–13.

56. Hofer, C. W. Toward a contingency theory of business strategy. *Academy of Management Journal*, 1975, *18*, 784–810.

57. Vraciu, R. A. Hospital strategies for the eighties: A mid-decade look. *Health Care Management Review*, 1985, *10*, 9–19.

CHAPTER 14

Creating and Managing the Future

Arnold D. Kaluzny
Stephen M. Shortell

The management challenges of the future must be placed in the context of future health system responses to societal change. Consider the following scenarios (1):

More of the Same

. . . the next fifteen years may well be much like the last fifteen, with continuing increases in the flow of revenues into the health care system. . . . Congress is likely . . . to avoid cutting back Medicare benefits. Few groups believe that federal expenditures can be contained. The exception is leadership of the American Hospital Association, which expects a strengthened DRG system to dampen outlays.

. . . . record numbers of physicians will enter the system and will influence demand for medical care. They will succeed in extending the boundaries of medicine to encompass a wide range of new services under the category of "wellness" and "aesthetics."

In the absence of a reduction of existing excess capacity, the proliferation of new health care delivery systems will tend to expand not reduce, total outlays.

Less of the Same

. . . . the accelerated development of HMOs will help to constrain total outlays for health care because they have a proven track record of reducing hospital admissions by a significant fraction. . . . If the public (and state governments) will allow many underutilized acute care hospitals to go under, and if the public finds these new prepaid ambulatory systems of care attractive, total outlays could be constrained.

At the same time, the federal and state governments would have to take a hard look at high tech medicine, especially the potential for expanded organ transplants and decide whether these and other technological benefits are to be made available to all. Authorities would have to look at two other issues: the conditions governing resort to life sustaining procedures and the use of high cost treatment for chronic patients dependent on alcohol and drugs.

A Radical Restructuring

. . . (While) the most recent opinion survey reported a low (about ten percent) percentage of the U.S. public favor a national health service . . . fifty-nine percent currently support national health insurance, a more modest proposal, despite the recent loss of interest by Congress.

. . . . a restructuring engendered by government is not impossible. It would require the following ingredients: the discontent of growing number of physicians, especially recent graduates with their prospects for satisfying professional careers; sufficient turmoil in the hospital areas as a result of declining utilization and price sensitive purchasing by third party pairs as well as accelerating competition from new ambulatory care providers that precipitate the merger, closure or bankruptcy of a substantial number of hospitals; and growing employer, physician, and community hostility to such closures.*

It is likely that elements of each will combine to influence the future provision of health care services. A number of sources will play a key role in the emerging health care system. In analyzing these scenarios, this chapter begins by considering changes likely to occur in the organization and its environment, discusses the future of individuals and groups within organizations, and ends with consideration of the managerial role. The intent is to be provocative yet realistic, building on issues developed in preceding chapters. A central theme is that health care organizations and their leaders can actively influence their environment and thereby create and actively manage their future.

THE ORGANIZATION AND THE ENVIRONMENT

Health care organizations, functioning g as corporate actors, are the major repository of power within the health care system. Health care expenditures represent a significant percentage of the gross national product, and as federal and state governments continue to be a major purchaser of care, the influence of health care corporate actors will increase. The collective decisions of individual hospitals, multihospital systems, alternative delivery systems, nursing home chains, regulatory groups, and other corporate actors within the health services field will significantly affect the basic structure and characteristics of services provided.

Moreover, these organizations will be operating in and affected by an increasingly complex and unpredictable environment, an environment characterized by the difficulty of predicting both the occurrence and content of change. For example, consider the interface between federal and state governments. At the federal level, cost shifting and pressures from commercial insurance companies and industrial coalitions will force states to increase regulation to contain cost and capital expansion. At the same time, the growing supply of physicians will encourage competition for patients among practitioners as well as among health care organizations.

---

*Adapted from Ginzberg, E. The restructuring of U.S. health care. *Inquiry*, 1985, 22, 279–280.

With increasing complexity and unpredictability of the environment will come a demand for greater organizational responsiveness and accountability from different groups. The organization will face the problem of reconciling incompatible objectives. For example, the federal government often defines accountability in terms of cost control, while local consumer groups may see accountability in terms of added facilities and services and greater consumer participation in decision making. Moreover, the emergence of for-profit organizations has challenged the orientation of not-for-profit organizations. As described by Sigmond (2, p. 38):

> The real problem is not the existence of the investor-owned hospitals, but rather the effect of their behavior on nonprofit community hospitals. Influenced by the investor-owned hospitals' recent spectacular success at "doing well" financially, will community hospitals increasingly concentrate their efforts on "doing well," or will they also give more explicit attention to "doing good"?

In short, the future involves major issues centering on the organization's ability to adapt to divergent demands. This effort will require innovation, the ability to manage external dependencies and, at the same time, the ability to restructure internal relationships. A number of major trends and their implications are presented below.

COST TRENDS AND COST CONTAINMENT

With increasing costs, cost containment efforts will remain a major issue facing health care organizations. National health expenditures currently represent nearly 10.7% of the gross national product ($387.4 billion) and are expected to increase to $660 billion and consume 11.3% of GNP in 1990 (3).

Cost containment efforts will involve an expanding group of actors and are expected to be an important focus for the foreseeable future. It is unlikely, however, that the effects of cost containment efforts will be equally distributed. Programs affecting the poor and the disabled will bear the biggest burden. As described by Mechanic (4, p. 454):

> When faced with competing claims on natural resources, government finds it easier to restrain growth in programs affecting the poor and disabled, who constitute relatively weak constituencies, than to reduce subsidies shared by large, articulate and sophisticated segments of the larger American public.

Perhaps the most immediate change will lie in the increasing direct involvement of industrial corporations in cost containment efforts as health care costs rise and employee benefit programs remain a major concern at the negotiating table. This involvement stems from growing recognition that corporations have substantial purchasing power and are increasingly concerned about escalating costs (5).

Recent developments indicate that involvement is likely to take two forms. First is the direct participation of large corporations in the operations of health service organizations at the local level. Under this approach large corporations establish specific departments concerned with health care utilization and quality and designed to generate long-term change in the health care system. For example, corporations may initiate audits and design benefit packages to ensure appropriate utilization and quality among subscribers. Industrial concern for cost containment and a determination to keep employees away from costly hospital care has spawned the development of new types of organizations involved in health services. In 1985, for example, approximately 150 medical review organizations—such as Intracorp, Medview, Cost Care, Quick Admit—emerged to handle preadmission certification, second surgical opinion programs for corporations and insurers (6).

A second form of involvement lies in the development of local coalitions. These coalitions, including representatives of community health providers, labor, and corporations in the area, have had relatively little influence to date. But coalitions may have greater impact in the long run as they act to unify business initiatives in health care cost containment and provide private-sector input into health planning and policy development. Most coalitions initially focus on gaining understanding of the local health care cost situation by means of data collection and analysis, followed by comprehensive review of service utilization. With this information, coalitions can develop or adapt programs designed to modify patients' use of and demand for services, such as health promotion campaigns, smoking cessation strategies, and fitness and exercise programs in addition to traditional benefit services.

The implications for health care organizations are substantial. First, health care organizations will need to develop proactive rather than reactive strategies toward cost containment. Undoubtedly, health care organizations will be under a great deal of pressure to control costs. However, the critical issue is the need to develop constructive and attractive approaches that go beyond simple incentive programs. These programs are likely to involve structural changes in services delivery and a renewed sense of leadership and collaboration among providers and third-party funding agencies.

Second, the magnitude of the cost issue will tend to overshadow other equally important aspects of health services, such as quality of care and access to services. It will be incumbent on providers and third-party funding agencies to balance the issues of cost, quality, and access. Too much emphasis on cost to the detriment of quality and accessibility will sacrifice the long-term credibility of health service providers.

Finally, with increasing involvement of industrial organizations and industrial consultants, health organizations will be more widely exposed to business management techniques. A major challenge lies in adapting these techniques to meet the specific needs of health care organizations. Inappropriate use of management techniques and strategies or failure to consider the context of their application may unintentionally limit the flexibility required to provide necessary services, particularly in emergency situations. Rising levels of expectation that cannot be realized can result in cynicism toward all managerial efforts.

CHANGING SOCIAL NORMS, EXPECTATIONS, AND DEMOGRAPHIC COMPOSITION

Increased attention to disease prevention and promotion of healthier life styles will redefine provider–patient relationships and consumer expectations of health care organizations. Patients will become more active in their orientation toward physicians and other providers, seeking greater sharing of information and more participation in these relationships. This will be particularly true for employer and health care business coalitions. Demands will be made of health care organizations for more personal, responsive, and coordinated care.

Perhaps the most far-reaching demographic change will be the increasing percentage of elderly people in the population. By the year 2025, 18% of the U.S. population is predicted to be over age 65. Particularly striking is the fact that individuals at age 72 now have the same future life expectancy as individuals at age 65 did 20 years ago. Between 1960 and 1980 there was an approximately 175% increase in the number of individuals 85 years and older (7). While there is growing concern that the nation will be dominated by an aged dependent population, recent estimates reveal that the vast majority of the elderly population appear to be free of dependency on other human beings for help in daily functioning. Despite these findings a doubling of nursing home population is projected, placing a great burden on the Medicaid program. The managerial challenge is to embark on a planning process for delivery of long-term care to those in need, but at the same time to reconcile the expectation that long-term care is so great a problem that it is simply best ignored (8).

Finally, the provision of medical care to the poor will be an increasing issue facing health services. Reduced governmental and philanthropic support and growing business and organized labor disenchantment with continuing cost subsidies, which in the past have financed a good share of care for the poor, has caused some critics to identify this as the single most critical issue in the 1990s (9). While many localities have made arrangements for providing and financing care to those uninsured, there is substantial evidence that basic needs are not being met. The data are impressive.

- Between 1979 and 1984, the number of people without health insurance in the United States increased by 22.3% from 28.7 to 35.1 million (10).
- Ten percent of the hospitals provide 40% of all care to the uninsured. However, these organizations are confronting cost containment and market pressures such that even they are unable to increase their uncompensated care sufficiently to meet the growing demand (11).
- Between 1980 and 1982, the number of poor people without health insurance increased by 20%, yet during the same period hospital uncompensated care increased by less than 4% (11).
- Even among individuals with health insurance, significant segments of the population can be excluded from insurance because of preexisting conditions (12).
- Increase in the number of interhospital transfers of patients to public general hospitals. Many of these patients were in unstable condition at the transfer hospital (13). For example, in Washington, D.C., transfers from private hospitals to District of Columbia General Hospital rose from 169 to nearly 1,000 annually between the years 1981 and 1984. At Cook County Hospital in Chicago the number of interhospital transfers has risen steadily from 1,295 in 1980 to 2,906 in 1981, 4,368 in 1982, and 6,769 in 1983. Moreover, in the Cook County data, 84% of the charges are attributed to the transfer patient where nonreimbursable and in 1983 this represented 12% of Cook's county's hospitals operating budget (13).

The continuation of this trend and an increasing realization that the existing system is unable to provide a level of basic care may stimulate restructuring efforts. For example, Florida has experimented with taxing hospital revenues to pay for indigent care and other states have instituted special insurance programs with adjusted premiums for people with preexisting conditions. Others believe that a broader base of support is needed to pay for such care with proposals ranging from a tax on liquor and cigarettes to setting aside a percentage of state lottery funds to pay for indigent care.

TECHNOLOGICAL DEVELOPMENT AND ASSESSMENT

Technological development will continue to have a major impact on health services in the future. The use of minicomputers and lithotripters, and the measurement of biochemical functions through such technology as nuclear magnetic resonance imaging will change diagnosis and treatment. Such developments will raise questions involving (1) who will have access to new technological developments, (2) to what degree the decision to use new technology will be decentralized, (3) what effect new technology will have on provider–patient relationships, and (4) what new ethical considerations must be considered.

New developments will change prevention and health promotion activities. Although it is not as dramatic and heroic as the hard technological developments, significant progress is occurring in the control of hypertension, coronary disease, cancer, and certain disabling forms of mental illness. For example, deaths due to heart disease decreased in the United States by 25.7% between 1970 and 1983; some of the decrease may be associated with disease prevention and health promotion efforts (14).

Future developments will be accompanied by a greater concern for assessment of cost and efficacy of both technological and programmatic innovations than has been evident in the past. There is growing recognition that technology that is "ineffective, superfluous, or unsafe" (15) contributes significantly to the increasing cost of health care. Aside from the obvious and direct cost implications of such assessment efforts, more systematic development of technology would reduce the uncertainty affecting health care organizations. Assessment permits allocation of scarce resources to technologies and programs proven safe and effective.

Efforts are already underway to deal systematically with many issues through the development of cooperative clinical trials, the operation of the National Institutes of Health's Office of Medical Applications of Research (OMAR), and research funded by the National Center for Health Services Research and Technology Assessment (NCHSR). Moreover, there is growing recognition that federal efforts may not be sufficient to meet the challenge. For example, a recent Institute of Medicine study (16) recommends the designation of a private–public organization with charter and financing to monitor, synthesize, and disseminate information and activities on technology assessment as well as develop the research agenda for filling gaps and knowledge relevant to assessment. It is further recommended that a portion of the health care dollar be allocated to existing public health service components already supporting research in medical technology assessment and that financial support for assessment should rise over the next 10 years to an annual level of $30 million greater (in 1984 dollars) than at present.

HEALTH PROMOTION AND DISEASE PREVENTION

Changing norms and expectations will enhance health promotion and disease prevention activities. Attention will be given to programs that promote wellness, including the identification and treatment of diseases or biological risks that lead to disease, such as hypertension and diabetes; behavioral change such as improved nutrition, physical fitness, weight reduction, and stress management; environmental changes that reduce exposure to hazardous or toxic substances or intolerable levels of stress; and educational efforts to increase awareness of the opportunities for self-improving and appropriate use of medical services. Analysis reveals that significant relationships exist between lifestyle and incidence of illness. For example, one UCLA study estimated the health effects of the following lifestyle practices: three meals a day, no snacks, breakfast every day, modest exercise two or three times a week, 7 or 8 hours of sleep per night, no smoking, moderate weight, and moderate alcohol consumption. After following 7,000 persons for several years, the study concluded that the average 45-year old male who observed 0–3 of the above practices had a life expectancy of an additional 21.6 years while the same person who followed six or seven of the rules would expect to live another 33.1 years—11.5 years longer (17).

While existing health care delivery organizations will be increasingly involved in providing such programs, increasingly industry will be the primary sponsor of these programs at the work site. Several factors will contribute to the implementation of these programs (18). First, illness generates expenses for health insurance, workman's compensation, reduced productivity, increased absenteeism, and turnover. Moreover, the work site offers opportunities to facilitate healthy behavior since most people spend at least one-third of their time at work. Finally, wellness itself relates directly to the product line of many of the large industrial organizations.

SOCIAL EXPERIMENTATION

Evaluation and experimentation will extend beyond technology assessment to encompass a wide variety of new approaches, programs, and organizations for delivering more cost effective health care. The demands for greater accountability under an environment of constrained resources will push the health care system further in the direction of Campbell's (19) "experimenting society," in which new demonstration programs are rigorously evaluated. Emphasis will be placed not only on results, but also on the process by which the results were obtained.

An important effect is that health care managers will increasingly become part of more formal program evaluation efforts. Examples include continued experiments in prospective reimbursement, case mix and outcome-based reimbursement, new ambulatory-care programs, and a variety of long-term-care demonstration initiatives. In these kinds of experiments, there are four areas in which managers will be called upon to play a major role (20): (1) initiation of the evaluation process, (2) facilitation of the evaluation process, (3) mediation of the relationship between the evaluators and program staff, and (4) implementation of the evaluation results.

In the initiation stage, managers will be responsible for determining the purposes of the evaluation. Is the organization willing to commit the resources required for a valid evaluation? What are the likely payoffs? Are ulterior or covert purposes involved? These are some of the question that managers will have to articulate and assess. In addition, managers will be faced with the issue of selecting an inside or outside group to conduct the evaluation. At the same time, the manager must determine whether and when the organization is ready for the evaluation. Premature evaluation serves no one's ends.

The manager will also play an important role in facilitating execution of the evaluation. This is particularly true in regard to formulating program objectives, which should be clearly understood by all involved.

The manager can also play an important role in mediating relationships between program staff members and evaluators. These relationships are frequently characterized by conflict. Program staff understandably view their activities as beneficial and as contributing to the organization's goals. Evaluators, on the other hand, are charged with maintaining the integrity of the evaluation design and taking an independent view as to whether or not and to what degree the program's objectives have been achieved. Further the evaluation may consume resources that program staff members feel may be better spent on direct services. Managers can help minimize these conflicts by ensuring that sufficient time is allocated for discussion and development of mutual understanding and by engaging in direct problem-solving and conflict-resolution strategies as needed.

Finally, managers play a key role in making use of the evaluation results. Managers who work closely with evaluators can help to ensure that the key questions are being answered in a manner that makes sense to the eventual users. This includes providing suggestions to the evaluators for writing the report in a language and format that is understandable to the intended audience.

ORGANIZATIONAL ARRANGEMENTS

While changes in social experimentation, social norms, and demography will affect organizational arrangements, other important developments will also affect the structure of health care organizations. For example, the growth of for-profit health maintenance organizations (21) and dramatic growth of preferred provider organizations (PPOs), which offer employers, pension funds, and other member groups fee-for-service health care at discount prices will have profound impact on delivery patterns (22).

Moreover, multihospital systems, both voluntary and investor-owned, are also likely to expand rapidly. In 1986 approximately 40% of hospitals belonged to a multi-institutional system. It is expected that by 1990 approximately 60% of the hospitals will belong to a multi-institutional system.

Many of these systems will be vertically integrated, comprising a wide range of out-of-hospital services including ambulatory surgery, occupational medicine, health promotion, home health care, preferred provider organizations, and health insurance. They will, thus, be the financier, planner, and provider of services. Further, corporate strategies will call for the continued integration of services at the local level. Systems will be working to position their hospitals, nursing homes, home health care agencies, ambulatory surgery centers, and related services in geographically concentrated areas in order to provide an integrated continuum of care.

System consolidation is taking place along six levels. The first involves the *large national hospital companies,* most of which are investor-owned. These include American Medical International, The Hospital Corporation of America, Humana, and National Medical Enterprises. These systems will become increasingly involved in vertical integration and diversification outside of the hospital line of business.

The second level involves large *voluntary affiliated systems.* These include American Health Care System, a consortium of voluntary multiunit hospital systems, and Voluntary Hospitals of America, an organization representing over 500 voluntary hospitals across the United States. Both of these "megaorganizations" provide members with access to capital, political clout, management expertise, joint venture opportunities, and linkages with health insurance services.

The third level involves *regional hospital systems.* These systems are largely voluntary. Examples include Health Central in Minneapolis, HealthWest in Southern California, Samaritan Health System in the Phoenix area, Intermountain Health Care System in the Salt Lake area, Southwest Health Care System in New Mexico, the Sun Alliance in North Carolina, and Baptist Systems in both Texas and Florida. They have no intention of becoming national systems and instead plan to focus on developing specialized market niches to best meet market needs in their own regions of the country.

The fourth level involves *metropolitan-based systems* centered in major SMSAs around the country. Examples include Henry Ford in Detroit, The New York Health and Hospital Corporation, Evangelical Health System in the Chicago area, and the Metropolitan Health System in the Portland area. For the most part, they plan to focus their efforts locally in their own area and do not intend to become regional or national in scope.

The fifth level is of particular interest because they often cross over with the metropolitan, regional, and to some extent national levels described above. These are the *special interest systems* organized along religious lines, teaching interests, or related special missions which drive their activities. Examples include such Catholic hospital systems as The Sisters of Mercy Health Corporation headquartered in Farmington Hills, Michigan and with hospitals in Michigan, Iowa, and Indiana; the Daughters of Charity headquartered in St. Louis and Evansville; the Providence Health Care System headquartered in Seattle and operating hospitals and other health care organizations on the west coast; and the Lutheran Hospital and Home Society headquartered in Fargo, North Dakota. Most of these are regional in scope, although networks of selective services are being put together on a national basis. The Adventist Health Care System is an example of a national special interest system.

In addition to the religious systems, teaching hospitals are organizing into systems. Some of these have been acquired by national investor-owned or voluntary systems while others have developed or will develop affiliation and consortia arrangements with each other. Still another special interest system is the Veteran's Administration, which continues to provide the majority of health services to the veteran population.

A final level of the health care system of the future will include some relatively *independent free-standing voluntary hospitals*. They will be located in higher-income communities with good health insurance coverage. In addition, they will be characterized by strong medical staffs, continuity of management, strong community support, and a history and tradition of voluntarism. To be sure, these hospitals will have linkages to some of the systems and levels described above (such as group purchasing arrangements and selected joint venture activities), but organizationally they will remain fundamentally as a free-standing independent hospital.

While these system levels have been described primarily in terms of networks of hospitals, it is important to note that other systems will center around health maintenance organizations, nursing homes, and other types of health care organizations. Kaiser–Permanente is an example of a national system of not-for-profit prepaid group practices. Maxicare is an example of an investor-owned national HMO system. Beverly Enterprises and Manor Health Care serve as examples of national investor-owned nursing home chains. As previously noted, most of the hospital systems described above have major components involving HMOs, nursing home care, home health services, and a variety of ambulatory-care services as well.

The net result of such activity is an increasingly consolidated health care industry replacing a cottage industry. These megasystems cutting across six levels constitute a "private" national health system involving a variety of different models serving different national, regional, and local values, traditions, and marketplace preferences.

The shift from an industry of single independent institutions to one of institutional networks will have significant effects on service delivery and on the analysis of health care organizations. The shift will require increased attention to the management of both horizontal and vertical interorganizational relationships. Issues will include how such relationships develop and how and why they are maintained over time. A number of managerial challenges are presented: (1) the need to market directly to a number of different groups, (2) the need to develop market niches, (3) the need to manage complex interorganizational relationships, (4) the need to link vertical and horizontal integration, (5) skill in capital formation, and (6) management of the price, quality, volume relationship for each major service line and target group.

While systems will develop increasingly complex horizontal networks, attention also needs to be given to the vertical dimensions of systems, or what Scott and Meyer (23) have termed sectors—groups of interrelated organizations providing similar or substitutible goods and services. Here attention is given to the specific focal provider organization and also the major organizations to which it relates, the organizations that contribute directly to or regulate the focal organization's activities. Thus vertical multi-institutional health systems include not only the organizations providing services, but also the formal/informal linkages with hospital supply organizations, educational institutions that train personnel, and financing and regulatory agencies.

The focus on vertical linkages takes us beyond the technical rationality of any single organization or multi-institutional system within the larger system. Moreover, the perspective also helps identify the unique opportunities for dominant and diversified systems to assume leadership in sector-wide service rationalization, including planning, development, and coordination of new and existing services. The nature of the relationship among the different levels becomes critical and even confusing since each level may be following a different rationality. As described by Scott (24, p. 134):

. . . Structure may appear as a waste and redundancy at the local (organizational) level but may enable the larger system to survive—and be responsive to simultaneous, conflicting

TABLE 14.1. Environmental Trends

	Past (1950–1970s)	Present (1980s)	Future (1990 & beyond)
Cost containment	Not an issue—retrospective reimbursement	Emergent concern and shift to prospective reimbursement	Continual cost concerns and development of a fully capitated system
Social norms demographic composition	Provider dominated. Aging of population not an issue	Changing consumer expectations. Aging an emergent issue	Provider/consumer/employer partnerships. Aging a major focus of activity
Technical development and assessment	Rapid development and implementation	Emerging efforts at assessment	Use of randomized trials and meta analysis
Health promotion/disease prevention	Not an issue	Emerging efforts	Major delivery efforts
Social experimentation	Emerging efforts	Pressure on accountability	Collaborative efforts between researchers and managers
Organizational arrangements	Cottage industry, large number of individual providers	Systems and consolidation	Mega systems both vertically and horizontally integrated

requirements. Rationality at the field level may require different structural arrangements than rationality at the subfield level

PAST, PRESENT, AND FUTURE

Table 14.1 presents each of the major trends involving the organization and the environment over time. As can be seen both the organization and environment are faced with increasing risk and uncertainty. Organizations are increasingly being challenged, requiring greater adaptability and creativity. The future obviously will involve activities that have not been done before and will require efforts that have not yet been tried.

INDIVIDUALS AND GROUPS WITHIN THE ORGANIZATION

As an organization functions within a larger environment, individuals and groups function within a larger organization. This interaction is critical to the overall performance of health care institutions. This applies to hospitals but is equally appropriate to all health care organizations:

> Organizational effectiveness depends upon social efficiency more than it does upon technical–economic efficiency, and the same may be said of reliable and high level performance on the part of the members—social efficiency entails personal goal attainment for the participants at all levels, and this includes meaningful participation in decision-making process, identification with the organization, opportunities for explicit behavior and satisfaction of intrinsic motives and psychological rewards—a great deal depends on the extent to which the various groups and members understand each other's work problems and needs; the degree to which work-relevant expectations, attitudes, motivations, and values of members and related jobs are congruent or complementary; the degree to which interacting groups and individuals are guided by informal norms of reciprocal trust and mutual helpfulness (25).

Several developments likely to affect the interaction of individuals and groups within organizations are discussed below.

CHANGING ROLE OF THE PHYSICIAN

Increased competition among hospitals and among physicians, continued regulation (albeit more at the state and local than at the federal level), physician surpluses in many areas of the country, the development of better measures of outcomes of care and health status, and newly emerging noninvasive technologies are all factors that are redefining the role of the physician. These changes are not likely to affect the basic position of dominance the physician has played in health services. The physician will retain legitimate authority to formulate standards and supervise and control most health care services. What is likely to change is the control over the allocation of resources to health care. As described by Friedson (26):

. . . There is no reason to believe that medicine's basic position of dominance, its key position in the health care system, will change. It will have considerably less control over the economics of health care, however, and will have to struggle to maintain a strong role in policy making and the governance of the organizations in which its members work.

The net result is likely to be threefold: a slight increase in the bargaining power of hospitals relative to physicians; an even stronger bond of dependence between the two than presently exists; and selectively greater competition between the two.

With the increased supply of physicians, hospitals can be more selective in granting staff privileges and defining criteria for reappointment. Given incentives to contain costs, physicians who are efficient utilizers of hospital resources will be favored over others. At the same time, greater attention will be given to maintaining an appropriate mix of primary care physicians and specilists. Hospitals will be in a position to demand more active physician participation in hospital management and governance. Hospitals will also be able to play a larger role in meeting some physicians' ambulatory-care practice needs in addition to supplying inpatient resources. One example is the development of hospital–physician sponsored preferred provider organizations (PPOs) designed to assist both the hospital and physician in maintaining or increasing market share. Another example is hospital-supported group practices which enable younger physicians to practice in a group setting with a greater variety of support services, such as social work, health education, nutrition, and counseling, than are generally available in other practice settings (27).

The new relationships, however, will be subject to greater scrutiny in terms of costs and, more importantly, in terms of cost effectiveness. The development of better measures of quality of care and health status makes it possible to imagine reimbursement based on outcomes of care, not merely costs of services. Simply put, hospitals that achieve better outcomes at the same cost or equivalent outcomes at a lower cost will be differentially rewarded. Closer integration of clinical and administrative decision making will develop, reflected in greater involvement of physicians as voting members of hospital boards; more joint participation of physicians, nurses, and managers on hospital committees; and more physicians with management training in high-level management positions. New forms of medical staff organization such as divisional and parallel designs may be needed to deal with the new challenges and opportunities (28). Evidence is accumulating that greater physician participation may be associated with lower costs and higher quality of care (see Chapter 12), owing to increased opportunities for sharing knowledge and information needed for taking corrective action and planning more effective programs and services.

Some, if not all, health care executives may perceive growing involvement of physicians in management as a threat. This perception is predictable and understandable, and it presents a challenge to enlightened health care management to overcome negative feelings and attitudes. Creative management will welcome the addition of trained executives who also possess clinical expertise. Existing data indicate that the investor-owned sector of the industry may be showing the way in this regard. Investor-owned hospitals have significant involvement of physicians as voting members of their governing boards and in some cases as key participants in important management decisions. A major issue facing all systems is how to best integrate physician input into corporate-level decision making.

CHANGING ROLE OF THE NURSE

The dominant coalition in health care management and leadership over the past 30 years or more has consisted of the governing board, the management, and the medical staff. Within the next 5–10 years it is likely that the nursing staff will join the coalition.

Two key features of the nurse's role have significantly influenced this trend. First, the nurse has become the day-to-day manager of the growing medical technology that pervades all hospitals. Second, the nurse is the primary resource coordinator of the vast array of specialists who practice in the hospital. Both features place nursing in the center of both the conceptual and methodological issues critical to assuring organizational productivity (29).

In their drive for professional recognition, nurses have come to recognize the power associated with nursing's increased responsibility and the growing demand on the part of hospitals, in particular, for their services. In a concerted fashion, they are beginning to demand a larger voice in management and governance. The challenge for management is to implement a more appropriate role for nurses, a role that recognizes their responsibility and provides the autonomy, participation, and rewards associated with the increased scope of responsibility.

Many possibilities exist, but three examples will be cited here (28). The first is development of a more coequal relationship between physicians and nurses in carrying out patient-care responsibilities. Examples of this kind of relationship can already be seen among physicians and nurse practitioners providing care in rural settings. In these settings, nurses are entrusted with responsibility and autonomy for delivering health care, using the physician as a resource in meeting patient needs. This relationship, which has proven itself in rural clinics, could be transferred in some cases to the inpatient hospital setting. A physician and nurse could have joint responsibility for the care of patients during the hospital stay and could work to coordinate the patient's health care upon discharge from the hospital.

A second possibility lies in further development of the nurse clinician role. Nurse clinicians would essentially be charged with managing the clinical affairs of a patient-care unit on a coequal basis with the physician head of that unit. This model appears to be particularly relevant for teaching hospitals.

While the first two suggestions relate to changes at the patient-care level, the third has perhaps more far-reaching implications for management and policy. This is the introduction of nurses into high levels of management and also into participation as voting members of hospital governing boards. Participation in high-level management will occur because of increased management training of nurses occupying senior management positions in nursing (30)—and also because many former nurses are being trained as managers and will increasingly occupy positions of responsibility.

There are many countervailing forces to these changes. In some cases new roles may not be workable or even wise to implement in many hospitals. In other cases a surplus of physicians may lead to physicians replacing nurses in some hospitals. Nonetheless, the challenge from the nursing profession will not go away. The need for more productive hospital–nurse–physician relationships is a significant problem and an opportunity for enlightened leadership.

ORGANIZATIONAL CULTURE

Growing concerns about productivity, commitment, and profitability have renewed interest in the human resource issues within health care organizations. The old closed-systems human relations approach has given way to a broader concept termed organizational or "corporate" culture. While the term itself is not well-defined, it generally refers to a shared system of beliefs, values, and norms about the way the organization functions—or as described by Deal and Kennedy (31)—"The way we do things around here."

The ability to manage culture depends upon the particular definition of culture (32). When the emphasis is on relatively superficial cultural manifestations such as work norms, rewards, and structures, the general conclusion is that structure can be managed to enhance the overall operations of the organization. When culture is defined as deeply rooted in emphasizing unconscious and historical dimensions, one tends to be less optimistic about efforts to manage culture to enhance overall organizational performance. Efforts to manage culture have taken on a variety of forms ranging from enhancing quality of work life (33) to more pervasive efforts to facilitate strategy making (34,35).

While the manipulation of culture will remain difficult, the challenge facing managers is to explore the cultural characteristics of their organizations and design programs, strategies, and actions that will best match the current culture with the organization's mission and environmental demands (36). Moreover, as described by Karl Weick (37), "Cultural contains premises, axioms, and first principles that define the nature of appropriate action." Culture provides coherence, order, and meaning, so that individuals know what is happening to them within the organization. The managerial challenge is thus to provide adequate attention to assure that culture provides meaning to individual activity.

ORGANIZATIONAL RESEARCH AND ASSESSMENT

One of the major problems of management is the lack of good indicators of organizational operations and performance. While increasing attention has been given to financial measures of organizational performance, there has also been a revitalization of interest in systematic assessment of the human aspects of organizations (38,39). Surprisingly, it has taken a long time to recognize that effective and efficient provision of health services depends on how well personnel function independently and collectively within the organization.

Specifically, *organization assessment* is defined as "the systematic measurement of organizational functioning from the perspective of the behavioral system, using scientific methods and procedures and characterized by the measurement of a range of variables encompassing the functioning of the total organization and making use of multiple methods of measurement over time" (40). Use of these data by health service managers has administrative and research implications. Administratively, organizational assessment provides managers with basic information to improve diagnosis of problems, design corrective interventions, and develop strategic plans, for example, through use of a long-term action research strategy involving systematic data gathering and feedback. Kaiser–Permanente was able to markedly improve physician involvement in many problems facing the organization as a whole (41). Specific accomplishments included development of new medical referral and consultation systems; initiation of new special-purpose meetings to facilitate physician–administrator communication; improved relationships with the board of directors, including open board meetings; and more involvement of physicians in the screening, hiring, and evaluation of support personnel. Unfortunately, managers have traditionally approached organizational behavior and design from an intuitive perspective alone, often resulting in inappropriate solutions, unanticipated problems, and missed opportunities.

Finally, development of valid and reliable assessment procedures provides the foundation for meaningful interaction among organizational researchers and health care managers. The availability of data and a shared conceptual understanding of the organization (42) provides an opportunity to transform the role of manager from that of an advocate of untested solutions to often imaginary problems to that of a diagnostician who identifies problems for action, considers alternative courses, and uses assessment data to evaluate options as they affect the organization (43).

From a research perspective, the availability of assessment data greatly enhances the understanding of organizational operations. The information base provides an opportunity to follow organizations over time and to note the impact of such changes as hospital-sponsored primary care or long-term-care activities on other aspects of hospital operation. Moreover, it provides the forum upon which researchers can interact with managers. Unlike research in the physical and biological sciences, people within the organization, including the managers, are an active part of the research process. As described by Lawler (44, p. 4):

> Theory and practice are not competing mistresses. Indeed research that is useless to either the theoretician or the practitioner is suspect. If it is useful to the practitioner but not the theoretician, then one must wonder whether it is a valid finding and whether it has addressed the correct issue. If it is useful to the theoretician but not to the practitioner, then one must wonder whether the research is capturing a critical issue. Indeed it can be argued that we should always ask two questions about research: is it useful for practice, and does it contribute to the body of scientific knowledge that is relevant to theory? If it fails either of these tests, then serious question should be raised. It is a rare research study that can inform practice but not theory or vice-versa.

DYNAMIC NATURE OF INDIVIDUAL AND GROUP CONFIGURATIONS

Effective management recognizes the dynamic nature of disciplinary and interdisciplinary work groups and individual interactions within the organization. This leads to the understanding that organizations frequently have ambiguous goals and criteria, sometimes use information to justify decisions after they are made as well as to make sense of events that have already happened, and are really coalitions of various interest groups whose designs are frequently unplanned and in part ceremonial (45).

The implications of this perspective are substantial. First, the recognition that health care organizations are composed of interest groups and coalitions that are constantly shifting in order to compete for resources provides an opportunity for managers to develop leverage between and among these interest groups and coalitions to enhance the overall operations of the organization. It also provides an opportunity to structure situations so that individuals and groups can more effectively monitor and control their own activities (46).

Second, the increasing role of interdisciplinary groups and work units in the provision of health services (e.g., oncology teams, pain clinics, tumor boards, etc.), raises the issue of work group effectiveness. The ability of these groups to function effectively is limited by the individuals' own disciplinary perspective and lack of appreciation for other disciplinary perspectives. The function of the group is constantly threatened by the discrepancies in members' expectations of each other and by the tendency of one disciplinary perspective to dominate. In fact Temkin-Greener's review of available research questions whether interdisciplinary health teams are real or illusionary. ". . . [Available data] challenge the notion of "interdisciplinary" or "interprofessional" team work as reflecting more of the impression of reality which some health care providers wish to foster than reality itself" (47).

Third, individuals within the organization will increasingly occupy boundary roles that span various work groups, interest groups, or coalitions. Spanning involves considerable conflict, since interest groups, coalitions, and work groups have different values and orientations that lead to conflict and increase occupational stress.

Moreover, much of what happens within the organization is the result of reactions of individuals to external events and of individuals' attempts to influence their environment directly. The characteristics and needs of individuals must be considered within the broader context and structure of the organization. There is a need to balance environmental demands with the organization's sense of its mission and the needs of its members. Changes in communications, decision making patterns, role relationships, reward systems, and many other areas need to be made with insight and sensitivity. Managers should avoid the psychological fallacy that the organization can change by simply changing the motivation, knowledge, or skills of its members.

But managers should likewise avoid the sociological fallacy that the organization can change by simply changing its structure. For example, one should not expect quality of care to improve simply as a result of consolidating medical staff committees. Rather, managers must pay attention to the interplay among individual, group, and organization-wide factors in designing solutions to problems and creating new opportunities.

Finally, recognition of the dynamic nature of individuals and groups within the organization and the context in which they function raises the question of the symbolic role of management within organizations. The manager of the work group or the organization, viewed as a symbol of its success or failure, provides the focus for a process of achieving stability (45). This process is likely to take on greater importance as organizations and groups are faced with increasingly complex external demands and si-

TABLE 14.2. Individual and Group Trends

	Past (1950–1970s)	Present (1980s)	Future (1990 & beyond)
Physicians	Solo practice	Group practice	Corporate practice and active involvement in managerial activity
Nurses	Clinical practice	Emerging as a political force	Active participation in managerial structure and policy
Organizational culture	Not an issue	Emerging issue	Integral part of managerial and organizational effectiveness
Organizational research and assessment	Not an issue	Increased recognition	Integral part of managerial and organizational effectiveness
Individual and group configurations	Individual and disciplinary groups dominate	Emergence of interdisciplinary groups	Dominance of interdisciplinary groups

multaneously forced to function under greater constraints. Managerial turnover may give the impression of doing something without substantially changing the basic structure of the organization.

PAST, PRESENT, AND FUTURE

Table 14.2 summarizes the trends dealing with individuals and groups within the organization. As with the environment and larger organizations, individuals and groups within organizations are confronting increasing complexity and uncertainty. The future will require the active participation of physicians and nurses, with the major challenge being to motivate and preserve human resources available to the organization. These resources will increasingly be involved in interdisciplinary groups and will require new designs and managerial strategies.

THE MANAGERIAL ROLE

Developments at the environmental–organizational level and the individual–group level of the organization provide a clue to future demands on managers. These demands involve three assumptions and three fundamental implications. The first assumption is that health care is *both* an economic and a social good. It is a service to be provided in the marketplace with increasing attention given to the price and quality aspects of that service. At the same time it is an intensely personal, human service which most Americans believe ought to be available to people in need who are without the ability to pay for the service. One of the major responsibilities and challenges of health care executives and managers of the 1990s will be to manage the inherent tension between health care as both an economic and a social good.

The second assumption is that the world will not become simpler but, if anything, more complex, ambiguous, and uncertain. Those who wish to return to the "good old days" or who wish to live in an orderly and stable world are in the wrong profession.

The third assumption is that health care executives and managers working together and with other health care professionals can create the future for themselves and their organizations. It is precisely *because* health care delivery will become even more complex, ambiguous, and uncertain that it is possible for managers to shape their destiny. The external environment not only influences managerial and organizational decision making, but the decisions made by managers on behalf of their organizations help to shape and influence the environment.

From the three assumptions mentioned above come three fundamental implications; each involves a major transition in mind set and behavior. The first is the need for health care executives and health care organizations to move from a production to a marketing orientation; from being passive producers of services to active managers of markets. In the past, under largely cost-based reimbursement systems and the model of the hospital as the "doctors' workshop," it was sufficient for hospitals and other health care organizations to simply be good technical producers of care to patients who were largely generated by physicians. In the new environment of prospective payment systems, increased competition, and changing consumer preferences, the needs and demands of multiple groups must be assessed and a portfolio of services developed to meet these needs and demands. These frequently involve alternatives to hospitalization and, more specifically, the development of service lines that emphasize wellness rather than illness. These "out-of-hospital" service lines must be profitable in their own right (and not merely contribute to hospital inpatient admissions) if the organization is to survive.

A second fundamental implication involves making the transition from care taking to risk taking. In the past, health care managers and executives have been largely caretakers of the institution, while trustees have played a similar role as "guardians or stewards" of the health care organization's assets. Again, cost-based reimbursement and the relatively benign environment demanded little more. But the new environment places a premium on taking risks. The winning organizations will be those that learn from their mistakes quickly and those who become prudent risk takers. Health care executives must be willing to challenge old assumptions, to develop new programs and structures, to work with changing value systems, and to channel conflict in positive directions.

The third implication involves making the transition from operational to strategic management. Operational management served well the production orientation of the past. In the new environment, effective internal operational management will be a given. What will distinguish the high-performing organizations (see Chapter 12) from the mediocre ones will be their commitment to and effectiveness in managing strategically at all levels of the organization. As developed in Chapter 13, strategic management emphasizes the development of a long-run, sustainable, distinctive competitive advantage. All decisions are made in the context of what one's current and future competitors are likely to do. Implementation of the overall strategic direction or vision of the organization is of central concern.

The ability of health care managers and executives to make these three fundamental transitions (from production orientation to a marketing orientation, from care taking to risk taking, and from operational management to strategic management) will have a significant effect on the future of health services. Managers will need to: *(1)* simultaneously manage various dimensions of accountability involving cost, quality, and access; *(2)* manage an increasingly complex and unpredictable environment; *(3)* develop marketing-oriented strategic plans; and *(4)* manage conflict among and between various groups of health professionals. The following sections describe a number of educational and training considerations that will effect the future of health care managers.

TRAINING CONSIDERATIONS

Management training for health care organizations has made significant progress since it first began at the University of Chicago in 1934.

• Training has entered the mainstream of management/organizational theory and methods. Historically health care training programs have been physically and intellectually isolated from larger developments in organizational and management theory; however, departments and programs are increasingly being linked to the conceptual and methodological developments relevant to the management of health care organizations. The inclusion of finance, accounting, organizational design and behavior, marketing, and operations research has improved the training of health service managers and their ability to meet the major challenges facing the field.

• Interdisciplinary squabbling among a number of programmatic orientations, such as medical care, hospital services, and public health, is at a minimum. The development of the generic term "health care management" has mitigated much of the interprogrammatic squabbling. Moreover, health services have developed a research focus that increasingly provides managers with the basis for analytic assessment of problems relevant to health services rather than to a particular service modality.

However, the fundamental changes occurring in health service organizations and environment have raised new issues and concerns for the education of health care managers.

• Indiscriminate adaptation of concepts and management strategies from industrial settings must be monitored. As health care managers are increasingly held accountable for the effective and efficient performance of health service organizations, there is a tendency to adopt indiscriminately concepts and management strategies from industry to the management of health care organizations. In part this trend reflects an inability to discriminate similarities and differences of health care organizations vis-a-vis other types of organizations as well as a tendency to demonstrate that something is being done to resolve problems. The indiscriminate adoption of concepts and methods has the potential of doing a great deal of harm to health care organizations while at the same time undermining the credibility of health care managers as responsible agents.

Moreover, the nature of the field has changed such that increasingly significant portions of the market are in search of managers—and only a secondary thought is given to whether there is expertise in health services. As we discuss in the last section of the chapter, major shifts have occurred in defining health care as an exclusively economic and industrial endeavor, rather than as a humanitarian effort. This shift has thus placed a premium on managerial skill and training—almost to the exclusion of knowledge and insight about health services as a humanitarian service. Failure to restore and maintain balance may lead to several undesirable outcomes, including gross inequities in both access and quality of care, decline in health services as a caring function, development and marketing of superfluous treatment, and increased litigation (48).

• Continual and major revision of graduate curricula makes it difficult to develop a base of support and identity even among recent alumni. While revision of the curriculum was needed to provide adequate preparation for the future management of health care organizations, changes created a substantial gap between alumni and graduates, making it difficult to involve alumni in clinical teaching directly relevant to the current academic curriculum. However, these changes make visible the responsibilities and challenges of continuing education programs to provide the basis for life-long learning.

• Curriculum innovations in content and format can enhance the education of future managers. In terms of content specifically relevant to the general area of organizational behavior, new course offerings need to be developed in organizational design, organizational development, strategic management, human resources management, ethics, management of professionals, and specialty courses in negotiation and conflict management. Moreover, these content areas need to be relevant to the management of multi-institutional systems.

In terms of format, attention needs to be given to an integrated approach utilizing a full range of educational strategies to accomplish multilearning objectives (49). Specifically, greater attention needs to be given to various exercises and forums by which students can develop skill in the management of health care organizations. Several options to be considered are listed below:

Simulation exercises. Students need an opportunity to practice skills and decision making under controlled conditions. While these opportunities have been well-developed in financial management (50) and health planning (51), there has been little development in the area of management, especially organizational behavior, design, and change. Several models are available for adaptation to health care organizations (52,53).

Under one approach, groups of students function as managers within a simulated hospital or health department for an 8-hour work day. Written and telephone communications confront the students with stimuli requiring immediate action. The proceedings are videotaped to allow evaluation of individual performance.

Use of videotapes. While tapes are often considered to be mere gadgets, the use of videotapes provides students with feedback to aid them in evaluating their performance. Managers spend a great deal of time in actions that are visible to subordinates, superiors, and co-workers. They need the ability to function under both stressful and nonstressful circumstances. To provide such appreciation and perhaps initiate corrective action when necessary, the use of videotapes as part of all classroom presentations is an important resource. Students and faculty members are given an opportunity to criticize routinely the substance of presentations as well as their delivery, thereby sharpening skills that are extremely important in the managerial role.

Experiential learning. Since health care management is a multidisciplinary activity, future managers will spend a great deal of time in interdisciplinary problem-solving groups. Managers need to know more than simply theory about operations. As described by Mintzberg (54):

> Our management schools have done an admirable job of training the organization's specialists, management scientists, marketing researchers, accountants, and organizational development specialists. But for the most part they have not trained managers.
>
> Management schools will begin the serious training of managers when skill training takes serious place next to cognitive learning. Cognitive learning is detached and informational, like reading a book or listening to a lecture. No doubt much important cognitive learning no more makes a manager than it does a swimmer. The latter will drown the first time he jumps into the water if his coach never takes him out of the lecture hall, gets him wet and gives him feedback on his performance. In other words we are taught a skill to practice plus feedback, whether in a real or simulated situation. Our management schools need to identify the skills managers use, select students who show potential in these skills, put the students into situations where these skills can be practiced, and then give them systematic feedback on the performance.

Experiential training provides an opportunity to structure situations to give students an opportunity to learn from experience. One such approach is to require students with different skills to practice as a team in the resolution of an organizational problem. For example, students with special expertise in operations research, quality assessment, and organizational behavior may be assigned or contracted to design and implement a quality-assurance program in an ambulatory care clinic. Over a 6- to 9-month period, this group may be required to develop the program, using the resources of the group, and present and defend a plan before clinic management as well as relevant faculty members. This experience would provide insight into the substantive problems of ambulatory-care quality-assurance programs as well as the interaction of interdisciplinary groups.

The variety of degree offerings mask the underlying curriculum content. Health services training is besieged by a variety of degree offerings (e.g., MBA, MHA, MPH, MSPH, and MSHA), a variety of schools (e.g., public health, medicine, allied health, business, and public administration), and a variety of program emphases (e.g., planning, management, and policy) (55). While historically an asset as experimentation was occurring within health services, this variety now has the tendency to create confusion among potential employers as well as students, undermining the credibility of the field. Although the actual curriculum has a generic core, the variety of degrees projects an image more accurate of past than of current training.

ROLE OF WOMEN IN MANAGEMENT

During the last decade there has been an increase in the ratio of women to men in middle-management policy and planning positions. This trend is likely to increase in the coming decade because the proportion of women students enrolled in graduate programs in health services administration is increasing. In 1965, 9.4% of the students were women; in 1981, women constituted 51.9% of the enrollment; and in 1983–1984, women constituted 56.3% of the enrollment (56).

Is the increasing number of women trained in management likely to affect the demographic composition of the managerial hierarchy of health service organizations? A review of nonhealth service organizations suggests that despite federal and state legislation against sex discrimination in employment, and even though job opportunities for women have been increasing, women are still experiencing difficulty moving into top management positions and making salary gains (57,58).

Several factors contribute to these difficulties. From the perspective of the organization, the introduction of women into high management positions is likely to increase uncertainty within the organization. Specifically, where the level of uncertainty inherent in a position correlates with the need for trust and understanding, it is not surprising that top management is dominated by males of similar training and social demographic status (59). The introduction of women into management positions reduces the level of social homogeneity. This poses a major challenge to current health care managers and other members of the organization.

While there is some question about the degree to which future managerial jobs can become more routine (thereby reducing uncertainty), the increased routinization of tasks and the objective measurement of output tends to make personal characteristics of workers less important. As the need for mutual trust decreases because organizational control mechanisms are adequate to ensure reliability in routinized performance, the elite group opens its ranks. Top executives become more subject to controls from within the organization or from external agencies and tend to lose power and privilege. Training in the skills and culture of management begins to take the place of membership in a social caste as a guarantee of reliability and trustworthiness (59).

From an individual perspective the factors are likely to be equally significant. As women assume managerial roles they are likely to encounter internal, interpersonal, and structural barriers (60). Internal barriers are those forces that, because of basic socialization, have traditionally disqualified women from assuming competitive, challenging positions within large corporate organizations. Historically, women have been socialized to assume a supportive position rather than intellectually aggressive or problem-solving positions.

A second barrier stems from the manner in which women are defined by significant others within the organization. One recent longitudinal survey of MBA students reports that male students were found to have a much stronger negative attitude toward women executives than women students and these attitudes did not change over the past decade (57). Negative attitudes are likely to be particularly acute within health care organizations where women have traditionally been involved largely in supportive capacities, such as social workers, nurses, and clerical workers. With the ascendancy of women into management positions, they assume a unique position with the organization and may experience considerable difficulty in interacting with other women as well as male counterparts. For example:

> Women's appearance in collegial networks as co-professionals often confuses men, because these women no longer fit their role definitions as being sweet, pretty, passive, and nurturing. Past standards for interaction are no longer appropriate or unambiguous. In meetings, attention often becomes focused on the uneasiness which everyone feels and on the need to define new ground rules for the situation rather than on carrying out the business at hand. Unable to engage in a collegial relationship with women, men may fall back on the traditional norms of male/female interactions or attempts to compensate by being overly solicitous, congenial, underdemanding or overdemanding. Thus, men may respond to a woman agency director as a woman and secondly as a director. Women are then confronted with the dilemma of how to respond to male colleagues in a way that will preserve their dignity and influence (60).

The final barrier involves the basic structure of the organization. This includes discrimination in hiring, promotion, nepotism, pay scales, and questions associated with child-care facilities and maternity leaves. These barriers, whether informal or formal, tend to minimize the effectiveness of the woman manager within the organization.

The resolution of barriers is likely to occur on two fronts. First, within graduate training programs in health services management, attention needs to be given to providing prospective women managers with the necessary skills to deal with internal, interpersonal, and organizational barriers. Training models are available and need to be integrated into the ongoing curriculum.

Moreover, continuing education efforts need to be developed to provide women currently involved in managerial positions in health care organizations with the necessary skills to deal with internal, interpersonal, and organizational matters. In part these may be considered remedial efforts, since it is unlikely that this kind of training was available in graduate programs even a few years ago. Continuing education should be considered supportive, since individuals operating within organizations require reinforcement to confront barriers successfully. Since a significant number of women already occupy management roles, it is likely that various professional groups of women in health care management will emerge to provide supportive networks and facilitate employment opportunities.

Second, any real substantive change must reflect larger structural changes in society. Specifically, the division of labor between the sexes relevant to work, child, family, and home responsibilities must change (61). What is clear at the level of society, the organization, and the individual is the need to confront the challenge directly, thus resolving barriers and assuring full utilization of available talent.

ROLE OF MINORITIES IN MANAGEMENT

Between 1970 and 1982 the number of members of minority groups enrolled in health care management programs increased significantly. In 1969–1970, less than 2% of the students enrolled in health service management programs were members of minorities, whereas by 1980–1981 13.1% of the enrollment consisted of members of various minority groups. However, in 1983–1984 the minority enrollment declined to 10.9% (56).

While there is little documentation of the actual number of minorities in management positions in health care organizations or the problems they encounter, studies in other settings show that minority individuals are disproportionately represented in managerial roles and either explicitly or implicitly receive fewer psychological, social, or material rewards per quantitative and/or qualitative unit of performance than comparable groups within the organization (62). For example, controlling for age, education, and experience, minorities are far less likely to supervise other employees in federal agencies (63). Similarly, in the private sector blacks are seldom seen in the ranks of senior management. While the number of blacks employed as midlevel managers has increased, blacks claim that they are channeled into staff positions from which few senior managers are selected (64).

Other studies indicate motivational problems for members of minority groups. For example, a study of one department in North Carolina state government shows that blacks and other minorities report less satisfaction with chances for occupational advancement within the department than their white colleagues. Moreover, significant differential pay-grade distributions by race were documented (65).

Future challenges center on the ability of management to provide leadership within the organization in such a way that resources are conserved or increased. The challenge goes beyond simply providing training opportunities for minority individuals, since these programs tend to perpetuate selection criterion inherently biased against individuals. For example,

> Potential employers, when asked about what they look for at interviews, respond "confidence, independence, ability to take charge." But when the people who act this way are minority people—they think of them as "pushy, aggressive, hostile/distant, and not team players" (66).

To ensure the successful integration of minority managers into health care organizations requires an affirmative action program at the local level that includes (67):

• A clear understanding of the situation at hand. Better theories and data about ways in which organizational discrimination is maintained and the way in which affirmative action programs succeed or fail.

• Clear organizational leadership for the affirmative action program. Specifically, people with power and privilege must demonstrate their commitment to the affirmative action agenda.

• Continued pressure for affirmative change from various constituencies and their allies.

• Development of support and survival training for affirmative action officers themselves. Experience to date indicates that these individuals require support in order to prevent burnout.

• A clear distinction between the problems faced by women and by members of racial minorities. There exist substantial differences between these two groups, not the least of which is the pace at which opportunity may become available and the relative ability to exploit opportunities once they appear. Failure to recognize differences inhibits the ability to design specific programs to facilitate change within the organization (68).

ROLE PERFORMANCE AND CHANGING VALUES

A major theme of this text is that health care managers will increasingly be expected to ensure the accountability of their organization and its relationship to the larger community. To meet this challenge successfully, managers will require a more analytic perspective—a perspective that takes into consideration multiple interacting factors (69).

Specifically, future role performance requires that managers examine an increasing number of factors simultaneously. As never before, the health care manager has to make sure that the organization's structure, forms of decision making, methods of coordinating work, employee selection, training, and socialization methods, and reward systems are well coordinated with each other. For example, it is dysfunctional to say that the organization promotes participative decision making but to have work schedules that do not permit time for such decision making. Likewise, it is dysfunctional to reward people based on individual merit and performance alone when one is trying to increase the productivity of interdependent units or teams. Thus health care managers will need to become more adept at simultaneously managing a wider scope of variables that influence performance. Human resource planning needs to be a central part of overall strategic planning and both need to be integrated into an ongoing process of strategic management.

Second, future role performance requires that managers consider the interactive nature of relationships that exist among factors or variables and the limited generalizability of these relationships to other situations. Nowhere is this more true than in attempting to anticipate the reactions of various segments of the medical staff to future administrative plans. For example, hospital-initiated ambulatory care programs may be strongly supported by specialists who hope to benefit from increased referrals, but strongly opposed by primary care physicians who fear increased competition for patients.

Third, future role performance requires that managers give greater emphasis to the long-term feedback effects of likely interventions. Managers will increasingly be called upon to think in system terms as decisions create complicated ripple effects. For example, the decision of a teaching hospital to develop an ambulatory care unit will have far-reaching effects throughout the community. From a community perspective, the ripples created by the decision of one executive may turn up as giant waves on the shores of another executive's hospital. While to some degree this has always been true, an increasing premium is being placed on the ability of the first executive to anticipate the other's response and deal with it effectively. This involves skills in marketing, strategic planning, and strategic management.

In the future, health care organizations and providers will be held increasingly responsible for a clear definition of service areas and will then be held accountable for the health status of people living in those areas. Accountability will require health care managers to pay attention not only to the financial status of their institution but also to the health status of the community they serve. Managers will need an increased ability to merge clinical and administrative data in making decisions. New kinds of integrated clinical/administrative information systems will be needed.

New dimensions of role performance are set within a context of values and expectations. There is concern that the ascendance of management represents a significant change from health care as a humanitarian effort to health care as an exclusively economic industrial endeavor with a new language and new values. As described by O'Rourke (70):

> The language that people use to describe their work is often an accurate indication of the way they conceive of themselves and their occupations. Whereas we used to speak about

TABLE 14.3. Managerial Trends

	Past (1950–1970s)	Present (1980s)	Future (1990 & beyond)
Training	Relatively isolated from mainstream management and organizational theory	Integrated and differentiated from industrial management	Fully integrated into management training and undifferentiated
Women in management	Emerging field of career opportunities	Continued career opportunities	Increased CEO responsibility and broader system impact
Minorities in management	Not an issue	Emerging enrollment	Expanding career opportunities and impact on the field
Role performance and changing values	Coordinating role subordinate to professional providers	Ascendence of managerial ability—financial and strategic expertise	Continued prominence of managers and recognition of role in managing human resources vs. simply financial resources

the profession of medicine or health care, we now speak of the health care industry. Whereas we used to speak about patients we now speak about consumers. Doctors, nurses, and hospital personnel have become providers. Health care professionals used to offer health care; they now deliver it. Medicine and medical procedures and practices used to be evaluated with regard to their power to alleviate pain or to heal; now cost effectiveness is all important, and the ultimate evaluation of medical practice is whether it enables people to become once again productive members of society.

Considering health care exclusively as a business destroys the basic meaning of health care. At the same time, ignoring the issues of cost containment and effectiveness is equally untenable. The critical issue facing health care managers is to maintain a balance between these different value orientations that takes into account the very nature of the field while recognizing resource limitations. As described by McNerney (71):

. . . There is more to health management than crisp efficiency. In the health field, perhaps more than in any other, management involves moral issues and ethical choices. It involves deep commitment and personal courage. It involves a resolve to be just and right, not only a resolve to win.

PAST, PRESENT, AND FUTURE

Table 14.3 presents the summary of trends dealing with the managerial role. As can be seen the role has made a number of major transitions—and more will be required to meet the challenges of the 1990s and beyond. The field is rich with challenges and opportunities—and as never before the manager is truly a significant player in determining the future provision of health services.

CONCLUSION

Returning to the initial three scenarios—more of the same, less of the same, and radical restructuring—managers are likely to face elements of all three as they deal with the organization and the environment, individuals and groups within the organization, and their own role. The challenge will be to identify tractable elements within each scenario and their inevitable combinations and to direct limited resources and energy to those elements that make a difference in the provision of health services. Issues of quality and efficiency will remain paramount, confounded by fundamental moral and ethical choices heretofore considered only in the abstract. Our ability—and contribution to determining the future provision of health services—will depend on a critical mix of abilities, insight, and courage. Failure to meet the challenge will sideline managers to simply observing rather than influencing the future.

DISCUSSION QUESTIONS

1. Recalling the three scenarios presented at the beginning of the chapter, speculate on the implications of each scenario as it affects efforts at cost containment, changing the organization's culture, and the role of management.
2. Design a training program for both incumbent personnel, women, and minority managers to enhance their overall effectiveness. Be specific about the types of problems you anticipate and how the training program will resolve or mitigate these problems.
3. Compare and contrast how a multiunit hospital system would be most likely to respond to the challenges outlined in this chapter. Compare the most likely responses of the hospital system with those of an individual hospital. Specifically address issues related to cost containment, changing social norms and demographic composition, technology development and social experimentation, changing roles of physicians and nurses, organizational culture, and the incorporation of women and minorities into management positions.
4. Select a health care organization (e.g., hospital, HMO, health department) and, drawing on the various chapters throughout the text and the challenges outlined in Chapter 14, suggest changes in the design and operations of the organization to enhance its ability to meet challenges. Be specific about the organization, the unit of analysis, and the specific strategies that are proposed to enhance performance.

SUGGESTED READINGS

Institute of Medicine. *For-profit enterprise in health care.* Washington, D.C.: National Academy of Sciences Press, 1986.
    Extensive report of an Institute of Medicine Committee which examined the implications of a growing for-profit orientation in health care on access, cost, quality, and hospital–physician decision-making. Contains 10 chapters and 15 commissioned papers addressing the issues.

Waitzkin, H. *The second sickness: Contradiction of capitalist health care.* New York: The Free Press, 1983.

A Marxist analysis of the problems affecting health services in the United States and other advanced capitalist countries. Problems of health care are linked to the underlying political, economic, and social structures of society. Chapter 8 reviews various reform proposals and concludes that only through a blend of theory, practice, study, and action directed at broader social change can current problems be resolved.

Smith, D. B., & Kaluzny, A. D. *The white labyrinth: A guide to the health care system* (2nd ed.). Ann Arbor: Health Administration Press, 1986.

A analytic view of how the health system is constructed, consequences of that construction, a description of organizational mechanisms underlying its operations, and strategies for change. First published in 1975, the book finds the system a continuing labyrinth with dramatic changes increasing the complexity and confounding managerial choices.

REFERENCES

1. Ginzberg, E. The restructuring of U.S. health care. *Inquiry*, Fall 1985, *XXII* (3), 272–281.

2. Sigmond, R. M. A community perspective on hospital ownership. *Frontiers of Health Services Management*, September 1984, *1* (1), 33–40.

3. *Health care financing review.* Baltimore: Health Care Financing Administration, Spring 1985.

4. Mechanic, D. Cost containment and the quality of medical care: Rationing strategies in an era of constrained resources. *Milbank Memorial Fund Quarterly/Health and Society*, 1985, *63* (3), 453–475.

5. Iglehart, John K. Health care and American business. *New England Journal of Medicine*, January 14, 1982, 120–124.

6. Kleinfield, H. R. When the boss becomes your doctor. *New York Times*, January 5, 1986.

7. Hughes, S. *Long-term care: Options in an expanding market.* Homewood, IL: Dow Jones/Irwin, 1986.

8. Weissert, W. G. Estimating the long-term care population: Prevalence rates and selected characteristics. *Health Care Financing Review*, Summer 1985, 83–91.

9. Blendon, R. J. Who will treat the poor? Paper presented at a symposium entitled U.S. health care system: A look to the 1990's. New York: Cornell University Medical College, March 7–8, 1985.

10. U.S. Bureau of the Census. *Current population survey*, 1984.

11. Feder, J. Hadley, J., Mullner, R. Falling through the cracks: Poverty, insurance coverage and hospital care for the poor, 1980–1982. *Milbank Memorial Fund Quarterly/Health and Society.* Fall 1984, *62* (4), 544–566.

12. Gottschalk, E. C. People with chronic diseases often find insurance is unaffordable— or unavailable. *The Wall Street Journal*, Tuesday, August 12, 1986, p. 31.

13. Schiff, R. L. Ansell, D. A., Schlosser, J. E., Idris, A. H., Morrison, A. & Whitman, S. Transfers to a public hospital: A perspective study of 467 patients. *New England Journal of Medicine*, February 27, 1986, 552–556.

14. Health United States: 1984. National Center for Health Statistics. PHS Publication No. 85-1232, Washington, D.C., 1984.

15. Relman, A. An institutional for health care evaluation. *New England Journal of Medicine*, February 18, 1982, 669–670.

16. Institute of Medicine. *Assessing medical technologies*. Washington, D.C.: National Academy Press, 1985.

17. Cummingham, R. M. *Wellness at work*. Chicago: Blue Cross Association, 1982.

18. Kiefhaber, A. K., & Goldbeck, W. B. Worksite wellness. Section 4: Background papers in proceedings of prospects for a healthier America: Achieving the nation's health promotion objectives. USDHHS, Public Health Service, November 1984.

19. Campbell, D. T. Reforms as experiments. *American Psychologist*, 1969, *24*, 409–429.

20. Michnich, M. E., Shortell, S. M., & Richardson, W. C. Program evaluation for administrators. *Health Care Management Review*, 1981, *6*, 25–35.

21. Ermann, D. Health maintenance organizations: The future of the for-profit plan. *Journal of Ambulatory Care Management*, May 1986, *9*, 72–84.

22. Rice, T., deLissovoy, G., Ermann, D., & Gable, J. The state of PPOs: Results from a national survey. *Health Affairs*, Winter 1985, *4*, 25–40.

23. Scott, W. R., & Meyer, J. W. The organization of societal sectors. In John W. Meyer & W. Richard Scott (Eds.), *Organizational environments*. Beverly Hills, Calif.: Sage Publications, 1983, pp. 129–153.

24. Scott, W. R. Systems within systems: The mental health sector. *American Behavioral Scientist*, 1985, *28* (5), 601–618.

25. Georgopoulos, B. S. Distinguishing organizational features of hospitals. In G. Wieland (Ed.), *Improving health care management*. Ann Arbor, Mich.: Health Administration Press, 1981.

26. Friedson, E. The reorganization of the medical profession. *Medical Care Review*, Spring 1985, *42* (1), 11–36.

27. Shortell, S. M., Wickizer, T., & Wheeler, J. *Hospital-sponsored primary care: Results and lessons from a national demonstration*. Ann Arbor, Mich.: Health Administration Press, 1984.

28. Shortell, S. M. The medical staff of the future: Replanting the garden. *Frontiers in Health Services Management*, February 1985, 3–47.

29. Hegyvary, S. T. Perspectives on nursing productivity: 1986. Paper presented at the National Invitational Conference on Nursing Productivity, April 17, 1986, Washington, D.C.

30. Leatt, P. Management education for nurses in Canada. *The Journal of Health Administration Education*, Fall 1985, 279–291.

31. Deal, T. E., & Kennedy, A. A. *Corporate cultures*. Reading, MA: Addison-Wesley, 1982.

32. Martin, J. Can organizational culture be managed? *In* Peter J. Frost, Moore, L. F., Louis, M. R., Lundberg, C. C., & Martin, J. (Eds.), *Organizational culture*. Beverly Hills, CA: Sage Publications, 1985.

33. Hanlon, M. D., Nadler, D. A., & Gladstein, D. *Attempting work reform: The case of "Parkside" hospital.* New York: Wiley-Interscience, 1984.

34. Bice, M. D. Corporate cultures and business strategy: A Health Management Company perspective. *Hospital and Health Services Administration*, July/August, 1984, 64–78.

35. Deal, T. E., Kennedy, A. A., & Spiegel, A. H. How to create an outstanding hospital culture. *Hospital Forum*, January/February 1983, 21–30.

36. Shrivastava, P. Integrating strategy formulation with organizational culture. *Journal of Business Strategy*, 1984, 5, 103–111.

37. Weick, K. Significance of corporate culture. In Peter J. Frost, Moore, L. F., Louis, M. R., Lundberg, C. C., & Martin, J. (Eds.), *Organizational culture*. Beverly Hills, CA: Sage Publications, 1985.

38. Van de Ven, A., & Ferry, D. *Measuring and assessing organizations*. New York: Wiley-Interscience, 1980.

39. Seashore, S. E. Lawler, E. E., III, Mirvis, P.H., & Cammann, C. *Assessing organizational change: A guide to methods, measures and practices*. New York: John Wiley & Sons, 1983.

40. Lawler, E. E., Nadler, D. A., & Cammann, C. (Eds.). *Organizational assessment: Perspectives on the measurement of organizational behavior and the quality of work life*. New York: Wiley-Interscience, 1980.

41. Stebbins, M. W., Hawley, J. A., & Rose, A. L. Long-term action research: The most effective way to improve complex health care organizations. In N. Margulies and J. D. Adams (Eds.), *Organizational development in health care organizations*. Reading Mass.: Addison-Wesley, 1982.

42. Tichy, N. M., & Hornstein, H. A. Collaborative organization model building. In E. Lawler, D. Nadler, & C. Cammann (Eds.), *Organizational assessment*. New York: Wiley-Interscience, 1980.

43. Staw, B. M. The experimenting organization: Strategies and issues in improving causal inference within administrative settings. In E. Lawler, D. Nadler, & C. Cammann (Eds.), *Organizational assessment*. New York: Wiley-Interscience, 1980.

44. Lawler, E. E., III. Challenging traditional research assumptions. In E. E. Lawler, III, Mohrman, Jr., A. M., Mohrman, S. A., Ledford, Jr., G.E., Cummings, T. G., & Associates. (Eds.), *Doing research that is useful for theory and practice*. San Francisco: Jossey-Bass Publishers, 1985.

45. Pfeffer, J., & Salancik, G. *The external control of organizations*. New York: Harper and Row, 1978.

46. Cohen, D. I., Jones, P., Littenberg, B., and Neuhauser, D. Does cost information availability reduce physician test usage? A randomized clinical trial with unexpected findings. *Medical Care*, March 1982, 286–292.

47. Temkin-Greener, H. Interprofessional perspective on teamwork on health care: A case study. *Health and Society Milbank Memorial Fund Quarterly*, Fall 1983, *61*, 638–641.

48. Levey, S., & Hesse, D. Bottom line health care? *New England Journal of Medicine*, March 7, 1985, *312* (10), 644–647.

49. Pointer, D. D. The alignment of learning objectives and educational methods: A commentary. *The Journal of Health Administration Education*, 1985, 3 (1), 47–53.

50. Starkweather, D. B. Financial management and regulation game. Berkeley, Calif.: Western Network for Education in Health Administration, 1985.

51. Holland, M., & Moore, J. *Community health care management simulator: Version two.* Atlanta: Georgia State University, 1985.

52. Miles, R. H., & Randolph, W. A. *The organization game.* Santa Monica, Calif.: Goodyear Publishing, 1979.

53. McCall, M., & Lombardo, M. *Looking Glass, Inc.: The first three years.* Greensboro, N.C.: Center for Creative Learning, 1979.

54. Mintzberg, H. The manager's job: Folklore and fact. *Harvard Business Review,* July/August, 1975, 61.

55. Pointer, D., Luke, R., & Brown, G. Health administration education at a turning point: Revolution, alignment, issues. *The Journal of Health Administration Education,* Summer 1986, *4* (3), 423–436.

56. Association of University Programs in Health Administration. Health services administration education, 1983–84: A report of AUPHA member graduate and baccalaureate programs and faculties. Office of Research on Student Affairs, Spring 1985.

57. Dubno, P. Attitudes toward women executives: A longitudinal approach. *Academy of Management Journal,* March 1985, *28* (1), 235–239.

58. Hymowitz, C., & Schellhardt, T. The glass ceiling. A special report: The corporate women. *The Wall Street Journal,* March 24, 1984, Section 4, p. 1.

59. Kanter, R. M. *Men and women of the corporation.* New York: Basic Books, 1977.

60. Hooyman, N., & Kaplan, J. New roles for professional women: Skills for change. *Public Administration Review,* 1976, *4,* 374–378.

61. Martin, P., Harrison, D., & DiNitto, D. Advancement for women in hierarchical organizations: A multi-level analysis of problems and prospects. *Journal of Applied Behavioral Science,* February 1983, *19* (1), 19–33.

62. Alvarez, R., & Lutterman, K. (Eds.). *Discrimination in organizations; Using social indicators to manage social change.* San Francisco: Jossey-Bass, 1979.

63. Lewis, G. B. Race, sex, and supervisory authority in federal white collar employment. *Public Administration Review,* Jan./Feb. 1986, *46* (1), 25–30.

64. *Business Week.* Progress report on black executives: The top spots are still elusive/ Blacks who left dead end jobs to go it none. Feb. 20, 1983, 104–106.

65. Neely, G. M. Institutional racism/sexism in North Carolina state government. *Interim to the final report of the affirmative action research project,* National Institute of Mental Health, Rockville, Md., 1981.

66. Neely, G. M. Affirmative action: Making change possible through self-interest. In *Consultation on the affirmative action statement of the U.S. Commission on Civil Rights* (Vol. 1). Washington, D.C.: U.S. Commission on Civil Rights, 1981.

67. Chesler, M., & Chertow, C. The affirmative action program and the organization: Structural conflict and role dilemmas. In *Consultation on the affirmative action statement of the U.S. Commission on Civil Rights* (Vol. 1). Washington, D.C.: U.S. Commission on Civil Rights, 1981.

68. Atkins, T. I. Statement. In *Consultation on the affirmative action statement of the U.S. Commission on Civil Rights* (Vol. 1). Washington, D.C.: U.S. Commission on Civil Rights, 1981.

69. Shortell, S. M. Managerial models. *Hospital Progress*, October 1977, 64–69.

70. O'Rourke, K. When health care becomes a business (letter). *New England Journal of Medicine*, February 18, 1982, 434.

71. McNerney, W. J. Managing ethical dilemmas. *The Journal of Health Administration Education*, Summer 1985, 331–340.

Author Index

Subject Index